UNDERSTANDING COMPUTERS

UNDERSTANDING COMPUTERS

Commodore Grace Murray Hopper
United States Navy

Professor Steven L. Mandell
Bowling Green State University

WEST PUBLISHING COMPANY
Saint Paul New York Los Angeles San Francisco

COPY EDITOR: Elaine Linden
ARTWORK: Barbara Barnett, John Foster, and David Pauly
COMPOSITION: Parkwood Composition Service, Inc.

50 West Kellogg Boulevard
P.O. Box 43526
St. Paul, Minnesota 55165

Printed in the United States of America

LIBRARY OF CONGRESS CATALOGING IN PUBLICATION DATA

Hopper, Grace Murray.
Understanding computers.

Includes index.
1. Electronic digital computers. 2. Microcomputers.
I. Mandell, Steven L. II. Title.
QA76.5.H67 1984 001.64 83-23429
ISBN 0-314-77946-9
1st Reprint—1984

CONTENTS IN BRIEF

CONTENTS

CHAPTER 1

AN INVITATION TO COMPUTERS 1

CHAPTER 2

THE MACHINE ITSELF: HARDWARE 29

CHAPTER 3

THE COMPUTER: WHAT IT IS AND HOW IT WORKS 73

CHAPTER 4

COMMUNICATING WITH THE COMPUTER: PROGRAMMING 99

CONTENTS

CHAPTER 5

CHAPTER 6

CHAPTER 7

CONTENTS

CHAPTER 8

COMPUTERS IN THE CLASSROOM 217

CHAPTER 9

COMPUTERS IN THE WORKPLACE 241

CHAPTER 10

COMPUTERS IN BUSINESS AND INDUSTRY 265

CHAPTER 11

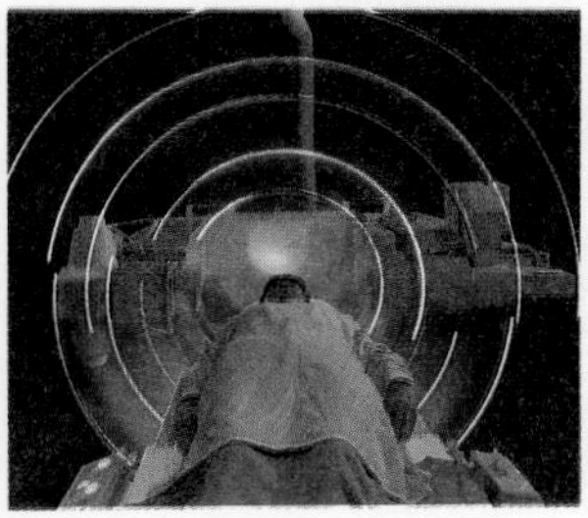

COMPUTERS IN SCIENCE, MEDICINE AND RESEARCH AND DESIGN 291

CONTENTS

CHAPTER 12

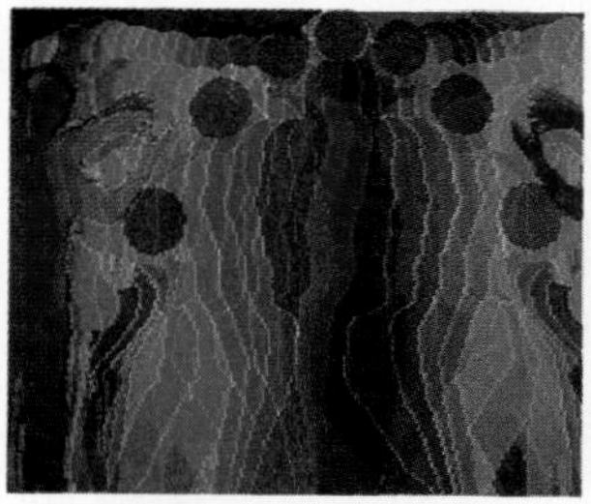

CHAPTER 13

CHAPTER 14

CONTENTS

COMPUTERS IN THE FUTURE 361

OUT THE AUTHORS

Commodore Grace Murray Hopper

B.A. Vassar College, Phi Beta Kappa
M.A. Yale University
Ph.D. Yale University, 1934

Active duty, U.S. Navy, 1944–46, when she assisted in programming the Mark I, the first large-scale digital computer, and 1977–present
Professorial Lecturer in Management Sciences, George Washington University, 1971–78
Staff Scientist, Systems Programming, UNIVAC Division of Sperry Corporation, 1964–71
Visiting Lecturer to Adjunct Professor, Moore School of Electrical Engineering, University of Pennsylvania, 1959–present
Systems Engineer, Director of Automatic Programming Development, UNIVAC Division of the Sperry Corporation, 1952–64
Senior Mathematician, Eckert-Mauchly Computer Corporation, 1949–52
Research Fellow in Engineering Sciences and Applied Physics, Computation Laboratory, Harvard University, 1946–49
Assistant Professor of Mathematics, Barnard College, 1943
Instructor to Associate Professor in Mathematics, Vassar College, 1931–43

Has received ten honorary doctorates
Published over 50 papers and articles on software and programming
Member ANSI Committee on standardization of computer languages, and presently serving on the CODASYL Executive Committee

Legion of Merit, 1973
Distinguished Fellow of the British Computer Society, 1973
Elected to membership in the National Academy of Engineering, 1973
Chosen by the Data Processing Management Association as the first Computer Sciences "Man-of-the-Year," 1969
Received the 1964 Achievement Award by the Society of Women Engineers

Professor Steven L. Mandell

B.A. Lehigh University
B.S. Ch.E. Lehigh University
M.B.A. Wharton School, University of Pennsylvania, IBM Fellow
D.B.A. George Washington University
Juris Doctorate, University of Toledo Law School

Associate Professor, Bowling Green State University, 1975–present
Director, Management Information Systems Institute, Bowling Green State University, 1977–81
Associate Director, ADP Management Training Center, U.S. Civil Service Commission, 1972–75
Captain, U.S. Army, ADP Plans and Operations Officer, 1970–72
Systems Engineer, IBM Corporation, 1969–1970
Financial Analyst, TWA, 1968
Engineer, U.S. Navy, 1967
Engineer, RCA, 1966

Published numerous textbooks in computers and data processing, and law
Holds Certificate in Data Processing from the Institute for Certification of Computer Professionals
Holds Certificate in Data Processing Education
Served as consultant to Bureau of Land Management
Served as consultant to the Agency for International Development
Member of Ohio Bar

PREFACE

Grace Hopper and Steven Mandell first worked together in 1972 in Washington, D.C. As associate director of computer specialist training with the U.S. Civil Service Commission, Mr. Mandell was responsible for interagency government training programs in advanced computer technology. Commander Hopper became the featured guest lecturer at the sessions and was an advisor to the program.

At George Washington University, Dr. Hopper served as the important link between Mr. Mandell and his dissertation research committee. Her active participation insured the success of the research project and led to a highly successful report published at international conferences on multinational corporate computer systems.

Together in 1974 Captain Hopper and Dr. Mandell organized the first government-wide conference on minicomputers and microcomputers. It was their belief that this new emerging technology was an important direction for future development. Some of the brightest young individuals in the country participated in this conference. For example, an instructor for the Naval postgraduate school demonstrated one of the first portable computers with a 4-bit Intel chip and a modified operating system. This instructor was Gary Kildall (see chapter 5) who is now president of Digital Research, and the operating system was the beginning of the current standard CP/M.

During the past several years, Commodore Hopper and Professor Mandell have appeared together on several panels at professional meetings. Her trips to Bowling Green to address his students have been a high point for many in their academic experiences. The nation-wide acclaim received by Commodore Hopper as a pioneer in the computer field and the success experienced by many of the textbooks authored by Professor Mandell provide the basis for this current project.

The computer revolution is having a profound impact upon us as individuals and as members of society. This fact has been brought home in a powerful manner by movies, books, television series, magazine articles, and newspaper stories. Some of the publicity is highly favorable and raises our hopes for a better life in the future. On the other hand, the negative messages are frightening and force us to continually reevaluate our position with regard to advancing computer technology. In such an environment it is essential for everyone to become computer literate so that we may all make knowledgeable choices in the future. This book has been designed to bridge the computer technology gap in an informative, exciting, and challenging manner.

In beginning this project, our first task was to determine what were the objectives of the book. This step caused us to examine our concept of computer literacy. We have decided to equate literate with educated and believe the broadest scope of coverage to be appropriate. Thus, the material included in this book is balanced between technology, applications, society, and programming. Only by understanding all these elements can intelligent decisions be made with regard to computers.

The basic pedagogical format found in this book is designed to aid in the clear, straightforward presentation of the material, while including motivational real-world examples. Each chapter begins with an outline that gives a frame of reference for the material to be presented. An interesting article from a current periodical is then used to maintain the reader's interest. A brief introductory section provides a logical link to the previous material. Throughout the text, there are marginal definitions to assist the student. At the conclusion of the chapter material, there is a point-by-point summary followed by review questions and discussion questions.

Two additional features in the pedagogical design warrant special attention. After the material has been presented, each chapter includes the presentation of a controversial, related societal issue. All sides of each issue are explored requiring the student to analyze some extremely important positions. Secondly, because of the importance of many individuals in the computer revolution, profiles of the people recognized are interspersed through the material. Students often find it easier to relate to humans rather than to machines.

Three highly important subject areas require special attention in appendices to the book. "Career Opportunities" is included to give students insight into computer-related careers. "Selecting Your Personal Computer" covers material highly relevant to many students in their family role as resident computer expert. "Flowcharting" supports the use of a programming module with the book.

Because programming is one element in a rounded computer literacy concept, a separate BASIC language supplement has been developed. This language section was geared to a microcomputer orientation and all programs were run on the IBM/PC. Because of the fundamental nature of the material presented, there will be no difficulty utilizing the text supplement with any other computer system.

We were very fortunate to have had several outstanding college educators serve as reviewers for this project. It is very difficult to fully express our thanks for their help and aid in shaping this project. Without the professional effort of the following individuals this book would not be nearly as effective a teaching resource:

George Beekman
Oregon State University

Beverly Bilshausen
College of DuPage, Illinois

Donald H. Cooley
Utah State University

Bill Griffith
College of San Mateo, California

Earl Jackson
North Texas State University

Ed Morris
Highline Community College, Washington

Perry Sanders
Indiana University, Northwest

Robert Schmiederer
Los Angeles Valley College

Michael Ward
Willamette University, Oregon

Susan P. White
Catonsville Community College, Maryland

Jean Wirsig
University of Wisconsin, River Falls

Louis Wolff
Moorpark College, California

SUPPLEMENTARY EDUCATIONAL MATERIAL

The Study Guide to accompany this text includes numerous materials for student reinforcement. Each chapter in the Study Guide includes the following: a narrative Summary of the chapter; a Structured Learning section; an extensive set of Questions and Answers (True/False, Matching, Short Answers). For each section in the language supplement there is: Summary, Structured Learning, Worksheet, and Programming Problems.

A complete instructor resource package has been designed to reduce administrative efforts. The classroom support includes: Learning Objectives, Lecture Outlines, Answers to Review and Discussion Questions, and Additional Review and Discussion Questions. For each section in the language supplement, there are an average of four programming problems; each problem is accompanied by a flowchart and list of any differences for microcomputers.

A Test Bank of nearly 1,000 multiple choice questions is also included in the Instructor's Manual. In addition, the WESTEST computerized testing service is available from West Publishing Company with these questions in machine-readable form.

Transparency Masters are provided. Most of these visuals are novel, and not mere reproductions of artwork found in the text.

A student-oriented audio cassette has been developed to support the text. The material on the tape parallels the coverage in the book with interesting examples included throughout. The appendix material in computer careers and selecting a personal microcomputer is given increased coverage.

An exciting new dimension in learning support is also available in the form of a microcomputer software. The disk contains four interactive programs designed to acquaint the students with some of the specific capabilities of the computer. These programs are completely user friendly and can be utilized in one laboratory session.

ACKNOWLEDGMENTS

Many individuals and companies have been involved in the development of the material for this book. Numerous corporations and government agencies provided the color pictures found in this book in addition to applications material. Many professionals provided the assistance required for a completion of a text of this magnitude: Edward Morris, Rhonda Raifsnider, Denise Weldon-Siviy and Patricia Cooke on student material; Robert Szymanski and Karen McKee with BASIC and Norma Morris, Donna Pulschen, and Candace Streeter in manuscript development. The design of the book is a tribute to the many talents of William Stryker. One final acknowledgment goes to my publisher and valued friend, Clyde Perlee, Jr., for his encouragement and ideas.

Steven L. Mandell

UNDERSTANDING COMPUTERS

CHAPTER 1
AN INVITATION TO COMPUTERS

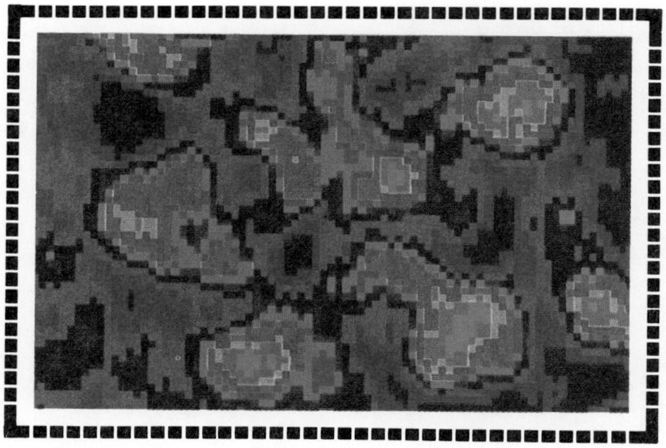

OUTLINE

ARTICLE

WITHOUT A COMPUTER, WILL KIDS FLUNK?

by Art Buchwald

The computer companies are now laying a real guilt trip on parents through TV commercials. They state that you're really cheating your children out of a chance to make it when they grow up if you don't go out immediately and buy them a computer. The kids see these commercials, too, and it's causing a lot of trouble between the haves and havenots in our school system.

"Johnny, where is your report card?"

"Here."

"Why did you get a D in math?"

"Wasn't my fault. You wouldn't buy me a computer."

"We can't afford a computer right now. They cost $200."

"Don't matter to me. The man on TV said if you don't want to give me a head start in life you'll have nobody to blame but yourself."

"That's a lot of television commercial nonsense. I did math without a computer."

"Maybe that's why you can't afford to buy me one."

"We didn't have computers in those days. Besides, it hasn't been proven yet whether computers are good or bad for children. There is a school of thought that they can be harmful to the learning process and kids should depend on their own brains instead of machines. The computer can tell you what 4 plus 4 is, but you don't know how you arrived at the answer."

"They don't care in school how you arrive at it as long as it comes out right."

"Let's forget math for a moment. Why did you get an F in deportment?"

"I hit Jill Gleason with a book."

"Why did you hit Jill with a book?"

"Because she's got a computer, and she wouldn't tell me the answers to the math problems."

"You can't go hitting people because they have a computer and you don't."

"You got to if they say your parents are too cheap to buy you one."

"Did Jill say that?"

"Yeh. She said you were depriving me of a chance to make something of myself and I should be taken away from you and put in a foster home."

"She couldn't have said that."

"The other kids heard her. Those that had computers laughed, and those that didn't all wanted to hit her too."

"What did your teacher do?"

"She sent me to the principal's office and he put my name in his computer and said if I did it again, I'd be kicked out of school."

"What about spelling? How do you explain the D in that subject?"

"I have to do all my own spelling. If I had a computer, it would check my spelling for me. When Jill Gleason hands in her paper, she never has a mistake on her printout. She says she gets her homework done five times as fast as I do."

"Yes, but is she learning how to spell."

"She said her father told her it doesn't make any difference because when she grows up computers will do all the spelling for you anyway."

"Her father apparently doesn't realize that the discipline you learn by doing your own work in school are far more important than whether you make a mistake or not in your papers."

"That's what Johnny Parks' father said. His father won't get him a computer either."

"Well, I'm not about to buy you one, so you'd better straighten out and come home with a better report card than this the next time, or you can spend your weekends in your room."

"I don't care. I'll probably wind up in jail anyway."

"Who told you that?"

"The guy on TV. He said if parents didn't buy their kid a computer, the kid would probably wind up sticking up liquor stores when he grew up."

Students are not the only ones using computers. Their parents and even grandparents are aware of and interested in the computer and the effects it will have on their lifestyles.

INTRODUCTION

Changes in attitudes toward the computer have kept pace with changes in the physical and logical makeup of computers. An industry saying that describes the extent of that change goes like this: "If the auto industry had done what the computer industry has done in the last thrity years, a Rolls Royce now would cost $2.50 and get two million miles per gallon. . . . It would also be only three inches long." Actually, unless you have seen early computers in operation, you can't really appreciate what today's computers can do. The increase in computer power and the decrease in its cost are combining to change our world and the way we live.

COMPUTERS TODAY
We've Come a Long Way

Today in the United States the citizenry watches shuttle flights with little more than casual curiosity. These shuttle flights absorb more than half of NASA's budget, each shuttle carrying five computers. The four main computers all process the same data, and all must agree for the systems they control to operate normally. If one computer doesn't agree, it is turned off and the remaining three govern the shuttle. Should one of these three change its mind, it too will be shut off. If for some reason the remaining two disagree, the fifth computer, the backup, is turned on and makes the final decision. The computers handled 324 billion instructions during the mission's first flight of just over 54 hours.

The computers have nearly total control of the shuttle flight from nine

Messages are sent by computer to and from the Space Shuttle and The Missions Operations Control Room.

Numerous computer devices are shown in this "fish-eye" lens view of the flight deck of the Space Shuttle Orbiter 102 Columbia. Each crewmember has his hand-controller to his immediate front for controlling the spacecraft. The controller provides information to the computer system which in turn records altitude changes. Between the two positions for the crewmembers are the flight computer and navigation aid console. Immediately in front of the console are the three cathode ray tubes (CRTs) used to display computer data and information for the crew.

minutes before lift-off until just before touchdown. During some parts of the flight, the computers must perform 325,000 operations a second. Some of the action is run by automatic **programs**; some is at the direction of a pilot. But even when a pilot "takes the stick," the computers are interpreting his or her actions and sending signals that make the shuttle react. These computers have made it possible for just four ground controllers to handle the jobs done by hundreds of personnel on the earlier Apollo flights.

PROGRAM
A series of step-by-step instructions that tell the computer exactly what to do.

Enhancing Our Daily Lives

Computers have quietly entered our national consciousness, performing tasks at all levels of usefulness, from the spectacular to the trivial. **Point-of-sale (POS) terminals** at many fast-food restaurants keep a running check on what is being sold and what is needed to keep the inventory stocked. The computer cannot guarantee the quality of food we get there, but it has a lot to do with how quickly we get served and how inexpensively the food is priced.

POINT-OF-SALE (POS) TERMINAL
A terminal that serves as a cash register but is also capable of relaying data to a central computer.

Recently, the Coca-Cola Company unveiled a talking vending machine. As is often the case with novelties, this one seems to be paying off. The machine greets customers, asks them for more money if enough hasn't been deposited, tells them if the soft drink they have selected is sold out, and cheerily invites them to "Come again" at the end of the transaction. Between these little chats, it plays musical standards. Bottlers who use the new dispenser report "tremendous" increases in sales.

The Yesterdays restaurant chain of Mobile, Alabama, places computerized cash registers at strategic spots in each of its food outlets. These station computers are hooked to the main computer at the firm's home office so that the sales performance of each restaurant is instantly accessible. From this constant monitoring, the company can determine such things as whether the sales are cash or credit, which stations within each restaurant are doing the most business, and whether the floor plans need to be rearranged to heighten the effectiveness of service. The station devices also assist in keeping up-to-the-minute food and drink tabs on a large number of customers, something that is difficult to do manually.

Although not all that apparent when you look at your daily newspaper, print journalism has been changed greatly by computer technology—at every stage from copy preparation to final production. Only a few years ago, typesetting was the task of an expert. This highly skilled (and usually unionized) artisan turned the copy the reporter had written and the editor had rearranged into columns of clean, correct, and graphically pleasing type.

Now the reporter is very likely to be his or her own typesetter. Using a terminal linked to a computer, the reporter can type in and edit the copy electronically instead of by hand. When the task is finished, the reporter presses a button and the copy on the terminal screen is transformed through computer adjustment into printed copy.

Changes at the production end of news reporting are just as remarkable. Such newspapers as the *New York Times*, the *Wall Street Journal*, and *U.S.A. Today* use the computer to turn out their national editions, which may be edited at one place but are produced at several. Commonly, the master page plates are laser read and then transmitted by satellite to regional receiving and printing stations. At each of these, a laser writer etches new page plates. These plates are then locked onto presses for the final printing. The regional locations have each of their plates etched simultaneously. The operation permits not only the transfer of written articles but also of color photo negatives, all at a very rapid rate.

On another level, Yale Security Group is using computers to change the locksmith trade. Yale has perfected a locking system for motel and hotel guest rooms that will require each new guest to use a personalized "key." The method promises improved security as well as diminished costs, since replacement of lost or stolen keys or locks that have to be changed for safety precautions will no longer be a problem.

The electronic security system is made up of a computer, a display screen, a keymaker, and a printer. As a guest registers, the information on the occupant and the room is fed into the computer, which, in turn, activates the keymaker. A punch-coded key that is valid only for that particular occupant is produced. When the new key is inserted into the room lock, the previous guest's code is automatically cancelled. If the computer in the door lock signals that the code on the key is correct, the lock will open. If the code is wrong, the lock stays shut.

Computers are frequently used to make things more fun. Baseball enthusiasts may search their record books high and low and never discover that Hank Aaron and Babe Ruth played in the same game together. But they did—in "computer land." An Apple computer was used to select two all-star teams from real statistics and then to project how they would

Point-of-sale terminals are commonplace in retail outlets. "Wraparound" light rays of a supermarket scanner read UPC stripes on merchandise held in various positions. This speeds service by allowing checkout personnel more freedom in guiding goods over the scanning window.

Have a Coke and a "thank you" is what customers will get when they purchase Coke from the new "Talking Vendor," a coin-operated vending machine that talks to customers through a computerized voice synthesizer.

fare against each other in a make-believe contest. The result was called "The Greatest Game Never Played," broadcast play-by-play from printouts on a network of radio stations. (The National League All Stars, assisted by a last-minute Aaron homer, took the game from the American League, 5–4.)

In the opening round of the 1982 PGA championship golf tournament—the real one—officials resorted to the computer to keep the game suitably difficult. By gathering detailed records on the top golfers and entering the statistics as these golfers progressed along the course, the tournament officials were able to determine whether the course was too hard or too easy. Based on their conclusions, the course actually was changed by shifting the pin (hole) placement on the putting green, according to the advice of the computer.

A less strenuous game is roulette. Kenilworth Systems Corporation has developed a remote roulette station called Roulabette. Consisting of two video screens connected to a central computer (one for showing the roulette table, the other for placing the bets), Roulabette permits the secretive gambler to play in relative privacy. The devices are installed in hotel rooms near the casino, in hotel lobbies, and in other special casino locations. A player bets using a special card encoded with the sum of money that was paid in advance to the casino cashier. The winning numbers on the wheel are flashed onto one of the video screens at the conclusion of each spin.

Fishing purists will gulp like their prey to discover that computers now on the market can take all the cunning out of fishing. One such device, the Pro Guide, has been programmed by professional fishers. With it an uncertain angler can select the best lure for each fishing situation by punching in such factors as water temperature (the computer has its own electronic thermometer), water depth, time of day, wind condition, and degree of water clarity. In less time than it takes to bait a hook, the computer suggests the right lure and how best to use it. Another fishing computer, the Lowrance X-15 Grayline Graph Recorder, locates where the fish actually are and exactly how deep they are running. The "big ones" may still get away, but now the angler can make the excuse, "My computer malfunctioned."

Around the World

In the industrialized countries, computers are the backbone of communications, banking, medicine, weapons systems, and dozens of other fields that affect us constantly in our daily lives. Because computers are so very adaptable to jobs and problems of all sorts, it is likely that very few inhabited regions of the earth will long remain outside the computer's influence.

Among all the nations of the world, perhaps none has embraced the computer with more passion and imagination than Japan. Here the creation of the most modern computers has become a national goal. This new generation of computers is expected to approximate the reach, flexibility, and utility of human intelligence. The capability to make inferences, judg-

Automated teller machines use increasingly sophisticated software to link customers and their home banks.

ments, and associations, just as the human brain does, is also a goal of computer technology. Enormous amounts of research funds are being assigned to this project in Japan, and scientists associated with it speak in terms of "when" the breakthroughs come, not "if."

In 1982 the FBI discovered several representatives of Hitachi and Mitsubishi, two major Japanese computer companies, offering to buy trade secrets developed by the American firm, IBM. What this event seemed to illustrate was that (1) American computer firms were worried about the research aggressiveness of other countries and (2) two companies, at least, were aggressive in seeking a technological edge on the rest of the computer-development world. Some observers, indeed, saw the whole affair as more a matter of politics than of law. In its own way, computer superiority has become as crucial an issue to all the industrial nations as military superiority. In fact, one kind of superiority may ultimately determine the other.

When it comes to **robotics**—the science of designing and building robots—Japan is without peer. An agency that monitors robot technology estimates that Japan has well over half the programmable robots now in existence. Essentially arms that are operated by a computer "brain,"

ROBOTICS
The science of designing and building robots.

these robots can assemble machinery, weld, paint—even make sushi, a Japanese food. Some factories have automated to the point that robots carry out virtually every mechanical operation, although still under the eye of a human supervisor (more on robotics in Chapter 14).

TELECOMMUTING
Computer hookups between offices and homes, which allow employees to work at home.

Scarcity of space and high office rents have helped to accelerate a business practice in Japan that also is becoming commonplace in America—conducting office work at home via a computer linked to a business's main computer. With such a setup, called **telecommuting**, the user can send and receive messages and feed in programs to do tasks without being bothered by such time-consuming and often nerve-wracking routines as commuting and parking and the distractions of office gossip.

Not all computer applications are as matter-of-fact as those just mentioned. At least one Zen priest in Japan has programmed his small personal computer to assist him in meditation by creating Sanskrit characters, images, and colors on a video screen.

VIDEOTEX
A service that provides two-way information capabilities using TV-like screens and computers.

France has especially distinguished itself in developing and popularizing **videotex** systems. Videotex allows the user to view on a video screen all sorts of information from distant computerized data banks by a phone connection. The applications of videotex seem endless and, so far, barely begun. In France it is being used for electronic telephone directories, financial services, access to classified advertisements, farm crop and equipment information, consumer rights data, timetables, restaurant guides, disease diagnosis, and more.

This is a sample screen of information available from Teletel, a videotex service in France. Consumers use their microcomputers to access information on a variety of topics including news, education, and leisure interests.

The French have also been forerunners in "smart card" development. These cards look like ordinary plastic cards. However, they have a tiny memory embedded in them that can accept nonerasable data and thus be customized to the card holder. Smart cards can identify their holders, initiate and record financial transactions, reveal (through electronic card readers) their holder's credit status, and free their users from such traditional banking chores as writing checks.

At the Unilever Company's Instrumentation, Control, and Automation Division in London, a scientist put the computer to use in designing a better bottle for household cleaners. "Better," in this case, meant a bottle that took about 8 percent less material to construct than former ones but that had the same volume at two-and-a-half times the strength.

Canada has computerized what might be called "cultural banking"—that is, keeping track of and guarding the treasures in its museums. The National Museums of Canada (NMC) organization has been developing a computerized catalog of the millions of artifacts in the country's 250 major museums. By late 1982 more than 35 million items had been cataloged. Museums belonging to the NMC will have computerized access to catalogs of the other member museums. In addition, they will be able to maintain their own individual inventories under an indexing system that has 3,000 separate classifications. One museum official said an information search that earlier might have taken as long as six days can now be done in 30 seconds.

China recently found itself in need of the newest technology when the government undertook a detailed census of its estimated one billion people. To get the operation underway, the Chinese government bought 29 American-made computer systems. The mammoth nose-counting campaign involved the services of 1,000 computer technicians, 4,000 data-entry personnel, a million census supervisors, and four million census takers. The actual counting took only 10 days to complete, but the coding and analysis of the gathered information is expected to take almost two years.

In Pakistan, a less-developed country, computers now play a part in many industries. In ship-salvaging operations, computers evaluate scrap metal prices and manage inventories; and, in the very different business of egg production, computers monitor and direct feed mixtures. Until late 1981 the only kind of computers legal in Pakistan were the expensive, larger ones. No one knows for certain why they were banned; one view is that the government didn't want the people buying a luxury item that would add to Pakistan's foreign exchange problems. However, the government has since lifted its ban on smaller, personal computers. So versatile are these computers that they can handle Pakistan's wildly fluctuating prices and the complex system of tax surcharges on products. Drawbacks, of course, persist: high computer prices, scarcity of computer technicians, and undependable telephone systems that make computer hookups hazardous.

Today the computer has become involved in so many aspects of our lives that remembering the skepticism about the computer technology of the 1950s and 1960s is difficult. How could only about 25 years make such a difference in our attitude toward computers? To understand, we must look at how this thing we call a computer—more than just a machine—developed.

TOWARD THE COMPUTER
Early Developments

COMPUTER
A general-purpose machine with speed, accuracy, and memory.

True **computers**—that is, electronically-based calculators—are relatively new, less than 40 years old. They are linked to a chain of calculating inventions that stretches back to prehistoric times. Knotted strings allowed ancient shepherds to keep tally of their flocks. Then came the abacus (Figure 1-1), whose rows of beads on wires allowed for rapid and accurate mathematical operations.

Blaise Pascal, the French mathematician, physicist, and philosopher, is credited with developing the first mechanical calculator in 1642. It manipulated numbers through a series of gears in much the same fashion as an odometer registers mileage. Pascal's mechanical calculator (Figure 1-2) was capable of adding and subtracting only. But by building on Pascal's invention in the late 1600s, Gottfried von Leibnitz, a German mathematician and philosopher, was able to create a device that also multiplied, divided, and yielded square roots (Figure 1-3).

These machines had to be prepared for each separate operation by its user; that is, if the machine was expected to add, its gears had to be physically positioned for that function, a tedious process at best. The next refinement in this chain of developments surfaced in the weaving industry in France during the early 1800s. There J. M. Jacquard perfected a series of **punched cards** to alter loom settings and create different weave pat-

PUNCHED CARD
A commonly used storage medium in which data is represented by the presence or absence of punched holes.

FIGURE 1-1 The Abacus

FIGURE 1-2 Pascal's Mechanical Calculator

FIGURE 1-4 Jacquard's Loom

terns without further human intervention (Figure 1-4). These punched-card instructions are recognizable forerunners of computer programs because they affected what the machine did without changing the machine in any way.

Theoretical—if not operational—refinements in computing and programming can be traced to the English inventor Charles Babbage. In the early 1800s, he designed and built an experimental model of a device he called the **difference engine** (Figure 1-5) to automate the calculation of roots of polynomials. Unfortunately, when Babbage tried to make a larger version of his difference engine, parts could not be manufactured to meet the precision needed in the machine. The man and his idea were ahead of the technology of that time. Later Babbage worked on an **analytical engine**, which was to be programmed by cards to perform even more com-

DIFFERENCE ENGINE
A machine developed by Charles Babbage to compute mathematical tables.

ANALYTICAL ENGINE
An invention by Charles Babbage that exhibited several ideas used in computers today.

FIGURE 1-3 Leibnitz's Machine

FIGURE 1-5 Babbage's Difference Engine

HOLLERITH CODE
The representation of numbers, letters, and special characters by the placement of holes in 80-column punched cards.

plex mathematical functions. This device would have made use of a memory unit, called the "store," to hold intermediate and final results separate from the computational area. The analytical engine too was not destined to be built by Babbage; he died before it could be constructed. However, using notes and drawings, his son put together a model of it which worked quite well. Because of these two inventions, Babbage is known as the "father of computers."

The United States' first significant contribution to the development of mechanical calculators came through Herman Hollerith who, as an employee of the U.S. Census Bureau, tackled the problem of speeding up the preparation of census reports, then being compiled by manual methods. In 1880 the census compilation had taken seven-and-a-half years, and the population in 1890 was much larger. To make the process more efficient, Hollerith designed a card the size of a dollar bill of that time. It had 80 columns and 12 rows into which could be punched coded information (**Hollerith code**). A machine automatically "read" that information from the cards (Figure 1-6). These inventions, first used in 1890, enabled the census tabulation time to be cut to two-and-a-half years!

Subsequently, Hollerith established the Tabulating Machine Company to make and market calculators for commercial use. Through mergers with other companies, Hollerith's firm eventually developed into the International Business Machines Corporation, or IBM. The present-day IBM punched card is a refinement of Hollerith's cards.

While Hollerith was perfecting his equipment, another American, William S. Burroughs, was refining his mechanical adding machine, a key-driven

FIGURE 1-6 Hollerith's Census Machine

PROFILE

ADA LOVELACE

Her father was Lord Byron, the most flamboyant and provocative of the English romantic poets; and it was evident to those who knew Lady Ada Augusta Lovelace that she had more than a fair share of her family's genius. Her share, however, inclined more to science than to poetry.

In 1842, when she was 27, she began working with inventor Charles Babbage on developing his Analytical Engine, a device for automatically making mathematical calculations from coded card instructions. Lovelace had first become interested in the invention after translating a paper describing it. Within a year after her collaboration with Babbage, she had invested the project with some of her own ideas—one of which is now called the "loop" concept. In her studies she had noticed that repeating the same sequence of instructions was often necessary in performing a single calculation. Lovelace then concluded that by using only a single set of instruction cards and a "conditional jump" facility to control repetitions, a calculation could be made with only a fraction of the original effort.

Because of her insight into the dynamics of this process, Lovelace is now considered history's first programmer. In honor of her achievements, a recent high-level programming language (used primarily by the government) was named "Ada."

and hand-cranked device that could record, summarize, and calculate numbers.

During the late 1920s and early 1930s, **accounting machines** evolved that could handle extensive record-keeping functions through the use of large quantities of punched cards, these plugboard-controlled machines handled America's business data processing load well into the 1950s. But what these machines had in common with all their predecessors—and what limited their speed, size, and adaptability—was their reliance on interacting moving mechanical parts to do calculations (Figure 1-7).

The advance that heralded the kind of computers now common was the creation in 1944 of an automatic calculator, the **Mark I**, by a team of researchers headed by Howard Aiken of Harvard University (Figure 1-8). Instead of relying on mechanical gears, the Mark I used electromagnetic relays and mechanical counters. This shift to electronics made a new language of directions (instructions) necessary. With mechanical devices, the wheels or gears could be positioned (by hand or punched card) to represent different numbers; but the electrical currents that operated the Mark I and its descendants had only two states—on or off—to represent numbers and characters. Thus, the present computer languages are based on the **binary number system**, which uses groups of ones and zeros (on and off) to convey data and instructions to the computer. Although few programmers today would write a program in binary code, this **machine language** is the only language upon which a computer can directly understand and act.

Two years after the development of the Mark I, the first true electronic calculator was constructed at the University of Pennsylvania. The project

ACCOUNTING MACHINE
A machine that could mechanically read data from punched cards, perform calculations, rearrange data, and print results in varied formats.

MARK I
The first automatic calculator.

BINARY NUMBER SYSTEM
The numeric system, used in computer operations, that uses the digits 0 and 1 and has a base of 2.

MACHINE LANGUAGE
A code that designates the proper electrical states in the computer as combinations of 0s and 1s.

FIGURE 1-7 Accounting Machine

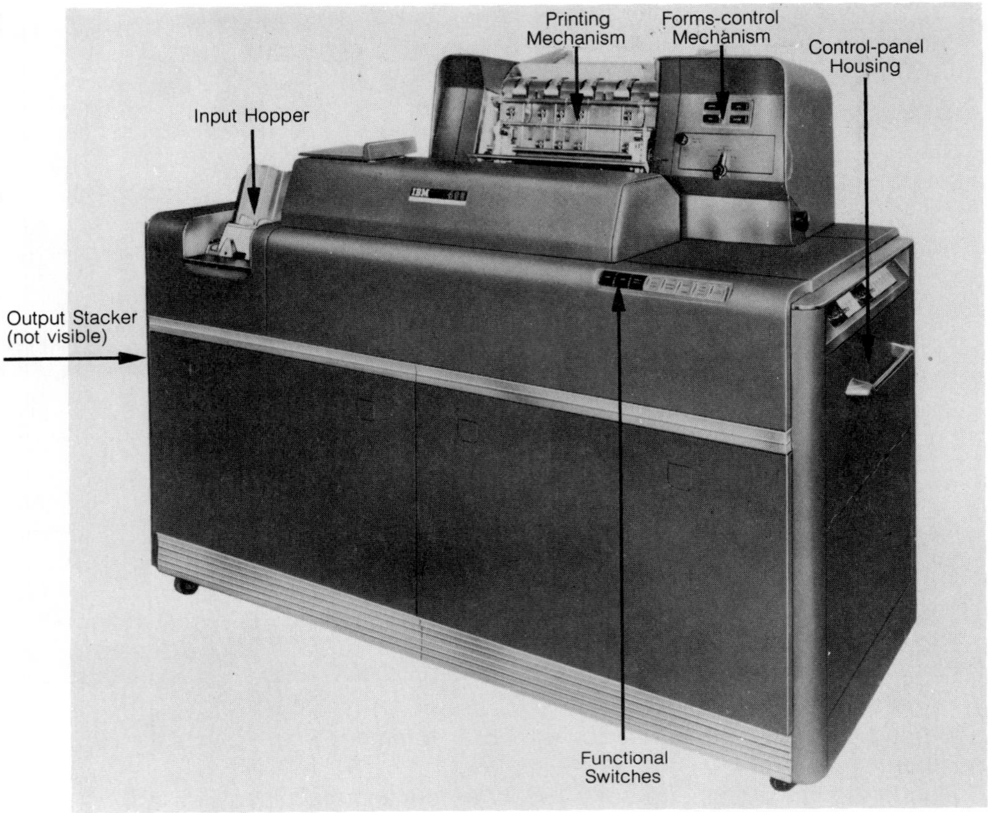

FIGURE 1-8 The Mark I

PROFILE

THOMAS J. WATSON, SR.

The most prominent company in the computer business is International Business Machines (IBM) Corporation, and IBM's success is largely due to the efforts of one man—Thomas J. Watson, Sr.

Watson grew up on a farm in Painted Post, New York. After attending the Miller School of Commerce in Elmira, New York, he held various sales positions, including one at National Cash Register (NCR) Corporation.

In 1914 Watson joined the staff of Computing-Tabulating-Recording Company (CTR)—the descendant of Hollerith's Tabulating Machine Company. Ten years later he assumed the position of chief executive and renamed the company.

Watson's strong and family-oriented leadership style directed the company through some difficult times. Watson refused to lay off employees during the Depression. Instead, he continued manufacturing tabulating machines, storing them in warehouses. This proved to be a profitable strategy and won IBM the contract as the equipment supplier for the newly established social security system.

IBM continued to build its reputation and fortune during World War II. Watson volunteered the company's services to the U.S. President. As a result, tabulating centers were established to keep track of the prisoners of war, intelligence information was collected for the U.S. State Department, and equipment was installed at Pearl Harbor that aided in breaking the Japanese military code. In addition, Watson was responsible for funding Howard Aiken's Mark I project—the first electromechanical machine—shifting the company into the computer age.

Watson died of a heart attack at the age of 82, but not before he saw his son, Thomas, Jr., take over as IBM chief executive officer. In his reign at IBM, Watson saw a 24-fold increase in assets and a 316-fold increase in business. Watson, in his life and career, represents the American ideal of integrity and achievement.

was financed with a $400,000 army contract and was under the direction of J. Presper Eckert, Jr., and John Mauchly. This machine was the *E*lectronic *N*umerical *I*ntegrator *A*nd *C*alculator, or **ENIAC**, and it was huge (Figure 1-9). ENIAC weighed 30 tons and covered 1,500 square feet of floor space. Although commissioned to be built to aid the war effort, ENIAC was not finished in time. ENIAC was, however, a success; it could perform, for example, the same multiplication function in three-thousandths of a second that took the Mark I about three seconds to complete. This was so fast that scientists felt that just seven computers like ENIAC could handle all the calculations the world would ever need.

ENIAC did not, however, store instructions as modern computers do. Instead, it had to be given directions through the manual setting of switches. The ability to store programming digitally in the computer and thus free it to work at its own speed was the contribution of mathematician John von Neumann. He collaborated with Eckert and Mauchly to build the *E*lectronic *D*iscrete *V*ariable *A*utomatic *C*omputer, or **EDVAC**. EDVAC is generally conceded to be the first **stored-program** computer. With the success of these pioneering efforts, the computer moved from an experimental novelty to a useful scientific and business tool.

ENIAC
***E*lectronic *N*umerical *I*ntegrator *A*nd *C*alculator; the first "electronic digital calculator."**

EDVAC
***E*lectronic *D*iscrete *V*ariable *A*utomatic *C*omputer; performed arithmetic and logic operations without human intervention by using stored programs.**

STORED-PROGRAM CONCEPT
The storage of instructions in the computer's memory in electronic form so the computer can process data at its own speed.

FIGURE 1-9 The ENIAC: J. P. Eckert, shown here, developed the ENIAC with John Mauchly.

First Generation: 1951–1958

FIRST-GENERATION
Computers that used vacuum tubes; faster than earlier mechanical devices but very slow compared with today's computer.

SYMBOLIC LANGUAGE
The use of mnemonic symbols to represent instructions; must be translated into machine language before being executed by the computer.

MAGNETIC DRUM
A cylinder with a magnetic outer surface on which data can be stored by magnetizing specific positions.

UNIVAC I
***UNIV*ersal *A*utomatic *C*omputer; the first commercial electronic computer; became available in 1951.**

First-generation computers were large, costly to buy, expensive to power, and often unreliable because of their delicacy and complexity. They used vacuum tubes for their internal operations; ENIAC, for example, contained more than 18,000 of these tubes and is rumored to have dimmed the lights of Philadelphia when it was turned on. Vacuum tubes, besides being bulky and using excessive power, generated so much heat while operating that they had to be cooled by special air conditioning.

Instructions and data were entered into these computers through the medium of punched cards. The instructions on the cards were coded in a **symbolic language**, which was easier for people to use than the 0s and 1s of binary code. The computer had to use another program to translate each symbolic language instruction into a machine language instruction. The machine code was recorded as a series of tiny magnetized spots on the outer surface of a rotating **magnetic drum**. Once all the instructions were translated, the computer could execute the program. Navy Commodore Grace Murray Hopper developed one of the first translation programs in 1952.

The first computer to embody all these features was the **UNIVAC I**, designed to process business instead of scientific data (Figure 1-10). UNIVAC I was the first commercially produced digital computer. It was, like ENIAC and EDVAC, a creation of Eckert and Mauchly.

FIGURE 1-10 A First-Generation Computer—The UNIVAC I

Second Generation: 1959–1964

The technology race began in earnest. The **second generation** of computers started when **transistors** began to be used instead of vacuum tubes around 1959. William Shockley led the team that developed transistors in the late 1940s at Bell Labs, but they had caught no one's attention at that time. (Shockley later shared the Nobel Prize for this invention.)

SECOND-GENERATION
Computers that used transistors; smaller, faster, and having a larger storage capacity than first-generation computers.

TRANSISTOR
A type of electronic circuitry; smaller, faster, and more reliable than vacuum tubes.

FIGURE 1-11 A Second-Generation Computer System—IBM 7070

MAGNETIC CORES
A type of computer memory; iron alloy, doughnut-shaped rings about the size of pinheads are strung on thin wires.

MAGNETIC TAPE
A storage medium consisting of a narrow strip of material upon which spots are magnetized to represent data.

INPUT/OUTPUT
Data submitted to or received from the computer.

HIGH-LEVEL LANGUAGES
English-language like coding schemes.

THIRD-GENERATION
Computers characterized by the use of integrated circuits, reduced size, lower costs, and increased speed and reliability.

INTEGRATED CIRCUITS
Electronic circuits etched on a small silicon chip less than 1/8-inch square.

SILICON CHIP
A small piece of silicon used to form the primary storage of third-generation computers.

Transistors greatly reduced the size of computers and the heat generated by vacuum tubes. Computers became smaller and more reliable and they had increased storage capacities. They also operated on far less electrical power (Figure 1-11).

Magnetic cores, invented by Jay W. Forrester, are rings of magnetic material strung on thin wires. This form of computer memory replaced the magnetic drums of the first-generation systems. Each magnetic core was placed at the intersection of a vertical and a horizontal wire. To "turn on" a core, one-half the electricity needed was run through each wire. Thus, only at the intersection of specific wires would a core become charged. About this time **magnetic tape** (similar to recording tape) largely replaced the cumbersome and time-consuming punched cards for **input/output** operations. Both of these media greatly increased the speed of processing and storage capacities.

Second-generation computers helped usher in more sophisticated programming languages too. These **high-level languages**, such as COBOL and FORTRAN, more like English than the earlier symbolic vocabularies, made programming easier.

Third Generation: 1965–1971

The **third generation** marked yet another era in which the computers got smaller while their capacities got larger. **Integrated circuits** on tiny **silicon chips** took the place of transistors (Figure 1-12). Hundreds of electrical components could be included on one silicon circuit chip less than ⅛-inch square. The chips were the brainstorm of Jack S. Kilby of Texas Instruments.

FIGURE 1-12 Four Generations of Computer Components

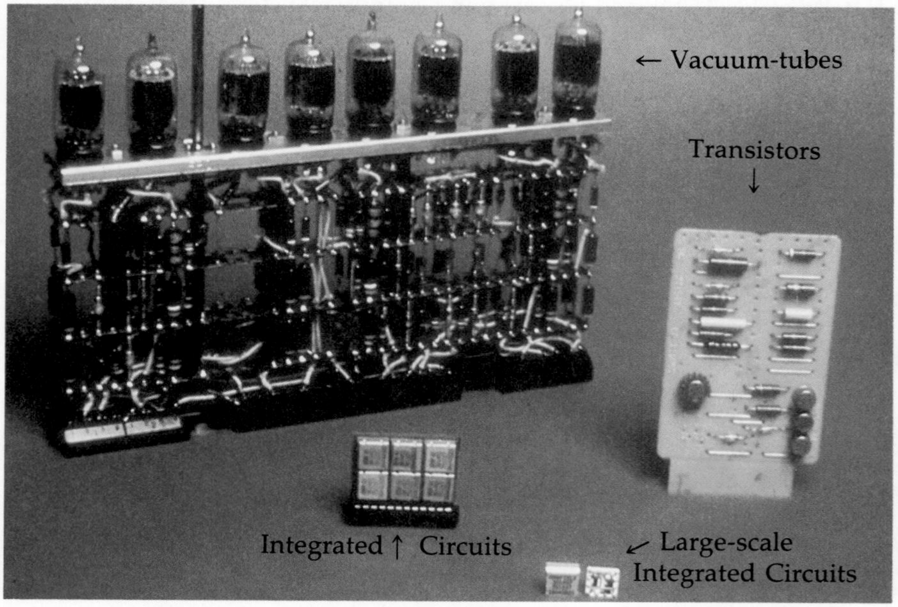

IBM's System/360, a series of six different computers with different **main storage** capacities, revolutionized the industry. For the first time, users could buy a computer and feel that their investment in **software** would not be wasted when the time came to move to a machine with a larger memory. This compatibility among computer models virtually assured IBM's dominance in the computer field, which has continued even to this date. Its features were mirrored in varying degrees by such competing manufacturers as RCA, Honeywell, Sperry, Burroughs, and others (Figure 1-13).

As solid-state technology progressed during this period, the production of the first **minicomputers** began. These devices boasted many of the same capabilities of large computers—but they were a lot smaller and had significantly less storage capacity (Figure 1-14). In 1965 Digital Equipment Corporation introduced the first commercially successful minicomputer—the PDP series.

Third-generation computers were the first to be accessible by **remote terminals**—input/output devices that are electronically linked to main computers but located at long distances from them. Such terminals are described as being **online**.

MAIN STORAGE
Memory that is inside the central processing unit.

SOFTWARE
Programs used to direct the computer for problem solving and overseeing operations.

MINICOMPUTER
A computer with the components of a full-size system but having smaller memory.

REMOTE TERMINAL
A terminal that is placed at a location distant from the central computer.

ONLINE
In direct communication with the computer.

Fourth Generation: 1972–?

Although the dividing lines between the first three generations of computers are clearly marked by major technological advances, historians

FIGURE 1-13 A Third-Generation Computer System—NCR V-8600

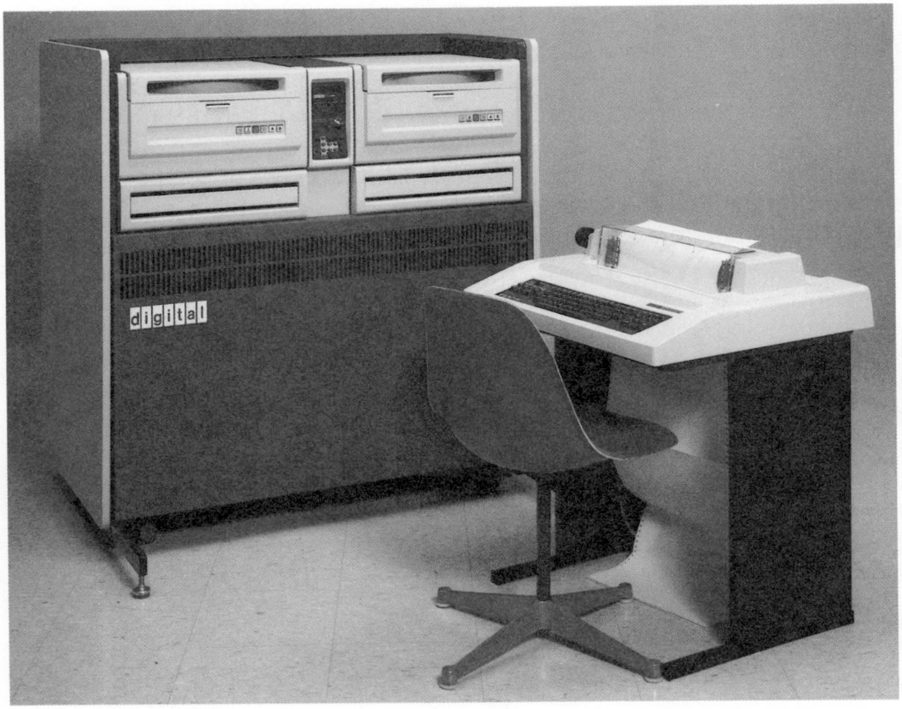

FIGURE 1-14 A Third-Generation Minicomputer using Miniaturization Techniques—DEC PDP 11/60

FIGURE 1-15 Microprocessor
The fourth generation marked steady progress in complexity and power of the microprocessor. This Bell Labs' chip has as much processing power as some minicomputers.

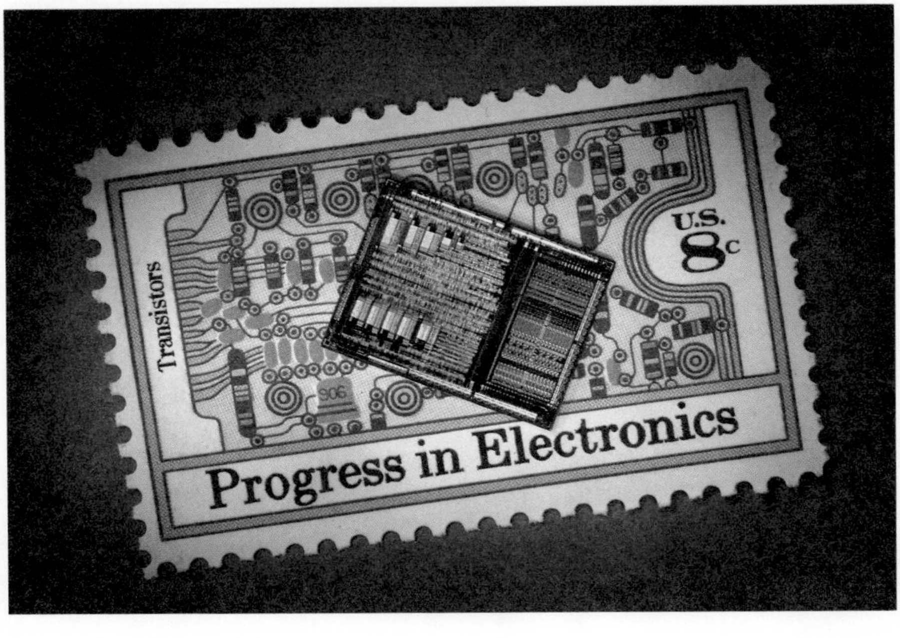

are not so clear about what characterizes the **fourth generation**, nor exactly when it began. That we are now living in the fourth generation—and have been since the early 1970s—is not disputed, though.

The third generation saw the emergence and growth of the silicon chip circuitry, but some computers at least partially relied on the older magnetic core. By the fourth generation, the core virtually had disappeared as a useful unit and chip circuitry was becoming increasingly miniaturized. **Large-scale integrated (LSI) circuits**, featuring thousands of transistors on a single chip, became the order of the day (Figure 1-15).

From LSI technology sprang the very tiny devices called **microprocessors**, which govern the functions of microwave ovens, sewing machines, thermostats, and automobiles. The same technology, employing the microprocessor, yielded the **microcomputer**, whose small size and almost infinite versatility have made the home computer market possible. LSI, as one might have guessed, has already progressed to the VLSI (Very Large Scale Integration) stage: more capabilities in smaller packages. Table 1-1

FOURTH-GENERATION
The computer era of large-scale integrated circuits and microprocessors.

LARGE-SCALE INTEGRATED (LSI) CIRCUITS
Circuits containing thousands of transistors densely packed in a single silicon chip.

MICROPROCESSOR
The central processing unit of a microcomputer; fits on a small silicon chip.

MICROCOMPUTER
A very small computer; often a special purpose or single function computer on a single chip.

TABLE 1-1 Generations of Computer Development

PERIOD	COMPUTER SYSTEM CHARACTERISTICS
First Generation 1951–1958	Use of vacuum tubes in electronic circuits Magnetic drum as primary internal-storage medium Limited main-storage capacity Slow input/output; punch-card oriented Heat and maintenance problems Applications: payroll processing and record keeping Examples: IBM 650; UNIVAC I
Second Generation 1959–1964	Use of transistors for internal operations Magnetic core as primary internal-storage medium Increased main-storage capacity Faster input/output; tape oriented High-level programming languages (COBOL,FORTRAN) Great reduction in size and heat generation Increased speed and reliability Batch-oriented applications: billing, payroll processing, updating inventory files Examples: IBM 1401; Honeywell 200; CDC 1604
Third Generation 1965–1971	Use of integrated circuits Magnetic core and solid-state main storage More flexibility with input/output; disk oriented Smaller size and better performance and reliability Emergence of minicomputers Remote processing through communication Applications: airline reservation system, market forecasting, credit-card billing Examples: IBM System/360; NCR 395; Burroughs B5500; DEC PDP-11 Series (minicomputers)
Fourth Generation 1972–?	Use of large-scale integration Increased storage capacity and speed Greater versatility of input/output devices Introduction of microprocessors and microcomputers Applications: mathematical modeling and simulation, electronic funds transfer, computer-aided instruction, and home computers Examples: IBM 3033; Burroughs B7700; HP 3000 (minicomputer); Apple II (microcomputer)

summarizes the generations of computers and features of each. Figure 1-16 shows the various types and sizes of today's computers.

SILICON VALLEY
Nickname for the high-tech area in the Santa Clara Valley south of San Francisco.

As you can see from this history, many slow years passed on the path toward computers until the middle of this century when progress grew amazingly rapid. This recent period of computer development is filled with interesting tales of the entrepreneur. More than one successful company actually got started in someone's garage, such as Apple, Inc., and Hewlett-Packard Company. (These firms and so many others are located in one area of California that the general locale is frequently referred to as **Silicon Valley**, in honor of the chip.) Progress toward the fifth generation is expected to be made quickly since we now have computers to help. However, some observers claim the day of the entrepreneur is coming to a close due to the corporate domination of computer research.

FIGURE 1-16 State of the art computers are represented by a variety of sizes and capabilities. (Continued on Facing Page.)

a. The Cray-1, the first supercomputer developed in 1977, is one of approximately 70 systems implemented worldwide. By definition, a supercomputer performs at least 10 million instructions per second. Supercomputers are the most powerful and most expensive computers in existence; the price ranges from $10–15 million. Applications requiring such sophisticated processing needs include meteorology, aerodynamics, seismology, and atomic and nuclear physics.

b. Mainframes are less sophisticated than supercomputers and are produced by a wide variety of manufacturers. They cost between $200,000 and $1,000,000 or more and are used primarily by businesses, hospitals, universities, and banks that have large processing requirements.

c. Minicomputers appeared in the early 1970s and were designed for specialized applications. The cost for these machines averages between $15,000 and $200,000. Many minicomputers can be connected together in order to share common resources. Typical applications of minicomputers include engineering, industrial automation, and word processing.

d. Microcomputers, the least expensive category, are available from $100 to $5,000. These general-purpose machines are used in unlimited applications including recordkeeping, inventory, and word processing functions in both business and in the home.

ISSUE

IS COMPUTER PHOBIA SEXIST?

Walk into an elementary classroom and it is unlikely you will see any boy or girl showing fear of the computer. But walk into a business firm and you are likely to find employees who do. This fear is known as computer phobia. One question being asked is whether computer phobia is sexist. In a study done at the University of Texas, women were found to be more likely to fear taking a computer course before it began than male students. But during the course, women enjoyed their projects as much as the men and the fear of computers soon disappeared.

Historical evidence shows very little sexism in computer areas. After all, the world's first programmer, born in 1815, was a woman, Ada Augusta Byron Lovelace (see Profile). She planned problems for Babbage's analytical engine, and invented the loop—a useful structure that makes programming more efficient.

Women entered the area of computers in the late 1930s. Thomas Watson, Sr., founder of IBM (International Business Machines), used women college graduates to sell computers to business people. The stereotype of women existed, but Watson had the insight to use it to his advantage. If a woman could operate a computer, he reasoned, potential customers—businessmen—could be more easily convinced that the equipment was not too complicated.

During World War II, women began to secure jobs as computer programmers. They were hired to program the first operational computer, the ENIAC, because this task was considered to be of low priority in the war effort. And COBOL, a high-level language developed in the 1960s, was standardized with the assistance of Commodore Grace Hopper. This development greatly advanced the progress of software development.

Women's interest in computers has continued to the present. Genevieve Cerf, an instructor in Electrical Engineering at Columbia University, believes that women make better programmers than men do, because they are more organized, more verbal, and more likely to take the end user into consideration while writing the program. Studies by biologists and psychologists support the premise that women are better than men at skills that involve the left hemisphere of the brain—these skills include verbal and communication skills and logical skills such as calculations. Logic skills, especially, are essential to computer programming.

Many women enter computer careers indirectly through jobs in the financial, educational, and secretarial areas. One of the benefits for women who do obtain a computer science degree and enter the field directly is pay. According to a recent National Science Foundation study, such women earn almost 100 percent of the amount that men holding the same type of jobs earn. This fact may seem trivial, but it is not. In some occupations even today, women earn as little as 59 cents for every $1 earned by men. Equal pay draws much interest, and may be one reason that women account for 26 percent of computer professionals. In 1980, the National Science Foundation reported there were 90,200 female computer specialists. Yet, that was a 44 percent increase from 1978, suggesting that women were just beginning to enter the area in force.

Yet, are girls getting the education that they need to fill those jobs? And, if not, is it because girls are afraid of computers, or because parents don't encourage girls to enter computer fields? Enrollment analysis of 23 summer computer camps and classes held in 1983 with a total of 5,533 students showed a male to female ratio of three to one. And the more advanced the class, the lower the percentage of girls. While girls accounted for 27 percent of beginning and intermediate classes, the figure fell to 14 percent for advanced classes, and again, to 5 percent for higher-level classes. Also, the more expensive the camp or class, the lower the percentage of girls overall. Yet, it is not possible to tell from these figures whether parents are simply more reluctant to pay for early computer education for girls, or whether girls are indeed afflicted with computer phobia.

The problem may not be fear of computers but the cultural perception of the computer world as a male preserve. Some computer stores, for instance, were once stores for electrical parts. Since many of these stores still handle electrical items as well as computers, women may feel uneasy about going into such stores. The salesperson (generally male) tends to speak computer jargon, and this too may keep women (and men) with little computer background away from the stores.

Software packaging itself may reinforce this cultural perception. In a study done on software, 28 men were found to be shown on game packages compared with only four women.

Another study used 157 junior high school students who rated 75 computer games. The students were asked whether the games appealed mostly to boys, girls, or both. The students felt that 35 percent of the games were aimed primarily at boys, while only 5 percent were designed to appeal mostly to girls.

To successfully adapt to the social changes being caused by the computers, we must change our cultural expectations and sexist biases. Girls in our elementary schools are already programming computers. This type of education will be instrumental in changing the attitude and outlook of the younger generation.

Already, many experts claim that because of early computer education, girls who are now under the age of fifteen will never be afflicted with computer phobia. Whether most of those over fifteen are or will be is still debatable.

SUMMARY POINTS

- The amazing quality of the computer is its versatility; its effects can be felt in every aspect of life.
- From journalism to restaurant service, record keeping to bank machines, computers are affecting how we work, stay informed, and use our leisure time.
- Japan has aggressively sought a role for itself in computer research and technology, giving the United States strong competition.
- People have always been preoccupied with calculating the answers to problems and keeping track of the results. Developments preceding the computer that illustrate this trend include the abacus, Pascal's and Leibnitz's calculating machines, and Babbage's difference engine.
- The weaving industry was the site of the first "programmable" machine, using punched cards to instruct the loom. Hollerith later applied this concept in processing census data, developing machines that could read data punched onto cards. Accounting machines applied the same techniques for processing business data.
- The Mark I was the first automatic calculator and it introduced the usage of the binary language; ENIAC was the first true electronic computer, even though it had no internal memory.
- Von Neumann proposed storing instructions in the computer using machine language. This breakthrough led the way for the development of EDVAC using internal memory and stored instructions.
- First-generation computers used vacuum tubes to control internal operations. These machines were very large, unreliable, and generated a lot of heat.
- Second-generation computers relied on transistors for controlling internal operations. Transistors were much smaller, faster, and more reliable than vacuum tubes.
- Third-generation computers used solid-state integrated circuits rather than transistors to obtain reductions in size and cost together with increased reliability and speed.
- Fourth-generation computers rely on large-scale integration and continue to offer improvements in size, speed, and cost.
- Present computers utilize binary language.
- Programs are not usually written in binary code; they must be translated to machine language before processing.

REVIEW QUESTIONS

1. What are the Japanese looking for in their fifth-generation computer research?
2. What has been France's main contribution to popular computer applications?
3. Explain telecommuting.

4. How may portable microcomputers help lessen rush-hour traffic and reduce the need for office space?
5. Which major computer company traces its ancestry to government statistician Herman Hollerith and his Hollerith card?
6. Before the Mark I was developed in 1944, what factors had limited all the calculating machines in speed, size, capability, and adaptability?
7. What was the first computer designed specifically for data processing rather than scientific use?
8. What scientific advance replaced the vacuum tube?
9. What advance replaced the transistors?
10. When and by whom was the first commercially feasible minicomputer introduced?
11. Which generation of computers was the first to use remote terminals?
12. How are computers important to the space shuttle program?
13. Describe some computer applications in the preparation and sale of food.

DISCUSSION QUESTIONS

1. Why do you think the general public of the late 1950s was so unwilling to accept the idea of space exploration as a real possibility?
2. Does a gender gap exist today in regard to computer use? What factors may influence the width of such a gap?
3. Are fifth-generation computers to be feared or loved if they embody the concepts of human thinking?
4. What types of research noted in this chapter are being enhanced by the computer's special capabilities?
5. Why is computer superiority important to the United States and other nations?

CHAPTER 2
THE MACHINE ITSELF: HARDWARE

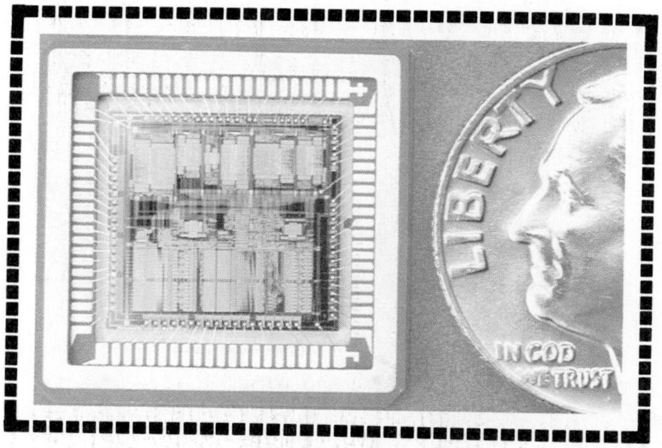

OUTLINE

ARTICLE

SAFETY PROMPTS COMPUTER USE IN DRUGSTORES

PAUL A. ENGELMAYER

Last spring, a customer entered a drugstore near Syracuse, N.Y., with a prescription for the drug Cyclapen. The drug could have seriously hurt her.

The woman was allergic to a Cyclapen ingredient, penicillin. Her new doctor didn't know that. But the pharmacist, by checking his new patient-records computer, found out. After consulting with her doctor, he substituted a penicillin-free drug.

"She was ecstatic that he caught it in time," recalls the pharmacist. "If she'd taken it, she would have been in shock by the time she was in the parking lot. Now, she's a regular here."

Such computers are the latest craze in drugstores. Hoping to cash in on consumer concern about medicines, chain drugstores are scrambling to install computers that tell pharmacists whether a particular drug is safe for a customer. . . .

EXTENDING LEGAL LIABILITY?

The computers worry some people. Some say the machines make it easy for outsiders to get private medical information. And some pharmacists worry that the machines will extend their legal liability.

But the computers have nonetheless become popular because bad prescriptions are such a big problem—last year they cost Americans more than $4.5 billion in hospital expenses and billions more in doctors' bills according to the Association of Chain Drugstores. Some drugs triggered allergies; others combined harmfully with other medications. Some people had only headaches or stomach cramps. But at least 100 died, estimates the Boston Collaborative Drug Surveillance Program, which has studied the effects of interactions.

The druggists' machines are ordinary computer terminals. Customers provide a detailed medical history, including a prescription record, a list of nonprescription drugs commonly taken and a history of dietary habits, chronic conditions and allergies. When customers come to any affiliated drugstore, their computer files are checked before prescriptions are filled. If any problems turn up, the pharmacist consults the doctor.

Pharmacists say most bad drug interactions occur when patients get prescriptions from different doctors. Medicare-Glaser Co., a 100-pharmacy chain based in St. Louis, estimates that every day, each of its stores prevents two or three severe interactions—ones that would have caused stomach pains, depression, internal bleeding or worse. . . .

By most accounts, Medicare-Glaser was first to develop a computer system. It installed the first 15 of its 47 drug-interaction computers in 1978. In 1981, it began aggressively advertising the computers on TV, radio and in newspapers.

The payoff was quick. At a time when the prescription-drug market had stopped growing, Medicare-Glaser's prescription volume shot up 10% in three months. "And those were the summer months, which are usually famine for us," says Vice President Ken Anderson. Sales are still climbing.

Now about half of the nation's 25 largest drugstore chains are installing or testing drug-interaction services. Among them are Fays Drug Co., Peoples Drug Stores Inc. and Longs Drug Stores Inc.

A NECESSITY FOR DRUGGISTS?

". . . The pharmacist who doesn't have this won't exist in five or 10 years," says an executive of a drugstore chain that is fighting to catch up. "We'll just have to have it to stay in the ballpark."

Drug chains say the boom in drug-interaction services began for two reasons. As computers got cheaper, drugstores started using them for billing and inventory. It was then relatively easy to add drug-interaction programs.

Consumers also started to demand more information about drug side-effects. "The major drug chains are banging down our door," says Robert Bachman, executive director of the National Council for Patient Information and Education, which supplies wallet cards and pamphlets with drug information. "Patient education is a way to make your pharmacy more popular than others."

Still, some customers decline to use the service, particularly those on psychiatric drugs, who worry about privacy. Many pharmacies concede it is impossible to secure their terminals from sophisticated computer thieves. But they play down the mischief a thief could do because the information isn't of much use.

Many doctors seem to appreciate that the computers double-check their prescriptions. Dr. William Choate, a general practitioner in Annapolis, Md., says pharmacists from Giant Food have called him three times in the last month to change prescriptions. . . .

But pharmacists say some doctors are peeved at being second-guessed. . . .

Dr. Choate says, "There are some physicians who feel intimidated, a little insecure. They feel the pharmacist is trying to practice medicine. I don't think that's true at all. It's simply a personality problem."

The drug chains worry that the computers cause legal problems. "If you have a system and you don't catch a bad interaction, are you liable? And if you don't have a good system, are you liable because you don't have the state of the art?" asks an executive at a drugstore chain. . . .

To pharmacists, however, those fears remain remote. "It's a good selling point," says one. "It allows us to practice even more professionally than we did before. It's good for business. It's beyond me how any body couldn't want it."

Patient-records computers in many drugstores are being used to lessen the possibility of a harmful drug interaction with patients. Much information on the various prescription drugs and the patient health records must be stored for later retrieval. The hardware, all the tangible parts of the computer, will be discussed in this chapter.

INTRODUCTION

The hardware of the computer is the physical devices that comprise the computer system: the central processing unit, the input devices, the output devices, and the storage devices. Basically, hardware includes all parts of the computer that are tangible. Hardware is *not* operating systems, concepts, or programs (these are software). Hardware consists of only those parts of the computer that one could reach out and touch.

THE CENTRAL PROCESSING UNIT

The **central processing unit,** or **CPU,** is the essence of the computer's hardware. It is the "brain" of the computer. It tells the other parts of the computer what to do; it decides what to do with the instructions that the programmer gives it; and it ensures that the tasks assigned to it are properly carried out.

CENTRAL PROCESSING UNIT (CPU)
Acts as the "brain" of the computer.

The CPU is composed of three separate units—the control unit, the arithmetic/logic unit, and the primary storage unit (Figure 2-1). The **control unit** is, quite literally, in control of the operations. It reads the actual instructions and tells the other computer parts what to do. The control unit directs the appropriate input device to send the necessary data. It keeps

CONTROL UNIT
Controls the execution of programs.

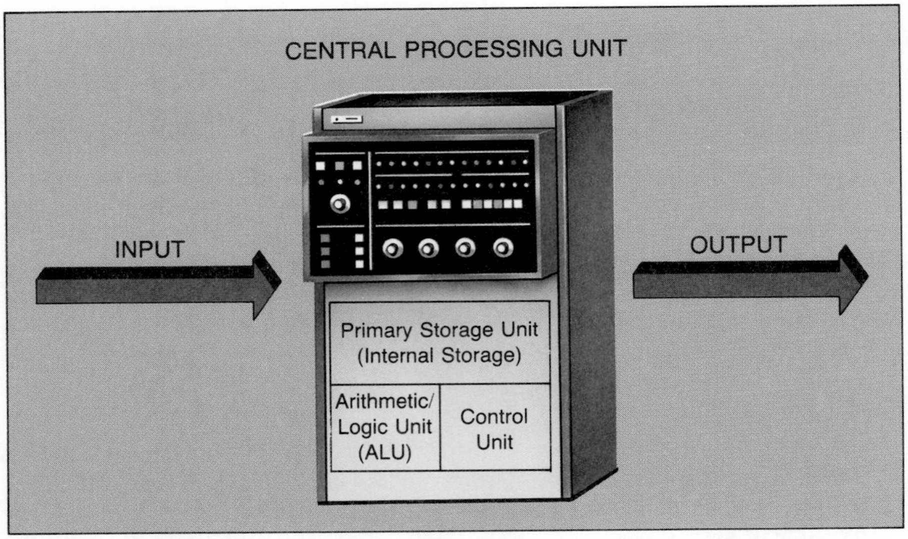

FIGURE 2-1 The Computer and Its Parts

track of what parts of the program have already been executed and which ones are left to be done. Finally, it controls the execution of the specific instructions, collects the output, and sends the output to the designated output device.

ARITHMETIC/LOGIC UNIT (ALU)
Executes mathematical and logic statements.

The **arithmetic/logic unit (ALU)** is the computer's own personal mathematician. It executes all arithmetic and logic statements. Logic statements aren't quite so straightforward as arithmetic statements, but they are equally easy to understand. A logic statement is a statement that makes a comparison and then does something based on the result. For example, if today is Friday, then pick up paycheck and go to the bank; if not, don't. Obviously, this isn't quite the type of logic statement that the computer would work with, but the idea is the same. More likely, the computer would want to know: If this is the end of the input data, then make the calculations and output the results. If not, read the rest of the input. Arithmetic and logic operations are the only type of instructions that the ALU can execute. But when you think about it, you will realize that almost everything you want the computer to do is either an arithmetic or logic problem. The only noticeable exceptions are reading input and printing output. (These are controlled by the control unit.)

PRIMARY STORAGE UNIT
The computer's internal memory.

The **primary storage unit** is in charge of storing data and programs in the computer's internal memory. It is very important to distinguish this internal memory, called primary storage, from external memory, called auxiliary storage. The primary storage unit is a part of the actual internal hardware of the computer. Without the primary storage unit, the computer could not work because it would not be able to store the programs. Auxiliary storage is not necessary for the computer to function; it is not part of its internal hardware. The CPU can access only primary storage; information between primary and auxiliary storage is transferred through electrical lines.

PROFILE

JOHN VINCENT ATANASOFF

It took 32 years before the matter was settled legally, but in 1974 a federal court finally declared that John Vincent Atanasoff was the true inventor of the electronic digital computer—a credit traditionally given to John W. Mauchly and J. Presper Eckert for the ENIAC. As is so often the case, necessity was also the mother of this invention.

Atanasoff first felt the need to have a computing machine while he was working on his doctorate in math and physics. After he completed his degree and accepted a teaching post at Iowa State, Atanasoff became even more acutely aware of the limitations in conventional calculating since, by this time, he had a number of graduate students whose work he had to monitor.

With the aid of his assistant, Clifford Berry, Atanasoff completed his prototype computer in late 1939. Three years later the two had their first working model, the "Atanasoff-Berry Computer (ABC)," a serial, binary electromechanical device. But Atanasoff could neither interest such companies as IBM or Remington Rand in his invention nor gain patent rights for himself.

In addition to serving in various industrial and governmental positions, he also established two companies of his own, Ordnance Engineering and Cybernetics. Atanasoff has also devoted more than a decade to another project—developing a new universal alphabet. Unfortunately, the rest of the world has not shown much enthusiasm with the project. Atanasoff, however, has thoroughly documented his ideas on the new alphabet to protect his idea. If the alphabet ever becomes adopted, there will be no confusion as to its founder.

Most current primary storage hardware consists of **semiconductors** which have their memory circuitry on silicon chips. The data are stored in **bit cells,** located on the chips, which can be in either an "on" or an "off" state. Each cell holds a BInary digiT (bit). The cells are arranged so that they can be written to or read from as needed.

Basically, the primary storage unit holds the program that is being executed, as well as its input, output, and intermediate results of any calculations. When a program is entered into the computer, the control unit sends the program to the primary storage unit. The control unit then retrieves one line at a time from the primary storage unit. Therefore, the pri-

SEMICONDUCTOR
A type of primary storage that stores data in bit cells located on silicon chips.

BIT CELL
Used in semiconductors; stores data by designating each cell as "on" or "off."

CHIP MAKING PROCESS

Integrated circuitry, synonymous with silicon chips, is the technology responsible for making computers perform faster and more economically. The chip-making process requires sophisticated engineering and manufacturing techniques. The following photographs show many of the steps involved in this complex process.

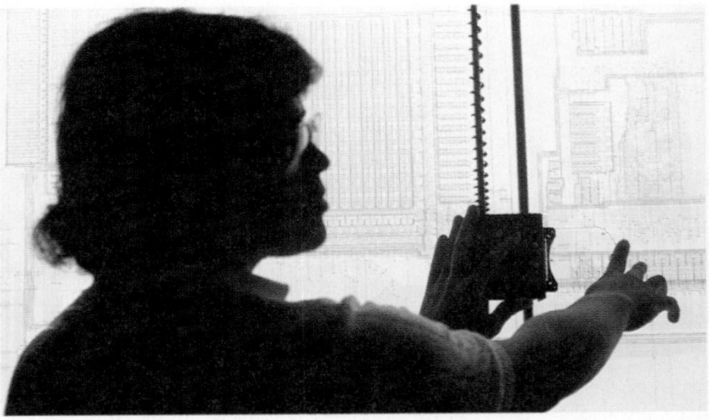

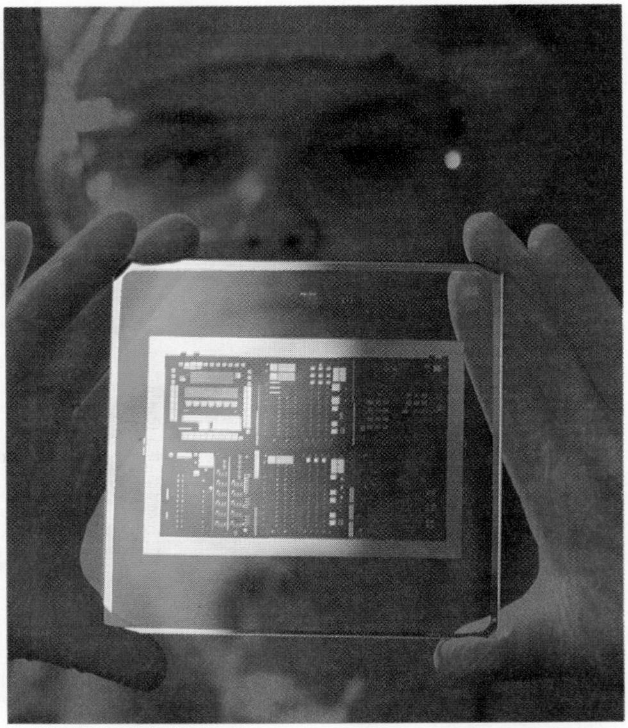

ABOVE
Traditionally, the design phase started with circuit designers drafting huge (8 sq. ft.) "blueprint-like diagrams" of the circuit. This hand-drawn information was then converted into computer memory by a process known as digitizing.

Today, experimental systems are being used to design circuitry directly on the computer. This is made possible by computer-assisted design (CAD) technology.

RIGHT
The model generated by the digitized or CAD process is then stored on tape and used to prepare a photomask. The reduced negative shown here is a photomask; it contains the same intricate lines as the hand-drawn diagram.

LEFT
The photomask is scaled down even further in this step. The final photomask is the size of a single chip—1/100 of a square inch. The photomask will be used in a highly refined photoengraving process that "etches" the circuitry onto a silicon wafer.

Meanwhile, silicon wafers, the foundation substance for all chips, have been prepared. The wafers (about three inches in diameter) are manufactured from silicon, an abundant element extracted from quartz rock. Wafers are then placed in ovens at a specific temperature to form oxides and other layers of minerals on the surface where the etching will be done.

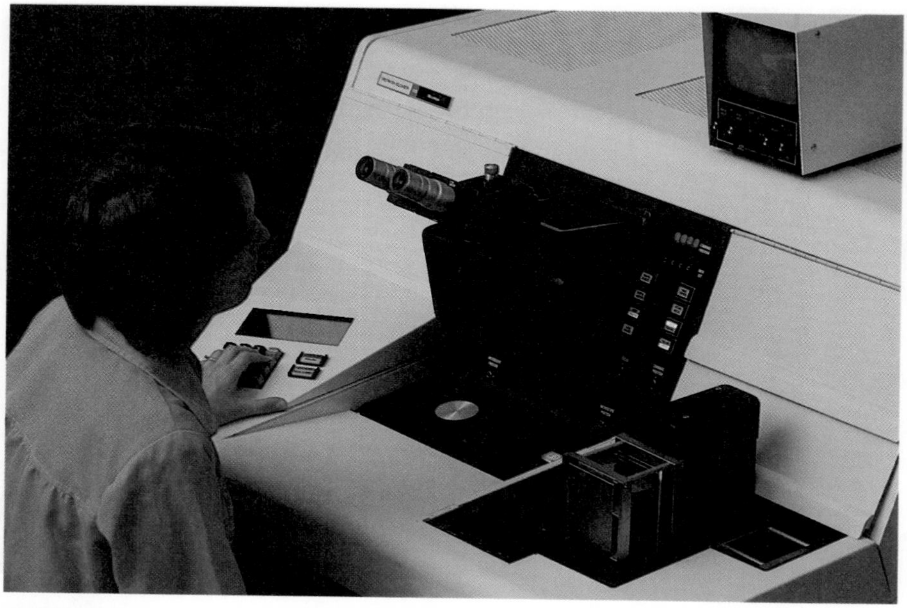

After the wafers are bathed in a type of photographic emulsion, called photoresist, the scaled-down photomasks are placed over each wafer. Shown here is a worker carefully aligning the mask over the wafer using a high-powered microscope to ensure perfect registration. Once the mask is in place, the wafer is exposed to ultraviolet light. The ultraviolet light causes the patterns from the photomask to be etched onto the wafer.

LEFT
The next step is the acid bath. At this step, parts not exposed to the ultraviolet light are washed away, leaving the layer of elements formed by the photomask.

BELOW
Here is a completed wafer containing three hundred chips. Upon close examination, you can see that each square has been engraved with circuitry.

Next, the wafer is cut apart into individual chips by a laser process. Laser beams are used for the necessary cutting precision.

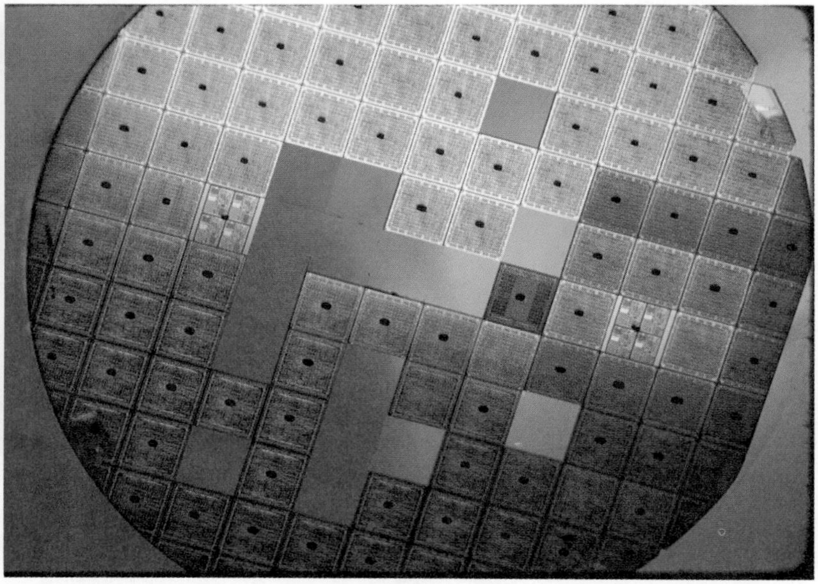

Here, selected chips have been cut from the wafer.

Now the chip is mounted onto a carrier. The gold wires surrounding the chip connect it to other chips and circuitry.

Finally, the chips (in their carriers) are assembled according to function onto circuit boards.

mary storage unit acts somewhat like a shelf upon which statements, instructions, and results are placed when they aren't being read by the control unit.

All three parts of the central processing unit work together to enable the computer to function. Together they are often called the "computer proper" because in some microcomputers, they *are* the computer. In any computer, the CPU is the central core.

Computers derive most of their amazing power from three features; speed, accuracy, and memory. Generally, computer speed is expressed as the time required to perform one operation. The following units of time apply:

UNIT	SYMBOL	FRACTIONS OF A SECOND	
Millisecond	ms	one-thousandth	(1/1,000)
Microsecond	μs	one-millionth	(1/1,000,000)
Nanosecond	ns	one-billionth	(1/1,000,000,000)
Picosecond	ps	one-trillionth	(1/1,000,000,000,000)

Today's computers can complete computations in a matter of **nanoseconds.**

NANOSECOND
One-billionth of a second.

A nanosecond is one-billionth of a second. The best way to comprehend just how small a nanosecond is is to compare it visually with one second. In the computer, computations are made electrically. The speed of electricity is approximately the speed of light. Thus, in one second the electricity used for computations will travel 186,000 miles. In one nanosecond that electricity will travel 11.8 inches.

MORE ON INTERNAL STORAGE
Storage Locations and Addresses

When the CPU stores programs, input data, and output, it does not do so randomly. These items are stored in specific memory locations that can then be accessed by their addresses to retrieve their contents.

To process information, the CPU's control unit must first locate in storage each instruction and piece of data. Computer storage can be compared with a large array of mailboxes. Each mailbox is a specific location and can hold one item of information. Since each location in storage has a distinct address, stored-program instructions can locate particular items by giving their addresses.

Suppose, for instance, the computer is instructed to calculate an employee's salary by subtracting TOTAL TAX from his or her GROSS PAY. Let's say that TOTAL TAX is stored at Mailbox 101 and has a value of $50 and that GROSS PAY is stored at Mailbox 108 and has a value of $260 (Figure 2-2). The calculation is then made by telling the computer to subtract the contents of 101 (TOTAL TAX) from 108 (GROSS PAY).

A better way of keeping track of storage locations for the programmer

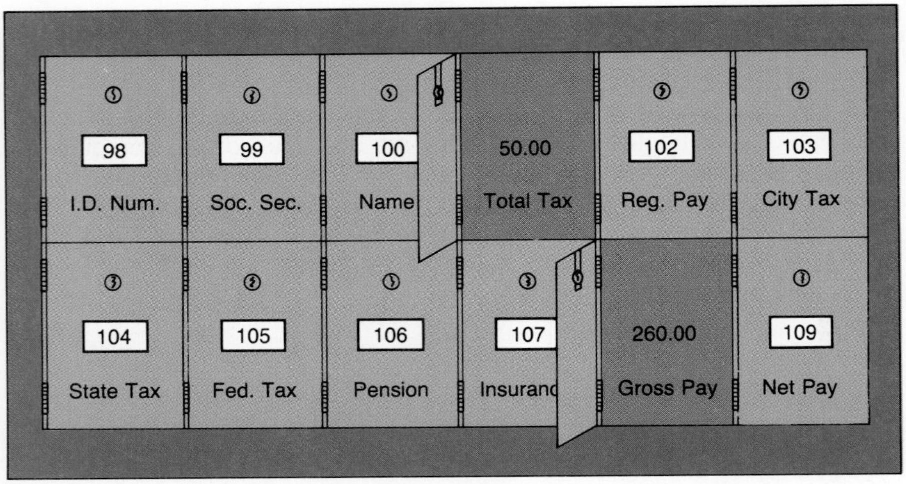

FIGURE 2-2 Each Mailbox Represents a Location in Storage with a Specific Address

FIGURE 2-3 Bubble Memory Section Magnified 1,500 Times

is to use symbolic names, or **variables,** such as TOTAL TAX or GROSS PAY, to represent the numerical storage addresses. Then, when the programmer tells the computer to subtract TOTAL TAX from GROSS PAY, the computer concludes that it should subtract the contents of 101 from the contents of 108.

Although the variable name (the storage address) itself does not change, the data stored at the location may. The value of TOTAL TAX and GROSS PAY are likely to change with each employee, but the addresses of TOTAL TAX and GROSS PAY will not.

VARIABLE
A symbolic name used to refer to a memory address.

Additional Memories

In addition to primary storage (internal memory) and auxiliary storage (external memory), there are a few types of memory that are difficult to categorize because of special properties. These are bubble memories, ROMs, PROMs, and EPROMs.

BUBBLE MEMORY
Potential alternate for primary and auxiliary storage.

Bubble Memory The **bubble memory** (Figure 2-3) is difficult to classify because it is being produced as a potential alternate for both primary and auxiliary storage. It uses magnetized spots, or bubbles, on a thin film of semiconductor material. To store data, the bubbles' positions are shifted on the surface of the material. These bubbles keep their magnetism indefinitely—and they can store much data. A bubble memory module that is only slightly larger than a quarter can store 20,000 characters of data.

Although some manufacturers use bubble memories in computers, the more common use of bubble memory is for providing limited storage in input/output devices. High cost and production difficulty have been the chief limitations to the wide use and acceptance of bubble memories.

Monolithic integrated circuits, better known as semiconductor or silicon chips, were invented by Jack Kilby in 1958.

Kilby began his work in the electronics industry in 1947 when he was hired by Milwaukee's Centralab Division of Globe-Union, Inc.—a manufacturer of radio and television components. His interest in technology grew when he heard of William Shockley's work on the transistor at Bell Labs in 1952. In fact, Kilby attended the first ten-day seminar that explained the transistor.

Soon after the seminar, Kilby joined Texas Instruments and was assigned to the Micro-Module project. The goal of the project was to interconnect miniaturized components (complete electronic circuits) by standardizing the size and shape, stacking them vertically, and running wires through the stack. Although a successful prototype was developed, Kilby realized that it would be more efficient to use a horizontal layout and more cost effective to use silicon instead of germanium. The company granted him $100,000 to build another prototype, and Kilby introduced the first silicon integrated circuit in September, 1958. By February, 1959, he received a patent, and the invention was released to the public.

The integrated circuit (IC) led to significant decreases in the cost and size of electronic equipment and created new applications for electronics in communications control and information processing.

Kilby was awarded the National Medal of Science in 1969 and was inducted into the National Inventors Hall of Fame in 1982. In addition to the IC patent, he holds another 30 patents for inventions—including an early handheld calculator and a solar-energy collection and conversion system.

PROFILE

JACK KILBY

Read-Only Memory (ROM) Computers can perform such complex functions as taking square roots and evaluating exponents. These functions can be built into either a computer system's hardware or software. Building them into the hardware creates the advantages of speed and reliability, since the operations are part of the actual computer circuitry. But building them into software allows more flexibility, even though carrying out functions built into software is slower and more subject to producing errors.

Functions built into the hardware are placed in **read-only memory (ROM).** Read-only memory instructions are **hard-wired**—that is, they cannot be changed or deleted by stored-program instructions. The only method of changing its contents is by altering the physical construction of the circuits.

A direct result of this characteristic is microprogramming. A **microprogram** is a sequence of instructions built into read-only memory to carry out functions (such as calculating square roots) that otherwise would have to be directed at a much slower speed by stored-program instructions. Microprograms are usually supplied by computer manufacturers

READ-ONLY MEMORY (ROM)
Special type of internal memory into which programs can be "hard-wired."

HARD-WIRED
A program permanently built into ROM.

MICROPROGRAM
A program hard-wired into ROM.

and cannot be altered by users. However, microprogramming allows the basic operations of the computer to be tailored to the needs of users. If all instructions that a computer can execute are located in ROM, a complete new set of instructions can be put in place by changing the ROM chip. This is, in effect, what happens when you change the game cartridge in your home computer.

PROGRAMMABLE READ-ONLY MEMORY (PROM)
Internal memory that can be programmed rather than hard-wired.

A version of ROM that can be programmed instead of hard-wired is **programmable read-only memory (PROM).** PROM can be programmed by the manufacturer or it can be shipped blank for the end user to program. Once programmed, however, its contents are unalterable. PROM enables the end user to have the advantage of ROM as well as the flexibility to meet special needs. A problem with PROM, though, is that mistakes programmed into the unit cannot be corrected. To overcome this drawback, **erasable programmable read-only memory (EPROM)** has been developed (Figure 2-4). This memory unit can be erased but only through certain processes, such as being bathed in ultraviolet light.

ERASABLE PROGRAMMABLE READ-ONLY MEMORY (EPROM)
Can be erased through special processes.

RANDOM-ACCESS MEMORY (RAM)
Plug-in storage that can input data as fast as one microprocessor can handle it.

Random-Access Memory (RAM) Chips **Random-access memory (RAM)** is the major type of memory used in primary storage. RAM can be either read from or written to and is a nonpermanent type of memory; that is, unlike ROM which is permanent, when the power is turned off, everything in RAM is automatically erased. Also, as the name would suggest, RAM can be randomly accessed.

The term "RAM chip" generally refers to additional RAM memory that is purchased once the computer is already in use to increase the capability of the machine. In some cases, the user can install the additional RAM chips simply by plugging them into the circuit board. (These RAM chips come with detailed directions explaining how this is done.) Other RAM chips must be installed by the manufacturer or service personnel. Whether the RAM chip can be installed by the user depends mostly on the design of the machine into which it is being installed. Because they are easy to use, plug-in RAM chips are commonly used to add memory to microcomputers.

Registers

REGISTER
Temporary holding area for instructions and data located in the CPU.

Registers are temporary holding areas for instructions and data. Even though they are located in the CPU, they are not addressed as or considered part of the primary storage. Registers can receive information, hold it, and transfer it very quickly as directed by the control unit of the CPU.

A register works something like a standard pocket calculator. The person using the calculator acts as the control unit by transferring numbers from a sheet of paper to the display (register) of the calculator. (The paper is similar in function to the primary storage unit of the CPU.) When the calculation is complete, the calculator displays the result. The person (control unit) then transfers the result shown on the calculator's display (register) back to the sheet of paper (primary storage).

ACCUMULATOR
A register that accumulates results of calculations.

There are various types of registers, each named for the specific function it performs. For example, an **accumulator** is a register that accumu-

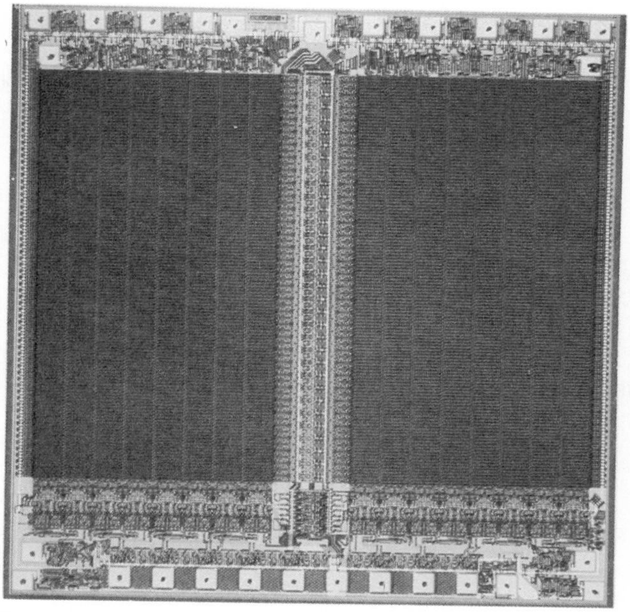

a.

b.

c.

FIGURE 2-4 EPROM

a. EPROM chip.
b. EPROM chip mounted in a plastic carrier with pins that allow it to be plugged into a circuitry board.
c. Once the chip is mounted into its carrier, it can be plugged into this device where it can be programmed.

STORAGE REGISTER
Holds information coming from or going to the primary storage unit.

INSTRUCTION REGISTER
Holds instructions being decoded by the control unit.

ADDRESS REGISTER
Holds the addresses of data called for by instructions.

GENERAL-PURPOSE REGISTER
Can be used as an accumulator or an address register.

lates results of computations (such as sums). A **storage register** holds information being sent to or taken from the primary storage unit. During program execution, each instruction is transferred to an **instruction register,** where it is decoded by the control unit. The address of a data item called for by an instruction is kept in an **address register.** Some computers have only **general-purpose registers,** which can be used for both arithmetic and addressing functions. The numbers and sizes of registers in computers vary.

Registers are used to complete all calculations and manipulations that are performed by the computer. However, unless you are programming in assembly language (a low-level language that resembles machine language), you will never need consciously to work with registers. Like the CPU, registers are invisible to the user; that is, although we know the hardware exists, we generally never see it.

AUXILIARY STORAGE

AUXILIARY STORAGE
Storage that is physically located outside the CPU.

SEQUENTIAL-ACCESS STORAGE
Storage that must be accessed sequentially, that is, read from the beginning.

DIRECT-ACCESS STORAGE
Data does not have to be accessed sequentially; it can be accessed directly.

Auxiliary storage (that which is outside the CPU) is used to store large amounts of data at a lower cost than primary storage. Access to data in auxiliary storage can be either direct or sequential. The method depends on the storage medium used (Figure 2-5). Magnetic tape and cassette tape provide **sequential-access storage.** This means that the computer must start at the beginning of the tape and read what is stored until it comes to the desired data. In contrast, storage media such as magnetic disks and magnetic drums do not have to be read sequentially; data can be accessed directly. Thus, these media are said to be **direct-access storage.** Direct-access media allow for faster retrieval than do sequential-access media.

Sequential Access

Magnetic Tape A magnetic tape is a continuous strip of coated plastic tape wound onto a reel. Its plastic base is treated with a magnetizable coating, usually iron oxide. Normally, the tape is ½-inch wide and is wound in lengths of 2,400 feet.

Data are stored on magnetic tape by magnetizing small spots of the iron-oxide coating. Although these spots can be read by the computer, they are invisible to the human eye. Large volumes of information can be stored on a single tape. As many as 1,600 characters per inch are common, and some tapes can store 6,250 characters per inch. A 2,400-foot reel of tape can store as much data as 400,000 punched cards.

TAPE DRIVE
Used to read from or write to magnetic tape

When a program calls for the information it contains, the magnetic tape is mounted onto a **tape drive** (Figure 2-6). The drive has a read/write head (Figure 2-7) that creates or reads the bits as the tape moves past it. When it is reading, the head detects the magnetized areas and converts them into electrical pulses to send to the CPU. When writing, the head magnetizes the appropriate spots on the tape while erasing any previously stored data.

FIGURE 2-5 **Auxiliary Storage for a Computer System**

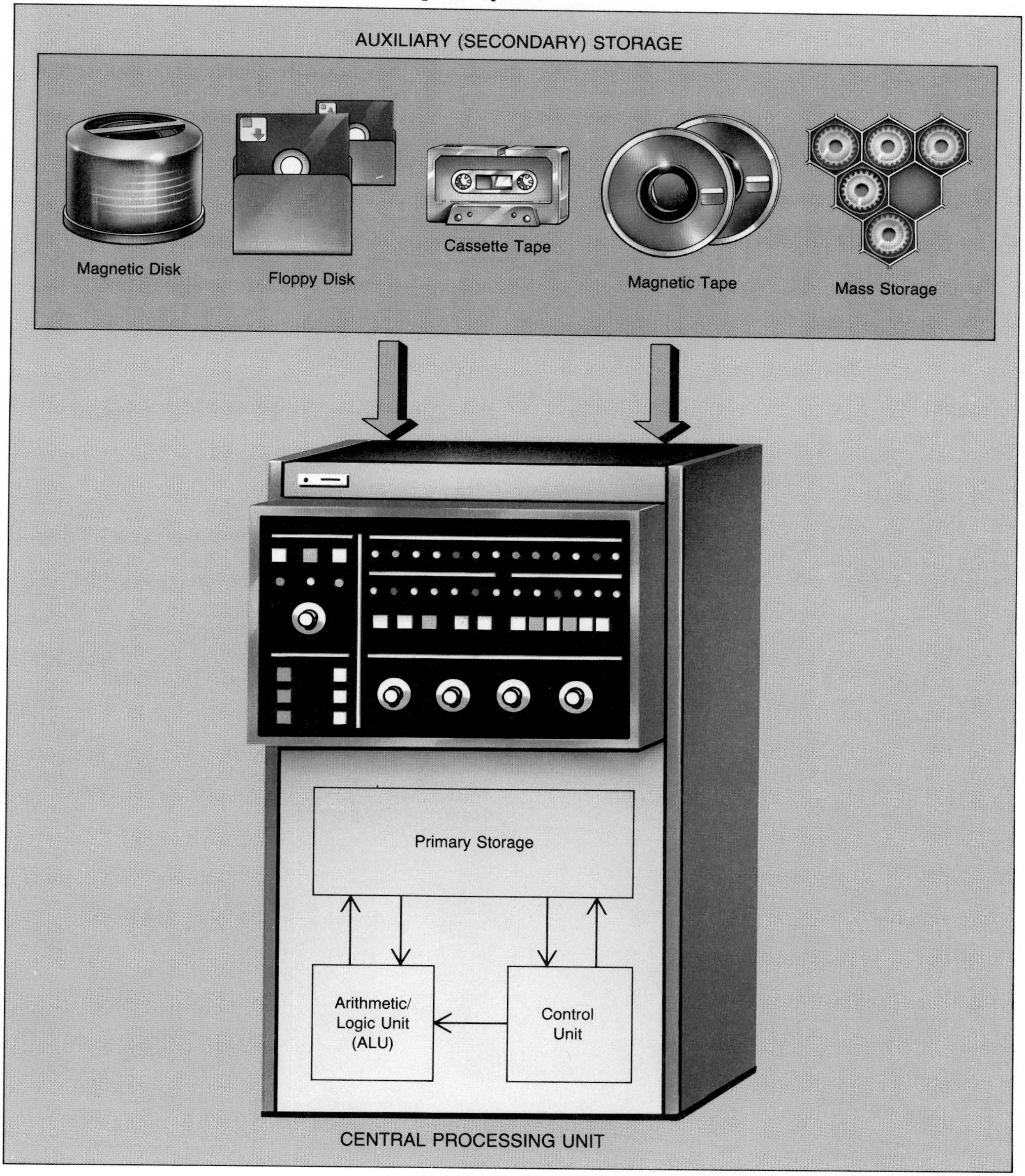

FIGURE 2-6 Magnetic Tape Drives

TAPE CASSETTE
A sequential storage medium; uses high-density digital recording tape to record data.

Cassette Tape For small computers that do not have a need for large amounts of auxiliary storage, **tape cassettes** have been developed. Tape cassettes look like those used in audio recording—and some can be used that way—but those made for storing data are constructed of high-quality, high-density digital recording tape (Figure 2-8).

The low cost and convenience of tape cassettes have greatly increased their use for input, output, and storage in minicomputer and microcomputer systems. Tape cassettes are an ideal storage system for

FIGURE 2-7 Recording on Magnetic Tape

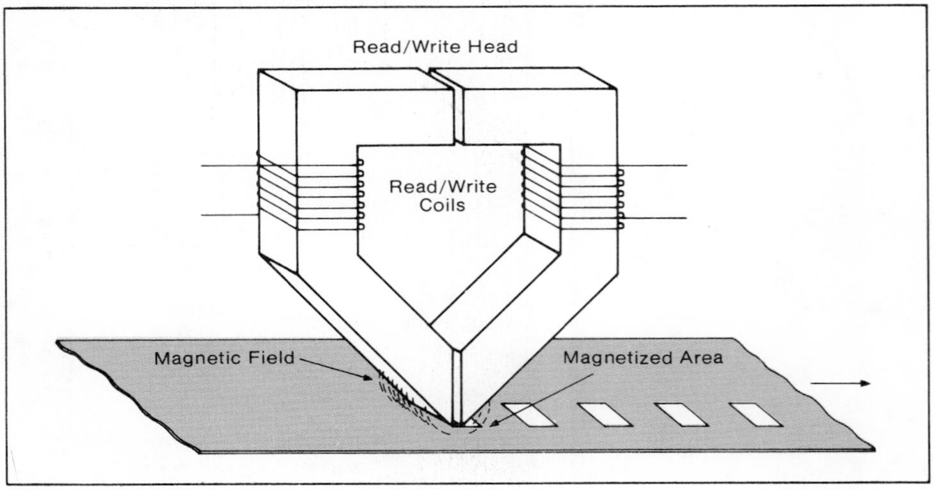

FIGURE 2-8 Data Tape Cassette

home computers. They can be used with a regular cassette player, are easy to store, and are easy to keep secure since the cassettes can be removed and kept with the user.

Direct Access

Magnetic Disk The **magnetic disk** is a metal platter usually 14 inches in diameter also coated on both sides with a magnetizable material. A magnetic disk resembles a phonograph record, but it has smooth surfaces instead of a record's characteristic grooves. Still, a disk unit does store and retrieve data in a manner reminiscent of a standard phonograph in operation. The disk is rotated while a read/write head is positioned above its magnetic surface. Instead of spiraling into the center of the disk, as a phonograph needle does, the data are stored in a set of concentric circles. Each circle is called a **track**. One track never touches another, as illustrated in Figure 2-9. A typical disk has 200 tracks on each surface.

In most disk storage devices, several disks are assembled to form a **disk pack** (Figure 2-10) and mounted on a center shaft. The individual disks are spaced on the shaft to allow room for a read/write head to move between them (Figure 2-11). The disk pack in Figure 2-11 has 11 disks and provides 20 usable recording surfaces. The extreme top and bottom surfaces are not used for storing data because they are likely to become scratched or nicked. A disk pack may contain up to six to 11 disks.

A disk pack must be positioned in a disk drive for the data it contains to be processed. The **disk drive** rotates all disks in unison at speeds of

MAGNETIC DISK
A coated metal platter, direct-access storage device.

TRACK
A concentric circle on a magnetic disk in which data is stored.

DISK PACK
A set of several magnetic disks mounted on a center shaft.

DISK DRIVE
A machine that rotates the magnetic disks for data processing.

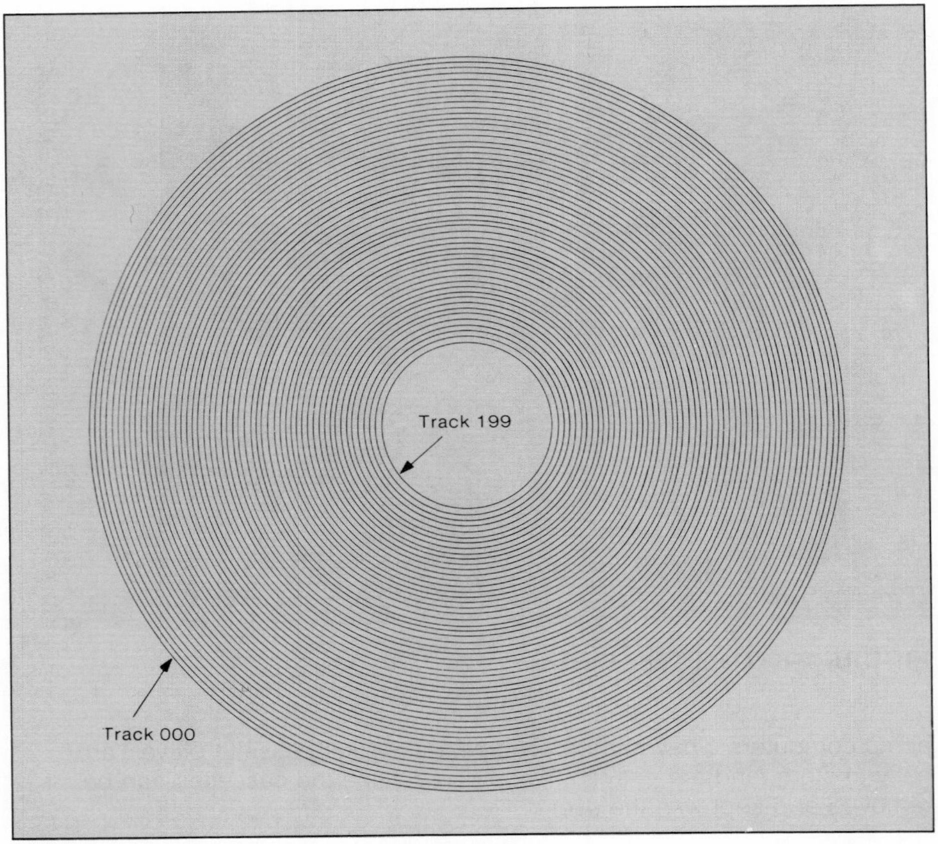

FIGURE 2-9 Top View of Disk Surface Showing Concentric Tracks

FIGURE 2-10 Disk Pack

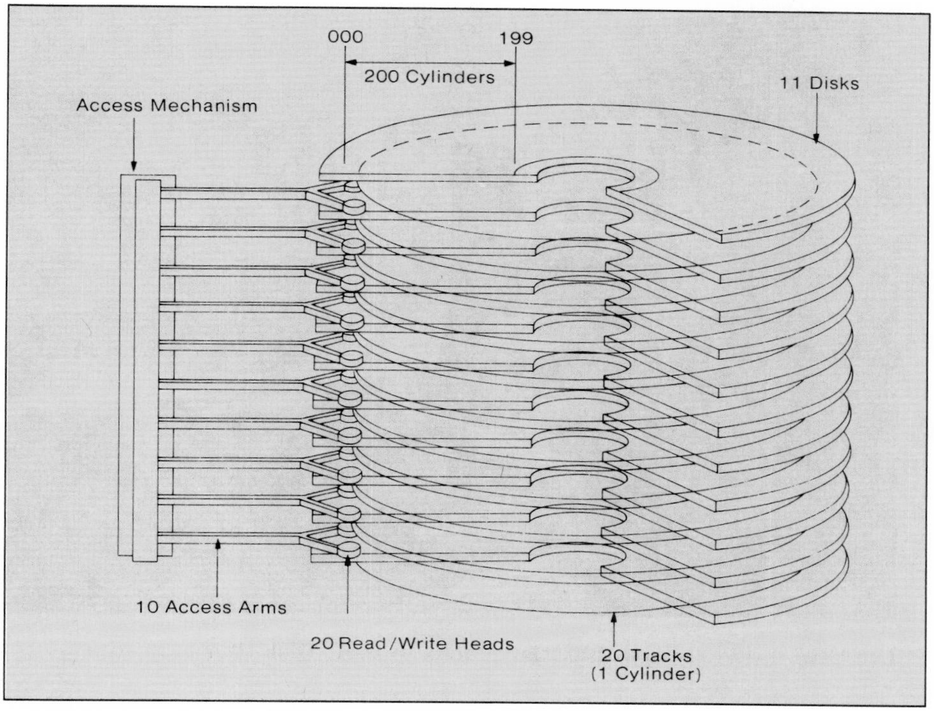

FIGURE 2-11 Disk Pack Showing Read/Write Heads

from 40 to 3,600 revolutions a second. In some models the disk packs can be removed (Figure 2-12); in others they are permanently mounted on the disk drive.

As we noted, data on a disk are read or written by read/write heads between the disks. Most disk units have one read/write head for each disk-recording surface. All the heads are permanently connected to an access mechanism. Some disk units have one read/write head for each track on each disk. The access time is much faster with this type of disk unit since the **access mechanism** does not need to move from track to track. But such units are rarely used because of their high costs.

ACCESS MECHANISM
Contains the read/write head that allows data to be read from or written to the disk.

Because disks provide direct access, they are routinely used to store data about which frequent inquiries are made. Depending upon the type of drive, transfer rates of up to 850,000 characters a second are possible.

Floppy Disk The **flexible disk** (also called **diskette** or **floppy disk**) was introduced in 1973 (Figure 2-13) to replace punched cards for data entry. But it can also store programs and data files. These disks are made of plastic and coated with an oxide substance and are available in two standard sizes—8 inches and 5¼ inches. Recently, a new 3-inch micro disk has been introduced. Because they are inexpensive, the disks are very popular for use with minicomputer systems, point-of-sale terminals, and personal computers. They are reusable, easy to store, and weigh less

FLEXIBLE (FLOPPY) DISK
A low-cost, random-access data storage unit made of plastic.

FIGURE 2-12 Removable Disk Packs in their Disk Storage Units

FIGURE 2-13 Eight-inch and 5¼-inch Floppy Disks

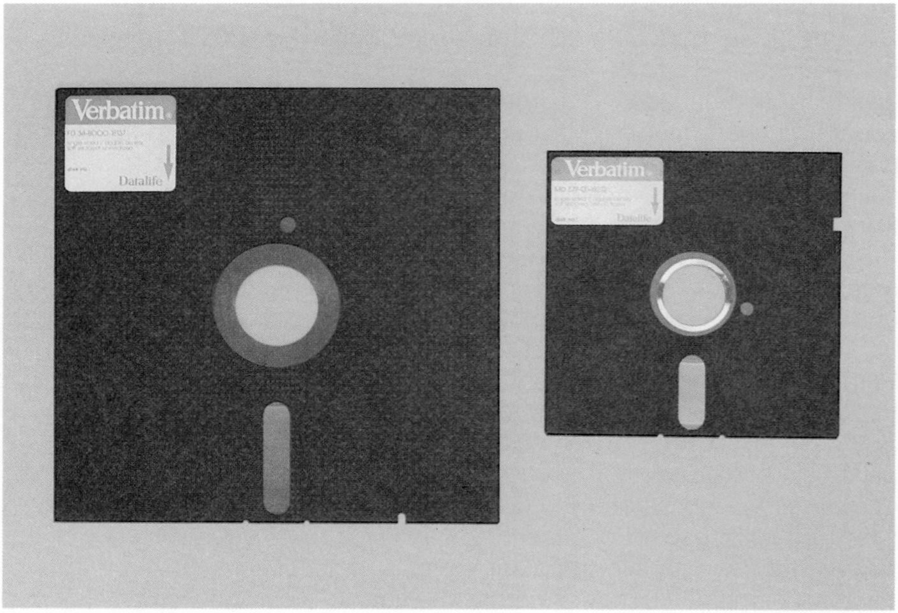

than two ounces each. They are readily interchangeable and can even be mailed safely. Since flexible disks can be removed from the systems that use them, they provide the system with added security. A typical floppy disk can store as much data as 3,000 punched cards, and the storage capacity is rapidly being expanded. Their capacity extends from 100 K to 1 megabyte (one million bytes) on the 5¼-inch disks and 125 K to 1.2 megabytes on the 8-inch disks. (**K** is an abbreviation for kilobyte. It stands for 1,024 bytes in computer terminology.)

K
Abbreviation for kilo; 1024 bytes in computer terms.

Mass Storage

Using primary storage is very fast because access to data is direct and requires no physical movement of parts. The speed of electricity is, in effect, the limiting factor. Primary storage is also very expensive. Disk storage is less expensive and provides direct-access capabilities at slower speeds. But even this form tends to be expensive when very large amounts of data must be stored for direct-access processing.

To meet this need, system designers have developed **mass storage devices**. These allow rapid access to data, although the time is much slower than that of primary storage or magnetic disk. Large files, backup files, and infrequently used files can be placed in mass storage at a relatively low cost.

MASS STORAGE DEVICE
Allows relatively fast access to data, generally infrequently used files, at a low cost.

One approach to mass storage uses a **cartridge tape** as the storage medium. The cartridges are similar to cassette tapes in design; however, the high-density tape used requires 90 percent less storage space than common magnetic tape. Cartridge tapes can hold the equivalent of up to 1,000 tape reels. The mounting of the cartridges is controlled and executed by the computer system (Figure 2-14) rather than by the operator, a factor that makes it faster than the traditional operator-controlled method.

CARTRIDGE TAPE
A mass storage medium using high-density tapes.

Mass storage is not limited to high-density magnetic tape, though. Recently, a mass storage system was introduced for minicomputers that uses small floppy disks for the storage medium. Unlike the cartridge system, most mass storage devices require extensive physical movement because the needed files must first be found and then mounted mechanically before data can be read or written. Although direct access is possible, the retrieval time is relatively slow.

FIGURE 2-14 Mass Storage. Because these data cartridges are stored in a fashion resembling a honeycomb, this type of storage is often referred to as honeycomb mass storage. It is well suited for applications with large volumes of data requiring slower access time.

TRADITIONAL INPUT DEVICES

Punched Cards

Traditionally, data from documents such as time cards, bills, invoices, checks, and the like were transferred onto punched cards and then read into the computer. Today many of these documents are punched cards themselves, with data being keyed directly onto the cards at their source. The most common example is the phone bill. These cards (bills) can be read directly into the computer, saving time and eliminating errors that may result from retyping the data.

KEYPUNCH
Typewriter-like machine used to punch data onto computer cards.

The standard punched card has 80 vertical columns and 12 horizontal rows (Figure 2-15). Data are recorded as a set of holes punched in a particular column to represent a given character. As we mentioned in Chapter 1, this coding scheme called the Hollerith code was developed by Herman Hollerith.

Usually, data are recorded on punched cards using a **keypunch** (Figure 2-16). An operator transcribes the data from a source document onto the cards by pressing keys on a keyboard that resembles an ordinary typewriter. The machine automatically feeds, positions, and stacks the cards. Even with these automatic functions, keypunching is still quite costly, both in time and personnel.

Key-to-Magnetic Media Systems

Because punched-card systems require much mechanical movement and have other limitations, new methods have been developed to record and enter data. These new methods use magnetic media, such as magnetic tape or magnetic disks. With magnetic media, data are entered through a keyboard—as with the keypunch—but they are stored as magnetized spots on the surface of the tape or disk. Because the spots retain their magnetism, the data can be stored and used indefinitely. Unlike punched cards, which cannot be repunched, old data on tape and disks can be replaced with new data. Tape and disks can also store much more data

FIGURE 2-15 Eighty-Column Punched Card and Hollerith Code

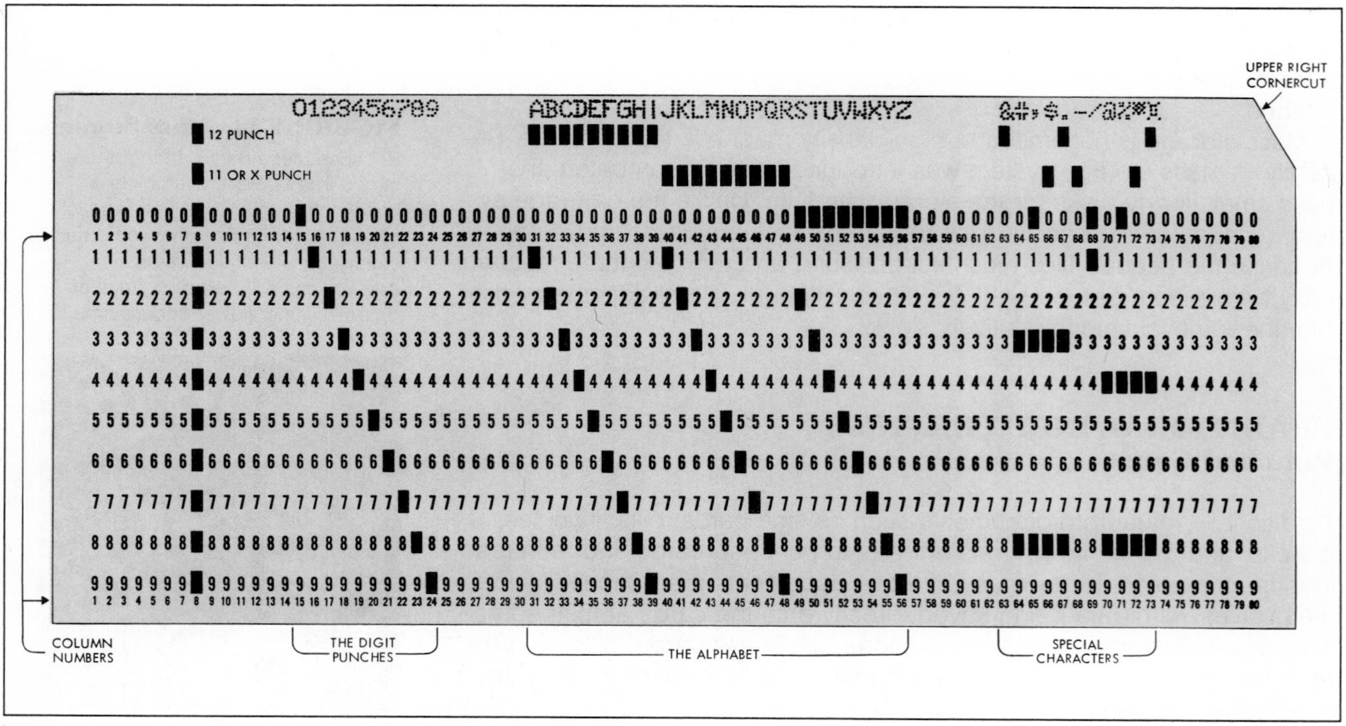

than cards and do so in a much smaller space. As many as 6,250 characters are commonly stored on one inch of magnetic tape. In addition, data stored on tape or disk can be read into the CPU hundreds of times faster than data on cards. Advances in disk technology, along with the fact that disks are easier to use and require even less storage area than tapes, will eventually result in most key-to-tape systems being replaced by key-to-disk (or -diskette) systems.

A typical **key-to-disk** system consists of several keying devices, all of which are connected to a minicomputer, that record data onto magnetic disks (Figure 2-17). But before that, the data are usually edited by the minicomputer. This editing is directed by the minicomputer's stored-program instructions. If an error is detected, the system interrupts the operator and "stands by" until a correction has been entered. The correct data are then stored on the magnetic disk for input into the computer.

An increasingly popular data-entry system is the **key-to-diskette** system. A flexible (or floppy) disk is used instead of the conventional hard disk. The data are entered through a keyboard, displayed on a screen for the operator to check, and then recorded on the diskette. While key-to-tape, -disk and -diskette systems offer many advantages over punched-card input, they also cost more.

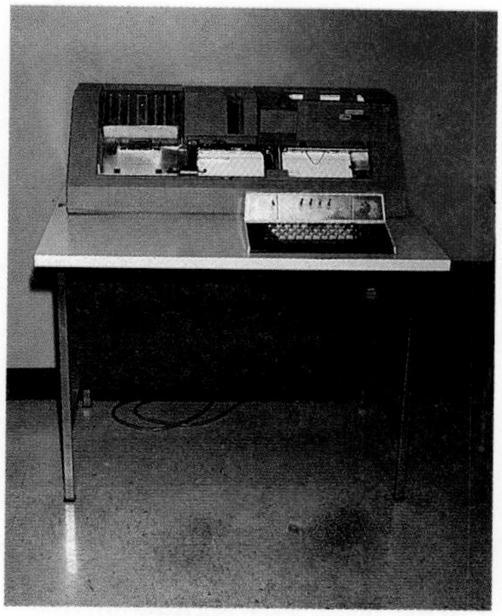

FIGURE 2-16 Keypunch

KEY-TO-DISK SYSTEM **Several keying devices connected to a minicomputer with a disk drive.**

KEY-TO-DISKETTE SYSTEM **Keyboard, display screen, flexible disk and drive.**

TRADITIONAL OUTPUT DEVICES

Once the data have been fed into the computer by card, tape, or disk, they are processed and then output in any of several ways best suited to

FIGURE 2-17 Key-to-Disk System Using Advanced Technology

SOFT COPY
Output that is not printed.

HARD COPY
Printed output

the user's needs. The output may, for example, appear as soft copy on a CRT screen or it may be printed as hard copy, which is the standard term for permanent printed copy. The type of output best suited to the user's needs determines the type of output device used. Most often, though, when we refer to output, we are referring to hard-copy output that has been produced by a printer.

Printers

IMPACT PRINTER
Presses print elements against paper to make the impression.

NONIMPACT PRINTER
Forms letters by signals; print elements never touch the paper.

To produce a copy, the printer (Figure 2-18) must first receive electronic signals from the central processing unit. With an impact printer, these signals activate print elements which strike the paper to make the impression. In the newer nonimpact printers, the signal activates heat, laser, or photographic actions to form the letters, numbers, words, and so on. Table 2-1 shows the difference in print speeds of impact and nonimpact printers.

PRINTER-KEYBOARD
Character-at-a-time impact printer resembling an office typewriter.

DOT-MATRIX PRINTER
Character-at-a-time impact printer that produces characters formed of combinations of dots; also called wire-matrix printer.

Impact Printers Impact printers come in a variety of shapes and sizes. Some print a character at a time, others a line at a time. Printer-keyboard, dot-matrix, and daisy-wheel printers are the three principal character-at-a-time devices.

The printer-keyboard (Figure 2-19) is similar to an office typewriter. All instructions, including spacing, carriage returns, and printing of characters, are sent from the CPU to the printer. The keyboard allows an operator to communicate with the system, such as by entering data or instructions.

Dot-matrix (also called wire-matrix) printers are designed something like the message display part of a football or basketball scoreboard. The ma-

FIGURE 2-18 Printer

TABLE 2-1 Printer Types and Speeds

PRINTER TYPE	APPROXIMATE PRINTING CAPABILITY
IMPACT PRINTERS	
Character-at-a-Time:	
Printer-keyboard	15 characters per second
Daisy wheel	50 characters per second
Dot-matrix (Wire-matrix)	120 characters per second
Line-at-a-Time:	
Print wheel	150 lines per minute
Print chain	2,000 lines per minute
Print drum	2,000 lines per minute
NONIMPACT PRINTERS	
Ink jet	200 characters per second
Xerographic	4,000 lines per minute
Electrothermal	5,000 lines per minute
Electrostatic	5,000 lines per minute
Laser	21,000 lines per minute

trix is a rectangle composed of pins. Usually, it is seven pins high and five pins wide. Combinations of pins are activated to represent characters. For example, the number 3 and the letter A are formed by a combination of pins being pressed against paper. The dot combinations, used to represent various numbers, letters, and special characters, are shown in Figure 2-20. Dot-matrix printers can ordinarily print up to 120 characters per second.

Daisy-wheel printers also resemble office typewriters. The daisy wheel (Figure 2-21)—the font, or type, carrier—has a set of spokes, each with a

DAISY-WHEEL PRINTER
Character-at-a-time impact printer with removable daisy wheels (font carriers); produces high-quality type.

FIGURE 2-19 Printer-Keyboard
This Dataproducts terminal provides a throughput of 50 characters per second.

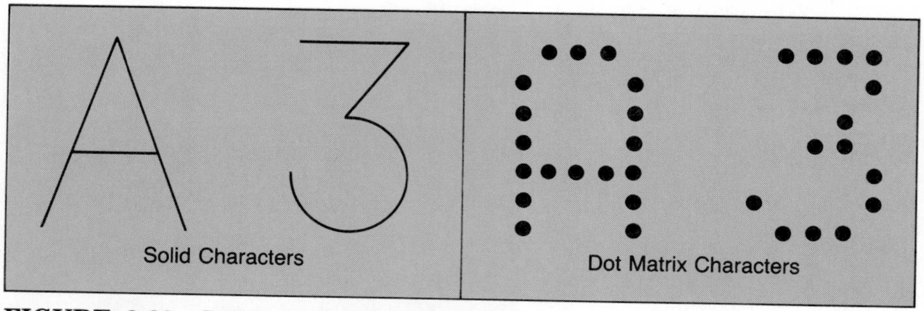

FIGURE 2-20 Solid versus Dot-Matrix Characters

single character at the tip. The wheel rotates to bring the desired character into position and is then struck by a hammer mechanism to form an image on paper. Daisy wheels come in several type styles. The daisy-wheel printer offers high-quality type and is often used on word processors to produce professional quality printing. It can print up to 50 characters per second, or 3,000 characters per minute.

PRINT-WHEEL PRINTER **Line-at-a-time impact printer, which has one print wheel for each print location on the line.**

Line-at-a-time printing devices include print-wheel printers, chain printers, and drum printers. A **print-wheel printer** usually has 80, 120, or 132 print wheels, one for each of the print locations on the line. Each print wheel (Figure 2-22) contains 48 characters—the alphabet, the numbers, and special characters—and rotates until the character called for moves into the right print position on the current print line. When all the wheels are in their correct positions, a hammer drives the paper against the

FIGURE 2-21 Daisy Wheel

"Since we switched to computer systems, J.B., McWilliams here wants to know if we might be able to buy a printer."

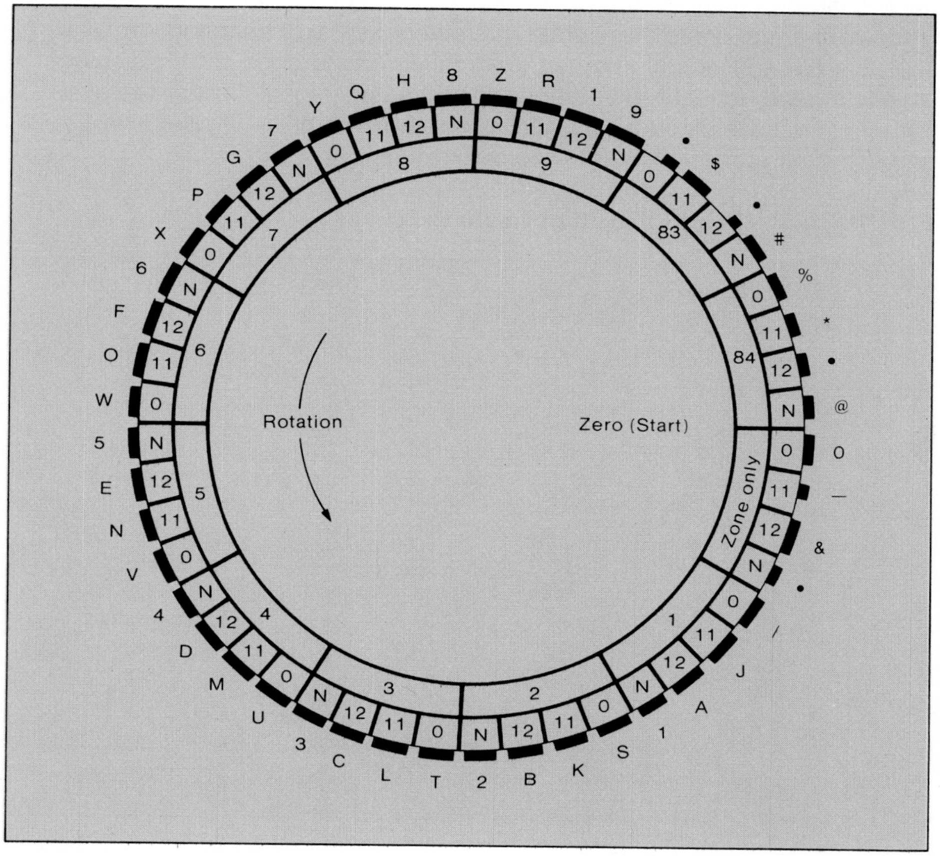

FIGURE 2-22 Print Wheel

wheels and an entire line of output is printed. Print-wheel printers can produce about 150 lines per minute (a comparatively slow output).

CHAIN PRINTER
Line-at-a-time impact printer, which has its character set assembled on a chain revolving past all print positions.

A **chain printer's** character set is assembled on a chain (Figure 2-23) that revolves horizontally past all print positions. There is one print hammer for each column on the paper. Characters are printed when hammers press the paper against an inked ribbon, which, in turn, presses against the right characters on the print chain. Type styles can also be changed easily on chain printers. Some of these devices can produce up to 2,000 lines per minute.

DRUM PRINTER
Line-at-a-time impact printer; uses a metal cylinder with rows of characters engraved onto it.

A **drum printer** uses a metal cylinder with rows of characters engraved across its surface. Each column on the drum (Figure 2-24) contains the complete character set and corresponds to one print position on the line. As the drum turns, all characters move past the print position. A hammer presses the paper against an inked ribbon and the drum when the appropriate character is in place. One line is printed for each revolution of the drum since all characters eventually reach the print position during each revolution. Some drum printers can produce 2,000 lines per minute.

ELECTROSTATIC PRINTER
Forms images with an electrically charged dot matrix and charged ink.

Nonimpact Printers An **electrostatic printer** forms an image of a character on special paper, using a dot matrix of charged wires or pins. The paper is moved through a solution containing ink particles that have an electrical charge opposite that of the image. The ink particles stick to each charged image on the paper and form the characters.

ELECTROTHERMAL PRINTER
Generates characters using heat and heat-sensitive paper.

Electrothermal printers generate characters by using heat and heat-sensitive paper. Rods are heated in a matrix. As the ends of the selected rods touch the heat-sensitive paper, they create images. Neither the electrothermal nor the electrostatic printer makes much noise in operation, and some can produce 5,000 lines per minute.

FIGURE 2-23 Print Element of Chain Printer

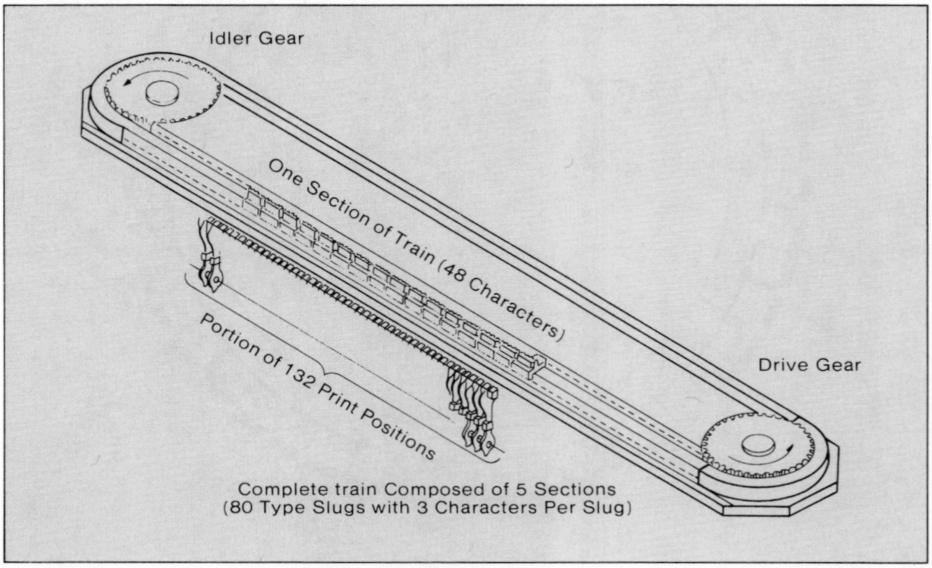

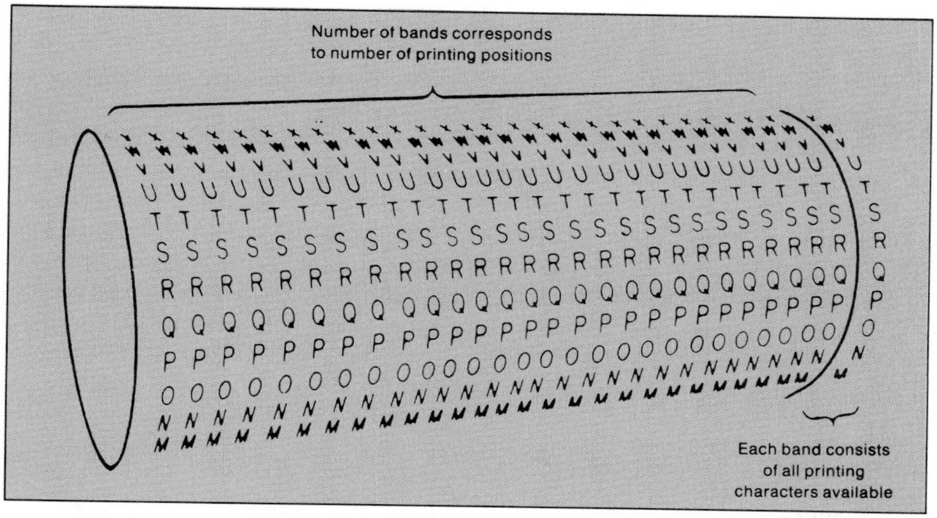

FIGURE 2-24 Print Drum

In an **ink-jet printer**, a nozzle is used to shoot a stream of charged ink toward the paper. Before reaching the paper, the ink must pass through an electrical field that arranges the charged particles into characters at a rate of up to 200 characters a second.

INK-JET PRINTER
Forms characters by spraying ink through an electrical field.

Laser printers (Figure 2-25) combine laser beams and electrophotographic technology to create images. A beam of light is focused through a rotating disk containing a full set of characters. The character image is

LASER PRINTER
Creates images with laser beams and photographic paper.

FIGURE 2-25 Laser Printer.
This one, made by Datagraphix, Inc., operates at speeds up to 21,000 lines per minute.

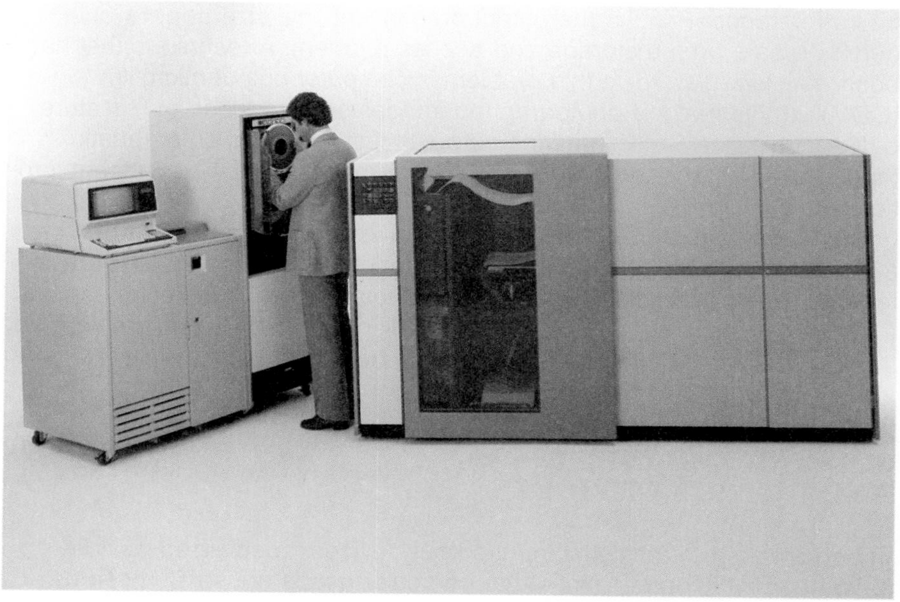

projected onto a piece of film or photographic paper, and the print or negative is developed and "fixed" like an ordinary photograph. Since the output is high quality, the process is often used to print books. Laser printers produce up to 21,000 lines per minute.

XEROGRAPHIC PRINTER
Uses the same methods as photocopying machines.

Xerographic printers use printing methods like those employed in common photocopying machines. For example, Xerox, the pioneer in this type of printing, has one model that prints on single 8½ × 11-inch sheets of plain paper. Xerographic printers can turn out 4,000 lines per minute.

Printing systems now being introduced combine many features of the printing process into one machine, including stacking, routing, hole punching, blanking out of proprietary information, and perforating. Some printers produce both text and form designs on plain paper. This reduces or eliminates the need for preprinted forms.

FIGURE 2-26 Plotter

Plotters

PLOTTER
A special printer used to print graphic images.

A **plotter** (Figure 2-26) produces hard copies of graphic images: lines, curves, complex shapes, bar charts, graphs, organizational charts, engineering drawings, maps, trend lines, supply and demand curves, and other useful graphics.

A plotter is composed of a pen, a movable carriage, sometimes a drum, and a holder for chart paper. Both the pen and/or paper can move up and down and back and forth. This allows for very detailed drawings. In some cases, the plotting pen can be positioned on as many as 45,000 different points within each square inch of paper. Some plotters can make their drawings in up to eight different colors.

Computer Output Microfilm

COMPUTER OUTPUT MICROFILM (COM)
Computer output produced on microfilm rather than on paper.

Sometimes large amounts of information have to be printed and stored for future reference. Printing the output on conventional-size paper would quickly create both a storage and access problem. A technique that has been developed to solve this problem is **computer output microfilm (COM).** In this method photographed images are produced in miniature by the computer. Sometimes the output is first recorded on magnetic tape and then transferred to 35mm. microfilm rolls or to 4 × 6-inch microfiche cards.

The COM system can store graphics as well as characters and records at a rate of 25 to 50 times the traditional printing speeds. Another advantage is that it costs relatively little to produce additional microfilm copies.

As marvelous and flexible as the foregoing input and output devices seem, improvements and adaptations are being made virtually every day.

SPECIALIZED INPUT AND OUTPUT DEVICES

In addition to the traditional input/output devices, specialized devices have been developed to meet the particular needs of users. These devices include several types of source-data automation and terminals.

Source-Data Automation

A real gain in computer input has come in the form of **source-data automation,** which allows data to be collected in computer-readable form where and when they occur (Figure 2-27). An example of this is the supermarket scanner that "reads" an item at the checkout counter, figures its price, displays the name and price on a screen and/or conveys it by a voice simulator, prints the name and price on a cash register tape (after calculating whether it is a taxable item and adding appropriate tax), and deducts the sold item from the store's inventory.

SOURCE-DATA AUTOMATION
Allows data to be collected in computer-readable form.

Source-data automation improves the overall time, accuracy, and efficiency of the input operation. Popular devices in the source-data automation category of input are the magnetic-ink character readers, optical readers, and remote terminals.

Magnetic ink is made with magnetized particles of iron oxide and is used to print characters that are readable by both machines and people. It was introduced in the 1950s within the banking industry as an aid to the quick processing of checks. Machines called **magnetic-ink character recognition (MICR)** devices can read and sort checks at the rate of 750 to 1,500 a minute. The sorting is on the basis of bank number at a federal reserve bank and by account number at the issuing bank. Figure 2-28

MAGNETIC-INK CHARACTER RECOGNITION (MICR)
Reads standard characters by reading magnetic particles embedded in the ink.

FIGURE 2-27 Common Methods of Source-Data Automation

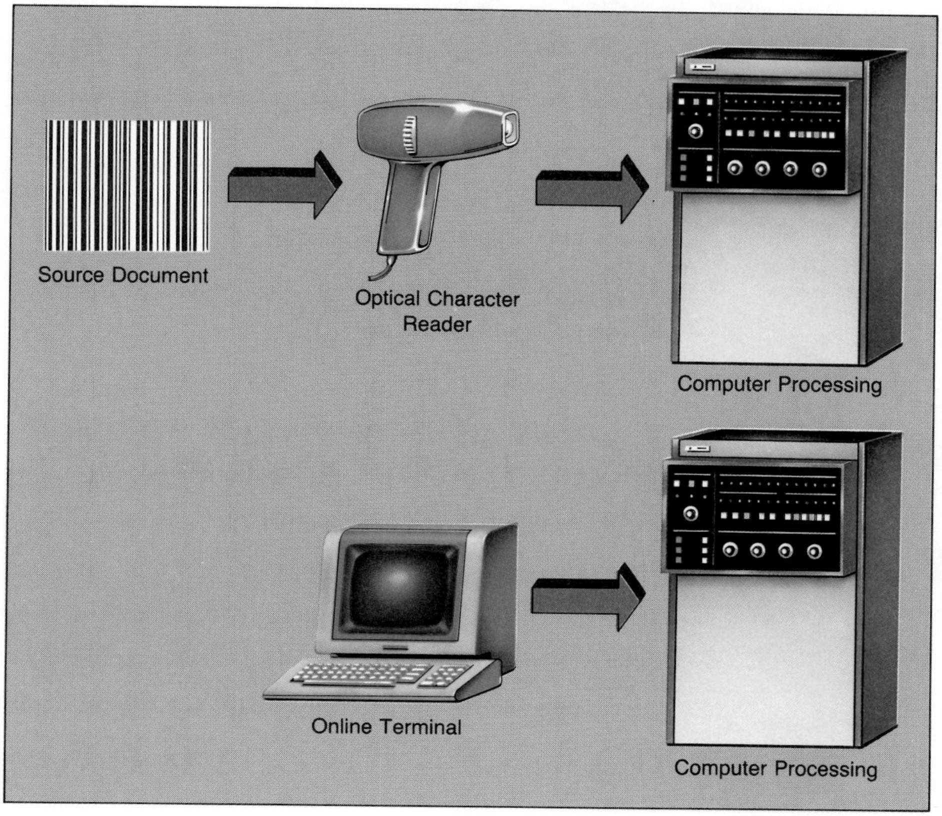

FIGURE 2-28 Magnetic-Ink Characters

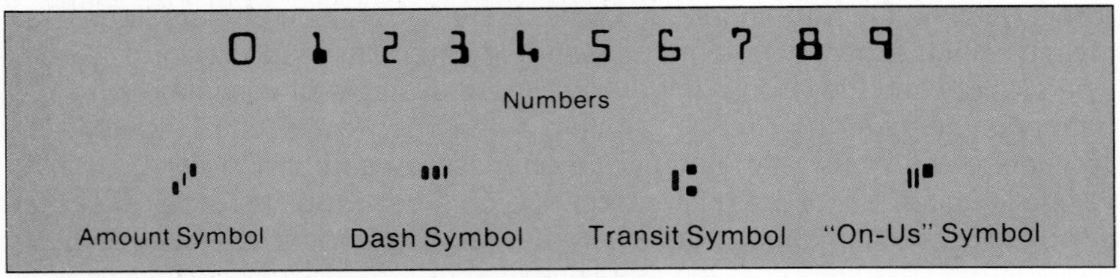

(a) Magnetic-Ink Character Set

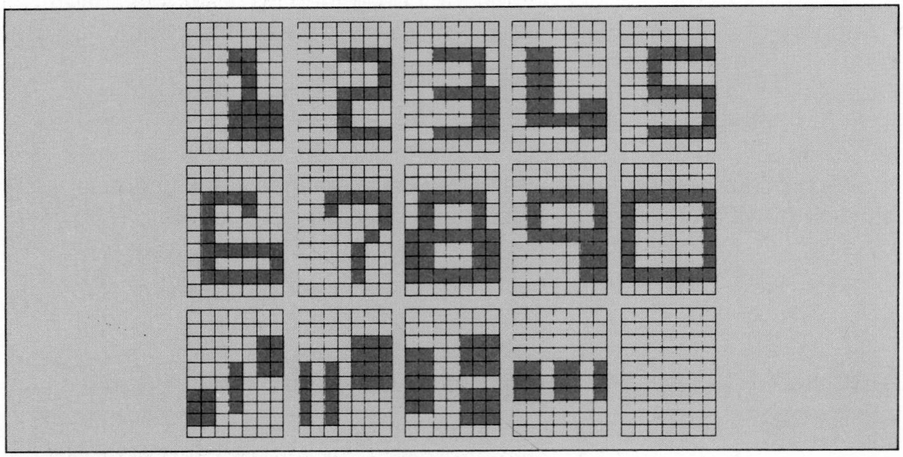

(b) Matrix Patterns for Magnetic-Ink Characters

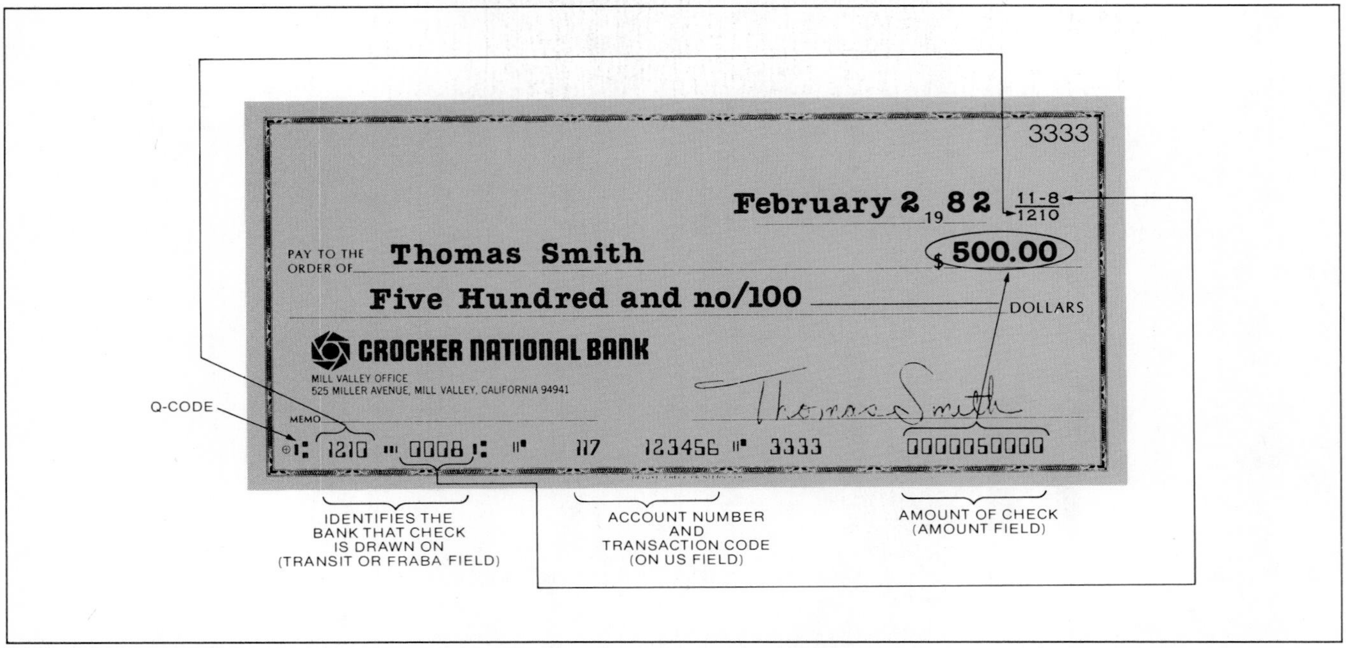

(c) Magnetic-Ink Characters on a Sample Check

shows what the magnetic-ink characters look like in close detail and how they are used on checks.

Optical readers, as the name implies, work on the same principle as the human eye rather than on magnetic properties embedded in the ink. What an optical recognition device "sees" is converted automatically into electrical impulses that can be sent directly to the CPU or stored for later use.

The simplest level of optical recognition is **optical-mark recognition (OMR)** or mark sensing. It is the method by which multiple-choice tests can be read and scored by machine (Figure 2-29). The machine relies not on the shape of the mark it is reading (the pencil mark) but rather on its location on the page. As the page is read, the data are converted directly into machine language. By connecting an optical-mark page reader to a computer, up to 2,000 documents (of the same type) can be read and processed in an hour.

OPTICAL-MARK RECOGNITION (OMR)
Converts marks into computer data by reading the position of marks on the page.

Bar-code readers can read the pattern of lines that form the code regardless of its location. Bar codes are useful in many situations, including point-of-sale (POS) and credit card verification. In a bar code the data are indicated by the width of the bars and by the distance between them (Figure 2-30).

BAR-CODE READER
Reads the pattern of lines forming the code, rather than their location.

The familiar **Universal Product Code (UPC),** which now marks most items sold in supermarkets, is made up of 10 vertical bars. Encoded within these bars is the name of the product's manufacturer and the identity of the item. The price is not encoded since that will vary from store to store.

UNIVERSAL PRODUCT CODE (UPC)
A standard bar code.

Optical-character recognition (OCR) devices can recognize specially shaped letters of the alphabet, both upper and lower cases and in different type fonts. (Type fonts are styles of type. For example, standard Ro-

OPTICAL-CHARACTER RECOGNITION (OCR)
Devices that read characters by their shape.

FIGURE 2-29 Optical-Mark Recognition (OMR) for Multiple-Choice Test

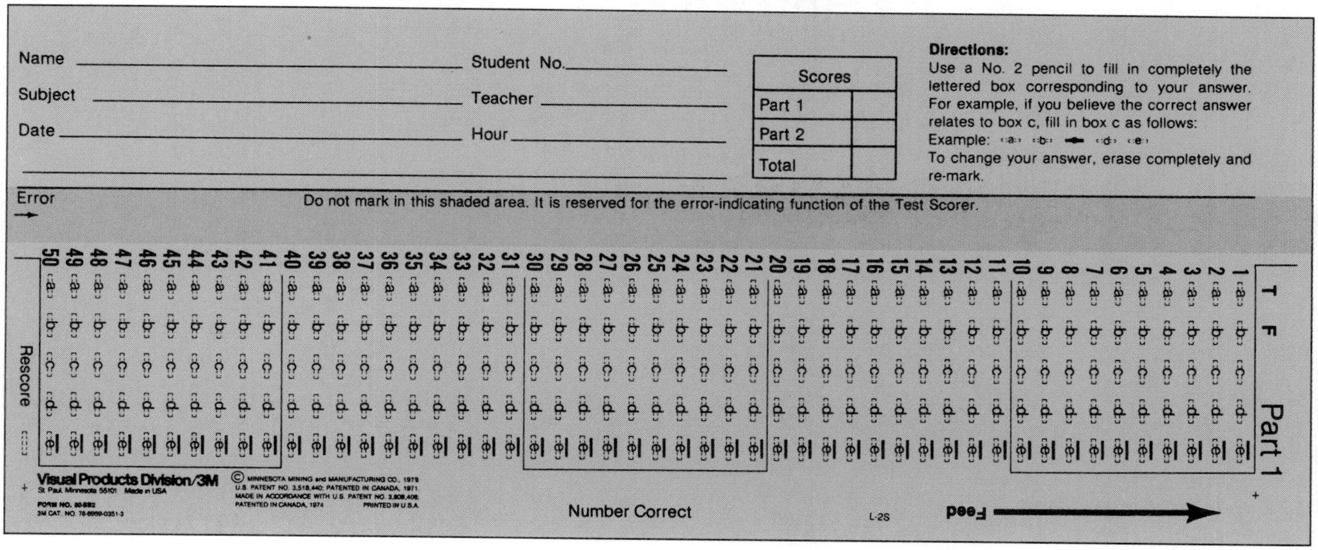
Name
Student No.
Subject
Teacher
Date
Hour

Scores	
Part 1	
Part 2	
Total	

Directions:
Use a No. 2 pencil to fill in completely the lettered box corresponding to your answer. For example, if you believe the correct answer relates to box c, fill in box c as follows:
Example: a b ▬ d e
To change your answer, erase completely and re-mark.

Error →
Do not mark in this shaded area. It is reserved for the error-indicating function of the Test Scorer.

T F Part 1
Rescore
Visual Products Division/3M
St. Paul, Minnesota 55101 Made in USA
Number Correct
L-2S
Feed

FIGURE 2-30 Types of Bar Codes

man characters and italic are two common type fonts.) Figure 2-31 illustrates the most common OCR characters.

VOICE-RECOGNITION SYSTEM
A terminal that responds to voice commands.

Voice-recognition systems (Figure 2-32) rely on the computer having been "trained" to understand the user's voice. Recognition is at a very limited level, so the user is restricted to the few patterns the computer has been programmed to acknowledge. Voice recognition is best suited to low volumes of data. Since data can be entered by use of commands in natural spoken language, greater accuracy in data entry may be obtained.

Terminals

TERMINAL
A device through which data can exit from or be entered into a computer.

A **terminal** is a device through which data can exit from or be entered into a computer. Remote terminals are located at a distance from the central computer that processes the data. In most cases, input and output are

FIGURE 2-31 OCR Characters

transmitted to and from the computer through communication channels such as telephone lines.

Touch-tone terminals (Figure 2-33) are remote terminals used together with ordinary telephone lines. They have a special keyboard through which data are entered. There are several types of touch-tone devices, including some that can read magnetic strips on plastic cards or combine with computer-controlled voice output.

Point-of-sale (POS) terminals are remote terminals that function as traditional cash registers and also capture sales data. Such devices have a keyboard for data entry, a panel to display the price, a cash drawer, and a printer that provides a cash receipt. Point-of-sale terminals are com-

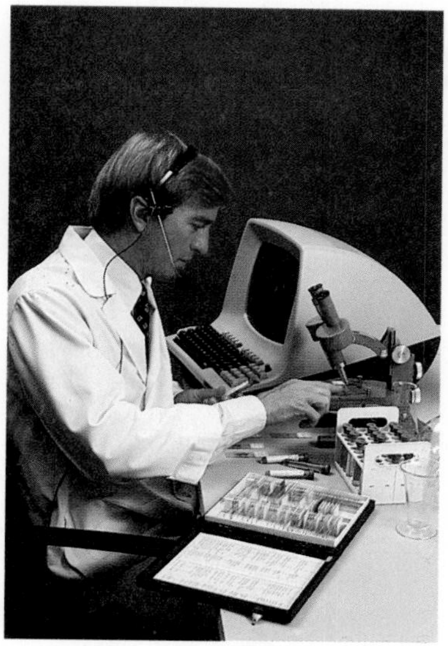

FIGURE 2-32
Voice-Recognition Terminal.
This lab technician is using a terminal made by Interstate Electronics for voice data entry. This replaces conventional keystroke entry, thereby keeping the user's hands free for other tasks.

FIGURE 2-33 Touch-Tone Terminal.
This device made by Anderson Jacobson combines voice and data communication.

TOUCH-TONE TERMINAL
Remote terminal that uses telephone lines to pass data.

POINT-OF-SALE (POS) TERMINAL
A terminal that serves as a cash register but is also capable of relaying data to a central computer.

FIGURE 2-34 Point-of-Sale Terminal with Fixed Scanner

monly used in retail businesses. Figure 2-34 illustrates a typical supermarket terminal.

VISUAL DISPLAY TERMINAL
A television-like screen used to display soft-copy output; sometimes called a CRT (cathode-ray tube).

Visual display terminals, similar to TV cathode ray tubes (CRTs), have been developed on which processed information in words and numbers can be flashed instantaneously (Figure 2-35). The resulting soft copy is well suited to those who need information immediately but who do not need to retain a permanent record of the information. The user may enter data on the keyboard attached to the visual display terminal and see them appear on the screen for verification as they are being keyed into the computer.

Although the use of a visual display output does not exclude the simultaneous use of a printer, the display has some advantages over a printer. Visual display terminals are faster (up to 10,000 characters a second) and quieter.

GRAPHIC DISPLAY DEVICE
Special visual display terminal used to display graphic images.

LIGHT PEN
A device used to modify graphics displayed on a screen by drawing on the screen.

The **graphic display device** (Figure 2-36) also shows its output on a video screen. It is generally used to make graphs and charts, but it can, in addition, depict complex curves and shapes. This makes graphic display devices particularly useful to designers and engineers in highly technical fields. Some of these terminals are coupled with a **light pen** (Figure

FIGURE 2-35 Visual Display Terminal

FIGURE 2-36 Graphic Display Device

FIGURE 2-37 Graphic Display Device with Light Pen

2-37) that enables the user to modify the graphics on the screen by "drawing" on the screen with the pen's light-sensitive tip.

INTELLIGENT TERMINAL **Remote terminal that can be programmed.**

Intelligent terminals are remote terminals that can be programmed by stored instructions, an ability the other terminals lack. Although they have the same kind of components found in full-size computers, intelligent terminals have limited storage space and are restricted in the instructions they can perform. Most of these have a visual display and/or a printer attached. They are useful for editing data prior to transmitting it to a central computer. The use of intelligent terminals will continue to grow as their cost continues to decrease.

ISSUE

JAPANESE IMPORTS: WILL THEY TAKE OVER?

With Japan's prowess in industrial manufacturing, predictions of an imminent takeover of the computer market have abounded. To discover whether this is a real possibility, we must examine the state of the market today and the experts' predictions for the future.

Presently, Japan is having a difficult time with its computer companies. Contrary to the popular scare myth, they are not proceeding with record profits. Hitachi exemplified this in 1981, squeaking by with a profit margin of only 7 percent—low by American standards. Fijitsu is even worse off, with a profit margin of barely 3 percent. Whereas U.S. companies hold 50 percent of the world's computer market, Japanese companies hold only 6 percent.

The reason for Japan's current lag in the computer market is not due to problems with hardware development or production; the Japanese are approaching us there. The problem is that for a computer to be useful, it must have software in addition to hardware, and Japan is failing miserably in the production of software.

There are two major reasons for this. The first is the structure of Japanese society. The traditional company loyalty that has produced admirable achievements in hardware development and production is proving harmful in the area of software. While the American entrepreneur who leaves his company to market his own software package and become a millionaire is feeding our market with an abundance of software packages, the lack of the entrepreneur ideal in Japan due to company loyalty is stifling the development of software. Without software, hardware simply does not sell.

The other major reason is the language barrier. Over the last few decades, English has become the primary language of world business. Currently, almost all computers are documented, labeled, explained, and programmed in English-like programming languages. The great difficulty in switching from Japanese to English (and vice versa) is definitely creating a problem.

Yet it would be naive to think that the Japanese have not made inroads in the American computer market. The Japanese share of the world market is definitely growing.

Current predictions indicate that the Japanese will increase their exports of computer products by 30 percent a year. By 1986 the Japanese will probably be exporting 20 percent of their computer products, amounting to approximately $2.5 billion. Even though American computer-related sales are predicted to be $60 billion in 1986, that $2.5 billion could do a good deal of damage. Obviously, this would not affect the larger computer companies such as IBM, DEC, and Hewlett Packard. But it could seriously affect the smaller companies. Companies that will be hit hardest are those manufacturing printers and hand-held computers because Japan is already ahead in these markets.

Most of the major doomsayers predict that the Japanese will exploit the market in the 1990s as software prices plummet in the fashion that hardware prices fell in the 1970s. This is a very contingent invasion. It could be that the Japanese will never catch up in software development, a necessity for wide-scale competition. And even if they do, there is no guarantee that software prices will actually drop. Hardware prices dropped due to improvements in manufacturing and increased demand. There is already a great demand for software, and unless someone devises a method for streamlining ingenuity, there will be no major advances in the way software is produced.

However, Japan does seem to be very determined to give U.S. computer companies serious competition. Their confidence has a realistic basis. The Japanese government gives

ISSUE

tremendous support to Japan's computer companies. Strict regulations are enforced to keep American computer companies from competing in Japan. When IBM opened their Japan branch, it was forced to sign away half of its profits for the privilege.

Japan is also very serious about research and development. Japanese business and government are spending literally billions of dollars on research for the development of fifth generation computers. Sharp Electronics, a Japanese company, gives money not only to its own research and development departments, but to American firms as well. In 1983, they provided funding for a small American firm doing research into developing biochips.

While we are watching, Japanese computer companies are moving some of their operations out of Japan. In particular, they seek alliances with the smaller American computer companies that would be hurt the most by intensive Japanese competition.

There is no doubt that the Japanese are putting forth every effort to increase their share of the world computer market. How successful they will be is the real question.

SUMMARY POINTS

- The CPU is the "brain" of the computer and is composed of three units: (1) the control unit, which controls execution of instructions; (2) the arithmetic/logic unit, which performs mathematical and logical calculations; and (3) the primary storage unit, which stores the instructions, data, and results of calculations.
- The primary storage unit is composed of semiconductors, which have their memory circuitry on silicon chips containing bit cells.
- Computers derive most of their power from three features: speed, accuracy, and memory.
- Storage locations in the primary storage unit are used to store instructions and data, and these locations are accessed by their addresses.
- Additional memories are those memories that either cannot really be called primary or auxiliary storage or may function as either. Additional memories include bubble memories and read-only memories.
- Bubble memories may function as either primary or auxiliary storage. They store data as magnetized spots, or bubbles, on a thin film of semiconductor material.
- Read-only memories are hard-wired by the manufacturer to perform specific functions. Some can be programmed by the user (PROMs) and others may be erased and reprogrammed using special procedures (EPROMs).
- Random-access memory (RAM) chips are one of the basic memory devices used by the CPU. Addition of more RAM chips can increase a computer's memory capacity.
- Registers are temporary holding places for instructions and data that are located in the CPU but are not considered parts of the primary storage unit. Types of registers include accumulators, storage registers, instruction registers, and general-purpose registers.
- Auxiliary storage is storage that is physically located outside the CPU. There are two types of auxiliary storage devices: sequential access and direct access.
- Sequential-access storage devices must be read from and written to sequentially—that is, from the beginning and in order. Common sequential-access devices are magnetic tapes and tape cassettes.
- Direct-access storage devices allow the user directly to access data at any point without reading sequentially. Common direct-access storage devices are magnetic disks and flexible disks.
- Mass storage devices are used to store files that are either very large, infrequently used, or are backups (copies of files). Mass storage is slower than primary storage or magnetic disks but is relatively inexpensive. A common mass storage device is cartridge tape.
- Traditional input devices include punched cards and key-to-magnetic media systems.
- Punched cards contain data that are coded by holes in the cards entered on a keypunch machine.
- Key-to-magnetic media systems use a typewriter-like keyboard that enters data magnetically onto either magnetic tapes, magnetic disks, or flexible disks.

■ Traditional output devices produce either hard or soft copy. Hard-copy output is printed on paper; soft-copy output is not.

■ The most common traditional output device is the printer. Printers come in two types: impact and nonimpact.

■ Impact printers create their images by pressing the print elements against the paper to create an impression. They print either one character or one line at a time. Common impact printers are printer-keyboards, dot-matrix printers, daisy-wheel printers, print-wheel printers, chain printers, and drum printers.

■ Nonimpact printers use a variety of means to create their images, but in all of them, the print element never touches the paper. Nonimpact printers include electrostatic printers, electrothermal printers, ink-jet printers, laser printers, and xerographic printers.

■ Plotters are special printers used to output graphic images. They can produce lines, curves, and complex shapes in up to eight colors.

■ Computer output microfilm (COM) is specialized output produced on microfilm rather than paper.

■ Source-data automation is a technique that allows data to be collected in computer-readable form when they occur. Most source-data automation systems use some type of mark or character recognition device. Common devices are magnetic-ink character recognition (MICR) devices, optical-mark recognition (OMR) devices, bar-code readers, and optical-character recognition (OCR) devices, and voice recognition systems.

■ A terminal is a device through which data can exit from or be entered into a computer. There are touch-tone terminals, POS terminals, visual display terminals, graphic display devices, and intelligent terminals.

REVIEW QUESTIONS

1. What are the parts of the CPU and their functions?
2. Explain how storage locations and addresses within the primary storage unit differ and how they are used.
3. In what way are bubble memories unique?
4. Differentiate among ROM, PROM, and EPROM.
5. How do RAM and ROM differ?
6. What are the types and uses of registers?
7. Explain the difference between sequential-access and direct-access storage. Give examples of each.
8. List and define traditional input devices. Give examples of each type.
9. What are the types of impact printers and how do they differ from each other?
10. List the nonimpact printers and explain how each creates the character images.
11. List some specialized input and output devices. What functions can they perform that traditional devices cannot, and in what situations would they be needed?

12. Explain how the different mark and character recognition devices recognize data.
13. List and differentiate the types of terminals. What tasks are best suited to each type?

DISCUSSION QUESTIONS

1. There are many types of printers available. What factors would you take into consideration when deciding which one to buy?
2. Choosing the appropriate methods for input or output depends on many factors—cost, time, user needs, and the like. After examining each method of input or output described in this chapter, discuss which situations (banking, retailing, and so on) would be best suited to each device.
3. Discuss the major advantages and disadvantages of the different memories available. List situations or specific jobs that would be best suited to each type.
4. Source-data automation has greatly affected business—in particular, retail stores and restaurants. Discuss how source-data automation has affected a business in your home town.
5. Read the issue section on American and Japanese production of computers. In your opinion, by the year 2000, who will be ahead? What are your reasons? Compare your answers with those of your classmates.

CHAPTER 3

THE COMPUTER: WHAT IT IS AND HOW IT WORKS

OUTLINE

ARTICLE

SCIENTISTS FIND NEW HIGH IN PRIME NUMBERS GAME

LEE DEMBART

Computer scientists using one of the world's fastest computers believe they have found the largest prime number yet—one that contains nearly 40,000 digits.

A prime number is one that has no divisors other than itself and 1.

Knowing a prime number larger than all others doesn't offer much benefit to society, nor anyone but a handful of mathematicians, but it is a feather in the cap of the supercomputer that finds it—in this case, a Cray XMP, which sells for about $9 million.

The new prime number, which has yet to be verified, is 2 raised to the 132,049th power minus 1, a number with 39,751 digits. . . .

The makers of supercomputers, which operate thousands of times faster than run-of-the-mill variety, view the search for large primes as a way of marketing their machines.

"It's like racing computers," said David Slowinski of Cray Research Inc. in Chippewa Falls, Wis., makers of the Cray XMP and its predecessor, the Cray-1.

Using these machines, Slowinski found the two previous largest primes as well as the latest one, which was found the other day on an experimental machine in the company's offices. . . .

The Cray XMP has two processors, each of which is capable of doing 200 million computations a second. One of the processors took 3,900 seconds (65 minutes) to find that 2 raised to the 132,049th power minus 1 is prime.

Slowinski said his new program for testing large primes is running about 12 times faster than the program he used last year to prove that a 25,692-digit number is prime. . . . Modern supercomputers are uniquely suited to the task. They run about 200,000 times faster than an IBM personal computer, for example.

Mersenne primes, named for a 17th Century monk who investigated them, are primes that are 1 less than a power of 2. They are generated by raising 2 to a prime power and subtracting 1. The first Mersenne prime is 3, which is equal to 2 raised to the second power (4) minus 1. The next Mersenne prime is 7, which is 2 to the third power (8) minus 1. The next Mersenne prime is 31, which is 2 to the fifth power minus 1. . . .

The advent of computers has greatly facilitated the search for Mersenne primes. The first four Mersenne primes (3, 7, 31 and 127) were mentioned in Euclid's Elements. The next one, 8,191 (which is 2 to the 13th power minus 1) was found in the 15th Century. The next two were found in the 16th Century, and one each was found in the 17th and 18th centuries.

As recently as 1963, only 23 Mersenne primes were known, the 23rd of which had 3,376 digits. Then the 24th was discovered in 1971 and the 25th in 1978 by Nickel and Noll. Noll found the 26th in 1979, the same year that Slowinski and Harry L. Nelson of Lawrence Livermore Laboratory jointly found the 27th in the series, a number with 13,395 digits.

Slowinski found the 28th last year.

Throughout the development of computers, they have become faster and can handle complicated tasks in less and less time. Finding new high prime numbers is just one application of how one of the world's fastest computers is being used. Although technological developments are responsible for the advances in computer hardware, it is important for us to understand how this hardware works.

INTRODUCTION

In the last chapter, we looked at the physical components of the computer—the hardware—examining in detail each of its parts, that is, the computer proper as well as the peripherals—input, output, and storage devices. We now turn to an examination of how those physical parts are used to process the information—how the computer works.

ANALOG VERSUS DIGITAL

Before discussing how the computer works, we must determine with what type of computer we are dealing. In general, there are two types of computers: analog and digital (Figure 3-1). **Digital computers** are those that operate by recording "on" and "off" electrical pulses. **Analog computers** are those that measure and display such continuous physical or electrical conditions as pressure, temperature, voltage, volume, and shift rotation. Gas pumps, for instance, employ an analog device to measure the volume of gas that has been pumped and, simultaneously, display the appropriate price.

Because of the major difference in the way digital and analog computers measure and represent data, it would be difficult, if not impossible, to represent both types of computers in describing the working of a computer. Therefore, we limit our discussion of computers in this book to digital computers.

DIGITAL COMPUTER
Operates by recording "on" and "off" pulses.

ANALOG COMPUTER
Measures continuous physical or electrical conditions.

BATCH PROCESSING VERSUS ONLINE PROCESSING

It is important to know whether a computer uses batch processing or an online (processing) system (Figure 3-2) for completing tasks. The differ-

FIGURE 3-1 Analog (left) versus Digital (right) Computers

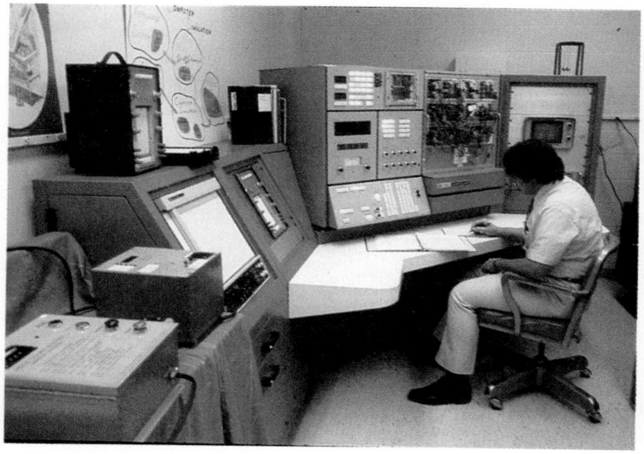

FIGURE 3-2 Online (left) versus Batch (right) Processing

ence determines not how the computer actually works but how it will process the jobs and whether it can use interactive software, or programs.

ONLINE (PROCESSING) SYSTEMS
Allow the user to interact with the computer during program execution.

INTERACTIVE PROGRAM
Asks the user to participate in the program execution.

Online (processing) systems place the user in direct communication with the computer. The best example of this is in using **interactive programs,** which ask the user to participate. For example, the electronic teller at your bank may use an interactive program. When you enter your account number or your banking card, the computer asks you to enter a transaction code and the amount of the transaction. What the computer does after that, whether it adds money to your account for a deposit or withdraws money and gives it to you, depends upon what you told the computer when it asked you for the transaction code and the amount of the transaction. In this way the computer is interacting with you and you are interacting with the computer. This is possible because in an interactive system, the computer runs in an online mode. It allows you to interact with the computer *once the computer has begun execution of the program.*

BATCH PROCESSING
Runs entire program at once, with no interaction.

Batch processing does not allow for interaction of the user with the computer. All of the information must be fed into the computer at once; that is, the program, the data, and any other information that may be used in the course of the program must be entered before the program begins execution. After this, input will not be accepted.

You can often tell what type of a system a computer is by the input devices it uses. Computers that use only punched cards for input are always batch-processing systems, whereas systems that use terminals with keyboard entry of data are almost always online systems. However, there may be exceptions. Some systems with terminals allow only batch processing.

Although the computer will process the information in the same basic manner regardless of whether it uses online or batch processing, there are certain tasks more suited for each system. An online system would probably not be used for processing a large number of bills because

PROFILE

GENE AMDAHL

Gene Amdahl has built a reputation as an expert architect of computer systems.

From 1952 to 1970, Amdahl held positions of chief designer as well as director of IBM's Advanced Computing Systems Laboratory in Menlo Park, California. During this time, he had a significant role in the design of the IBM 704, 7030, and System/360 computers—creating an architectural revolution. In 1970 he introduced the concept of plug-compatible mainframes, but IBM did not pursue the project.

Confident in the potential of his idea, Amdahl left IBM and founded Amdahl Corporation with the goal of marketing industry-compatible mainframes. The next years were spent soliciting investors and designing the equipment. In 1975 he shipped the company's first computer. Among his early clients were AT&T and NASA. Advertising was primarily done by word of mouth from satisfied customers, and praise of Amdahl poured forth. His machines were not only smaller, faster, and less expensive than the corresponding IBM models, but they were also compatible with other brands and previous models, allowing longer life for initial software investments.

Amdahl resigned from Amdahl Corporation in 1979 after a disagreement with the other owners and formed a new business, Trilogy Systems Corporation, with his son. Amdahl's new frontier is the design of macro chips—silicon wafers equivalent to 100 regular chips—and the ultimate goal of using the macro chips to build a competitive supercomputer.

there would be no need for interaction when performing such a task. In addition, having to enter the information from each bill through a terminal as the program is executing would be an extremely inefficient and costly use of CPU time. On the other hand, a batch-processing system would never be used to play games or to answer "what if"-type questions because it allows for no interaction between the user and the computer once the program has begun execution. In the case of games, it would be useless to write a game if one were not allowed to interact in its play—the only one playing the game would be the computer. In the case of "what if" questions, for example an airline reservation system, one would probably wish to ask additional questions based on the outcome of earlier questions. If you were using batch processing, this would mean running the same program over and over again for each additional question. Thus, when using a particular system, you should keep in mind the tasks for which it is suited.

MACHINE LANGUAGE

It is essential to understand that a computer is capable of recognizing only a code composed of 0s and 1s, known as **machine language**. The computer cannot perform instructions directly from an English-like programming language (such as BASIC or COBOL). Sometimes programmers tend to credit the computer with more capability than it actually has,

MACHINE LANGUAGE
A low level language using combinations of 1s and 0s to designate the "on" and "off" electrical states in the computer.

assuming that the computer recognizes words like "READ" or "MULTIPLY". All other languages must first be translated into machine language before the computer can execute the instructions. (More on translation in Chapter 4.)

This machine language of 0s and 1s is also called binary representation and will be explained later. Various combinations of 0s and 1s are used to tell the computer what operation to perform. This same type of code provides the addresses in memory where the necessary data are stored. Everything in a digital computer is stored as "on" and "off" electrical states, which parallel the two states of 1 and 0.

Machine language is probably the least-used language among programmers because it is very difficult to use. Although machine language is explicitly clear to the computer, it is almost entirely incomprehensible to people—or even to other brands of computers. Another reason why machine language is not widely used for programming is that the programs are not portable—they cannot be used on different brands or models of computers. So if a programmer learns to program in machine language on one type of computer, he or she could not use the same machine-language program on another type of computer. Each computer manufacturer uses a different machine language. Although all of the computers speak only machine language, they do not all speak the same "dialect."

ASSEMBLY LANGUAGE
A low-level language that uses abbreviations and codes rather than 0s and 1s.

Although most people do not program in machine language, some do program in a language that closely resembles machine language, called **assembly language**. Assembly language consists of abbreviations and codes rather than 0s and 1s, making it much easier for the programmer to understand. Assembly language requires less complex translation for the computer to understand and operations are performed more quickly than if a higher-level language were used.

Not long ago, most programs were written in assembly or machine language because they execute much faster than high-level languages, and because computer time was very expensive. However, today, because programmers' time often costs more than the hardware being programmed, it is considered more efficient to use an English-like language so the programmers can write programs faster and with fewer errors, rather than write entire programs in machine language to shave a few seconds off the execution time.

DATA REPRESENTATION

For the computer to work, it must be given information in a form it can understand. Binary representation is one way to do this. There are also other methods that build upon the binary code. Most of the common methods of data representation are discussed in this section.

Binary Representation

As we noted, data are represented in the computer by the electrical state of the machine's circuitry: "on" and "off." We symbolize these on and off states by a code composed of 0s and 1s that is called the **binary** (base 2) **number system.** The binary system is similar to the familiar **decimal** (base 10) **number system.** For example, the decimal number 3,568 can be analyzed like this:

BINARY NUMBER SYSTEM
A base 2 system; uses only zeroes and ones.

DECIMAL NUMBER SYSTEM
A base 10 system; uses digits zero through nine.

3 5 6 8

$8 \times 10^0 = 8$
$6 \times 10^1 = 60$
$5 \times 10^2 = 500$
$3 \times 10^3 = \underline{3{,}000}$
3,568

or

3	5	6	8
10^3	10^2	10^1	10^0

Each position represents a certain power of the base 10. The progression of power is from right to left—that is, digits farther to the left in a decimal number represent larger powers of the base 10 than digits to the right (Figure 3-3).

The same principle holds for binary representation. The difference is that in binary representation each position in the number represents a

FIGURE 3-3 Decimal Place Values

←	10^5	10^4	10^3	10^2	10^1	10^0
←	100,000	10,000	1,000	100	10	1

FIGURE 3-4 Binary Place Values

2^6	2^5	2^4	2^3	2^2	2^1	2^0
64	32	16	8	4	2	1

power of the base 2 (Figure 3-4). For example, consider the decimal number 11. In binary the value equivalent to 11 is written as follows:

1 0 1 1

$1 \times 2^0 = 1$

$1 \times 2^1 = 2$

$0 \times 2^2 = 0$

$1 \times 2^3 = \underline{8}$

11

or

1 0 1 1

2^3 2^2 2^1 2^0

BIT
A digit position in a binary number.

As indicated by the preceding example, the binary number system uses combinations of 1s and 0s to represent various values. Each digit position in a binary number is called a **bit.** A 1 in a bit position indicates the presence of a specific power of 2; a 0 indicates the absence of a specific power. As in the decimal number system, the progression of powers is from right to left.

Computer Codes

4-BIT BINARY CODED DECIMAL (BCD)
Represents decimal numbers in binary one digit at a time, rather than as a whole binary number.

Many computers use coding schemes other than simple binary notation to represent numbers. One of the most basic coding schemes is called **4-bit Binary Coded Decimal (BCD).** Instead of representing a decimal number as a string of 0s and 1s (which becomes increasingly complicated for large numbers), BCD represents each decimal digit in a number by using four bits. For instance, the decimal number 19 is represented by two groups of four bits, one group for the 1, the other for the 9. Here are the representations of 19 in the 4-bit BCD and in binary (note the leading zeros are not shown):

0 0 0 1	1 0 0 1	4-bit BCD
1	9	Decimal
10011		Binary

The representation of a three-digit decimal number in 4-bit BCD consists of three sets of four bits, or 12 binary digits. For example, the decimal number 548 is coded like this:

0 1 0 1	0 1 0 0	1 0 0 0	4-bit BCD
5	4	8	Decimal
	1000100100		Binary

Another approach to data representation is an 8-bit code known as **Extended Binary Coded Decimal Interchange Code (EBCDIC).** The 8-bit EBCDIC can be used to represent upper-case and lower-case letters and additional special characters, such as the cent sign and the quotation mark. The EBCDIC bit combinations for upper-case letters and numbers are given in Figure 3-5.

The **American Standard Code for Information Interchange (ASCII)** is a 7-bit code developed cooperatively by several computer manufacturers whose objective was to develop a standard code for all computers. Because certain machines are designed to accept 8-bit rather than 7-bit code patterns, an 8-bit version of ASCII, called **ASCII-8,** was created. ASCII and EBCDIC are similar. The key difference is in the bit patterns used to represent certain characters.

Because bits are very small units of data, it is often useful to combine them into larger units. A fixed number of adjacent bits operated on as a unit is called a **byte.** Since eight bits are sufficient to represent any character, 8-bit groupings are the basic units of memory. In computers that accept 8-bit characters, a byte is a group of eight adjacent bits.

The symbol K (mentioned in Chapter 2) is often used to describe large amounts of storage. Generally, one K equals 1,024 (2^{10}) units (in this case, bytes). Thus, a computer that has 250K bytes of storage can store 250 × 1,024 or 256,000 characters.

EXTENDED BINARY CODED DECIMAL INTERCHANGE CODE (EBCDIC)
An 8-bit binary code used to represent the letters of the alphabet.

AMERICAN STANDARD CODE FOR INFORMATION INTERCHANGE (ASCII)
A standard 7-bit binary code.

ASCII-8
An 8-bit version of ASCII.

BYTE
Eight adjacent bits.

Code Checking

Computers do not always function properly. Errors do occur. To enable the user to detect when an error has occurred, most computers have at

FIGURE 3-5 EBCDIC Representation: A–Z; 0–9

CHARACTER	EBCDIC BIT CONFIGURATION	CHARACTER	EBCDIC BIT CONFIGURATION
A	1100 0001	S	1110 0010
B	1100 0010	T	1110 0011
C	1100 0011	U	1110 0100
D	1100 0100	V	1110 0101
E	1100 0101	W	1110 0110
F	1100 0110	X	1110 0111
G	1100 0111	Y	1110 1000
H	1100 1000	Z	1110 1001
I	1100 1001	0	1111 0000
J	1101 0001	1	1111 0001
K	1101 0010	2	1111 0010
L	1101 0011	3	1111 0011
M	1101 0100	4	1111 0100
N	1101 0101	5	1111 0101
O	1101 0110	6	1111 0110
P	1101 0111	7	1111 0111
Q	1101 1000	8	1111 1000
R	1101 1001	9	1111 1001

PARITY (CHECK) BIT
Bit used to indicate a character miscoding error.

each storage location an additional bit called a **parity (check) bit.** Internal circuitry in the computer constantly monitors operations to ensure that the required number of bits are present in each location. If a parity error is detected, the system may reattempt the read or write operation that was occurring when the error was detected. If additional attempts are unsuccessful, the system informs the computer operator that the error has occurred. The checking circuitry of the computer can only detect the presence of an error; it cannot correct the data.

CHECK DIGIT
A digit in an input number used to catch input errors.

Similar in function to the parity bit is the **check digit.** Like a parity bit, a check digit is used to catch errors. However, whereas one parity bit indicates an error in internal representation, the check digit is used to catch input errors through program instructions. Check digits are generally used to catch errors after input but before processing. Credit cards, banking cards, and employee ID cards regularly use check digits. For example, a check digit in the following employee ID may be the last digit, a nine: 292449692<u>9</u>.

DATA PROCESSING

For the computer to be truly useful, it must do more than represent, or even store, data. It must process them. The advent of the computer has not fundamentally altered the ways data are processed. However, the manner of the processing has progressed from manual to automatic (machine-assisted) to electronic. **Electronic data processing**, or **EDP**, is simply shortened to data processing and refers to completely machine-executed data processing.

ELECTRONIC DATA PROCESSING (EDP)
Computer-assisted data processing.

All data processing, whatever its manner of execution, involves converting raw facts into configurations of information upon which decisions can be made. Although common definition holds that "data" and "information" are synonyms, in the computer world they are distinctly different. **Data** refers to raw, unorganized facts. **Information**, on the other hand, is facts that have been organized and are thus useable and meaningful (Figure 3-6).

DATA
Raw, unorganized facts.

INFORMATION
Meaningfully organized facts.

INPUT
Collecting, verifying, and coding the data for processing.

PROCESSING
Classifying, sorting, calculating, summarizing, or storing the data.

OUTPUT
Retrieving, converting, and communicating the results of processing.

Information must be accurate, complete, timely, relevant, and delivered to the right person at the right place if it is to be useful. Computers can help in all these areas. But they have to deal with the material in a logical and unvarying three-part sequence: input, processing, and output. **Input** means gathering the relevant data, translating them into a form the computer can understand, and submitting the data to the computer. **Processing** refers to the steps in the computer's task of arranging the data and making the desired manipulations with them. Finally, **output**, as we noted, means producing these results in a way that will be understandable and meaningful to the user. These three steps are required for all types of electronic data processing. Figure 3-7 shows the data flow.

To get the original data into the computer, input, requires a three-step process. First, data must be collected. Second, the data must be verified to see if they are accurate, complete, and relevant. Careful verification is essential. If the data going into the computer are incorrect, all the computer's results will also be incorrect. Third, the data must be coded so that they can be machine read and inserted into the data-processing system.

Depending on what the user asks for, the processing link in the chain may entail classifying, sorting, calculating, summarizing, and storing of data. Classifying simply means organizing the raw facts according to

FIGURE 3-6 Data versus Information

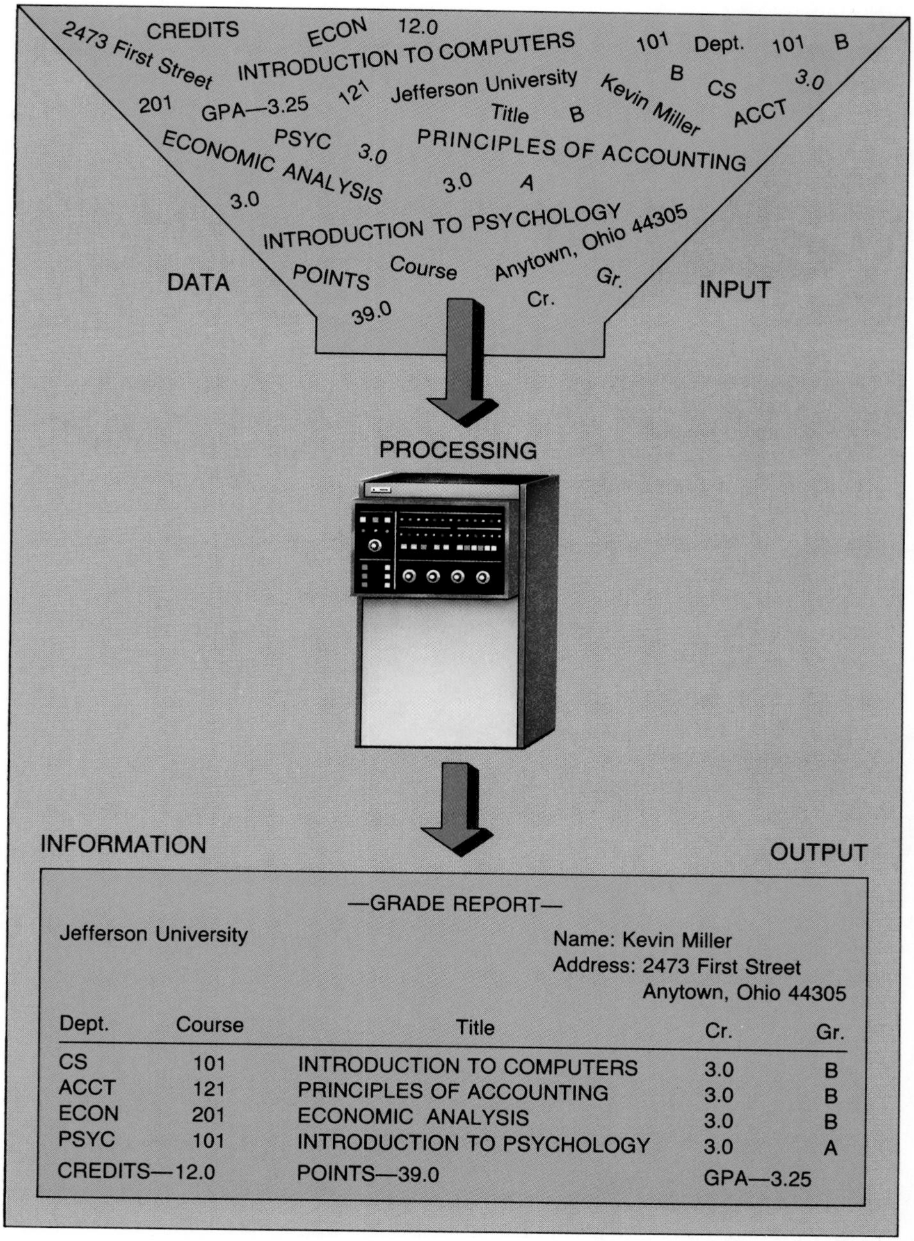

FIGURE 3-7 Flow of Data

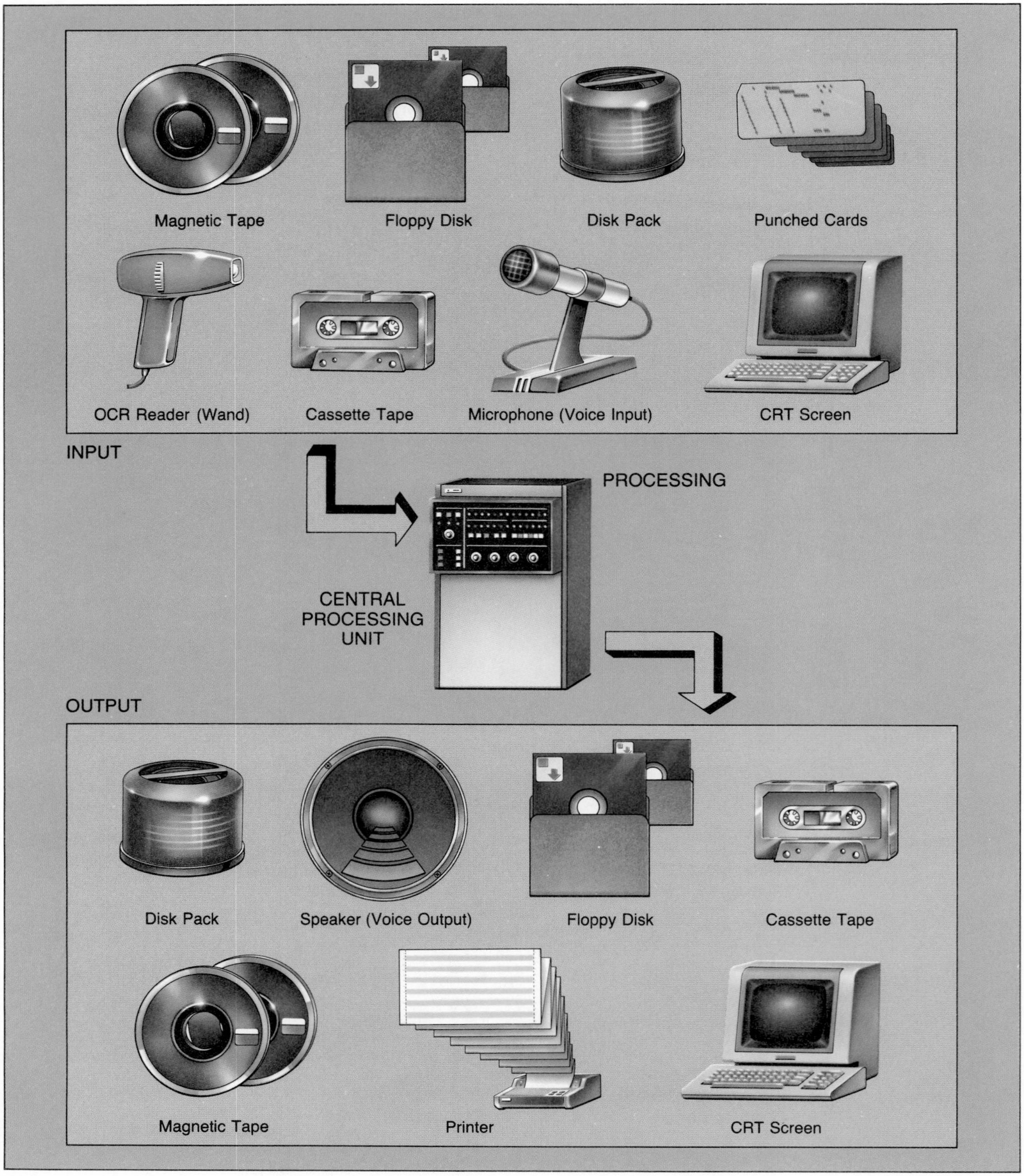

characteristics that are sensible to the user. Daily bank transactions, for example, may be classified in the categories of deposits, withdrawals, and payments. The next step may be sorting, which involves putting data into a sequence to make processing easier. To continue with the bank example, if the deposits are sorted by account numbers, the processing can be speeded up. A calculation may be needed to determine a customer's checking account balance. Summarizing is used to reduce large amounts of data to a concise, usable level upon which management decisions can be made. For instance, a bank's manager may be interested in a summary of customers who defaulted on loans and their previous credit records and income levels. Finally, storing data is an essential part of the processing mode so that the data may be easily available for later processing or retrieval. See Figure 3-8 for more examples of these functions.

Output, the last link in the chain, is—like input—a three-step process. The first step is retrieving the processed information from the computer's storage devices. The second step is converting the information from the form used to store it (binary) into a form understandable by the user. The final step is communicating that information to those who need it when they need it. Usually, this is done through a terminal display or a hard copy.

THE STORED-PROGRAM CONCEPT

A major advance in computer technology took place when a way was devised to store instructions in the computer's memory. Before this, instructions had to be supplied—slowly and carefully—by the computer programmers before each data-processing operation. The programmers either had to wire the instructions into control panels that were plugged into the computer or read in the instructions by way of punched cards. Both methods seriously limited the computer's ability to provide information rapidly.

Under today's **stored-program concept**, instructions are read into the computer's memory. They stay there, ready to act upon relevant data, until they are erased. Since the instructions can be called upon and activated instantly, the computer can work at its top speed. Instructions can be fed in initially by cards, tapes, disks, or keyboards.

STORED-PROGRAM CONCEPT Allows all instructions and data in a program to be stored in memory.

To write an effective set of instructions, called a program, one must first know how the computer uses it. Once the instructions have been converted to machine language, the computer carries them out in the sequence they were submitted unless it was told to do otherwise. This quality makes it necessary for instructions to be placed in the computer's memory in consecutive locations, allowing the computer to move from one location to the next in executing the instructions.

Because input data have to be brought into the memory for processing, a separate area must be set aside for them. This keeps the computer from being confused between what are data and what are instructions

FIGURE 3-8 Processing Functions

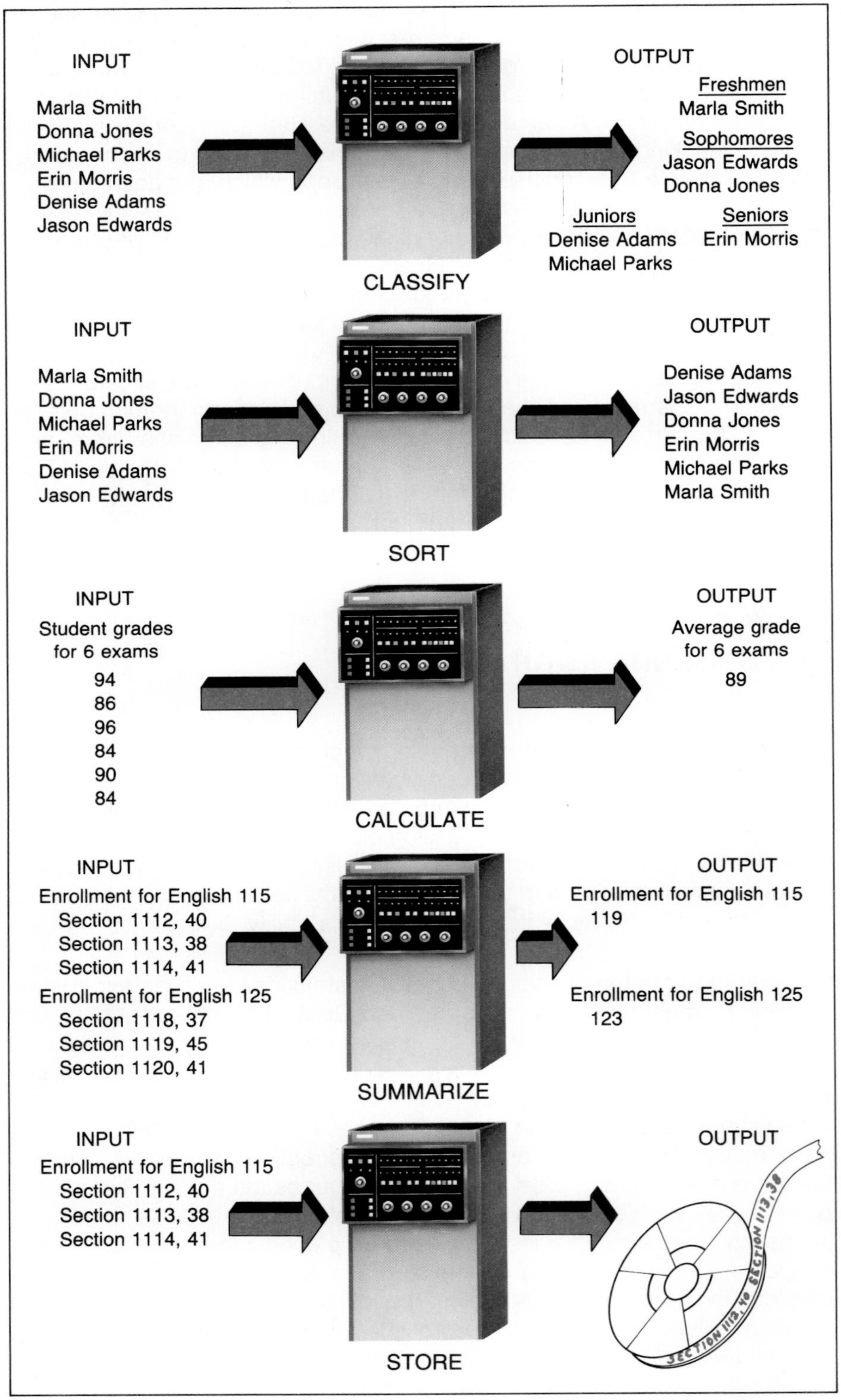

about the data processing. Output is also separated from instructions for the same reason. Figure 3-9 illustrates this memory segmentation.

LOGIC PATTERNS

Basically, the computer can understand and carry out only four logic patterns. They are simple sequence, selection, loop, and branch (Figure 3-10).

SIMPLE SEQUENCE Sequential or ordered logic pattern.

Simple sequence is a series of consecutive statements of instruction given by the programmer and then executed by the computer. It is by far the "simplest" logic pattern. With simple sequence, if a program has three instructions that are numbered 1, 2, and 3, the computer will execute instruction 1 first, instruction 2 second, and instruction 3 third, exactly in the order, or sequence, in which they appear.

SELECTION Logic pattern in which the computer makes a choice based on an evaluation.

Selection calls upon the computer to make a choice between two possibilities (or between several with certain program languages) or items by deciding that one of them is equal to, less than, or greater than another one. For an example of a selection logic pattern, consider how a bank's computer would process a savings account withdrawal. First, the computer would subtract the amount of the withdrawal from the balance in your savings account. Then, it would compare the resulting balance with zero. If the resulting balance would be less than zero, the computer would elect not to process the withdrawal or give you the money. If the resulting balance would be greater than or equal to zero, the computer would elect to process the withdrawal and give you the money. All selection logic patterns work basically that same way. The computer compares two items and then selects a response based on the result of the comparison.

FIGURE 3-9 Memory Segmentation

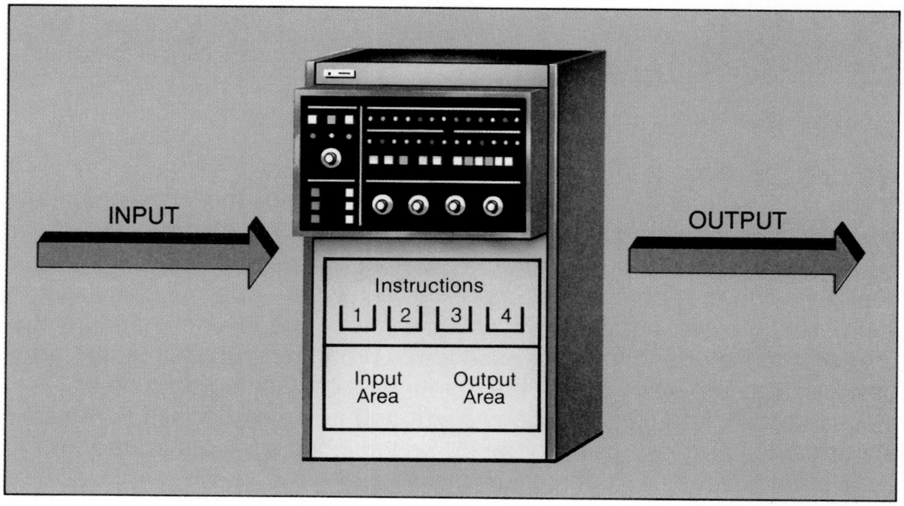

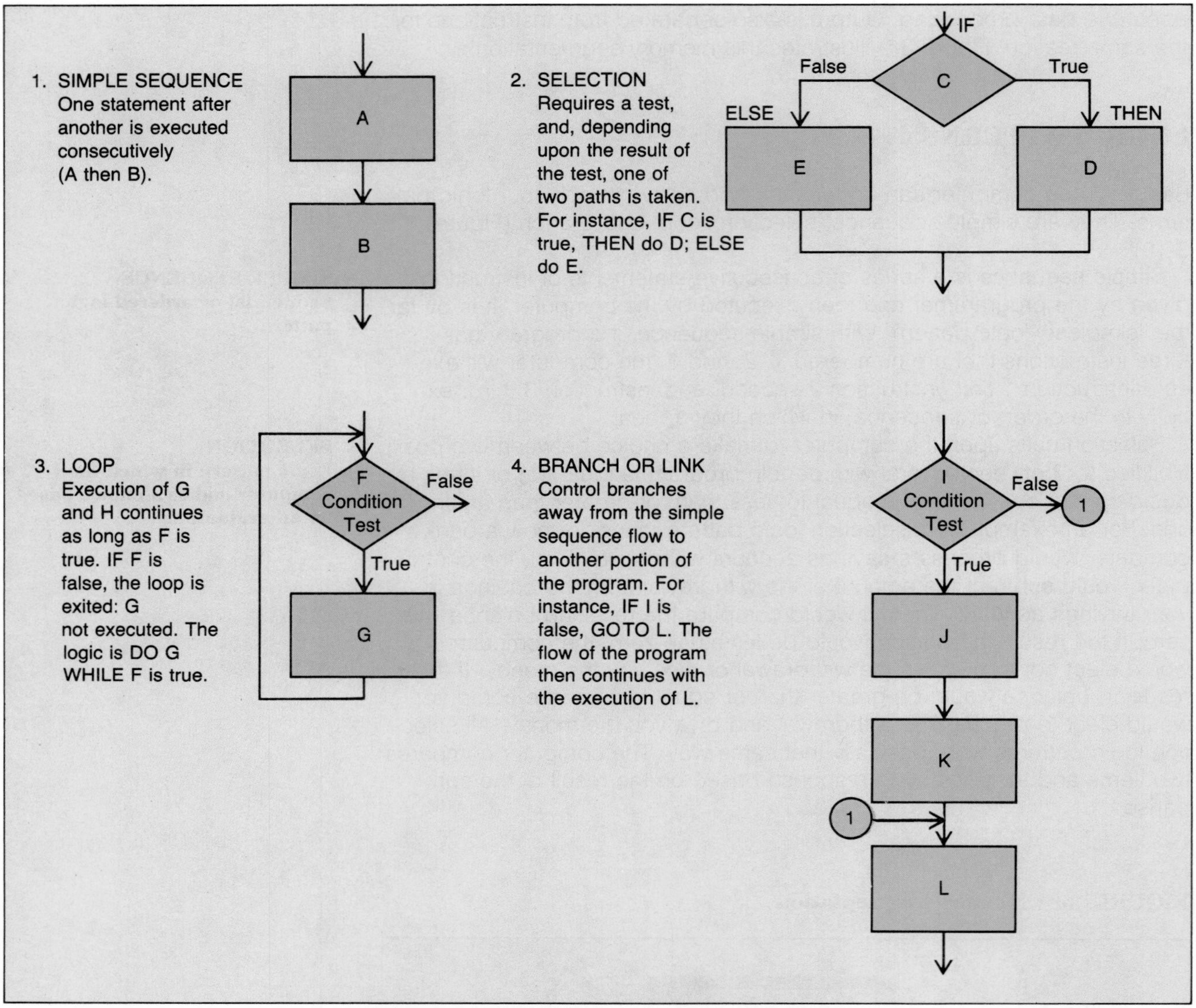

FIGURE 3-10 Four Program Logic Patterns

LOOP
Logic pattern in which the computer repeats a series of instructions.

The third logic pattern is the loop. A computer uses the **loop** action to return to an earlier step in its programming and repeat the same sequence over again but usually with new data. By looping, a programmer avoids having to repeat, for example, the same set of payroll calculation instructions for each employee being paid. Many people have accurately pointed out that the loop is the essence of programming. Computers are best at doing repetitive tasks. The loop allows the computer to do just that—repeat the same instructions again and again and again. For example, a payroll program using properly written loops will work equally well for five employees or 5,000.

PROFILE

CLIVE SINCLAIR

Clive Sinclair will undoubtedly be remembered as the man most responsible for making personal computers accessible to almost everyone. The self-taught English inventor introduced his Timex Sinclair 1000 into the United States in 1982 at a list price of $99. But since discounting reduced that figure by a third, it made the tiny 12-ounce unit the least expensive major brand available anywhere.

Sinclair has been an imaginative inventor since he was a boy. He built miniaturized mechanical calculators when he was 12. By the 1970s—when he was still in his thirties—Sinclair was turning out pocket calculators capable of doing sophisticated mathematical functions, as well as digital wristwatches and TV sets with 2-inch screens. With the success of his inventions he founded Sinclair Research, Ltd. in Cambridge, England and Boston, Massachusetts.

Sinclair's most popular products to date are the ZX81 and Spectrum personal computers. The mass-market Sinclair computers were developed with only 2K of memory, but that was enough to power video games, calculate math problems, and handle home budgets. Most important, these machines were very affordable—retailing for approximately $100.

Currently, Sinclair is involved in designing a flat-screen television capable of producing high-quality images. Such a screen would be a major breakthrough; it would promote a new generation of portable computers and enable consumers to take advantage of a low-cost monitor opposed to the standard models presently available.

Sinclair's research is not limited to only computers– he is also working on a prototype of an electric vehicle.

The last logic pattern is the branch, which has been criticized by some programmers as being inefficient and confusing to those who had no hand in the original programming of a particular program. The **branch** pattern allows the computer to skip over (branch around) some statements in a program instead of following them consecutively. Jumping from one part of the program to another is more time consuming—and thus less efficient—than sequence following. Also, because it does not follow the usual order of programming, it is difficult for other programmers to understand. In most cases, if common sense is applied, branch statements can be used effectively, but the rule of thumb is to use them sparingly.

BRANCH
Logic pattern that allows the computer to skip (branch around) instructions.

This is easily seen in the use of the "GO TO" statement, used in many high-level languages such as BASIC, Pascal, and COBOL. The GO TO tells the computer to "go to" another line. For example, if the program was on the second line in Figure 3-11 when the computer read the GO TO statement, it would tell it to go to line 60. In that way the computer would "branch around" or skip lines 30 through 50.

The GO TO statement has its place in programming; however, the problem with branch logic patterns such as the GO TO is that beginning programmers tend to misuse them, as in this program segment. The program shows very bad use of the GO TO statement. While this may be an extreme example, it serves to illustrate the point that too many GO TOs can make the program logic difficult to follow or understand. To avoid this

```
10 INPUT "ENTER X,Y";X,Y
20 IF X < Y THEN GOTO 60
30 IF X > Y THEN GOTO 80
40 IF X = Y THEN GOTO 100
50 GOTO 999
60 PRINT "X < Y"
70 GOTO 120
80 PRINT "X > Y"
90 GOTO 120
100 PRINT "X = Y"
110 GOTO 50
120 GOTO 10
999 END
```

FIGURE 3-11 Example of Branch Logic Pattern Using GO TO Statements

problem, branch structures such as the GO TO statement should be used carefully and sparingly.

TELECOMMUNICATIONS

So far we have been looking at the computer and its input and output devices as a closely clustered system; that is, at how a single computer works. But many times, computers in different locations work together, and even more often, the input/output devices for a computer are located in a different building, city, or even country than the computer itself. Need and refined technology have made all sorts of remote (away from computer) linkups possible. Advanced processing techniques increasingly use remote input/output devices that are in direct communication with the computer. As we learned in Chapter 2, point-of-sale (POS) terminals can communicate sales data directly to the computer as they occur and furnish up-to-date sales and inventory figures. Magnetic-ink character readers process checks at incredible speeds, using the computer to keep track of checks and dollar amounts. CRT terminals are used to input data as well as output information. Whatever the form, direct communication with the computer can provide fast, current information by reducing delays in the collection and transfer of data.

Communication Channels

COMMUNICATION CHANNEL
A pathway that allows remote input/output devices to communicate with the computer.

TELECOMMUNICATIONS
The combined use of communication facilities and data-processing equipment.

Remote input/output devices communicate with the computer by a pathway called a **communication channel**. Such channels include telegraph lines, telephone lines, microwave links, communication satellites, and laser beams.

In a data communication system, data are transmitted between terminals and a central computer or even between two or more computers. The combined use of communication facilities, such as telephone systems and data-processing equipment, is called **telecommunications**.

COMSAT's Launch Control Center. Located at COMSAT's headquarters in Washington, DC, the LCC is the world's only commercial facility designed and optimized for monitoring and controlling spacecraft during the launch phase of the mission through injection into synchronous orbit. The Center has provided launch and transfer orbit support for satellites in the INTELSAT, COMSTAR, and Satellite Business Systems series.

Analog versus Digital Message Transmission

Data can be transmitted over communication channels in either analog or digital form. Transmission in continuous wave form is called **analog transmission**. This is the type of transmission used on normal telephone lines. An analog transmission is like waves created in still water. Here the "waves" of messages are sent down a wire electronically. In the past, analog transmission was the main method of relaying data over a long distance, largely because of the type of communication lines provided by American Telephone and Telegraph (AT&T). **Digital transmission** involves transmitting data as distinct "on" and "off" states and represents data in the same form as the computer does (Figure 3-12).

ANALOG TRANSMISSION Transmission in continuous wave form.

DIGITAL TRANSMISSION Transmission as distinct "on" and "off" states.

FIGURE 3-12 Analog and Digital Transmission

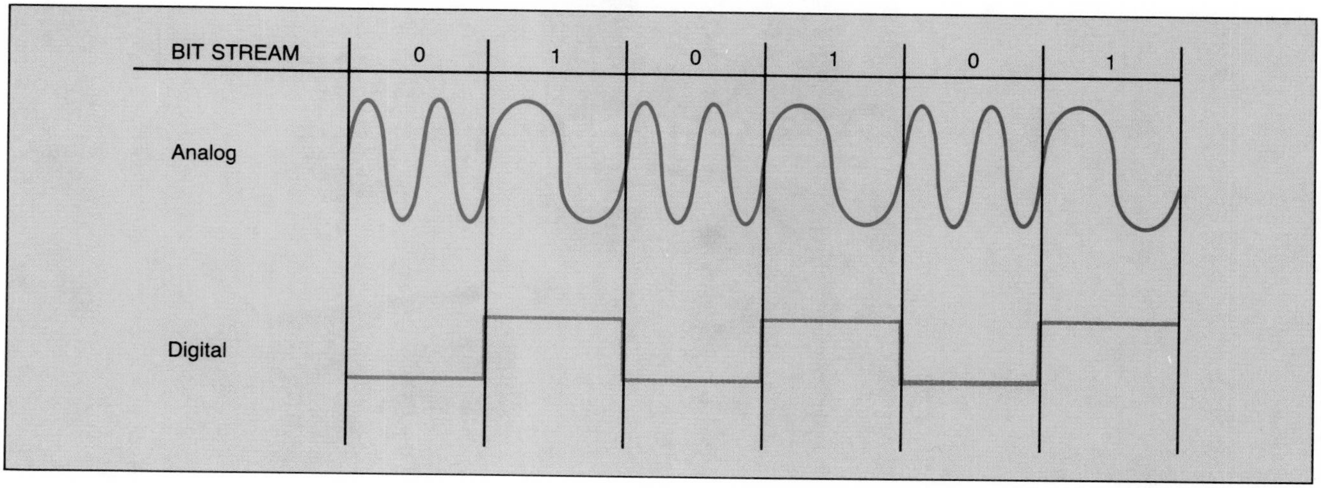

MODULATION
Conversion of data from digital to analog form.

DEMODULATION
Conversion data from analog to digital form.

MODEM
Device used to modulate and demodulate data.

Analog transmission requires that the sender convert the data from the digital (on and off) form in which they are stored to analog (wave) form before transmitting them. This conversion process is called **modulation**. The opposite conversion—from analog to digital—is necessary at the receiving end before the data are entered into the computer. This conversion is called **demodulation**. Both modulation and demodulation are accomplished by devices called **modems** (Figure 3-13).

Digital transmission requires no data conversion since the computer stores data in on/off pulse form. This reduces the time required to send messages. It also results in fewer transmission errors than with analog transmission.

Modes of Transmission

A method of classifying communication channels is by the mode of transmission they use. Depending on the application and the terminal equipment, channels operate in one of three basic transmission modes (Figure 3-14):

SIMPLEX
Mode used for one-way data transmission.

HALF-DUPLEX
Mode that allows two-way transmission; one way at a time.

FULL-DUPLEX
Mode that allows simultaneous two-way transmission.

A **simplex** channel provides for unidirectional (one-way) data transmission. A terminal that transmits by a simplex channel can either send or receive but cannot do both.

In the **half-duplex** mode, communication can flow in both directions but in only one direction at a time. This type of transmission is common in telephone services and networks.

A **full-duplex** channel can transmit data in both directions simultaneously and is the most versatile mode of transmission.

FIGURE 3-13 Modem

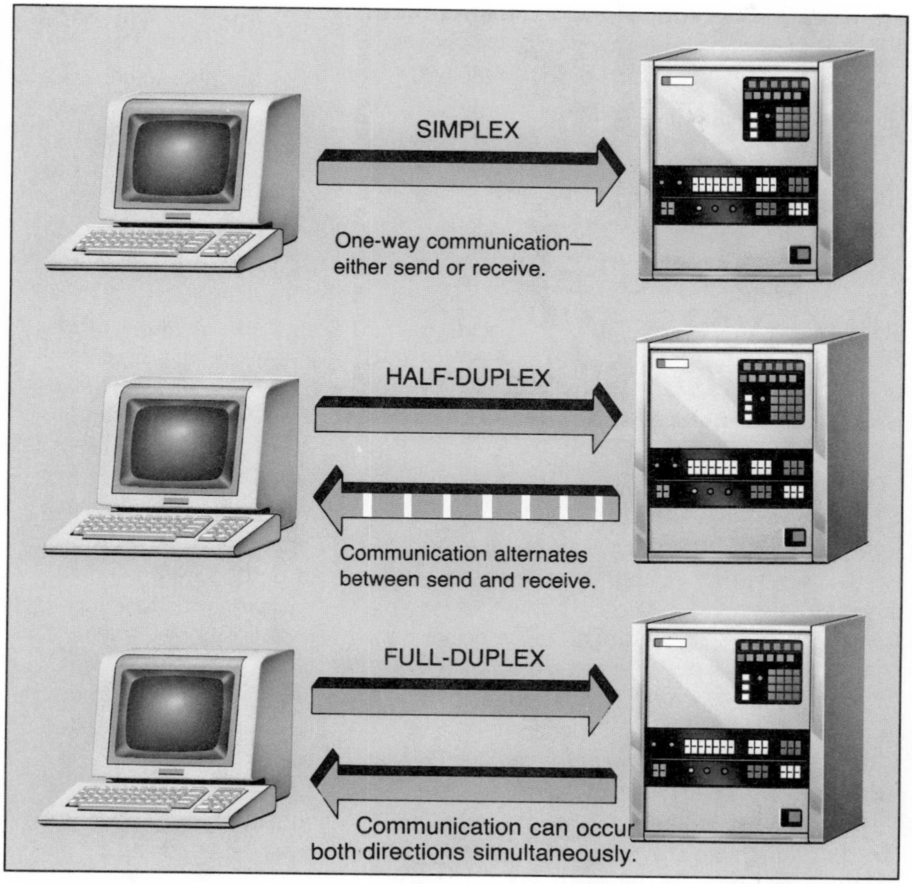

FIGURE 3-14 Channel Transmission Modes

ISSUE

COMPUTER MISTAKES: WHO IS RESPONSIBLE?

We have all heard the story about the man who was declared dead because of a computer error. Social security payments stopped, pension benefits ceased, and the infamous red tape set in. "So sorry, but if the computer claims you're deceased—you *are* deceased. Computers don't make mistakes . . ."

Of course, computer errors do happen, as many of us have discovered to our annoyance. If we have this unhappy experience, what we want to know is (1) Who actually made the mistake? and (2) Who is responsible for it?

There are four common ways to generate a computer error. By far the most common is using incorrect input. If the data going into the program is wrong, the information coming out will be just as wrong. Incorrect input can come from two sources: (1) the typist or keypuncher mistypes the input or (2) the person who gathers the input records it wrong to begin with.

Another common cause of computer errors is that the program doesn't anticipate every possibility. For example, if a program doesn't take into account the possibility that it may be leap year, its customers could lose one day's interest because of the error.

Sometimes this type of error can occur on the system level. That is, rather than a program that leaves out a possibility, you can have a system that leaves out a program. The courts recently faced such a situation.

One of North American's drivers became fatigued after driving for over seventy hours in an eight-day period, a violation of an Interstate Commerce Commission rule. The fatigued driver was involved in an accident in which a motorist was killed. The motorist's widow sued North American for negligence because their computer system did not include a program to detect violations of the "seventy-hour" rule. The justices agreed with the motorist's widow, and she was awarded $10,000,000.

The third type of error occurs when the input is right and the program is right—but the answer is wrong. These errors can be generated by not taking into consideration the limitations of real and integer arithmetic. Similar errors could also be generated by a power surge. Theoretically, even cosmic rays can interfere with computer operations, but that possibility is very slight.

The fourth way to generate a computer error is to unintentionally design a program that would not give the same response as a human being in the same situation.

A prime example of this involved a stop payment order on a check. A corporate customer of a large bank ordered a stop payment on check number 896 dated February 27 for $1,844.48, on account number 02042178315. However, the actual amount of the check was $1,844.98. When the computer processed the check, it noted the $.50 difference and issued payment on the check.

This resulted in a lawsuit in which the judge ruled that because a human operator would not have issued payment on the check, the bank was liable for the amount.

However, there is little legal guidance in the area of dealing with computer mistakes. Because the area is so new, many states have few, if any, laws pertaining to them. Court decisions are often based on Uniform Commercial Code regulations that have to be newly applied—and rulings are by no means consistent.

Thus, although computer errors are fairly obvious, the answer to the question of who is responsible for them is not. Is the programmer personally responsible for any errors that are written into the program? Or does the company using the program assume responsibility when it purchases the program? Should the typist be held personally responsible for input errors? Or is it management's responsibility to check the information once it is processed? Can we really expect computers to function as human beings would?

ISSUE

The answer to the question of responsibility is crucial. Computer errors can be far more serious than most people think.

Businesses die from computer errors. An insurance company survey showed that 90 percent of all business depending on computers that experience a major loss of service due to a computer error go out of business after that loss.

Computer errors have done more than ruin businesses. Computer errors have endangered people's health. They have ruined reputations and they have killed. Because of the potential for error, it is essential that we determine who is responsible.

If you live in a large city, chances are that many of the traffic lights are computer controlled for efficiency. If an error occurs, you could be injured in an auto collision. If the computer at your heating company decided that your bills were overdue, you could freeze. Many water treatment plants also use computer controls . . . the possibilities are terrifying. And they are especially terrifying because the issue of responsibility is so muddled.

SUMMARY POINTS

■ There are two types of computers: (1) digital computers, which operate by measuring "on" and "off" electrical pulses and (2) analog computers, which work by measuring continuous physical or electrical conditions.
■ Computer systems may either be online or use batch processing. Online systems place the user in direct communication with the computer and allow the user and computer to interact once the program has begun execution. Batch-processing systems process all instructions and data at once and allow for no interaction during program execution.
■ Machine language is composed of electrical states, often represented by the binary system, and is the only language that the computer recognizes. All other languages must first be translated into machine language before the computer understands them.
■ Because computers understand only machine language, programmers have devised codes to represent data to the computer. Binary is the simplest of those codes; it uses base 2. Because binary is tedious, coding schemes have been devised that offer shorthand methods of representing binary. These coding schemes are 4-bit Binary Coded Decimal (BCD), Extended Binary Coded Decimal Interchange Code (EBCDIC), American Standard Code for Information Interchange (ASCII), and ASCII-8.
■ A bit is a position in a binary number. A byte is eight adjacent bits, and the parity or check bit is used to indicate a character miscoding error.
■ Information processing consists of three steps: (1) input, (2) processing, and (3) output. Input involves collecting, verifying, and coding the data. Processing may include any combination of the following: classifying, sorting, calculating, summarizing, and storing. Output consists of retrieving, converting, and communicating the results.
■ The stored-program concept allows the entire program, along with the data, to be stored in memory. (A program is a set of instructions.)
■ There are four logic patterns that the computer may use when executing a program. They are simple sequence, selection, loop, and branch.
■ Telecommunications refers to the combined use of communication facilities and data-processing equipment.
■ In telecommunications, data can be transmitted in either analog form (as a continuous wave) or digital form (as distinct "on" and "off" states). Modulation converts digital data to analog form; demodulation converts analog data to digital form. Modems are used for modulation and demodulation.
■ There are three modes of transmission used in telecommunications: (1) simplex, which allows one-way data transmission; (2) half-duplex, which allows two-way transmission; and (3) full-duplex, which allows simultaneous two-way transmission.

REVIEW QUESTIONS

1. How do digital and analog computers differ?
2. Give an original example of a program that would work on an online system but wouldn't work on a batch-processing system. Explain why it wouldn't work.
3. Why don't people program in machine language?
4. List the standard coding schemes and explain what they are used for and how they differ.
5. Define the terms "bit," "byte," and "parity bit."
6. What is the difference between data and information?
7. List the steps involved in input and explain the purpose of each one.
8. What operation may be used in processing?
9. What is a program?
10. What are the four logic patterns and how do they differ?
11. Why is use of the branch pattern criticized by some programmers?
12. Why are loops essential to programming?
13. Define telecommunications and give some examples of types of communication channels.
14. What is the purpose of a modem? (Be specific and give an illustration of how it is used.)

DISCUSSION QUESTIONS

1. In electronic data processing, information processing requires many steps. Which of these would not be needed to process information manually?
2. The idea of a stored program was a significant discovery. Explain the concept and explain how programs were processed before this advance occurred.
3. Even though the computer can only use four logic patterns, its limitations in solving problems are very few. Try to think of a problem that could *not* be solved using some combination of these logic patterns.
4. Telecommunications is more than sending information from one place to another. It is changing the way businesses operate and the way executives travel (or don't travel). Think of two businesses that use telecommunications. How has it affected their operations?
5. Computer errors can range from merely frustrating to fatal. Discuss some computer errors that you have either experienced or heard of. How do you think they could have been avoided?

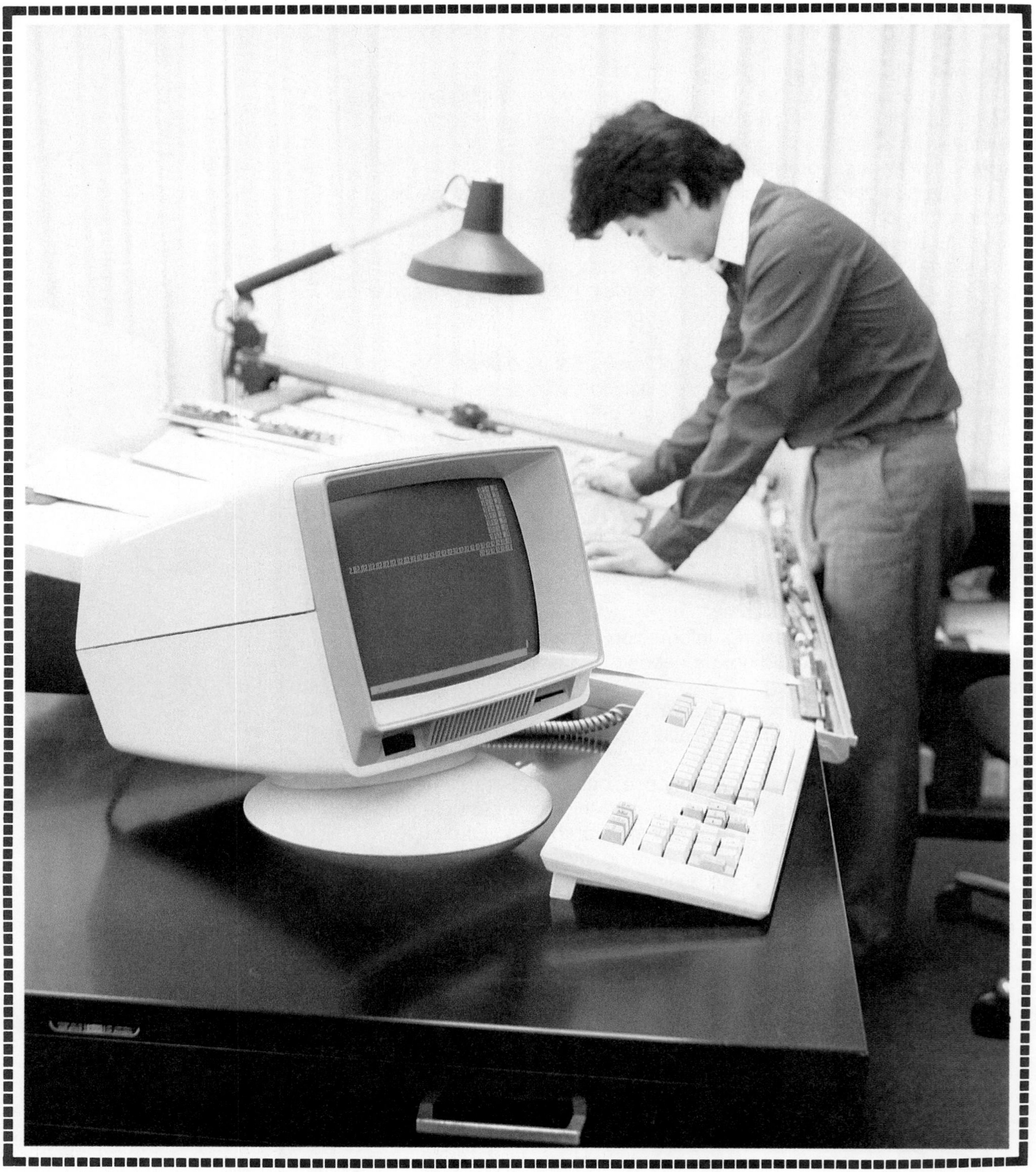

CHAPTER 4
COMMUNICATING WITH THE COMPUTER: PROGRAMMING

OUTLINE

ARTICLE

COMPUTER PROGRAMMING: WHAT'S IN IT FOR YOU?

Paul Bonner

Computer programming is for nerds, right? You know: those funny looking guys with thick glasses who wear white shirts buttoned at the collar (with no ties) and fill their breast pockets with ball-point pens; long-haired, bearded refugees from the love-and-peace-generation who traded in their electric guitars and amps for S-100 buses and surplus circuit boards. People with nothing else to do. Those are the only ones who waste their time trying to program a . . . computer, right?

Wrong. By a mile.

Today, businessmen with plenty of other things to do with their time are studying the art of programming and taking advantage of the wide variety of software, books, and specialized computers. Some of these people are driven by pure curiosity, others by an inability to find software that meets their needs, and still others by the belief that learning to program will give them a competitive edge.

The curiosity angle is easy to figure. After you've been working on a . . . computer for some time, it's natural to wonder how it works. Programming, the means by which you put a computer through its paces, goes a long way towards satisfying that curiosity.

It's also easy to understand how people can become frustrated by the idiosyncrasies of commercial software, or by an inability to find a commercial program that exactly meets individual needs. It's been said that you can't write a job description for any job worth doing. That implies that any challenging job is unique, making it difficult for a manufacturer who wants to sell thousands of copies of his program to supply a tool that fits the unique requirements of such jobs. It also suggests that the person doing such a job is unique, thinks uniquely, and works in a unique way. That may be why you can read a glowing software review, only to find when you buy the program that its command structure and the way it works don't seem logical and natural to you. Learning to program helps solve these problems, since you'll be able to write applications programs tailored to fit your needs and preferences.

Finally, there's the possibility that knowing how to program will give you an edge in business. Understanding more about computers than can be learned solely by using commercial applications programs may enhance your value to a company.

So, there are good reasons to be interested in learning how to program.

As computers become more prevalent in our society, more and more people are either learning elementary programming or learning about programming—what it is, how it works, and who needs it.

INTRODUCTION

Programming is the process by which the user communicates with the computer. More importantly, it is the process we use to get the computer to execute the task we want it to do.

Before jumping into programming, the user should consider several factors. In what language would he or she like to program? What languages are available for the particular computer? Finally, the most important question: How does one program a computer?

THE PROGRAMMING PROCESS

Within their physical limitations, computers will do what they are told. But the telling has to be done in special languages used to program instructions to the computer. Some programming is permanently built into the circuitry of the central processing unit (CPU) of the computer (its "brain"), and some is fed in through such media as punched cards and magnetic tapes and disks.

A Texaco programmer and geologist work together aboard the *Acadian Seafarer* using state-of-the-art technology to find crude oil and natural gas far beneath the bottom of the sea.

PROGRAMMER
Person who writes computer programs.

Sets of instructions, programs, that are compiled by a **programmer** to make the computer solve specific problems or carry out specific tasks are referred to as software—in contrast to the computing machines themselves, the hardware. Just as human languages have evolved to fit the needs of particular groups of people, so have computer languages been tailored to different functions. All humans don't speak the same languages and neither do computers.

Levels of Language

As computers have evolved in sophistication of functions, so have the programming languages they use. There are three levels of language: machine language, assembly language, and high-level languages. Each level of language has special virtues and drawbacks.

Machine Language As mentioned earlier, machine language is the code that designates the "on/off" electrical states in a computer. Old as the computer itself, this language is expressed as combinations of 0s and 1s. This is the only language to which the computer can respond. Each type of computer has its own machine language, which is not transferrable to another type of computer. Each instruction in machine language must state not just the operation required but also the storage locations of the data items. Since these requirements—plus the nature of the language itself—make machine language programming extremely complex, tedious, and time consuming, other languages have been developed.

Assembly Language Assembly language is a little more understandable (readable) to the user than is machine language. With it, programmers still must specify both the operations to be performed and the storage locations. But people can understand assembly language more easily. It replaces the 0 and 1 groupings of machine language with more convenient symbols and abbreviations. For example, "STO" may stand for STORE and "TRA" for TRANSFER. Nonetheless, programming in assembly language remains a cumbersome and cryptic task.

High-level Languages High-level languages are designed so that a programmer's primary attention can be on the problem itself, rather than on the peculiarities of computer operations. Many high-level languages are English-like and use common mathematical terms and symbols. These qualities reduce the time and effort needed to write a program, and such programs are easier to correct or modify.

High-level languages least resemble the 0 and 1 combinations of machine language. Figure 4-1 shows the difference between a simple statement in BASIC, a high-level language, and its equivalent in machine language. Although one assembly language instruction is generally equivalent to one machine language instruction, there is a one-to-many relationship between a statement in a high-level language and a machine language instruction. Because of this, it may take five or six machine-level instructions to accomplish what is done by a single BASIC statement.

PROFILE

TED HOFF

Eleven years after Jack Kilby's invention of the integrated circuit, a new development in computer technology entered the market—the microprocessor. The first microprocessor was invented in 1969; however, there is some question as to its real inventor. Intel Corporation supports Ted Hoff for the 4004 microprocessor while Datapoint Corporation defends Victor Poor for the 8008 microprocessor. Even though the debate has not been officially resolved, Marcian E. "Ted" Hoff, Jr., is usually recognized as the man behind the microprocessor.

After receiving his Ph.D. from Stanford University, Hoff joined Intel in 1968 as its twelfth employee. There he was assigned the project of developing chips for a family of high-performance, programmable calculators for Busicom (a now defunct Japanese calculator manufacturer). The original plan outlined 12 chips for the calculator's various functions, but Hoff proposed the idea of creating a single chip capable of performing all the functions. Furthermore, the chip would be a general-purpose processor—not limited to just calculator-type processes. By the fall, Hoff's idea materialized. The chip, the 4004 microprocessor, contained approximately 2300 transistors. More importantly, it had all the components of a full-size CPU; hence, the phrase "microcomputer on a chip" accurately describes the microprocessor.

Intel negotiated with Busicom and gained the rights to sell the chip to other companies for various applications. The first advertisement for the 4004 appeared in an issue of *Electronic News* in November, 1971. By 1974, Intel sold more microprocessors than the entire population of mainframes and minicomputers.

Since then, several other more sophisticated models of the microprocessor have been developed to keep current with the state-of-the-art technology. This invention has not only reduced the price of computers, but also created uses for computer technology in a number of consumer products.

Language Translation

Assembly and high-level languages cannot be executed directly by computers. The set of instructions written by the programmer, the **source program**, must be converted into machine-executable form by a **language translator program**. The resultant translation, known as the **object program**, is the same as a program originally written in machine language.

SOURCE PROGRAM
Instructions written by the programmer.

LANGUAGE TRANSLATOR PROGRAM
Translates the source program into the object program.

OBJECT PROGRAM
Machine language program used for high-level languages.

FIGURE 4-1 One BASIC Statement and Corresponding Machine Language Instructions

(a) HIGH-LEVEL LANGUAGE (APPLE-SOFT BASIC)

```
100  C = A + B
```

(b) MACHINE LANGUAGE (MOS-TECH 6502 MACHINE LANGUAGE)

```
1010  0000  0000  0000  0000  1101
1010  1101  0000  1110  0000  1101
0111  1001  0110  0000  0000  1100
1101  1000
1000  1101  0011  1111  0000  1100
```

ASSEMBLER PROGRAM
Language translator program used for assembly language.

INTERPRETER
Translates source programs to machine language—one instruction at a time.

COMPILER PROGRAM
Language translator program used for high-level languages.

The translator program for assembly language is called an **assembler program**, and a high-level language translator is called either an **interpreter** or a **compiler program**. Translator programs are designed for specific machines and languages. A compiler that translates a program written in FORTRAN into a machine language program, for example, cannot translate COBOL statements. Figure 4-2 illustrates the different levels of language.

During the translation process, the object program is generated and the programmer receives a listing that indicates any errors detected dur-

FIGURE 4-2 Language Levels

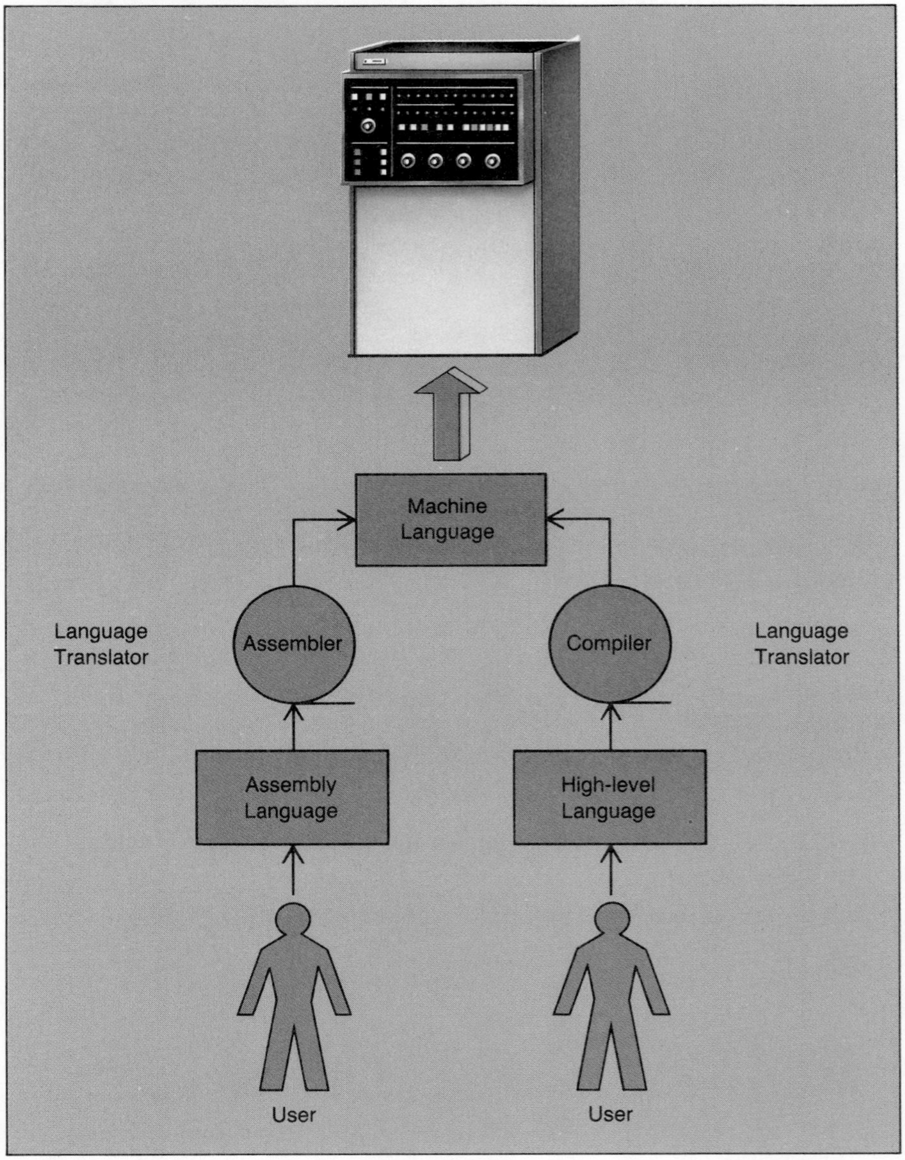

ing translation. Such errors are usually violations of the rules of a particular programming language. These are called **syntax errors**. For example, an error warning will be generated if such language keywords as "WRITE" or "COMPUTE" are misspelled. The error-message listing may give the number of each statement in error and also describe the nature of the error (Figure 4-3). The object program is fed into the computer for execution only after all detected errors have been corrected. Several attempts at error correction may be needed.

SYNTAX ERROR
A violation of the rules of a programming language.

Complex programs are often tested in separate sections. This way errors can be isolated to specific segments of the program. To correct all the mistakes, or **debug** the program, the programmer may have to run and rerun a specific unit before the cause of the error can be discovered. Once this is done, the programmer must rewrite the parts in error and resubmit them for another test. The programmer must be careful to see that the correction of one logical error does not cause the creation of several others.

DEBUG
To remove errors from a program.

Each section of a program—even those that will be used infrequently—must be tested. Costly computer errors may result from not checking all possibilities. If instructions for handling exceptions are part of the program, then the sample input data should include items that test the program's ability to spot and reject improper data items. The programmer often resorts to **desk checking** (desk debugging), whereby he or she "pretends" to be the computer by reading each instruction and simulating how the computer would process a data item. Sometimes as an additional safeguard, programmers trade their partially debugged programs among themselves. A programmer who goes through a "fresh" program may uncover mistakes in logic to which the original programmer was oblivious.

DESK CHECKING
Debugging technique in which the programmer "pretends" to be a computer.

Solving Problems with the Computer

Solving problems with the computer is what is often referred to as programming. We have decided not to use the term programming because too many people associate programming with coding. **Coding** is translating the program design into the particular programming language being used. To be sure, coding is a part of programming, but it is not the only part, nor is it the most important part.

CODING
Translating the program design into a programming language.

FIGURE 4-3 Compiler-Detected Errors

Statement Number	Error Message
2061	Invalid or no program heading
2399	Identifier already declared
2480	Identifier not declared
2491	Illegal symbol
2601	Type conflict of operands
2621	Minus sign not preceded by a space. Assume space.

Solving problems with the computer is a four-part process. These parts are (1) defining the problem, (2) designing a solution, (3) coding the program, and (4) compiling, testing, and debugging the program.

Defining the Problem The first part of problem solving with the computer is built upon the answers to a number of questions. Who needs information? What kind is needed? What data are needed to yield the information and where can it be found? Will the data have to be accumulated in a certain order? In what form must the data be fed into the computer once they have been gathered? In what form will the output be most useful to the intended users?

All these questions—as well as many others—are vital; and it is clear that not all of them can be answered by a programmer alone. Some help and guidance will be needed from management, the information users, or a specialist called a **system analyst**. The analyst can be expected to develop an overall view of the system's aims, organization, priorities, and needs. (Chapter 6 discusses system analysis in more detail.)

SYSTEM ANALYST
A specialist who evaluates the aims, organization, priorities, and needs of the computer system.

Designing a Solution Once the information-processing problem has been analyzed, the analyst and/or programmer can begin designing the computer-assisted solution. Because even the most advanced computer is rigidly limited in the logical patterns it can apply to a problem, the design will require considerable creativity from the programmer.

To guard against the writing and use of faulty programs, programmers should carefully formulate their algorithms before they begin coding their programs. An **algorithm** is an outline of the logic used to solve the problem. It outlines the desired sequence and details of instructions so they can be prechecked for errors and omissions. The two most popular ways to represent algorithms are the pseudocode and the flowchart.

ALGORITHM
An outline of the logic used in writing the program.

Pseudocode is simply a brief set of instructions written in sentence form in the order that the instructions will appear in the actual programming. Pseudocoding allows the program planner to write out the details quickly without having to pay meticulous attention to programming demands. Pseudocoding is to writing a program what an outline or a rough draft is to writing a term paper.

PSEUDOCODE
A written description of the algorithm.

Figure 4-4 shows a pseudocode of the steps in calculating a depart-

FIGURE 4-4 Example of a Pseudocode

```
Start
Begin Loop  <-----------------------------+
  Read Price of Clothes                   |  LOOP (Until There Are
  Add Price to Total Bill                 |  No More Items)
  If There Are More Clothes               |
    Then Goto Beginning of Loop           |
  Else                                    |
    If There Are No More Clothes          |
End Loop  <-------------------------------+
Print Total Bill  <-----------------------+  SIMPLE SEQUENCE
Stop  <-----------------------------------+
```

ment store bill and demonstrates the programmer's adherence to the logic patterns.

Like pseudocode, the **flowchart** is a skeleton of the real thing. It is a diagram of the necessary steps instead of a prose statement of them. (Other names for the flowchart are block diagram, logic diagram, and logic chart.) Figure 4-5 shows the pseudocode example as it would appear in flowchart form.

FLOWCHART
A diagram of the algorithm.

Accurate flowcharts, both in their original and updated forms, are good visible records of programs and how they were designed. Because of the reference value of flowcharts, programmers should use the standard flowchart symbols established by the American National Standards Institute (ANSI) and keep flowcharts complete, up-to-date, and legible. Figure 4-6 illustrates the major ANSI-sanctioned symbols, as well as the off-page connector, a non-ANSI-sanctioned symbol recommended by IBM.

Coding the Program Coding is translating the algorithm into a programming language. The language used will depend on what the program is expected to do and what facilities are available to the programmer. We will not discuss the actual coding of a program, because that would be impossible without using a particular programming language. However, there are general rules that should be followed to ensure that the program is well written.

Getting the right answer or response is not the only requirement of a well-written program. That, alone, can be done in different ways. But one program can be better than another. The programmer should strive for these qualities in any program:

FIGURE 4-5 Example of a Flowchart

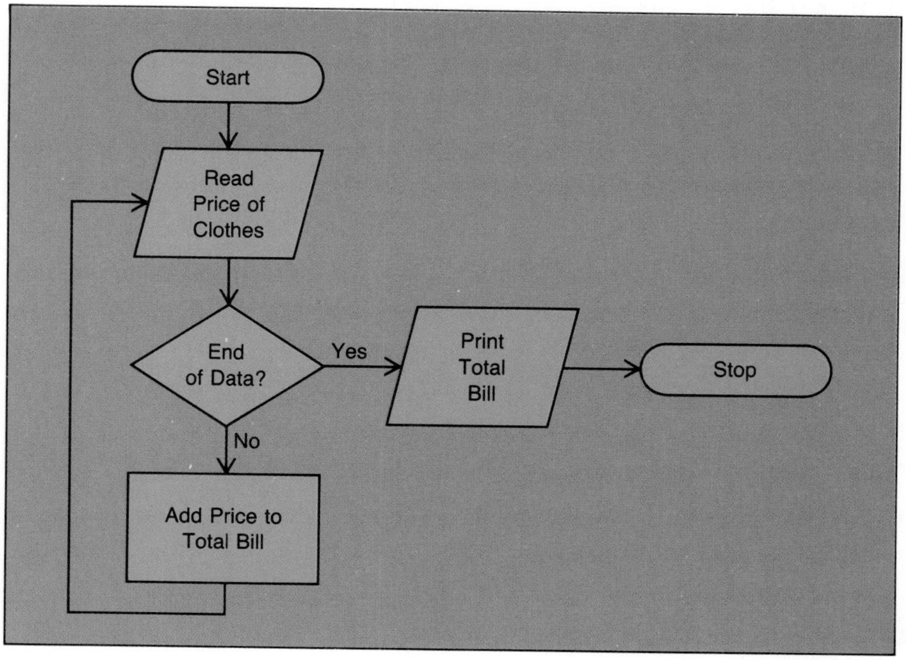

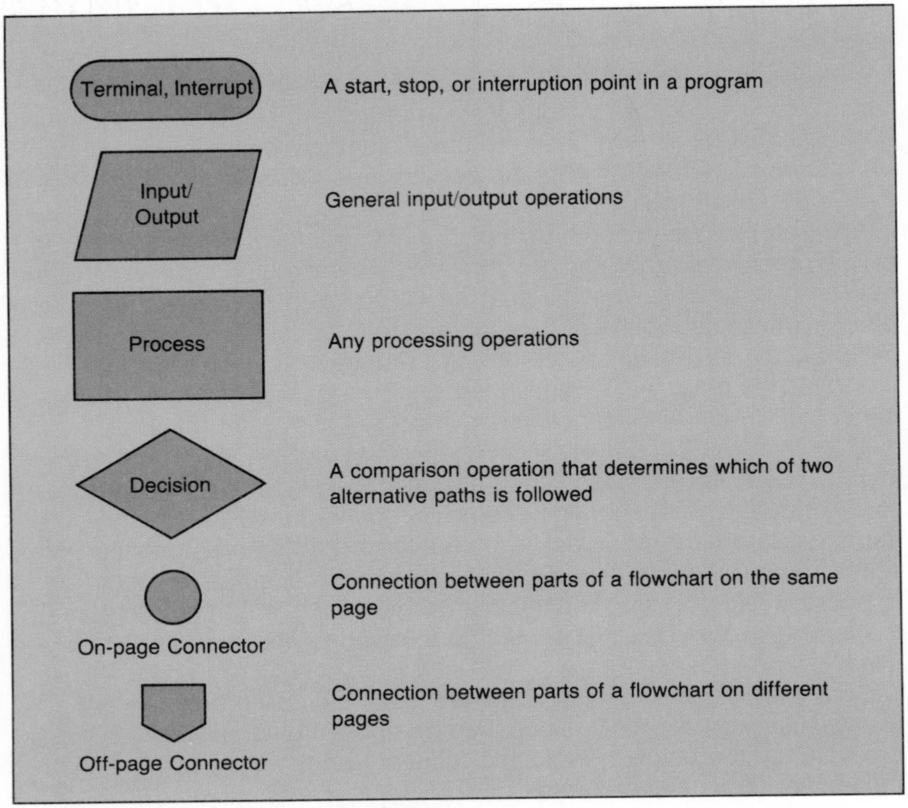

FIGURE 4-6 Flowchart Symbols

- Ease of reading and understanding. The program should be written so that another programmer will be able to see quickly what is happening.
- Reliability. The program should consistently produce the right output.
- Workable under all conditions. Reliability is not the only factor of a satisfactory program. Even when internal logic is correct, incorrect or inappropriate input data ("garbage in") can result in incorrect or inappropriate output ("garbage out").
- Ease of modification and updating. Programs should be constructed in independent segments so that a change in one segment does not mandate a change in others.
- Portability, that is, its ability to be used on other computers without modification.

Compiling, Debugging, and Testing the Program Before the coded program can be executed, it must be translated into machine language. This can be done by either a compiler or an interpreter, as mentioned earlier.

Once the program has been translated, the first thing the programmer will probably notice is some error messages. This does not indicate that the programmer has poor coding skills. Rather, it exemplifies Murphy's first law of programming: A program seldom works the first time. It must be debugged.

The term "debugging" came into use in the summer of 1945, when scientists were working on one of the earliest computers, the Mark II. The computer had stopped for no apparent reason, and the programmers were trying to figure out what was wrong with it. They finally discovered that a moth was caught in one of the relays. They removed the "bug" and the computer worked fine. Since then computer scientists have used the term debugging to refer to removing any type of error or malfunction from either a computer's hardware or software.

In general, there are three types of computer errors. They are syntax errors, run-time errors, and logic errors.

Syntax errors, discussed earlier, are errors that violate the rules of grammar of a particular programming language. These must be corrected before the compile step can be completed successfully.

Run-time errors occur when you tell the computer to do something that it cannot do. For example, if you told the computer to add 12 numbers but only gave it 11 numbers, a run-time error would occur as the computer tried to read data that was not there. Another common run-time error is asking the computer to divide something by zero. The common factor in run-time errors is that they are detected while the program is running. Unlike a program with a syntax error, a program with a run-time error will compile. It will simply stop running when the error is encountered.

RUN-TIME ERROR
An error that stops the program's execution once it has begun.

Logic errors are the worst type of errors. With syntax errors and run-time errors, at least the compiler or interpreter will tell you that there is an error; and, in most cases, it will also tell you what the error is and where it is located. Logic errors produce no error messages. A program with a

LOGIC ERROR
An error in designing the solution; the end result is that the solution doesn't solve the problem.

A programmer at work in a computer center at Hilheim, West Germany. The opportunities available to skilled programmers are truly international.

logic error will compile and execute as if everything were working fine. Rather than return an error message, the computer will simply return the wrong answer. A logic error indicates that the logic the programmer used to write the program did not solve the problem. Therefore, it is very important to carefully formulate algorithms and record them in either pseudocode or flowchart form. These records can then be used to locate a logic error if one should occur. Using these design tools will usually spotlight logic errors before the coding step itself.

Testing is the final part of writing a good program. Testing begins once everything else has been done and the program appears to be working fine. When the programmer tests the program, an attempt should be made to test every possibility. The programmer should test each possible input, as well as incorrect input to see how the program reacts. Testing will never prove that the program will work in all situations for all input, but it will decrease the chances that it won't.

A Programming Case Study

Let us say that a homeowner wishes to calculate his average monthly heating bill and verify the gas company's charges. The first step is to define the problem and decide whether a computer could help in solving that problem. If the solution is computable, then a program can be designed, coded, and finally compiled, debugged, and tested.

Defining the Problem Our homeowner has been faithfully recording his meter readings throughout the year. But the readings alone do not give him the information he needs to make his financial budget for the next year. So his problem is one of turning raw data into information. This is called processing the data. The information he requires is the average monthly bill and a check of the gas company's billing. Looking at the problem more closely, we can see that it will include calculating each monthly bill and keeping a running total to arrive at a yearly average.

Designing a Solution To design a program solution, he must determine what output the problem requires. In this case, it is a monthly billing amount and an average. To accurately derive these outputs, the proper inputs also must be determined. For the gas user, it will be his meter readings and the current rate for gas. To get the output from the given inputs, a certain amount of processing is required.

The needed steps are as follows:

1. Subtract beginning from end-of-month meter reading to calculate gas consumption.
2. Multiply consumption by gas rate to get monthly bill.
3. Total monthly bills and divide by 12 to get average monthly bill.

Here you can see the general information flow for this problem:

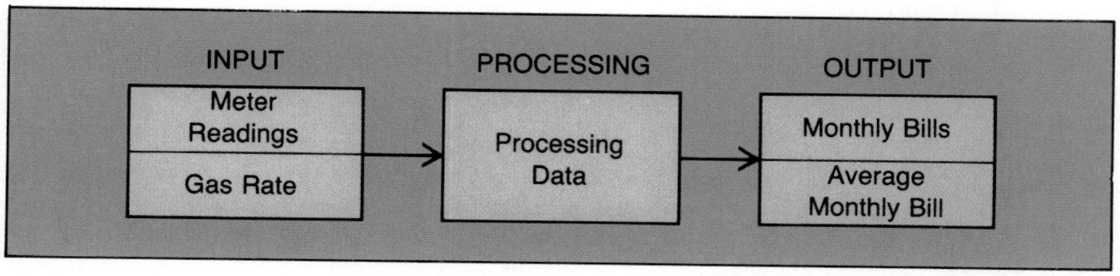

The next step in the design process is determining the algorithm required to complete the processing. The algorithm would consist of these steps:

1. Declare variables and constants.
2. Read in 13 meter readings.
3. Initialize variables and print headings.
4. While Month $\leq$ 12, do steps 5 through 9.
5. Calculate consumption.
6. Calculate monthly bill.
7. Write monthly bill information.
8. Add bill to total for year.
9. Increment month.
10. Calculate average monthly bill.
11. Write average bill.
12. Stop.

Once the programmer constructs the flowchart (Figure 4-7), it must be traced through by hand to verify the logic.

Coding the Program After verification the homeowner codes the program into a programming language—in this case Pascal. The completed source program can then be entered into the computer by the programmer. Figure 4-8(a) shows the source listing for the program. Figure 4-8(b) shows the data that are input to be processed.

Compiling, Debugging, and Testing the Program Once the program has been written, it is submitted to the computer to be compiled into machine language. Then a listing of the source program and notification of any errors detected by the computer can be generated. Finally, the program is executed. Figure 4-9 shows the program's output.

SOFTWARE
Programs

Within the category of function, there are two basic types of programs: **system programs** to coordinate the operation of computer hardware and **application programs**, which solve particular problems for the computer user.

System programs directly affect the operation of the computer. They facilitate the use of hardware and help the computer run quickly and effi-

SYSTEM PROGRAM
Coordinates the operation of the computer's hardware.

APPLICATION PROGRAM
Solves problems for the computer user.

FIGURE 4-7 Flowchart for Case Study: Calculation of Average Monthly Gas Bill

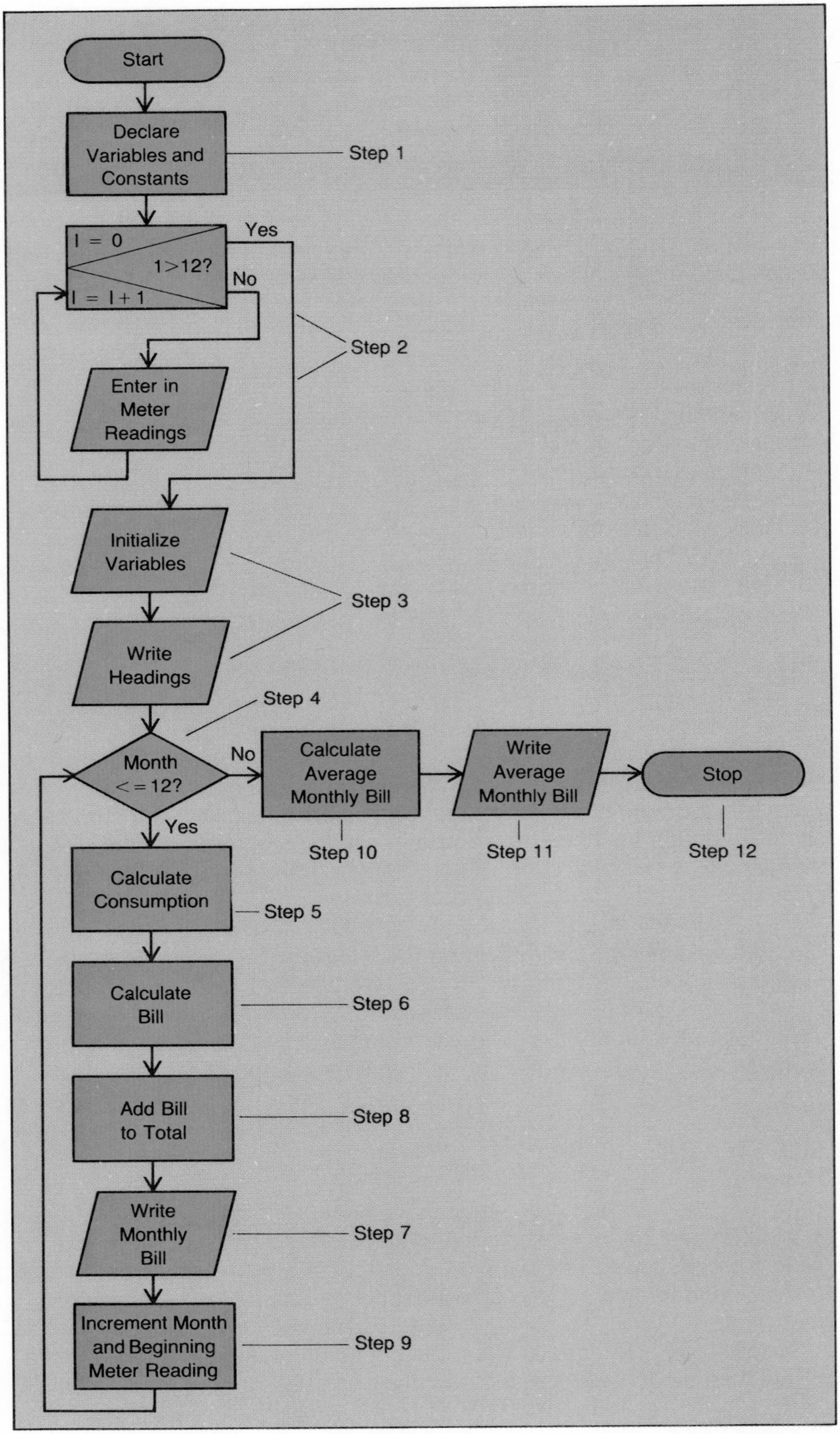

```
PROGRAM BILLCALC(INPUT,OUTPUT);
   (* THIS PROGRAM IS DESIGNED TO CALCULATE MONTHLY GAS
      CONSUMPTION AND THE BILL. IT WILL THEN DETERMINE
      THE AVERAGE MONTHLY BILL FOR THE YEAR. *)

      CONST       RATE = 0.52;

      VAR
                  CONSUMPTION : REAL;
                  BILL : REAL;
                  MONTH : INTEGER;
                  I : INTEGER;
                  READINGS : ARRAY [0..12] OF REAL;
                  TOTAL : REAL;
                  AVG : REAL;
BEGIN
  FOR I := 0 TO 12 DO
    BEGIN
      WRITELN(TTY,'ENTER METER READING');
      BREAK(TTY);
      READ(TTY,READINGS[I]);
      BREAK(TTY)
    END;
  MONTH := 1;
  TOTAL := 0;
  WRITELN(TTY,'MONTH':10,'AMOUNT':10,'RATE':10,'BILL':10);
  WRITELN(TTY);
  WHILE MONTH <= 12 DO
    BEGIN
      CONSUMPTION := READINGS[MONTH] - READINGS[MONTH - 1];
      BILL := CONSUMPTION * RATE;
      WRITELN(TTY,MONTH:10,CONSUMPTION:10:2,RATE:10:2,BILL:10:2);
      TOTAL := TOTAL + BILL;
      MONTH := MONTH + 1;
    END;   (* WHILE *)
  AVG := TOTAL / 12;
  WRITELN(TTY,' ');
  WRITELN(TTY,'  YOUR AVERAGE MONTHLY BILL IS .. ',AVG:10:2);
END.
```

FIGURE 4-8a Source Listing for Gas Bill Program

FIGURE 4-8b Data Entered for Gas Bill Program

```
TO CONTINUE, HIT THE RETURN KEY *
ENTER METER READING
123.5
ENTER METER READING
199.5
ENTER METER READING
300.5
ENTER METER READING
423.5
ENTER METER READING
523.7
ENTER METER READING
678.9
ENTER METER READING
756.1
ENTER METER READING
845.0
ENTER METER READING
900.2
ENTER METER READING
1054.7
ENTER METER READING
1132.6
ENTER METER READING
1234.5
ENTER METER READING
1322.7
```

MONTH	AMOUNT	RATE	BILL
1	76.00	0.51	39.51
2	101.00	0.51	52.51
3	122.99	0.51	63.95
4	100.19	0.51	52.10
5	155.20	0.51	80.70
6	77.19	0.51	40.14
7	88.90	0.51	46.22
8	55.19	0.51	28.70
9	154.50	0.51	80.33
10	77.90	0.51	40.50
11	101.89	0.51	52.98
12	88.19	0.51	45.86

YOUR AVERAGE MONTHLY BILL IS .. 51.96

FIGURE 4-9 Output for Gas Bill Program

ciently. System programs are written specifically for particular types of computers and cannot be used (without modification) on different machines. System programming is normally provided by the computer manufacturer or a specialized programming firm.

Application programs are written to perform specific data processing or computational jobs. They can be developed by the user or purchased from software firms. When they are written in a standard high-level language, many can be used on other machines. Examples of application programs are those used for inventory control and financial accounting and those used by banks to update checking and savings account balances.

Operating Systems

When computer systems were in their infancy, human operators monitored computer operations, decided the order in which the programs would run, and handled the input and output devices. But as the processing speeds of CPUs increased, the speed of human operators stayed the same, giving rise to time delays and errors. Operating systems were developed in the 1960s to help this problem of mismatched speed between machine and human. An **operating system** is a collection of programs the computer uses to manage its own operations, a control system that can operate at computer speeds. Thus, operating systems fall in the category of system programs.

Each program, as a subsystem of the operating system, performs specific duties. Since all operating system programs work as a team, the CPU time is used more efficiently. Operating system programs are usually stored in an auxiliary known as the **system residence device** (tape, disk, or drum) and are called into primary storage when needed (Figure 4-10). Two types of programs comprise the operating system: **control programs** and **processing programs**.

OPERATING SYSTEM
Set of programs the computer uses to manage its own operations.

SYSTEM RESIDENCE DEVICE
Auxiliary storage used to store the operating system programs.

CONTROL PROGRAMS
Oversee system operations.

PROCESSING PROGRAMS
Help programmers simplify program preparation.

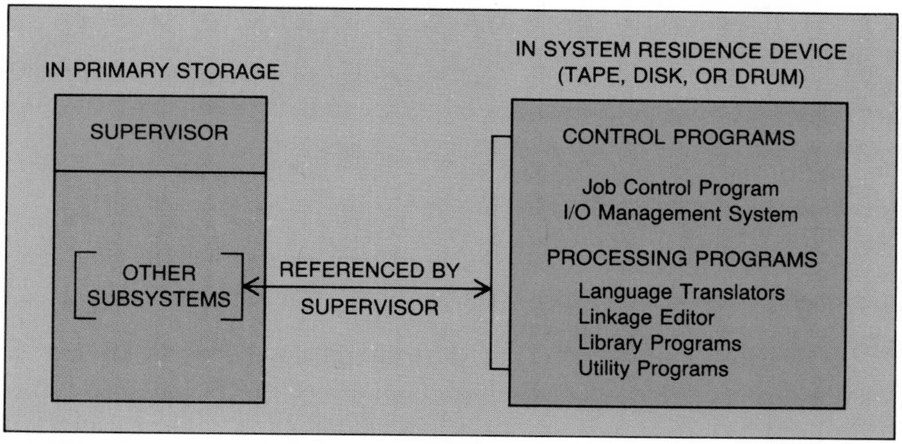

FIGURE 4-10 Operating System in Primary Storage and System Residence Device

Control Programs Control programs oversee system operations and perform such tasks as input/output, scheduling, and communicating with the computer operator or programmer.The **supervisor program** (also known as the monitor or executive) is the major part of the operating system and coordinates the activities of the system's other parts. When the computer is first put into use, the supervisor is the first program to be transferred into primary storage from the system residence device. The electronic supervisor schedules input/output operations and allocates resources to various input/output devices. It also sends messages to the human computer operator to indicate the status of particular jobs, error conditions, and so on.

SUPERVISOR PROGRAM
Coordinates the activities of the operating system.

Processing Programs Processing programs are executed under the supervision of control programs and are used by the programmer to simplify program preparation for the computer system. The principle processing programs include language translators, library programs, and utility programs.

As noted earlier, a language translator program (also known as a compiler or interpreter) translates English-like programs (such as FORTRAN or COBOL) written by humans into an object program of machine language instructions. A **librarian program** maintains a directory of programs in auxilliary storage and contains procedures for adding and deleting programs.

Utility programs perform specialized functions, such as transferring data from tape to tape, tape to disk, card to tape, or tape to printer.

LIBRARIAN PROGRAM
Maintains directory of programs in auxiliary storage.

UTILITY PROGRAM
Performs specialized data transfer functions.

Programming Languages

Programming languages may be divided according to the overall goal or by the orientation of the language. **Machine-oriented languages** seek the most efficient computer use. **Procedure-oriented languages** concentrate on the various processing steps in a particular application and are de-

MACHINE-ORIENTED LANGUAGES
Concentrate on efficient computer use.

PROCEDURE-ORIENTED LANGUAGES
Concentrate on the processing steps.

PROBLEM-ORIENTED LANGUAGES
Concentrate on the desired results.

signed to make it easier for the programmer to direct the computer to perform these tasks. **Problem-oriented languages** are designed to solve processing requirements with minimal programming effort—that is, they allow the user to focus on the desired results rather than on the individual steps needed to get the results.

Machine-Oriented Languages

MACHINE LANGUAGE. Machine language, as already noted, is the only language that the computer can recognize and respond to. The programmer using machine language must specify absolutely everything to the computer—which means that the programmer must know exactly how the computer works. Actual numerical addresses of storage locations must be specified for instructions and data, requiring knowledge of every switch and register (the temporary storage areas for holding data and instructions).

MNEMONICS
A symbolic name to specify machine operations.

ASSEMBLY LANGUAGE. To lessen the disadvantages of machine-language programming, programmers developed assembly languages. In these, the programmer uses symbolic names—or **mnemonics**—to specify machine operations. Mnemonics are English-like abbreviations for the machine language instructions. Table 4-1 shows some common arithmetic operations coded in an assembly language and in binary.

Many of the operations listed in Table 4-1 use registers. Further, the mnemonic codes for assembly language instructions differ depending on the type and model of computer. Thus, assembly language programs, like machine language programs, can be written only by persons who know the internal operation of the specific computers. Figure 4-11 shows a program written in assembly language calculating student grades.

COBOL
Business programming language.

Procedure-Oriented Languages

COBOL. **COBOL** (COmmon Business-Oriented Language) is a frequently used business programming language. COBOL had its specifications established in 1960 by the CODASYL (COnference of DAta SYstems Languages) Committee, and the first commercial versions of the lan-

TABLE 4-1 Examples of Assembly Language Mnemonic Codes

OPERATION	ASSEMBLY-LANGUAGE MNEMONIC CODE	TYPICAL BINARY CODE
Add memory to register	A	01011010
Store accumulator in memory	STA	01001001
Compare memory locations	CLC	11010101
Branch on carry clear	BCC	00110010
Load from memory into register	L	01011000
Multiply register by memory	M	01011100
Compare register to memory	CPY	10010111
Subtract memory from accumulator	SBC	10110011

FIGURE 4-11 Student Grades Program in Assembly Language

```
* THIS PROGRAM CALCULATES THE AVERAGE OF THREE TEST SCORES FOR FIVE
* STUDENTS AND ASSIGNS A LETTER GRADE
         BALR  12,0              SET UP BASE REGISTER
         USING *,12
         LA    3,5               LOAD REGISTER 3 WITH A 5
         XPRNT HEADER,27         PRINT HEADING
         XPRNT PRTOUT-1,31       PRINT BLANK LINE
LOOP     XREAD NAME,30           READ IN DATA CARD
         XDECI 4,TEST1           CONVERT TEST1 TO BINARY AND PUT IN REG 4
         XDECI 5,TEST2           CONVERT TEST2 TO BINARY AND PUT IN REG 5
         XDECI 6,TEST3           CONVERT TEST3 TO BINARY AND PUT IN REG 6
         AR    5,4               ADD CONTENTS OF REG 4 TO REG 5
         AR    5,6               ADD CONTENTS OF REG 6 TO REG 5
         SR    4,4               ZERO OUT REG 4
         L     6,=F'3'           LOAD REG 6 WITH CONSTANT 3
         DR    4,6               DIVIDE CONTENTS OF REG 4 BY REG 6
         MVC   PRTOUT(15),NAME  MOVE NAME TO PRINT AREA
         C     5,=F'90'          COMPARE AVERAGE IN REG 5 TO 90
         BM    B                 IF MINUS (AVERAGE < 90) BRANCH TO B
         MVI   PRTOUT+23,C'A'  MOVE LETTER GRADE A TO PRINT AREA
         B     PRINT             BRANCH TO PRINT
B        C     5,=F'80'          COMPARE AVERAGE TO 80
         BM    C                 IF AVERAGE < 80 BRANCH TO C
         MVI   PRTOUT+23,C'B'   MOVE LETTER GRADE B TO PRINT AREA
         B     PRINT             BRANCH TO PRINT
C        C     5,=F'70'          COMPARE AVERAGE TO 70
         BM    D                 IF AVERAGE < 70 BRANCH TO D
         MVI   PRTOUT+23,C'C'  MOVE LETTER GRADE C TO PRINT AREA
         B     PRINT             BRANCH TO PRINT
D        C     5,=F'60'          COMPARE AVERAGE TO 60
         BM    F                 IF AVERAGE < 60 BRANCH TO F
         MVI   PRTOUT+23,C'D'  MOVE LETTER GRADE D TO PRINT AREA
         B     PRINT             BRANCH TO PRINT
F        MVI   PRTOUT+23,C'F'  MOVE LETTER GRADE F TO PRINT AREA
PRINT    XPRNT PRTOUT-1,31       PRINT NAME AND GRADE
         BCT   3,LOOP            BRANCH BACK TO READ AGAIN
         BR    14                STOP
* DECLARE VARIABLES
HEADER   DC    C'1 STUDENT NAME        GRADE'
NAME     DS    CL15
TEST1    DS    CL5
TEST2    DS    CL5
TEST3    DS    CL5
         DC    C' '
PRTOUT   DC    CL30' '
         END
               =F'3'
               =F'90'
               =F'80'
               =F'70'
               =F'60'
```

```
 STUDENT NAME        GRADE

JOANN WEISS            A
TOM FARR               D
ANN BLASS              B
BOB WILLS              F
JANIS MAYS             C
```

"By Jove . . . this is written in COBOL!"

guage were offered later that year. One of the objectives of the CODASYL group was to establish a language that was machine-independent—that could be used on any computer. When several manufacturers began offering their own modifications and extensions of COBOL, the need for standardization became apparent. In 1968 the American National Standards Institute (ANSI) established and published guidelines for a standardized version of COBOL that became known as ANSI COBOL. Six years later ANSI published a revised standard in which the language definition was expanded.

Another key objective of the designers of COBOL was to make the language look like English so that a program written in COBOL would be understandable even to casual readers. The success of that goal can be partly judged by the COBOL-coded application in Figure 4-12.

Well-written COBOL programs tend to be self-explanatory. Moreover, the language has a strong file-handling capability, supporting as it does

FIGURE 4-12 Student Grades Program in COBOL

```
IDENTIFICATION DIVISION.
PROGRAM-ID. GRADES.

ENVIRONMENT DIVISION.
CONFIGURATION SECTION.
SOURCE-COMPUTER.  IBM-370.
OBJECT-COMPUTER.  IBM-370.
INPUT-OUTPUT SECTION.
FILE-CONTROL.
    SELECT CARD-FILE ASSIGN TO UR-S-SYSIN.
    SELECT PRINT-FILE ASSIGN TO UR-S-OUTPUT.

DATA DIVISION.
FILE SECTION.
FD  CARD-FILE
    LABEL RECORDS ARE OMITTED
    RECORD CONTAINS 80 CHARACTERS
    DATA RECORD IS GRADE-CARD.
01  GRADE-CARD.
    02  STUDENT-NAME   PIC A(15).
    02  TESTONE        PIC 999.
    02  TESTTWO        PIC 999.
    02  TESTTHREE      PIC 999.
    02  FILLER         PIC X(56).
FD  PRINT-FILE
    LABEL RECORDS ARE OMITTED
    RECORD CONTAINS 132 CHARACTERS
    DATA RECORD IS PRINT-REC.
01  PRINT-REC.
    02  OUT-LINE       PIC X(132).
WORKING-STORAGE SECTION.
77  TEST-TOTAL         PIC 999.
77  AVERAGE            PIC 999V99.
77  HEADING1           PIC X(32) VALUE
                       ' STUDENT NAME       LETTER GRADE'.
77  BLANK-LINE         PIC X(132) VALUE SPACES.
01  LINE-FORM.
    02  NAME           PIC A(15).
    02  FILLER         PIC X(11).
    02  LETTER         PIC X.
```

sequential and direct-access files. Since COBOL is standardized, companies may purchase new computer equipment with little or no rewriting of existing programs needed.

COBOL's disadvantages are that it tends to be wordy and its computational capabilities are limited. This makes it undesirable for scientific applications.

FORTRAN. **FORTRAN** (FORmula TRANslator) is the oldest high-level programming language. It began to be formulated in the mid-1950s when most programs were written in either assembly or machine language. The goal was to develop a programming language that resembled English but that could be translated into machine language by the computer.

FORTRAN
Scientific programming language.

Early FORTRAN compilers contained many errors and inefficiencies. Also, to compound the difficulties, several manufacturers offered variations of FORTRAN that could be used only with their own brand of com-

FIGURE 4-12 Continued

```
PROCEDURE DIVISION.
BEGIN.
    DISPLAY HEADING1.
    DISPLAY BLANK-LINE.
    OPEN INPUT CARD-FILE,
         OUTPUT PRINT-FILE.
    PERFORM WORK-LOOP 5 TIMES.
    PERFORM FINISH.
WORK-LOOP.
    READ CARD-FILE
      AT END PERFORM FINISH.
    ADD TESTONE, TESTTWO, TESTTHREE GIVING TEST-TOTAL.
    DIVIDE TEST-TOTAL BY 3 GIVING AVERAGE.
    IF (AVERAGE IS GREATER THAN 90 OR EQUAL TO 90) THEN
      MOVE 'A' TO LETTER
    ELSE IF (AVERAGE IS GREATER THAN 80 OR EQUAL TO 80) THEN
      MOVE 'B' TO LETTER
    ELSE IF (AVERAGE IS GREATER THAN 70 OR EQUAL TO 70) THEN
      MOVE 'C' TO LETTER
    ELSE IF (AVERAGE IS GREATER THAN 60 OR EQUAL TO 60) THEN
      MOVE 'D' TO LETTER
    ELSE MOVE 'F' TO LETTER.
    MOVE STUDENT-NAME TO NAME.
    WRITE PRINT-REC FROM LINE-FORM AFTER ADVANCING 1 LINES.
FINISH.
    CLOSE CARD-FILE,
          PRINT-FILE.
    STOP RUN.


 STUDENT NAME        GRADE

JOANN WEISS            A
TOM FARR               D
ANN BLASS              B
BOB WILLS              F
JANIS MAYS             C
```

PROFILE

JOHN BACKUS

John Backus, developer of the FORTRAN programming language, was one of the first programmers in the computer industry. After graduating from Columbia, Backus chose to work for IBM, where he was assigned to lead a group of engineers working with the FORTRAN project. In 1957, Backus introduced the first high-level, Englishlike programming language. FORTRAN was oriented toward the mathematical and scientific communities—the users of the early number-crunching computers.

After FORTRAN Backus developed a syntax—an orderly arrangement of the grammatical elements of a sentence—known as Backus Normal Form. Backus applied the syntax when participating in the development of Algol, another programming language. Backus is still employed with IBM. Although his new project remains undisclosed, it is likely to deal with programming languages.

puters. For these reasons ANSI decided to lay the groundwork for a standardized FORTRAN. In 1966 two versions were standardized: ANSI FORTRAN and Basic FORTRAN, both similar to two earlier versions, FORTRAN IV and FORTRAN II. A more recent version, FORTRAN 77, has enhanced the language's usefulness and supports structured programming, which uses modular and mostly nonbranching logic patterns. (Structured programming is discussed in more detail later in this chapter.)

A group from Ontario's University of Waterloo developed a subset of FORTRAN—WATFOR (WATerloo FORtran)—specifically for the beginning programmer. When improvements were made in WATFOR, the new version was dubbed WATFIV. But regardless of the attempts to standardize FORTRAN, most computer manufacturers continue to offer their own versions, and the compatibility of FORTRAN with different computer systems remains a problem.

When FORTRAN was first released, the computer was used primarily by engineers, scientists, and mathematicians. Naturally enough, FORTRAN was designed to meet their needs, a purpose that has remained unchanged. FORTRAN is a procedure-oriented language that has extraordinary mathematical capabilities. Being most applicable in situations where complex arithmetic calculations are necessary, it is ill-suited to programs for file maintenance, data editing, or document production. Figure 4-13 shows the sample student grades program in FORTRAN.

PL/I
Procedure-oriented language for science and business.

PL/I. **PL/I** (Programming Language One) was developed as a procedure-oriented language suited for both scientific and business applications. Increased use of management science techniques—such as linear programming and regression analysis—demonstrated to the business

```
C THIS PROGRAM CALCULATES THE AVERAGE OF THREE TEST SCORES FOR FIVE
C STUDENTS AND ASSIGNS A LETTER GRADE
      INTEGER TEST1, TEST2, TEST3, I
      REAL  AVG
      CHARACTER  NAME*15, GRADE
      WRITE (6,100)
 100  FORMAT ('1',1X,'STUDENT NAME',7X,'GRADE')
      WRITE (6,200)
 200  FORMAT (' ')
      DO 500 I = 1, 5
      READ (5,300) NAME, TEST1, TEST2, TEST3
 300  FORMAT (A15,3I3)
      AVG = (TEST1 + TEST2 + TEST3) / 3.0
      IF (AVG .GE. 90) GRADE = 'A'
      IF ((AVG .GE. 80) .AND. (AVG .LT. 90)) GRADE = 'B'
      IF ((AVG .GE. 70) .AND. (AVG .LT. 80)) GRADE = 'C'
      IF ((AVG .GE. 60) .AND. (AVG .LT. 70)) GRADE = 'D'
      IF (AVG .LT. 60) GRADE = 'F'
      WRITE (6,400) NAME, GRADE
 400  FORMAT (1X,A15,7X,A1)
 500  CONTINUE
      STOP
      END


 STUDENT NAME       GRADE

JOANN WEISS           A
TOM FARR              D
ANN BLASS             B
BOB WILLS             F
JANIS MAYS            C
```

FIGURE 4-13 Student Grades Program in FORTRAN

programmer the need for a language with greater computational capabilities than COBOL. Similarly, scientific programmers needed a language with greater file-handling ability than FORTRAN. PL/I combines both COBOL and FORTRAN features. It was introduced in the early 1960s for use with IBM System/360 computers and is still an IBM-sponsored language.

All the languages discussed previously require strict coding rules. PL/I, in contrast, is a free-form language with very few coding restrictions and is usable by both novice and expert programmers. The PL/I program in Figure 4-14 is actually written in PL/C, a subset of PL/I developed at Cornell University.

PL/I's greatest strength is its power. PL/I is powerful because it is a flexible language, supporting many options and applications. A language with many features, PL/I is most attractive in its ability to support structured programming. Being less wordy than COBOL, it is well suited for short programming projects. But because it is such a broad, powerful language, its compiler requires a large amount of storage, keeping it from being usable in smaller computers. However, as minicomputers and microcomputers become more powerful, subsets of PL/I may become workable.

```
GRADE:  PROCEDURE OPTIONS (MAIN);
/* THIS PROGRAM CALCULATES THE AVERAGE OF THREE TEST SCORES FOR FIVE */
/* STUDENTS AND ASSIGNS A LETTER GRADE                                */
DECLARE (NAME) CHARACTER(15);
DECLARE (LETTER) CHARACTER(1);
DECLARE (TEST1, TEST2, TEST3, I) FIXED DECIMAL(3);
DECLARE (DUMMY) CHARACTER(56);
DECLARE (AVERAGE) FIXED DECIMAL(5,2);
PUT PAGE LIST (' STUDENT NAME        LETTER GRADE');
PUT SKIP;
DO I=1 TO 5;
  GET EDIT (NAME, TEST1, TEST2, TEST3) (A(15), F(3), F(3), F(3));
  GET EDIT (DUMMY) (A(56));
  AVERAGE = (TEST1 + TEST2 + TEST3) / 3.0;
  IF AVERAGE >= 90 THEN LETTER = 'A';
    ELSE IF AVERAGE >= 80 THEN LETTER = 'B';
      ELSE IF AVERAGE >= 70 THEN LETTER = 'C';
        ELSE IF AVERAGE >= 60 THEN LETTER = 'D';
          ELSE LETTER = 'F';
  PUT SKIP EDIT (NAME, '           ', LETTER) (A(15), A(11), A(1));
END;  /* DO */;
END;


 STUDENT NAME         GRADE

JOANN WEISS             A
TOM FARR                D
ANN BLASS               B
BOB WILLS               F
JANIS MAYS              C
```

FIGURE 4-14 Student Grades Program in PL/C

RPG
Problem-oriented language used to generate reports.

Problem-Oriented Languages

RPG. **RPG** (Report Program Generator) is a problem-oriented language that was designed to produce business reports. Essentially, a programmer using RPG must describe the kind of report desired but need not specify much of the logic involved. Acting upon the description, a generator program can build a program to produce the report. Little programming skill is necessary.

RPG was first meant to support the logic of punched-card equipment, which is why it is used primarily with small computer systems. Many firms that once used electromechanical punched-card processing equipment have upgraded their data-processing operations to small computer systems. Such a system using RPG can significantly improve data-processing operations.

Instead of coding statements, the programmer completes specification forms, such as those shown in Figure 4-15. All files to be used by RPG must be defined once through the specification forms. After the files have been defined, the programmer has only to enter the operations to be performed and the content and format of the desired output. Entries on the RPG forms are keypunched, combined with job control cards and submit-

FIGURE 4-15 RPG Program Specification Forms

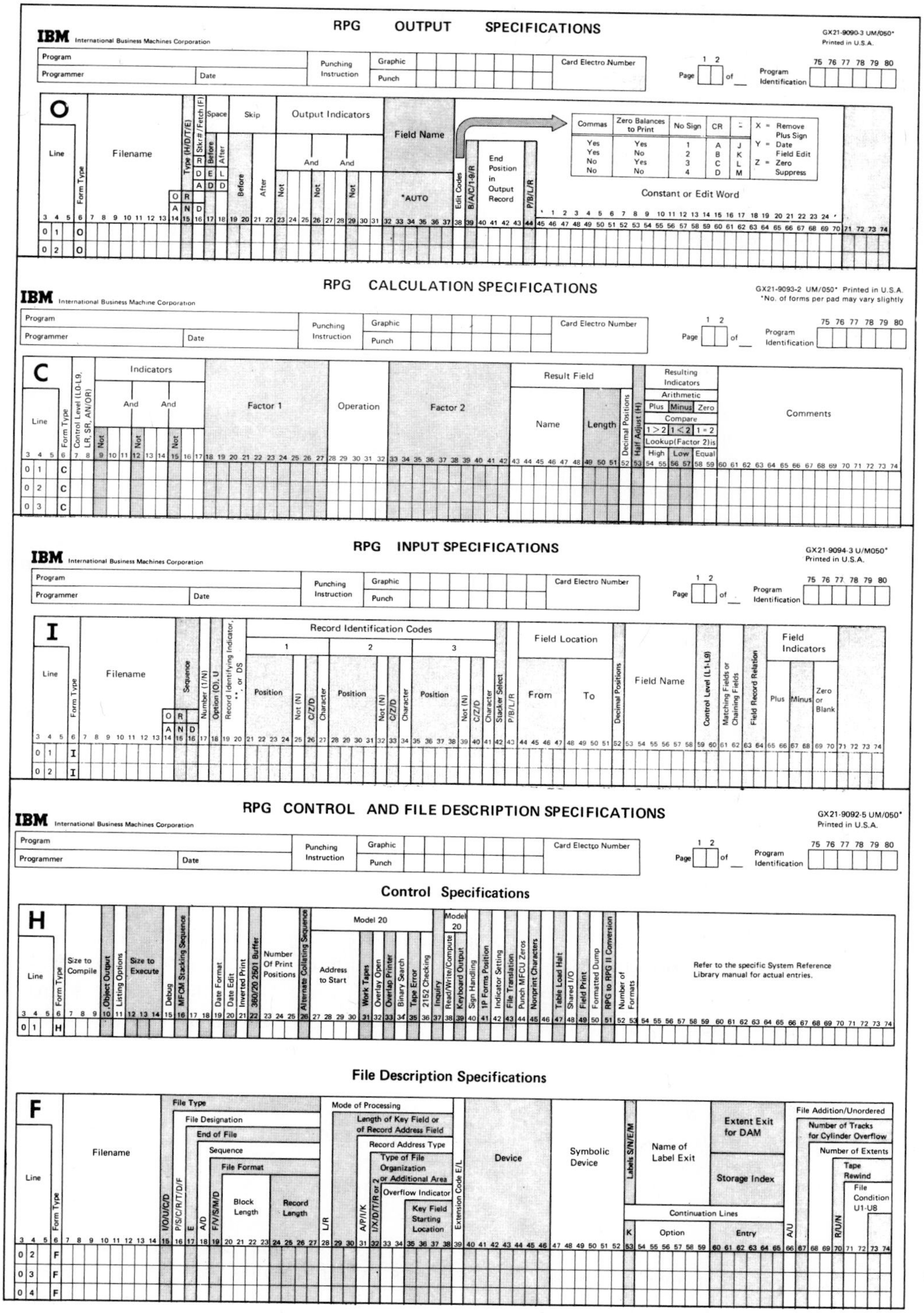

ted to the computer. The RPG generator program then builds an object program that the computer executes.

Because RPG requires little main storage space, it is one of the primary languages of small computers and minicomputers. But it has shortcomings, among them that its computational capabilities are limited and that it is not standardized. RPG programs written for one computer may require significant changes to be used on another computer.

Interactive Programming Languages Interactive programming languages are made to use immediate input from either the programmer or user to direct the processing. The computer can respond to the input instantaneously. Some traditional batch programs (such as COBOL and PL/I) are being modified to accommodate interactive capabilities.

A number of interactive languages on small computer systems use an interpreter rather than a compiler to translate source program statements to object program code. Unlike a compiler, which translates an entire program into an object code at one time (for later execution), an interpreter evaluates and translates program statements one instruction at a time. The interpreter takes one source program instruction, translates it into machine code, and then executes it. It then takes the next instruction, translates it, executes it, and so on. An interpreter can save space because the interpreter program itself can be quite small. The need to store the program's translated object code in the computer is also eliminated. The interpreter, however, can be inefficient since program statements that are used many times must be translated each time they are executed.

BASIC
Very simple, interactive interpreter language.

BASIC. **BASIC** (Beginner's All-purpose Symbolic Instruction Code) was developed at Dartmouth College for use with time-sharing systems. The language is easy to learn and can be used by people with little or no programming experience. Beginners can learn to write fairly complex BASIC programs in a matter of hours.

The growth of time-sharing systems has resulted in an increase in the use of BASIC. Most computer manufacturers offer BASIC support on their computers. Although it was originally intended for instructional purposes at the college level, many companies have adopted BASIC to their data-processing needs. The increasing popularity of microcomputers in homes is also furthering the use of BASIC. BASIC's most attractive features are its simplicity and flexibility. Although it was intended as an interactive language, it is finding increased use as a batch language.

Manufacturers offer many different versions of the language. A BASIC standard was established in 1978, but it covers only a small subset of the BASIC language. This means that BASIC programs written for one system may have to undergo substantial modification before being used on another. Figure 4-16 shows a program written in BASIC.

PASCAL
Highly structured, conceptual language suited for batch and interactive modes.

PASCAL. **Pascal** is named after the French philosopher and mathematician, Blaise Pascal, inventor of the first mechanical adding machine. Niklaus Wirth, a Swiss computer scientist, developed Pascal between 1968 and 1970. The first Pascal compiler became available in 1971. Like

```
10 REM THIS PROGRAM CALCULATES THE AVERAGE OF THREE TEST SCORES
20 REM FOR FIVE STUDENTS AND ASSIGNS A LETTER GRADE
25 PRINT
26 PRINT
30 PRINT "STUDENT NAME       GRADE"
35 PRINT "------------       -----"
36 PRINT
40 FOR I = 1 TO 5
50   READ STUDENT$,TEST1,TEST2,TEST3
60   LET A = (TEST1 + TEST2 + TEST3) / 3
70   IF A < 90 THEN 100
80   LET G$ = "A"
90   GOTO 200
100  IF A < 80 THEN 130
110  LET G$ = "B"
120  GOTO 200
130  IF A < 70 THEN 160
140  LET G$ = "C"
150  GOTO 200
160  IF A < 60 THEN 190
170  LET G$ = "D"
180  GOTO 200
190  LET G$ = "F"
200  PRINT STUDENT$;TAB(18);G$
210 NEXT I
220 DATA JOANN WEISS,83,96,91,TOMM FARR,61,78,69
230 DATA ANN BLASS,93,82,87,BOB WILLS,43,56,62
240 DATA JANIS MAYS,73,84,71
999 END



STUDENT NAME      GRADE
------------      -----

JOANN WEISS       A
TOMM FARR         D
ANN BLASS         B
BOB WILLS         F
JANIS MAYS        C
```

FIGURE 4-16 Student Grades Program in BASIC

BASIC, Pascal was developed to teach programming concepts to students. But it is rapidly finding increased acceptance in business and scientific applications. Pascal is well suited for both batch and interactive modes, but most Pascal business applications are batch oriented.

Although the language is relatively easy to learn, like BASIC, it is powerful, like PL/I. But unlike PL/I, Pascal is available on microcomputers and seems to be a good alternative to BASIC.

Probably the major drawback to Pascal is that it is not yet standardized. Some critics say, moreover, that Pascal has poor input/output capabilities. Figure 4-17 shows the student grades program in Pascal.

FIGURE 4-17 Student Grades Program in Pascal

```
PROGRAM GRADES;
VAR
  NAME:STRING;
  TEST1,TEST2,TEST3,I:INTEGER;
  AVERAGE:REAL;
  GRADE:CHAR;
BEGIN
  FOR I := 1 TO 3 DO
    BEGIN
      WRITELN('ENTER STUDENT NAME');
      READLN(NAME);
      WRITELN('ENTER SCORES FOR TESTS 1,2,AND 3');
      READLN(TEST1,TEST2,TEST3);
      AVERAGE := (TEST1 + TEST2 + TEST3) / 3;
      IF AVERAGE < 90 THEN
        IF AVERAGE < 80 THEN
          IF AVERAGE < 70 THEN
            IF AVERAGE > 60 THEN
              GRADE := 'D'
            ELSE GRADE := 'F'
          ELSE GRADE := 'C'
        ELSE GRADE := 'B'
      ELSE GRADE := 'A';
      WRITELN;
      WRITELN;
      WRITELN;
      WRITELN('STUDENT NAME      LETTER GRADE');
      WRITELN(NAME:11,GRADE:10);
      WRITELN;
      WRITELN;
      END;
  END.


ENTER STUDENT NAME
JOANN WEISS
ENTER SCORES FOR TESTS 1,2,AND 3
83 96 91



STUDENT NAME      LETTER GRADE
JOANN WEISS           A


ENTER STUDENT NAME
TOMM FARR
ENTER SCORES FOR TESTS 1,2,AND 3
61 78 69



STUDENT NAME      LETTER GRADE
  TOMM FARR           D


ENTER STUDENT NAME
JANIS MAYS
ENTER SCORES FOR TESTS 1,2,AND 3
73 84 71



STUDENT NAME      LETTER GRADE
 JANIS MAYS           C
```

APL. **APL** (A Programming Language) was conceived in 1962 by Kenneth Iverson and described in his book of the same name. APL became available to the public through IBM in 1968. Many businesses now use APL as their main programming language. It functions best when used for interactive processing through a terminal.

A programmer can use APL in two modes: execution and definition. In the execution mode, the terminal can be used like a desk calculator. An instruction is keyed in on one line and the response is shown immediately on the following line. In the definition mode, a series of instructions is entered into the memory and the entire program is executed on command from the programmer. Its two-mode capability makes APL unlike any of the high-level programming languages discussed so far.

APL can be used to perform some very complex operations with minimal coding (Figure 4-18). Its lack of formal restrictions on input and output and its free-form style make it a very powerful language.

This language has a few disadvantages as well. It is difficult to read, requires a special keyboard, and is unsuitable for handling large data files. It also requires a large storage space for its compiler and lacks support documentation. Figure 4-19 shows an APL keyboard and Figure 4-20 illustrates an interactive APL session. Table 4-2 compares all the batch and interactive languages discussed in this chapter.

APL
Interactive language that can be used in execution or definition modes.

Multiprogramming, Virtual Storage, Multiprocessing

System programs—like application programs—have become more sophisticated over the years. The early systems were plagued by inefficient

FIGURE 4-18 APL Coding

APL CODING	ENGLISH TRANSLATION
A + B	A plus B
A←25	A = 25
A⌊B	Finds the smaller of A and B
V1←2 5 11 17	Creates a vector of 4 components and assigns the vector to V1
⌈/V1	Finds the maximum value in the vector V1

FIGURE 4-19 APL Keyboard

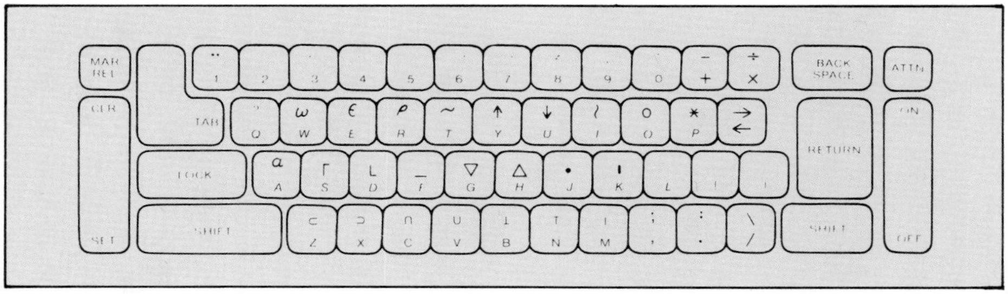

FIGURE 4-20 Student Grades Program in APL

```
         ∇GRADE[⎕]∇
      ∇  GRADE
[1]    ⍝ THIS PROGRAM CALCULATES THE AVERAGE OF THREE TEST SCORES
[2]    ⍝ FOR THREE STUDENTS AND ASSIGNS A LETTER GRADE
[3]     I←0
[4]    LOOP:I←I+1
[5]     →(I>3)/OUT
[6]     ' '
[7]     'ENTER STUDENT NAME:
[8]     NAME←⍞
[9]     'ENTER SCORES FOR TEST 1,2,AND 3:
[10]    SCORES←⎕
[11]    AVG←(+/SCORES)÷3
[12]    →(AVG≥90)/A
[13]    →(AVG≥80)/B
[14]    →(AVG≥70)/C
[15]    →(AVG≥60)/D
[16]    →(AVG<60)/F
[17]   A:'GRADE:  A'
[18]    →LOOP
[19]   B:'GRADE:  B'
[20]    →LOOP
[21]   C:'GRADE:  C'
[22]    →LOOP
[23]   D:'GRADE:  D'
[24]    →LOOP
[25]   F:'GRADE:  F'
[26]    →LOOP
[27]   OUT:
      ∇
       GRADE

ENTER STUDENT NAME:
JOANN WEISS
ENTER SCORES FOR TEST 1,2,AND 3:
⎕:
       83 96 91
GRADE:  A

ENTER STUDENT NAME:
TOM FARR
ENTER SCORES FOR TEST 1,2,AND 3:
⎕:
       61 78 69
GRADE:  D

ENTER STUDENT NAME:
ANN BLASS
ENTER SCORES FOR TEST 1,2,AND 3:
⎕:
       93 82 87
GRADE:  B
```

TABLE 4-2 Comparison of Programming Languages

FEATURE	ASSEMBLY LANGUAGE	FORTRAN	COBOL	PL/I	RPG	BASIC	PASCAL	APL
Strong math capabilities	X	X		X		X	X	X
Good character manipulation capabilities	X		X	X		X	X	X
English-like			X	X		X	X	
Available on many computers	X	X	X		X	X	X	
Highly efficient	X							
Standardized		X	X	X		X		
Requires large amount of storage			X	X				X
Good interactive capability						X	X	X
Procedure oriented		X	X	X		X	X	X
Problem oriented					X			
Machine dependent	X							

use of resources—either because excessive human assistance was required or because system programs were not sophisticated enough to allocate computer resources well. Among the developments that have greatly increased the efficiency of the computer are **multiprogramming**, **virtual storage**, and **multiprocessing**. Multiprogramming allows the computer to work with more than one program at a time. Virtual storage makes primary storage work as if it were larger than it is. Multiprocessing allows simultaneous execution of programs submitted by several computers.

MULTIPROGRAMMING
Allows computer to work on more than one program at a time.

VIRTUAL STORAGE
Allows program execution on only a section of the program in primary storage at a time; also called virtual memory.

MULTIPROCESSING
Use of more than one CPU to speed up processing time.

Multiprogramming When the CPU is very active, the whole system is more efficient. But when input/output devices are slow in providing data or instructions the CPU frequently remains idle as it must wait until input/output operations have been completed before executing the instructions. This is because the CPU can operate on only one instruction at a time and can do this only on data that are in primary storage.

Multiprogramming helps by allocating computer resources to offset slow input/output speeds. In multiprogramming, several programs stay in the primary storage unit at the same time. Although the CPU can execute only one instruction at a time, it can execute an instruction from one program, then one from another, and so on. As long as all the programs do not require data flow to or from the same input/output device, the rotation can happen so quickly that the execution of all the programs seems simultaneous.

Virtual Storage Multiprogramming increases system efficiency because the CPU can concurrently execute several programs instead of waiting for the completion of input/output operations on each program. There is a limitation to multiprogramming, though, which is that all the instructions of a program are kept in primary storage throughout its execution, needed or not. A large program may have many instruction sequences that are seldom executed. As processing requirements increase, the physical limitations of memory become a critical weakness.

To alleviate the problem, an extension of multiprogramming, virtual storage, has been developed on the principle that only a portion of a program has to be in primary storage at any time. The rest of the program and data can be kept in auxiliary storage. Since only part of a program is in primary storage, more programs can be placed there at one time and more programs can be executed within a given time.

REAL STORAGE
Primary storage.

A direct-access storage device, such as a magnetic disk unit, is used to implement virtual storage (or virtual memory, as it is sometimes called). The term **real storage** is usually given to primary storage within the CPU, whereas virtual storage refers to direct-access storage located outside the CPU. Both real and virtual storage locations are given addresses by the operating system. If required data or instructions are not in the primary storage area, the portion of the program containing them is transferred from virtual storage to primary storage. Meanwhile, another portion currently in primary storage may be written back to virtual storage. This process is known as **swapping**.

SWAPPING
Data transfer between real and virtual storage.

A major limitation of virtual storage is the requirement for extensive online auxiliary storage. Also, the virtual-storage operating system is highly sophisticated and itself requires significant amounts of internal storage. If virtual storage is not used wisely, much valuable time can be spent simply swapping portions of a program in and out of primary storage.

Multiprocessing Multiprocessing involves the use of two or more CPUs linked together for a coordinated operation. Stored-program instructions are executed simultaneously but by different CPUs. The CPUs may execute different sections of the same program or from totally different programs.

Multiprocessing systems are designed to achieve particular objectives, one of which is to relieve a large CPU of such tasks as scheduling, editing data, and maintaining files. Thus, the CPU can continue high-priority or complex processing without interruption. To do this, a small CPU (often a minicomputer) is linked to the large CPU. All work coming into the system from remote terminals or other peripheral devices is first channeled through the small CPU, which coordinates the activities of the large one. Generally, the small CPU handles all input/output interrupts, while the large CPU handles the "number crunching" (large mathematical calculations). This type of multiprocessing is illustrated by Figure 4-21. The small CPU in Figure 4-21 is commonly referred to as a **front-end processor**. It operates as an interface between the large CPU and peripheral devices like online terminals.

FRONT-END PROCESSOR
Small CPU used in multiprocessing.

Coordinating the work of several CPUs demands careful planning and highly sophisticated software. Scheduling the workloads for the CPUs means making the most efficient use of computer resources. Implementing a multiprocessing system is time consuming and may require the help of special consultants as well as those provided by the equipment manufacturers. The payoff from this effort is a system with capabilities extending far beyond those of a single CPU system.

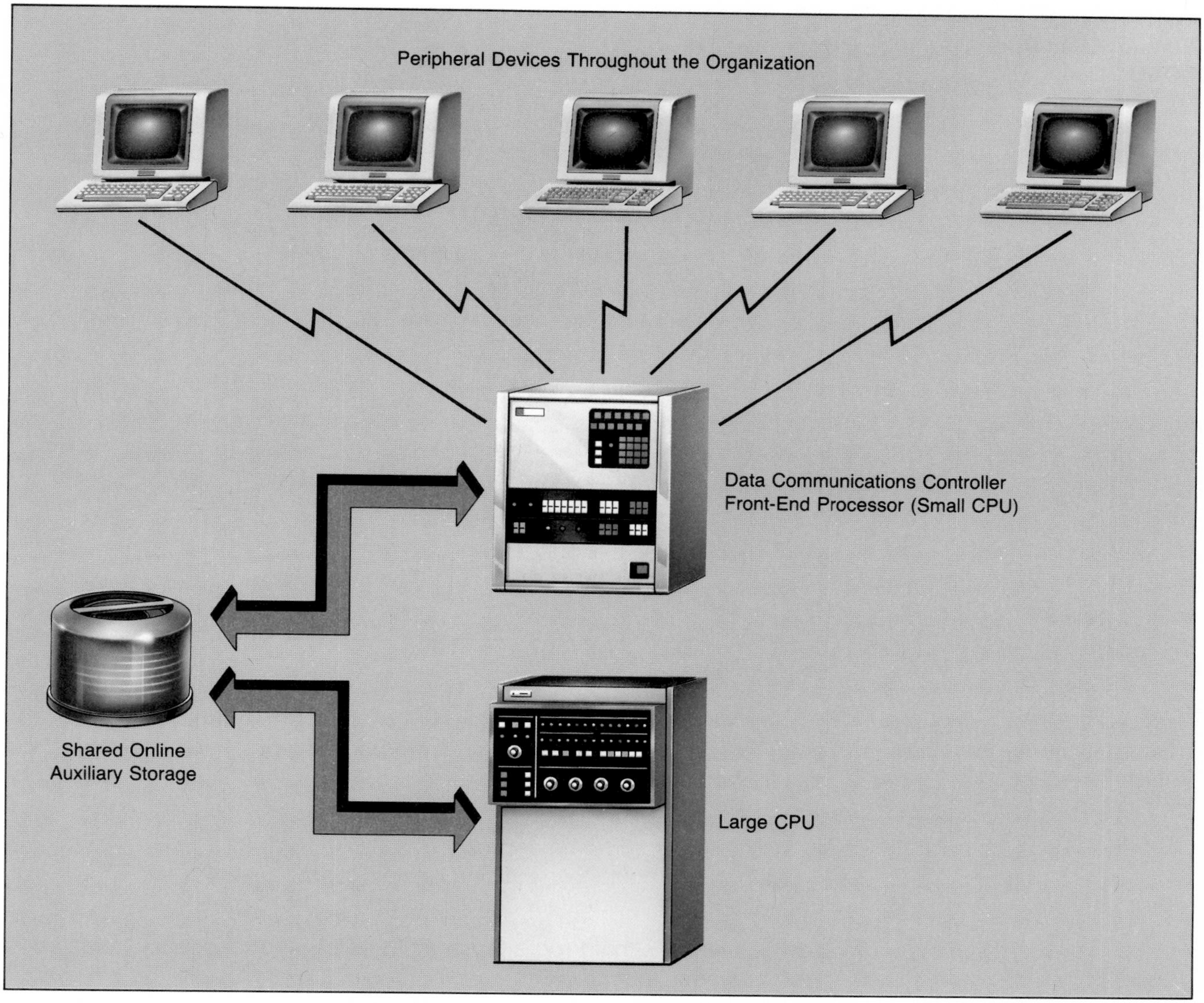

FIGURE 4-21 Multiprocessing System with Small Front-End Processor and Large Mainframe

STRUCTURED PROGRAMMING

Emphasis on programming as an art and on the flexibility of high-level languages sometimes encourages poor programming techniques. As an example, programs may contain numerous branches that continually alter the sequential flow of processing. Although these programs may work successfully, their logic frequently is understood only by the original programmer. Such situations increase the costs and difficulties of program maintenance. Also, without a standardized method of approaching a problem, a programmer may spend far more time than necessary to de-

FIGURE 4-22 Unstructured Versus Structured COBOL Code

```
PROCEDURE DIVISION.
BEGIN.
    DISPLAY HEADING1.
    DISPLAY BLANK-LINE.
    OPEN INPUT CARD-FILE,
         OUTPUT PRINT-FILE.
WORK-LOOP.
    READ CARD-FILE
      AT END GO TO FINISH.
    ADD TESTONE, TESTTWO, TESTTHREE GIVING TEST-TOTAL.
    DIVIDE TEST-TOTAL BY 3 GIVING AVERAGE.
    IF (AVERAGE IS GREATER THAN 90 OR EQUAL TO 90) THEN
      MOVE 'A' TO LETTER.
    IF (AVERAGE IS GREATER THAN 80 OR EQUAL TO 80) AND
      (AVERAGE IS LESS THAN 90) THEN MOVE 'B' TO LETTER.
    IF (AVERAGE IS GREATER THAN 70 OR EQUAL TO 70) AND
      (AVERAGE IS LESS THAN 80) THEN MOVE 'C' TO LETTER.
    IF (AVERAGE IS GREATER THAN 60 OR EQUAL TO 60) AND
      (AVERAGE IS LESS THAN 70) THEN MOVE 'D' TO LETTER.
    IF (AVERAGE IS LESS THAN 60) THEN
      MOVE 'F' TO LETTER.
    MOVE STUDENT-NAME TO NAME.
    WRITE PRINT-REC FROM LINE-FORM AFTER ADVANCING 1 LINES.
FINISH.
    CLOSE CARD-FILE,
          PRINT-FILE.
    STOP RUN.
```

(a) Unstructured

STRUCTURED PROGRAMMING Uses mainly the simple sequence, loop, and selection logic patterns.

termine an appropriate solution and develop the program. To counter these erratic tendencies, **structured programming** has been developed. It has four objectives:

1. To reduce testing time.
2. To increase programmer productivity.
3. To increase clarity by reducing complexity.
4. To decrease maintenance time and effort.

All this means is that programs ought to be easy to read, easy to maintain, and easy to modify.

Structured programming encourages well-thought-out program logic and uses three of the four available logic patterns: simple sequence, selection, and loop. Branching may be used only under special conditions, described later. Basic to the concept of structured programming is the construction of programs in modules, with each module being an independent segment that performs only one function. Naturally, the modules should be small to facilitate programming and debugging. Each module should have only one entry point and one exit point. This allows the flow of control to be followed easily by the programmer. When the modular approach is used, the one-entry/one-exit guideline is easier to incorporate into the program. A program that has only one entrance and one exit is called a **proper program**. Figure 4-22 compares two program segments—one structured and the other nonstructured.

PROPER PROGRAM Has only one entrance and one exit and performs a single function.

Structured programs are characterized by other special features, such as the liberal use of comments, statements, and remarks. Variable names

```
PROCEDURE DIVISION.
BEGIN.
     DISPLAY HEADING1.
     DISPLAY BLANK-LINE.
     OPEN INPUT CARD-FILE,
          OUTPUT PRINT-FILE.
     PERFORM MAIN-LOGIC 5 TIMES.
     PERFORM FINISH.
MAIN-LOGIC.
     READ CARD-FILE
       AT END GO TO FINISH.
     PERFORM AVG-CALC.
     PERFORM GRADE-CALC.
     PERFORM GRADE-PRINT.
AVG-CALC.
     ADD TESTONE, TESTTWO, TESTTHREE GIVING TEST-TOTAL.
     DIVIDE TEST-TOTAL BY 3 GIVING AVERAGE.
GRADE-CALC.
     IF (AVERAGE IS GREATER THAN 90 OR EQUAL TO 90) THEN
       MOVE 'A' TO LETTER.
     IF (AVERAGE IS GREATER THAN 80 OR EQUAL TO 80) AND
       (AVERAGE IS LESS THAN 90) THEN MOVE 'B' TO LETTER.
     IF (AVERAGE IS GREATER THAN 70 OR EQUAL TO 70) AND
       (AVERAGE IS LESS THAN 80) THEN MOVE 'C' TO LETTER.
     IF (AVERAGE IS GREATER THAN 60 OR EQUAL TO 60) AND
       (AVERAGE IS LESS THAN 70) THEN MOVE 'D' TO LETTER.
     IF (AVERAGE IS LESS THAN 60) THEN
       MOVE 'F' TO LETTER.
GRADE-PRINT.
     MOVE STUDENT-NAME TO NAME.
     WRITE PRINT-REC FROM LINE-FORM AFTER ADVANCING 1 LINES.
FINISH.
     CLOSE CARD-FILE,
           PRINT-FILE.
     STOP RUN.
```

(b) Structured

are definitive; for example, if a variable computes city tax, it is called CITY TAX—not CT. In addition, attention is paid to the indentation and spacing of program statements to improve readability.

The branch pattern, characterized by the GO TO statement, is not recommended for structured programming. A GO TO statement causes an unconditional branch from one part of the program to another. Excessive use of GO TO statements results in continual changes in the flow of execution, and often the flow is transferred to totally different logical sections of the program. Programs that contain many GO TO (branching) statements are difficult to modify because they are obscure and complicated. A programmer may not know how a change in one part of the program will affect processing in other parts. This is not to say that a structured program may not have *any* GO TO statements—just that they should be used only to implement structured logic. GO TO statements should never cause a branch outside of the program module in which they reside.

Some programming languages are better suited than others to structured programming. Especially well suited are Pascal, COBOL and PL/I. FORTRAN and BASIC lack some features essential for structured programming.

ISSUE

PROGRAMMING: ART OR SCIENCE?

Programming is the voodoo that is performed to make the computer do what you want it to. In the early days of programming and even with the advent of higher-level (more English-like) languages such as COBOL, programming was seen as a mysterious art practiced by a strange breed called the "programmer."

There may have been two reasons for this: (1) it was believed that the ability to program took special talents, and (2) at the time, there were no standards or systematic methods for programming.

In these early days of programming, management saw the programmer as an individual with special creative talents that needed a special environment in which to put these talents to work. To ensure that the programmer would not "abandon ship" leaving the organization with a program or programs that no one else could decipher or modify, management made certain concessions to the programmer.

In general, programmers were subject to less management control than any other people in an organization. In fact, it was not an uncommon sight to see a programmer going to his/her job in jeans and a sweatshirt while everyone else was required to wear a business suit.

Another reason for the lack of management control might stem from the fact that management, having no experience with programming, had no guidelines to measure or control a programmer's performance. Because of this lack of quantitative measures, many believe as William Thomas, Lord Kelvin who wrote, "When you can measure what you are speaking about and express it in numbers, you know something about it; but when you cannot measure it, when you cannot express it in numbers, your knowledge is of a meager and unsatisfactory kind; it may be the beginning of knowledge, but you have scarcely in your thoughts, advanced to the stage of a science."

Some attempts in recent years at quantifying a programmer's productivity have been made, for example, counting lines of code or the number of written instructions per a set period of time. But these attempts have fallen short of giving any insight into what makes the programming process productive or how to increase that productivity. A major fault of this attempt of quantitative measurement is that it assumes that one line of code is equivalent to any other line of code and that one software developer is interchangeable with another. Also, it ignores the quality of the program in favor of quantity.

Because of the lack of any systematic methods or standards of programming, many programs were of the "shoot from the hip" variety. Often solutions were not designed until the actual coding was taking place, and problems were dealt with as they were encountered. This method of creating-as-you-go often got the job done, but just as often led to a roundabout means of accomplishing a program goal. This approach often led to unnecessarily complex programs, making it difficult for any one but (and sometimes including) the original programmer to understand or make modifications to the program.

Another result of this create-as-you-go type of programming was that the programs were very inefficient in terms of execution time and required storage (memory) space—two very important cost considerations in the early days of computers.

Because of these problems with this "artistic" approach to programming, many organizations reevaluated their method of programming. As a result, a more logical and systematic approach emerged known as structured programming. Structured programming not only refers to how the program is to be coded but also to the methods used in designing, documenting, and testing programs—three areas that had been more or less neglected in the past. Because structured programming follows a specific system of methods from program design to program testing and because results can be controlled, many of its proponents claim that the techniques have brought programming into the realm of a science and refer to it as the "scientific" method of programming. Many organizations have adopted the structured programming methodology finding it much more efficient and cost effective than the "artistic" method.

Another argument for the scientific viewpoint is the fact that there is a strong revived movement towards granting software patents, which are given for protection of something that furthers scientific advancement instead of the traditional copyright, which is issued to protect a literary or artistic expression.

Use of the more structured approach appears to be the trend in the business programming environment. However, with the advent of the home computer many novice programmers, unaware of the techniques of structured programming, are giving new life to the idea of programming being an art.

It is said that history repeats itself; we will have to wait and see whether or not the home programmer, too, will make the move toward the structured approach. It may be that, to the home programmer, the most important thing is the *results* rather than the *efficiency of the methods* used to achieve those results. With the decreases in hardware and memory cost, the home user is not faced with the same cost constraints that affected the early business users. Different situations lend themselves to different approaches and the old addage "if it works use it" may be a useful model for the home programmer.

Looking at programming as either an art or a science may not be an appropriate means of analysis. While a case may be made for either viewpoint, many feel that it is of necessity a blend of the two, in the same way that a piece of classical music might be viewed as a blend of artistic talent and musical "scientific" theory. There is indeed a great deal of creativeness and artistic endeavor in the creation of a musical piece, however, it can be broken down and analyzed in quantitative terms, as is done in the science of musicology. Programming, also, appears to show characteristics of both disciplines and perhaps should not be placed into one or the other category.

SUMMARY POINTS

■ There are three levels of language: (1) machine language, (2) assembly language, and (3) high-level language. High-level language is the most English-like and the most used.
■ Before the program written by the programmer (the source program) can be executed, it must be translated into machine language (the object program) by a language translator program. There are three types of language translators. Two of these translate the entire program at once. They are assembler programs, used to translate assembly language programs, and compiler programs, used to translate high-level languages. The third type of language translator translates one instruction at a time rather than the entire program at once. It is used with some interactive high-level languages and is called an interpreter.
■ Syntax errors are violations of the specific rules of a programming language. The process of going through a program and removing the errors is called debugging.
■ There are four parts in solving a problem using the computer. They are (1) defining the problem, (2) designing a solution, (3) coding the program, and (4) compiling, debugging, and testing the program.
■ A program is defined by asking questions about its purposes and requirements. Then an algorithm is formulated that describes the logic used to solve the problem. Algorithms can be represented in two ways: (1) in a sentence form using pseudocode or (2) in diagram form using a flowchart.
■ A well-written program should be readable, reliable, workable under all conditions, and easy to update and modify.
■ Coding the programs is translating the solution into a programming language.
■ The last part of problem solving using the computer is compiling, debugging, and testing the program. When the program is compiled, the compiler will report any syntax errors in the program. Once these have been eliminated, the programmer will continue to debug the program—removing any run-time or logic errors that may be present. Once the program is running properly, the programmer will test the program to try to ensure that it will work under all possible situations.
■ There are two types of programs, or software: (1) system programs, which coordinate the operation of the computer's hardware, and (2) application programs, which solve a particular problem for the computer user.
■ The operating system is a collection of programs the computer uses to manage its own operations. They are stored in an auxiliary called the system residence device.
■ The supervisor program, or monitor, coordinates the activities of the operating system.
■ Two types of programs comprise the operating system: (1) control programs, which oversee system operations, and (2) processing programs, which help the user to simplify program preparation for the computer system.
■ A librarian program maintains a directory of programs in auxilliary stor-

age. Utility programs do specialized functions like transferring data from, for example, tape to disk.

■ The most often-used types of high-level languages are procedure-oriented languages, problem-oriented languages, and interactive languages.

■ The most common procedure-oriented languages are COBOL, used for business applications; FORTRAN, used for scientific applications; and PL/I, used for both business and scientific applications.

■ A problem-oriented language is geared toward solving a specific problem in the easiest way possible for the user. An often-used problem-oriented language is RPG (Report Program Generator), designed to produce business reports.

■ Interactive languages sometimes use an interpreter rather than a compiler. One such language is BASIC, which is often used to teach beginners how to program a computer. Pascal is also interactive, but it uses a compiler rather than an interpreter. Pascal is often used because it is a very structured language and its compiler is small enough to be used on microcomputers. APL is mainly a business programming language and can be used in two modes: execution and definition. This allows it to function as a calculator and as a computer at the same time.

■ Multiprogramming, virtual storage, and multiprocessing are sophisticated system programs. Multiprogramming helps the computer to work with more than one program at a time. Virtual storage lets the computer store only part of the program in primary storage during execution, allowing more programs to be run. Multiprocessing uses a front-end processor, a smaller CPU, to handle smaller jobs such as interrupts, while the larger CPU concentrates on executing the program.

■ Structured programming uses logic patterns that encourage the production of proper programs—single-entry, single-exit programs, while discouraging the use of unconditional branches.

REVIEW QUESTIONS

1. What is a program and what does it do?
2. What are the three levels of language? Name some characteristics of each.
3. What are the differences among a translator, a compiler, and an assembler?
4. Compare pseudocode and program flowcharts.
5. What is the importance of debugging?
6. What is the major difference between system programs and application programs?
7. Name the two types of programs that comprise the operating system and explain the function of each.
8. What are the common procedure-oriented languages and for what purposes are they used?
9. What is the purpose of a problem-oriented language?

10. Which interactive languages are interpreted and which are compiled?
11. Why was multiprogramming developed?
12. How does virtual storage make storage seem larger than it is?
13. In what way does multiprocessing speed up computer processing? On what type of system would it be used?
14. What are the rules and objectives of structured programming?

DISCUSSION QUESTIONS

1. Why do you think a company might be upset at a programmer who did not use structured programming?
2. Why is it essential to plan your program before you begin writing it? Would it be possible to write a program without first formulating an algorithm? If so, would it be advisable?
3. You are a system analyst for a company that has asked you to look into how it might make more efficient and cost effective use of its computer. The main problem has been an inefficient use of CPU time. Your job is to recommend ways of increasing the efficiency and thus reducing the cost of CPU time. What techniques might you suggest to acomplish this? How would each of these help?
4. Your boss has asked you to make a presentation to some nonprogramming personnel. She wants you to explain the programming process and how it relates to other personnel in the firm who must rely on the computer for information. What would you talk about?
5. You have been asked to write a program for a multinational corporation. Your program will use large files and involve lengthy calculations. Your output should be a clear and concise chart of all results. What programming language would you use and why?
6. You are now writing the program described in question five. Are you functioning as an artist, a scientist, or both? Explain your answer.

HEATH
data systems
CONDOR
HEATH
data systems
MULTIPLAN
HEATH
data systems
COBOL-80
HEATH
data systems
MSDOS
HEATH
data systems
FORTRAN-80
HEATH
data systems
CP/M
HEATH
data systems
MBASIC
HEATH
data systems
BASIC Compiler

CHAPTER 5
MICROCOMPUTER REVOLUTION

OUTLINE

ARTICLE

COMPUTER LAB OR CARIBBEAN CRUISE?

"Micro People" sounds like the name of a raucous new-wave group, but it's actually a business that provides computer instruction aboard spacious sailboats roaming Caribbean coves. The Micro People are three Washington, D.C., entrepreneurs: William Trayfors, Noel Berge, and Nancy Berge. Trayfors doubles as ship's captain and chief computer instructor, and Noel Berge also pulls double duty as a deck hand and teacher.

The Micro People's week-long floating workshops cost roughly $1500 per person (exclusive of airfare to Florida), and the number of students is determined by the size of the sailboat. The first Micro People voyage was to the British Virgin Islands aboard a beautiful 46-foot sloop fully equipped with creature comforts such as fluffy towels, private cabins, snorkeling gear, a dinghy with an outboard, and a well-stocked spirits locker—not to mention the generator that powered the Apple IIs and Kaypros secured below. Gourmet meals were prepared by Nancy, who is computer-literate enough to be a teacher if either Bill or Noel falls overboard.

On that first cruise, mornings were devoted to workshops on computerized spreadsheets, database management, and word processing. Around noon, Trayfors and crew would set sail for the next secluded cove. After dropping anchor in mid-afternoon, the students were free to swim, snorkel, or venture inland. After dinner, students could either resume the computer sessions or mix a tropical rum drink—or both.

Student John Grierson, who plans to use microcomputers in his management job in the Philippines, felt the voyage was worth every penny. "We worked in splendid isolation from the twentieth century," he recalls. "No phones, no traffic, no telexes—the setting enabled us to immerse ourselves in the twenty-first century. It was incredible!"

Classmate Jim Parker has pleasant memories of his week as a saltwater hacker. "In terms of programming know-how, I'm now lightyears ahead of where I was when I got on that boat. And I even learned a little bit about sailing as I was considering the meaning of SYSGEN."

The Micro People's most recent voyage was aboard a 70-foot motor sailer. The trio schedules one workshop a month, and more details are available from The Micro People, 805 Devon Place, Alexandria, VA 22314; (703) 548-3849.

Although a Caribbean cruise sounds like an inviting and enjoyable way to learn about microcomputers, not everyone need do that to be successful at using one. Microcomputers offer numerous opportunities to users. Now, let's take a closer look at the microcomputer and the technology behind it.

INTRODUCTION

Throughout this book we repeatedly refer to microcomputers and the many functions they now perform in the home, business, education, science, and industry. But microcomputers merit a closer look, not just because of what they represent in electronic advancement, but also for the way they are making computers accessible to everybody.

Even after microcomputer technology became firmly established in the late 1970s, it took several more years before the hardware became widely known outside of specialist or hobbyist circles. By 1982, though, newspapers and television programs were filled with ads for microcomputers of all sorts, as well as with stories about their applications. Figure 5-1 shows some of the more popular microcomputers. Most of the ads were aimed at people who had little or no background in computing. The attempt was to reach the home and small business market.

Computer manufacturers had several reasons to believe they could open up these previously untapped markets. For one thing, the price of microcomputers had decreased to the point that most people could afford to buy at least a basic model. Microcomputers were also being designed to be **user friendly**. They came with simple, easy-to-understand instructions, and, most important, even people who could not program could operate the new microcomputers thanks to the availability of commercial software. Finally, microcomputers had already been entering the home and educating the family in the guise of video games. The mystery that had long made the computer seem an instrument reserved for the scientific elite was being banished.

USER FRIENDLY
Easy to use.

Advertising agencies seized on these qualities and turned out commercials that made micros seem as approachable as typewriters and as handy to have around as a four-blade pocket knife.

Elementary school children, in the meantime, were being introduced to microcomputers and were learning to accept them as just another part of the classroom hardware.

In short, by the early 1980s, the microcomputer had become reasonably well domesticated.

One of the newest, and most awaited, entries in the microcomputer market—the IBM PCjr.

HARDWARE

As remarkable as their capabilities are, microcomputers are not just compact versions of mainframes and minicomputers. To get the size, price, and simplicity of today's microcomputers, developers had to make tradeoffs in the speed and number of functions available, memory capacity, and peripheral options.

A microcomputer is built around a **microprocessor chip** (Figure 5-2) that is a single, integrated circuit. Built into the circuit are the arithmetic/logic unit, the control for memory and input/output access, and the primary storage unit. Larger computers have central processing units (CPUs) that are made up of a series of integrated circuits. Therefore, the CPU can hold

MICROPROCESSOR CHIP
A single, integrated circuit containing one ALU, control unit, and a primary storage unit.

FIGURE 5-1 Popular Microcomputers Include the Apple IIe, the Commodore 64, the IBM Personal Computer, the DEC Rainbow 100, and the TRS-80 Model 4

Apple IIe

Commodore 64

DEC Rainbow 100

IBM Personal Computer

TRS-80 Model 4

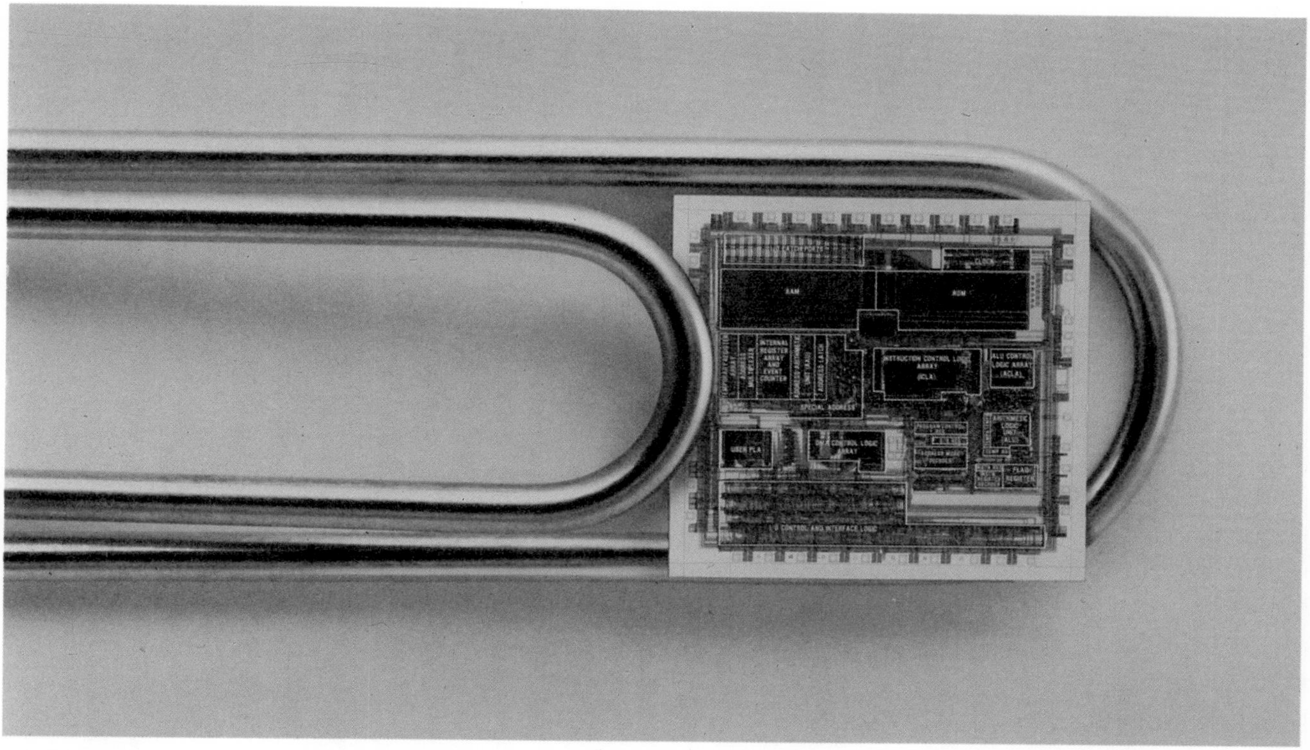

FIGURE 5-2 This Tiny Chip Is A Microcomputer with Functional Parts Identified.

more complex sets of instructions and carry them out faster than can the microchip.

Other differences between the large and small computers include the number and size of registers, **word size** that can be accommodated, and the number of users that can be accommodated at one time. Registers, as we noted in Chapter 2, are storage locations that receive and hold information while the computer is in operation. Word size is based on the size of the registers. This factor limits the complexity of the operations that microcomputers can perform and the speed at which they can perform them. Micros not only have smaller registers but also fewer of them than larger computers. Large computers, for example, can handle word sizes of 64 bits. But micros are generally restricted to word sizes of eight, 16 or, recently, 32 bits. Most micros are restricted to one user at a time because they generally have only one communication channel between the tape or disk unit and the computer itself. Mainframes, however, have several such communication channels, which allow many users to work at the same time.

WORD SIZE
Based on the size of the registers and decides on the complexity of operations that can be handled.

In spite of these differences, microcomputers should not be considered inferior to the larger machines. They are simply different machines with different purposes.

PROFILE

STEVEN JOBS and STEPHEN WOZNIAK

Perhaps the most publicized success story in the computer world concerns the two adventurous spirits who founded Apple, Inc.—Steven Paul Jobs and Stephen Wozniak.

Jobs, the marketing wizard of the Apple computers, attended college for only one semester. His interest in technology landed him a job with Atari, and prompted him to attend meetings of the Homebrew Computer Club. There he ran into an old friend, Stephen Wozniak.

Wozniak built a small computer using state-of-the-art technology scaled down for the small user. Jobs, impressed by his friend's invention, believed that producing the computer for public use would be a profitable venture. After persuading Wozniak to leave his job at Hewlett Packard, Jobs sold his Volkswagen and Wozniak's scientific calculator to raise $1,300 to build the first microcomputers. Jobs and Wozniak named the machine the Apple after a memorable summer they spent working together in an Apple orchard. The Apple II was officially unveiled in 1977 and by 1982, Apple, Inc., collected revenues of $664 million.

Steven Jobs has been the primary advocate behind the microcomputer revolution. Through lectures across the country, he has convinced thousands of individuals and businesses of the benefits new technology can offer, emphasizing the easy-to-use nature of the Apple microcomputers. Currently chairman of the board at Apple, Jobs has recently introduced two new microcomputer models—the Apple IIe and Lisa. Initial responses look very good, and it is likely that Jobs, who already has a net worth of $210 million, will secure his status as one of the world's wealthiest computer entrepreneurs.

Wozniak, although still a major stockholder in the company, left Apple and founded UNUSON Corporation—the corporate sponsor of the successful US Festivals.

Steven Jobs

Stephen Wozniak

Storage

Because microcomputers have relatively little internal memory capacity, they are nearly always used in conjunction with peripheral storage devices. The most common devices used for secondary storage with microcomputers are magnetic tapes, floppy disks, cartridges and hard disks (Figure 5-3).

Magnetic Tapes The magnetic tape used for data storage with microcomputers is generally housed in a tape cassette. Tape cassettes are becoming fairly common because they are very inexpensive. Most can be used with a standard cassette player, the same one on which you could

FIGURE 5-3 Various Storage Media Available for Microcomputers

later listen to your favorite music tape. This aspect makes them popular, because they require no expensive disk drive. Also, because the technology used with them is already familiar to most people, they don't seem as intimidating to the first-time user.

Although tapes are very inexpensive and are commonly used, they have a major drawback. Much like the music recordings they resemble, they have to be read sequentially. If, say, on an album tape, you want to listen to song three, you have to fast forward (quickly read past) songs one and two. This also applies to data that are stored on these tapes. Also, because they have to be read sequentially, they are excruciatingly slow. For this reason, tapes are best suited to short programs such as games.

Cartridges Cartridges used for computers are also common and are used extensively for video games. The cartridges are exceptionally easy to use. You simply plug them in, much as you would insert an eight-track tape into a tape player. Cartridges contain random-access memory (RAM) or read-only memory (ROM). Game cartridges use ROM, so it is nearly impossible to damage the data short of physically abusing the cartridge. Memory expansion cartridges, on the other hand, use RAM to temporarily expand the internal storage capacity of a microcomputer.

CARTRIDGE
Plug-in plastic containers holding either ROM or RAM depending on its function.

Floppy Disks Floppy disks, or diskettes, generally come in two sizes, 8 inch and 5¼ inch, and can hold much more data than cassette tape. Storage capacity on the floppies range from 100K to 1 megabyte (one million bytes) on the 5¼-inch disks to 125K to 1.2 megabytes on the 8-inch disks. In addition, there is a third size of floppy, which has only re-

PROFILE

GARY KILDALL

Gary Kildall designed the industry standard for microcomputer operating systems—CP/M.*

Kildall served as an instructor of computer science at the Naval Postgraduate School in Monterey (California) after receiving a Ph.D. from the University of Washington. Kildall first came in contact with the microprocessor in 1972 when he noticed an advertisement for the Intel Corporation's 4004 microprocessor (the first microprocessor developed by Ted Hoff in 1969) posted on the campus bulletin board. He was interested in using the $25 chip for the development of a navigation calculator, so he inquired about it. The microprocessor intrigued him so much that he arranged a four-month consultantship with Intel Corporation by the end of 1973.

There, Kildall developed a simulator as well as a systems implementation language—PL/M (Programming Language for Microcomputers) for the 8008 microprocessor. From this concept he began designing a variation of PL/M, called CP/M (Control Program for Microcomputers), for the 8-bit 8080 microprocessor, the chip that replaced the 8008 and started the microcomputer revolution.

Intel, however, chose another operating system over Kildall's. So Kildall formed his own company, Intergalactic Digital Research, later to be renamed Digital Research Corporation, and began selling CP/M to hobbyists for $70.

CP/M became a popular program for two reasons: it eliminated the need for manufacturers to design individual operating systems, and CP/M was the first operating system designed to control floppy disk drives. As a result, CP/M became a standardized component of major microcomputers, allowing the advantage of software compatibility.

*CP/M is a registered trademark of Digital Research, Inc.

cently entered the market. This is the sub-4-inch floppy, which stores considerably less data than the 8-inch or 5¼-inch variety. Although their smaller size makes them easier to use, they are not yet standardized; sub-4-inch may refer to anything from 3 inches to 3¾ inches. Naturally, the 3-inch floppies require a 3-inch disk drive and will not work with a 3¾-inch disk drive. However, the trend in hardware has consistently been toward miniaturization, and the sub-4-inch floppies will undoubtedly catch on big once a standard is set.

Data are stored on the disks in the form of magnetized spots arranged in concentric tracks, which can be scanned by track number and sector. The amount of data that a floppy disk can store depends on how the disk is **formatted**. Disks may have data on both sides or on one side only. Another format variation is "double density," which means that double the amount of data has been recorded in the same space, whether on one side of the disk or on both. These variations produce four disk formats: single sided/single density; single sided/double density; double sided/single density; and double sided/double density. The kind of disk drive will determine which of the formats can be used.

FLOPPY DISK FORMAT **Indicates the density of information and whether it is stored on one side or both.**

Floppy disks have another major advantage over magnetic tape; that is, the data can be accessed randomly as needed, instead of being read or written sequentially. For this reason data transfer (reading from or writing to the floppy) is much faster than with magnetic tape.

The major drawback of using floppy disks is that they require the purchase of an additional hardware device. Although it would not be unusual to find a cassette player lying around the house, it is not very likely that one would find a disk drive; and disk drives are considerably more expensive than cassette players.

Hard Disks Hard disks are useful for people needing a great deal of storage space, since hard disks can store much more data than can floppy disks. Perhaps the most familiar application is word processing. If you were to write a novel, it would be far less complicated to store the entire work on a single hard disk rather than have most of the chapters on separate floppies. This would also make it much simpler if you decide that you want to move material, say, from the beginning of the book to the end.

HARD DISK
A rigid platter used for random-access data storage with greater storage capacity than floppy disk.

The hard disks come in two configurations: the fixed hard disk that is sealed and allows no user access, and the removable hard disk pack. Figure 5-4 shows a cutaway view of two different fixed hard disks. The removable disk pack is the more expensive but also the more versatile of the two, particularly when it comes to copying and using backup data. However, removable disk packs have more mechanical problems than fixed hard disk units.

Hard disk drives are considerably faster than floppy disk drives, yet again the price is also correspondingly higher. Also hard disks are not usable with some personal computing systems. It is apparent that the more data a device can store and the faster it can transfer that data into memory, the more expensive it will be.

FIGURE 5-4 Cutaway View of Two Different Fixed Hard Disks

New Alternatives Two other alternatives in storage media have been developed, although they are not yet widely used for microcomputers. They are the optical laser disk and the RAM chip. The **optical laser disk** can hold 5,000 bits of data in a line one inch long. Data are recorded on the disk by way of microscopic laser burns, or "pits." A 12-inch optical disk can hold the equivalent of 1,735 average books on just one side. Because these disks cannot be erased or used for rerecording data, they are used primarily for long-term storage and data retrieval.

OPTICAL LASER DISK
New high-capacity device for data storage using laser technology.

The random-access memory (RAM) chip is the only storage medium, besides ROM, that can input data about as fast as the microprocessor can handle it. A new storage device that uses RAM chips, the **RAM card** (Figure 5-5), can be plugged into the same slot that the disk drive uses. Microsoft's RAM card, made for use with the IBM Personal Computer, has 256K of memory and is 50 times faster in data retrieval than a disk.

RAM CARD
Recently developed storage medium for microcomputers.

Input/Output

Users can input their data into microcomputers and receive their output using a variety of devices. Some of these devices are standard; that is, they are used commonly both on micros and on larger computers. Other devices are not standard; they are almost exclusively used with microcomputers.

Standard Input/Output Devices The standard input/output devices are those used not only with microcomputers but also with most computers. The most predominant input device is the keyboard. The keyboards used with microcomputers may be similar to those on a regular typewriters with

FIGURE 5-5 RAM Card

keys that move up and down or they may be pressure-sensitive membrane keyboards. **Membrane keyboards** are flat, with keys that are activated by just being touched rather than by being pressed. Figure 5-6 compares a regular keyboard with one type of membrane keyboard. Some micros have keyboards divided by functions: one part for entering letters, another for numbers, and a third part for special functions. Some have keys, each of which can perform several functions, depending on the mode into which it is shifted. Almost all microcomputers use some type of keyboard as a way of entering data.

MEMBRANE KEYBOARD
Flat, pressure-sensitive keyboard.

Standard output devices for micros include printers, display screens, and plotters. (For additional information, refer to Chapter 2.) A continuing problem with microcomputers that are connected to printers has been that the computer processes information much faster than the printer can reproduce it. A new device, called a **hardware spooler**, or **buffer**, can be connected between the computer and printer to hold the processed data and feed them to the printer at its own rate, enabling the computer to continue being used. It is important to note that a spooler or buffer used by a microcomputer is a hardware device as opposed to the software used to simulate buffers in large computers.

HARDWARE SPOOLER (BUFFER)
Holds processed data being fed to the printer to enable the computer to complete other tasks.

Because storage devices can be written to and read from, they also function as input/output devices. Therefore, floppy disks, hard disks, and magnetic tapes are also standard input/output devices.

Special Input/Output Devices These special input/output devices include joysticks and game paddles, electronic drawing pens, light pens, graphics tablets, spatial digitizers, voice recognition and voice output systems, and "mouse" systems. These input/output devices are used almost exclusively with microcomputers, although some are also used with larger computers.

Joysticks and **game paddles** (Figure 5-7), common to video games, simply control the movement of cursors on a TV screen by inputting electrical responses. A **cursor** is a mark that indicates where you are on the

JOYSTICK AND GAME PADDLES
Control cursor movement by inputting electrical response.

CURSOR
Indicates current location on display screen.

FIGURE 5-6 Regular Keyboard versus Membrane Keyboard

FIGURE 5-7 Joysticks

screen. If you are doing word processing, the cursor may be shown on the screen as an "at" sign (@) or as a flashing box. On games, the cursor is whatever you are moving with the joystick or paddle. For instance, if you are playing a tennis game the tennis paddle is the cursor.

ELECTRONIC DRAWING PEN AND LIGHT PEN
Allow the user to create or alter designs by drawing directly on the screen.

Electronic drawing pens and **light pens** (Figure 5-8) represent unique input devices that are used to create computer graphics. They allow the user to "draw" and alter designs on the display terminal, similar to drawing on paper with regular markers.

FIGURE 5-8 Light Pen

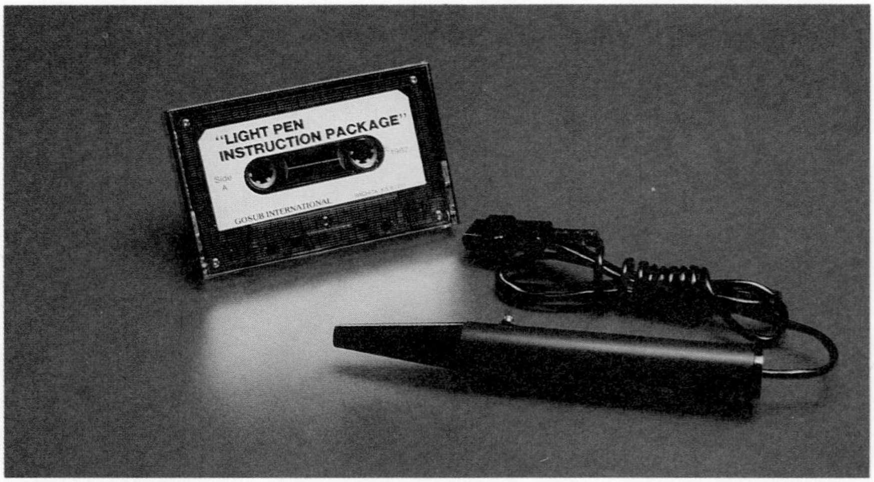

Graphics tablets, are similar in use to light pens but the user draws on the tablet rather than on the screen (Figure 5-9). The results are still shown on the display screen.

Spatial digitizers are also commonly used in creating computer graphics. With a spatial digitizer, the user can input the x, y, and z coordinates of any three-dimensional object by tracing the object with its arm-like appendage. The image will appear on the display screen in simulated three dimension.

An upcoming input device for microcomputers is the voice recognition device. It is also the most futuristic of the unique input devices. Voice recognition systems and voice synthesizers are being used for vocal in-

GRAPHICS TABLET
Allows the user to create or alter designs on the display screen by drawing on the tablet.

SPATIAL DIGITIZER
Simulates three-dimensional objects.

FIGURE 5-9 Graphics Tablet

VOICE RECOGNITION SYSTEM
Allows the computer to accept spoken input.

VOICE SYNTHESIZER
Produces spoken output.

MOUSE
Hand-held input device.

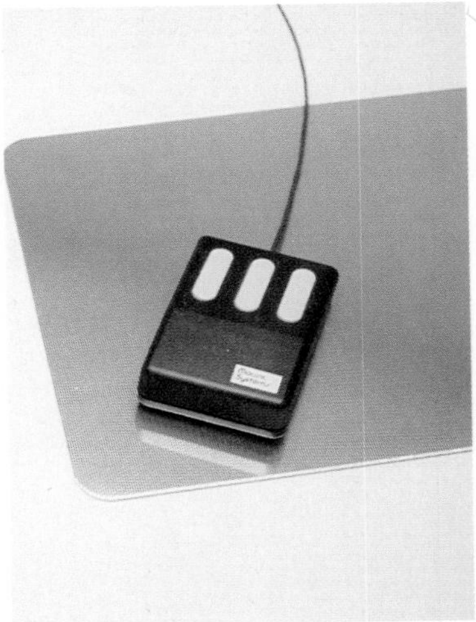

FIGURE 5-10 A Mouse

BUSINESS SOFTWARE
Packages specifically designed for business functions such as payroll or word processing.

put and output. **Voice recognition systems** activate the computer to do specific tasks according to the vocal sounds fed into it. This allows you to instruct the computer by simply talking to it. The system is adaptable to a variety of personal vocal variations. However, because of the vocal differences among people, it will only respond to the *one* person's voice that it was "taught" (programmed) to recognize. As this manner of entry is refined, it holds many possibilities for computer uses by handicapped people or those whose jobs prevent them from using their hands for keyboard or other manual input. In the same category, many microcomputers can be equipped with **voice synthesizers** to provide vocal output as well.

The **mouse** (Figure 5-10) is a hand-held input device that controls the position of the cursor on the screen. It is connected to the computer by an input cord. The mouse is rolled on a flat surface; it sends electronic signals through the cord, back to the computer to move the screen's cursor in direct proportion to its own movement. It allows you to move the cursor to any point on the screen quickly and easily. The mouse, when used with the proper software, serves to make the system more user friendly, allowing the user to bypass the keyboard when entering instructions. Although the mouse was invented in 1964, it has just recently received public notice, thanks mainly to the use of the mouse in Apple's Lisa.

SOFTWARE

So far we have said little of the software designed for microcomputers—yet this is probably the most exciting part of the whole system since speed and memory alone are rather limited qualities without the software to make them functional. There are literally thousands of ready-made programs for the micro user, having applications in business, home management, education, and games.

Business Software

Business software can cover a variety of areas, from tasks like accounting, budgeting, planning, and tax calculation to more sophisticated fields such as stock portfolio management.

By far the most commonly used software package in business is word processing. It has obvious benefits for business correspondence and text preparation, but it is also being used increasingly by writers as a replacement for typewriters. A good word-processing package can provide the writer with quick and flexible editing capabilities as well as speed up the composition process itself. Some packages even offer automatic spelling correction.

Other common packages are programs for payroll, spreadsheet, inventory, chart and graph generation, and reports.

Home Management Software

HOME MANAGEMENT SOFTWARE
Designed to help inventory, organize, and manage domestic matters.

Home management software embraces everything from budgeting, coupon management, and meal planning to energy control and security. One company offers a computerized cookbook that is a recipe storage file, nutritional calculator, calorie counter, shopping list generator, and portion calculator.

Foremost among the home management packages are the inventory programs. First, there is the standard electronic address book, which helps you to inventory your friends' and relatives' addresses. There are also wine cellar and coin collector inventory programs. Theoretically, anything that can be counted or listed can be inventoried by computer, and sooner or later someone will write the software to do it.

Other home management programs are home budget, income tax, and résumé writers. Hobbyist programs are often placed in the home management category; these cover everything from astrology and genealogy to computing bowling averages for the team.

Home management software assists this user in budgeting household finances.

Educational Software

EDUCATIONAL SOFTWARE
Geared to drill, tutor, or instruct the user.

Educational software is demonstrating its value at every level of learning since it can be tailored to the level of difficulty and pace that is most appropriate to the learner.

The interactive and nonjudgmental qualities of educational software make it an extremely effective teaching device. Also, as the learner's skills increase in sophistication, so can the software.

Software packages are available on every level from preschool to college, and on subjects ranging from algebra and geometry to English grammar and advanced organic chemistry.

Educational software packages generally fall into one of three categories based on the method they use to present the material: (1) drills, (2) tutorials, and (3) simulations.

DRILL PROGRAM
Repeats questions to test the user's knowledge.

Drills are educational packages that present short passages of material and then drill the learner on the contents. They are often repeated and/or timed. Some drills present no material at all. These are most likely to be mathematical packages that function somewhat like electronic flashcards.

Educational software published by SRA, IBM's educational division, incorporate CAI techniques in teaching elementary school mathematics.

Selected packages allow you to input the learner's age or grade level and then gear the drill to material most appropriate to that level. These levels are not restricted to children. Drill packages in, say, mathematics can cover anything from addition to advanced calculus.

Tutorial programs provide more material for the learners to absorb before testing their retention of it. The material is geared toward explaining concepts or steps. For example, a foreign language tutorial in Russian may concentrate first on the forms in the Russian alphabet and then advance to an explanation of pronunciation. Tutorials are used in a wide variety of subjects including English grammar, foreign languages, science, and even typing. Some computer tutorial packages will even tutor the student in computer history, applications and specifications of computer science theory, and computer programming. Depending on the nature of the material, tutorials may or may not include drill sections.

TUTORIAL PROGRAM
Explains new material.

SIMULATION PROGRAM
Simulates a specific machine or situation.

The third category of educational programs contains the **simulation programs**. Simulation programs teach the learner how to operate a piece of machinery or how to react in a certain situation by imitating that machine or situation. The most common simulation program is the flight simulation. A flight simulation program presents all of the controls found in the cockpit of an airplane to the learner, on the video screen. The student uses either a joystick or keyboard (or sometimes a combination of the two) to manipulate the controls. Thus, he or she can have the "plane" take off, fly through fog, execute day or night flights, land, or crash. All of the results are based on the student's manipulations of the computerized cockpit controls. Many flight schools now require practice with these programs before allowing would-be pilots in the air. Simulation programs enable students to make major mistakes with minimal consequences.

DENNIS the MENACE

"I THINK IT LIKES ME!"

Computer Games

Because computer games are the most popular form of software for microcomputers, they are also the most prolific and fastest selling (Figure 5-11). There are three types of computer games.

The first type is the arcade-like "shoot-'em-up" games, commonly referred to as **video games**. They are characterized by fast action and excellent graphics. Into this category fall such infamous creations as Donkey Kong, Frogger, Space Invaders, and Pac Man. This is the fastest-moving type of computer software, both in play and in sales. Yet sales cannot be used exclusively in judging the overall popularity of this software. Because these games are easily learned, people tire of them quickly and replace them often.

VIDEO GAME
Fast-action computer game.

The second type, **adventure games**, are word games that may or may not incorporate graphics. They are long-playing games because they require their users to make careful decisions about their possessions, their surroundings, and their companions (real or fictional). These games require anywhere from two to 64 hours to play, depending on the user's skill and the complexity of the game.

ADVENTURE GAME
Long-playing, decision-making game.

Some of the adventure games are exceptionally complex. One series of games called Zork even allows the user to input compound-complex En-

FIGURE 5-11 Computer Games

glish sentences provided they stay within the bounds of the game's predefined vocabulary.

EDUCATIONAL GAME Combines learning with game play.

The last type of computer game is the **educational game**. This is an ambiguous area, with some people categorizing such software as education, others as games. Obviously, they fit well—and belong—in both categories.

Educational games are also varied. Some educational software present their subject using the popular simulation technique. Other programs allow the user to create something, such as synthesized music. The music so created is not of performance quality, but it is of sufficient complexity to sharpen the user's compositional, arranging, and performing skills, and the process itself is an enjoyable form of recreation. Educational games are also often disguised as tutorials and drills.

PROGRAMMING LANGUAGES

Micros can be programmed in several languages, but BASIC is currently the most popular because of its interactive quality and the fact that it is comparatively easy for novices to use. Moreover, the BASIC language requires less memory than do some other languages such as COBOL.

However, since there are a number of variations of BASIC, no one form of it works on all micros. The BASIC that is closest to being universal is Microsoft's BASIC in ROM.

Pascal vies with BASIC for popularity, but it requires a good deal more memory. Like BASIC, it is interactive and its structure demands that the programmer be systematic in his or her program writing. As personal computers increase their memory size, Pascal is expected to gain in usage.

Other programming languages have some usefulness in microcomputers, especially such new educational languages as LOGO and Pilot. Both are well suited to graphics and can be taught to children. COBOL, FORTRAN, and RPG—because of the memory required—are only marginally relevant to microcomputers. But this is likely to change as micros enlarge their capacity.

A continuing concern of language developers is that the language be user friendly. Lacking that quality, the language will have limited usefulness with micros aimed at varied markets.

NETWORKS

One of the most exciting developments in microcomputing is the linking of computers into a **network** for sharing messages and information. Some networks are relatively small and simple, such as those within a school or a classroom that connect students with students and students with teachers in lesson situations. Other networks are national or even global.

NETWORK
Links computers for sharing messages and information.

In the classroom a student may carry out learning tasks on a micro, check the correctness of his or her responses, and make inquiries through the network to teacher-operated computers. For their part, teachers can monitor student progress and give instruction and assignments from their computer stations. In addition, students may link to each other to carry out joint projects.

Apple, Commodore, and Radio Shack are already active in educational networking. Systems available are marketed under such names as Schoolbus, Omninet, Classroom Monitor, Radio Shack Network 2 and 3, Questar, Mupet, and VIC Switch.

Although educational networking is growing in popularity and versatility, it is still somewhat hampered by cost and scarcity of software.

Commercial networks for conveying news and reference data are well established. The largest of these **data banks** are The Source, the Dow Jones Information Retrieval Service, the Knowledge Index, CompuServe, and Bibliographic Research Service, (BRS). These are described in Chapter 7.

DATA BANK
Commercially available databases for conveying news and reference data.

Noting the success of the QUBE interactive cable TV system in its home base of Columbus, Ohio, CompuServe has established a cooperative experiment with QUBE and Atari. The initial experiment involved connecting Atari 800 micros to TV sets; the first linkup was between the users and Columbus' City Hall to see if the interactive technology could contribute to the quality of municipal operations.

Whether a network is confined to a classroom or a continent, it offers the users the means of rapidly and accurately exchanging information without enduring footwork and delays that were an inevitable part of the old search and transmit processes.

CONCLUSION

In spite of the rapid advances, microcomputers have not reached their most advanced form or that their uses have been exhausted. In the future we may see micros that are much smaller (and much more capable) than today's models, that "talk" back to us, and that can perform functions like making on-the-spot medical analyses and monitoring the ongoing state of our health.

Information retrieval—from finding a phone number to researching for a dissertation—will be made easier through micros. The refinement of leisure and business networks will allow people to conduct as much of their lives from their homes as they wish. No more going to the bank or the store unless one does it for the exercise.

Microcomputers will teach small children concepts and ways of visualizing that are beyond the ability of the best human teacher unaided by technology.

Although we can only guess at the forms and applications microcomputers will have, it seems certain there will be more of them, doing more tasks, in smaller spaces, for less cost, and with more ease of operation.

ISSUE

THE GREAT MICROCOMPUTER GIVE-AWAY

In Greek mythology, there is a story about a horse that was given to the city of Troy as a gift. An invading army was secretly housed in the horse. The Trojan horse story led to the saying, "Beware of Greeks bearing gifts." Recently, this warning might be applied to the great give-away by computer companies.

In the spring of 1982, Steven Jobs, cofounder of Apple, Inc., announced that if Congress would increase the tax breaks, he would give a computer to *every* school in the country. This would amount to $200 million worth of free computers for America's schools. That is quite a substantial amount, and the obvious question is "Why"? Was this a humanitarian offer or a business proposition?

The humanitarian aspect of the offer is in keeping with Apple's policies. In 1979 the Apple Education Foundation was established to provide donations of hardware for educational research. By February, 1983 they had also made 150 grants for software development in addition to publishing the *Journal of Courseware Review*.

Apple is not the only microcomputer manufacturer engaged in educational activities. Radio Shack offers an annual $500,000 grant program to fund teacher training and software development, in addition to donating equipment to educational research and development projects funded through the National Science Foundation. IBM began donating equipment to schools by providing 84 public and private schools in New York, California, and Florida with a total of 1,500 personal computers. This type of give-away program, which is becoming more common, has both business and humanitarian ramifications.

Computer give-aways received widespread public attention through the computer contributions bill of 1982. Although the bill was passed in the House of Representatives by an overwhelming majority, it was defeated in the Senate. The business aspects of computer give-aways were the underlying reasons for that defeat.

One of the major complaints was the contention that Apple would use the give-away to rid itself of surplus computers while writing off most of the loss as educational donations. Apple was working on a new version of the Apple II and the give-away would afford them the opportunity to unload the old Apple IIs, which would be obsolete and virtually unsalable. But even that was not the major objection.

Tax breaks proved to be the breaking point for the computer contribution bill. The bill would have allowed companies to deduct for each computer the value halfway between the manufacturing cost and the retail price. Who sets the retail price? The computer companies, of course.

The final deciding factor in the death of the bill was a clause raising the current maximum corporate charitable donation from 10 percent to 30 percent of the year's profits. This would increase the loss of tax revenue—possibly forcing the taxpayer to make up part of the difference through increased tax rates.

Although the profit motive is certainly a factor in give-aways, the fact remains that $200 million worth of hardware would also represent one monumental effort to upgrade educational resources in this country; and if Apple began a give-away on that scale, other manufacturers would have to follow suit to retain viability in the educational market.

Those give-aways would help to provide computers to poorer school districts that would not otherwise have access to them. The publicity accompanying a national give-away might encourage schools receiving the computer at least to make an effort to develop programs for implementing the computers in their curricula. This would help to eliminate the seemingly random manner in which computers are being used in today's schools. And perhaps schools would be motivated to establish

ISSUE

teacher-training programs to help orient teachers, most of whom are not computer trained.

From a company's sales viewpoint, it is likely to realize future profits from the donation of computers. These profits could perhaps come from sales of peripherals and software to the schools, repair and service, and even new sales of computers to those who have become familiar with their brand of computer.

Peripherals and software compatible with that particular computer would probably eventually be bought by the school to take advantage of all the capabilities of the computer; they would be likely to be purchased from the same company for flexibility.

The question of who pays for repair and service to the donated equipment—the school system or the company—is still sometimes unclear.

And finally, the fact that a child or teacher may already be familiar with a particular brand of computer would likely influence them to purchase a computer of that brand.

There is no doubt that both humanitarian and profit motives are operating in this area. The question is one of degree. The computer contribution bill will most likely be reintroduced in the near future. When it is, we will be forced to answer the following question: Given the combination of motives and potential effects, should the government treat the donations of microcomputers to schools primarily as a humanitarian offer—or as a business proposition?

SUMMARY POINTS

- Microcomputers are more than just tiny computers. They use a microprocessor chip rather than a CPU. Micros also have smaller registers, fewer of them, and have to use smaller word sizes.
- Standard storage devices for microcomputers are magnetic tape, cartridges, floppy disks, and hard disks.
- Magnetic tape is used with cassette players and must be accessed sequentially.
- Floppy disks come in 8-inch, 5-inch, and sub-4-inch sizes and are direct access media. They can be formatted in four ways: (1) single-sided/single-density, (2) single-sided/double-density, (3) double-sided/single-density, and (4) double-sided/double-density. Acceptable disk format is determined by the type of disk drive used.
- Hard disks are used for large amounts of storage and come in two configurations: (1) fixed hard disks and (2) removable disk packs.
- New alternatives for storage are optical laser disks and RAM chips. Optical laser disks utilize laser technology and can store virtual libraries in the space of a single disk. RAM chips add large amounts of memory and are the only storage devices that can input data as fast as the microprocessor can handle it.
- Standard input/output devices that can be used with microcomputers are keyboards, display terminals, printers, and plotters. Many printers use spoolers, which hold data while they are waiting to be printed to enable the microcomputer to complete other tasks.
- The special input/output devices include joysticks, game paddles, electronic drawing pens, light pens, graphics tablets, spatial digitizers, voice recognition, and voice output, and mouse systems. These devices are used almost exclusively with microcomputers.
- Many different kinds of software packages are available for microcomputers. The major categories of software are business, home management, education, and games. However, some software packages may fit into two or more categories.
- Business software packages generally perform tasks such as accounting, tax calculation, and word processing.
- Home management packages perform inventory, security, and budgeting tasks for the home.
- Educational packages are available for all levels and come in three basic types: (1) drill, (2) tutorial, and (3) simulation.
- Computer games are the most popular form of microcomputer software. Types available are arcade games, adventure games, and educational games.
- The choice of programming languages for microcomputers is very limited because of the small size of available memory. The most common language used is BASIC. Other languages that can be used are Pascal and the educational languages LOGO and Pilot.
- An exciting aspect of microcomputers is that they can be linked into networks to share messages and information. Commercial data bases, called data banks, offer services ranging from reference data to at-home electronic banking and shopping.

REVIEW QUESTIONS

1. What differentiates microcomputers from their larger counterparts?
2. List the standard storage devices for microcomputers and their advantages and disadvantages.
3. What are the advantages of optical laser disks?
4. Why are RAM chips preferable to cassette tapes?
5. List the standard input/output devices that can be used with microcomputers.
6. How do joysticks and game paddles work? What are they used for?
7. How are electronic drawing pens, light pens, graphic tablets, and spatial digitizers similar?
8. What jobs are business software programs used for?
9. What types of software are included in the home management category? Give examples.
10. What is a simulation program?
11. List and define the types of computer games available for microcomputers. How do they differ?
12. What computer languages can be used with microcomputers?
13. What is a computer network and what are its uses?
14. What services are offered by data banks?

DISCUSSION QUESTIONS

1. Spatial digitizers offer the option of representing a three-dimensional object. In what situations would this be useful?
2. Optical laser disks can store vast amounts of information. As they become more commonly used with microcomputers, to what uses do you think they will be put?
3. Drills and tutorials are two different approaches to educational software. For what subjects would each be preferable? Why?
4. What problems would you run into if you decided to rewrite an encyclopedia using word processing software and floppy disks?
5. Answer the question in the issue section: Are microcomputer manufacturers acting as humanitarians or business people in giving microcomputers to schools?

CHAPTER 6

SOLVING PROBLEMS USING COMPUTERS: SYSTEM ANALYSIS

OUTLINE

ARTICLE

SWITCH TO MINIS NETS VICE-PRESIDENCY

WHEN ANALYST TALKED, E. F. HUTTON LISTENED

Jeffry Beeler

New York—To a great extent Vincent Pica owes his current job to a report he wrote in 1976 while he was still working as a "cost analyst" for E. F. Hutton Co., the Wall Street brokerage house. . . .

A careful analysis of Hutton's time-sharing costs eventually convinced Pica that some 60% of the company's externally processed jobs could be performed just as effectively and much less expensively in-house.

The problem with trying to reduce the firm's dependence on time-sharing support was that Hutton's existing host processors were already heavily burdened and lacked the capacity to shoulder a large number of extra jobs. So Pica proposed an alternative: He urged the company to install its first in-house minicomputers and use the machines as a partial replacement for the outside time-sharing resources. . . .

The results of the time-sharing cost analysis were later detailed in a report that eventually caught the eye of Hutton's executive vice-president of operations. So impressed was the vice-president by the study's recommendations that he approved the minicomputer installation plan outright and appointed Pica to oversee its execution. . . .

The adoption of Pica's minicomputer proposal marked a turning point in The adoption of Pica's minicomputer proposal marked a turning point in the evolution of Hutton's computing facilities and helped catapult the former cost analyst into his current position as vice-president of the company's management information systems (MIS) operations.

Today, at the age of 27, Pica already heads two parts of the three-level systems hierarchy that constitutes Hutton's in-house computing department. . . .

The formation of Hutton's MIS operations group reflects the company's—and Pica's—guiding philosophy of continually trying to streamline internal corporate activities and trim costs whenever possible.

"No matter how profitable we are, I say there's always some place where we can be more efficient or save one more dollar through the use of automation," Pica said. "That personal philosophy happily coincides with the company's own. On that point, the firm and I are simpatico." . . .

In practice, the firm's philosophy of ever-increasing efficiency and economy has manifested itself in a nearly uninterrupted stream of new automation projects that have brought computing power to a wide variety of formerly manual administrative tasks.

In the back office, for example, "we're striving to automate every function that can be routinized, and we're starting with jobs that promise the greatest potential for savings," Pica explained. "Our unofficial motto is, "If it doesn't require discretion, it ought to be computerized." . . .

The fact that an analyst moved into the vice presidency of a major company is not surprising. System analysis is becoming an important part of business, a part that can make or break whole businesses—not just vice presidents.

INTRODUCTION

Computers have made the task of storing data so easy that we are amassing great stores of information. Yet we rarely look at the value of that information. Many experts are concerned that we will continue to find pieces of hardware on which to put programs when what we should be doing is determining the significance of the information we have. We should look at the total flow of information through the organization or activity and then decide which information is the most valuable. We need to put our best equipment on the most valuable information. The way to do this is through **system analysis.**

SYSTEM ANALYSIS
The analysis of information systems.

Theoretically, system analysis could take place without any reference to computers. As long as there have been businesses, methods have been available to give people the information they needed to keep their businesses going. Computers are latecomers in this field, and even now a few sizable businesses do not use computers to gather systemwide information.

But practically speaking, computers are destined to play an increasingly larger role in organizations of all types by providing the multilevel information they need to survive and prosper. Today information, so essential to the decision-making process, is too detailed and plentiful to be assimilated without computers.

In this chapter we use the word "system" dozens of times. Sometimes it is the *thing* described (such as management information system) and sometimes it helps to *explain* or *clarify* the thing described (such as a system of implementation). Whatever its context, however, the word fits this definition: A **system** is a grouping of organizationally related elements working toward a common goal. The elements may be individual employees or entire departments within a company, for example, and the common goal may be as grand as record profits or as practical as simple survival.

SYSTEM
A grouping of related elements working toward a common goal.

Naturally, each system has its own inputs, processes, and outputs, just as a computer operation does. A system receives data from within that system and from without, then it processes these data and outputs them as relevent information that may aid in achieving, say, lower costs, higher production, and greater profits. Besides input, output, and process, there is a fourth element in system dynamics: feedback. **Feedback** refers to the responses and reactions to what is happening within a system. The feedback may be requested, required reports, for example, or spontaneous (customer praise or complaints). Essentially, feedback is a guidance and correction mechanism to keep a system on its stated course. Figure 6-1 outlines these system characteristics.

FEEDBACK
Responses and reactions to what is happening within a system.

Systems are self-contained entities, yet they also are elements within larger systems. The system analyst who wants to streamline and maximize a unit's information-gathering and dispersing process must keep this relationship in mind. A department, for example, is a system within a company; a company is a system within a country's economic system; and a country's economic system is an element within the worldwide economic system. Each system gathers data from within and/or without and,

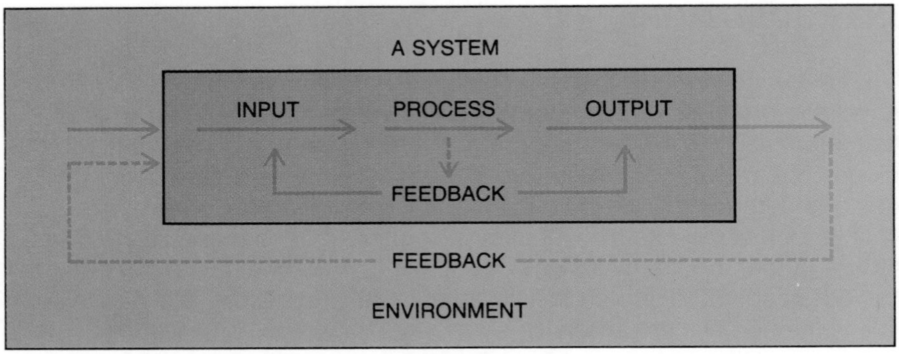

FIGURE 6-1 A Simple System with Feedback

in turn, provides data to the other systems. So a big part of analysis is taking into account this constant and shifting state of interdependence. The anatomy of a hypothetical company's interaction is illustrated in Figure 6-2.

FIGURE 6-2 Interacting Systems

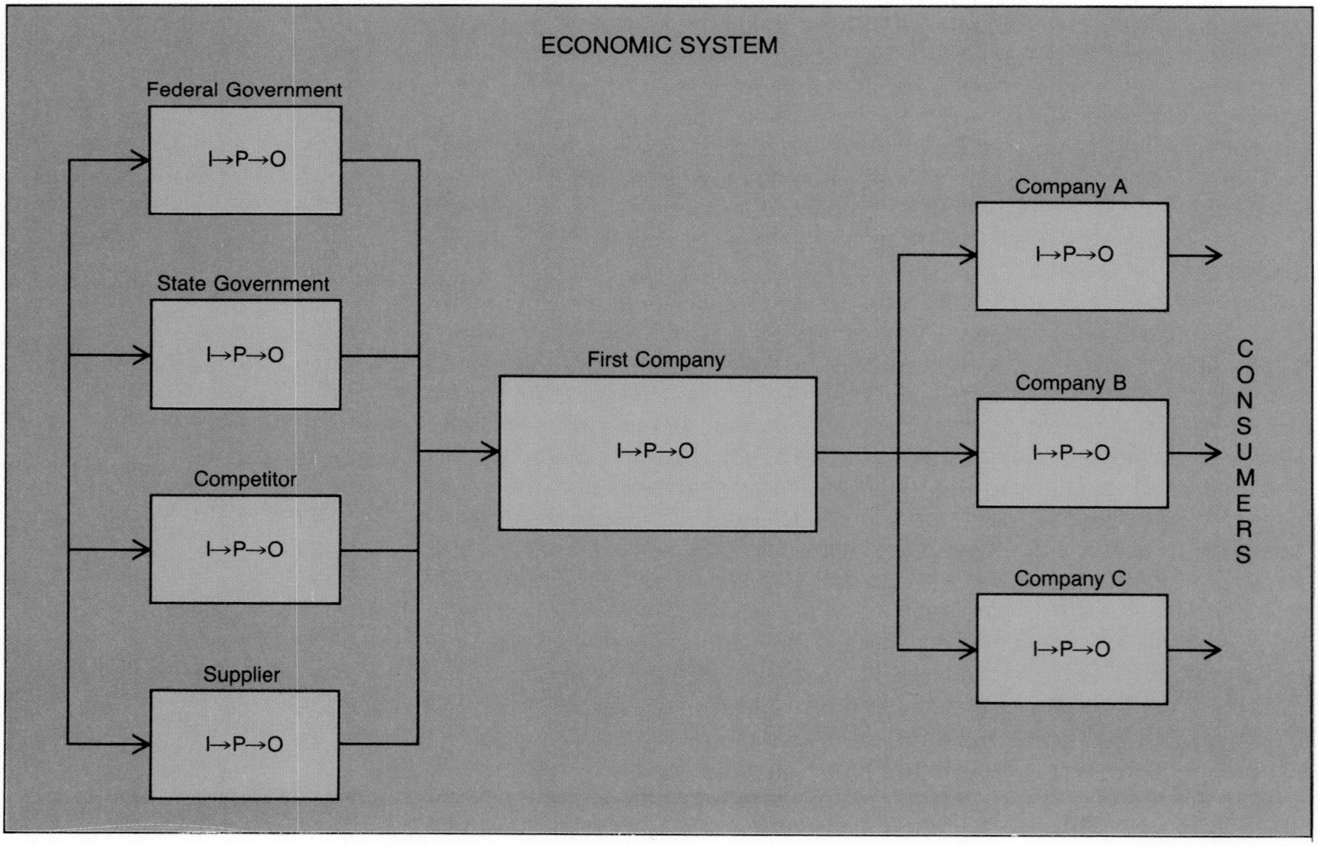

Inside a particular company, the interdependence of departments on an **information system** might go like this: The production department turns to the sales department for sales forecasts to estimate how much should be produced. The sales department projects its forecast after examining records of what has been sold in the past and by assessing customer feedback from the marketing and/or public relations departments. Both sales and production confer with the purchasing department to determine the availability of raw materials for making the company's products. Purchasing must consult with the finance department to discover how much money will be allocated for buying and transporting the raw material. Clearly, the need for information goes on and on; and just as clearly, today's information will have to be updated tomorrow to continue to be useful to decision makers. Figure 6-3 shows how departments within a company are information linked.

INFORMATION SYSTEM
A subsystem specializing in processing information.

What happens when company management decides more, better, or more timely information is needed to operate at peak efficiency? Perhaps

FIGURE 6-3 The Company as a System

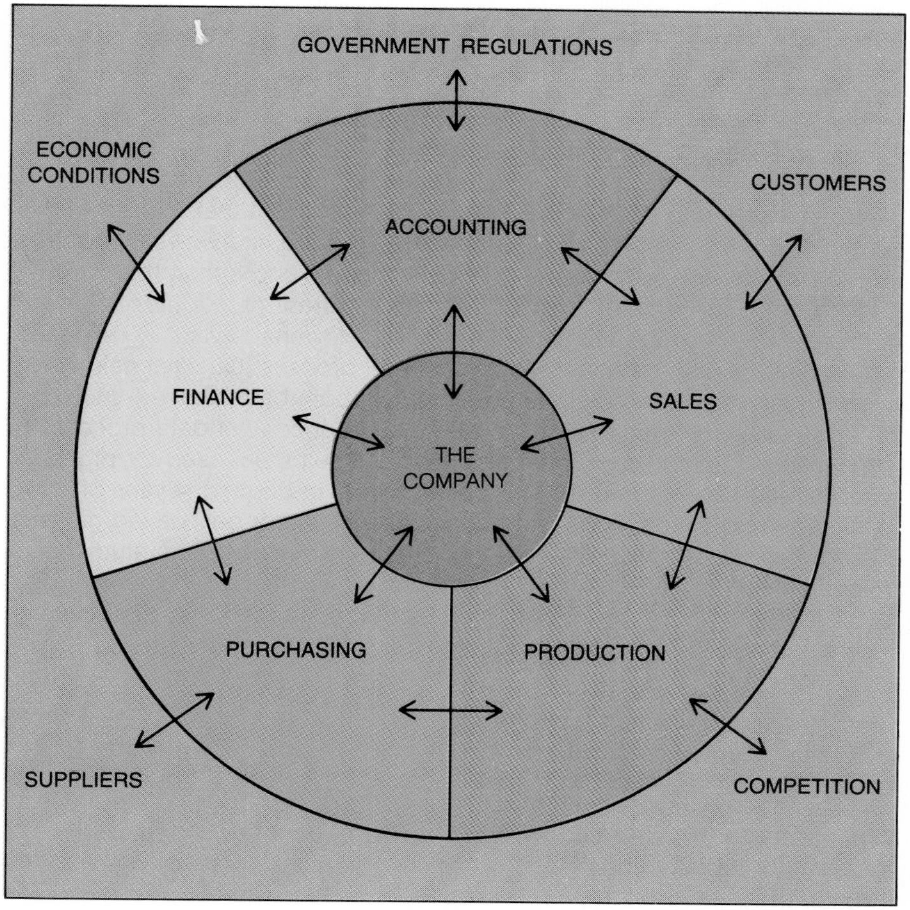

the information shortcomings could be remedied in a random fashion by replacing personnel, creating new departments with new duties, or buying computers in the hope that effective uses will appear. A more rational approach, and one more likely to succeed, is to have the information system examined by a system analyst who is trained to develop and suggest new methods for getting the job done.

THE PROCESS

Developing an information system is a three-step operation: system analysis, system design, and system implementation.

System Analysis

To understand how an information system is succeeding and failing, an analyst has to examine how the system works at every level, while keeping in mind what the users are asking (or should be asking) from it. Maybe new problems are arising so that demands are being made that the old information system was never intended to meet. Maybe the company has grown so much that new technology (a new or more effective computer setup, for example) is called for. Perhaps the company has branched into areas uncontemplated when the old system was set in place. The reason for the analysis will determine how wide, detailed, and thorough such analysis should be.

An initial examination of the system requires data gathering from sources inside and outside the member of the system that requested the study. The usual sources of internal information are interviews, flowcharts of the system as it now operates, questionnaires, and formal reports. Interviews give the system analyst data about current procedures and what the users think the system should be doing. Flowcharts visually relate the current information-gathering and transferral process. Questionnaires, if properly prepared and distributed, can yield both broad-based and detailed data about such pertinent matters as frequency of data processing, processing time and personnel, and kind of equipment used for processing. Formal reports are useful for documented, in-depth analyses of specific segments of the processing chain, as well as for delineating goals.

Some sources of external data that affect the system being studied might include books on system operations, case studies of other systems, business periodicals, product brochures and specifications, customers, and suppliers. Analysts may also examine similar companies to see how their information systems work.

Once the internal and external data have been collected, they have to be organized and examined as to their functions within the entire system. The focus in data analysis is on *why* certain operations and procedures are being followed. Several analytical aids have been developed and refined to make this step easier. They include system flowcharts, grid charts, input/output charts, and decision-logic tables. These aids are illustrated in Figures 6-4 through 6-7.

A **system flowchart** (Figure 6-4) traces the movement of data within an information system from their point of origin to their point of use. This kind of flowchart, although still useful for giving an overall view, is much less detailed than the program flowchart discussed in Chapter 3. Many operations on the system flowchart may be shown by one process symbol.

SYSTEM FLOWCHART
Traces data movement within an information system.

Analysts use the **grid chart** to indicate the relationship among different components in a system. In the example shown in Figure 6-5, the grid lists various documents that are commonly used by the company and the departments that routinely receive particular documents. Having this information in an easily understood tabular form allows the analyst to raise

GRID CHART
Indicates the relationship among different components in a system.

FIGURE 6-4 A System Flowchart

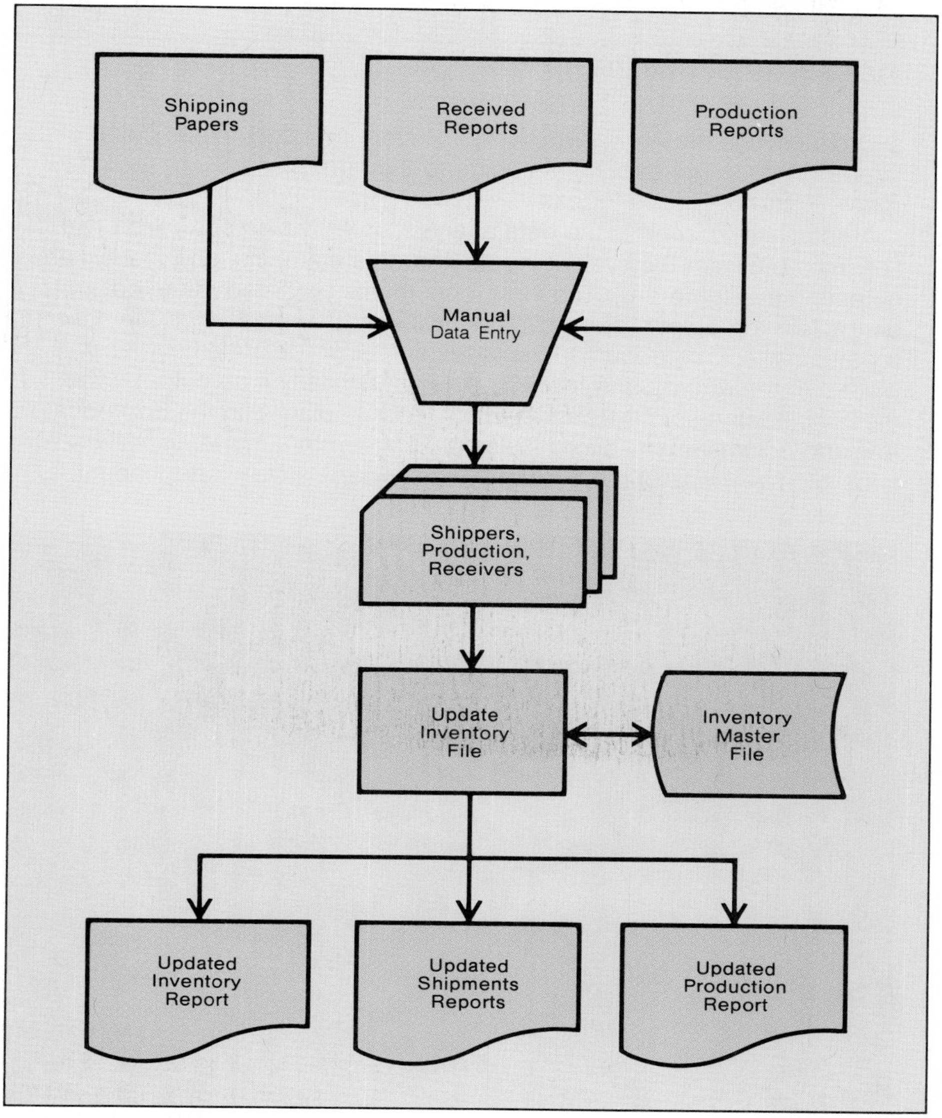

DOCUMENT \ DEPARTMENT	Order Writing	Shipping	Billing	Inventory	Marketing	Accounts Receivable
Sales Order	X				X	
Shipping Order	X	X	X	X		
Invoice			X		X	X
Credit Authorization					X	X
Monthly Report					X	X

FIGURE 6-5 A Grid Chart

such questions as: Are there enough or too many documents being circulated? Are the right documents going to the right places? Are the documents in the best form for easy use?

DATA ANALYSIS SHEET Highlights the relationships between system inputs, data elements, and system outputs.

A special grid chart is the **data analysis sheet**, which shows the relationships between the system inputs, the data elements, and the system outputs (see Figure 6-6). The input documents are listed in the columns on the left; the output reports are identified in the columns on the right. If a particular source document includes a specific data element, an X is placed in the appropriate row and column. Similarly if an output document includes a specific data element, an X is placed in the appropriate row and column intersection. These charts help the analyst to identify subsystems—parts of the system that may be relatively independent.

System analysts have gathered data and are determining whether a new information system is necessary.

FIGURE 6-6 A Data Analysis Sheet

____ of ____ sheets	DATA ANALYSIS SHEET	AREA: TITLE VII
INPUT	ELEMENTS OF DATA	OUTPUT

CLASS OF DATA	CODE
FIXED ELEMENTS	
IDENTIFYING	I
QUANTITATIVE	Q
VARIABLE ELEMENTS	
REPORTED	R
GENERATED	G
CONSTANTS	C

DOC. NAME INPUT/OUTPUT DATA	Form 1	Form 3A	Form 3B	Form 4	Referral			DATA CODE	DESCRIPTION	NR CHAR	A/N	DEC	Form 2	Form 5	Form 6	Form 7	Form 8	Form 9			
CODE																					
GEN FLOW REF																					
VOL																					
FREQ																					
	X								DATE/INITIAL PARTICIPATION												
	X		X	X	X				NAME				X	X							
	X			X					SOCIAL SECURITY NUMBER												
	X			X	X				ADDRESS				X	X							
	X								DATE OF BIRTH												
	X			X					RACE												
	X			X	X				SEX												
	X				X				PHONE NUMBER												
	X			X					MEANS OF TRANSPORTATION				X								
	X			X					DOCTOR												
	X			X					DOCTOR'S PHONE NUMBER												
	X								EMERGENCY CONTACT												
	X								EMERGENCY PHONE NUMBER												
	X								PHYSICAL HANDICAP												
									WEEKLY CALENDER TRANSPORTATION				X	X							

SELECTING APPLICANTS		RULES				
		1	2	3	4	5
CONDITIONS	Age < 18 Years?	Y	N	N	N	N
	High School Education?		N	N	Y	Y
	Experience > 1 Year?		N	Y	N	Y
ACTIONS	Reject	X	X			
	Interview			X	X	
	Hire					X

FIGURE 6-7 Decision Logic Table

DECISION-LOGIC TABLE
Lists conditions under which certain actions can be taken.

A **decision-logic table** lists conditions under which certain actions can be taken, as shown in Figure 6-7. This table shows the logic of hiring by listing minimum qualifications applicants must have and by cross-referencing possible personnel actions, ranging from rejecting to hiring the applicant.

Following the data collection and analysis, the next phase for the system analyst is submitting a report of findings to management. Such a report will cite the system objectives, describe the system now in use, suggest feasible alternatives to the present system, and estimate the resources and money necessary to change the present system or design a new one.

System Design

SYSTEM DESIGN
Developing solutions to problems uncovered in system analysis.

Should management accept the report's conclusions and authorize the analyst to continue, the next step is designing another system. **System design** is a necessarily time-consuming process. Using a hastily conceived and installed system could be more costly than retaining the old one.

At the design stage, the analyst reappraises the goals of the new system, creates a system model, develops alternatives, assesses any organizational restrictions, estimates what the cost/benefit balance is likely to be, and prepares a design report and recommendation.

The goal review phase focuses attention on who will use the system the most and on what they need from it. Applications may be suggested that the users haven't considered. The model will show the system's major components, as does the example of the accounts receivable system in Figure 6-8. Even the best planning will be for nothing if the analyst fails to take into account restrictions imposed by the organization. Among the inevitable restrictions are size of budget, available personnel, computer capabilities, and time.

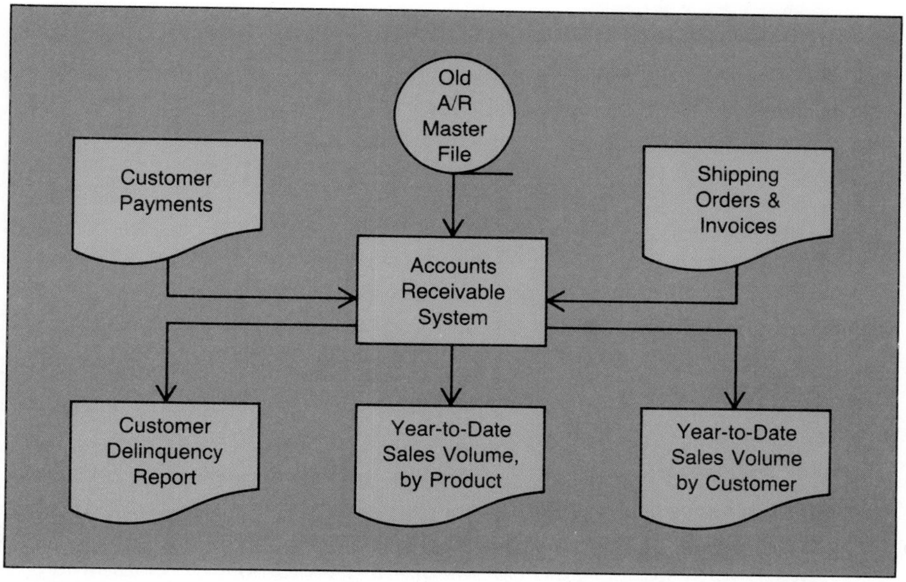

FIGURE 6-8 Model of an Accounts Receivable System

Because no one system is likely to be accepted by management as originally designed, the analyst should prepare, in rough form at least, several alternatives to the proposed system. These alternatives will be especially welcome options if the cost/benefit calculations of the preferred system show costs that are too high compared with the benefits. Finally, the analyst prepares a report for management summarizing the findings and suggestions. Management can then accept the recommendations, approve them with alterations, or reject them entirely. If one of the suggested systems is accepted, the analyst proceeds to the implementation stage.

In the system design stage, representatives from the prospective user groups meet to discuss goals and objectives of the system, develop a system model, and consider specific processing needs.

SYSTEM IMPLEMENTATION
Replacing the old system with the new system.

PARALLEL CONVERSION
Installing and operating the new system side by side with the old system.

PILOT CONVERSION
Converting a small part of the business to the new system.

PHASED CONVERSION
Gradually implementing the new system as the old system is retired.

CRASH CONVERSION
Putting the new system into use immediately and entirely.

REVIEW
Analyzing the new system's performance.

System Implementation

System implementation involves replacing the old with the new. It is difficult at best and traumatic at worst. Computers will have to be reprogrammed and programs will have to be debugged; personnel will have to be retrained in the new system procedures; and the system must be thoroughly pretested. After these preliminaries are over, the conversion from old to new takes place, generally in one of four ways: (1) **parallel conversion,** where the new system is installed and operated side by side with the old one until the new has proved itself; (2) **pilot conversion,** which involves converting only a small part of the business or firm to the new system to see how it works; (3) **phased conversion,** in which the new system is put in place gradually as the old system is retired gradually; and (4) **crash conversion,** in which the new system is put into use immediately and entirely and the old one removed.

The last stage of this process, as far as the system analyst is concerned, is the **review.** It is carried out only after the conversion is complete and the new system has had a chance to demonstrate its strengths and flaws. The system should be flexible and adaptable to handle the changes of data and demands common to any organization. The analyst will assess the system by asking such questions as: Does it perform the way it was planned and yield the benefits anticipated? Do the controls that have been established for input, processing, and output of data work effectively? Does the system suit its users? Do they use it effectively?

Eventually, the monitored and modified system will shape itself to the organization's needs. But as the organization changes in size, function, and needs, it will again outgrow the system, and the analysis/design/implementation process will have to start all over.

Training is an important part of the system implementation phase.

MANAGEMENT INFORMATION SYSTEMS

A well-designed and -implemented system providing timely and complete information will not ensure that an organization will have good management, but the lack of such information will almost certainly lead to bad management. As computers have become more vital in producing the kind of information management needs at all levels, a specialized area of business study has evolved: **management information systems (MIS).** By definition, an MIS is an information-gathering and -dispensing network that uses the computer to help managers make wiser decisions.

Different levels of management have different duties within an organization. The nature of these duties tells the system analyst more precisely what kind of information should be available to the users and in what form.

MANAGEMENT INFORMATION SYSTEM (MIS)
A computerized information-gathering and -dispensing network to aid in management decisions.

TOP-LEVEL MANAGEMENT
Persons who make strategic decisions.

MIDDLE-LEVEL MANAGEMENT
Persons responsible for tactical decisions.

LOWER-LEVEL MANAGEMENT
Persons controlling operational decisions.

Levels of Management

There are three fundamental levels of management: **top-level management** for strategic decisions, **middle-level management** for tactical decisions, and **lower-level management** for operational decisions (Figure 6-9).

Top-level Management This is the level where good judgment plays a big part, not only in time spent, but also in matters that will determine whether the organization fails or prospers.

What will be the business and governmental climates in which the organization must function? Should the organization diversify its financial interests or concentrate them? Should new services or products be offered? What should be the size of next year's budget? Should new

FIGURE 6-9 Levels of Decision Making

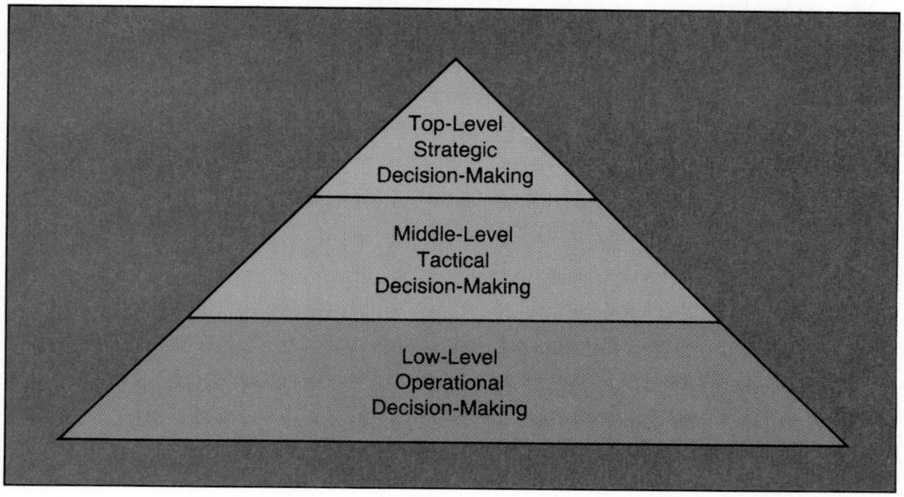

"Call it a hunch, but I get the feeling you've run into a problem."

markets be developed or should current ones be exploited more thoroughly? Should physical facilities be built, rented, or cut back? What assets are there—and how should they be used—to ensure an adequate flow of capital? These are all typical top management questions, and they are the most difficult ones for which to find answers, with or without computers.

At this level of management, the focus is on the future. The problems and possibilities do not stay the same day after day, and they can't be faced with formulas. Usually, top-level decisions involve one-of-a-kind conditions and require one-of-a-kind responses. Current data that have been transformed into general, understandable, and relevant information can allow management to make statistically supported decisions instead of off-the-cuff ones. Top-level management requires information that has been sifted of nonessential details and presented in a form that helps with long-range planning. Top-level management seldom needs to know what an individual employee is being paid, what his or her qualifications are, and what he or she does for the organization. What it needs to know is whether the organization is maintaining, for example, a satisfactory ratio between salaries and benefits paid out and goods or services produced. A change in the ratio could lead to substantial hirings, firings, layoffs, expansions, diversification, or cutbacks.

Few information systems are—or can be—complete enough to make decisions at this level fail-safe. But the more rapidly a system can gather the data and make sense of it (from the ultimate user's point of view), the more likely that decisions will be ones with which the organization can prosper.

Executive desk-top computers are an invaluable aid to top-level managers in analyzing information used for making long-range corporate decisions. This Compass computer is a convenience for executives because it is portable.

PROFILE

WILLIAM NORRIS

The history of the computer industry, like that of the early automobile industry, is made up of highly individualistic men who "seized the day" to launch their enterprises. One of the most successful is William Norris, who founded Control Data Corporation.

Norris, an ambitious and resourceful Nebraska farm boy, graduated with a degree in electrical engineering from the University of Nebraska during the Depression. He briefly served as a sales engineer for Westinghouse until he joined the navy in 1941. There he was assigned to the top-secret operation of cryptography.

After the war, at the government's suggestion, Norris and other technical specialists found private financing and formed Engineering Research Associates (ERA), which specialized in producing customized data processing equipment for the navy. ERA was purchased by Remington Rand (now Sperry) in 1952; however, rivalry between the two groups caused Norris to venture out on his own.

Many members of his original staff joined Norris in forming Control Data Corporation in 1957. Although the company's primary objective was to provide research and development for military projects, Norris also wished to produce a line of computer components and accessories.

Norris took advantage of a competitor's failure in producing a scientific computer by introducing the 6600, then the most powerful computer on the market, in August 1963. Other models of supercomputers, designed by staff engineer Seymour Cray, soon followed, and CDC gained a reputation in the mainframe business. Meanwhile Norris continued to build his empire by developing a strong line of peripherals; two service bureaus—scientific-oriented Cybernet and business-oriented Service Bureau Corporation; and TECHNOTEC, a technology information service. Norris's more recent efforts are directed toward the educational area. The company has made substantial investments in the development of the PLATO system—computer-aided educational hardware and software.

Middle-level Management At this level the decisions made at the top start to be carried out. Top management says what must be done, middle says how. Top management will, for example, set production quotas, while middle management will schedule resources and personnel to meet the quotas. When top management decides what the organization is to do and how much money will be allocated, middle management solicits, screens, hires, and establishes pay rates for the personnel.

Thus, the middle level demands an entirely different kind of information. Also, because decisions must be made more quickly than at the top, middle management may need its information faster and in greater detail. Again, computer-provided information cannot solve all management problems at this level, but since the demands for information are more precise, the computer can be counted on to furnish a greater amount of relevant facts than can be supplied the top level.

Lower-level Management On this level are first-line supervisors and foremen and -women. These managers require information aimed at getting specific jobs done. Such jobs might include keeping inventory rec-

A Boise Cascade foreman monitors production of the company's wood products via computer.

ords, assigning tasks to workers, preparing invoices, and determining material needed. Top decides what, middle decides how, and lower does. Essentially, lower-level management controls the organization's output. Results must be kept in line with plans.

Being concerned with immediate actions and results, lower-level management must have a steady flow of reliable and relevant information. The information used here (and then transmitted upward in a digested form) is basic to the entire MIS. If information is faulty or distorted at this basic level, decisions at all subsequent stages will be tainted and misdirected. For instance, if lower-level management, acting on deficient information, fails to correlate personnel with available material and production orders, then middle management won't be able to make the best use of factory resources and top management won't be able to set quotas.

Table 6-1 illustrates the differences among the three decision-making levels of management.

TABLE 6-1 Characteristic Differences in Levels of Decision Making

CHARACTERISTICS	LEVELS OF DECISION MAKING		
	Operational	Tactical	Strategic
Time Horizon	Daily	Weekly/Monthly	Yearly
Degree of Structure	High	Moderate	Low
Use of External Information	Low	Moderate	Very High
Use of Internal Information	Very High	High	Moderate/Low
Degree of Judgment	Low	Moderate	Very High
Information Online	Very High	High	Moderate
Level of Complexity	Low	Moderate	Very High
Information in Real Time	High	High	High

PROFILE

GEORGE TATE and HAL LASHLEE

The popularity of dBASEII, a data-base management system designed for microcomputers, can be attributed to George Tate and Hal Lashlee.

Tate, born in 1943, developed his technical education on the job. In 1973 he moved to California and worked as a repairman for Computer Mart, the second or third largest computer store in the country. At the same time, he bought an Altair microcomputer kit and joined the Southern California Computer Society where he met his future business partner, Hal Lashlee.

Tate realized the potential of the hobbyist market and was convinced that a competitive software dealership would be a profitable venture. So in January 1980 Tate and Lashlee formed Discount Software, a software mail-order house. By the summer of that same year, the company started receiving phone calls about software called Vulcan. Neither Tate nor Lashlee had heard of this product but subsequent research about the product led them to Wayne Ratliff.

Ratliff, a systems designer at Jet Propulsion Laboratory (a development laboratory for NASA), designed Vulcan in 1977, but he had had little marketing success with it—only 50 copies had been sold in 1978.

In the following months, the three men negotiated a deal and Tate and Lashlee initiated an advertising campaign. The software was renamed dBASEII, a term implying its capabilities as well as suggesting an improved version. A new company, Ashton-Tate, was established to sell the product. By the end of 1981, 50 copies of dBASEII were being sold daily. The success of dBASEII has made Tate and Lashlee prominent dealers in the software business.

Decision-oriented Reporting

Management information systems supply various kinds of reports, each of which has its own purpose and form. The four most common kinds are scheduled reports, exception reports, prediction reports, and demand reports.

SCHEDULED REPORT
Produced at a regular interval to monitor ongoing functions.

Scheduled reports are produced at regular and agreed-upon intervals and are useful for monitoring the ongoing functions of an organization. Scheduled reports can keep managers informed about production, individual use of work time, raw materials on hand, inventory, and so on. Although these reports are useful in themselves, their data are frequently used as the basis for other kinds of reports. An example of a scheduled report—two pages from a business payroll journal for one pay period—is shown in Figure 6-10.

EXCEPTION REPORT
Provides information on unexpected situations.

Exception reports are generated in response to any deviation from expected results. They ignore all normal events and focus management's attention on abnormal situations that require special handling. An exception report might be generated in response to an unexpectedly low production rate, in response to an excessive drop in the quality of a product, or if an employee has an abnormal amount of sick days.

PREDICTIVE REPORT
Answers hypothetical "what if" questions.

Predictive reports are designed to give management some insight into the future so that they may better plan for that future. By manipulating the variables that go into making the report, management can answer the question, "What if . . .?"

FIGURE 6-10 Scheduled Report

Autopay I Payroll Journal

COMPANY CODE	COMPANY NAME	PAY DATE	WEEK NO.	BATCH			
662	M&M PRODUCTIONS	030183	09	4863	BL	3	0036

ADP

PERIOD ENDING DATE	PAGE NO.	COMPANY CODE
022483	0006	662

EMPLOYEE INFORMATION / YTD ACCUMULATIONS / CURRENT PAYROLL INFORMATION

1

** EMPLOYEE RECONCILATION ** ACTIVE TERM LOA TOTAL

PREVIOUS CONTROL 19 2 21

ADD NEW HIRES & REHIRES
LESS TERM & LOA

PRESENT CONTROL 19 2 21

** RATE CONTROL TOTALS **

	SALARY	RATE-1	RATE-2	NO. EMP
PREVIOUS TOTALS	3,398.32	95.3100	16.0000	
NEW HIRES	.00	.0000	.0000	
NET CHANGES	.00	.0000	.0000	
PRESENT TOTALS	3,398.32	95.3100	16.0000	

2

** PAY DISTRIBUTION ** ACTIVE TERM LOA TOTAL

NO OF EMPLOYEES PAID 12 12
NO OF EMPLOYEES NOT PAID 7 2 9
NO OF PAYS IN EXCESS OF ONE
NO OF PAYS THIS PERIOD 12

** NUMBER OF PAYS BY RANGE OF GROSS EARNINGS **

0-099 2
1-199 2
2-299
3-399 2
4-499 2
5-599 1
6- 699 2
7- 799 1
8- 899
9- 999
10-1499
15-1999
OVER 1999

3

** FEDERAL TAXES **

FEDERAL INCOME TAX 509.89
EARNED INCOME CREDIT ADVANCES .00
FICA EMPLOYEE AMOUNT WITHHELD 299.73
FICA ER TXBL 4473.32 X 6.70 299.71
FEDERAL DEPOSIT LIABILITY 1109.33
FUTA TXBL 4473.32 X .8 PCT 35.79

** CITY TAXES **

TAX CODE 114B 67.08

** STATE TAXES **

OHIO INCOME TAX 58.87
OHIO SUI TXBL 4473.32 X 3.000 PCT 134.20

4

5

6

Occasionally, management at all levels will want information that neither addresses a deviation from the norm, as in exception reports, nor addresses a hypothetical situation, as with predictive reports. A **demand report** may be needed to confirm or contradict a management suspicion. As the name suggests, they are produced only on request. For example, is the cost of rent, insurance, and security for a leased warehouse off the company's premises more expensive in the long run than the construction of an on-premises storage building? Or a demand report might address advertising or marketing strategies. For example, a company may demand an immediate report on whether the recent newspaper and television advertisements were cost-effective; did the revenue they generated in new sales exceed their expense? The key word is "demand." A management information system cannot come close to anticipating all the demands that will be made of it. Therefore, the system has to be developed with the reach and flexibility necessary to make it capable of dealing with most one-of-a-kind management decisions.

DEMAND REPORT
Specific report needed for one-of-a-kind management decisions.

Management and MIS

Managers know they constantly need information. But they don't always know what kind of information, how much they need, how it should be presented, or how quickly it should be available. Some look upon decision making as an activity that requires a little information and much intuition. Others, finding that a little information is helpful, conclude that a wealth of information is better—and drown in the deluge.

What information is relevant to the task that must be done? This is the ever-present question for both the MIS user and designer.

DATA ORGANIZATION

To furnish concise, relevant information to the various levels of management, the system analyst must examine how the data are to be organized once they have been gathered. The organization of the data dictates how that data can be used.

There are two common ways to organize large amounts of data: files and data bases.

File Organization

One traditional method of organizing data is in computer files. Files can hold a great deal of information for a business. For example, a business may want to maintain such specific facts about its employees as address, social security number, wage per hour, number of dependents, and withholding tax. Each one of these items is a **field**. Therefore, an employee's address is a field.

A collection of fields that relate to a single unit is a **record**. All of the fields concerning an employee (the address, social security number, wage, and so on) constitute the employee record. A collection of all the related records is a **file**. In our example, that file would contain the records for all of the employees of the business (Figure 6-11).

FIELD
An item in a record.

RECORD
A collection of fields related to a single unit.

FILE
A collection of related records.

Traditionally, each function or department of a business has maintained separate files, resulting in much duplication of data and problems with data accuracy. When several files are being kept that contain a particular piece of information, it is difficult to ensure that a change made in one file will be reflected in the others. Recently, the development of more sophisticated software has made it possible for businesses to develop their information systems using a **data base.**

DATA BASE
Provides central data organization independent of specific applications.

Data-Base Systems

In the past an organization commonly had at least as many data files as it had departments. But with an MIS, the focus has shifted to the centralized storage of data in a way that will allow all authorized users to draw information from it. This arrangement is a data base. In this system data are independent; they are organized according to their own characteristics instead of associated with a specific application. This allows for many uses, yet avoids duplication of data. Efficiency is also promoted. If a particular item needs to be updated, the change has to be made only one time. With separate files, a time-consuming and error-producing multiplicity of changes may result. In a data base, data are structured in a manner that allows a wider variety of information needs to be satisfied, while reducing data redundancy and increasing data accuracy (Figure 6-12). Besides these virtues, the integration of all related data makes the system more flexible—information can be provided from one source that earlier would have had to be gathered from several separate data files.

PHYSICAL DATA DESIGN
Data-base design that focuses on how data are kept in and retrieved from storage devices.

LOGICAL DATA DESIGN
Focuses on relationships among the data.

Three kinds of designs are used in organizing data for a data base: physical, logical, and application. The **physical data design** looks at how the data are kept in storage devices and how they are retrieved from them. **Logical data design** concerns how the data are viewed by application programs or individual users. Logical data design is created by the system analyst and the data analyst, the latter of whom analyzes the rela-

FIGURE 6-11 File Organization

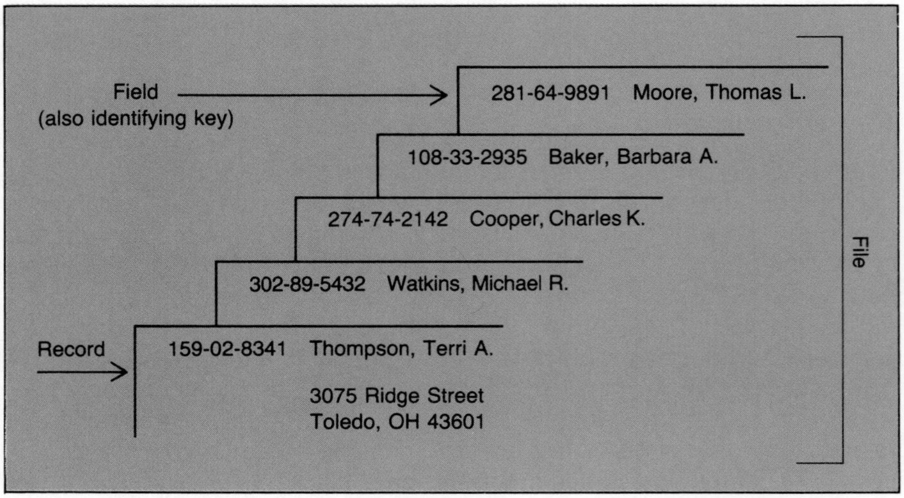

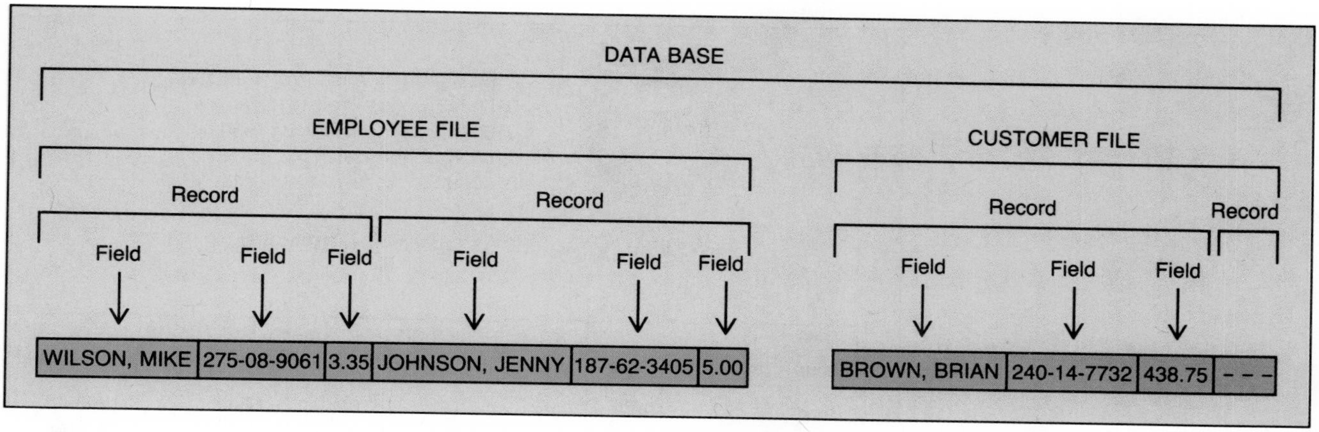

FIGURE 6-12 Organization of a Data Base

tionship of data to the data base. Logical designs should be made independently of physical storage considerations. Physical designs may be constructed by a data administration department, which can implement the logical design within the physical records. The **application data design** examines how the data will actually be used by application programs. In keeping with flexible design, an application design should consider not only current but also possible future applications.

APPLICATION DATA DESIGN
Looks at how the data will be used in application programs.

What seems a logical unit of data to one user may include data from more than one physical file. Conversely, one physical file may have parts of several logical units of data. One user's logical unit may include only a student's name and grade-point average, whereas another may include only the student's age and home address. In both cases, the data may be part of only a single physical file: the student file.

Figure 6-13 shows the physical, logical, and application views of data design using a file with inverted structure. This type of file is well suited for handling a number of inquiries quickly and efficiently. For instance, we might need a list of all the female assistant professors employed. The user would type in the request and the computer would check the attribute list (value) until it found a female. Next the computer would go through the attribute list and locate assistant professors. The record address for both of these values would be compared. If any of these addresses match, the computer would then go to each of the matching addresses in the master file and return the name.

Data-Base Management System

A **data-base management system (DBMS)** is a set of programs that makes the data-base contents easily accessible to its three chief users: the programmer, the operating system, and the information user. A ready-made DBMS eliminates the need for an organization to develop its own detailed data-handling capabilities. One of the major purposes of the DBMS is to bring about physical data independence. That is, it allows the physical layout of data fields to be altered without necessitating changes in application programs. The programmer, therefore, does not

DATA-BASE MANAGEMENT SYSTEM (DBMS)
The set of programs that makes the data base accessible to its users.

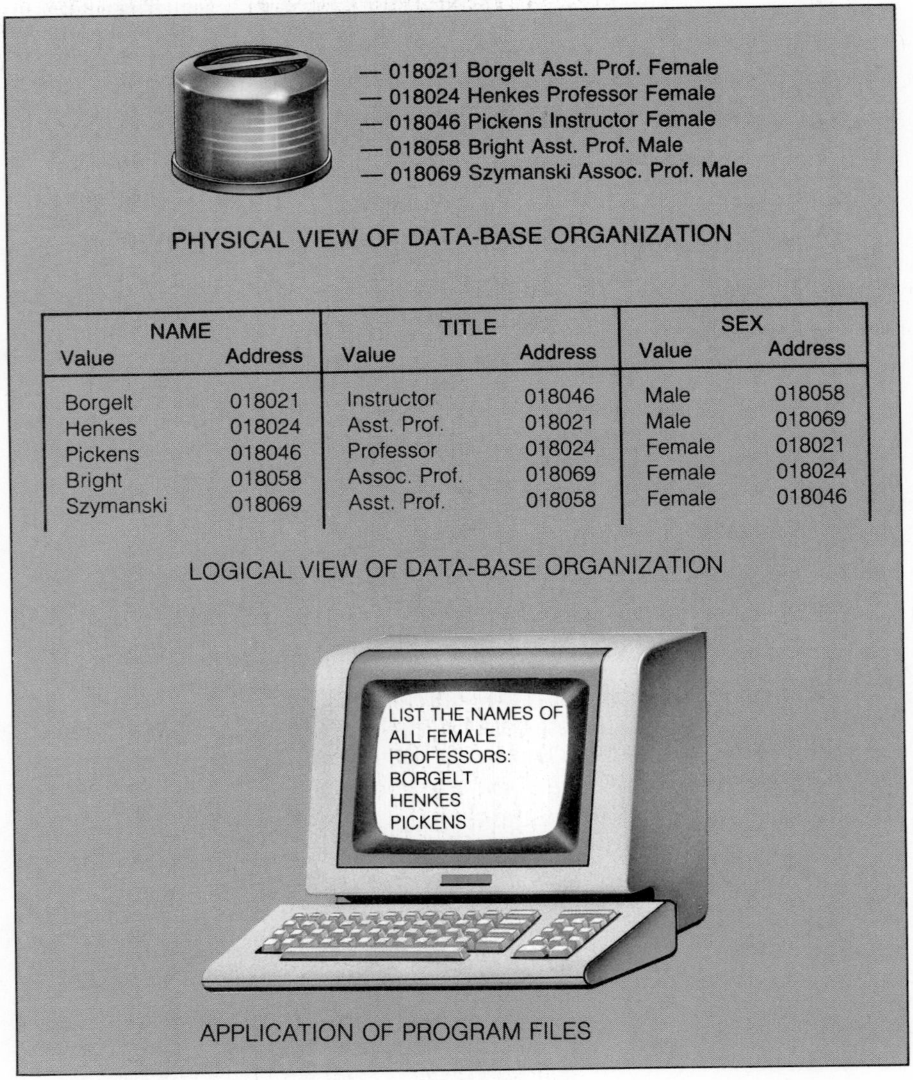

FIGURE 6-13 Physical, Logical, and Application Views of Data

need to pay attention to the physical nature of the file but simply refer to the specific data that is needed by the program.

DISTRIBUTED COMPUTING

CENTRALIZED APPROACH **Locates all data-processing resources in a single location or department.**

The systems we have described so far for organizing information within an organization use a **centralized approach;** that is, all data-processing resources are located in a single physical location or department (subsystem) within the organization. Generally, this subsystem is the MIS or the data-processing department. However, the centralized approach is not the only way to organize a management information system. An increasingly popular alternative is distributed computing.

In the **distributed computing approach**, the data-processing resources are located at the various departments that will be using them. In this way, data-processing hardware and personnel are distributed throughout the system. For example, the processing of payroll may be done through the personnel department rather than through the central data-processing department. The function of the central department is changed to supervising the overall performance of data processing throughout the other departments and coordinating the overall hardware resources of the organization. Figure 6-14 compares a centralized system with a distributed computing system.

DISTRIBUTED COMPUTING Locates data-processing resources at the various departments that will be using them.

FIGURE 6-14 Centralized versus Distributed Computing Approach

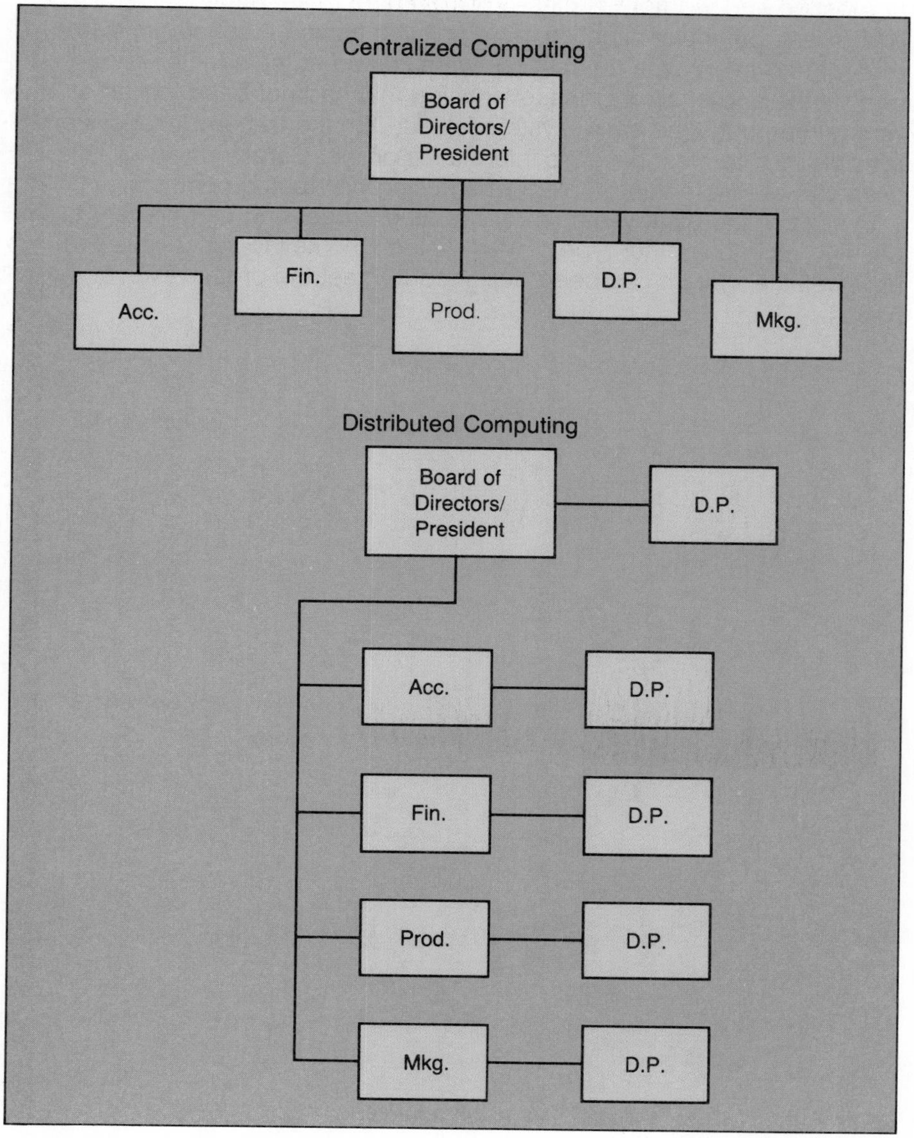

There are advantages to using distributed processing. It allows for diversity in management style and output and gives the users more responsibility and authority over their data processing. When used properly, distributed processing enables easy adaptations to be made within departments to solve individual needs. In addition, because distributed processing breaks up the data-processing resources into smaller units, they are easier to manage.

There are also disadvantages to using distributed processing. A great deal of central planning is required to ensure that the different departments are not duplicating each other's efforts and to avoid duplicating personnel, computer facilities, and data.

Another problem with distributed computing is that unnecessary information may be kept online. Many people consider being online a matter of prestige and will fight endlessly for the right to keep their material online. In one particular situation, an employee tucked a counter in every record, and every time the records were looked at the counter added one. At the end of six months, everything that had not been looked at was printed out. One entire system fell out. Yet the owner of that system insisted that he must have his information online. Careful planning is necessary to eliminate this problem when using distributed computing.

In spite of the disadvantages, distributed processing can be very successful. As in any other type of MIS system, the key to success lies in how well the system has been designed to meet the organization's needs.

ISSUE

TRANSBORDER DATA FLOW: WHO NEEDS A PASSPORT?

Information is managed through systems. There are systems of all sizes and shapes. More often than not, a large system is composed of several smaller systems, while that large system itself is a smaller system within an even larger, more encompassing system. Although this may be confusing at first, it becomes easier to comprehend if we view the world in which we live as an information system. In fact, an information system is exactly what it is.

Our global economy is a large system that is composed of smaller systems—countries—which are, in turn, composed of even smaller systems—territories, states, cities, and so on. Each of these systems, being in the information business, produces huge amounts of data. These data are stored in some form, then transported and integrated within the larger system. Of course, not all of the data are moved. Factors like national security and economic planning (import taxes, export restrictions, and the like) dictate to a large degree not only what data get out but also where these data go.

But do they? With the advent of satellite communications, advanced telecommunications, and networks, can anyone really regulate where information is going? Or even what information is going?

This is a problem that has gained international attention in recent years because of its potential for economic disaster. It is commonly referred to as transborder data flow, meaning data flow across national borders.

The major users of transborder data flow are large multinational corporations, which use satellites on a regular basis to beam information to their various offices and headquarters around the globe. In doing so, they avoid the expense of sending representatives around the world to deliver the information personally.

The receiving countries have little concern about the loss of travel revenue from those company representatives. What they are upset about is the loss of software tariffs. Tax revenues, or tariffs, are routinely collected when software is brought into the country. For a small spreadsheet program, this is not a serious problem. However, multinational corporations have been using their satellites to beam million-dollar database management systems in and out of countries, avoiding a substantial amount of tariffs. Currently companies are not able to exert control over the information flow either. When information was personally delivered, the representative at least had to carry a passport. Then there were visa applications and customs checks. With data flowing in and out of countries electronically, there is little hope of preventing it from reaching its destination until the appropriate import taxes or tariffs have been paid.

Some companies even use transborder data flow to transfer funds between countries to avoid paying income taxes. Sweden has enacted strict laws governing transborder data flow to eliminate that problem and Denmark has also addressed the problem through legislation.

These considerations are of monumental importance right now. We are beginning to realize that information is a method of control in our global economy. We are deluged by information, increasingly gathered and used for every decision from the mundane to the essential. Information is in such high demand because our economy, and that of most of the world, is increasingly geared toward service—information service, in particular. It has been estimated that close to half of our gross national product is information related. With information at such a premium, it may soon be that information will become a form of economic or even political control.

Information on prices transmitted transborder could be used to reroute oil ships midroute to the country paying the highest price. Multinational pharmaceutical companies could likewise use transborder data flow to ensure that their products reach the best-paying markets.

This, again, could affect the amount of control that nations have over multinational corporations with offices within their boundaries, that is, if those nations have *any* control over the multinational corporations.

Take, for example, the following hypothetical situation. Let's imagine that there is a multinational pharmaceutical corporation with a manufacturing plant located in Brazil that produces the serum for small pox vaccines. Almost simultaneously, small pox epidemics break out in Brazil and in Africa. The Brazilian market is able to pay $5 per bottle for the vaccine. The African

ISSUE

market will pay $10. Who will the company sell the vaccine to?

Would they have done the same thing before the advent of transborder data flow? Probably, but not to the same extent. The lag time involved in communications before satellite information would have prevented them from mobilizing any massive reallocation of the vaccine within the same time frame. Although they still would have moved some of the vaccine, merely due to proximity they probably would have sold more of it to Brazil first, at the lower price.

In addition, with transborder data flow, the decision of what to do with the vaccine would most likely have been made outside of Brazil by a surprisingly small number of corporate employees. For reasons such as these, many nations wish to see transborder data flow regulated.

However, regulation of information systems could produce even more difficulties than it could prevent. Historically, regulation of products has produced large monopolies, protected and entwined within even larger bureaucracies. These tend to stifle creativity and technological advances—a situation that would be especially intolerable in an increasingly important segment of our economy like information systems.

The multinational corporations, of course, agree. They ask, "Whose data is it anyway?" This is a question that the United States must face. The United States has been host to several proposals to deal with the matter, but as yet has been reluctant to legislate in the area, the only notable exception being electronic funds transfer. As usual, we tend to watch the market and let it take care of itself. Capitalism, in theory, prevents us from interfering too heavily.

But some experts say it may not be possible to maintain this neutral stand indefinitely. It may not even be advisable. If we are entering a new era that is controlled by information, we should certainly be more aware of where ours is going—with or without a passport.

SUMMARY POINTS

- Developing an information system is a three-step process: (1) system analysis, (2) system design, and (3) system implementation.
- System analysis is the study of how one system processes information and includes gathering internal and external information. Internal information is gathered through interviews, system flowcharts, questionnaires, and formal reports. External information can be obtained through books, case studies, periodicals, brochures, specifications, customers, and suppliers.
- Several analytical aids have been developed to simplify system analysis. They are system flowcharts, grid charts, and decision-logic tables.
- The system design step takes the results of the system analysis into account in designing a new system free of the inadequacies of the old one.
- The system implementation step puts the new system into effect. System implementation can be achieved by one of four methods: (1) parallel conversion, (2) pilot conversion, (3) phased conversion, or (4) crash conversion.
- A management information system (MIS) is a computerized information network to aid management in decision making.
- There are three basic levels of management: (1) top-level management, (2) middle-level management, and (3) lower-level management. Top-level management makes strategic decisions; middle-level management is responsible for tactical decisions; and lower-level management handles operational decisions. The MIS should recognize these levels and furnish appropriate information to each, corresponding to the type of decisions to be made.
- In many cases, information to be used in decision making is provided in the form of reports. Common types of reports are scheduled reports, exception reports, prediction reports, and demand reports.
- Appropriate data organization is essential in MIS. The two common methods of organizing data are files and data bases. Files are geared toward specific applications, while data bases offer data independence.
- A data-base management system (DBMS) is the set of programs used to make the contents of the data base accessible to the programmers, operating system, and information users.
- Management information systems may organize information using either the centralized approach or the distributed computing approach. The centralized approach groups all data-processing resources in a central location or department. The distributed computing approach scatters data-processing resources throughout the departments that will have use of them and uses a small central department to coordinate processing.

REVIEW QUESTIONS

1. Define "system" and give an example showing how a system is interdependent with both smaller and larger systems.
2. What are the responsibilities and functions of the system analyst?
3. What restrictions may be imposed on the system analyst who is designing a new system?
4. List and briefly explain the three steps in developing an information system.
5. What are the similarities and differences among system flowcharts, data analysis sheets, grid charts, and decision-logic tables?
6. What must be taken into consideration when designing a new information system?
7. What are four methods of system implementation? When would one be more desirable than another?
8. What is a management information system?
9. List the levels of management and their functions. Why must the system analyst take this information into consideration when designing a system?
10. What types of reports are commonly provided by a management information system? How do they differ?
11. Why is an MIS essential to management?
12. What are the major differences between files and a data base?
13. What differentiates physical and logical data design? What is a DBMS?
14. Compare the centralized approach and the distributed computing approach.

DISCUSSION QUESTIONS

1. System analysis is integral to maintaining an edge on the market in a constantly changing society. What economic and social changes have you observed in the last 10 years that would seem to mandate system analysis?
2. Each method of system implementation has some disadvantages. Yet crash conversion could be especially detrimental to a business. Why?
3. Incorrect or inadequately organized information at the lower management level causes a chain reaction that can endanger the validity of decisions made in top-level management. How?
4. Currently, data-base implementation is the trend in data processing. Yet there are situations where file systems are more feasible—both organizationally and economically. What are some situations where files would be preferable?
5. Transborder data flow is a serious international issue. The information passed through one satellite is a part of a company's MIS and is essential to their management decision making. Yet countries are concerned about controlling information flow. In your opinion, which side of the issue has the most merit? Why?

WEBSTER'S
DICTIONARY
UNABRIDGED
sailing illustrated

CHAPTER 7
COMPUTERS IN OUR DAILY LIVES

OUTLINE

ARTICLE

COMPUTERS CHIP INTO FAMILY LIFE

GEORGIA DULLEA
New York Times News Service

NEW YORK—From California's Silicon Valley comes word that a Universal Life minister is joining couples in electronic matrimony. Instead of "I do," which means nothing to a computer, the bride and bridegroom type "yes" into the machine. Instead of wedding pictures, they get printouts of the ceremony. Will they live happily, electronically, ever after?

One wonders. Computers can break as well as make marriages, according to mental-health professionals who are seeing an increase in divorce and family stress as home computers command more and more of a spouse's time and attention.

The so-called "computer widow" and, to a lesser extent, the "computer widower" are becoming familiar figures in psychotherapists' offices. Their complaint: their mates cling like barnacles to the machine, staring for hours at illuminated characters on the screen. They are withdrawn, unresponsive, uncommunicative. In extreme cases, the computerized spouse begins giving commands to family members as one does to the machine.

On the other hand, there is some evidence that friendships, even love, may bloom amid silicon chips. Shy students are using college computers to exchange mash notes. Home computer operators communicate via electronic bulletin boards devoted to such subjects as politics, music, or literature. Faces are unseen, voices unheard, real names unknown, while computers "crosstalk," as they say, long into the night. . . .

Working with the computer can be habit forming. The "lost mates" of this article discovered the attraction of a very logical, patient, knowledgeable companion. For those who enjoy using computers, they can be used for a variety of applications in the home environment.

INTRODUCTION

If you talk with people who have used or been affected by computers, you will observe two basic attitudes: They loved the computer or they hated it. Most people enjoy computing and can think of ways the computer would be useful at home. Once purchased, the computer's success depends largely upon how well the purchaser's expectations were met. What can we expect from a home computer?

This couple uses their Residence Energy Management terminal to keep track of how much electricity and natural gas they have used in their home.

DEDICATED SYSTEMS

A microcomputer can be dedicated to one particular job or several microcomputers together could be used to handle many of a home's physical functions. In Arizona a computer-controlled house has been built as a showcase of automated systems. Called Ahwatukee (a Crow Indian word meaning "house of dreams"), this house is described as the state of the art in technology, ecology, and sociology. Visitors come by the thousands each month to view the house in a half-hour tour for $2. (The money goes to charity.)

Five microcomputers are linked to run the five systems in the house. Heating, cooling, and the opening and shutting of doors and windows is the province of the environmental control system. The security system protects against intruders through the use of TV cameras, sensors, and a password-controlled front door. The sensors also watch for fire and will sound a warning if necessary. The electrical switching system uses the sensors to note people moving through the house and adjusts lights as appropriate. Cost-efficient use of electricity is assured with the energy management system, and an information storage and retrieval system is provided for personal or home business needs.

Ahwatukee, truly the house of dreams, is home to no one. But along the Hudson River are some homes where dreams have come true. These luxurious, high-tech condos are filled with computer gadgetry and priced at a not-so-modest $400,000 to $750,000 each. Computers in the Terrace, as these Fort Lee, New Jersey, pleasure domes are called, monitor smoke detectors for fire prevention, noise detectors for security, and even run a talking elevator, presumably for amusement. The elevator doesn't just talk, though; it also lectures. Activated by a tenant's key, the elevator recites current stock market quotations and weather data. It will even allow the user to tape a memo in the morning going down and then will play it back to him or her in the evening going up.

Houses are now routinely designed to rely on computer assistance for their maintenance. Linked to sensors, computers can precisely control temperatures at locations throughout the house and make the best use of energy. They can raise shades, activate fans and switches, and turn on security lights (which go from an energy-saving dimness to an alarming brightness if a sensor detects an intruder). They can also dial the police should a break-in occur and activate the video camera that monitors the area of break-in.

Of course, not all **dedicated computers** in the home operate on such a

DEDICATED COMPUTER
A computer that has a specific function determined by its hardware.

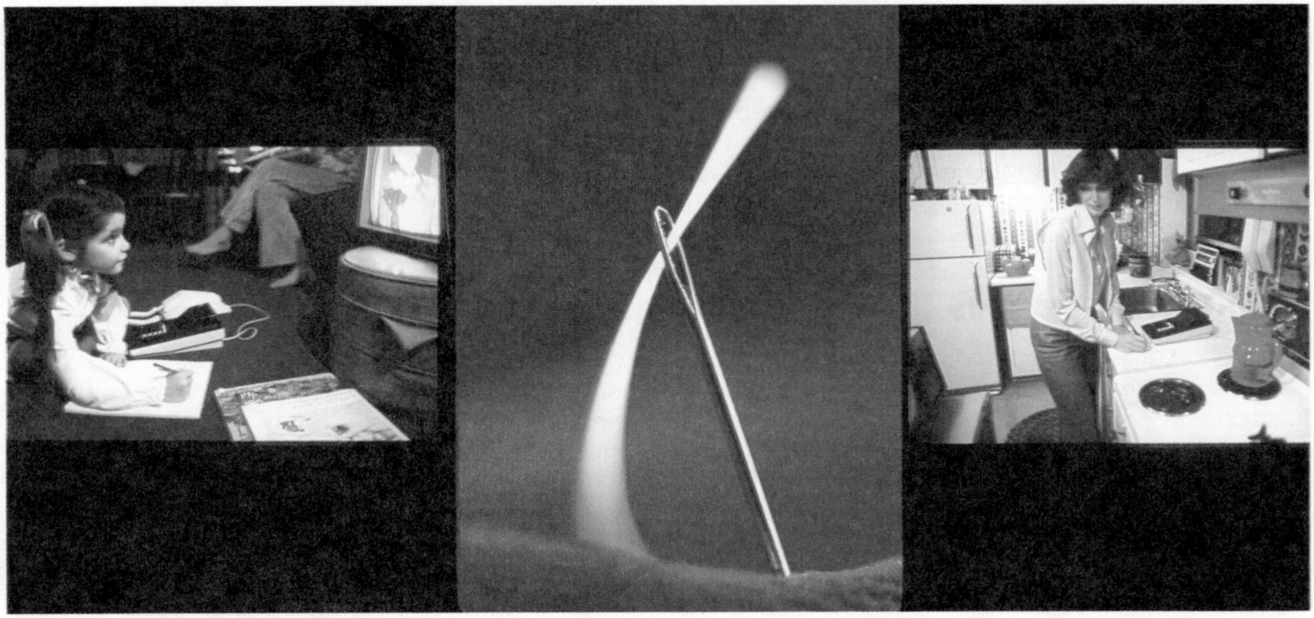

Fiber optics (center) is a technology that improves the quality of communication necessary for using computers in the home (left and right).

grand scale. Microprocessors are routinely built into appliances like sewing machines, microwave ovens, and stereos. One product recently introduced is a microelectronic screening system, which hooks into your telephone and squelches many unwanted calls. An incoming call is answered before the phone rings by a synthesized female voice chip who asks the caller for an access number. If the number is valid, the call is completed, the phone rings, and the caller's access number is registered on a digital read-out. Thus, the owner knows before answering who the caller is. If the caller has no valid access number—as would an obscene caller or someone with the wrong number at 3 A.M.—the phone never rings.

Probably the most common computer in homes today is the video game machine (Figure 7-1). Such systems as those offered by Atari, king of the video hill with 150 different games, and Intellivision are designed specifically to play games. Although technically such game systems are computers, few can support other applications. Their makers use much of the built-in, limited memory to program graphics and sound capabilities. Also, most game systems have joysticks, not keyboards, for input. Now game companies are developing and selling add-ons to turn your electronic game machine into a general-purpose computer.

GENERAL-PURPOSE COMPUTERS

Most home, or personal, computers were purchased to play games. However, their owners were smart enough to realize that for just a little extra

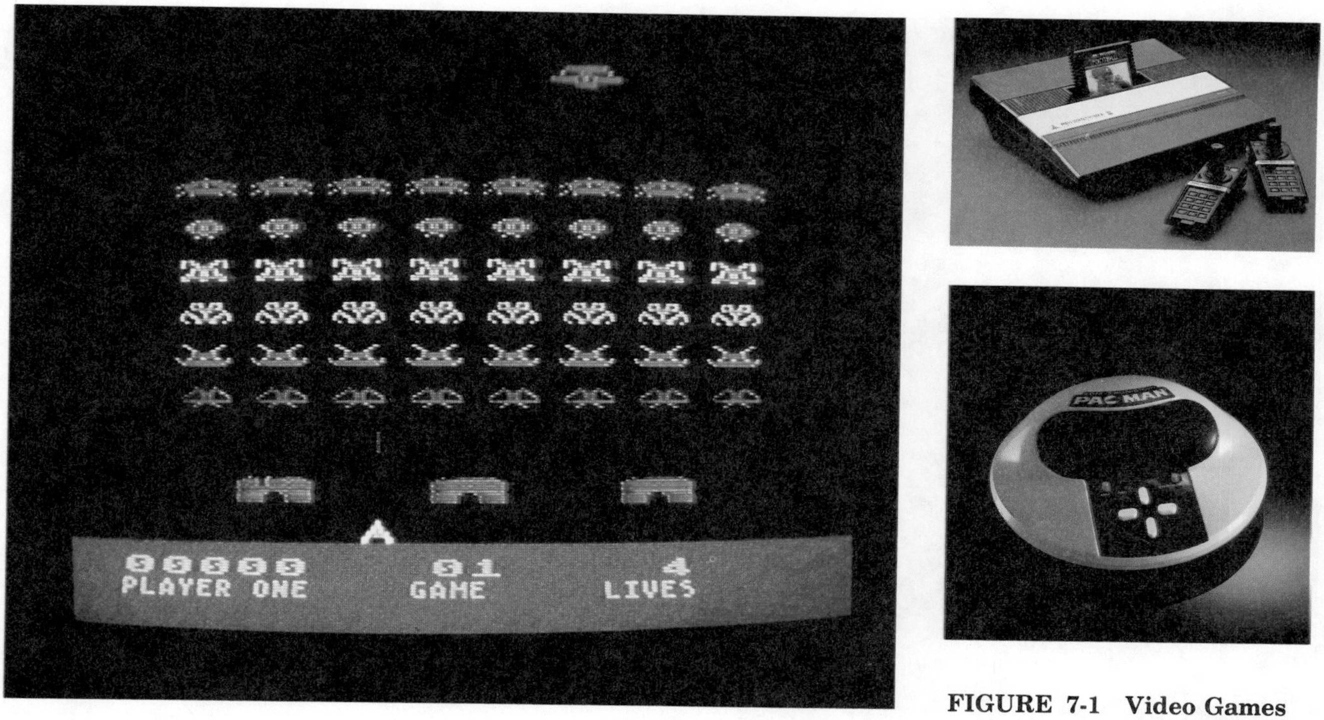

FIGURE 7-1 Video Games

money, they could have much more. Personal computer manufacturers have been caught up in a price war for the past few years. With sales, rebates, and trade-in allowances, even quite powerful computers like the Commodore 64 can be bought for much less than the current $599 list price; and the VIC-20, the Timex-Sinclair, and Texas Instruments' TI-99/4A, for instance, are priced below $100.

If a customer can spare a few thousand dollars, the variety of machines available becomes astounding. How to choose? Generally, the home computer should be selected to fit the tasks the owner wishes it to handle. (See Appendix B for a more detailed discussion of choosing a personal computer.) Let us take a look at some of the current software for, and uses of, general-purpose microcomputers at home.

Software and Support

Glorified Games Even Sally Ride, the first American woman astronaut, plays games on her Apple computer. Her favorite games are Zork, which she says she never comes close to winning, Air Traffic Control, and, not surprisingly, Flight Simulator. She is not alone. Home computer sales in 1982 alone were 2.5 million units, and games were the most common software sold for use on these machines.

One advantage of having so many computers in homes is the opportunity to play games with other people without the limitations of geography or time. If your computer system includes a modem and the proper soft-

PROFILE

JOHN V. ROACH

Tandy Corporation's Radio Shack division released the first official microcomputer—the TRS-80—available on the consumer market by September 1977. The quick action was due largely to John V. Roach, at that time vice president of Radio Shack Manufacturing, the management person most interested in and supportive of the microcomputer movement. His interest in computers had been almost accidental, however.

In June 1961 Roach graduated from Texas Christian University with a degree in physics and math. A job as a general engineer at the navy's Pacific Missile Range in Point Mugu, California, influenced him to return to school and pursue a degree in business. Roach received his MBA in January 1965 and became data-processing manager for a consumer finance company.

Originally hired by Charles Tandy for the position of general manager of Tandy Computer Services, Roach was soon promoted to vice president of Radio Shack Manufacturing. Roach persuaded Tandy to manufacture a microcomputer and market it through the Radio Shack division. Roach followed the project through—a task accomplished in less than a year.

The public response to the TRS-80 was more favorable than anticipated and the sales reflected this. As a result, Tandy's Radio Shack division has become a leader in the microcomputer market, having sales of $466.2 million by 1982. Roach's success has corresponded to that of the company's. He became president of Tandy in 1980, chief executive officer in 1981, and chairman in 1982—an impressive record accomplished by hard work and insight.

Roach realizes the importance of research and development and supports a strong program of developing future products. His current research is being directed toward robots and satellite TV reception.

ware, a game is just a phone call away. Several firms offer interactive, multiplayer games. The most well known is the PLATO system, which offers Dungeons and Dragons. Up to 60 players at one time from around the country can team up, each through his or her own computer. They explore the maze in groups, searching for treasure and adventure—all the while, of course, dodging dragons and monsters. Another successful game is Megawars, offered through CompuServe, where you can choose to be a good guy (a Colonist) or a bad guy (a Kyron) in the race to gain control over the universe. During play you can talk with your allies or enemies over subspace radios. Up to 10 people can play at once, and games may vary from less than an hour to many hours. If you dial up the game, and no one else is playing, the computer will take you on as its adversary. Playing such games, however, is not cheap. Usually, you must pay the network service a fee (CompuServe's lowest charge is $5 an hour) and maybe long-distance phone charges in addition.

Educational games are gaining in popularity, particularly with the younger set and with parents. The whole realm of educational software has progressed with games that are fun, visually attractive, thought provoking, and nonviolent. For instance, Facemaker, a game by Spinnaker, allows children to build a face and then make the face move (wink, smile, cry, frown, even stick out its tongue) or to play a memory game with it, complete with sound effects. While playing, children become familiar with the computer keyboard, **menus,** (the lists of choices) and simple programming.

MENU
A list of choices the user can select on a computer keyboard.

Finances For adults the traditional function of the home computer is to control the budget and checkbook. Since most people do not program their own games, the financial area is the first where this major decision must be faced: Where will you, as the owner, acquire the software? There are four choices: (1) you learn to program; (2) you hire a programmer; (3) you buy the software; or (4) you find a source of free software. Many people choose to learn programming because keeping financial records seems a simple task with which to start. Keep in mind, however, that if you can't balance your checkbook without a computer, programming the computer to do it will be neither fast nor easy.

Experiments in banking and shopping at home by computer have already been pronounced successful (Figure 7-2). The know-how exists to make us all homebodies. If movement in this direction seems slower than predicted, it is mainly because the widespread application of computers is still too expensive. In addition, some consumer resistance needs to be overcome. After all, when you shop at home, you can't actually touch the product on which you are about to spend your money and you may not be able to determine its quality or appropriateness. Also, when you bank

FIGURE 7-2 Home Information System

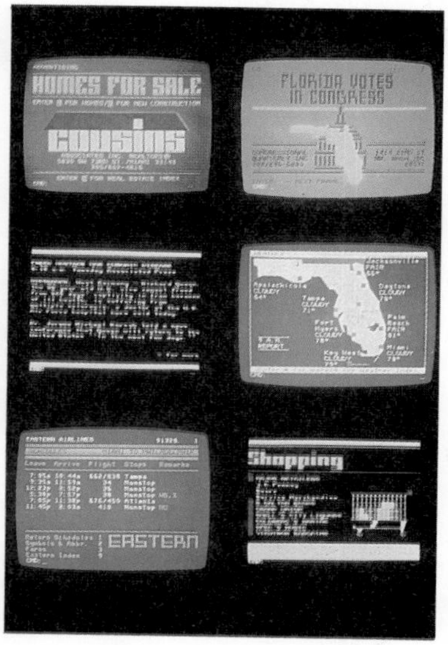

at home by computer, you may feel that the transaction is too impersonal or may fear that your finances may be revealed to unauthorized eyes.

Once this initial resistance is overcome, though, the advantages of home-based shopping and home-based banking become clear. When shopping by computer, the customer avoids the cost of driving to the stores, the irritation of traffic, and the exposure to ignorant or indifferent sales personnel. Also minimized are the dangers of impulse buying and the prospect of being mugged. Shoppers can call up catalogs from different stores on their video terminals and select the items for purchase. By inserting a keyed charge card into the terminal and pressing a button, the order is placed for home delivery or pickup.

With in-home, 24-hour banking, customers can instantly and as often as desired get the same kind of details about their accounts that is now available only from the mailed monthly statements. The bank-linked computer will allow the user to pay bills automatically by instructing the bank's computers to transfer money out of the designated account and send it to designated creditors.

Unfortunately, there is a major concern in the area of computerized financial services. The same arrangement that allows people to reach out of their homes by computer also enables privacy invaders to gain electronic entry. Currently, the threat is not as real for homes as it is for businesses. However, the danger may increase as more people buy computers for transacting financial affairs. Robert Ellis Smith, publisher of the monthly newsletter *Privacy Journal,* contends that "all elements for an Orwellian society are in place." Stopping the leaks in personal privacy will call for both new legal and technological safeguards.

Personal Record Keeping Software is available, too, for keeping all those lists and files that help run an orderly home. Addresses and phone numbers, insured assets, charge card numbers, recipes, Christmas card and birthday records, investment information—the types of information that can be stored for convenient retrieval are nearly unlimited.

This may all sound pretty dull. But with the help of a program, for example, that correlates nutritional and caloric data with recipes, planning dinner may be more efficient and easier (Figure 7-3). You could push a few buttons and ask your computer to list all the stored recipes that could be prepared in one hour using the leftover roast, potatoes, and the broccoli that needs to be used tonight. Or you could have it list what you should eat for supper to satisfy the nutritional and caloric requirements of your diet, taking into account what you have already eaten that day. Although this may sound like a line from a sales brochure, the fact is that the utility of a home computer is only hindered by the user's imagination.

Hobbies The fun of hobbies can be greatly increased by computer involvement. We saw in Chapter 1 several sports-related examples of computer software. New programs for special interests are being written and developed rapidly. Most of this software comes in a range of prices, depending upon how deeply you wish to pursue the interest. For example, a program to help coin collectors record data and produce investment and

FIGURE 7-3 Electronic Recipe File

tax reports dealing with the collection costs about $95. If the collector wants quarterly updates, he or she may have to pay an additional $25 for each update.

Music, a medium that most of us appreciate in one form or another, is the object of some intriguing new software. Electric Duet, for use on the Apple II, offers a complete system for creating, editing, storing, and playing musical compositions for less than $30. When in the "piano mode," you can sound notes by pressing keys on your computer keyboard; the top keys are higher notes and the bottom keys are lower notes. The software is built for multivoice compositions, so two voices can sound at the same time.

A second musical software product should appeal to serious hi-fi listeners. It is called Audio Spectrum Analyzer, made by Radio Shack and

PROFILE

JACK TRAMIEL

Commodore Business Machines has been a leading company in the personal computer market since 1977 under its founder and president, Jack Tramiel. A resourceful and feisty character, Tramiel has maintained company growth over some rough times.

Born in Poland, Tramiel survived an experience in a German concentration camp during World War II. At the first opportunity after the war, he emigrated to the United States. For a short while he drove a cab but soon he found employment with a typewriter repair business in Brooklyn. Tramiel expanded the business assembling and selling adding machines first in Canada and later in the United States. Tramiel has been quoted as the first to predict that calculators would one day be sold for $10 in drugstores.

By the mid-1970s calculators were the main product for Commodore. As new competition entered the market, Commodore was left with an oversupply of calculators. Tramiel sought ways to compensate. He bought two companies, one of which was MOS Technology, a semiconductor manufacturer in the process of developing the 6502 microprocessor. His insight proved to be most rewarding, for the 6502 is the microprocessor used in several major microcomputers today including Apple, Atari, and of course, his own products.

Introduced in January 1977 at the Consumer Electronics Show, the Commodore PET is the largest selling personal computer in Europe and one of the big five in the United States. Tramiel's insistence on offering more affordable models to home users also has resulted in the production of such strong-selling Commodore models as the VIC-20 and the Commodore 64. In addition to the standard research and development, Tramiel is designing a variety of software specifically for the C-64.

priced less than $20. This software provides a real-time analyzer (RTA) for visual display of the frequency composition of the music being played. RTAs previously available to consumers cost around $250 as a separate component.

Educational Pursuits If a person had the time, a computer could help him or her learn a wide variety of things—math, foreign languages, rapid reading, air navigation, or geography, to name a few. Sometimes the learning is in the form of a game, other times it is tutorial—the computer instructs, questions, and corrects your response (Figure 7-4). The nice thing about **computer-assisted instruction (CAI)** at home is that you can initiate the lesson whenever you wish—no appointments with teachers; no getting showered, shaved, and appropriately dressed; even a lesson very late at night is okay.

COMPUTER-ASSISTED INSTRUCTION (CAI)
Direct interaction between a computer, acting as instructor, and a student.

Religion can now be studied at home with a piece of software called the Word Processor. Not to be confused with word-processing equipment or software, this package has the entire King James version of the Bible and a study program on eight double-sided floppy disks. Bible students can search the text for specific words, suffixes, or prefixes. It can be read on the screen as a regular, paginated Bible or a personalized reference index can be made. The Word Processor is superior to most concordances (large alphabetical listings of major words, phrases, and refer-

FIGURE 7-4 Educational Games

ences) in the extent of its listing of key words, topics, or phrases in any part of the Bible, as well as in the ease of the information search.

Probably the major topic of educational interest to home computer buffs today is the computer itself. Just learning to run it successfully is an educational experience. Bookstores have responded to the wave of interest by adding to their stocks of "how-to-compute" manuals. New magazines are aimed at the personal computer market with advice from those who have learned the hard way.

Some of these magazines are even made to be used on the computer. *CLOAD,* for example, is a popular magazine for TRS-80 users. It arrives monthly, but to browse its contents you have to turn on your computer. *CLOAD* is on disk, not paper. Each *CLOAD* issue usually has an animated cover and contains six to eight programs of general, nonbusiness interest. The great appeal of the disk-based magazine is that to try a program, you don't have to type lines and lines of program code into your machine; a few keystrokes are all that is necessary.

A second disk magazine, called *Diskazine,* is for Apple users and takes a slightly different approach. *Diskazine* is more like a traditional magazine—it has a cover, a table of contents, an editor's page, feature articles, regular departments, and letters to the editor. Subscribers can send in their own articles and, if accepted, may receive up to $100 for one.

Both of these magazines are also available in cassette form, and both are rather expensive when compared with traditional paper magazines. They are, however, more fun.

To dispel the perplexity that surrounds learning to use home computers, computer clubs have sprung up in most large cities. These clubs can be useful to both beginners and experts; they offer a mixture of friendly companionship, useful information, and sympathetic support. Although many of the clubs specialize in a particular brand of computer, most meetings follow the same general pattern: a feature program about a topic of general interest with speakers, demonstrations, or panel discussions; a question-and-answer period; and a time for the club to meet in special-interest groups. Dues are usually low, and the meetings are especially helpful to beginning computer users or to those who want to make professional contacts aimed at a career in the computer industry.

Networks

One of the joys of computer ownership is being able to keep up with the changing world beyond your doorstep without leaving home. Research data that were once available only at the local public or university library can now be accessed in the home. Subscription to home information services can give the user video versions of major newspapers, stock market reports, restaurant listings, recipes, and movie reviews. Control Data

"The computer can talk to terminals all over the country. Bentley is convinced it's talking about him."

Corporation, through its PLATO learning center, is offering some of its educational courses to home users. By subscribing to an **online service**, customers can access these types of data bases and more.

Before going further, terminology must be clarified. The information that people would like to access is compiled and stored in huge hard-copy data bases by the **data-base producers.** Other companies, called online services, buy the rights to this information and put them in electronic storage. They then sell the opportunity of accessing the information to customers. Similar to the online service is a videotex firm (that provides services on the larger, more visually complete, home TV-like screen instead of a small computer monitor.) These online services are provided by a **telecommunications network.** For example, *Better Homes and Gardens* magazine is produced by Meredith Corporation. CompuServe, an online service, buys from Meredith the rights to electronically send *BHG* to subscribers of CompuServe. To get *BHG* on your home terminal, CompuServe uses the telecommunications network of Tymnet in some areas and CompuServe's own network in others.

The popularity of online services is evidenced by the growth in their numbers. In the fall of 1979, only 59 services were listed in the *Directory of Online Databases*. By the fall of 1982, the listings had jumped to 213. Two of the current major data bases that provide in-home information are The Source in McLean, Virginia, and CompuServe in Columbus, Ohio.

In most cases, these services can be accessed by the home user with a local phone call, since the three major telecommunications networks—Telenet, Tymnet, and Uninet—have spun their webs through all of the major American cities. One of the major functions of the network is error checking. While phone line static may cause little problem with an ordinary phone call, it is a major problem with digital transmission. Through technology, the files you request are checked for errors at regular points along the way from the online service to your home.

Since information often is equated with power, the value of the online service cannot be denied. One of CompuServe's more exciting recent additions is an online encyclopedia. The entire 21-volume (28,000 articles, 9 million words) Grolier's *Academic American Encyclopedia* is now available to subscribers. A topic can be researched by requesting a list of articles with the topical key word in the heading. The cost is CompuServe's normal charge ($22.50 an hour weekdays between 5 A.M. and 6 P.M., and $5 an hour at other times) for connecting plus a $5-an-hour surcharge. While expensive, the cost is considerably less than an encyclopedia set.

The most popular items supplied by CompuServe and other online services are **electronic bulletin boards** on which you can exchange or post messages. The reason for this popularity may be that although people like to communicate, they are most comfortable doing so from behind a terminal where they can wear a mask. In fact, electronic bulletin boards are so popular that they are frequently set up by independent personal computer operators on a smaller scale and at no charge. Sometimes these local systems have a specific interest or will feature electronic articles.

ONLINE SERVICE
A company that sells computerized access over networks to information in data bases and other services.

DATA-BASE PRODUCER
A company that assembles information into data bases to sell to others.

TELECOMMUNICATIONS NETWORK
A means by which one or more mainframes is linked to other computers for communication.

Microcomputers are enabling more people to work from their home. Here a real estate agent uses a computerized online multiple listing system and computer-generated photo listing books to provide more efficient and accurate service to prospective buyers.

ELECTRONIC BULLETIN BOARD
An electronic clearinghouse for messages that travel via networks.

CONFERENCE TREE **A type of bulletin board structured around topics.**

An offshoot of the private electronic bulletin board is a new form of amateur telecomputing called **conference trees.** One software package is by Communitree and was written to appeal especially to people with home computers and an interest in community activism. A conference tree starts out with a trunk, the list of main subjects, and offers the tree climber a choice of branches. Each branch will give someone a chance to give his or her ideas about the initial subject or respond to the contents of a previous branch. As Steven Levy, writing for *Popular Computing,* describes it:

> By following branches, you could trace the give-and-take of a heated discussion, full of yes-buts, hold-on-heres, well-puts, and you're-full-of-its. Ultimately, the branch ends with the anticlimactic "No Submessages," at which point the user may provide his or her own capper or return to the trunk or a previous branch. (May 1983, p. 72)

Trees cover a wide range of topics, and their "caretakers" occasionally must prune the outdated notices or obscene comments. Approximately 200 trees are in operation today; many more are expected to crop up as home computers gain ground.

New Developments

As computers have become more common in American homes, new developments have made them more versatile, easier to use, and easier to fix. Some of these developments are the "mouse," home robots, and hardware diagnostic tools.

The mouse is a desktop input innovation. By remembering where the mouse was and noting how it has moved positions on a flat surface, the computer can tell the cursor on the screen to move in a corresponding manner. As we noted in Chapter 5, using the mouse simplifies input and makes computers easier to use. For this reason mice are being used in many new computers, such as Apple's Lisa.

Robots too are showing up in homes. Mostly built by hobbyists, the robots can perform small tasks, such as welcoming guests, acting as a sentinel, or fetching a small object. Heath Company now has a personal robot kit for $1,500 that allows you to assemble your own Hero I. Hero can be programmed by cassette or ordered about with a joystick linked to the robot by a cable. Although robots have a long way to go before they are household fixtures, they probably will be useful in the home as well as in the factory.

Hardware diagnostic tools help you to determine what you can do when your computer—as invariably happens sooner or later—gets "sick." Most new operators panic first (thinking they broke the machine) and seek help second. When this happens, finding out where the problem lies is the first order of business. Hardware diagnostic tools are programs that help diagnose the problem. One of these, Diagnostics II, can determine if the "sickness" abides in the memory, microprocessor, disk drive, terminal, or printer. Finding an appropriate cure is then easier.

Microcomputers even provide consumers with graphic capabilities.

COMPUTER CONTACTS

Whether your home is computer equipped or not, you are very likely to be aware of the machine's presence in our society. The telephone directory assistance for which you ask probably is given to you through a computer-activated voice synthesizer; and when you ask for time and charges on a long-distance call, this same kind of system does the calculations and announces them as soon as the call ends.

Computers may be phoning you to sell you something, conduct a survey, or make a political pitch. Some of these automated phoning systems can make 3,000 calls an hour and even remember to call back if a particular number is busy on the first try. They automatically tally the results of the calls and give them to the user in hard copy form if requested. Former president Jimmy Carter used computerized phoning in his 1980 bid for the presidency. Department stores use the system to notify catalog customers when their orders are ready. Bill collection agencies use them to remind delinquent payers. Schools use them to check on absentee students.

Just as television and automobiles changed the daily lives of people the world over, so will computers. We have been through the start-up of the computer industry. We now have the Model T. It's a bright beginning for what will be the largest industry in the United States as future computer applications are nearly limitless.

ISSUE

COMPUTER NETWORKING: SHOULD YOUR FINGERS DO THE WALKING?

One of the most exciting prospects of owning a personal computer is the wide reach you can gain when you also have a modem connected to your telephone. Read the ads in some computer-related magazines. Services offered are abundant: electronic magazines, national news wires, worldwide weather, current movie reviews, electronic banking, shop-at-home services, bulletin boards, CB simulators, electronic mail, file retention, games, puzzles, financial information—the list goes on and on.

Although such options sound great, some problems must be solved before the systems work as planned. Prospective subscribers would do well to be careful. They may not get what they expected from the service, and the cost may be a problem.

Let us start with the cost. Shopping at home may sound simpler and cheaper than a trip to the store, but not after paying for the electronic catalogs. First, you need the hardware. A videotex terminal used in a U.S. test market in 1984 was offered at a special price of $600; or you could purchase a decoder to add on to your own television set for $250–$450. Your third choice is to purchase a home computer and a modem to use with your telephone, which would likely cost even more.

After getting your hardware ready to go, you need to subscribe to the service you have chosen. Sometimes this is a one-time fee, but usually it is a regular monthly charge. The range is wide, but for the more economical online or videotex services, the subscription fee may be from $15 to $40 a month.

Finally, you may have to pay for connect time or for pages (screenfuls of material) viewed. These charges vary too, depending upon time of day and the service to which you subscribe. In some locales you might even have a long-distance phone bill if you are using your phone lines for transmission. When all these factors are taken together, the total cost of "letting your fingers do the walking" may be more than you care to pay.

If it is not, you must then consider your particular information need. Is the information you want available? If it is airline schedules, stock market prices, baseball scores, or this week's horoscope, you will probably find it. But, if you are researching a lead for a term paper or looking into the background of a political office seeker, you may be in for a surprise. Finding some information is complicated by the unavailability of data before a certain date. For example, June 1980 is the earliest issue of the online *New York Times* on its own information service. A second complication is the inadequate search function offered by some services. Frequently, what is made available in the information bank is the current week's news or a summary of the issue surrounding your topic.

For example, the Knowledge Index, a network service available to home users, has article summaries available for review on the screen. To get a copy of the complete text of the article, you can then go to your library or you can order it from Knowledge Index. A set fee plus a cost per page are charged for each article ordered.

However, if you are fortunate enough to find a full-length article, you may have no way of knowing, before reading it, how long it is. You might find it difficult to concentrate on a fairly long article knowing that the cost is adding up all the while you read.

Most people who have read George Orwell's *1984* shudder at the thought of two-way video screens in the homes of the public. No one wants Big Brother keeping his eye on us. Can this happen with videotex and similar services?

Certainly, the potential for abuse exists. Perhaps the screen cannot watch us as we go about our private lives, but records of the transactions made and data we access electronically can be kept. In fact, most companies

ISSUE

routinely generate such records for billing purposes or, in the case of at-home shopping, to protect against claims of error. These records are usually collected in one large data bank for—you guessed it—easy access. If you think of how sending away for just one catalog can flood your mailbox for years with unwanted circulars because the catalog producer's lists containing your name have been bought by other firms, the prospect of others gaining access to sensitive personal data kept in these centralized electronic files is truly frightening.

As a case in point, the owner of a theater in Columbus, Ohio, was on trial for showing obscene movies. In his defense he subpoenaed lists of people who had watched these "adult" movies on a cable-TV channel equipped with two-way service. This list was made possible because of this two-way service.

Currently, the law does little to protect citizens from such misuses. Some states have taken the lead and enacted laws, but these vary from state to state. The lawmakers also need to look at the potential for eavesdropping; wiretapping legislation currently in effect does not seem to cover data transmissions. The industry itself is trying to provide some self-regulated protection to its subscribers. With their business just getting under way, the videotex and online services do not wish to scare away potential customers.

Finally, there is an individual issue that must be addressed. Technology will soon advance to the point where receiving only the information you want will be possible. You will define your areas of interest, and the software will screen the news. If we allow ourselves that luxury, will we become more narrowminded and limited in our viewpoints?

"Letting your fingers do the walking" may not be all that you expect.

SUMMARY POINTS

- Dedicated computer systems can control some of the physical functions in a home. Security and energy conservation are common computer applications.
- The most common computer in a home today is a game system.
- General-purpose computers may not cost much more than game systems, while providing many other applications.
- Educational games are becoming more fun, visually attractive, thought provoking, and nonviolent.
- Many home computers are used for keeping financial records. This application may be the one chosen by the user who wants to learn to do his or her own programming.
- Home banking and shopping are changing the way some people handle their money, although privacy can be an issue.
- Computer games can be enjoyed by many players in separate homes through networks and phone links.
- Computers can enhance hobbies, record keeping, and learning. Prices of software and services vary according to the depth of user involvement.
- Networks and online services allow computer users to communicate with others outside their immediate environment and provide access to large amounts of information.
- Data-base producers are compiling vast information banks.
- Magazines now are being published on disks and cassettes, rather than on paper, for the personal computer user.
- Robots may become useful in homes as well as factories.
- Software is available to diagnose your malfunctioning system.
- Computers will likely enter your daily life through such innovations as computerized telephone directory assistance and sales phone calls.

REVIEW QUESTIONS

1. What is a dedicated computer? Name some examples.
2. What is the most popular type of computer software?
3. What is an interactive, multiplayer game?
4. When selecting a computer, what should be the primary consideration (other than money)?
5. What qualities of educational games set them apart from other games?
6. What is a danger of in-home banking that the industry needs to consider?
7. What types of home files can be easily computerized?
8. How could software aid in meal planning?
9. What hobbies named in this chapter have software support available?
10. How is computer software used to help compose and analyze music?
11. How do magazines such as *Diskazine* and *CLOAD* differ from conventional magazines?

12. Distinguish among these terms: online service, videotex, network, data-base producer.
13. What can a home computer operator do if his or her computer doesn't work properly?
14. How may the computer be used as a reference tool?

DISCUSSION QUESTIONS

1. Why do some people prefer dealing with computers to dealing with people?
2. How might shopping by computer improve the general atmosphere in cities and stores?
3. Why and when would having information be equated with having power?
4. How does a conference tree promote intelligent dialogue?
5. Do you feel that automated phoning systems are an invasion of privacy? Why?

CHAPTER 8
COMPUTERS IN THE CLASSROOM

OUTLINE

ARTICLE

IN PITTSBURGH: HACKING THE NIGHT AWAY

ROBERT T. GRIEVES

The hour approaches midnight on the campus of Carnegie-Mellon University in Pittsburgh, but in Wean Hall, C.M.U.'s computer center, it might as well be high noon. On the fifth floor, two dozen undergraduates pound computer terminal keyboards, complete class assignments or work on research projects. In a glass-walled room two floors below, 20 students are seated at terminals. . . .

Welcome to the world of the computer hacker. As midnight wears on to 3 A.M. and then 6 A.M., the hum of conversation dies and Wean Hall becomes very quiet. But the lights burn on, the soft-drink machine on the third floor continues to dispense 16-oz. bottles, and nocturnal computerniks still sprawl before green screens, clack-clacking their instructions into the memory of a DEC-20 system. . . .

[A] hacker . . . is a member of an intense, reclusive subculture of the computer age that has cropped up at the nation's top universities. The term hacker derives from "hack," meaning a subtle, sometimes elegant fix for a flaw in a computer program. Hackers spend hours typing commands on terminal keyboards to learn as much as possible about the strengths and weaknesses of a particular program or network. They tinker for the sheer fun of it, delving deeper and deeper into the mysteries of software. . . .

Like all enthusiasts, hackers have developed their own argot, handed down from the first computer zealots of the early 1970s. To "gronk out," for example, means to go to sleep; to "frobnicate" or "frob" means to fiddle with the controls of a computer. Hackerese changes along with computer technology; even the term hacker is under revisionist pressure. At Carnegie-Mellon, some hackers contend that "wizard" is a more appropriate moniker for those adept at programming. . . .

"Flaming" is another favorite hacker activity. To flame means to speak rapidly or obsessively on a variety of subjects both significant and trivial. Hackers flame by typing opinions, gossip, and mad rantings into a computer file reserved as a community bulletin board. Those wanting to know what is on the mind of computerniks all over campus can call up the board on their terminals and read the latest flame. . . .

Hackers, wizards, nerds, frobnicaters, computerniks—names abound for those who seem afflicted with the latest terminal disease, computer addiction. The disease can attack anyone, but those under 25 succumb most easily.

INTRODUCTION

Typical of the student population, these children are enthusiastic about computer programming courses.

People who are old enough to remember what life was like B.C. (before computers) are uneasy about the rising computer generation, but most realize that knowledge of computers will be vital to the adult success of today's youngsters. Thus, we find ourselves on the threshold of an exciting technological age—not quite sure how to meet it but knowing that it must be met. Parents are demanding from their public schools courses that will prepare their children for this complex technological world. Schools, eager to please, are buying computer equipment and software. Teachers are surprised when they discover that no master plan has been made for computer education. No one is sure just what computer literacy is. But children are eager to use the computer systems—they know that they—and computers—are the future.

COMPUTER APPEAL

Why do students of all ages feel so at ease with and attracted by these machines? Students stay after school and give up free time to get computer time. Some psychologists feel that the answer is a fascination with control. Children, particularly, do not entertain the notion of the computer as a miracle worker. They quickly realize it is just a machine that does only what it is told to do. Therefore, if the output seems miraculous, the student knows where the credit belongs—with himself or herself. Not only is this a good feeling but also it may be the first situation the child ever really controlled.

Computers in education are not new. Some schools have had com-

A workroom in Brown University's new Gould Laboratory provides computer science students with a variety of equipment, including high-resolution color monitors for computer graphics projects.

puter equipment since the mid-1960s. Most often these schools have used the computer primarily as a glorified flashcard system to teach such things as state capitals or the multiplication tables. Computer-assisted instruction (CAI) in its traditional format rarely teaches skills that are new and seldom presents the material in an unusual manner, but advantages still exist (Figure 8-1). Each student receives instruction adapted to his or her learning pace, immediate feedback, and motivation from sound and graphics. Also, the teacher-learner relationship is unintimidating. The computer is the ultimate in patience and good nature; it does not scold or yell. Even very young children can learn how to be at ease with teaching machines. In the long run, gaining this familiarity with computers at an early age may be the most durable lesson.

The question that has arisen, following several years of CAI, is whether children who use this mode of learning are becoming computer literate. The answer from parents, educators, and students alike is a resounding "No!"

FIGURE 8-1 Computer-assisted instruction (CAI) is gaining in popularity among U.S. school systems.

COMPUTER LITERACY

Now comes the rest of the story, and this part of the story is a bundle of questions: (1) Just what *is* computer literacy? (2) Why is it so important? and (3) How do we achieve it?

What Is Computer Literacy?

Not everyone agrees on a definition of **computer literacy**, but most feel that being comfortable with using computers to solve problems of both an academic and a personal nature is important. This implies that students at least must gain a knowledge of simple programming techniques and the functions of various hardware components.

COMPUTER LITERACY
Knowing how to use computers and understanding their societal implications.

In Tennessee, Governor Lamar Alexander made computer literacy in the schools a keystone in both his successful election campaign for a second term and his subsequent plan for improving the state's educational system. An advisory committee, which recommended the immediate introduction of a computer literacy program in the state's middle schools, outlined its definition of computer literacy: Students "will know how to turn a computer on and off, run simple programs, and use different software programs, such as word processing and learning programs." Tennessee's response was a typical one throughout the United States in the early 1980s.

Many literacy courses are being designed so that students also gain an understanding of how computers work, for instance, by examining chips or circuit boards and by taking apart hand calculators, digital watches, and computer games. This way students learn to identify the parts of a computer; they can follow the path that electricity takes, and they learn about the practical need for and the use of the binary number system.

In Hampton, Virginia, high school students have developed a daily dialogue with a computer to widen their academic horizons.

DOONESBURY **by Garry Trudeau**

To prepare students for adulthood in a highly technical society, literacy courses often examine the effect of computers upon society. Knowing the history of computers, examples of current uses, and projected future trends are all important to understanding how computers are changing our lives.

Educators are also realizing that some form of computer manners must be taught. Students need to learn that invading business files, making unauthorized use of communications networks, and pirating software are all unethical. Many students have turned to computers as a sort of rebellion against authority figures, who so often speak of the evils of video games and machine logic. Computer crimes among juveniles are not unusual.

Why Is Computer Literacy So Important?

In May, 1983, the Federal Commission on Excellence in Education, proposed new guidelines to stem the "rising tide of mediocrity" in our society. Among these was a suggestion that all students be required to take a half year of computer science in high school. Among all the controversial opinions generated by this report, the wisdom of that suggestion was questioned by few poeple. Why?

The most likely answer is that parents and other adults have seen the computerization of their own workplaces and realize there is no turning back. Schools cannot be allowed the option of ignoring computers, because these machines alter jobs, entertainment, and home lives so radically. It is becoming evident that those who learn about computers are advancing in their jobs, whereas those who avoid the use of computers are forfeiting promotions and even job security. Naturally, a problematic job future is not what parents would select for their children.

How Can Computer Literacy Be Achieved?

Social Issues How do children become literate in reading and writing? Of course, they study reading, writing, and spelling. The key to literacy, however, seems to lie in the fact that students are required—indeed they want—to use these new skills in other classes and in their personal lives. Their culture supports and uses language skills in many ways. So too with computers. Computing techniques can be taught, but they must be reinforced by the entire culture with which the child interacts.

This means that our elitist, traditional practice of providing computer training to only the bright, gifted-in-math students must be replaced. All children, regardless of sex (see the issue section in Chapter 1), academic achievement, or the financial resources of the school district, must be provided with computer training. Otherwise, a cultural split between those who can compute and those who cannot will arise. Such a split has already been observed in many high schools and colleges; the math and science departments, but not the humanities, have long been using computers. Most colleges are only now beginning to see that computers will affect all lives and that, because of this, all students must become familiar with the new technology.

With so many cuts in federal and state aid, investing in a great deal of new computer hardware and software is next to impossible for the poorer schools. Computers are not like movie projectors; only one or two children can be taught at a time with just one terminal. Thus, acquiring

Geology students at Brown University in Rhode Island use computers to analyze crater distribution on earth's moon and to study NASA images of the planets. Brown is the NASA data center for New England and has datasets from almost all NASA missions.

Student and instructor looking on as another student uses the computer for CAI.

enough state-of-the-art technology is a significant capital investment for a school. Realizing this, government, industry, and parents have worked to get computers in the children's hands. Parents in Florida have held bake sales, carnivals, tree plantings, car washes, and bike-a-thons to raise money. More than two-thirds of the computers in Utica, Michigan, were purchased through parent fund-raising efforts.

A bill was introduced in Congress in 1982 to give tax breaks to computer companies donating equipment to elementary and high schools. Although that bill didn't become law, the idea is not dead (see the issue section in Chapter 5). At least one state, California, has passed a bill giving tax credits for computer donations. Also, some companies are giving equipment to schools anyway. Tandy Corporation awards $500,000 annually for teacher training and software development, and Apple Computers has donated nearly $1 million in computers and equipment to schools across the nation. Other companies are following; they all realize that the type of equipment a student uses in school will most likely be what that person buys for personal use later.

Teaching Arenas Teaching about computers, usually, first occurs in classrooms and not just at secondary and postsecondary levels. Some schools are introducing kindergarteners to the world of computers with good results. Children, like the college students described in the opening article of this chapter, frequently become so entranced that they stay after school or come early to work on their own computerized projects. Many begin to frequent local computer stores and learn more about bits, bytes, disk drives, and interfaces than their teachers know.

Parents are doing their part by buying home computers and educational software. Children now swap software as they once did baseball cards. Although a good share of students' recreational time with computers goes toward playing games, many are attending the computer camps that have mushroomed across the country. They join computer clubs and write their own programs for science fairs. Girl and boy scouts now can earn badges for computer-related activities.

Colleges were the first to make extensive educational use of computers—simply because students at that level could come to terms with computers when those machines were still unusual and difficult to operate. More and more, colleges are requiring students to have their own microcomputers, just as the students must have textbooks (Figure 8-2). Such personal computers, the educators point out, are not only useful for many different classroom applications but also can be linked to college data banks to retrieve (and input) a variety of information.

West Point installed a $16 million computer-based instructional support system in 1982 with, among other features, computer-aided design and interstudent communication capabilities. These users do not own the computers but have access to terminals in barracks, instructors' offices, laboratories, and classrooms.

Some colleges are so anxious to help students get computing power that they finance the cost or arrange hefty discounts ranging from 18 to 30 percent off the retail prices. In Springfield, Massachusetts, at Western

FIGURE 8-2 Several colleges are predicting that each student will be required to have a computer in order to complete coursework.

New England College, staff members are motivated to keep ahead of students by a program that offers them three-year, interest-free loans *and* 18 to 20 percent discounts.

Training Teachers Teachers need incentive for computer training because computers have not been—and still are not—welcomed universally by teachers and administrators. Some fear the technology is too difficult to learn themselves, much less teach to others. Some see the emphasis on computers as gimmick-ridden and profit oriented. Some honestly wonder if the computer isn't put to negligible use when it is brought out of the laboratory or the business school. But whether these fears are honest or self-serving, most people agree that computers are becoming more portable, affordable, easy to use, and suitable for solving real problems. This direction was summed up in an editorial in *InfoWorld* magazine that spoke to the reluctant educator: "Our message to those who fear the introduction of computers on a wide scale in society is, keep an open mind. A computer can be like the most adaptable wrench in your tool kit: Some day you'll find a job for every setting" (August 9, 1982, p. 24).

Because the tool is so versatile, *all* teachers—just like all students—need to have some computer training. To meet this need, teachers are attending classes and then returning to their schools to lead in-service workshops for other teachers. In many cases, teachers are also learning from their students—situations that, when approached with a good attitude, can be of mutual benefit.

In the area of computer training, perhaps the hardest fact to accept is

Faculty member explains an image to a student in a color video studio at the School of Film/Video, California Institute of the Arts.

that such education is never over. Technology has reached no plateau, and no one expects one soon. Teachers, children, adults, engineers—nearly everyone who wants to stay computer literate—can *never* stop learning.

SOFTWARE SUPPORT

In the area of software support, the educational field is lacking. There are two reasons for this. First, educators have felt so much pressure to rush into computer education that they have rarely stopped to judge the scope of the field. They fought to get the latest technology for the least money and often found themselves without a well-thought-out plan for using their purchases. Second, most educational software on the market is sadly unimaginative because, hurrying to be the first to get their products on the market, most software publishers neglected software design. Administrators who wanted to get the computers in use had little choice but to purchase these inadequate packages. Recently, however, some new programs have become available that make the situation brighter.

Purchased Software

A Digital Equipment Corporation product, HMRABI (for Hammurabi) livens up social studies. With this program a student can be the leader of ancient Babylon, conduct trade in arms, and distribute wheat to the people. As long as his or her decisions lead to a strong military, adequate food supplies, and a stable economy, the student enjoys power. Exile is the alternative because if a wrong move occurs, the peasants revolt and the next student takes the seat of power.

The Learning Company has an intriguing product, called Juggle's Rainbow, for children from ages three to six. The package comes with a blue cardboard strip to divide the keyboard into two areas, above and below. The screen then can become active with an animated juggler shown above or below a blue line, depending on where the child presses a key on the keyboard. Soon the computer takes over and tries to guide the child to press a key either "above" or "below." By challenging the youngster with very appealing visuals—a rainbow, butterfly, windmill, or large question mark—he or she may experience several variations on the above-below, left-right theme.

In an educational experience called Capture the Flag published by Apple Computer, Inc., children play in pairs against four little machines controlled by the computer. The children must defend their flag and try to get the machine's flag while the machine tries to do the same thing. Two features make this game a good learning experience. First, children can freeze the action at any time by pressing a button; thus, they can work out strategies. Second, by pressing another key, they can actually hear the computer "talking" to its little helper machines in binary code. By converting this code—which is a number corresponding to some part of the

PLATO® computer-based education is designed for the individual, offering personal, one-to-one learning with infinite patience and personalization.

Honeywell's CAN-8 is a computer-assisted instructional (CAI) software system for schools and industry that allows non-programmers to develop courses. Honeywell's CAN-8 is adaptable to the needs of schools at all levels, from elementary grades through college.

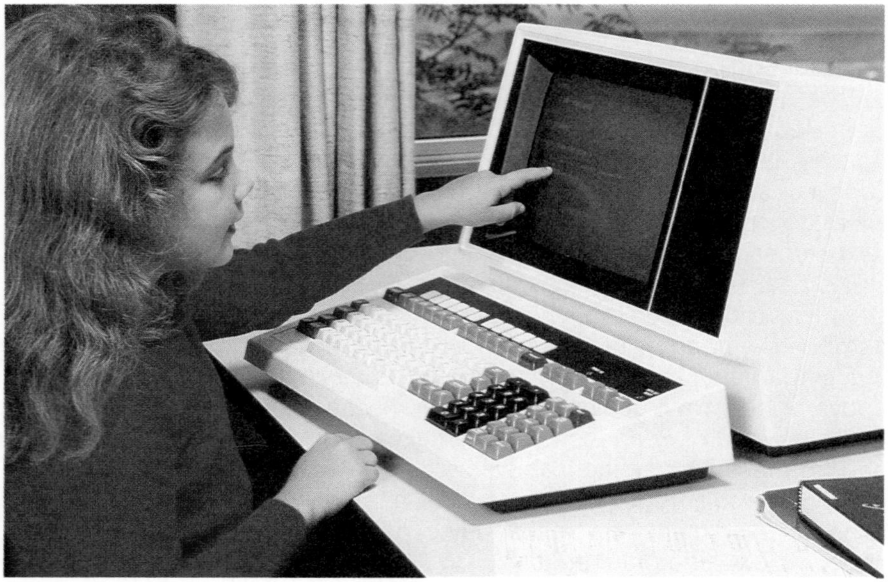

playing grid—to the decimal system, the children can spy on the machine's moves. They can even pretend to be one of the computer's helpers and ask the computer a question. The answer may help them determine its overall strategy.

Perhaps the most novel uses of computers in education have been made by the Chicago's Institute for Computers in Jewish Life. Although the applications of new technology to such ancient traditions of law and religion may not be immediately apparent, many exist. Programs designed by the institute teach 13-year-olds the text and chanting for the bar mitzvah. A game called Jewish IQ Baseball demands that the successful hitter have a knowledge of Jewish history and traditions, since home runs, stolen bases, and the like depend on the right answers being fed into the computer. A video screen displays the baseball field and the game actions. One program, made to teach the significance of Rosh Hashana, The Jewish New Year, can even simulate the sound of the ram's horn, or shofar.

Computers using Ibycus software at the University of Texas at Austin are helping students of ancient literature analyze writing styles. The software can do character string searches of the entire *Iliad* in just seven seconds. By using it, students settled a debate about whether a portion of a poem written on a piece of Eygptian papyrus dated back to the third century A.D. They found the passage in the Greek version of the *Iliad* by string searching.

Now word processing is available for children, and the software is so convenient that adults are enjoying it too. Called Bank Street Writer and developed by Intentional Educations, Inc., it uses three basic steps: write, edit, and transfer. The software is easy and self-explanatory; most children are writing after just half an hour of instruction. It comes with good documentation, which is rarely needed with this program. The package includes suggested activities for integrating word processing into a traditional language arts class. Word processing seems to help children write sooner and better, in part because the tedious process of making multiple rough drafts is eliminated.

Grolier Electronic Publishing's computerized encyclopedia, mentioned in Chapter 7, combines pictures and sounds, plus the actual text on the screen. The encyclopedia will be age coded so that a child inquiring about elephants, say, will be given a much more basic lecture than will an adult.

Since computers never become fatigued, frustrated, or impatient, they have become a boon in the teaching of retarded students. These students can control their computer environment and feel a sense of success and control they may never have felt before. With special programming, the computer can talk to the student, present interesting graphics, gently announce that the student has given a wrong answer, and urge another try. Its variety can make repetition of lessons more tolerable; and its mechanical nature guarantees that no impatience or weariness, such as might be shown by a human teacher, will occur.

Colleges recommend an introductory computer course for many of their students.

The summer program at this school offers a computer class for six-year olds.

Languages of Learning

Computer learning has had positive effects even on so-called "bad kids." Through a group called the Los Angeles Committee for the Transformation of Street Gangs, a computer store owner has been working with adolescents from the slums using Commodore computers, which are on loan from the company. To play games or run programs, these young people have had to learn to read. Some are now ready to go to work in computerized offices and, it is hoped, can thereby break out of slum and gang life.

Such results like these are the rule, not the exception, when students start learning to program. Two languages are widely used with beginners: BASIC and Logo.

BASIC Developed at Dartmouth College in the 1960s, BASIC was designed so that even the least mathematical students could write fairly complex programs with little instruction. It is meant to be used with interactive computing. Most microcomputer software for home and business use is written in a form of BASIC, and it is the first programming language most people learn.

BASIC is still too complex for very young children, and it is not well suited for structured programming.

Logo
A powerful programming language that allows even small children to define new commands and explore many concepts.

LISP
***LIS*t *P*rocessing; a programming language primarily used in artificial intelligence research.**

Logo Because of BASIC's deficiencies, many schools are starting to use the language **Logo,** whose name is derived from the Greek word for "reason." It was developed under the leadership of Seymour Papert at MIT. Logo stems from an earlier language called **LISP** (*LIS*t *P*rocessing), which is used by many researchers in the field of artificial intelligence. Logo combines LISP's list-processing capabilities with a syntax that children can readily understand and use (Figure 8-3). It is well suited to structured

PROFILE

JOHN G. KEMENY

A new wave of user-oriented programming languages was initiated by the work of John G. Kemeny. Born in Hungary in 1926, Kemeny emigrated to the United States in 1940. As an undergraduate at Princeton, Kemeny served in the army's Manhattan Project, which designed the first atomic bomb. Kemeny's interest in science and mathematics was enhanced from 1948–49 when he worked as a research assistant for Albert Einstein at the Institute for Advanced Study while working toward his Ph.D.

Upon graduation, Kemeny taught mathematics at Princeton and Dartmouth. Subsequent promotions within the department plus the introduction of computers into the curriculum made Kemeny an early advocate of computer literacy.

He designed an introductory computer course in 1963 and soon realized that the existing batch-processing systems were inadequate for the course assignments. With a team of assistants, Kemeny developed the first prototype time-sharing system.

Next Kemeny and a colleague, Thomas Kurtz, developed the language, BASIC, the most common language used on microcomputers today.

Kemeny has published several books on computers and the BASIC language. In addition to consulting, Kemeny has served on a variety of significant committees including the U.S. Commission on Mathematics Instruction, the President's Commission on the Accident at Three Mile Island, and the Consortium on Financing Higher Education. Currently, Kemeny is the president of Dartmouth College.

programming. Although it is usually associated with children, Logo's potential use need not be so limited. (Logo software now comes in many forms, some more suitable for particular ages, applications, and equipment than others.)

FIGURE 8-3 Texas Instruments was the first computer manufacturer to make the children's programming language, Logo, available to consumers.

PROFILE

SEYMOUR PAPERT

The Logo programming language, created by Seymour Papert with the collaboration of countless other people including computer scientists, classroom teachers, and even the students themselves, is designed as a learning environment in which people easily progress not only to computer literacy, but computer *fluency*.

Papert studied mathematics and philosophy in his native South Africa, at Cambridge University in England, and in Paris, France. There he met Jean Piaget, beginning a long and fruitful interaction which focused his interest in the influence of environment on learning. Following five years which he spent in Geneva with Piaget, Papert came to MIT in 1963, and became Co-Director with Marvin Minsky of the Artificial Intelligence Laboratory in 1967. At this time, he began designing a computer language that would be suitable for children. The first implementation of the language was done at the research firm of Bolt, Beranic and Newman, and subsequent implementations at MIT where the language grew into its modern form.

The past dozen years has seen many expansions and refinements of Logo, as well as the development of microcomputers both powerful enough to use Logo and inexpensive enough to allow school systems to provide each child with a microcomputer within the foreseeable future. Papert's book *Mindstorms*, published in 1980, describes both Logo and the philosophies which led to its development. Because Logo is especially well-suited to learning environments, it is very likely to replace BASIC as the best means of introducing students (of all ages) to computer programming.

The differences between BASIC and Logo are important. David Yukol, an instructor for Computer Camp International, described the distinction in these terms: "Some of the kids are hardware-rich and imagination-poor. I had a kid last week who told me he knew all about BASIC. He really needed a strong dose of Logo. He didn't understand the difference between following someone else's rules and making his own" (*OMNI*, April 1983, p. 141).

Logo uses the computer as a control device. To program, you teach the computer your own commands called **procedures.** Even three- and four-year-olds can write simple procedures and create drawings on the video screen using **turtle geometry,** in which a simulated turtle acts as a pen and follows instructions. By doing so, they learn geometric concepts that used to be introduced in junior high school.

PROCEDURE
A Logo command defined by the programmer.

TURTLE GEOMETRY
A Logo method of drawing on the video screen in which a simulated turtle acts as a pen and follows instructions.

For example, if a youngster wants to make a square, these commands could be used:

```
FORWARD 50
RIGHT 90
FORWARD 50
RIGHT 90
FORWARD 50
RIGHT 90
FORWARD 50
RIGHT 90
```

The number 50 tells the turtle how far to move; RIGHT 90 tells it to turn 90 degrees. This sequence can be simplified by instructing the computer to

REPEAT 4 [FORWARD 50 RIGHT 90]

Then, to have square making become a procedure, the student simply needs to define it as

```
TO SQUARE
REPEAT 4 [FORWARD 50 RIGHT 90]
END
```

After this, telling the computer to SQUARE will get the expected shape.

Sprite procedures are another intriguing feature of Logo. Programmers can determine the shape of a sprite, how many sprites they want, and their colors. The sprites can be moved across the screen to make startling, exciting graphics.

Logo has commands that allow input to be entered from a keyboard, joystick, or game paddle. Even music compositions can be programmed. This language is expected to change the way both math and music are taught and learned.

A day at computer camp means waking up in a college dormitory, slipping into a t-shirt and shorts, eating a hearty breakfast, and then sitting down at your computer to work through your learning packet. Here, a CompuCamp curriculum director helps a student work through a lab project.

SPRITE
Small blocks that can assume user-defined shapes and colors and that can be moved rapidly across the screen using the language Logo.

INNOVATIONS

In Hartford, Connecticut, a specialized learning tool called Urban Adventure was developed as a project of Encendiendo Una Llama (Lighting a Flame). This program combined the adventure game concept with the real urban environment to help children in grades 3 through 6 explore their city.

The children first explored landmarks of the city. Then using a light pen and an Apple Graphics Tablet, they drew the landmarks and stored them in the computer's memory. They programmed an exploration game to go with the graphics, and a speech synthesizer was programmed to say certain words and phrases about the landmarks in both English and Spanish. Although the game they developed is a good learning activity for all children in this age group, the children who created it learned the most—about their city, speaking in both languages, how computers work, and working with others on a complex project.

At the University of Iowa, teachers are experimenting with a teaching device that combines computer and videodisc technology. The videodisc,

Student at computer of motion control camera at the Film Graphic Department, School of Film/Video, California Institute of the Arts.

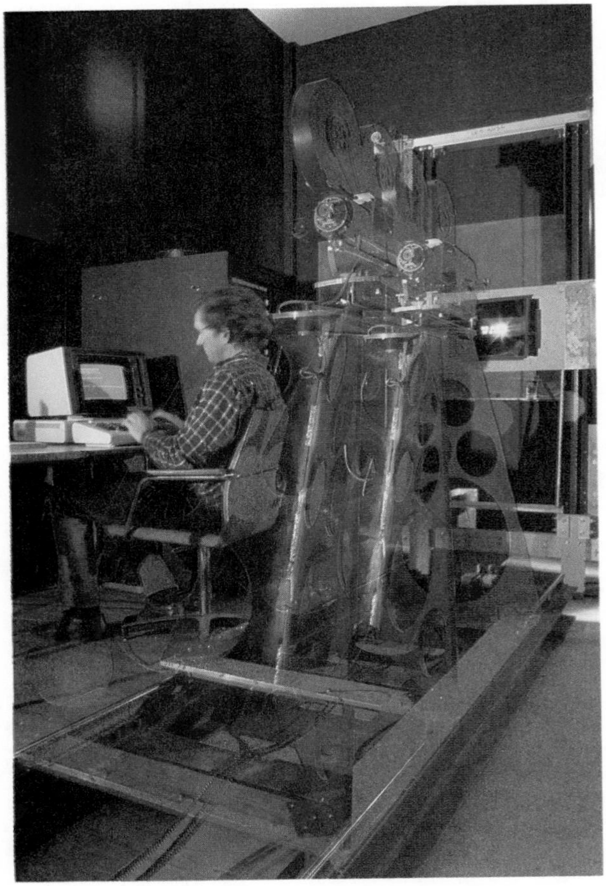

An electronic blackboard.

unlike videotape, can be immediately accessed at a chosen point. Working through computerized controls, students have access on the discs to visual stills, sound tracks, or computer texts and graphics in a number of combinations. According to Joan Sustik, director of the school's Intelligent Videodisc Research and Development Project, "Motion sequences can be shown in slow motion or still frame to observe critical details. It is also possible to overlay computer text and graphics on top of projected videodisc images. This allows highlighting, cuing, and other visual techniques."

The system can operate automatically or at the direction of the student user. Teachers have so far used the system to teach dance students 190 ballet positions—plus their names and how they are spelled. For architecture students, a program shows moving and still pictures while an interview with Frank Lloyd Wright is carried on the sound track.

As you can see from the issues and examples in this chapter, from preschool to graduate school, the computer is a looming educational challenge. How we meet it will determine the course of the future.

ISSUE

COMPUTERS: HELPING OR IMPEDING CHILDREN'S GROWTH AND DEVELOPMENT?

Just about everyone today realizes that a social revolution is occurring—one that will be as important as the Industrial Revolution and in which children currently are participating more heavily than adults. This revolution was brought on by computers—microcomputers, particularly. Children interact with the powerful machines as a matter of course—at home, at school, and elsewhere. What effect is this interaction having on them?

When looking for answers to this question, most people think first about game arcades where children frequently get their first computer experiences. Arcades can be family oriented, but most are more like yesterday's poolroom, dark and dominated by males. Children plug their quarters into the machines and wage battles of destruction or play electronic versions of aggressive sports. The real war here, though, isn't the one depicted by the flashing lights. The war that is being fought today is mind versus body—and not just with arcade games but also with general-purpose computers.

The computer is sneaky, no doubt about it. With it, some battles are won; others are lost. Caught by the subtle seduction of a difficult, but beatable, game or problem, a person can remain nearly as motionless as a puppet without a string. Computers do not promote physical activity. To spend time on them, children forego school recess, street basketball, and natural exercise of all kinds. At a computer camp in Connecticut, counselors were faced with the problem of their charges not getting outdoors enough. Now they routinely demand that students turn in their diskettes and get into the pool.

The computer acts so quickly that users learn to live in the moment. Indeed, it changes the whole notion of space and time. A message sent from Calcutta is received almost immediately in Chicago. After working with computers for a while, the 10-second wait while a program loads or a routine is executed may be excruciating. Impatience thrives; attention spans become shortened. One lecturer on the school circuit claims that now he must change topics at least once every 30 seconds to hold his audience. Some say that children are learning to have little thought for the future or the past. Without such insight, will the theoretically correct decisions best serve humankind?

In return for the sacrifice of bodies, the computer lets the mind roam free. When Einstein was young, he used to wonder how it would feel to ride a wave like a surfer. With the graphic effects computers can create, children will come close to knowing. They are learning to juggle many variables as they search for strategy and knowledge. They can program away natural laws that keep the body here and now.

The digital awareness created by computers gives children a new sense of precision. Ask for the time, and the reply is, "1:28," not, "half past one" as children of another age would have said. This is a sign of a completely different relationship with the environment, one that grows by learning to program.

Programming promotes, even demands, sequential thinking—logic as we sometimes call it. Children learn new languages and terms. But to use them, to gain that important sense of mastery over the machine, strict rules must be followed. Children learn to follow those rules in writing sequential, step-by-step instructions to accomplish the tasks assigned. In this way, regardless of what programming language they are using, the children learn to focus on the *process* involved in performing a given task, rather than the end result. They then describe that process in step-by-step logical instructions that adhere to the rules of the language they are using.

Teenagers especially accept the rules of the programming language while rejecting the rules of

ISSUE

society. Rebellious behavior has new avenues—pirating programs in disregard of copyrights, "unlocking" telephone lines, accessing other systems illegally. The movie, *War Games,* effectively depicted the new kind of status being enjoyed by young people who are skilled at accessing school records or breaking into company files, enabling them to show off their electronic know-how.

Perhaps worsening the situation, the computer's role as a communication broker makes actions less personal, with mixed results. Recent research at Carnegie-Mellon University has pointed at how electronics communications over networks shapes human communications. In the test situation, whenever a discussion was held anonymously by computer, the sessions took longer before a decision was reached, arguments were common, and the students were frequently abusive to one another. However, computer discussions turned out to be more fair with each participant getting his or her share of time. The highly vocal individuals held less sway than in a group where people talk in person.

Used in appropriate ways, the knowledge of science, math, and technology is beneficial. Unleashed by rebellion or an ignorance of ethical behavior, the same knowledge wreaks havoc. This has always been true, but the computer's ability to shrink geographic space by assembling data from far and wide into accessible data bases has made the effects much more pronounced. What will the world be like when this social revolution is complete?

SUMMARY POINTS

- Younger people have little fear of computers.
- Schools have been buying computers without really knowing how they should use them.
- Computers are attractive because they can be controlled; provide individual instruction, feedback, and motivation; and do not intimidate the learner.
- Computer-assisted instruction is not equivalent to computer literacy. To be computer literate, a person should be able to work with the computer to solve problems and should understand how the computer works and its effects on society.
- A code of computer ethics should be taught.
- Parents, governments, and computer companies are helping schools get computers.
- Computer literacy implies the need for a computer-literate culture to support the education of the young.
- All children and all teachers must be taught to use computers so that we do not have a knowledge gap between groups.
- Software support has been of poor quality in the past. The situation is beginning to improve.
- BASIC was the first programming language for learners and is still used extensively.
- LOGO is a more recent language for educational use. It is powerful and can support very creative programming by all age groups.
- New input/output devices are also helping schools learn new ways to teach about computers and other subjects.

REVIEW QUESTIONS

1. What are some nicknames for people who spend much time with computers?
2. Why are parents anxious to have their children work with and learn about computers?
3. What is computer literacy?
4. How were computers first used in education?
5. What are some unethical computer-related practices?
6. What computer-related requirement was suggested by the Federal Commission on Excellence in Education?
7. Why can't schools be allowed to put off computer education?
8. How are schools financing computers for themselves? How are they helping others to get computers?
9. Why are some teachers afraid of the computer revolution?
10. Why has software for education been so poor in the past?
11. What skills are being improved with some of the new software now available?

12. What special groups of people can also benefit from computer use? How and why?
13. What are the shortcomings of BASIC?
14. What are some distinguishing features of LOGO?

DISCUSSION QUESTIONS

1. Why does the present generation of young people have little fear of computers compared with people born before 1960?
2. What skills might children learn by using computers?
3. What negative results might occur when people become addicted to computers?
4. What qualities are necessary in a piece of software to make it educationally beneficial?
5. Do you believe video games help or hurt children?

CHAPTER 9
COMPUTERS IN THE WORKPLACE

OUTLINE

ARTICLE

HORSE BREEDER CORRALS HIS DATA BASE

Computerized dating services nowadays hardly qualify as news. Lovelorn Americans have been turning to digital matchmakers for years. But when someone uses a computer to match horses instead of humans, that's news—and that's what Brad Baker is doing at Moondrift Farms, a Colorado horsebreeding ranch, with the help of data-base management software. . . .

To increase the likelihood of success, detailed information is kept on all horses who come to the ranch. For example, when a mare comes to Moondrift to be settled, her past history is carefully noted. "We want to know when she was last in heat, what she's been fed, the history of her foaling, how many times she's been bred to settle, and even a little bit about her personality," says June Baker. . . .

Arming himself with an Apple II with two disk drives, an Epson MX-80 printer, and Software Publishing's PFS data-base management software, Baker began to make order out of chaos.

"PFS has just been super," says Brad. "I've set up several programs, the first of which is a total medical history of all our horses.

"Then, I have a program for mares—really everything we need to know in connection with breeding. I'm working on a similar program for stallions. We have a sophisticated laboratory on the premises, so we'll want to know things like the motility of a stallion's sperm."

Mare owners will be able to check the background of any stallion they are interested in. For example, a mare's owner might want to breed her with a descendant of a certain sire. At the push of a button, the names of all such horses may be recalled.

And it's exactly this rapid recall capability that has been so useful at Moondrift. "I can recall information in about 30 or 40 different ways," says Brad. "I can get a complete price list"—Moondrift's Morgans fetch anywhere from $35,000 to $50,000—"or I could call up the names of all horses who need their teeth worked on."

Brad is also using PFS to stay abreast of show performances by Moondrift horses, and to keep track of work that has to be done on the farm's equipment.

"We're enjoying and learning," says June Baker. Adds Brad, "It's done wonders for the way we do business."

Computer-assisted horsebreeding is only one example of the changes that have occurred in the workplace since the introduction of computers. On the farm and in the city, in offices of every description, computers are revolutionizing the way we work.

INTRODUCTION

The farm with its fields of crops, stables of horses, and pastures of dairy cattle is experiencing the effects of computers, as is its city counterpart—the business office. On the farm, the computer stores animal health records and assists farmers with feed selection and bookkeeping. In the city computers store information on houses and buildings for the fire department, and newspaper reporters use desk-top terminals rather than traditional typewriters to enter stories for the morning edition. The office, however, is probably the area of greatest change and offers the greatest potential of full-scale automation.

COMPUTERS CHANGE THE FARM

Microcomputer applications, like those previously mentioned, have meant increased sales of microcomputers to farmers. For the farmer, the microcomputer is a good investment. If the farmer uses the computer to make a choice about what to do with barren beef cows, it could easily pay for itself in a single day. Also, devising a low-cost feed program is difficult to do without the aid of a computer. The existing software for feed programs determines the most nutritious and cheapest blend of feed consisting of 50 to 100 ingredients.

Studies of the agricultural market show dairy farming to be more record oriented than cattle or crop farming (Figure 9-1). For example, Mountain

FIGURE 9-1 Computers on the Farm. This farmer examines a printout giving information on his dairy operation.

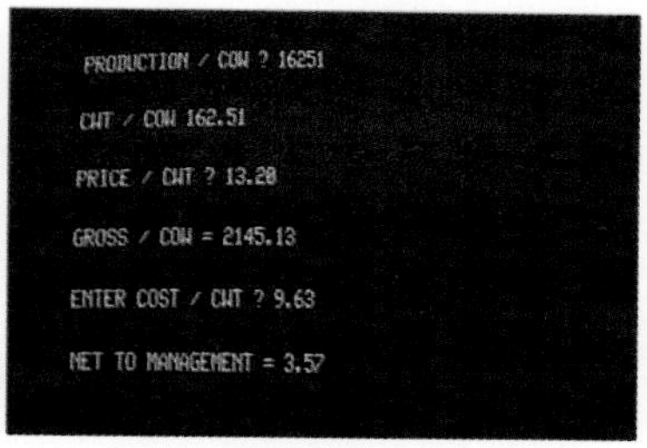

Dairy in Connecticut has turned to the personal computer to keep track of the 8,000 to 9,000 quarts of milk processed daily. In ways like this, farmers are able to reduce operating costs and improve management.

Outbreaks of disease and pests can be forecast by computers early enough to halt the threat before it gets out of hand. Computers are being used to control such outbreaks as apple scab, a disease that can destroy an orchard within two years. The computer receives information from sensors, which continuously monitor factors like date, time of day, air temperature, wetness of the leaves, and humidity. When conditions are right for outbreaks, the computer will indicate when the trees need to be sprayed. With apple scab, the trees must be sprayed within eight hours of detection of adverse conditions. By using the computer monitoring system, the number of sprayings can be reduced by two-thirds to three-fourths, in turn reducing environmental hazards and spraying costs.

COMPUTERS ENTER THE FIRE DEPARTMENT

Fire fighting is becoming more efficient as a result of computers. Many fire departments in larger cities are using computers to handle emergency calls. Before fire fighters arrive at the scene, the system provides detailed information about a burning structure (Figure 9-2).

Before the computerized system, many fire stations had used a card file to record information about major buildings. This card included infor-

FIGURE 9-2 Computers in the Fire Department. Graphic computer terminals installed in fire trucks improve fire departments' ability to respond to emergencies.

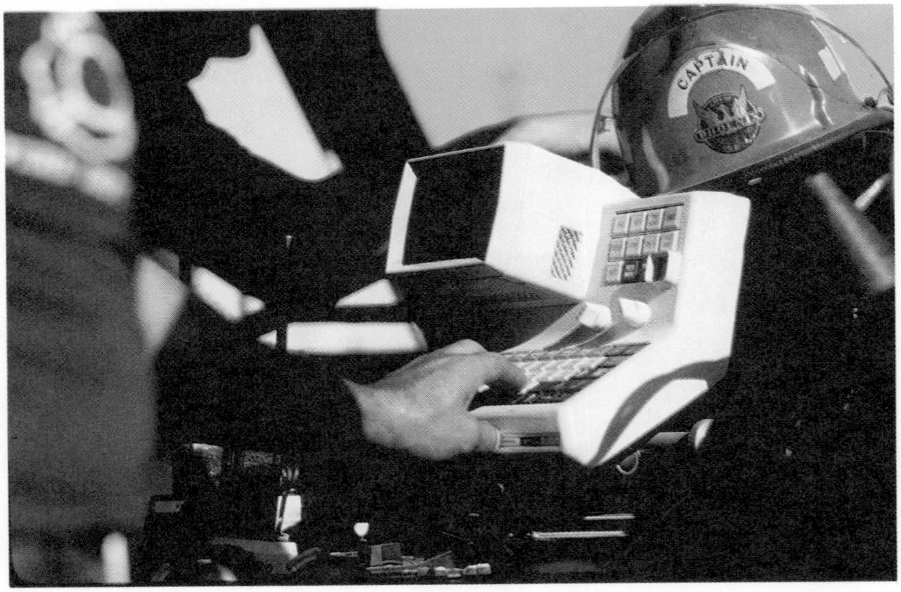

mation about the type and layout of the building, and the type and location of any flammable materials that might be stored there. With the new system, this information is provided by the computer while the dispatcher is at the switchboard, and the details of the building can be immediately flashed on a video screen.

Additional information can be sent to the fire fighters, such as persons to be notified in case of emergency, and the location of special facilities. A fire department could have information in a computer file for every residential and commercial structure within their district.

COMPUTERS IN THE NEWSROOM

Many newspaper reporters, especially in the last few years, have begun entering their stories on visual display terminals in the newsroom. Gone are the desk-top typewriters; in their place are computer keyboards and screens. All wire copy, such as AP (Associated Press) and UPI (United Press International), is received by satellite or over the phone lines. The transmitted data can be directly handled by the computer. The actual typesetting procedure has been made easier also. Usually, copy is accepted up to one and a half hours before press time; however, with the satellite, wire copy on a late-breaking story can be put directly into the computer and transferred to the typesetting room until one hour before press time. In case the system breaks down, some newspapers have a backup system, usually one used by another department, for example, the business department.

THE OFFICE OF YESTERDAY, TODAY, AND TOMORROW

Consider the office of the past. There were chairs, desks, and telephones. File cabinets loomed in the distance and the sound of typewriters could be heard. Usually, within easy reach of the typist were sheets of carbon paper.

The earliest indication of office automation can be traced back to Frederick W. Taylor and his principles of scientific management, which were introduced in the early 1920s. These principles were used to analyze and categorize duties and establish performance standards to promote factory-like productivity. As machines (typewriters, adding machines, and bookkeeping machines) entered the office, the unorganized clutter associated with roll-top desks was replaced with order and efficiency.

A significant change in office organization occurred when punched-card equipment was introduced. A special tabulating center was set up, complete with a staff of specialists to operate the equipment. When computers became available, they were also installed in the technology center—now referred to as the data-processing department. Again, all transactions requiring computer processing were performed in this department

"Do you enjoy working with machines?"

PROFILE

ADAM OSBORNE

Realizing that computerization can change the professional's work role, former chemical engineer Adam Osborne introduced the portable computer, offering executives computing flexibility.

Bangkok-born Osborne, an active and respected consultant in computers, wrote and published the first book on microcomputers, *An Introduction to Microcomputers,* that was so successful it enabled him to found his own publishing company (purchased by McGraw-Hill in 1979). With a reputation as an accomplished technical writer, Osborne started writing a column for *Interface Age* in 1976. This position enabled him to observe the strengths and weaknesses of the then-emerging microcomputer revolution. Osborne's chief criticism was that microcomputers could not satisfy the average consumer's needs. His solution was obvious—produce an inexpensive product that was industry compatible in both hardware and software.

It took just four months for Osborne to build a prototype. His microcomputer, the Osborne 1, released in 1981, received favorable response. The innovative portable computer was compact and affordable; the $1,795 price included five software programs. The Osborne 1 was well suited not only to the typical business functions, but also to a variety of applications—it was used in computing statistics for the TransAmerican Tennis Tournament in 1982.

Although Osborne Corporation is no longer in business, Adam Osborne made a significant contribution to the computer industry. The portable computer is a valuable convenience, and other companies have obviously recognized this by introducing their own versions of the portable computer.

WORD PROCESSING
A program that allows text material to be entered, corrected, added or deleted, and printed.

by trained specialists. **Word processing** followed the same pattern. However, because word processing involves text manipulation, rather than data manipulation, it became necessary to decentralize the structure so individual users throughout the company could directly interact with the operator.

Today's office illustrates the transitions taking place as a result of computer technology. Word processors are commonplace. Jane Pauley, in hosting a "Today" show segment from Hewlett-Packard, noted with wry amusement that amid all the high-tech wonders of the place, she had difficulty finding a typewriter on which to prepare her script. In addition to word processors, other forms of office automation are available. Although full-scale office automation may not be feasible or practical for the average office at this time, some of the larger corporations are experimenting with the technology and are on the road to a "paperless office."

If we believe the advertisements on television and in business magazines, the office as we now know it is doomed. Gone will be the typewriters, the bulky desks, the cumbersome filing cabinets, the impromptu "conferences" at the water fountain, and the endless rows of clerks and secretaries. In their place will be high-speed word processors, multifunction work stations, disk files, and a few employees who are able to interact with their office from their homes by way of personal microcomputers. Gone, too, will be the bulky mailroom, replaced by an **electronic mail** sys-

ELECTRONIC MAIL
Messages sent at high speeds by telecommunication facilities and placed in a special computer storage area.

tem. Gone will be the executive rushing through the office to catch a flight, since **teleconferencing** is almost as effective as meeting face to face and is far less expensive.

Writing about the automated office in an advertising supplement of the October 3, 1982, *New York Times,* Randy J. Goldfield, president of the Omni Group, drew this rather rosy picture of things to come:

> You're pondering a purchase decision, so with a couple of keystrokes, you request information on your company's current holdings. It appears on screen instantly. Next you get records of your firm's position last year at this time, arranged in bar charts. Now you check trends in commodities prices, displayed as a line chart. Everything looks OK to go ahead and buy, but you should check with senior management.
>
> Your terminal tells you that Smith is in Rio, Jones in Detroit. You send them priority electronic mail messages asking for confirmation of your decision to buy; you send your supporting data and charts.
>
> In moments, you get an OK from Jones—and a "must talk first" from Smith. The three of you teleconference. Smith's data says prices are dropping, so you should wait to buy.
>
> You place a hold order with your broker via the terminal, and at the proper time, the purchase is made.

Portable computers, such as this one by Hewlett Packard enable professionals to process information away from the office.

TELECONFERENCING
Conferences using electronic and/or image-producing means to communicate.

Welcome to the modern office. You've accomplished in minutes what once took days, and your executive workstation has helped save your company a few hundred thousand dollars.

This is an intriguing picture, and, technologically speaking, all the capabilities cited exist. Teleconferencing, whereby people communicate from diverse locations by computer terminals, is not so widespread as to be commonplace, but it is a working reality. Electronic mail, where a message is sent from one computer user to another by terminals, has demonstrated its value in some—if not all—situations. Quick data retrieval has long been a matter of facts; and, as mentioned earlier, it is nudging its way into the executive suite.

Some barriers to the automated office do exist. Price is one of them. Incompatibility of equipment is another. Human resistance to change is a third—and very compelling—barrier, particularly when no overriding need to make the change is apparent.

OFFICE AUTOMATION

OFFICE AUTOMATION
The integration of computer and communication technology with traditional manual procedures in the office.

Office automation is a generalized and comprehensive term for the processes that integrate computer and communication technology with the traditional manual procedures of office work. To better understand the concept, office automation can be divided into four categories: (1) word/data processing, (2) communication, (3) information retrieval, and (4) support systems.

Word Processing

Because word processing is the most solidly established technology, it has assumed the role of leader in the advance of office automation. Word processing manipulates text data to achieve a desired output (Figure 9-3). A typical system consists of a keyboard, a visual display device, a storage unit, and a printer. Like data processing, word processing relieves workers of time-consuming and routine tasks, thereby increasing standards of productivity and quality. It is estimated that, depending on how much typing a secretary does, the secretary's productivity can be increased 25 to 200 percent using word processing.

Word processing bypasses the difficulties and shortcomings of traditional writing and typing. A word-processing program not only produces finished copy in a form that is as readable and attractive as typewritten copy, but it can also produce the final copy much faster. The secretary or other user may edit, rearrange, insert, and delete material—all electronically—until the text is exactly as it should be. Then the text can be stored on tape or disk and/or printed for later use. Each copy of the text that is printed is an "original." Thus, the output of a reliable word-processing system is of a consistently high quality.

If there are numerous form letters to be typed, the secretary only has to type a single letter. Through the use of special codes, addresses and

FIGURE 9-3 Word Processing System

phrases can be merged into the original letter, creating personalized correspondence.

There are definite advantages to using a word processor rather than a conventional typewriter. Word processors offer many functions to increase efficiency in the text manipulation process. Standard features include automatic centering, boldfacing, automatic pagination (page numbering), automatic alphabetizing, search and find, and automatic justification of type.

In addition to the typical functions of the word processor, some options offer more versatility; one option, a dictionary, can include up to one million words and is available in languages other than English. Misspellings and hyphenation on the copy are checked by the machine at the rate of 10 seconds per page. Depending on the type of program, it may even correct misspelled words when they are located. Specialized dictionaries are available for legal and medical offices.

Several word-processing systems offer flexibility. For example, word processors using special software can also perform data-processing functions. (The word processor is, after all, just a computer with word processing software and external storage.)

Optical character recognition (OCR) devices allow an alternative to keying in information directly to the word processor. With an OCR scanner, typewritten pages can be read into the computer—a process that saves considerable input time. Consider, for example, that the average operator keys in text at a rate of 60 words per minute from typed (prepared) copy.

PROFILE

JOHN OPEL

John Opel can take much of the credit for making IBM a force to contend with in microcomputers, instead of just maintaining its eminence in the mainframe market it pioneered.

Opel, the son of a German hardware store owner, studied at Westminster College and received an MBA from the University of Chicago. In 1949 Opel began working as an IBM salesman in his hometown of Jefferson City, Missouri. Ten years of outstanding sales records secured his promotion to the corporate headquarters in Armonk, New York, where he served as administrative assistant to the chief executive officer. Opel quickly rose to become president in 1974 and chief executive officer in 1981.

Under Opel's leadership, IBM began opening retail stores that would ultimately become outlets for its computer products. He also oversaw the development and production of IBM's first microcomputer—the IBM Personal Computer, introduced in August 1981.

Less cautious than his corporate predecessors, Opel authorized IBM to use computer components and software made by other companies. The payoff for his calculated risk taking resulted in $500 million worth of microcomputer sales for 1982.

The OCR can input the same prepared copy at more than 1,000 words per minute. This type of source-data automation means that editing needs to be done only at the processor's keyboard. Also, input to the word processor can be done by others—each at his or her own work station—relieving the company of the expense of training them specifically on the word processor. This procedure also relieves the trained user from simple, time-consuming activities and allows him or her to assume more challenging duties.

Another example of flexibility is in phototypesetting. Here, word-processing equipment can be connected by a modem to phototypesetting equipment, avoiding the middle step of rekeying information (Figure 9-4). In addition to improved turnaround time, this capability allows greater control over copy and reduces costs by 10 to 40 percent.

Communication

Another area of office automation is communication. Communication may be accomplished through several forms: electronic mail, voice mail, teleconferencing, and telecommuting.

Electronic Mail Electronic mail is already being used by many businesses as a supplement to regular mail, and some look for it to eventually replace regular mail. Commercial electronic mail services are offered by the United States Postal Service (E-COM) and GTE Telenet (Telemail), among others.

Electronic mail, now used mainly for internal communication, is the sending of messages at high speeds using telecommunication facilities (Figure 9-5). One user of the service can send a message to another by

FIGURE 9-4 Computerized Phototypesetting System

FIGURE 9-5 Electronic Mail System

placing it in a special computer storage area. The recipient user can receive the message by retrieving and displaying or printing it through his or her terminal. People using such systems need not be at the same location or be online at the same time.

Electronic mail in its present form has several advantages, including virtually assured express delivery via terminal-to-terminal setups; terminal access from the business office to Western Union Mailgram service; the reduction of telephone, paper, and duplicating costs; the capacity to be sent as certified mail; and less cost for next-day delivery than with conventional private carriers. But some drawbacks are evident too. Most systems require the recipient of electronic mail to have a terminal; also, there may be no way to notify the recipient of a pending message until he or she turns the terminal on. Photos and graphics can't be transmitted quickly. Also, some systems have a minimum-use requirement that may reduce the savings otherwise offered.

VOICE MAIL
Message spoken into a telephone, converted into digital form, stored in memory until recalled, then reconverted into voice form.

Voice Mail A variation of electronic mail is **voice mail.** It is computer-based, but the end product is a recorded message, not hard copy. The spoken message is converted by the voice mail system into digital form and stored in the computer's memory. Using a telephone, the message can be recalled by the receiving party and reconverted into voice form. Several characteristics distinguish voice mail from standard answering machines. Recipients can fast-scan the messages, keep them, or forward them to a third party. Senders can edit their messages. Voice mail also allows for longer messages than do answering machines.

Teleconferencing The feasibility of teleconferencing has existed for about a decade; however, despite the benefits of teleconferencing, it has not yet received wide acceptance. Teleconferencing allows two or more locations to use electronic and/or image-producing means to communicate (Figure 9-6). (Images may be still frames or full video.) It appears to have many benefits. It encourages managerial productivity because managers do not have to spend long hours traveling. It also reduces travel costs. Finally, teleconferencing appears to give a corporation a competitive edge.

However, despite these benefits, cost has been the main drawback to teleconferencing's success. For example, Atlantic Richfield Company (Arco) has spent approximately $20 million to upgrade its teleconferencing capabilities. Not too many organizations are willing or able to make that kind of investment. It should also be noted that the primary factor in the high cost of telecommunications is the cost of the communication line itself.

In addition, many executives have expressed skepticism about teleconferencing, feeling that they do not appear as businesslike on the screen as they do in person. On the television screen, they are more aware of trivial things like disheveled hair.

Telecommuting Probably the most exciting prospect for the automated office is employees commuting to the office by computer rather than in

FIGURE 9-6 Teleconferencing

person. Telecommuting, using a computer hookup between office and home, is already being tried by some companies on an experimental basis. The system has many advantages in areas where office rent is high and mass transit systems or parking facilities are inadequate and in situa tions that do not require frequent face-to-face meetings among the office workers. Telecommuting provides greater flexibility for disabled employees and working parents.

Being such a radical departure from past practices, telecommuting is not universally approved, even theoretically. Employees are not sure they have the discipline to work as well at home as they do among congenial office surroundings. Managers fear that out of sight may mean out of control. Thus, telecommuting is likely to appear first at the managerial level and filter down as it demonstrates its worth. Salespeople, who are routinely away from their offices, have been demonstrating the utility of telecommuting with the portable computers and tiny printers that accompany them on their sales trips.

The portable computer can be used to type memos, correspondence, or reports. In addition, some portable computers have editing capability similar to that of a word processor. With a portable computer and a modem, the person can send information over the telephone lines (Figure 9-7). Once the information has been received at the office, phone messages, edited copy, or other such information from the office can be sent back.

Also, a salesperson can enter orders into the computer's memory; receipts are printed and the computer at the office has the information to update inventory and customer records and make out shipping instructions. All this is done with no clerical personnel; therefore, day or night, salespeople can keep in touch with their office.

COTTAGE KEYERS
People who work at home and transmit work to the company by cassette tapes or other means.

Blue Cross and Blue Shield of Columbia, South Carolina, has been experimenting with a form of telecommuting it calls **cottage keyers**—workers who process claims at home on personal computers and then transmit them, by cassette tapes, to the company's central computers. Reports are that the experiment is very successful.

FIGURE 9-7 Telecommuting Terminal

William Bates, an independent computer consultant, is also a cottage keyer. Bates does all his work at home. He does free lance work for Atari and is author of *The Computer Cookbook—How to Create Small Computer Systems That Work for You*. His updated version of *The Computer Cookbook*, written on his terminal, will be sent from his home computer to a computer in Japan via satellite. When his copy reaches Japan, a word processor at the book's publisher will produce a copy of the manuscript. The copy will be ready to photograph for the photo-offset printing process.

Obviously, the nature of the business will always dictate whether telecommuting is an option and to what degree it can be used. One futurist, Jack M. Nilles, director of interdisciplinary programs at the University of Southern California, estimates that by 1990, 15 to 20 percent of American workers will be working from their homes.

Information Retrieval

Because computerized information is stored in a manner not easily transcribed by the users, information retrieval is an important part of office automation. In the past, users often had to copy entire reports to locate information they needed. To avoid this expensive and time-consuming process, an electronic file management system was necessary.

Data-base management and text management systems have been designed to allow users direct access to company information. The information may be in data, text, image, or voice form and users may locate the specific item they want.

Information retrieval is not limited to internal sources. Companies may subscribe to online information services (Figure 9-8). By accessing the

FIGURE 9-8 Online Information Service.
Here an office worker accesses one of the databases available from The Source.

online data bases, workers receive additional information and save considerable research time.

Support Systems

The last area of office technology is support systems. Basically, there are two types of support systems: personal support systems and management support systems.

Personal support systems allow individuals to use computers to keep track of personal work-related information. These systems have little value to the overall operation of the company other than organizing individual employee activities. One popular application of a personal support system is an electronically-posted list of "things to do." Other examples are time sheet reporting and keeping track of one's own travel expense reports or insurance claims.

Management support systems, like personal support systems, are also administrative oriented. However, they are used within the company operations. Common examples of management support systems include appointment calendars and business-related diaries. These records are usually prepared by office workers for management use.

LOCAL AREA NETWORKS: INTEGRATION OF CAPABILITIES

LOCAL AREA NETWORKS (LANS)
Linking computer systems in adjacent offices and buildings for intercomputer communication.

Some office designers contend that automation is a meaningless concept unless it involves integration of capabilities.

This integration is accomplished through **local area networks (LANs).** As you recall from Chapter 5, networks imply a linking of CPUs and terminals by a communication system. A local area network is a special type of network that operates within a well-defined and self-enclosed area such as a small office building. The communication stations are usually linked by cable and are generally within 1,000 feet of each other.

The major advantage of LANs is that users at different terminals are able to share files, devices, and programs (Figure 9-9). Under this approach, work stations become multifunctional with word and data processing, communication, information retrieval, and support capabilities. LANs eliminate needless duplication of equipment, data bases, and actions. As a result, LANs provide the potential for maximum operating effectiveness by reducing time and cost factors. In addition, as companies grow they may find LANs necessary to keep competitive and up to date.

There are presently a few disadvantages with LANs. Although the technology exists. They are not widely adopted. Implementing a local area network is not cost effective in most cases. Finally, because the technology is relatively new, some compatibility problems are blocking the goal of attaining intercomputer communication. However, it is likely that in time the disadvantages will be reduced and the advantages will lure companies into full-scale office automation.

ERGONOMICS

Office automation systems, versatile as they are, still are less than perfect. Constant checking of the text on the CRT screen can create eye strain, leading to fatigue. The issue of whether the small amount of radiation given off by the screen is hazardous has not been resolved to the satisfaction of all concerned. As a result of such problems, the new field of ergonomics is growing rapidly.

Ergonomics, formerly termed "human factors engineering," is the science of changing the work conditions to suit the worker. For example, studies of people using computers for data processing have found that stress resulting from computer use is related to absenteeism and a high annual turnover rate.

ERGONOMICS
The science of changing working conditions to suit the worker.

In addition to creating stress, working at computer terminals may cause physical problems. Recently, Verbatim Corporation, a supplier of magnetic data storage media, sponsored a study using a sample of 1,263 office workers in companies of various sizes across the nation. The leading

FIGURE 9-9 Local Area Network

FIGURE 9-10 Ergonomic Workstation

complaints among the workers were eyestrain and backstrain. A high percentage of those working with automated machines requested better lighting, and a majority of workers were in favor of periodic rest breaks.

To overcome some of the physical problems created by standard office equipment and computer terminals, specially designed hardware and furniture are being introduced, such as terminal display screens that tilt to user preference and detachable keyboards to reduce muscle fatigue (Figure 9-10).

Work stations should be large enough to accommodate computer terminals, and there should be diffuse lighting over the work station. Most people, however, are unaware that different lighting conditions are needed for VDT work compared with general office work.

ISSUE

ARE COMPUTERS BREAKING DOWN INTERPERSONAL COMMUNICATIONS?

The most vital function of any office is communication, and effective communication depends on timely, accurate, and relevant information. Specific benefits have been realized as a result of the implementation of computers in the workplace; however, other, potentially threatening human factors are surfacing.

Office automation has enhanced the communication process through improved access to information, increased information reliability, and faster movement of information. Together, these factors result in greater white-collar productivity.

According to a study conducted by the international consulting firm, Booz, Allen and Hamilton, the average office worker wastes 25 percent of the working day on such activities as waiting for meetings to start, making travel arrangements, and attempting to get associates on the telephone. The firm estimated that office automation could raise average office worker productivity by 15 percent. This increased productivity translates into an increase in net income that is more than enough to cover high-tech equipment expenses.

The current emphasis on the network approach of integrating office technologies offers even greater possibilities of operating effectiveness and flexibility. Multifunction work stations can allow access to word and data-processing capabilities, electronic mail services, information retrieval from the company data base or online data bases, and teleconferencing or videoconferencing.

The new technology has had a major impact on the office worker. The most evident change is in the nature of the work. Since office automation is technically oriented, workers must concentrate more on the activities being performed. Workers focus their attention on reading and manipulating the symbols required to communicate with the machines. As a result, unnecessary office conversations are greatly reduced. Furthermore, there is no need to leave the multifunction work station to deliver memorandums or locate reports; therefore, other opportunities for interacting with coworkers are also limited.

Over time such computerized employee services may block interpersonal relationships. For example, electronic bulletin boards containing notices and news items may eliminate the social gatherings associated with the conventional bulletin board. Likewise, employee services could also take on a different dimension. Reservations for special vacation packages offered through the company via the work station, may eliminate the chance of socializing with others while waiting in line. The exchange of useful information on projects or performance and the establishment of friendships, characteristic of traditional work settings, may be severely diminished.

Office automation may also lead to significant behavior changes in workers. To study the effects of human/machine relationships, a new field of psychology, "tech psych," has emerged. Even though tech psych is relatively new, some interesting observations have been made indicating that computer communication could be a barrier to overall communication.

Computer communications seem to suggest a loss of the human connection; instead of a personalized touch, messages are transferred from machine to machine in a structured and routine fashion. Communicating by machines is usually a one-way process; a message is either sent or retrieved. Immediate feedback is not received. For interaction to occur, additional electronic transactions are necessary. The parties involved are unable to interpret the nuances of meaning conveyed in face-to-face situations by tone of voice and nonverbal signals.

Valerie Geller of Bell Labs conducted an

ISSUE

experiment that measured the "psychological arousal level" of various communication alternatives. In order of importance, face-to-face communications ranked highest and typewritten messages the lowest. The study found that business people prefer face-to-face communications, especially for important exchanges. The other alternatives, videoconferences and telephone conversations, ranked better than the typewritten message—but still were inadequate substitutes.

Another experiment, conducted by Sara Kiesler at Carnegie Mellon University (described in the issue section of Chapter 8), indicated that although computer discussions permitted strangers to break initial communication barriers more easily and provided an equal opportunity to air opinions, the parties tended to be more argumentative and abusive than in face-to-face conversations. This verbal overkill, known as "flaring," caused by anonymity as well as by unintended distortions, creates problems in the communication process.

As workers spend more time communicating with machines rather than interacting in human conversations, there is a danger that general communication skills will weaken—a phenomenon observed among computer buffs, video arcade enthusiasts, and other high-tech specialists. The potential long-range effects of this behavior are frightening. Workers could become as functional as the machines they operate; in essence, extensions of the machine.

As projects become more individualized due to the integrated capabilities of the multifunction work stations, organizational goals such as teamwork, participative management, and other group-oriented practices could suffer by the deterioration of human-to-human communication. More important, though, is the question of whether a reduction of social outlets will affect the overall quality of job performance, the worker's job satisfaction, and his or her ability to relate to others outside the work environment.

Because work is a major activity in most of our lives, and because computers are becoming such an important part of the workplace, it is essential that we become aware of the implications and any effects of increased automation in the job world.

SUMMARY POINTS

- Software is available to assist the farmer in finding a low-cost feed program. Environmental hazards and spraying costs can be reduced because computers can be programmed to detect outbreaks of disease and pests in the farmer's fields and orchards.
- Fire fighting is more efficient in departments using computers to handle emergency calls. Information about storage of hazardous materials and persons to be notified in case of emergency can be stored in the system to be available if the building or residence catches fire.
- Newspaper reporters are using desk-top terminals instead of typewriters to produce copy.
- Word processing has become the most solidly established part of the automated office of today.
- It is estimated that a secretary's productivity can be increased 25 to 200 percent using word processing.
- A dictionary option is available for most word processors; some programs correct misspelled words when they are located.
- Typewritten copy can be input into the word processor many times faster by optical character recognition (OCR) than by manual input.
- Electronic mail and voice mail are being used in office communications to store and display messages.
- Teleconferencing is being used by executives to reduce travel costs and long hours on the road.
- Telecommuting allows individuals to work away from the office using a computer hookup.
- One objective of local area networks (LANs) is to bring about intercomputer communication within the office.
- Persons using computer terminals are complaining of stress and physical problems; as a result, ergonomics—altering the work environment for the benefit of the workers—is a growing issue among office workers.

REVIEW QUESTIONS

1. Name several ways computers are being used on the farm.
2. How can computers help fire fighters?
3. Name the ways computers are being used in the newsroom.
4. What are some of the common predictions about the effects of the computer on the workplace?
5. Why is it unlikely that the office as we know it will change its appearance much over the next few years?
6. Why does office automation not necessarily mean office integration?
7. What will probably be the chief features of the automated office?
8. How does word processing differ from simple typing and copying?
9. What are the advantages within the office for optical character recognition (OCR)?

10. How does electronic mail differ from voice mail?
11. Why is there managerial resistance to telecommuting?
12. How large a percentage of the American work force may be telecommuting by 1990, according to one futurist?
13. What are "cottage keyers"?
14. Explain ergonomics and give examples of physical problems caused by computer terminals.

DISCUSSION QUESTIONS

1. Do you believe the benefits of multifunction work stations outweigh what could happen to interpersonal relations among office workers? Why?
2. Keeping in mind the present technology, predict the office of the future. How close are we to the office of the future?
3. Although teleconferencing is feasible, do the benefits outweigh the cost?
4. With office workers using a computer hookup between office and home or office and travel, will this eventually create problems in communication between managers and staff?
5. What attitude should the employer take to ergonomics? Keep in mind that work conditions may have to be changed to prevent computer terminal operators from developing physical problems.

CHAPTER 10

COMPUTERS IN BUSINESS AND INDUSTRY

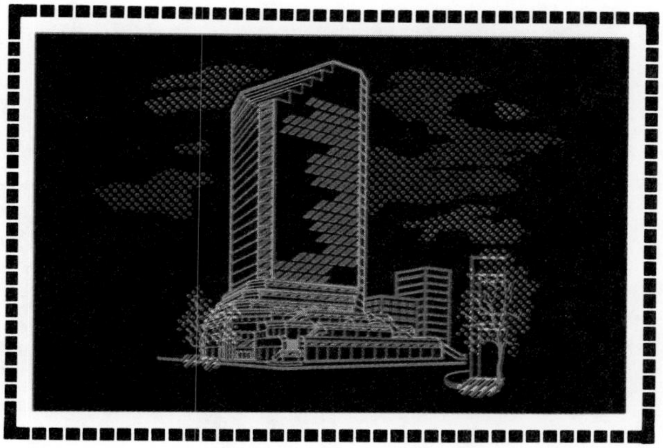

OUTLINE

ARTICLE

WELCOME TO THE HOTEL INTERACTIVE

"Touch Me," flirts an unusual television screen in the lobby of the Boston Sheraton Hotel. Curious guests take up the offer and immediately find themselves interacting with a computerized video information system called Teletouch.

In place of the screen's beckoning invitation comes a listing of categories—such as sight-seeing attractions in the city and suburbs, current entertainment around town, where to shop, and airline schedules. If you're interested in buying gifts, just touch "Shopping" and a menu of major department stores flashes onto the screen. Another touch brings a specific store's address and the type of merchandise it carries. And you don't have to search for your notepad to jot down the address: the system can even provide you with an instant hard copy of the video information.

Aimed primarily at helping business travelers, the Sheraton system is part of a microcomputer-controlled video network being tested by Interaction Systems Inc. . . .

Following the local trial, Interaction intends to place its terminals nationwide. Walter Winshall, Interaction president, says plans are in the works to add a range of other material to the system such as news, sports, and ski reports.

The idea of making interactive systems available to travelers has caught the interest of hoteliers. Hilton—the chain calling itself "America's Business Address"—plans some day to offer these services right in its private guest rooms. . . .

Imitations of the "hotel interactive" have been springing up around the country and have been a great hit with business travelers. The success of hotels with computer capabilities illustrates the degree to which our businesses and industries are beginning to use, expand, and depend on their computers.

INTRODUCTION

As computers have infiltrated American society, nowhere have they had more impact than in business and industry. Part of this is due to the fact that using computers speeds operations, reduces mistakes in calculations, and gives companies efficient, cost-effective analyses that would be nearly impossible with manual operations. Another major reason for the great impact of computers is the domino effect. If Business A speeds up its operations through the use of computers, then Business B must also computerize to compete. The same applies to the use of automation in industry. Once one factory incorporates automation, they set a standard to be imitated and repeated.

These factors have caused a phenomenal increase in the number and types of computer applications in business and industry. Some experts even claim that these computer applications are helping to trigger a new type of industrial revolution.

COMPUTERS IN BUSINESS

Because businesses are so varied in purpose and structure, it is nearly impossible to examine all business uses of computers. However, it is possible to look at how computers are used in most businesses or at least the average business. Of course, specific businesses will have special uses of computers. For example, a retail store might be interested in

Computers greatly enhance the architectural design process.

computerizing inventory, whereas a stock brokerage would be more interested in computerizing the files of its customers. In general, though, there are four areas in which computers are used in most businesses: (1) finance, (2) management, (3) sales, and (4) publishing.

Computers in Finance

In the past, financial transactions were tediously calculated, either by hand or by calculator, and recorded using pencil and paper. This method has rapidly become obsolete as computers have moved into virtually every area of finance. To illustrate this point, let us examine how computers are being used in the areas of general accounting, financial analysis, and information management.

General Accounting General accounting software is a very popular type of business software. In fact, it was the first business software to be offered for personal computers.

Some of the most common uses of general accounting software are in preparing checks, reports, and forms. Forms, because of their repetitive nature, are well suited to computer processing. Form-oriented accounting packages are responsible for the great number of "personalized" form letters travelling through the U.S. Postal Service. For example, general accounting packages that output reports keep you informed of everything from your grades to your monthly gas bill. Checks seem to be the most popular type of form output by these programs—at least with those who receive them.

These examples are of simple accounting programs. Each program performs basically one task. A check writer writes checks, but it does not

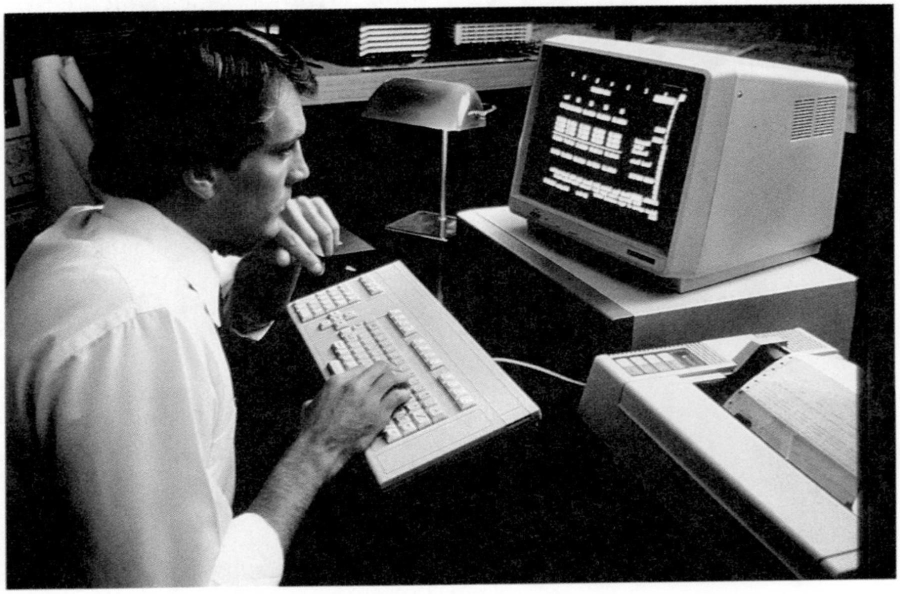

This executive uses his computer to analyze financial information.

provide productivity reports on the worker being paid. In the same manner, report programs always report on your grades, but rarely include information on your school status or tuition. This is not the case with all general accounting software.

In addition to the standard accounting functions, such as inventory control, general ledger, payroll, and accounts receivable, many programs are designed to incorporate more than one task. These more sophisticated packages are especially useful to businesses that have computerized most or all of their accounting processes. For example, a wholesaler may have an accounting program that records sales, maintains inventory, and handles billing as well. These types of programs help to eliminate repetition of incoming data and also eliminate confusion by performing related tasks at the same time.

Millwide information systems provide production management with concise, up-to-the-minute information about the entire production operation of a pulp and paper mill. Such systems allow managers to make quicker, better decisions about running their operations.

There are, however, advantages to single-purpose accounting programs. In particular, they can be used to ease the transition from manual to computerized processing by allowing the business to computerize one task at a time. This prevents problems arising from a crash conversion that would require immediate and intensive retraining of personnel. The gradual introduction of single-task accounting programs allows the business to implement the conversion in subtle stages.

Although this section focuses on general accounting programs, it should be noted that there are also specific accounting programs designed for specific businesses. These packages take into account any special reports or terminology that might be used in, for example, dentistry or retailing.

ELECTRONIC SPREADSHEET **A large computerized grid divided into rows and columns; used for financial analysis.**

Financial Analysis Today the most common use of the computer in financial analysis is the **electronic spreadsheet**. VisiCalc, developed by Daniel Bricklin (see profile), and introduced in October of 1979, was one of the first of the electronic spreadsheets and became the best-selling business application program ever introduced.

A spreadsheet is a large grid that is divided into rows and columns (Figure 10-1). Such spreadsheets are used to design budgets, record sales, produce profit-and-loss statements, perform general accounting and bookkeeping, and aid in financial analysis. Although electronic spreadsheets are useful in many areas of business, nowhere are they as helpful as in financial analysis where projections must be made to determine profit margins, sales, and long-term strategies. The reason for the great impact of the electronic spreadsheet in this area is its ability to quickly and accurately answer "what if" questions. This is accomplished

FIGURE 10-1 Electronic Spreadsheet

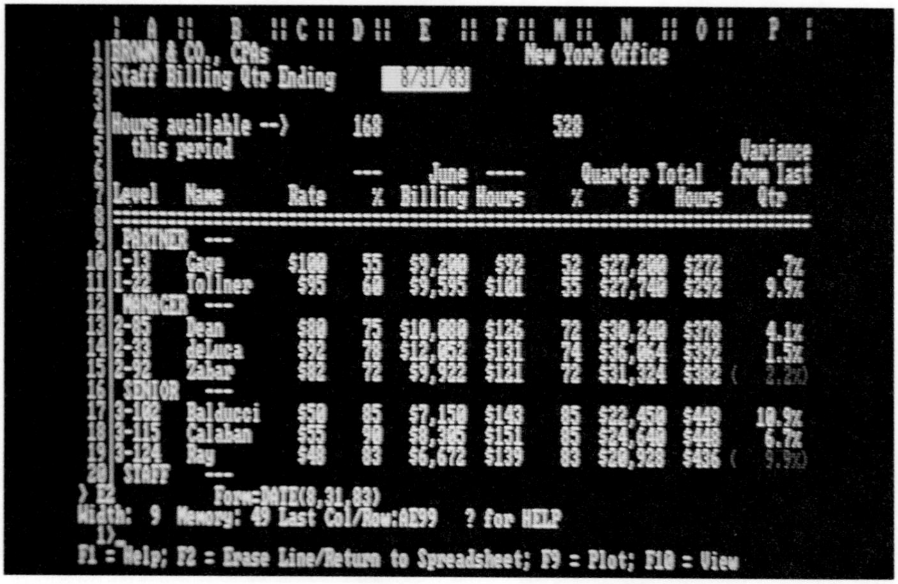

PROFILE

DANIEL BRICKLIN

VisiCalc is a software package that helps businesses in their financial planning by showing the overall results of various shifts in capital. This "electronic spreadsheet" was created by Daniel Bricklin to simplify the process and minimize the kind of errors that are common when calculations are done manually.

Bricklin, who had worked with computers from the time he was in his teens, came up with the idea for VisiCalc in 1978 while he was a student at the Harvard Business School. He and his friend Robert Frankston developed the software. (Its name stands for "visible calculator.")

As useful as VisiCalc was, its invention earned little attention and even less excitement in the business and computer communities until Daniel Fylstra was put in charge of marketing. In 1982 Bricklin's company, Software Arts, of Wellesley, Massachusetts, had sales of $7 million; and by early 1983 approximately 400,000 copies of VisiCalc were in consumer hands.

by recalculating all figures dependent on the variable changed.

For example, let us imagine that the financial planner for Company X has just worked out a projected profit margin for the third quarter. The projection shows that profits will be down and the business will be in serious financial trouble. The financial planner could then enter a series of "what if" questions using the spreadsheet to determine the most effective way to eliminate or reduce the loss. He or she could tell immediately the effect of laying off say, 10 workers, by entering a new figure for employee wages. On the other hand, if the company were doing well, the planner could check the effects of giving all workers a 10 percent raise or a special Christmas bonus. In any case, the virtue of the electronic spreadsheet is that once the initial figures have been entered, it takes only a matter of seconds to answer "what if" questions because the only thing that must be reentered is the variable (such as pay rate) that the financial analyst has changed for the new calculation. Before computerization, each change meant filling out a new spreadsheet—a time-consuming task that served to restrict the number of "what if" questions that analysts would ask. Of course, the more limited the number of questions, the more limited the possibilities and the less chance that the optimum solution would be found.

Information Management Information management software for business computers gives them the capability of an electronic filing system. Data entered into selected categories can be retrieved by specifying, for example, those files on employees receiving a certain salary or employees hired on a certain date. Such a system makes file retrieval faster and more flexible, in addition to decreasing the amount of storage space required.

Bell Operating Companies are increasing their use of an interactive computer graphics system (shown here) to design electronic central offices.

"Intergraph" graphics work station used for automated maping of gas and electric service facilities. Through a data base management program these work stations provide all the information necessary for Pacific Gas & Electric's major facilities reports.

Small information management software packages designed for personal computers enable a person's appointments to be recorded and recalled as necessary. Some systems in this category also maintain expense account records.

Computers in Management

The essence of business is communication, and computer graphics are becoming an essential part of business communication. In the average business, computers are used to produce graphs that keep management informed and up to date on company statistics, sales records, and the like.

It is well known in business that executives make 80 percent of their decisions based on 20 percent of the data, that 20 percent representing the core data necessary to run their businesses. Finding that data can be difficult for managers if they are presented with pages upon pages of data. Graphically displayed data makes the task much easier. It is widely agreed that such displays can help managers to make better decisions. Also, comparisons, relationships and trends, and essential points can be clarified more easily with graphics. Finally, computer graphics are the most cost-effective means of presenting the manager with that 20 percent core data.

"Let's see if the computer can tell us why we're losing money."

Business graphics have come a long way from the once standard black line bar graph. Although bar graphs are still used, they are generally brightened up a bit. Pie charts, bar graphs, line and area graphs that are brightly colored and clearly marked can be especially effective in communicating core data (Figure 10-2). Executives prefer receiving their information through graphics not only because graphs are attractive but also because they are quick and effective. Like the engineers and artists

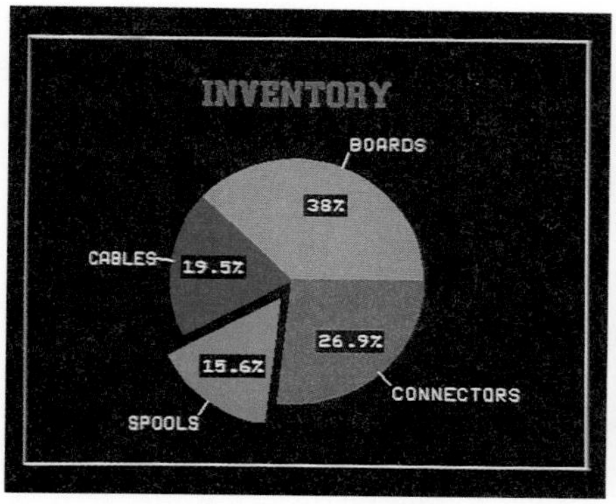

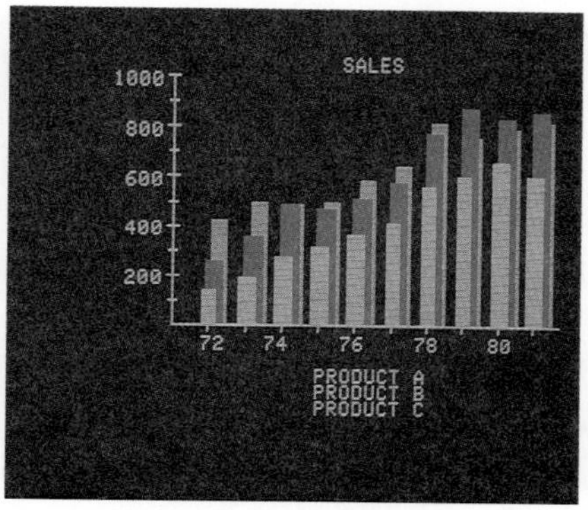

FIGURE 10-2 Business Graphics

who use the computer's graphic capabilities, executives also feel that a picture is worth a thousand words.

Because these graphs play such a vital role in decision making, many software packages have been developed for use by managers in the business area. The first graphics software package for the personal computer became available in 1979, and the popularity of business graphics software has been growing ever since.

The computer graphics packages for businesses vary. Some packages display the bar graphs and pie charts directly on the visual display screen. Other packages allow for the drawing to be printed directly by a

Through a central computer facility in Findlay, Ohio, headquarters of Marathon Pipe Line Company, specialists operate a complex, 4,200-mile pipeline network. At the touch of a few keys on the computer terminal console, the operators control more than 500 valves and 200 pumping units that move crude oil and refined products from Wyoming, Louisiana and Texas across much of middle America.

PROFILE

FRANK R. LAUTENBERG

Automatic Data Processing Inc., a national giant in payroll services, was founded by Frank R. Lautenberg and Henry Taub.

Born in 1924 in Patterson, New Jersey, Lautenberg was a studious youngster. After graduating from high school, he served in the army during World War II. With the aid of the G.I. Bill, he attended Columbia University and earned a bachelor of science degree in 1949.

During Lautenberg's first job with Prudential, he encountered Henry Taub, who operated a small business that performed manual payroll services. In 1953 Lautenberg was offered and accepted a position moonlighting for Taub's company. Later the company was renamed Automatic Data Processing (ADP) and converted to computerized equipment to perform the payroll services. ADP was the first large-scale service bureau that incorporated the use of batch processing, a relatively new concept.

Lautenberg, a multimillionaire businessman always active in community affairs, won election to the U.S. Senate from New Jersey in 1982.

SLIDE SHOW PACKAGE
A computer graphics package that displays the graphics in a timed sequence on the terminal; similar to a slide show.

printer or plotter. A third type of package is the **slide show package**, which allows entire series of graphs to be sequenced in timed intervals for display on the computer screen. Some of the packages even comeequipped with various typefaces or borders, which can be used to further enhance the charts.

Computers in Sales

Businesses use computers in a variety of ways to facilitate sales, record sales, update inventories after sales, and make projections based on expected sales. In addition to these standard functions, some computers are also being used in customer contact.

The Helena Rubenstein cosmetic firm served as a triggering force in the movement of computers onto the sales floor. The cosmetic computer assisted customers in their decisions about perfumes, makeup, and colorings. The firm's effort was very successful and inspired similar applications by other companies.

Robert J. Hennessey is the man responsible for a computer system that assists vinyl flooring salespeople in selling their product. Hennessey got his idea after reading about the electronic selling approach used by Helena Rubenstein in 1978. Hennessey noted that the same decisions had to be made by customers looking at vinyl flooring, and in 1981 he began work on his idea. It became reality in May 1982 and he named his system Compu-flor. In addition to the computer, the system includes a slide show featuring television personality Ed McMahon. The computer prompts the customer by asking questions like "What is the predominant style of furniture in your room?" and providing such possible answers as modern, traditional, antique, and so on. On the basis of the customer's answers, Compu-flor presents only 10 samples of flooring.

Sporting goods stores, such as this one, are taking advantage of the effectiveness computers offer in recording sales and inventory of merchandise.

The questions were developed after a long process of interviews and surveys with retailers and salespeople. Still in its testing stages, the success of the program hasn't yet been established. However, several salespeople feel it helps customers decide more quickly. In fact, one salesperson added, "It's crazy, but people seem to be more likely to believe what the machine tells them than what a salesman tells them."

Computers in Publishing

Almost all businesses require some type of publishing, whether it be customer information pamphlets, quarterly reports, or entire books. Publishing itself is one of the largest businesses in this country.

Publishing, consisting of a series of discrete operations culminating in a final product and using language as its medium, is a prime candidate for computerization.

First, the original manuscript may be written on a word processor. This is often the case in business because when many people have to approve a document, many revisions are usually required. Word processing makes these updates easier and faster.

Once the manuscript has been written on the word-processing equipment, the writer can either transmit the manuscript over the phone lines

AccuRay 1180 MICRO Paper Machine control system monitors and controls the complex process of making paper from wood fiber and water.

via a modem to the publisher's computer or simply mail the floppy disks or tapes. The publishing company can then proceed to edit the material on its word processor and send the edited version to the typesetter's computer. Once that computer has typeset the manuscript, it may be printed out by a high-quality printer, such as a laser printer. The manuscript need never be written on paper until it is actually printed for distribution.

Unfortunately, this is an idealized account of the process. Although this sequence of events does occur, it is rare because of problems with hardware/software compatibility. The major problem is that a writer may work on any one of 150 word processors, none of which are compatible with each other. So if the author has a different word processor than the publisher, the publisher's computer will not accept the material. In the same way, the publisher's computer must be compatible with the one used by the typesetter. In addition to the technical problems, some editors are opposed to word processing because they fear losing their jobs. Sean Morrison, assistant professor of communications at Boston University, estimates that 40 to 60 percent of an editor's time is spent on repetitive tasks. The computer is eliminating many of these tasks.

For example, where an editor may go through an entire manuscript changing the spelling of "recieve" to "receive," the computer could do this in one step. The editor would simply enter a command telling the computer to change every occurrence of "recieve" to "receive."

Some writers complain that they are unable to get a full 8½ × 11-inch page onto the terminal screen at one time. These people prefer to see their work on paper and they still use typewriters. Problems can also occur with phone lines. Random House used an Osborne computer to send files by phone to typesetters and found dozens of errors in the printed copy. The errors were the result of static on the telephone lines.

Not all publishers, however, are opposed to becoming computerized. Time, Inc., McGraw-Hill, and Reader's Digest Association, the three leading publishers in the United States, have already computerized the editorial operations of their book divisions. These three companies, especially Reader's Digest, already had standard formats for their work, enabling them to computerize more quickly than other companies.

COMPUTERS IN INDUSTRY

The financial and bookkeeping uses of computers apply to both business and industry. However, industry also uses computers in designing and manufacturing products. It does this in two ways: (1) with the use of CAD/CAM and (2) with robotics.

CAD/CAM

One of the fastest growing areas of computer use in industry is **computer-aided design (CAD).** CAD allows the engineer to design, draft, and analyze a prospective product using computer graphics on a video terminal (Figure 10-3). The designer, working with full-color graphics, may easily make changes, so he or she can test many versions of a product before the first prototype is ever built. The system is also able to analyze the designs for poor tolerance between parts and for stress points. This can

COMPUTER-AIDED DESIGN (CAD)
The use of the computer in the design process.

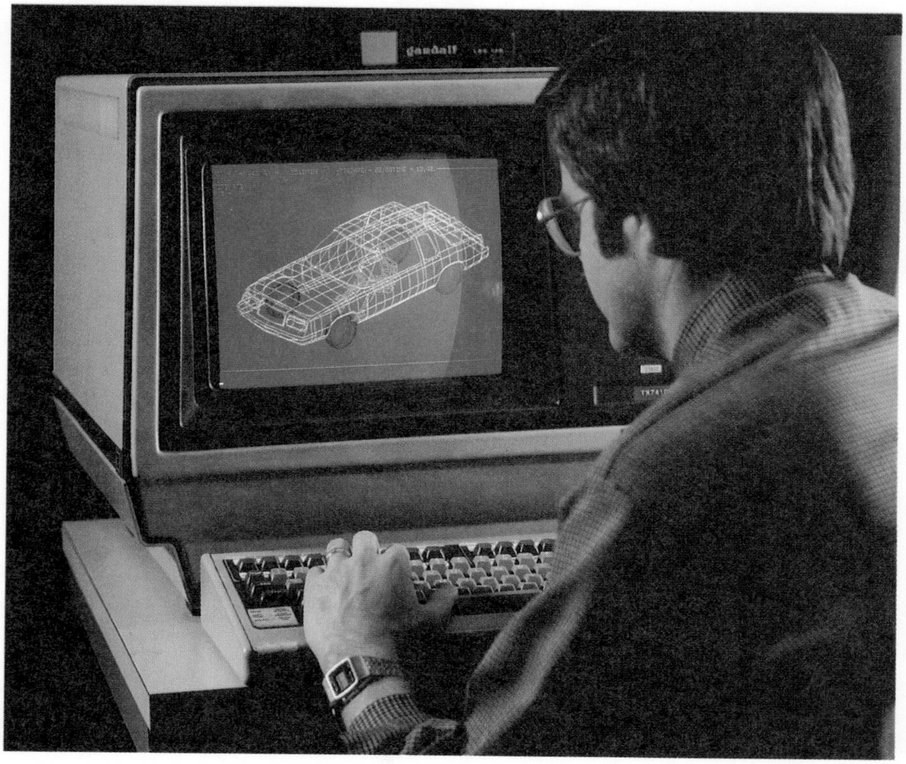

FIGURE 10-3 CAD

Computer-aided design, an increasingly important tool for many development areas, helps an engineer visualize a possible terminal for the Information Age.

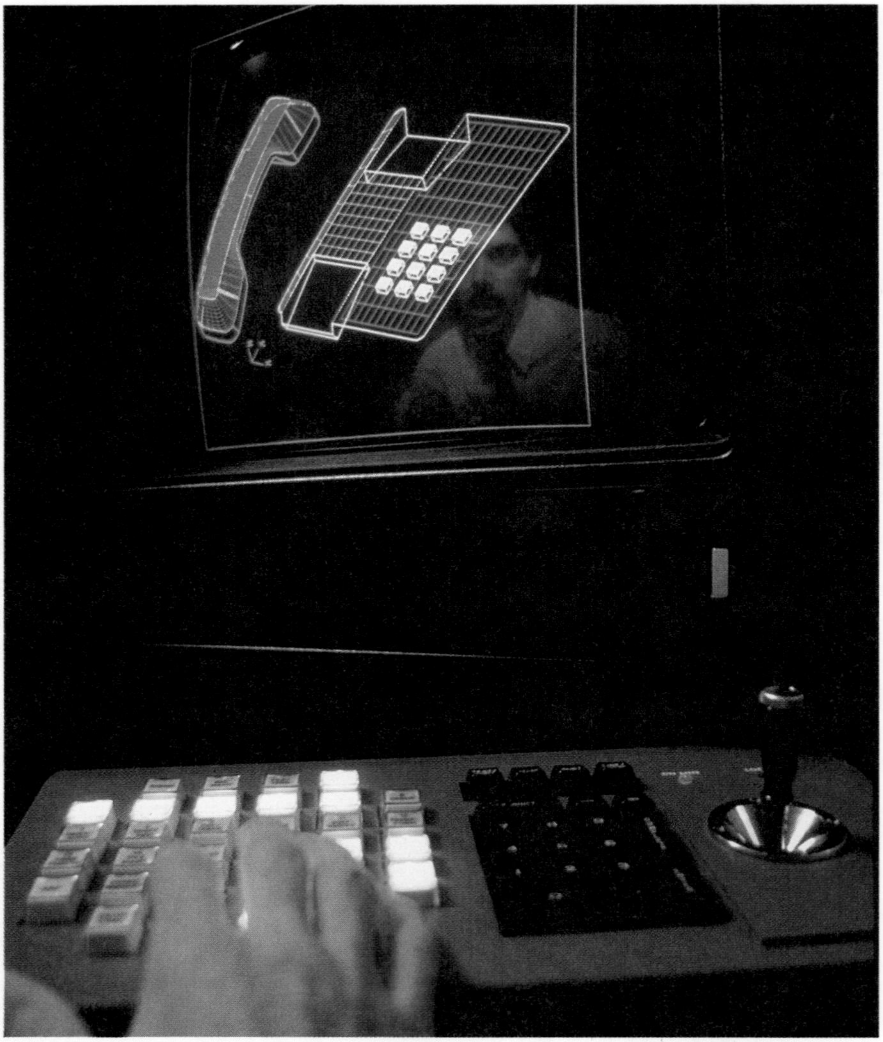

COMPUTER-AIDED MANUFACTURING (CAM)
The use of the computer in the manufacturing process.

save a great deal of money by eliminating defective designs *before* the money is spent to build them.

Computer-aided design is often coupled with **computer-aided manufacturing (CAM)** and the combination is referred to as CAD/CAM. Using CAD/CAM, the engineer can analyze not only the product but also the manufacturing process.

Once the rough design of the product has been entered into the computer, the engineer can have the computer simulate any manufacturing step (Figure 10-4). For example, if the product must be drilled, the engineer can create a computerized drill. This drill can be guided, either by the engineer or the computer, and simulate the drilling process. This can be very helpful in two ways. First, it should indicate any major problems that may be encountered on the assembly line—*before* it is even set up.

FIGURE 10-4 CAM

Second, the computer will record exactly how the tool moved and will store that information on magnetic tape. If that factory uses robotics and computer-controlled machines as part of its CAM system, those tapes can be used to drive the actual machines in manufacturing the product. In this way CAD/CAM can take the engineer from idea to final product.

The CAD/CAM market has exploded in recent years. Between 1976 and 1980 worldwide sales of CAD systems quadrupled. To best examine the impact of these systems, let us look at the companies that are using them.

The leaders in this field have been the aerospace and automotive industries. In the manufacture of airplanes, CAD/CAM has proved to be especially cost-effective. McDonnell Douglas used to employ 12 people to manually bend tubing for a single F-18 fighter. Now only three are required: one to watch the machine and two to assemble the tubing. Formerly, as many as 100 tubes per aircraft didn't fit. Now, using CAD/CAM, only four have to be readjusted. Most significant, before CAD/CAM the tube-bending process took six weeks. Now it takes 18 minutes.

In auto manufacturing CAD/CAM is being used for a variety of purposes. It enabled Ford to design a highly efficient engine for its new Escort and Lynx subcompacts in "record time." At Fisher Body computer-designed cars hit computer-designed bumps on the terminal screen, while engineers look on, checking for design flaws. General Motors has used CAD/CAM to cut the production time for car body components in half.

The production of VLSI (Very Large Scale Integrated circuits) is so detailed that it almost requires CAD/CAM. Using traditional methods, designing a microprocessor took at least four people a year. CAD allows one person to complete the job in four months. In addition, checking the

CAD/CAM AT NIKE

In an industry as competitive as the modern athletic shoe industry, the speed with which a new shoe model can be designed and manufactured is critical. Speed and accuracy in producing a new shoe model at NIKE is made possible in part by CAD/CAM (computer-aided design/computer-aided manufacturing). While CAD/CAM technology has been commonplace for years in the automotive and aerospace industries, its use by NIKE in the athletic shoe industry is revolutionary. It is a unique tool serving the Product Development area by decreasing the time necessary to bring a new design into production.

In the CAD stage of the development process, the designer inputs the specifications of the new shoe pattern into a computer graphics terminal (photo a). Each graphics terminal is connected to a sophisticated host computer. CAD technology permits a designer to create and modify computer-generated visual displays of new designs quickly and accurately. The image shown on the screen (photo b) is an air-sole mold. The final results of this process far exceed what could be expected from a conventional draftsman (photos c and d).

(a)

(b)

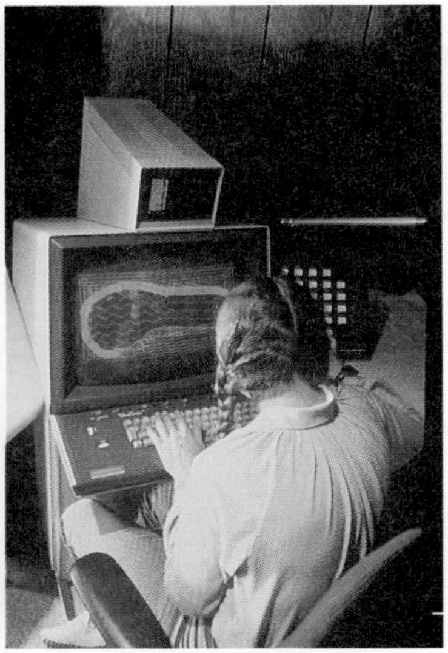

(c)

(d)

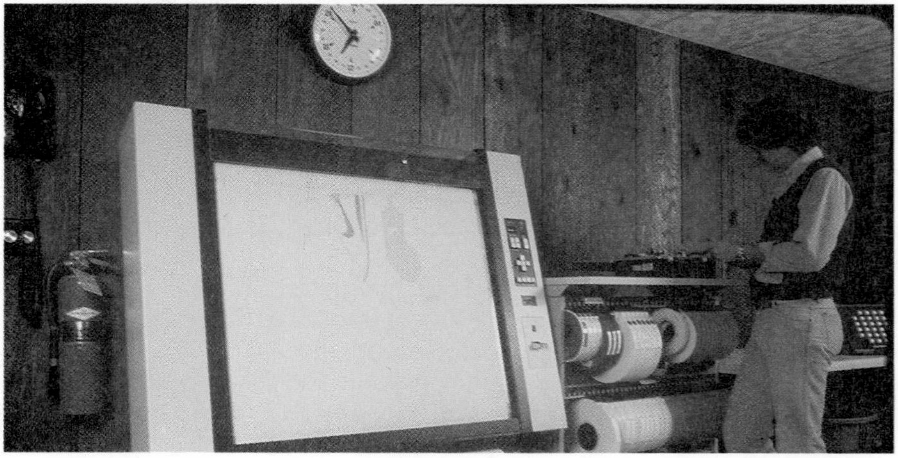

(e)

(f)

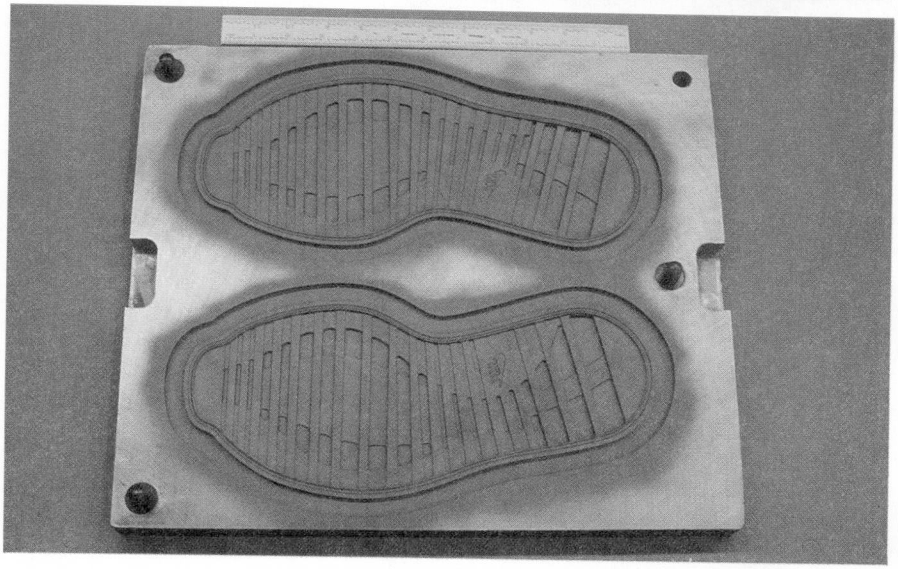

(g)

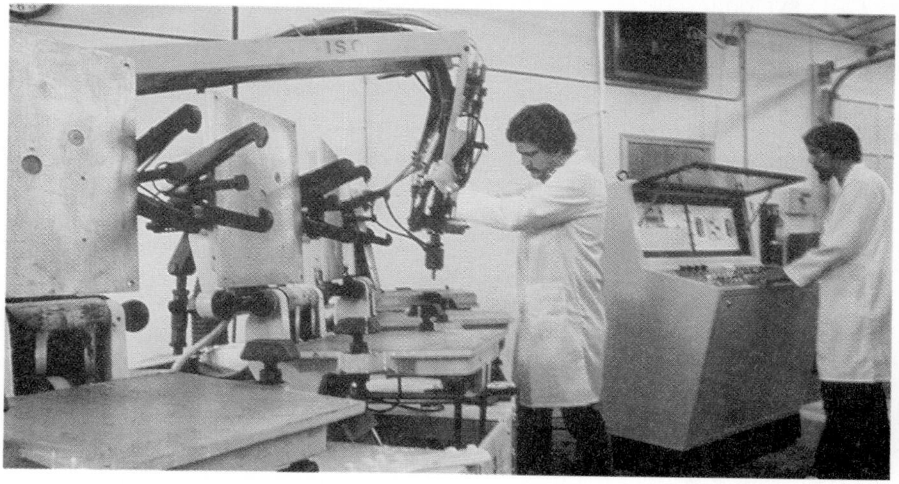

At the appropriate time, all pertinent information pertaining to the manufacture of the mold is passed from the CAD area to the CAM area. A computer in the CAM area instructs a numerical control milling machine how to machine the mold block (photo e). First, the milling machine mills out a sample of the design from a block of low-cost test material. This test milling is inspected to ensure the accuracy of the pattern. If everything is satisfactory, a finished part is milled out of metal (photo f). After the milling mold is completed, a four station open-pour polyurethane machine is used for manufacturing sole units (photo g).

Computers are also used to test the new shoe. By measuring the energy cost of running on a treadmill, researchers can compare the effect of various shoe designs on running efficiency (photo h).

(h)

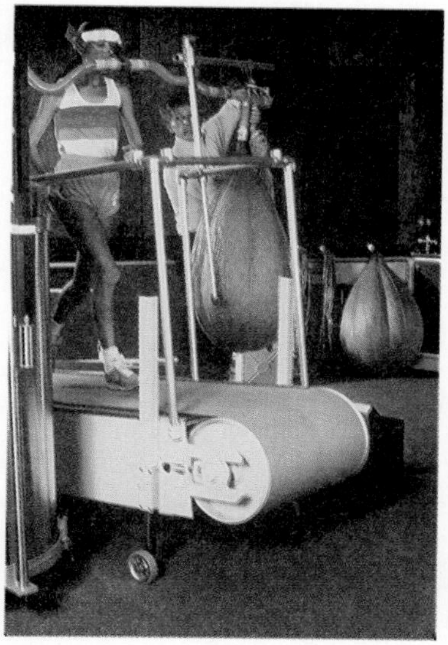

Computer-aided Manufacturing. Computer monitors and controls finishing treatment of fabric for apparel.

design for errors is extremely difficult and tedious. This process once took a team of engineers 22 weeks; it is now done completely by computer in 30 hours.

In general, there are six types of problems that are best solved with CAD systems. They are (1) mechanical drafting, (2) engineering, (3) printed circuit board design, (4) architecture, (5) cartography mapping, and (6) photogrammetry (the use of photographs to make precise measurements). Most of the uses we have discussed so far fall under one of these six categories. However, CAD/CAM has been turning up in some very unexpected places. NIKE recently used a CAD system to design the pebbling for the soles of tennis shoes. The same system (belonging to the MCAUTO consulting agency) was used to design the grips on the handle of one of John Deere's weed cutters and also to design the lens curvatures for a new line of sunglasses. Unique as these applications may sound, they are cost-effective. The sunglasses design that was completed in two days would have taken four months to do manually.

Another area in which computer-aided design is particularly effective is in pharmaceuticals. Several drug companies are now using computer models to design new drugs and simulate their reactions with different chemicals and enzymes. American Hoechst has had a good deal of success in this area, taking a particular compound from computer design to actual product. It should be noted, however, that due to the recent nature of these experiments, none of the computer-designed drugs are yet ready for human consumption.

CAD/CAM has found applications that range from the awesome to the obscure. The effects of CAD/CAM on industry have been so profound that some experts are calling it the dawn of a new industrial revolution. Most of the revolution is linked to the increase in productivity. Since the 1960s worker productivity per hour has been declining. Yet, users of CAD/CAM systems have found that the productivity of their designers increased five to 20 times.

The market for CAD/CAM is spiraling, with an estimated growth of 25 percent per year. According to Reginald H. Jones, chairman of General Electric Company, is a staunch believer in the benefits of CAD/CAM, a sentiment often echoed by executives.

On the other hand, a full-scale CAD/CAM system including robotic stations can run upward of $25 million. That could make for a rather exclusive revolution.

Robotics

Almost everyone has heard of the terminology given workers: those who perform management-level jobs are referred to as white-collar workers; those performing unskilled tasks or factory jobs are called blue-collar

Cincinnati Milacron's electric-driven robot performs a welding operation on stainless steel golf club heads.

workers. However, the influx of computers into the working world of the factories has created another category: the steel-collar worker. The steel-collar workers are nonhuman, and human workers are beginning to fear this new work force—the robots.

ROBOTICS
The science dealing with the construction, capabilities, and applications of robots.

The science fiction writer Isaac Asimov coined the term **robotics.** Robotics is the science that deals with robots, their construction, capabilities, and applications.

Currently, American factories have some 6,000 robots hard at work (Figure 10-5). However, this figure is expected to increase rapidly, reaching nearly 150,000 robots by 1990. General Motors, General Electric, and Westinghouse are the three leading users of industrial robots. Already, General Motors has approximately 1,700 robots. These steel-collar workers perform standard jobs, such as spot welding and spray painting, as well as more complex jobs like fitting light bulbs into the dashboards of cars. The automobile industry is the leading user of robots in the United States.

The steel-collar worker is not always as efficient as one may think. Robots perform well on the factory floor, but they have been known to go berserk. Swinging its powerful steel arm, a robot can deliver blows to anything within its reach; the problem—a crossed wire. Also, robots lack

FIGURE 10-5 Robotics

common sense and intelligence. For example, consider the case of a robot that drills holes in the doors of cars as they pass on the assembly line. If the car is not in the right position, the robot will still drill holes—and very nice ones at that—but, perhaps in the fuel tank.

Two generations of robots have appeared so far. The first generation possesses mechanical dexterity but no external sensory ability; that is, they cannot see, hear, touch, or smell. Second-generation robots, however, possess more humanlike capabilities, including tactile sense or crude vision; they can "feel" how tightly they are gripping an object, or "see" whether there are obstacles in their path.

Robots are appearing in places other than the factory, such as the area of sales. In Aurora, Colorado, an office supply store has robots for salespersons. They will, for example, tell customers about the specials within the store while pointing to the wares displayed.

Robots are also appearing in the office. A robot receptionist greets people entering the office of Davidson Aluminum and Metal Corporation on Long Island, New York. The performance of the robot receptionist, however, is controlled by human employees watching on closed-circuit televisions. The robot greets people by blinking its eyes, turning its head, and speaking. Another kind of robot delivers internal mail at the regional offices of the State Farm and Prudential Insurance companies in Westlake Village, California. As the "senses" (sight, sound, and touch) of robots become more advanced, robots will move into even more areas of business and industry. Unfortunately, the common sense required to make steel collar workers more compatible with their white and blue collar counterparts is still a long way in the future.

ISSUE

INDUSTRIAL ROBOTS: IMPROVING WORK OR ELIMINATING WORKERS?

With the unemployment problems that plague the 1980s, industrial robots have become a topic of heated controversy. Workers claim that the robots are eliminating their jobs. Management claims that the workers are only being temporarily displaced to other positions, not permanently replaced. And factory owners claim that robots are an economic necessity if they are to compete with the foreign market.

The management-owner faction and the worker faction are convinced that the other is unreasonable, untrustworthy, or, at the very least, simply "wrong." Obviously, neither side is entirely correct. Each makes very good points; but each either misinterprets or neglects to present the entire issue.

First, let us look at why the factory owners invest in industrial robots. The cost of these robots ranges from $5,000 to $125,000, with most at the higher end of the scale. Although this sounds expensive, robots are, overall, cheaper to pay for and maintain than workers. Studies show that the average industrial robot costs the factory about $4.80 an hour, whereas the worker—who is displaced by the robot—had cost the company almost $15 an hour.

Why this differential? Simple. Robots can work 24 hours a day. They are never absent, and so they never require sick pay or replacements. They never take maternity leave, nor do they show up for work with occasional hangovers. They don't require health insurance or fringe benefits. They have no difficulties relating to management and exhibit no signs of boredom, exhaustion, or irritability on the job. Because robots don't get tired, they are ideal for jobs where human workers tend to perform poorly later in the shift due to fatigue. Robots are *always* at 100 percent productivity. They produce 100 percent predictable quality work. One of the first uses of robotics was in high-risk jobs where employee injuries were a frequent problem. Robots can be used safely in areas containing high levels of harsh fumes. They can work with toxic chemicals and can't develop debilitating diseases for which the company might be held legally responsible.

Perhaps even more economical for the company, robots don't form unions and they *never* go on strike. This is important to management, which blames the unions for workers being replaced by robots. They claim that if the unions had not been so demanding, they would not be required to turn to automation to make a profit.

Union workers rightly claim that, although they cost more than the robots, most robots don't have families to feed, rent to pay, or refrigerators to fill. The main question is not whether robots are more effective; they undoubtedly are in some situations. The real question is whether automation should be given the go-ahead knowing that, although it may put American businesses back on their feet, it may also put American workers out on the streets.

The fact is that robots are being used more and more by companies simply to cut down on expenditures by cutting down on employees. Increasingly, robots are moving into companies that run several shifts because they are especially cost-effective there. In those situations a single robot can replace several workers and save a company several salaries.

This is not to say that the companies are heartless. They are hurting too, and they have to cut back. Inexpensive imports have drastically cut their profits and companies are being forced to seek the quickest, most efficient ways to bounce back from the slump in the economy. Unfortunately, the question of what to do with the displaced workers has not been answered.

Already workers are being replaced by automation. Almost 50 percent of the factory jobs in our automotive industry have been eliminated by

ISSUE

robotics. The secondary effect of robotics is just as painful. Many American workers in the steel industry have been laid off because the industry cannot compete with the automated Japanese steel industry. Some of the major steel companies have told their workers that those with less than 10 years of seniority will probably never be recalled. Where will they go for work?

Add to that the 18 million young Americans who will come of working age between now and 1990. All of those people will not find jobs making, maintaining, or supervising robots.

The effects that automation, with full-scale use of robotics, could have on this country have not been examined carefully. However, a study was done in Austria in 1982 on the possible effects of robotics on that country. The estimates were not encouraging. The study projected that full-scale automation without a reduction in the work week would result in 38 percent unemployment by 1990.

Experts in the field of robotics maintain that between 65 and 75 percent of America's factory workers could be displaced by robots were we to implement unrestricted, full-scale automation. Officials in companies that wish to automate assure their unions that this type of mass unemployment will never materialize. Companies claim that they will retrain and relocate workers who are temporarily displaced by robots. But will they be able to relocate them all?

Unions also need to be concerned about those workers who remain after automation, since our status in the community is derived from our jobs. Will working a computer, or working with a computer, elevate or lower the self esteem of the American assembly-line worker? Keep in mind that workers like to think that they make a difference in the resulting product.

The fact that American factories have problems is obvious. So do American factory workers. The real problem lies in finding a solution to this dilemma that will be beneficial to both groups or—at the very least—will help one group without hurting the other.

Some degree of automation will probably be required to keep American factories afloat. But care must be taken not to drown the workers in the process.

SUMMARY POINTS

- Software packages are being developed for use by business managers to be used for visual display of data; the visual displays include pie charts, bar graphs, and line graphs.
- In financial analysis, forecasting, a "what if" function, is done using electronic spreadsheets.
- Software can be purchased for business computers, allowing them to have the capability of an electronic filing system.
- Computer graphics are often used in business to condense large amounts of data into charts and graphs that are understandable at a glance. The use of computer graphics helps managers make accurate and timely decisions.
- Salespeople are being assisted by computers in the vinyl flooring industry and in the cosmetic industry.
- Computers are being used in all phases of the publishing process.
- CAD/CAM systems allow the engineer to design, draft, and analyze a prospective product and analyze the manufacturing process using computer graphics on a video terminal.
- Users of CAD/CAM systems have found that the productivity of designers increased five to 20 times.
- American factories have over 6,000 robots hard at work.
- The automobile industry is the leading user of robots in the United States.

REVIEW QUESTIONS

1. List some functions of the computer in general accounting.
2. Define electronic spreadsheet.
3. Explain how electronic spreadsheets can be used for forecasting.
4. How are the graphic capabilities of the computer being used by managers?
5. What is information management?
6. Why are computer graphics so important to management?
7. Salespeople are being assisted by computers. What are some applications of computers in this area?
8. Explain CAD. How is it used?
9. Explain CAM.
10. In what ways does CAD work with CAM?
11. Who coined the term "robotics?"
12. Which industry is the leading user of robots?
13. What are the two generations of robots and their characteristics?
14. Describe some nonindustrial applications of robots.

DISCUSSION QUESTIONS

1. Describe how the role of the finance department is changing as a result of computers.
2. Explain the reasons for both the positive and negative attitudes toward using computers in book production.
3. What effect will CAD/CAM have on industry?
4. In the future what are the tasks that robots will do?
5. To what degree will robots replace workers in industry, and should management have an obligation to those displaced workers?

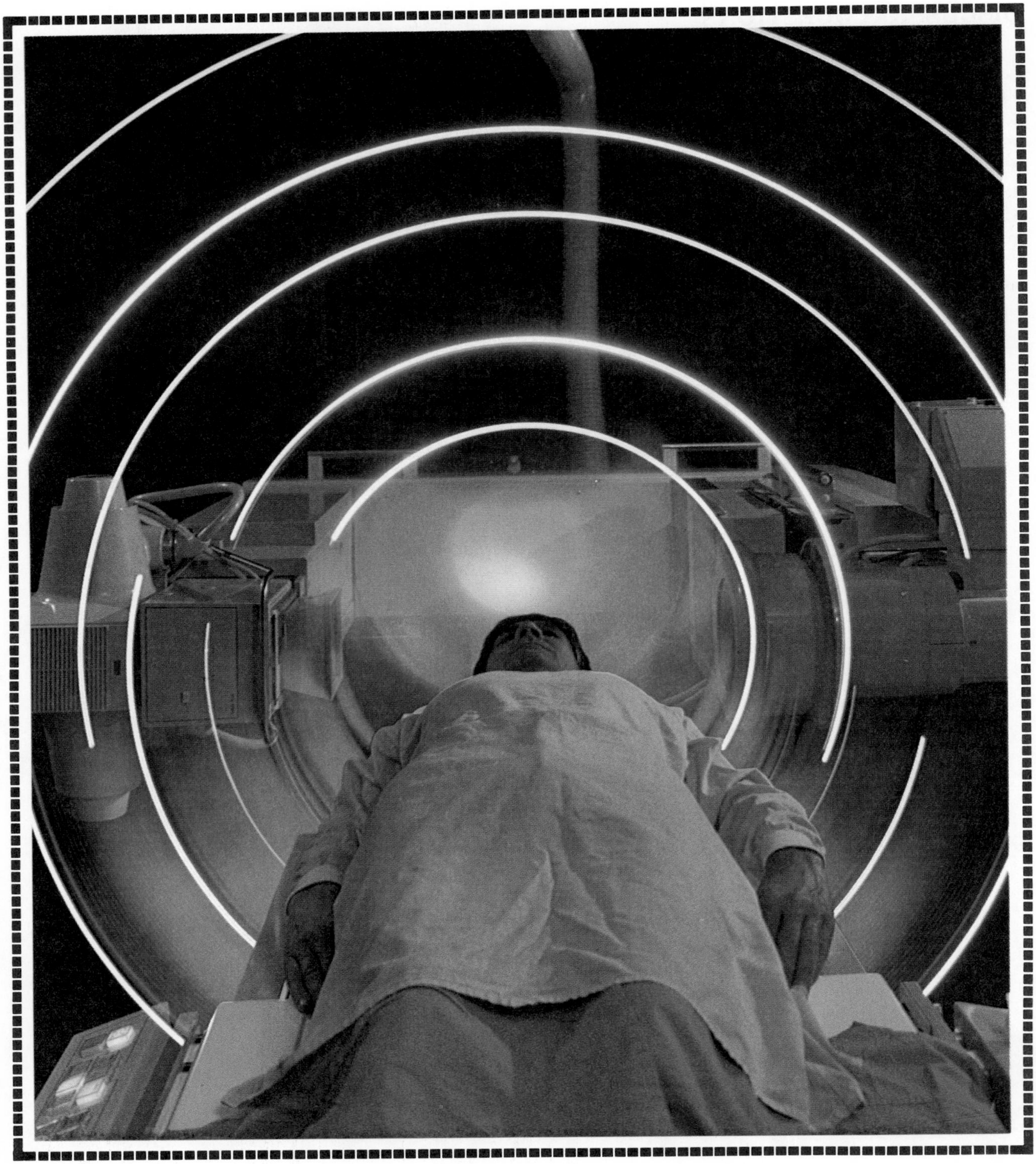

CHAPTER 11
COMPUTERS IN SCIENCE, MEDICINE, AND RESEARCH AND DESIGN

OUTLINE

ARTICLE

PROGRAMS UNDER THE SKIN

Elisabeth Rosenthal

Computers may soon give diabetics the insulin that is prescribed to maintain their blood sugar at normal levels; many diabetics produce little or no insulin of their own. These watchdog computer programs will not be located in a massive hospital computer bank or even stored in a desktop Apple II. Instead, a tiny computer, with its associated insulin pump, will be inserted directly into the patient's abdomen.

The Implantable Programmable Infusion Pump (IPIP) is being developed at the Johns Hopkins Applied Physics Laboratory under grants from NASA and the National Institutes of Health. "We have tested four devices in dogs, and they have worked very well," says Kermit Sanders, an electrical engineer working on the project. "Someone will probably try human implants by the middle of this year."

If all goes well, the small device—about three and a half inches in diameter—will be placed in the patient during a simple surgical procedure. The pump's insulin reservoir is refilled every few months by injecting the substance through a membrane in the IPIP, which will lie just under the patient's skin. Once in place, the pump's only links with the outside world are the radio waves that flow between the physician's computer terminal and the abdomen to program, reprogram, and monitor the device.

By holding a computer-controlled transmitter over the patient, the doctor sends his orders to a receiver in the implant. The technique, called radiotelemetry, "is exactly the same technology used to program satellites once they're in space," Sanders explains. Using this invisible link, the physician instructs the pump to deliver insulin on a certain schedule throughout the day. The patient, who has his own small transmitter, can signal any temporary change in the delivery pattern of insulin—less after exercise, more following a meal.

Just as satellites can transmit as well as receive, so too can the insulin pump report back to the physician. If, for example, a patient says he feels "run down," a doctor might want to reach back into the computer's memory to see whether the patient has been administered extra insulin correctly; the implanted microprocessor keeps tabs on its user for up to a 21-day period.

Because the IPIP can be programmed to dole out insulin on a "continuous basis," diabetics gain more stable blood sugar levels than they would from single injections. But flexibility is IPIP's biggest boon. It is simple for the doctor to alter the dose schedule. So simple, in fact, that if the patient has the proper communications equipment, the doctor can transmit new instructions—direct from office to abdomen—over the telephone.

As can be seen by the remarkable IPIP device, computer technology and computer applications work hand in hand with science, medicine, and research and design. This chapter focuses on applications in these areas.

INTRODUCTION

Until the last 30 years, scientists, medical personnel, and research and design specialists relied heavily on pencil and paper to record data, make calculations from lab results, and sketch out new ideas. The results were checked and rechecked for accuracy. Although this checking was critical, it took time away from creative ventures.

Especially in research and design, large amounts of money and time were used to build prototypes for testing. Often these prototypes were abandoned for better ideas later on and the investment was lost.

Since computers have entered these fields, much of that time and money is being saved. Computers make mathematical calculations and projections in seconds that human beings couldn't complete unaided in months. Computers gather, compile, and sift statistics for those similarities and differences that lie too deep for human detection. They can turn raw data into graphic representations. Using computers, the scientists' conclusions are made easier, because the data can be retrieved, classified, and displayed much more quickly. Computers can generate models and make projections without the subjectivity that humans inevitably bring to such tasks.

Computer applications in the area of science perhaps have the widest range. Let us look at some of these first.

SCIENCE

Computers can do a variety of tasks in the broad area of science. These tasks can be placed in several categories: (1) large-scale mathematical computations, (2) real-time computations, (3) simulation and modeling, and (4) control of laboratory instruments and devices.

Computers are used in the field of astronomy for several purposes including the analysis of planetary orbits.

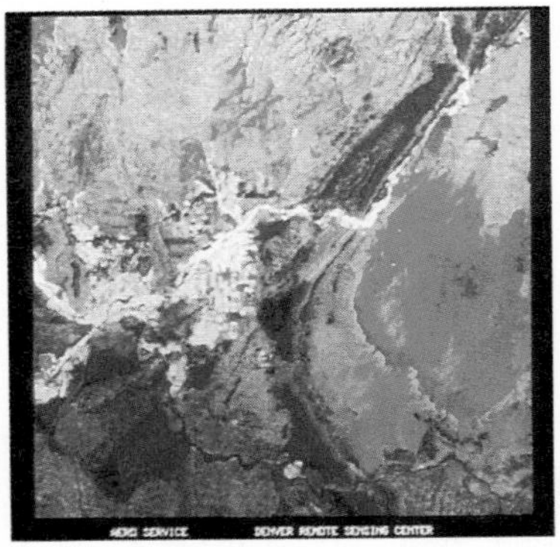

This computer-generated output of the earth's layers aids geologists in the interpretation of earth exploration data.

Large-Scale Mathematical Computations

Vast amounts of data are collected, for example, from satellite photographs. The data are entered into the computer and output in a form that is easily read and interpreted. This and other examples of areas in which computers are used for large-scale mathematical computations follow.

From a Satellite's View Five hundred and seventy miles above us orbit two Landsat satellites launched by NASA. Although four of these satellites have been launched into space since 1972, only two remain operational. Like a "candid camera" orbiting in space, each Landsat takes pictures. Approximately 30,000 overlapping scenes must be recorded to get a view of the whole earth. Of these 30,000 photos, 12,000 of them are taken over land. Although the Landsats shoot pictures of the world's largest cities, nothing on the ground smaller than the length of two football fields can be disclosed (Figure 11-1), unlike the spy satellites whose keen "eyes" can even detect individual cars and people on the ground. Each Landsat photograph covers an area 115 miles wide.

In addition to light we can see, infrared radiation from the sun that is reflected by the earth can also be detected by the computer. Healthy or sick vegetation can be spotted by examining such infrared radiation pat-

FIGURE 11-1
Landsat Picture
From 570 miles above Tokyo, Japan, this computer-generated Landsat picture defines subtle details in surface geology. Urban areas appear as light blue surrounding the dark blue area—Tokyo Bay. Land under cultivation appears in red.

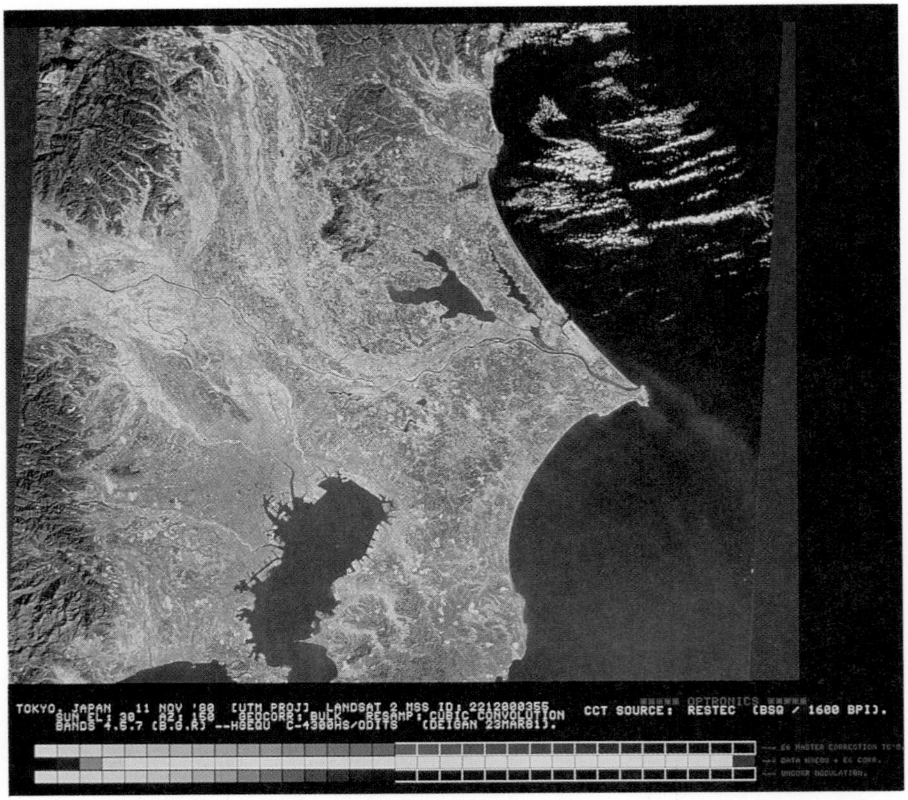

terns. Infrared radiation directly emitted by warm objects on the ground is also detected by the newest Landsat.

Each scene photographed is electronically composed of 32 million tiny squares called picture elements, or **pixels**. The wavelengths and intensity of light in a Landsat photograph are measured and then converted into digitized electrical impulses. These impulses are then stored in magnetic memory. When a ground receiving station comes into range, the pictorial data stored in memory are broadcast to the station. Once received on Earth, the data are entered into a computer system. Experts reassemble the tiny pixels into photographs with the aid of the computer. Color intensities and tints reveal hidden characteristics of the landscape.

PIXEL
One of the many image points comprising a graphic display.

Because of the altered color (red), the photographs do not show Earth in the same hues that we perceive our natural environment. Since infrared radiation is invisible to our eyes, it must be made visible by color. A special color scheme has been adopted. A photograph with red areas indicates healthy vegetation, such as forests and wheat fields because plants emit high levels of infrared radiation. Heavily populated areas emit low levels and are shown as a greyish-blue.

The results of this NASA venture are available to 130 countries. Experts can examine the colors and tints to detect mineral deposits, urban areas, regions of insect infestation or droughts. Landsat photos can even help pick out the best locations for oil drilling.

Microscopic Structures in 3-D Electron microscopy (EM), in which individual electrons can be used to view biological material about the thickness of a baby's eyelash, has been in use for nearly a quarter of a century. However, only recently has a computer system been devised to

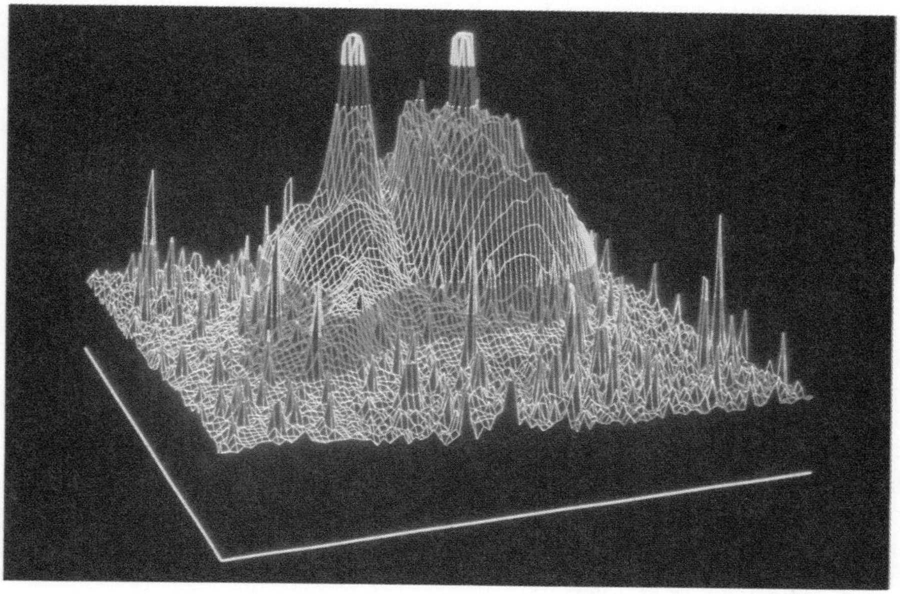

A single frame from a computer-generated movie. This movie is an astronomical study of a complex double galaxy, M51. The height represents brightness; the different colors represent different levels of intensity; the two peaks represent the centers of the two galaxies; and the spikes represent the light intensities of individual stars.

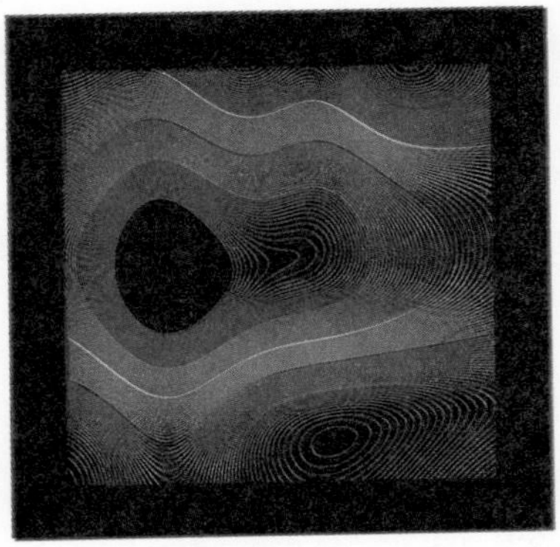

A topographical map made of color-coded contour lines is an easy task for computers. Color-elevation relations plus an accompanying key replace the small numbers printed on the contour lines of conventional maps. Graphic representations such as this provide scientists with a clearer understanding of the mathematical relationships of the variables under analysis.

accompany the EM techniques and to provide a three-dimensional image. This system, developed by scientists at Oak Ridge National Laboratory, Oak Ridge, Tennessee, will be used to determine the three-dimensional structure of biological specimens.

The negatives of the photographs taken with the electron microscope are viewed with a scanning television camera attached to a computer. The computer displays a representation of a three-dimensional structure on the television screen. Special glasses must be worn to view the image.

Recently, new synthesized ribonucleic acid (RNA) in a gene of a water insect has been viewed using the new technique. The technique is referred to as electron microscope tomography, as it is based on a similar technique used in medicine—computerized tomographic (CT) scanning—discussed in the section on medicine.

Prediction and Control of Industrial Waste Another environmental application of computers helps the Department of Health and Human Services predict and control the effects of industrial waste on rivers and streams. Computers first calculate the amounts of oxygen and chemicals in the waterways. From this data, they determine the degree and kind of life-sustaining ability that remain in a given area. Similar air quality assessments are also done by computer to provide the essential knowledge base for environmental cleanup and correction.

Real-Time Mathematical Computations

REAL TIME
Online processing.

Real-time mathematical computation ability refers to the way the computer can process collected data so fast that it gives what appears to be instantaneous feedback. As a result of their speed, real-time systems are used as emergency systems to warn of potential or actual danger. Computerized emergency systems are now in use in the chemical industry and nuclear power plants. Other types of real-time systems are found in such areas as space flight operations, air traffic control, and medicine.

Emergency Management Systems Crises, like the much-discussed Three Mile Island incident, may be brought under control more quickly as a result of emergency management systems that rely on computers. Form & Substance, Inc., in Westlake Village, California, has developed one such emergency management system (Figure 11-2). The system was designed for the chemical industry and contains information such as the properties of the chemicals manufactured at the particular plant site, evaporation rates of the chemicals, the influence of the surrounding land on wind patterns and flow, and backup plans for any number of possible accident situations. The computerized data bank is constantly updated with information supplied by chemical sensors around the plant. These sensors keep track of wind velocity and direction, temperature, and toxin levels.

In the event of an emergency, the system will supply instructions and appropriate emergency telephone numbers. A light pen makes the system easy to use. When a computerized map is displayed on the screen,

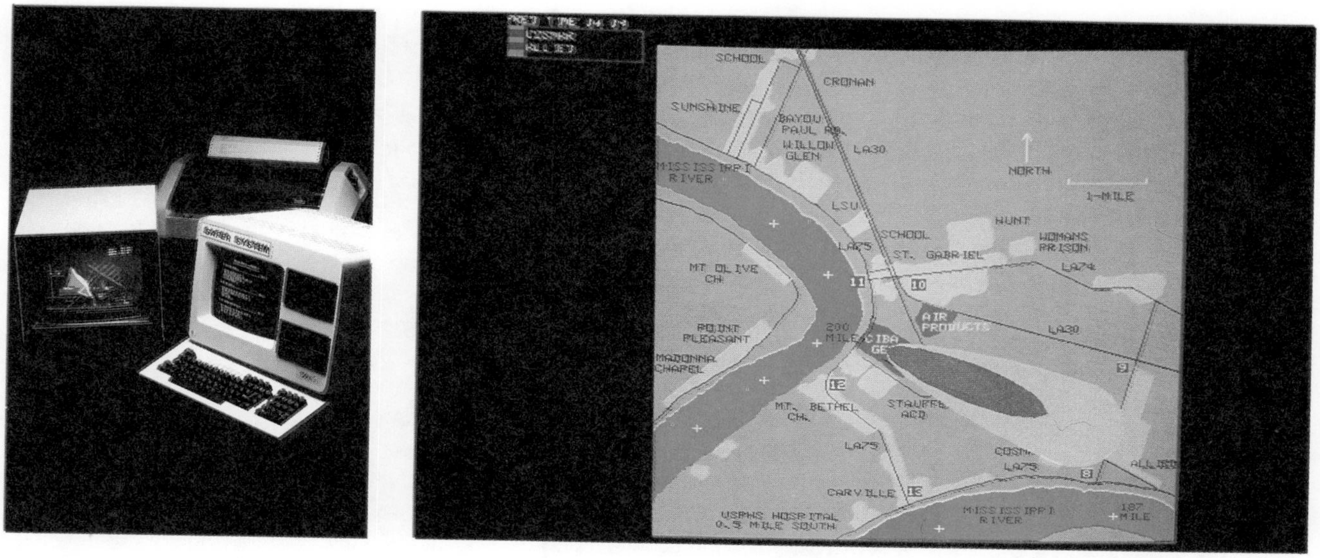

FIGURE 11-2 Emergency Management System

The SAFER system (left) is an emergency response system that alerts industrial companies of toxic releases that could pose potential harm to the employees and neighboring area. The system displays actions to take in a variety of emergency situations. The display frame (right) illustrates the essential graphic information helpful in an emergency situation.

the user touches the pen to the area where a chemical spill has occurred or uses the pen to answer questions displayed on the screen about the spill. Nearby residents are warned automatically through a prerecorded telephone message. While the residents are being warned by the computer, the necessary plant personnel are free to work with civil defense people and to mobilize resources within the plant itself.

Chemical plants are not the only places emergency management systems are used. Such systems are now required in nuclear power plants by the Federal Nuclear Regulatory Commission. Although an emergency management system will not guarantee that a crisis can be resolved, it will make emergency evacuation and response much more efficient.

Simulation and Modeling

Computers are used for **simulation** and **modeling** in science. The computer is programmed to consider certain facts (stored in its memory) and come to a decision. Sometimes a system of simulation and modeling is referred to as an **expert system**, because it involves decision making using the same information as would an expert in the field.

SIMULATION AND MODELING
A technique in which mathematical data are analyzed and the results used to generate models or to make projections.

EXPERT SYSTEM
Contains programmed facts to imitate human decision making.

Modeling in the Automotive Industry Computer modeling is widely used in the automotive industry. The computer uses complex mathematics to form a model, a technique that can simulate all aspects of a car's performance. The computer also helps evaluate the effect of changes on any one part of the automotive system. Finally, when a part (or system) is

PROFILE

SEYMOUR CRAY

Tremendous number-crunching capabilities are required to process scientific data. Seymour Cray was determined to build superfast and superpowerful computers to meet these needs.

Hired by Control Data Corporation (CDC), Cray convinced the company president, William Norris, to build such equipment. Cray's first project, the 1604 computer, was so successful in the scientific community that CDC built a private laboratory for Cray in his hometown, Chippewa Falls, Wisconsin. There Cray continued his work and in 1963 introduced the powerful 6600, a machine that was immediately adopted by the U.S. Weather Bureau and the Atomic Energy Commission.

By 1972 Control Data Corporation began shifting its priorities from Cray's work to more service- and peripheral-oriented projects. Cray therefore gathered investors and founded Cray Research in 1976. Four years later he introduced the world's first supercomputer, the Cray-1. (A supercomputer performs at least 10 million computations per second.)

Cray's reputation for product excellence has given his company 70 percent of the nation's supercomputer business. Of the 65 supercomputers in use to date, 50 are Cray computers; the remaining 15 belong to CDC. The machines are used in a variety of operations including engineering support, weather forecasting, and designing special effects for the film industry.

Currently, the Cray-2 supercomputer is in the research and development stage. When available the Cray-2 will be at least six times faster than any existing computer and one-tenth the size of the Cray-1. In the meantime, the X-MP has been introduced as an intermediate machine between the Cray-1 and the Cray-2. Use of the X-MP and introduction of the Cray-2 should ensure Seymour Cray a future that will be as profitable as his past.

redesigned, the computer can evaluate the effects of such a change on the entire automobile before any parts are manufactured or tested.

Oil Drilling Not only are computers used by experts to interpret satellite data to find the best locations for oil drilling, but also they will soon be used to assist oil companies in other ways. For example, computer software firms are developing expert systems for oil drilling. Oil companies will no longer have to rely on the dipmeter, a tool that can be dropped down a hole to measure local geological conditions. The expert system is much needed here since human specialists who read dipmeters are few.

An expert system has already programmed into its memory the knowledge of human experts. The capability exists for the computer to support its judgments by giving an explanation of the reasoning used. Therefore, the expert system designed for oil drilling will assist the oil companies in analyzing geological data and advise them where to drill.

A year of development went into the Dipmeter Advisor—six months of work with oil-drilling specialists and six months of system development. Teknowledge, Inc. programmers tested their system by inputting details of previous accidents taken from drilling log books. The recommendations of the computer were then compared with those of humans. The system tested well, although it is unable to address as many problems as

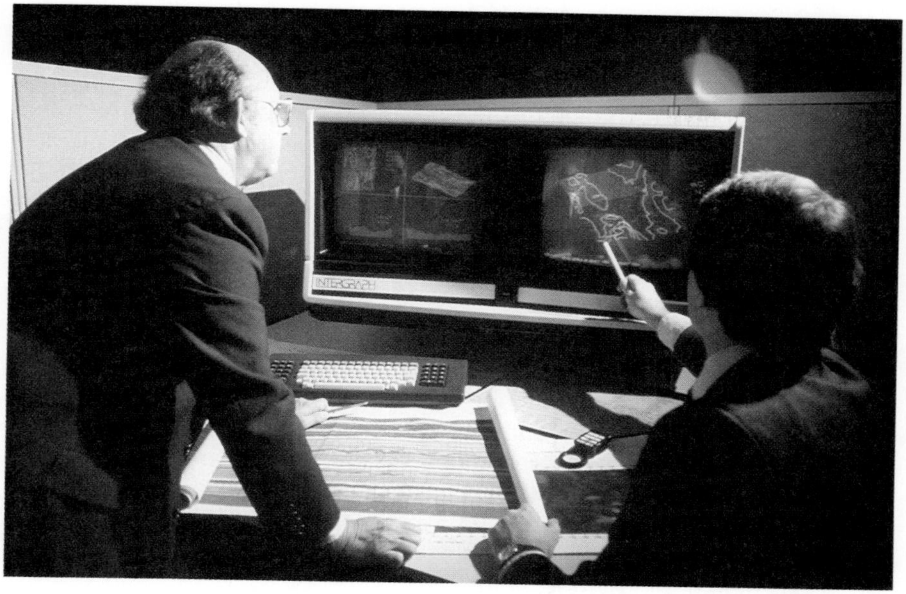

Geophysicists examine a computer-generated contour map of a three-dimensional plot of the earth's interior. Geophysicists use special tools and techniques to remotely sense and measure characteristics below the earth's surface. Computers such as this have magnified the geophysicists' ability to interpret remote measurements.

the human experts. A marked advantage of such a system, is that it is as good, consistently as the experts are only at their best.

The cost of an expert system like Dipmeter Advisor is estimated at $1 million. Although this may sound very expensive, the cost of operating a drilling rig for one day may be around $100,000. An expert system might pay for itself in a matter of weeks.

PROSPECTOR: A Geology Program A computer program developed by geologist Alan Campbell and computer scientist Peter Hart recently led to the pinpointing of a huge deposit of molybdenum by shifting through a set of probabilities. Called PROSPECTOR, the program imitates the reasoning process of a trained geologist with a series of IF/THEN statements: "IF this type of rock formation is present, THEN this is a probable site." Using this technique, the program asserted that a molybdenum deposit existed near eastern Washington's Mount Tolman. Subsequent tests demonstrated that the program was right.

Control of Laboratory Instruments and Devices

Computers also control various pieces of laboratory equipment. A properly written program enables the equipment to operate both quickly and "intelligently." The computer can analyze data and store data that are necessary. The use of computers in this area allows the researcher to spend valuable time conducting other experiments rather than overseeing the instruments.

The World of Cells In the biology department at the California Institute of Technology, Pasadena, computers are being used to study the minute world of cells. DNA (deoxyribonucleic acid) is a chemical that carries the genetic code. Strands of DNA used to be synthesized—or cloned—using a manual process; this procedure cost $2,000 to $3,000 and took many weeks and sometimes months. However, using computers to perform the same task takes less than one day and has a price tag of $2 to $3. Dr. Michael Hunkapiller, a senior research fellow, commented that the manual procedure was very intensive and since it involved much repetition, it was easy to make a mistake. By turning the task over to a computer, the mistakes were eliminated and the procedure became more economical.

Volcano Monitoring The May 1980 eruption of Mount St. Helens drew much attention, including the attention of scientists. The U.S. Geological Survey recently began a monitoring system on Mount St. Helens. Tilt meters, built by scientists in a Vancouver, Washington, laboratory, send data into a large computer every 10 minutes. When the data are analyzed, they show trends in the tilt of the crater floor. Because the meters are inside the crater, eruptions of the volcano can be predicted within 30 minutes; this allows time for scientists working near and on the volcano to be quickly evacuated by helicopter.

Geologists use computers to analyze the compound elements found in rocks.

Before the installation of this system, analysis of the data was always a few weeks behind the activity of the volcano; thus the predictive ability of the old system was limited. But although the computerized monitoring system has been helpful in keeping track of volcanic activity, there is still one difficulty. The monitoring instruments are wiped out each time the volcano explodes or when lava oozes from the side of the dome.

MEDICINE

Computers have many uses in medicine. Most of these applications are found in hospital settings. With the area of medicine growing at a fast rate—especially since the 1950s—computers have become essential for the health care profession.

Computer-Assisted Diagnosis

Computer-assisted diagnostic techniques evaluate numerical data and compare them with normal or standard values (Figure 11-3). In this way a diagnosis can be reached. There are many applications of computer-assisted diagnosis. Two examples of **computer-assisted diagnosis** being used in clinics and hospitals are multiphasic health testing (MPHT) and computerized tomography (CT) scanning.

COMPUTER-ASSISTED DIAGNOSIS
Using computers to evaluate medical data to show variations from normal.

Multiphasic Health Testing When a patient goes to a center that does multiphasic health testing, he or she is asked to complete questions concerning family history. These data are put in computerized form. The results of the battery of tests that are then run, including perhaps eye, hear-

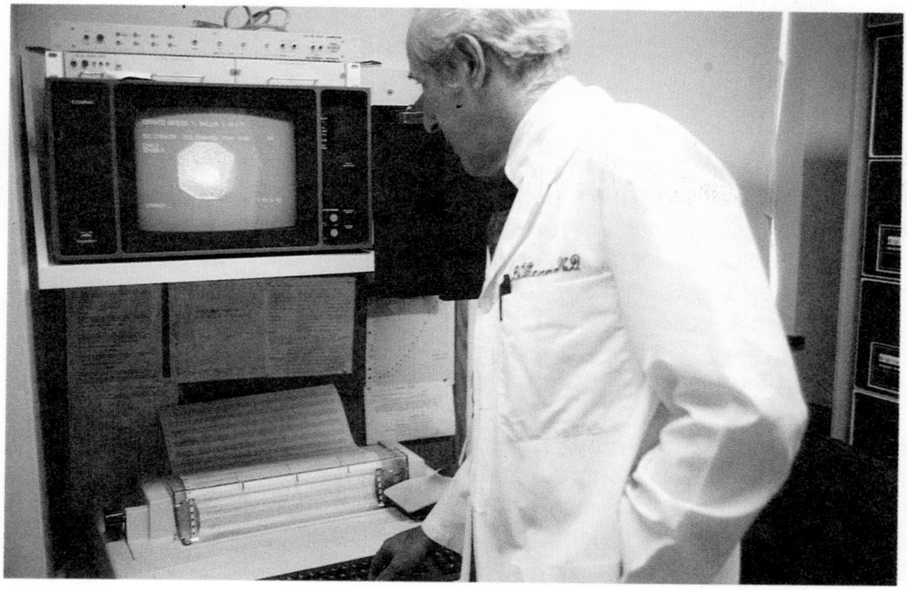

FIGURE 11-3
Computer-assisted Diagnosis
Radiology departments in hospitals are using computers to assist doctors in diagnosis. Here, a radiologist views a computerized image and reviews a printout of information regarding the image.

Medical testing is made easier with computers.

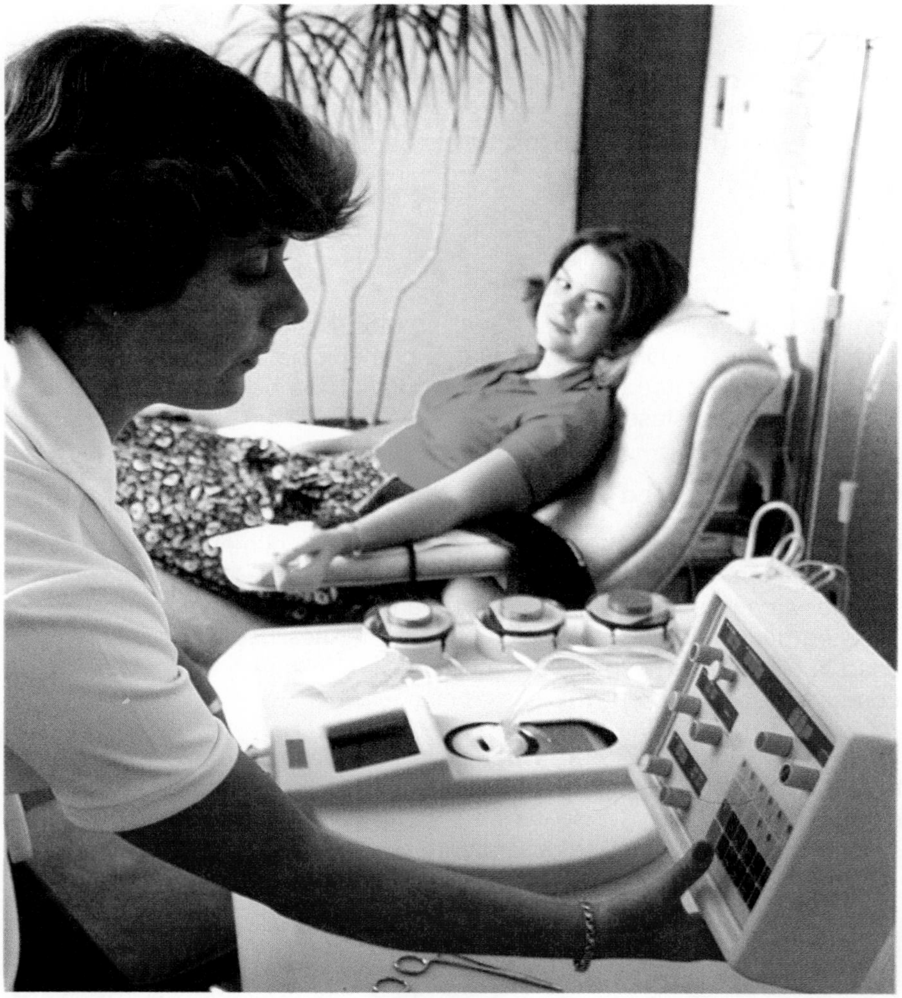

ing, pain tolerance, chest X-ray, and blood tests, are also computerized. The computer can then compare a given test value against established "normal limits" or a mean. A printout of the test findings is then made, including any abnormal test results and necessary information from the patient's medical history. The tests are administered by nurses and the printouts are reviewed by a trained physician. The final results, along with the physician's recommendations or remarks, are then sent on to the patient's family physician. A consultation with the family physician about the results can then be arranged by the patient.

Computerized Tomography A major advance in health care technology has been achieved through computerized tomography (CT or CAT) scanning, a method that combines X-ray techniques and a computer for quick and accurate physical diagnosis (Figure 11-4). Although the equipment is still expensive to hospitals, and thus to patients, costs for scanning can

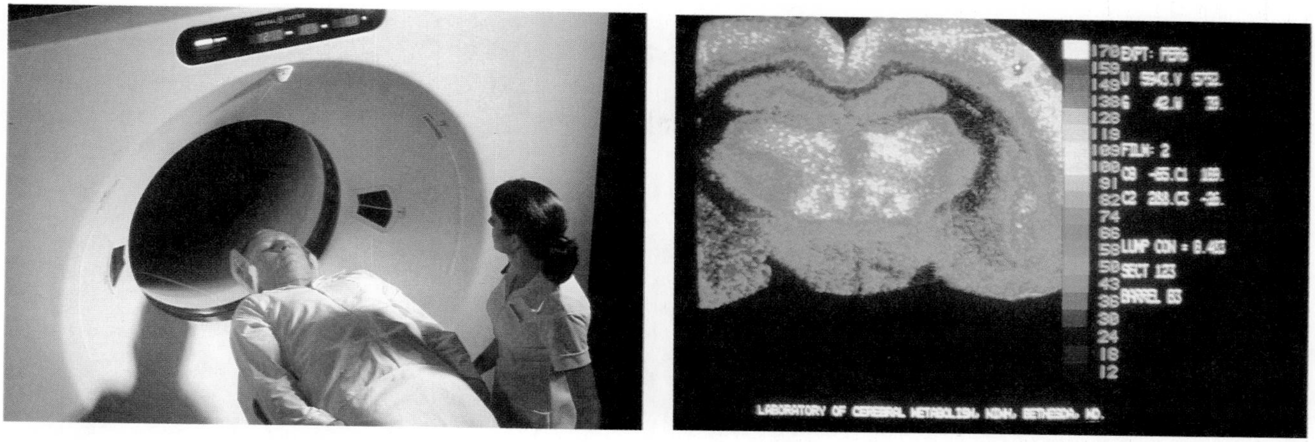

FIGURE 11-4 Computerized Tomography

Computerized tomography is used for many diagnostic purposes. Shown here are the patient undergoing brain scan (left) and a resulting image (right). This image depicts area of brain activity using special tests. Colors shown indicate different levels of brain activity.

be cut by linking several scanning units to a central computer. When this linking was done by three hospitals in Kansas, each one saved approximately $500,000 without impairing the quality of the diagnoses. Because of this, the computerized tomography scan is becoming a common procedure in today's hospitals.

Computerized tomography can assist in surgery. For example, a child born in September 1982, was found to have a congenital deformity of the skull. After 39 CAT scans, a three-dimensional composite of the skull was assembled by computer. A lucite model of the child's skull was made us-

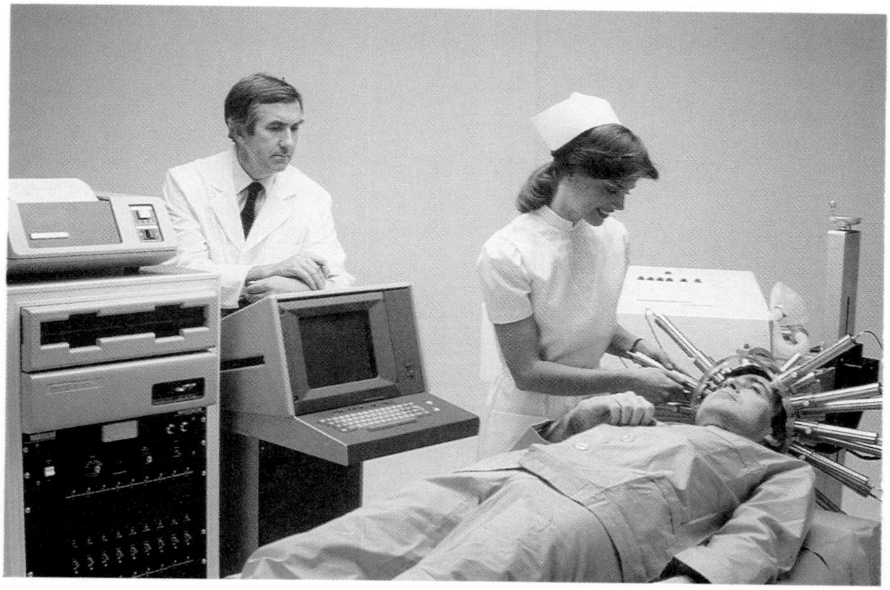

Here, a special system tracks and measures blood flow through the brain enabling physicians to diagnose blood flow impairments in the brain; it discloses the area and the extent of the damage.

PROFILE

HARRY POPLE AND JACK MYERS

Dr. Jack Myers and Harry Pople, Jr., are pioneering a new and exciting frontier in medicine.

Myers, a professor at the University of Pittsburgh's School of Medicine, was interested in finding a way to assist with the information overload heaped on medical professionals. Pople, an alumnus of Carnegie-Mellon's artificial intelligence group, was concerned with analyzing the methods used in the diagnostic process. Together, they developed a computerized medical consultation system called CADUCEUS. Applying artificial intelligence principles, Pople programmed information and decision processes supplied by Dr. Myers.

CADUCEUS contains an information library on 600 diseases and 2,500 manifestations (disease symptoms, laboratory data, and so on). By cross-referencing these two categories, the user has the option of retrieving information on a particular disease or entering symptoms that can be linked to a disease. Patient data such as age, test results, and family history are also factored into the final computer-generated diagnosis.

Although CADUCEUS is not widely adopted, it has been reviewed favorably in medical journals and hospitals are beginning to experiment with the system. The groundwork made by Pople and Myers will be a valuable tool in the development of additional diagnostic programs.

ing the computer to plot the contours of each cross-section onto lucite sheets. Similar to slices in a loaf of bread, these sheets were placed on top of each other to result in a life-sized replica of the child's skull. The surgeon noticed the left side of the patient's head appeared to be normal. His task then was to make the right side match the left. Using the computer, the surgeons could see the probable results of their surgery—which was a success—before lifting a scalpel.

'The Doctor Is Out. At the Sound of the Tone Open Wide and Say "Ahhh" Into the Computer . . .'

It is interesting to note that the computer graphics system used in this patient's case was the same system used to design the F-15 and other aircraft at McDonnell Douglas Corporation, St. Louis.

Life Support Functions

Only a few years ago, 24-hour nursing was needed for a critically ill patient. But now computers are being used in the intensive care and coronary care units to acquire and digest the patient information. Mainly, computers monitor physiological variables such as heart rate, temperature, and blood pressure. The computer is also used in some cases to monitor the patient's urine output; whenever the output goes below a predetermined quantity, the computer can activate a pump to infuse a diuretic agent.

The computerized monitoring system frees the nurse from constant watch over the critically ill patient. The computers provide an immediate alarm if any abnormality occurs, allowing the nurse to react promptly. Usually, information on as many as eight patients can be displayed at the nurse's station.

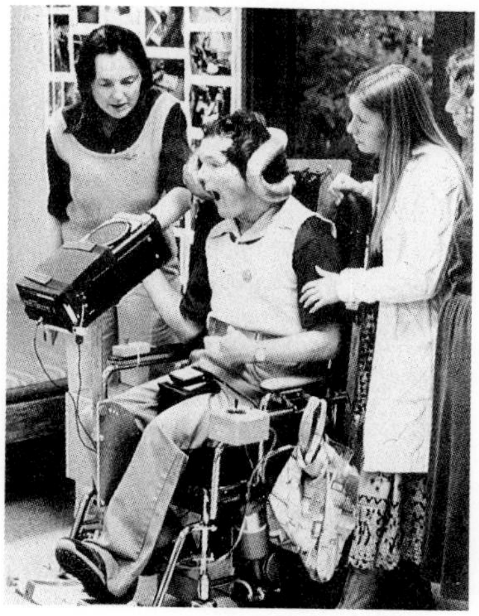

The disabled young man pictured is unable to speak, but he is communicating by means of an electronic system which produces highly intelligible synthesized speech. Known familiarly as the "talking wheelchair" and formally as the Versatile Portable Speech Prosthesis (VPSP), the system incorporates technology developed by Ames Research Center for advanced aircraft communications.

Information Storage and Retrieval

Because of the vast amount of information kept on patients, including medical history, laboratory tests, doctor's notes, and adverse reactions to drugs, computers are used to make this information easy to enter and retrieve. In some cases, for example, a medical emergency, complete information with quick retrieval allows faster and more effective patient care.

COMPASS: Comprehensive Pharmacy Administrative Support System Computers are changing the role assigned to the local pharmacist. Recently, Honeywell, Inc., a computer manufacturer, launched COMPASS (*COM*prehensive *P*harmacy *A*dministrative *S*upport *S*ystem). Using the system, the pharmacist enters the patient name and prescription into the computer terminal (Figure 11-5). A list of all generic equivalents is displayed on the screen if the prescription specifies a brand name drug.

The computer then checks the patient file to see if the new medication will conflict with one already being taken. Because of the time this procedure requires when not computerized, few pharmacists have performed this service in the past.

COMPASS also prints the prescription label and keeps track of transactions from inventory to ordering. Many COMPASS systems have already been installed in chain drugstores nationwide.

Patient Records At the Jules Stein Eye Institute in the UCLA Medical Center, Los Angeles, computers are used to record, store, and access patient information to aid in both diagnosis and treatment. The system was made simple to use so that doctors would be as comfortable with it as they had been with the paper reports and records. Doctors use the

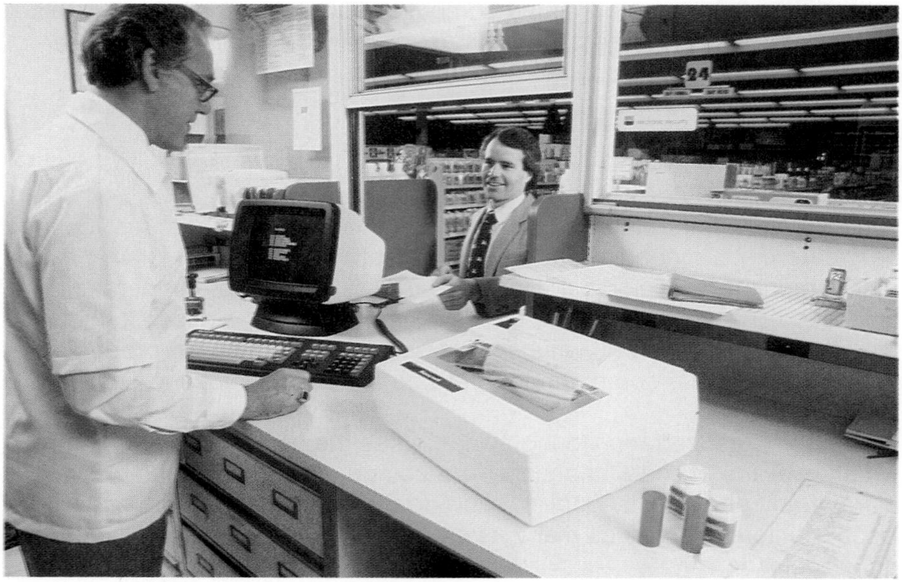

FIGURE 11-5
Computerized Pharmacy System

Computers assist the local pharmacist. Not only are computers helpful for drug inventory, but patient files are stored in memory to check for a conflict of a new prescription with medication already being used.

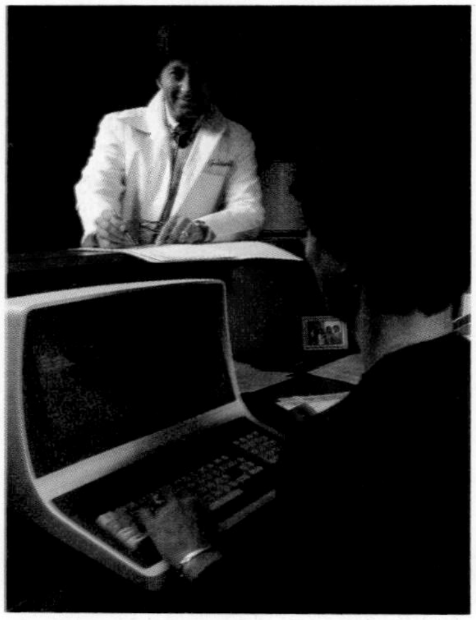

FIGURE 11-6
Medical Administration

Computers are used extensively in the health-care profession. Large amounts of patient information can be stored (such as medical history and test results), and then be retrieved by the physician as needed.

system (which includes a word processor) to prepare operating room reports, enter and store examination data, and conduct research of medical literature produced at the Institute. It also helps the staff keep track of patients who should have follow-up examinations or treatment.

Clerical and Administrative Functions

Computers are used for the clerical and administrative functions in both hospitals and doctors' offices. Patient billing, personnel payroll, and drug inventories are done more easily and faster using the computer (Figure 11-6). Computers can also be used to schedule the use of operating rooms.

RESEARCH AND DESIGN

The area of research and design is closely linked to science and medicine. The computer has now replaced the manual data-recording and analysis in research, and the light pen and graphic display terminal have taken the place of manual techniques in design.

The Imaginary "Stroll"

In the 1960s Cornell University architect Donald Greenberg designed a computer graphics program that took one on an imaginary "stroll" of the Cornell campus. Greenberg designed his building-by-building simulation of the campus after viewing the General Electric visual simulators used for astronaut training. Greenberg was able to use his program to show the other architects how a proposed art museum would change the looks of Cornell's campus.

Greenberg sees a great advantage to such capabilities. The computer simulation, he says, will be able to review the plans of unconstructed buildings and screen out structural weaknesses. Currently, Greenberg's program uses color to show structural stresses—the greater the stress, the deeper the color.

Other programs like Greenberg's have been designed; one is a "walkable" simulation of all of Chicago's downtown area and another is the simulation of a four-block area of Manhattan's Time Square as it was a half-century ago. These programs could be useful to city planners wishing to build up a functional and aesthetic downtown area.

Joint Design

Computers assist in the design and manufacture of artificial human joints that can be surgically implanted to replace defective ones. Developed at New York's Hospital for Special Surgery, the complex mechanisms include a digital computer that reads the patient's X-ray in three dimen-

A chemist uses an Apple computer in the laboratory for recording data gathered from experiments.

FIGURE 11-7
Joint Design via Computer
This hip prosthesis (an artificial hip bone) was designed by a computer to maximize resistance to stress.

sions and creates for the surgeon a "picture" of what the suggested implant looks like. Further, the computer feeds into its calculations and design such factors as the patient's age, ambulatory (walking) condition, allergies, level of activity, and any other relevant details in the patient's medical history before suggesting a particular design for a joint.

Formerly an expensive and time-consuming process, the design stage of the artificial joint can now be completed in a few minutes. The surgeon has the final say, of course, as to whether the design suggested is actually manufactured (Figure 11-7). Once the design is approved, the surgeon instructs the computer to manufacture the joint by producing directions for the machines, as was described in Chapter 10, using CAM. This process has cut the patient's waiting time for these artificial devices almost in half.

Automotive Design Turns to CAD

Computer-assisted design is also used by the automotive industry to design many of the cars produced. Because CAD relies on numerical representation in displaying a system or a part, the computer can change it, test it, draw it, break it, or even tell a machine how to manufacture it. Once the computer has displayed a car, driver, and passengers onto the screen, it can calculate the center of gravity and weights. The computer can even be programmed to show parts of the car in movement, for example, the windshield wipers. In this way the designer can see if the design will meet manufacturer and government standards.

Aerospace Industry

CAD aids preliminary design in the aerospace industry too. Before CAD it was difficult to envision and evaluate a design, as only two dimensions could be seen from the drawings. Wood or clay models were the only way a product could be evaluated in three dimensions.

With CAD a three-dimensional representation can be seen and rotated. A dimension can be changed easily and other dimensions altered accordingly. Jerry Lavick, director of CAD/CAM at McDonnell Automation, St. Louis, says, "CAD techniques lead to a higher-performance product, developed in less time, and with more reliability."

The Lockheed-Georgia Company designs and builds an electronic ground support system when it begins building an airplane. The support system provides for maintenance of navigation equipment, radar systems, and communication radios. Lockheed's Ground Support Equipment Group uses CAD to support system design.

Before CAD, the design process was carried out by time-consuming and repetitious sketching. Productivity increased markedly following implementation of the new design system. A graphic display terminal visualizes the diagram and can focus on a portion of the design. A plotter prints that portion in a blowup format. Drawings presented by the plotter have a high quality. In fact, quality of detail of drawings done by the plotter is better than the handmade drawings.

Other advantages of Lockheed's CAD include ease in moving components during the development stage and the need to draw fairly common components only once. These components can be stored in a library in the system to be called out again at a later time. The company reports a 97 percent productivity increase in the inking of a drawing and a 50 percent increase in sketching and layout, the design phase. No manual ink drawings are now produced at Lockheed-Georgia's plants.

Technical Publications

In the production of technical publications and documentation at Hewlett-Packard Loveland Instrument Division, CAD was found to be very helpful. Prior to CAD the technical illustrators occupied their time with erasing and redrawing shapes when orders were changed, copying penciled drawings in ink, and other time-consuming, repetitive work. At a time when the Instrumental Division felt its staff would have to be increased by four times to handle the workload, CAD solved many of their work problems. The new system allows for greater accuracy and speed, especially reducing the design time.

In addition to drawing, their system has text-editing capability. Where necessary, text can even be incorporated into the illustration itself.

ISSUE

WHO SHALL PLAY DOCTOR: THE PHYSICIAN OR THE COMPUTER?

Computers are already being used in medical diagnosis by general physicians and specialists. The old question "Who shall play God?" can be rephrased in this context with "Who shall play Doctor?"

As computers begin to prove both their worth and cost in the field of medicine, it is time for the public to decide whether or not they are indeed worth it. What are the advantages of using the computer in medicine? If the computer is to be used in making a diagnosis, how should it be used? How will the increased use of computers in medicine affect doctor training? What will be the effects on the quality of health care? Will computer-assisted diagnosis raise or lower the cost of health care? And finally, what about the privacy and security of the patient's files?

The advantages of using computer-assisted diagnosis for the patient are fairly obvious. First, computers do not forget. While no human being could really be expected to remember every minor symptom of every known disease or ailment, a computer could easily do so. The analytic and monitoring capabilities of computers could be used to improve overall health care. More patients will be able to be cared for than if everything were done manually. Computers also keep much better hours than physicians. Computers don't play golf on Wednesdays and they are always in their offices.

The next consideration is how computer-assisted diagnosis should be used. These diagnostic machines could be used only for hard-to-diagnose cases. However, that might be seen as denying the best possible care to those people with other problems. It is also important to make sure that "hard-to-diagnose" does not come to be synonymous with "able-to-pay." Using a different approach, the diagnostic computer could be used as a routine screening device. It could do the mass-screening, selecting only those people who are truly physically sick, thus saving the doctor valuable time. However, much of a doctor's function is in caring for the emotional side of patients as well. Often, we feel better after seeing our doctors even before we take the medication. The reassurance and caring—that "human touch"—are very important. Sometimes, as with anxiety and tension, that human touch is all that we need. And even if those things are treated purely as physical symptoms, people may be uncomfortable seeing a computer rather than a doctor.

Next, we wonder how computer-assisted diagnosis will affect the physicians. One worry is that new doctors will be less skilled because of heavy dependence upon computers during their training. We know that skills waste away when they are replaced with new technology. One concern is that physicians coming out of medical schools will rely too heavily on computerized diagnostic techniques. On the other hand, outdated skills are generally replaced or eradicated swiftly and with few side-effects. It is possible that the ability of the computer to output diagnoses and the possible treatments will free the doctor from monotonous memorization, enabling him or her to spend time in medical matters requiring more thought, such as research or new treatments. And even if the doctors are well-trained, it is still uncertain whether the increased use of computer-assisted diagnosis will affect the quality of health care.

Can the computer actually do as good a job as a doctor can in screening patients? It is true that the diagnostic computer CADUCEUS has passed the American Board of Medicine's certifying examination. However, that is a test of book knowledge. How that knowledge will be applied in actual practice is quite another thing. It is highly debated whether a computer can really mimic the thought processes of a doctor.

Also, consider the importance of bed-side manner. For decades, we

ISSUE

have all become used to having our own personal physician, the family doctor. He or she is not only a doctor, but someone that you can trust—a family friend. Are we ready to give up that personal attention that we get from our own doctors? Sometimes the sympathy and understanding is almost as important as the medication. Could a computer do that?

Even ignoring the bedside manner, and assuming that the computer did learn to humor us, it is not known whether the computer will be able to recognize signs of emotional stress. Psychiatric problems may be more easily and accurately diagnosed by our family doctors who have known us for years and are aware of our normal emotional states. A large number of psychiatric cases are referred for treatment from their family doctors. It is difficult to believe that the computer could learn the nuances of tact and the careful questioning required in diagnosing and prescribing for an emotionally ill person.

We also need to consider how the older generations will react to computerized medicine. They may be repulsed and frightened by the mechanical treatment. This could lead them to even further shun the medical treatment they need. And we can't forget those unfortunate few with either no family or one that's uncaring, for whom that monthly trip to the doctor's office is one of their few contacts with other human beings. How will they react when they are referred by that "nice young doctor who always smiles" to just sit in the hall and wait for the computer to attend them? "Don't worry, it'll send you back here if there's anything seriously wrong. If not, we'll see you next month."

Also, the use of computer-assisted diagnosis will surely have some effect on the cost of health care. It is possible that by reducing the amount of time that patients spend with physicians, health care costs could be reduced. Yet, it would cost a great deal of money just to install the computers in the first place. And have you ever heard of health care costs going down?

It is also not certain whether computer-assisted diagnosis will improve health care or simply skyrocket costs by testing for every possible disease a patient might have. Perhaps the new machines will save some lives by testing for and isolating obscure occurrences of rare diseases, but it is also possible that the overall cost of health care will increase so much that it would negate any good the machine might have done. Some people might no longer be able to afford any physician—particularly an electronic one.

Perhaps it is possible that the doctor and the computer can share the role of physician. We could envision a perfect balance where the computer provides diagnoses and recommends treatments while the doctor tends to the emotional and human side of the patients. Thus diagnostic accuracy would be increased and the doctor would remain in the position of family friend and comforter. Yet, how often does reality reflect the perfect balances we imagine?

Even assuming a perfect balance, all of this may also affect the patient's degree of privacy. Many patients feel anxiety at the thought of their medical histories being put into a computer bank. They are more comfortable with the traditional physician-patient relationship. But perhaps more important is the possibility that unauthorized persons might gain access to the patient file and the unauthorized modification of patient data. Security is a major concern because many of the plans for computer-assisted diagnosis include the use of a centralized computer facility.

Once we have initiated a computerized health service, how long will it be until our records are online, that is, accessible through a central computer? Knowing how difficult it is to protect online data, do we really want our private medical records online?

On the other hand, online information is timely, and in medicine, time can mean saved lives. Would we want to die because our information couldn't be located quickly?

The more we look at the issue the more obvious it becomes that there is no easy answer to the issue of if, how, and when to let the computer play doctor.

SUMMARY POINTS

- Computers are used for large-scale mathematical computations in analyzing data and reporting them in a form that can be easily interpreted.
- Real-time computations are being used in emergency management systems because they provide instantaneous feed-back.
- Simulation and modeling in the sciences saves time and money. It is used to test a device before manufacturing or to see what effect changing one dimension will have on another.
- Computers are used to control laboratory instruments and devices, freeing researchers for other tasks.
- Computer-assisted diagnosis is becoming more common. Test data are entered into the computer, which compares the results against established normal limits.
- Computers are being used to monitor information on patients in intensive care and coronary care, freeing nurses from constant attendance.
- Patient information is kept on computer by many doctors and hospitals, making such information easily accessible in time of an emergency.
- Patient billing, personnel payroll, and drug inventories are also computerized.
- The light pen and graphic display terminal have taken the place of manual techniques in research and design in the areas of urban design, design of artificial joints, automotive design, and aerospace design.

REVIEW QUESTIONS

1. What are some patient benefits of computer-assisted diagnosis?
2. Why is computer design helpful in architecture?
3. Name some applications of real-time mathematical computation?
4. How is the computer being used to design and manufacture artificial joints?
5. Explain computerized tomography scanning and its advantages over other forms of diagnosis.
6. What are the differences between large-scale mathematical computation applications and real-time computation applications?
7. Explain the use of computers with satellites.
8. What qualities does the computer possess that make it an especially valuable scientific tool?
9. Explain how information storage and retrieval can be used in areas other than medicine.
10. Why is CAD (computer-aided design) less expensive for an industry than building prototypes?
11. In addition to car design, what are some specific uses of the computer in the car industry?
12. In what other scientific fields are computers used?
13. What features enable a computer to predict?

DISCUSSION QUESTIONS

1. Will expert systems eventually take the place of humans? Why or why not?
2. Computer-assisted diagnosis might increase speed and accuracy of medical diagnoses. It may also pose great threats to the patient's privacy and the physician's familiarity and recall of diagnostic information. All of these factors must be considered before implementing computer-assisted diagnosis. In your opinion, are the advantages or the disadvantages weightier? On what do you base your answer?
3. Do you feel computer-aided design limits or expands a designer's creativity?
4. Discuss possible problems with emergency management systems.
5. Productivity in the automotive and aerospace industries has been dramatically increased by the use of computers. What other industries could be similarly affected and how should their computers be used to maximize productivity?

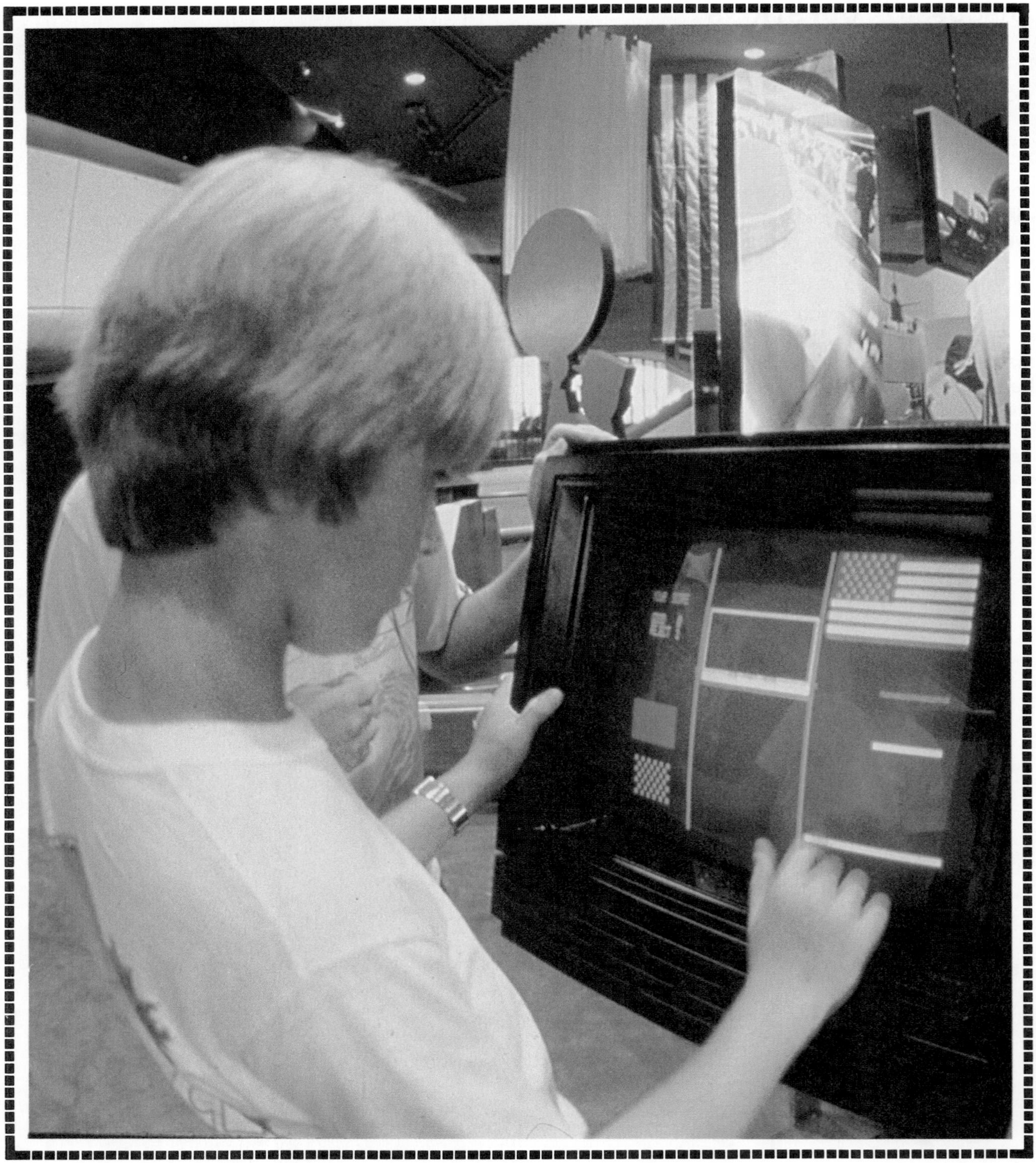

CHAPTER 12

COMPUTERS IN SOCIETY: ART, ENTERTAINMENT, AND LEISURE

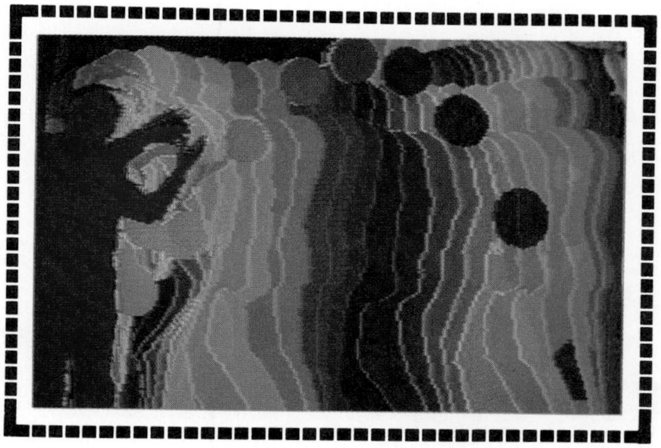

OUTLINE

ARTICLE

CALTECH AT IT AGAIN

CREDIT BEAVERS FOR SABOTAGING ROSE BOWL SCOREBOARD

In the fourth quarter, UCLA was leading Illinois, 38–9, but the scoreboard read: Caltech 38, MIT 9.

In another Rose Bowl prank, the geniuses of Caltech struck again. In 1961, they took over the card stunts during the Washington-Minnesota game. This time, they took over the scoreboard.

Earlier Monday, they flashed other messages on the board, including, Go CIT! (California Institute of Technology), and a matrix picture of an arrow pointing to two beavers, the Caltech mascot. Later, they had planned to flash 1984 Beaver Bowl, but the scoreboard was turned off with four minutes left in the game.

Virgil Lubberden, manager of the Rose Bowl game, said there wasn't enough time to get re-control of the scoreboard.

"They had shorted out one of the scoreboards," he said. "We would have had to send somebody up into the scoreboards to fix them."

Of the whole affair, he said: "It was just a prank. They'll do it every time."

Although it was a prank, it also was serious business. The project took about 15 months, and some of the 15 Caltech students who worked on it will get class credit.

Ted Williams, a Caltech senior majoring in applied physics, said they took control of the scoreboard via radio control, using two microprocessors that they controlled from a vantage point about two miles away.

"We had the ability to send both text and pictures," Williams said.

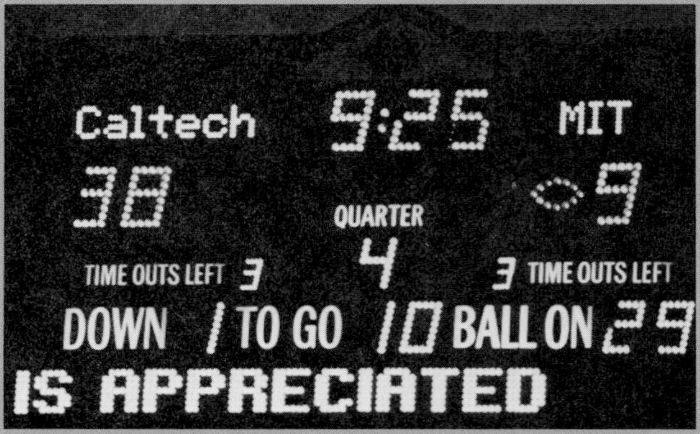

He added: "Pranks at Caltech always start with ideas, and somebody decides if they are of such magnitude that we could get class credit for them."

In 1961, Caltech students sabotaged the Washington card tricks. When a Washington spellout was called for, it came out Washington spelled backward. The next time it was called for, instead of Washington, the cards spelled out Caltech.

Times columnist Jack Smith, recalling the prank in his Monday column, wrote: "I suppose it can't ever happen again. Security is so good these days.

"But don't count on it."

While computer pranks are certainly entertaining, the fact that these students were given college credit for their efforts raises serious ethical questions. True, such ingenuity and talent should be recognized, but can our educational institutions teach responsible computer use and at the same time reward such behavior?

INTRODUCTION

Computers are not only used in the world of work, but they are also being used in perhaps more enjoyable pursuits: the arts, entertainment, and leisure. Computer features that are being used in these areas include word processing, graphic capabilities, sound production, and data manipulation. Some of these features are combined, for example, as in dance.

COMPUTERS IN THE ARTS

Computers have many uses in the arts, from controlling stage lighting to writing and editing through word processing. The word processing capability is revolutionizing many of the arts. Choreographers employ word processing in dance notation (dance steps both graphically displayed and explained in a written type of shorthand) as do writers and editors in their craft.

Broadway's Computer Debut: *A Chorus Line*

In 1976 computers made their way to Broadway in the hit *A Chorus Line.* A Tony Award was given to the show's lighting director, Tharon Musser; her company used a computer lighting system—Light Palette. Since that time other Broadway presentations have employed computer-controlled lighting. House lights and footlights, particularly, are controlled by the computer (Figure 12-1). The spotlights are handled by the electricians.

The Broadway musical *Dream Girls* also used computer-controlled lighting for scenery. The backdrop was a fiberglass prop, transformed into a luminous staircase by the use of computer-controlled lights. By us-

FIGURE 12-1
Computer-Controlled Lighting
Strand Century's Light Palette Control Console allows complex lighting changes to be programmed in advance and played back exactly as recorded, or modified for the immediacies of live performance. Here the Light Palette and its operator control the lighting of a concert at Universal Amphitheatre in Los Angeles, California.

ing lights in this way, maintenance problems and costs were reduced. *Dream Girls* too received a Tony Award.

Computers Illuminate the Metropolitan Opera

Gone are the days when 39th Street was the location of New York City's Metropolitan Opera House. Even more remote are the days when the old Opera House was illuminated by gaslight. Today the Metropolitan Opera has a new home—the Lincoln Center. The lighting for opera, as for the Broadway plays, is controlled by computer, using the Light Palette. The software makes available well over 30,000 lighting "presets" from which a single operator can select. Although the computer adds to the efficiency of the lighting designer, computers do not remove the human element from the opera. Even after the lighting controls are set during dress rehearsal, many of them are edited later. Also, the computer operator must watch the stage and will not always rely on the commands displayed on the computer screen.

Revolutionizing *Swan Lake*

Like theater and opera, ballet is lighted by computers. Computers also assist ballet in another way—in dance notation.

In a few years at least one version of the ballet *Swan Lake* may be notated by computer. Many choreographers speak of dance as the illiterate art because no permanent record exists. Traditionally dancers have been individually instructed by the choreographers. When the choreographer dies or the company folds, the works can no longer be produced or danced as designed.

Dance has had a notation for describing elaborate patterns, but notation methods have not proven adequate and are laborious to do. Filming and videotaping to record and convey the essence of dances have been tried but were found unsatisfactory. Shot from one angle, only parts of the dance are captured. In addition, the stage lighting, which is essential to creating mood, is frequently too dark for the camera to catch images and nuances. Coming to the rescue, however, is a computer graphic system, still in its experimental stage (Figure 12-2). The system records dances by analyzing movements and translating the data into a moving human figure on a computer screen, to be studied and stored.

Computer graphic notation in dance began in the mid-1970s and it is still in its early stages. But it has already made significant progress. Previously, it took six hours of notation to record one minute of dance. Now dance can be notated almost as fast as one can type. An additional feature of one system even allows repetitive steps to be recalled so they do not have to be redrawn each time. Also, the score can be instantly edited.

Computers Challenge Great Poets of the Past

The computer has already been programmed to emulate the works of famous poets. The following example was cited in *Popular Computing*

FIGURE 12-2 Dance Notation
By using a microcomputer and a video display screen, choreographers may combine the best aspects of written and visual recording techniques.

(February, 1983, p. 171);

APOLOGIES TO EMILY DICKINSON

The bird covets her own victory;
Then guesses the company;
In her silent truth buzz no more.

The definition presumes her own thing;
Then covets the victory;
Of her condensed journey buzz no more.

The thing presumes her own civility;
Then advocates the nectar;
With her forbidden victory perish no more.

Other great poets like William Shakespeare and Robert Frost are also being imitated. Computers aren't exactly poets, however. The computer requires a program and accompanying data (vocabulary) to produce poetry.

Famous words from well-known poets are entered into a fixed skeleton representing a poem's format. The poetry generator consists of three parts: a vocabulary in which each word has been entered according to its part of speech; a random number generator to select the words to be included in each poem; and a format to determine the sequence of the parts of speech—nouns, verbs, and adjectives. As evident in the above sample of computer-generated poetry "Apologies to Emily Dickenson," the quality of the poetry leaves something to be desired. At present, poetry generators are used mainly for amusement.

Writing a Novel on Computer: The New Hemingway

The written word is now becoming the electronic word. Books were once written longhand or typed on a typewriter. With computers some authors

PROFILE

LESTER KILPATRICK

Before Lester Kilpatrick invented the electronic plotter, the computer was limited to number-crunching operations. Kilpatrick, a native of Oklahoma, received a degree in electrical engineering from Texas Tech in 1948 and a master's degree from MIT. He directed the development of the first airborne digital computer at North American Aviation; however, the contribution that he is most noted for revolutionized the computer industry.

As an engineer Kilpatrick noticed that there was a weak link between the design and production stages of a product. Computers were capable of generating lists of numerical information that described physical objects, but there was no method of visually displaying the information to users. Kilpatrick solved this problem in the late 1950s by designing a machine that could convert the numerical descriptions into line drawings. This machine, the electronic plotter, operated with great speed and accuracy and became a vital tool in the field of engineering. Kilpatrick's idea also opened the door to state-of-the art graphics and CAD/CAM.

Kilpatrick formed California Computer Products, Inc. (Calcomp), and began marketing his electronic plotters. However, a lawsuit against IBM caused Kilpatrick to resign from the company in 1977.

Currently, Kilpatrick and his son operate Newport Securities, a financial consulting service company in Orange County, California.

let the word-processing capabilities of the computer help write their works. Because computers are becoming more widely used, they are contributing to a change in the writing process itself.

Burke Campbell is known as an electronic novelist. Campbell, author of *Blind Pharaoh,* wrote his work in less than three days using the computer. The novel is in public domain and can be read over a computer network, The Source. However, reading the electronic novel directly from the display screen can make one's eyes ache. The alternative is printing the novel before reading. This would produce a mile-long roll of paper and would be far more bulky and inconvenient to read than a paperback version. Also, The Source charges a fee for printing the novel and the average paperback would be less expensive.

Computers are opening avenues for the multi-author novel as well, in which each chapter is written by a different author. Several multi-author novels are currently in the creation stages on computer networks.

COMPUTERS IN ENTERTAINMENT AND LEISURE

We would probably think we were in the year 2001 if we could see all the ways computers are already being used in the areas of entertainment and leisure. The field of sports generally uses the computer as it was originally intended—to calculate statistics. Hollywood, however, is using computers to their fullest to create and manipulate sounds, produce graphics, allow machine control over camera movement, and perform word processing.

Computers in Sports and Recreation

Baseball: A New Pitch Currently, the manager of the Chicago White Sox baseball team is using a computer. Many other teams are joining the ranks. According to a Texas Ranger statistician, "Baseball people are definitely seeking out new and more meaningful ways to scientifically analyze the game."

Computers determine batting averages and runs batted in. They also examine how certain pitchers and hitters work together. To keep up with such statistics, teams are employing computer operators to record pitch-by-pitch accounts of each game (Figure 12-3). A computer located elsewhere stores the information received from the ballpark via a telephone hookup.

FIGURE 12-3 Computerized Baseball Statistics
Here, a New York Yankees Baseball Operations Department official uses an Apple Computer at Yankee Stadium. During the games, he records every pitch, play, etc. for later analysis.

"I know you've struck out the first twenty-six batters, Fernando, but the computer says we have to take you out."

In addition to statistics kept on team players and the team as a whole, computer-generated graphics are also used. The graphics show the path of all fly balls hit by Chicago White Sox players during the previous season.

Although computers are entering the sport of baseball, their use is not expected to markedly change the spectacle of baseball. During the game, the computer is infrequently used. Consulting a computer to determine the probabilities of success for doing things one way or another would be too time consuming.

Computers Tackle Football The National Football League (NFL) is using computers to prepare game plans, monitor collegiate players, and log player injuries. As a result football has been made much more strategic. The computer has even been useful in scouting. Statistics on every player currently or previously signed by an NFL team are kept by the United Scouting Combine (USC). Also, information on college players is pooled by the USC. Reports on approximately 1,000 college players can be accessed. These reports contain information on height, weight, grades, speed, and profiles for each player.

However, the use of computers in football is not always met with enthusiasm. The NFL already has set up rules: no use of computers during the game—either in the coaching booth or on the sidelines. Football knowledge and intuition will still be the basis for coaches' decisions.

Football scoreboards are computer-controlled.

Computers "Love" Tennis During the 1982 TransAmerica Tennis Tournament, the official statistician's job was eased as the result of a portable microcomputer. In the TransAmerica championship's 93-year history, this was the first time a microcomputer was used for scoring.

Percentages for first serves in and first serves missed are automatically figured by the computer's program as data are entered. The computer gives both computer screen viewers and spectators a more detailed analysis of the game. Players can get reports on performance following the game.

Computers Schedule the Professionals On Staten Island, New York, Holly and Henry Stephenson use a microcomputer to schedule professional baseball, basketball, and soccer games. The two have written programs to draft playing schedules for the National and American baseball leagues, the National Basketball Association, and the outdoor and indoor soccer leagues. Not only does the appropriate day for each game have to be scheduled but also the hour and turf. This brings some problems. The Baltimore Orioles, for example, must play out of town during the Preakness horse race. The Canadian teams demand home games on their national holidays but prefer the United States for their games on the Fourth of July. Each season the baseball leagues play a total of 2,106 games. Developing the program for the baseball leagues alone required 18 months of work.

The amount of work saved by computer scheduling of 3,565 games annually for the four leagues is tremendous. Before the Stephensons and their computer took over the job, Eddie Gottlieb, former coach and owner of the Philadelphia Warriors, had scheduled the NBA games since the association began. When Gottlieb manually scheduled all 23 of the NBA's teams and 943 games, it took him six months each year. Five computer

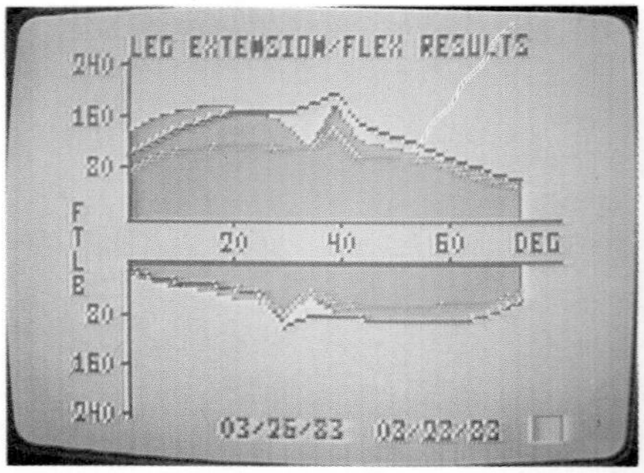

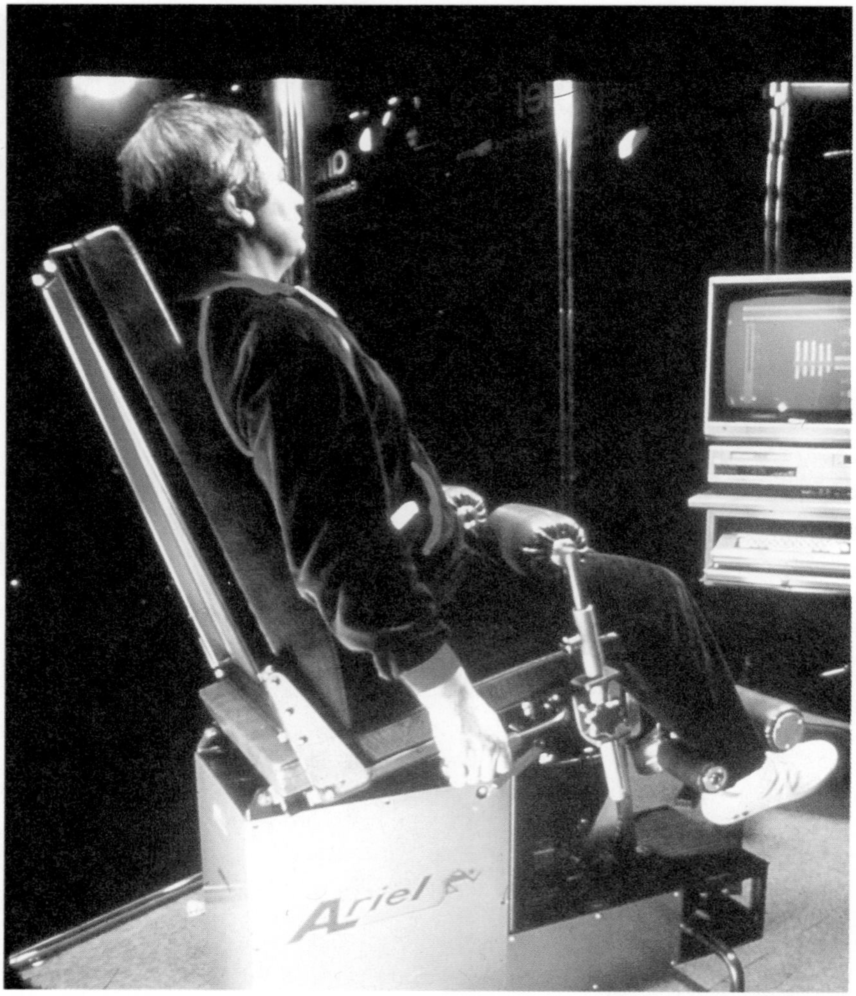

Physical fitness is taking on increased significance in our society. Through the use of high-tech equipment, The Coto Research Center in California has implemented one of the most effective exercise and training programs in the country. The ARIEL 4000 (right) uses a computer to monitor and produce instant feedback on an individual's performance. Above is a sample output produced by the ARIEL 4000. This analysis compares current performance to optimal performance or training goals.

companies tried and failed to write a scheduling program for the NBA, but the Stephensons managed to succeed.

Cycling on New Avenues For 100 years bicycling has remained the same, but it is now changing as a result of computers. Cyclists may now have sensors attached to the front wheel. Computers collect data from these sensors and compute speed and distance. This method is more accurate than mechanical speedometers and odometers. Some computers even calculate the cyclist's estimated time of arrival.

The new bicycle computers are lightweight, some weighing less than one pound. Prices vary but are generally under $100. Add-on options are available, for example, the heartrate monitor, which has sensors connected to the computer to keep track of the rider's heartrate.

Computerized Roller Coasters At Walt Disney World computers are used with the roller coasters. Although the excitement of the ride is the only immediate benefit, the coasters demonstrate a system of computer pacing and spacing that may work equally well in systems of mass transportation. The double roller coasters in the RCA Space Mountain run adjacent to each other on two virtually identical courses. To ensure safety, the cars on each roller coaster track must be kept at least 18 seconds apart. If one car approaches the one in front of it too quickly, a computer automatically slows down the approaching car.

Computers Go Hollywood

Hollywood, well known as the home of the film industry, is becoming known for its use of computers in movie production (Figure 12-4)—in scriptwriting, sound effects, and special effects. Computers are used in television work as well, even in the production of television commercials.

Computers and Hollywood Scripts According to one screen writer, the scripts for screenplays should come out exactly 116 pages long. An average script for a situation comedy or sitcom, averages 30 pages per half-hour episode. The scripts for sitcoms can go through seven or more

FIGURE 12-4 Computers in Movie Production
The film industry relies on computers for creating special effects in motion pictures. Computers had an active role both on and off screen during the making of *War Games*.

drafts. Because of the need to constantly retype the scripts, Hollywood is turning to the computer.

"DUKES OF HAZZARD": A FIRST. Keeping up with production of the vast number of scripts is a reason for both television and film script writers to use computers. The first Warner Communication television show to automate was the "Dukes of Hazzard." The computerization of "Love Sidney" followed. The scripts for these shows are written and keyed into computers in Burbank, California, and are sent for filming to New York using a modem.

However, there is at least one disadvantage to the procedure. Because it is no longer necessary to retype the document for each change or edit, writers may change words more often than before. The fact that word processing has a tendency to prompt rewriting is a danger.

Michael Crichton, author, screen writer, and director, feels that too much emphasis is placed on word processing, which he describes as "just glorified typewriting."

BEHIND THE SCENES. Computers are being used behind the scenes for sound effects and expanding artistic capabilities, and industrial uses of computer-aided design have been modified for use by the film industry. Because Hollywood is turning out twice as much film as it did 10 years ago, computers are taking a larger role in the filmmaking process.

The Black Hole, produced by Walt Disney Studios in Burbank, California, used a special computer system—Automated Camera Effects System (ACES). It consisted of a computer-controlled model platform coordinated with a computer-controlled camera platform. This system gave the viewer the effect of observing a mile-long space colony; the colony was

Programmed by computer, the robots at Pizza Time Theatre franchises entertain patrons.

PROFILE

NOLAN BUSHNELL

Video games are the most popular form of computerized entertainment. Nolan Bushnell is acknowledged as the person who started this trend with the introduction of Pong in 1972.

Bushnell, a creative genius, grew up in Clearfield, Utah. His interest in science and technology was evident in his childhood experiments and pranks. Games too had an important role in Bushnell's life. He supported himself through college by directing the games department at a Salt Lake City amusement park. After briefly working at Ampex, Bushnell founded his own company, Atari, in 1971 with a $500 investment and began marketing Pong—the first commercially successful video game. The game was so successful that Warner Communications bought the company for $28 million in 1976. As part of the deal, Bushnell signed a contract restraining him from competing against Atari for seven years.

Since games were temporarily out of his life, Bushnell began developing other ideas—robotics in particular. In 1977 he opened the first Pizza Time Theatre Restaurant in San Jose, California. It offered an arcade of coin-operated games and miniature amusement park rides, but the real attraction of the restaurant was entertainment provided by Muppetlike robots. Like Pong, Pizza Time became an instant hit; by 1983 there were 200 franchises.

Meanwhile Bushnell also established Catalyst Technologies, an organization to provide facilities and financial support for entrepreneurial companies, including Androbot, which recently introduced one of the first personal robots perhaps creating the next revolution in the home market. Another venture, Sente Technologies, has been formed to research second-generation video games. Since Bushnell's agreement to stay out of the video game market ended in October of 1983, it is expected that he will soon announce introduction of a new frontier in video games making use of the new videodisc technology.

really a 10-foot scale model. Safety was also considered by ACES' designers. The system's software has been designed so that when it detects a hazard (possible damage to props or persons), execution of that move is halted automatically.

Star Trek, produced at Paramount Studios, also used special effects done by a computerized camera system, called COMPSY—Computerized Multiplane System. It uses an updated version of the multiplane imaging first developed in the early 1930s at Disney Studios. In this technique eight or ten sheets of glass, each having different details painted on it, were stacked. When the camera moved past the stacked sheets of glass, the images nearest the camera appeared in the foreground. The images on the sheets farther back from the camera appeared as the background.

Sound Editing Sound editing of films, the addition of sound effects, has been in existence since 1970. ACCESS, a microcomputer-based disk library and editing system, is one of the most complete computer sound libraries. The system contains a complete sound effects library, which includes such sounds as an automobile crash and chirping crickets. Because unsightly wires and microphones would have to be placed in the camera's field of view, certain sound effects, like sirens, bells, and even footsteps, must be added after the filming. These sounds can last up to 30 seconds and can be shrunk or stretched as needed. ACCESS was designed at a cost of $.5 million.

Animation Imagine a flight simulator being used to generate animation for commercial television spots. An award-winning animation house, Robert Able & Associates, specializes in such a system and the base price of the system is just under $150,000. A total of 1,440 individual frames need to be filmed for one six-second animated television spot. Once difficult for an artist, the task is simplified by the computer. In fact, commercials in the form of line drawings can now be filmed directly from a 21-inch graphic display unit. Three views of the object to be animated must be drawn by the artist—right side, front, and top. The drawings are then translated into numerical points by a digitizer. These points are stored in the memory of the computer, and the processor presents an image of the object that can be rotated in space or moved farther away or closer.

In 1938 Walt Disney Studios released its first feature-length film, a conventional animation—*Snow White and the Seven Dwarfs*. In 1982 they released *TRON*, which used computers in the production phases. TRON's writer and director, Steven Lisberger, used computers to offer sights that no camera—or eye—had ever before seen. More than half of the film's 96 minutes contained fantasy sequence backgrounds generated by computer. Also, animation for half of the show was achieved by electronic means.

As one can imagine, the actor's performance was changed because of the use of computers. With only a neutral backdrop and a bare stage, the actors had to perform some complicated actions. They were filmed in black and white and color was added electronically.

Ben Franklin and Thomas Jefferson in a computer-controlled scene from *The American Adventure* at Epcot Center.

Using computer simulation, no physical limitations are placed on objects. For example, one object can pass directly through another. Nothing like this could be performed with conventional means of filming. *TRON* is somewhat of a breakthrough in the movie industry, displaying not only a new area of technology but also a new way of seeing.

Disney computers can also approximate the motions of the human body by a specially designed and patented system called Audio-Animatronics. The system is so refined that it not only simulates movement but it also coordinates it with voices, music, and sound effects. Whatever its origin or original purpose, such a technological breakthrough becomes a part of science's "tool box," ready to use when the next need or idea comes along.

Computers in Music: Symphonies Produced by Computer?

The popularity of the computer—especially the microcomputer—extends to the area of music (Figure 12-5). French composer and former music director of the New York Philharmonic Orchestra, Pierre Boulez, used computer technology to produce an 18-minute work, *Repons*. The piece uses 24 musicians, six soloists, and a computer to alter and transform the musical sounds produced by the soloists. These altered sounds are carried over six loudspeakers, which are stationed around the performance hall.

The late John Lennon used computer editing during the recording of his last album, *Double Fantasy*. Lennon would reject take after take while making the album. Finally, his producer, Jack Douglas, had the idea of using the computer as an editor. The best portions of the takes were pulled and the computer merged them. The computer successfully com-

FIGURE 12-5 Microcomputer Music System

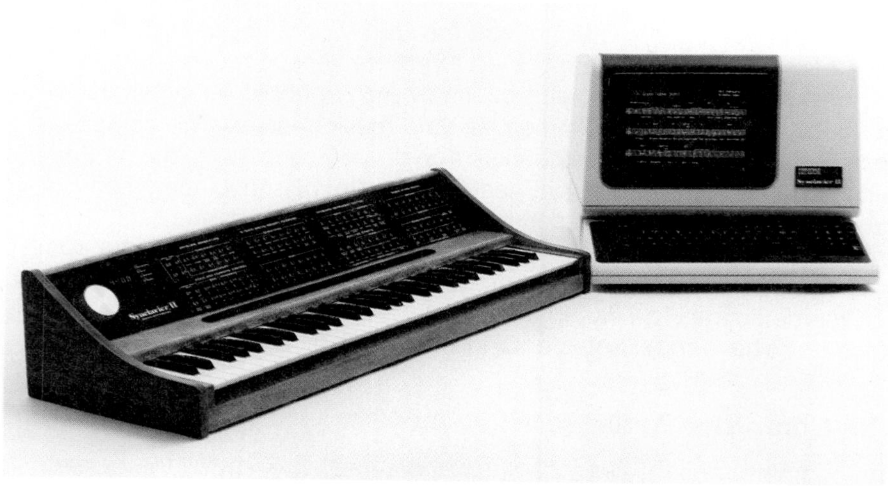

Complex programming procedures are needed to produce computer art. This example shows a pattern of color and lines.

pleted the editing in 10 minutes. Lennon was very pleased with the results.

Besides being able to reproduce sounds of specific instruments, computers also produce other sound effects such as stones scraping pavement or breaking glass. The sounds are stored on a floppy disk. These stored sounds can also be modified to imitate various moods.

Computerized music is being heard by many people—sometimes unknowingly—in television commercials and music themes. The computer-designed music for TV commercials appears on such spots as Dr. Pepper, Club Med, and Kentucky Fried Chicken. In TV show theme songs, the theme from the hospital series "St. Elsewhere" heads the list.

The main advantage of computerized music is economic. Before computers, musicians were hired to produce the music for TV commercials and theme songs. The studio computers save money and time, as musicians don't have to be selected and paid for their performance.

The Computer Artist

The computer artist (Figure 12-6) does not need to know all the details about computers but he or she must be knowledgeable about program-

FIGURE 12-6
Computer Artist
Here Hewlett Packard 2703A is used in a typical commercial art application.

ming. This expertise is equivalent to knowing about different types of brushes and paints.

One of the leading microcomputer artists is Saul Bernstein. Although his art career goes back to the early 1960s, Bernstein began his work in computerized art in 1978 after receiving a microcomputer. The terminal became a tablet for his paintings. Bernstein has won an Emmy Award and has gained nationwide recognition as a result of his work in microcomputerized animation. In addition, he was commissioned by Hewlett-Packard to "paint" portraits of Prince Phillip and Queen Elizabeth using his computer. The Queen is reported to have had difficulty telling the computer images from photographs.

CONCLUSION

Computers are definitely with us in the areas of art, entertainment and leisure. The next time we read a poem or novel, listen to a television commercial for fried chicken, tour an art gallery, or ride a roller coaster, we will undoubtedly be experiencing the effects of computers. They are offering us a new way of seeing and experiencing our environment.

ISSUE

CREATIVE COMPUTERS: IS MICHELANGELO THREATENED?

Within the past few years, artists in various fields have begun turning to the computer as a means of enhancing their creativity. Painters, musicians, writers, filmmakers, script writers, and designers have all been finding computers useful.

Creative people, it is believed, possess the characteristics of curiosity, flexibility, originality, and sensitivity to problems. The creative person is usually keenly aware of the smallest details of his or her surroundings, seeing much more than the obvious.

Keeping these characteristics in mind, let us look at how creative people—painters, musicians, and writers—use the computer to express their ideas.

For artists, the light pen may now be used in place of the brush and a visual display screen may take the place of the canvas. Using this medium allows the artist a new flexibility. Unlike Picasso, the artist will not have to draw two versions of the same subject to see which best meets his or her goal without destroying the finished product. The screen allows the artist to experiment with various ideas; if the finished product is unsatisfactory, it can be selectively erased so the artist can begin again.

A Chinese artist, Pang Yun-Jie, for example, works in an art form similar to that done in his country in the sixteenth century. His art, however, uses computers. Pang is a computer scientist; only recently did he begin to experiment with using the computer for image making.

Pang's images are unique, although they duplicate the 2,000-year-old technique of Chinese painting. Rather than making geometric shapes and patterns, he uses the computer to create brush strokes—a result of programming. The strokes can be overlaid to create such objects as trees and pagodas. Each piece of art is different. The variety of shapes is nearly unlimited as his program randomly alters details of each object, for example, bamboo branches and leaves. Yet, it is the computer that is creating the variations, not Pang. Is he really in that sense an artist?

Music has also become one of the more popular arts that use computers. This may be partly because one does not have to know how to read music to compose music on the computer.

Ed Walsh, a New York session musician, uses computers on various projects, including albums and television commercials. Walsh feels the computer systems make the creation and storage of music easy. The work of an entire orchestra can be done by one man at a keyboard. Other musicians, such as jazz great Herbie Hancock and pianist Peter Nero, also write music using computers.

In addition to musicians (and nonmusicians) composing music with the computer, the computer itself can also compose music. Using a random number generator, it produces a series of numbers representing pitches and durations of notes. When portions of the generated music do not conform to certain composition rules, the computer rejects these musical portions. Therefore, except for the restraints of the composition rules based on principles of melody and harmony, the end composition is generated totally at random.

But if a computer can do that all by itself, who needs the artist?

Computers can also be used to generate plots for writers. There are a number of programs available for this purpose. One program in particular is capable of generating 7,728 different plots. And for each of these, variations can also be introduced. For a science fiction novel, the number of monsters can be changed, and for a murder mystery, the number of victims can be altered. A computer has not yet produced any masterpieces of poetry or fiction. But attempts are being made in these areas.

If computers, then, can randomly alter details of

ISSUE

paintings, be used for music synthesis, and generate plots for writers, how much of the final product can be attributed to the user's creativity? Is it the artist or the computer that is producing the artwork? Will computers stimulate an artist's creativity by leading the user to new concepts and new ways of using concepts? Will they allow the artist to take a different perspective on his or her work? Finally, does computer creativity threaten artists?

The real issue then is whether the user of the computer art program is truly acting as an artist. Is the computer being used by that person as a medium for artistic expression, or to actually generate the art?

For example, a painter uses paint as an artistic medium with which to communicate his or her art; yet the paint itself is not capable of making itself into a picture without help.

The computer on the other hand, causes a special consideration in this area. A properly written program can, in effect, create art without any intervention from the user aside from plugging in the machine and inserting the disk with the program on it. In that case, how creative is the person using the machine being? Or, is it the computer which is really creating the art?

The issue is further muddled when we consider that not all computer art programs work this way. Some allow the user to interact; others, graphics tablets in particular, simply allow the user to erase and redraw or change colors. They are similar to having a notepad that remembers what you have drawn and can redraw it for you. Or, one that erases itself. In these cases, it would really be exaggerating to say that the computer is creating art.

If the self-generating artist programs are to become popular, what will become of the traditional artists? Will not computer art be cheaper and of similar quality? Will Michelangelo be threatened?

SUMMARY POINTS

- Computer-controlled lighting is used in Broadway shows, at the Metropolitan Opera House, and in ballet.
- Dance notation in ballet is more useful than other recording techniques, such as filming and videotaping.
- Computers are generating poetry, but require appropriate programming and accompanying data (vocabulary).
- Writers are using the word-processing capabilities of computers to write novels.
- Multi-author novels are being created on computer networks.
- In baseball, batting averages and runs batted in are being determined by computers.
- Computer-generated graphics are being used by the Chicago White Sox baseball team to show the fly balls hit by their players during the previous season.
- The United Scouting Combine (USC) keeps statistics on approximately 1,000 college players.
- Cyclists are using computers to compute speed and distance; an additional option for cyclists is a heart-rate monitor.
- Programs have been written that are used to draft playing schedules for the National and American baseball leagues, the National Basketball Association, and both the outdoor and indoor soccer leagues.
- Scriptwriting for some television shows is now being done using computers.
- Computers are used behind the scenes in Hollywood for sound effects and expanding artistic capabilities.
- Computers are used in the area of music to edit recordings, reducing recording time for musicians.
- Computer graphics, used widely in the areas of manufacturing and engineering, are being used by computer artists.

REVIEW QUESTIONS

1. Explain how computers are used in the arts. What aspects of the computer are used?
2. How is word processing assisting potential authors?
3. Explain how poems such as "Apologies to Emily Dickenson" are created with the computer.
4. Will baseball become a science with the increasing use of computers in the sport?
5. Why was "Dukes of Hazzard" a first?
6. List several different areas in art, entertainment, and leisure in which word-processing is being used.
7. What are the new applications of computers for bicycling?
8. How is computer-aided design (CAD) being used in Hollywood?
9. How is the flight simulator used for commercial television spots?

10. How does the production of Disney's *Snow White and the Seven Dwarfs* differ from the production of *TRON*? Be specific.
11. How are computers used at Disney World?
12. How were computers used for the late John Lennon's album, *Double Fantasy*?
13. What are some applications of computer music in the television world?

DISCUSSION QUESTIONS

1. Do you think that the graphic capabilities of the computer will overpower the artist's creative contribution to a work? Why?
2. The computer was named "Man of the Year" ("Machine of the Year") by *Time* in January 1983. Will the computer become the "Poet of the Future?"
3. Complete notation has not existed until recently for ballet. Before notation, ballets were taught by the choreographer or by members of the ballet company. What effect will computers have in ballet?
4. With computers being used by the National Football League (NFL) to monitor collegiate players and generate reports on all players, will the issue of privacy become a controversy?
5. Computers are used in the movie industry to create special sound effects and special scenery. What do you see in the future of computer use in the movie industry?
6. Does word processing really assist people or does it just promote additional editing?

CHAPTER 13

COMPUTERS IN SOCIETY: GOVERNMENT, PRIVACY, AND CRIME

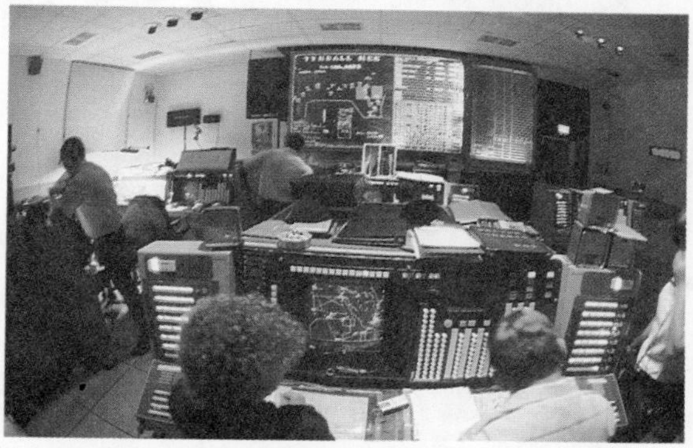

OUTLINE

ARTICLE

KEEP THE COMPUTERS FROM TELLING SECRETS

In the movie *War Games*, a teen-age computer whiz taps into a military computer and nearly starts World War III.

Last week, life imitated art: A dozen Milwaukee high school hackers were caught infiltrating computers at places like New Mexico's Los Alamos National Laboratory, where nuclear weapons are made, and at New York's Sloan-Kettering Cancer Center.

Are the nation's computers really so vulnerable? Experts say that national security information is heavily coded and guarded—that the *War Games* script is fantasy.

But the security of government computers is deteriorating, recent studies conclude—which means that sensitive information about every one of us could become as easy for computer criminals to play with as a video game.

There are no valid statistics to measure computer crime, but the losses are enormous. Guesses range all the way from $100 million a year to $2 billion.

One thing we do know: As more valuable information is stored in computers, the crimes are becoming more spectacular. Last year a boxing promoter was convicted of stealing $21 million from Wells Fargo Bank computers—the largest bank embezzlement in American history.

Often the thief wants information, such as the economist caught tapping the Federal Reserve Board computer last winter for secret data on the nation's money supply—data that could have made his "predictions" come true.

Whether the object is money or information, stealing by computer is just like breaking into a house or a company filing cabinet—only neater, cleaner and harder to trace.

And the most vulnerable victim of computer crime may be not government, not corporations, but you.

As an ordinary citizen, you may think you're anonymous. But computers know a great deal about you. The Internal Revenue Service knows how much money you make and where it comes from. Law enforcement agencies know if you've ever been arrested. Your credit card company knows how much you buy and when and where you buy it.

If a clever, persistent high school student can tap into the computers that store this information, a criminal can, too. So could an employer, a landlord or a credit bureau. Then, you might as well wave goodbye to your privacy.

The first line of security, of course, is to question whether sensitive information needs to be in a computer at all. But if it does, it must be protected. Security must come first. And existing laws, framed before computers existed, need to be modified to make computer crime easier to prosecute.

Up to now, advances in computer technology have far outpaced advances in computer security. If we value our privacy and the security of our institutions, we'd better close that gap fast.

Much valuable and important information is being stored in computers. Although computer crime is not new, amateurs are making it more apparent that the data stored in the computers are not safe from intruders. Because government has the most data on us, privacy is a growing concern.

INTRODUCTION

The government collection and use of information and the issues of privacy and crime have taken on new meaning with the advent of computerization. Computers are used by government to collect and process scientific data. Computers are also used to gather data on individuals. When we complete the census, fill out our income tax statement, apply for a credit card through a major department store, or attend a university, information is collected on us as individuals and filed in a computer system for later recall. Because access to such information is made easier through the use of computers, the protection of privacy becomes an important concern. Also, data within the computer can be manipulated by others; therefore, computers have made possible crimes that would have been impossible without the computer. At the same time, because of their ability to provide rapid access to information about court cases and criminal records, computers are assisting us in solving crimes.

GOVERNMENT

The federal government is the single largest user of computers in the United States. As such, it gives rise to some of the worst fears (such as those generated by *War Games*) and the highest hopes (space exploration) computer observers can imagine.

Two major categories in which computers are used in government are simulation and modeling, and data bases.

Simulation and Modeling

Computers have long been a mainstay in the Department of Defense weapons development program, doing everything from simulating wars (Figure 13-1) to designing and testing weapons to actually guiding mis-

FIGURE 13-1 War Simulation
This participant uses the computer for War Games simulation exercises. The display screens represent various situations that may be encountered in an actual war.

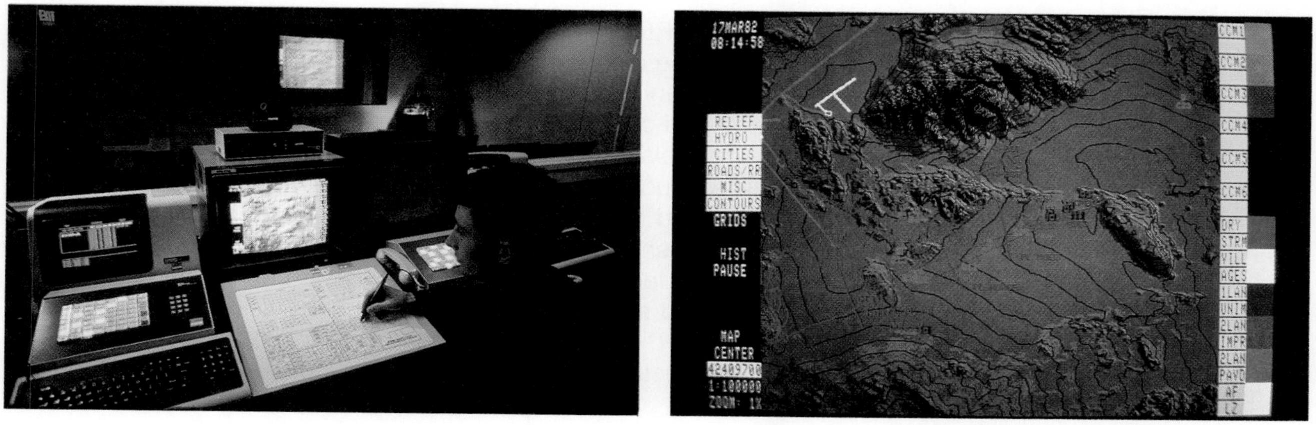

Control console computer for a multiple launch rocket system.

siles. As computers have nudged their way into the civilian school system, so have they advanced into military training programs.

Military

U.S. NAVY TRAINING DEVICE. The U.S. Navy is currently experimenting with a training device called NAVTAG (*Navy Technical Action Game*). The game is equipped with three terminals: one for "them," one for "us," and one for the referee. In addition to the several tactical scenes built into the game, players can invent their own. Essential information—such as target location and fuel on hand—is flashed onto the display terminals in written or graphic form. Players access the information and plan their battles accordingly. The referee can add factors into the game to make it more difficult. The game teaches not only tactics, but provides the players with real information, such as real ship names and data on accuracy and range of weapons.

U.S. ARMY PREPARES FOR NUCLEAR WAR. It was a clear day. A 15-square-mile slice of land could be visualized from the vantage point of United States military officers. Blue rivers could be distinguished along with mountains and cities. Within moments, tanks could be seen rolling through the pastureland toward a nearby town. The tanks stayed close to the woods. The opposing forces opened fire. Flashes of white resulted from exploding land mines, helicopters flew overhead, and artillery fire—like laser beams lashing out—opened across the land.

One officer decided to attack and "go nuke." A bomb exploded in a flash of orange and a white circle appeared. The officer momentarily rejoiced as he noticed that he had killed the enemy. Looking around, he realized he also destroyed his own troops; his weapon had been too powerful.

This experience—a computer simulation of a nuclear war—took place in 1981 in the Lawrence Livermore National Laboratory at the request of the Pentagon. The computer simulation, Janus, was used as part of a five-week session initiating the $2.45 million Army nuclear war-simulation project. The Janus program was named after the two-faced Roman god believed to guard Rome in war-time.

The U.S. Army War College in Carlisle, Pennsylvania, is now using Janus to train high-ranking officers for command positions. Janus executes two million programming instructions per second, providing real time results. Preprogrammed, the flight time of artillery shells has been calculated to the millisecond. So precise is Janus, it even calculates how fallout will blow and how fast a fireball will spread, taking into account humidity, temperature, and wind speed.

The Defense Department states that the nuclear war simulation will teach officers to consider more clearly both the benefits and the costs of battlefield strategies. So far, all officers in training seem surprised at the rapidity of casualties.

An expert on the psychological impact of computer games, Professor Sherry Turkle, at Massachusetts Institute of Technology, stated: "The computer is confronting us with something we tend to repress: the brute fact that we are playing with the survival of the planet."

Shown here is a data tag with coded information to replace the old "dog tag."

National Bureau of Standards Works to Prevent Fires Computer modeling techniques are being tested by the National Bureau of Standards to

The operating position in the Washington Terminal of the Washington-Moscow Direct Communications Link.

help with fire prevention (Figure 13-2). Such models answer questions about, for example, how quickly a fire spreads, how material burns, and how intense a fire must be before the fire alarm goes off. For maximum model effectiveness, many variables must be considered, such as the type of furnishings, construction materials used in the building, and the chemical makeup of the air.

Models can also be used to devise evacuation paths for people in the buildings and to aid fire fighters in predicting the areas where the fire is likely to spread in a burning building.

U.S. Bureau of Land Management Uses a Lightning Alert Facility In California the computer has been drafted to minimize the effects of an age-old hazard of nature: the lightning strike and its devasting effect on forests. At its present stage, the strike detection system is used mainly to guide exploratory aircraft to the site of the strike. But plans are for the system to eventually provide fire fighters with such additional information as the type of land on which the strike occurred, the topography, and the kind of vegetation.

Developed for the U.S. Bureau of Land Management, the lightning alert facility uses sensors located throughout the state to scan for the positive electrical charges that occur when lightning hits the ground. From this information, the computer calculates the approximate locations and pinpoints it on a map for the exploratory flyovers. The information can also

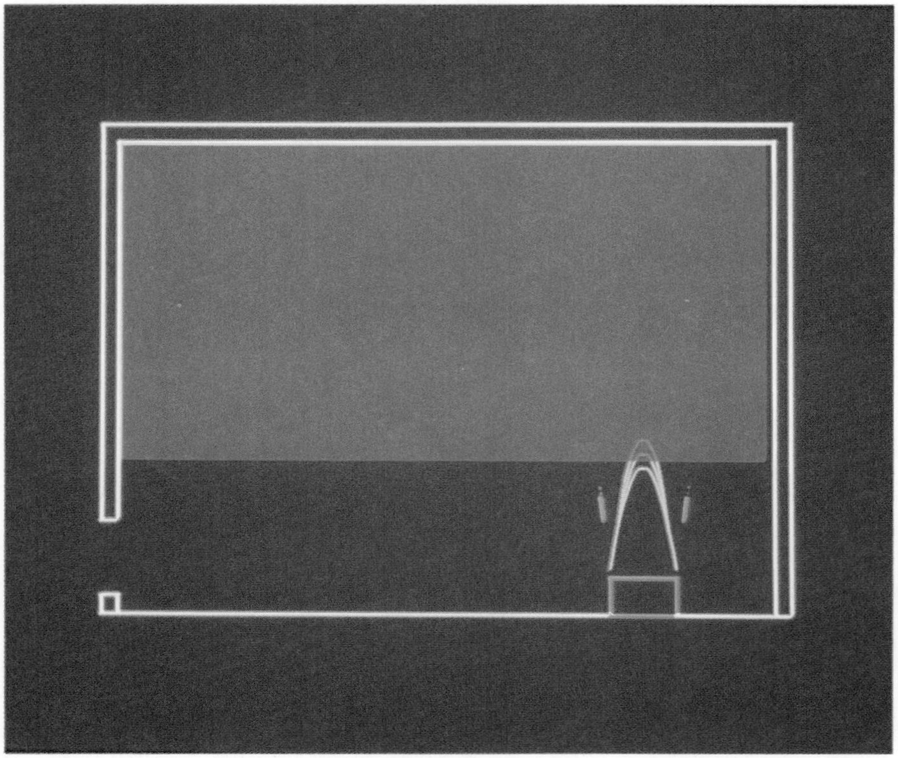

FIGURE 13-2 Fire Model

A simple single compartment fire model shows the hot upper layer in red, the burning object in green, the flame in orange, and the fire plume in blue. Fire researchers at the National Bureau of Standards use computer models to take what is known about fires and predict what would happen if a particular fire were to break out in different-sized rooms or under different conditions.

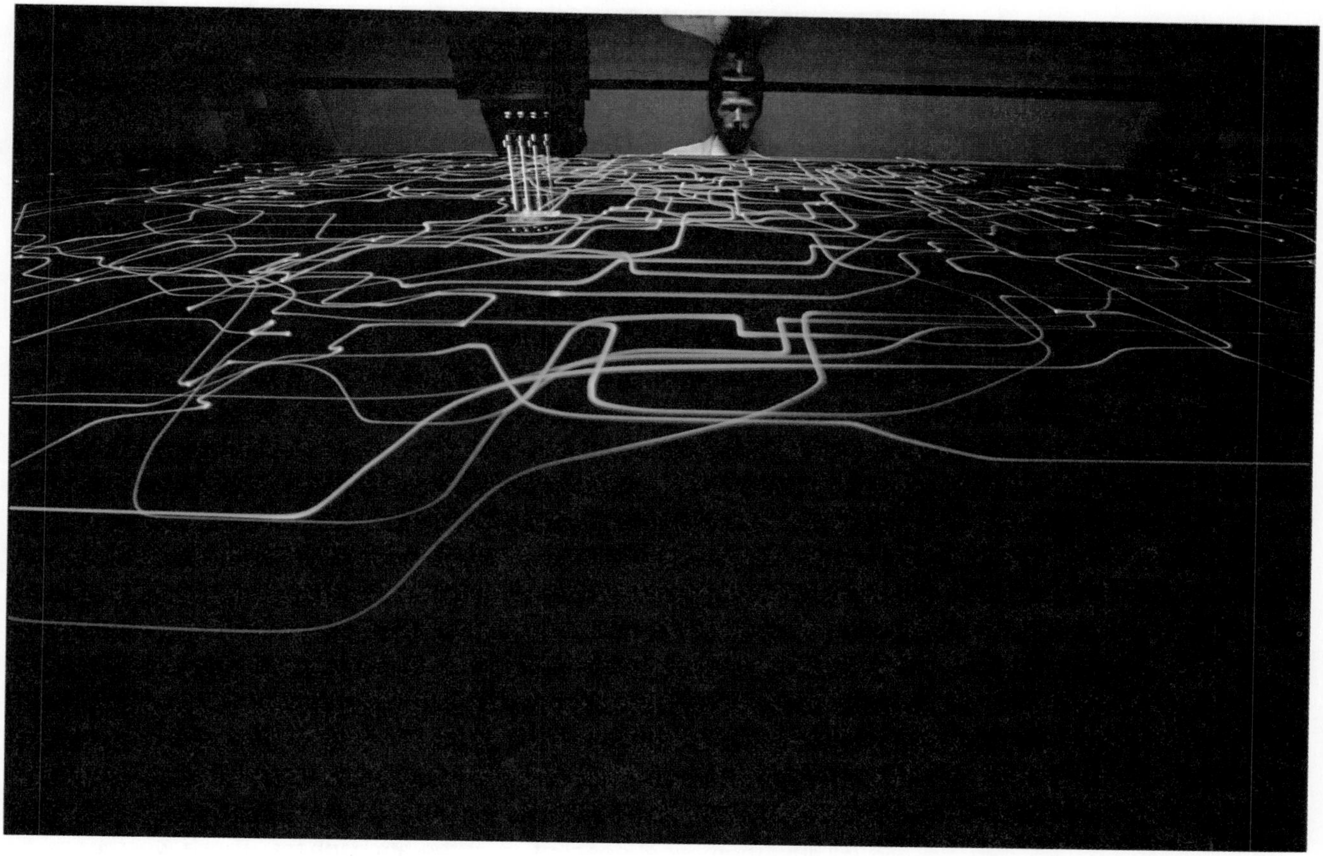

Computer-controlled color plotter is part of a multicomputer system developed by Planning Research Corporation of McLean, Virginia, for the Defense Mapping Agency to improve map production. System will permit both automated and interactive editing of digitized cartographic data.

be relayed to ground-based fire fighters. The entire process takes about five minutes.

National Weather Service Forecasting: Up to the Minute Using Computers The forecasting of weather is one of the most interesting applications of computers in government. Several variables, such as air pressure, velocity, humidity, and temperature, are input into huge computers for the processing of complex mathematical equations. The equations describe the interaction of these variables. Combining these data with mathematical models, forecasters can predict the weather.

The world's weather information is collected by the National Weather Service in Maryland from a variety of locations: hundreds of data-collection programs (DCPs), which are placed on buoys, ships, helium-filled balloons, and airplanes; about 70 weather stations; and four satellites. Of the four satellites, two orbit the Earth over the poles to send pictures revealing the movement and shape of clouds. The remaining two satellites are stationary and photograph the Earth above the equator.

Although local forecasters use radar data directly, they also rely on the weather service information. The service's "brain" consists of 14 computers housed at the meteorological center. These computers receive in-

Weather satellite computer display of a hurricane system.

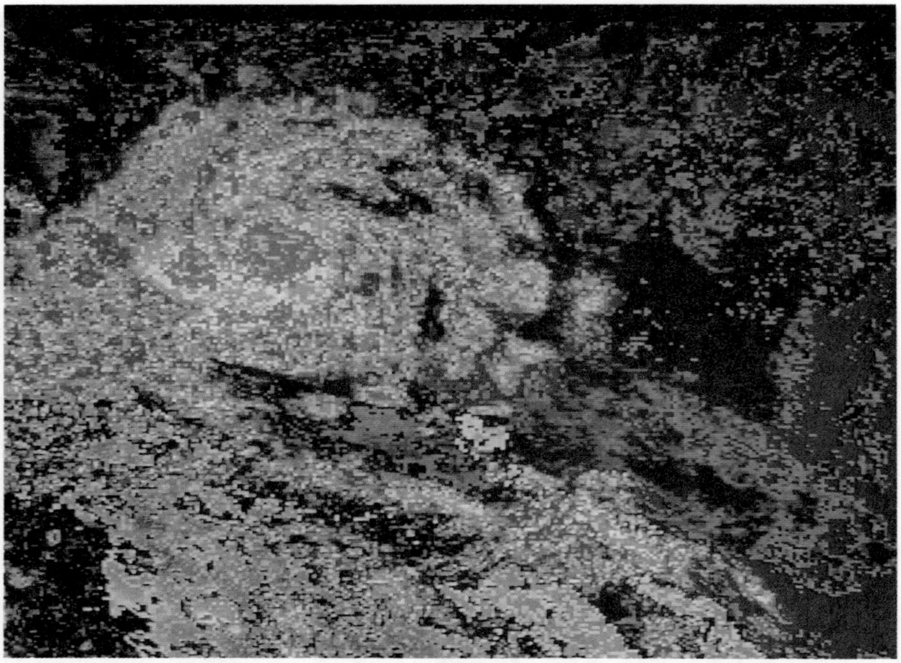

formation from some of the DCPs whose data are beamed up to the two stationary satellites above the equator. The computers also receive information from other DCPs; the information travels from ground station to ground station. The 14 computers use all of this incoming data to construct a mathematical description of the atmosphere. These weather reports—2,000 daily—are then sent to local weather offices.

Processing and analyzing demographic and economic data collected in the 1980 census of population and housing.

Data Bases

Data bases, large information files kept on individuals and documents, are most prevalent in the government. Much of the information in these data bases is acquired from the census returns filed each decade and the income tax returns filed annually. Three of the largest data bases are in the Library of Congress, the FBI, and the IRS.

Library of Congress The work of the mammoth Library of Congress has been radically changed by the computer. The library's storage, retrieval, and printing system now converts library cards into digital images on optical disks developed by Xerox. Under the old system, the library's file cabinets of catalog cards ran the length of a football field. The same information can now be stored on about 30 14-inch optical disks. Each disk holds about 200,000 library cards.

FBI Another keeper of enormous records is the Federal Bureau of Investigation. The bureau's master index alone contains nearly five million index cards. To make its records more useful, the FBI has organized sev-

The government depends on information to formulate public policy on such matters as unemployment, inflation, resource utilization, and pollution. Jay Forrester is a leading authority on using computers in such applications.

Forrester got his start in the computer business at MIT's Digital Computer Laboratory while working on the Whirlwind I computer project. The Whirlwind's purpose was to experiment with real-time aircraft simulation; therefore, speed and reliability were a must. Forrester, the laboratory chief, devised a new internal memory, the magnetic core, to accomplish this objective.

PROFILE

JAY W. FORRESTER

Magnetic cores were the internal memory medium of second-generation and third-generation computers.

In the late 1950s Forrester became absorbed in a new effort—system dynamics. System dynamics uses computer simulations to study human social systems by analyzing factors contributing to the problems of inflation, unemployment, and the like.

eral computer-accessed data bases and is working toward having all of its 500 or so offices connected to the data bases by the end of the 1980s.

Among the bureau's new information setups are the Organized Crime Information System (OCIS), the Investigative Support Information System (ISIS), and the Foreign Counter Intelligence System (FCIS). OCIS has information on about 50,000 habitual criminals and is organized to discover associations among the criminals that might not be detected through regular avenues of research (Figure 13-3). ISIS coordinates the thousands of leads that are common in complex criminal cases. And FCIS tracks the movements and associations of suspected foreign spies and international terrorists. Although terminals for retrieving material from these files are in only a handful of offices, the bureau visualizes the time when terminals can be located in the agents' cars or even hand held.

IRS Every person living in the United States who earns more than a minimal amount of money must report to the federal government for tax purposes. In addition, corporations and businesses file annual tax returns on their businesses. The Internal Revenue Service (IRS) receives millions of tax returns each year. Computers are used by the IRS to monitor these returns and record the information (Figure 13-4). Without the aid of computers, it would take many years to process just one year's worth of returns.

The IRS also performs audits on selected returns. Computers are used to randomly select tax returns for audits and perform some of the preliminary operations. This reduces the number of manual operations required to perform the audits, increasing the number of audits that can be performed each year.

FIGURE 13-3 FBI's OCIS Terminals

The IRS recently lived up to its own publicity when one of its computers detected that a taxpayer had made a one-cent underpayment of his taxes, because of an error in math. The computer automatically fired off a letter demanding payment of the penny, plus a fine of $159.78. "Obviously, the computer has gone berserk," an IRS agent admitted.

FIGURE 13-4 IRS Tax Return Processing

Other Computer Applications

Automating Air Traffic Control The nation's air traffic control system is expected to become more fully automated over the next decade at a cost of $85 billion. This cost includes new computers, advanced radar systems, airborne collision avoidance equipment, and other technology. By building elements of the ground control system into the plane's cockpit, the required number of controllers and technicians will drop by a third. The display screens currently monitored by two or three controllers will be monitored by one controller with a wider area of air space in his or her control. By the year 2000, it is estimated that more than $20 billion will be saved.

Medicaid Assisted by Computers After a computer took over payment of federal Medicaid costs for the Office of Medical Assistance, Pennsylvania's Department of Welfare recently realized a $12 million savings. The state's 29,000 doctors annually produce 22 million invoices for the system, which services 1.1 million Medicaid recipients. The savings were achieved by a reduction in the number of erroneous, fraudulent, and duplicate health claims.

Before the Office of Medical Assistance obtained a Univac computer, the incoming doctors' bills were paid manually, making it practically impossible to identify duplicate bills. The system also made it difficult to spot Medicaid recipients who were overusing the system with too-frequent doctor visits.

Computers Link State's Public Schools In Florida an ambitious plan is underway that will computer-link all the state's public schools—from kindergartens to universities—by 1986. One of the major benefits will be an ability to forward student data from one level to the next without the tedious form filling and form keeping still common in most systems. Transcripts will be called up and printed instantly. All information can be passed on electronically from one school or college to the next.

PRIVACY

With computers being used as the main means of storage of personal information on credit, employment, taxes, and other aspects of a person's life, the issue of privacy is becoming a growing concern. Since the early 1970s, regulations and laws regarding the protection of privacy have been enacted. These regulations and laws control the collection, use, distribution, and transmission of personal data.

Data Bases

Because of large data banks kept on individuals in the government (especially by the IRS), the workplace, banks, credit unions, and universities, many people feel that individual privacy is threatened.

PROFILE

KENNETH OLSEN

Digital Equipment Corporation (DEC), recognized as a giant in the computer industry, was founded in 1957 by Kenneth Olsen.

Olsen, a native of Stratford, Connecticut, earned his B.S. and M.S. degrees in Electrical Engineering from Massachusetts Institute of Technology. In 1950 he joined MIT's Digital Computer Laboratory as a research assistant and worked with Jay Forrester on the Whirlwind Computer project for four years. The Whirlwind proved to be such a success that in 1954 the Air Defense Command awarded MIT with another project, the SAGE system—a computer and radar network designed to detect enemy aircraft. Under the leadership of Olsen, the computer for this project was developed in less than a year.

Olsen remained involved in the SAGE project for the next few years. In 1957, with a $70,000 investment from American Research and Development, Olsen founded a company in an old woolen mill. The company's early products were circuit modules originally used for testing purposes and later for designing the company's first computer—the Programmed Data Processor (PDP). Refinements to the PDP led to the development of minicomputers in the mid 1960s. As the name implies, minicomputers were smaller and less expensive; thus they were ideal for small-business applications. More importantly, the machines were interactive; the user could communicate with the computer via a video or keyboard terminal. As a result, DEC has become the world leader of the minicomputer industry.

Still serving as the company president, Olsen has established a museum to preserve the historical aspect of the computer industry. When he learned that MIT was disposing of the Whirlwind in 1974, he hurried to rescue it. The Whirlwind along with other computer artifacts and memorabilia, dating from Napier's Bones to the more recent experimental robots, are now on display at The Computer Museum in Marlborough, Massachusetts.

Because information is both easier to obtain and easier to store as a result of computers, there are more data being collected on individuals. An individual's data are stored in one main file and can be easily accessed by entering his or her social security number.

Also, the increased ease of obtaining information tempts organizations to collect more information than is really necessary. People then have less control over who has access to their personal information. They are unaware of whether their personal data files are complete and accurate. They may not even be aware that such information is being kept about them at all.

The major concerns about privacy can be summarized:

- Too much personal information about individuals is being collected and stored in computerized files. The possibility of file integration exists because many of the systems use social security numbers as a common means of identification. This permits the various users to link files, easily correlating and matching scattered bits of data.
- The accuracy, completeness, and currency of the information may be low.
- Much of the personal information data may be irrelevant for the purposes for which they will be used.

- Decisions are often made by organizations solely on the basis of these computerized records.
- The security of stored data is a problem.

Despite the negative aspects of this type of computer use, it does reduce cost and add to efficiency. It is helpful, say, for a business to have adequate financial information about an individual before issuing credit. However, there must be an appropriate balance between the need for information by an organization and the rights of individuals to maintain their privacy.

Privacy Legislation

Efforts to protect our privacy have led government, particularly at the federal level, to pass several laws and regulations. The major legislation has been the Privacy Act of 1974, which covers information gathered by the federal government. This act, applying only to federal agencies, provides that:

- Individuals must be able to determine what information about themselves is being recorded and how it will be used.
- A way for individuals to correct wrong information must be made.
- Information collected for one purpose should not be used for another without consent of the individual involved.
- Organizations creating, manipulating, using, or divulging personal information must ensure its reliability and take precautions to prevent its misuse.

Although the act did not extend to state and local governments, many states have followed suit with similar legislation. States are also becoming aware of the need to protect individuals from privacy invasion by private businesses. Recently, California, Illinois, and Wisconsin have passed privacy laws. Six other states are currently considering such laws. However, the laws vary from state to state, as does their potential effectiveness.

The lawmaking process is slow on this issue, perhaps partly due to the lack of litigation over privacy. Since the data may be disclosed without the knowledge or consent of the subjects, most people will not realize their privacy has been breached. If they did know, many still would not go to court for fear of making public the very information they wanted protected.

CRIME AND CRIMINAL JUSTICE

Crime is another area in which computers play both a beneficial and a detrimental role. As we noted, computers have aided in preventing and solving crimes and, in addition, have strengthened the court system by allowing easier access to laws and decisions already on the books. However, there is a reverse side. People having a good understanding of computers have begun to use them as a means of illegally transferring funds to their possession. Such frauds are difficult to uncover. Programmers as well as "outsiders" have been involved in such frauds, making computer security very difficult.

Crime Prevention

The computer's ability to make statistical analyses has been called on in New York City to help authorities pinpoint buildings that are likely targets for arson. Several agencies contribute information to the computer about fires, and further data are available on fires in the recent past. Out of this mass of data, the computer constructs profiles of the most probable targets of arsonists. The city can both keep a watch on the building "candidates" and tell their owners how to lessen the risk of fires. The program is also intended to decrease the owners' incentive to burn the buildings to collect the insurance proceeds. Part of the data mix fed into the computer is the names of landlords who are behind in their taxes or who have been cited for safety or occupancy violations.

Another computerized crime predictor, this one maintained by the FBI, has drawn a good deal of criticism—some of it from members of Congress. No complaints are heard about the system as it pertains to tracking known criminals. What worries people is that the Justice Department is using the system to monitor people who are considered a threat to officials but who have never been convicted of a crime. Under the plan, the Secret Service can place in the FBI's National Crime Information Center computer the names of persons considered to be threats to the president, vice president, presidential candidates, visiting heads of state, or anyone else the Secret Service must protect (Figure 13-5). Among the most elaborate communication systems in the world, the National Crime Information Center is linked to 64,000 federal, state, and local justice agencies.

Computer technology has become an important tool for police work.

The head of the FBI said the Secret Service receives about 9,000 reports a year about people who might constitute a danger to public figures. Of these, 300 to 400 are considered dangerous. By putting these names in the bureau's massive computer, the Secret Service is able to learn immediately if any of its suspects are arrested and thus can keep track of their movements. In addition, any local law enforcement agency can quickly determine if a person they are considering arresting or have arrested is a Secret Service suspect. The fear that civil libertarians express about this system is that anyone's name might find its way into the computer, possibly causing damage to an innocent person.

Computer-aided Detection of Crimes

Not only have computers aided in crime prevention, but computers have also made some headlines in crime detection. A far-ranging computer system helped put an end to the string of child killings in Atlanta. Using two IBM computers and several data bases, the Atlanta police department was able to pinpoint Wayne Williams as the prime suspect in the 28 killings and ultimately convict him for the murder of two.

Because 10 different law enforcement agencies were involved in the

FIGURE 13-5 FBI's National Crime Information Center

Atlanta cases, officials agreed early in the investigation that a system was needed for handling and cross-checking the great volume of investigative data and tips that poured in. The computer system was designed so that key words could be fed into it to generate a printout of all other data that contained those words. For example, if someone reported seeing a blue van in the area where a body was discovered, operators could ask the computer to bring up all other references to "blue" and "van." Through such repeated uses of the computer, Williams was finally apprehended. When Williams went to trial, the computer system was used to check defense testimony against prior statements and the results were factored into the cross-examination.

Recently, after a machine gun raid on a Jewish restaurant in Paris, French President François Mitterand announced that his country was developing an antiterrorist data base to systematically put an end to this type of activity. The French antiterrorist data base holds information from a number of legal agencies, among them those having to do with border security, military security, and terrorism. It is modeled on a similar data base in Austria.

Computers in the Court System

Computers are widely used in the court systems across the United States. Some of the computer capabilities used include word processing, data-base capabilities for researching court cases, and special program packages designed for keeping track of juvenile charges and offenders, scheduling of court dockets, and many other tasks pertaining to the functioning of the court system.

In the American judicial system, computers not only gather and compare evidence for trial, as in the Williams case, but they are also employed in jury selection, record keeping, and searches for legal precedents. The United States Supreme Court, which considers more than 5,000 cases a year, has installed a word-processing system with 65 terminals. Available to the justices, clerks, and secretaries, the terminals are streamlining the court's burden of drafting, writing, and rewriting as many as 150 opinions a year. It is not uncommon for an opinion to go through 10 or 15 rewrites before being accepted by a majority of the justices. The system's speed and editing flexibility save the court a lot of time.

One of the most time-consuming processes in law has been searching through past court decisions for precedents that might have bearing on current cases. To address this problem—and others—West Publishing Company in St. Paul has created a research service for lawyers and judges called WESTLAW. Since about 50,000 new cases are reported in the United States each year, keeping abreast of them, much less finding relevant information in the accumulated cases of many years past, is impossible by normal means. WESTLAW has in its data bases the full text and headnotes (brief explanations) of all opinions of the United States Supreme Court from 1925 to date, of the United States Court of Appeals from 1945 to date, and of the United States District Courts from 1950 to date. The full text and headnotes of all reported opinions of the state courts are available from 1967 to present years in most states and earlier than that in others.

Both state and federal cases are added to the data base as decisions are reported. Besides finding specific cases, the system can also find references to specific judges, witnesses, products, companies, medical terms, and unusual legal terms. These items are not usually indexed in law books.

Inslaw, a Washington, D.C., software company, has created program packages to streamline the ponderous administrative task of keeping track of people who pass through in the judicial system. One package is for juvenile charges and offenders. It tracks their referrals, offenses, delinquency charges, court appearances, parents or guardians, supervisors, witnesses, and the police officers and caseworkers involved. Another package schedules court dockets, keeps track of cases and the names of litigants, and maintains a record of each case from filing through final disposition. The third package monitors people who have been jailed. It covers the facts of the booking, calculates the automatic release date, accounts for inmate funds, aids in visitor control, lists reported incidents, and keeps a record of the facts surrounding the inmate's imprisonment.

Computer Crime

Law enforcers and lawbreakers alike are rallying to the computer with almost equal zeal. As we have seen, computers can amass, assess, and deliver large amounts of information on crime with much ease; this makes them the great hope of many law enforcers. However, for some, computers are the vehicles to a perfect crime, particularly if it only involves getting money or information that can be sold for money.

A lot of crimes committed with a computer, such as money and data theft, are never reported—perhaps because these crimes are among the hardest to discover or because the institutions that have suffered the losses may fear that disclosure will undermine investor confidence.

In 1977 a most original financial crime was committed using a computer. At Florida's Flagler Dog Track, a computer was used to figure the dog-racing odds. Because the races were so short, it was not until after the race was over that the odds could be completely figured. A computer operator, with the help of another, developed a system. The operator was informed of the race results by the cohort who had observed the race. The operator would then stop the computer program in progress and deduct a number of losers; in the losers' place, a corresponding number of winners was added in the computer storage. The program was restarted and shortly finished its run. False winning tickets, printed by the computer, were redeemed the following day. The loss went undetected because the winners were paid from a pool formed by the losers' money. Therefore, each winner's share was slightly less than it should have been.

The crimes that generally do come to light are those that seem bizarre or silly. A California man used the automatic teller machines at his bank to build up his account from $1.17 to $4.4 million—then stoutly maintained that his good fortune was a miracle of God. His method of operation was to punch in phantom deposits to his account and then withdraw real money. A built-in limitation on the amount that could be withdrawn within a single day kept the bank's actual loss at $2,000.

It is not trained experts only, though, who have demonstrated they can crack computers almost at will. High school students who have become hooked on computer capabilities routinely make games of these electronic raids. A student in Los Angeles did a quarter of a million dollars in damage to a leasing corporation by raiding its computer system, causing the system to collapse. Estimates are that a corporation will lose the ability to function properly if deprived of its computer system for more than

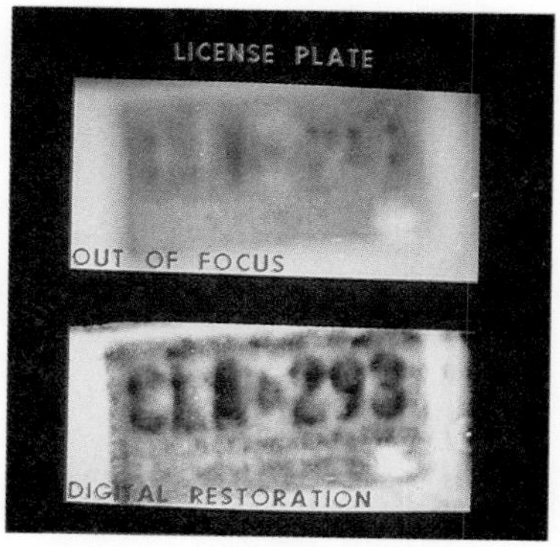

Image enhancement techniques sharpen a blurred photograph of a license plate. The top picture is the digitized image of a blurred photograph; the lower picture is the resulting image after it has been improved through image restoration.

"I know I don't have to wear a mask. I just can't pull a heist without one."

4.8 days. In New York four 13-year-olds electronically broke into several corporate computers in Canada, destroying some files at one and instructing another company, which did data processing for Pepsi-Cola, to send them 10 cases of Pepsi.

At a Social Security office in Baltimore, a clerk stole more than $100,000 by temporarily changing the addresses of those who were due additional payments and directing the checks to be mailed to her own post office box. Once this was done, she would restore the correct addresses in the computer and delete the phony ones.

A growing concern is that computers themselves will become the target of terrorists because of the crucial roles computers fill in the conduct of a nation's business and military affairs. The awareness that a criminal in one country could tap into the computers in another country and have them switch goods or funds to a third country is raising questions of law as well as questions of security. In fact, the ease with which computers can act across national borders is creating a security dilemma of a dimension all its own.

Several reasons may explain the recent rash of computer crimes: lax security in data-processing areas once a person gets past the front gate; the intrinsic flexibility of computers; the spread of microcomputers and their simplified operating instructions; computer skill being taught to students at an early age; the ease with which a lot of sensitive data can be stored; and more.

Computer Security

No matter how complex a computer's security is, the inventive spirit can find a way to get around it; and, it seems, each time one hole in the system is plugged, another opens. For a time in the early 1970s, the United States Department of Defense recruited teams of experts to make mock raids on the department's computers. Almost without exception, these teams, called tiger teams, were able to access the protected information. Their success became so frighteningly routine that the tiger teams were eventually disbanded.

To guard against computer abuse, systems may encode their data automatically to keep it from being understandable without a key. Also, some companies are making more restrictive rules about the portion of company data a data-processing worker may obtain. Some terminals are made to shut off and lock if their operators ask for data they have not been cleared to receive. The terminals can only be unlocked by a supervisor, who is thus alerted. In the final analysis, however, no computer system can be made more secure than the honesty of the people authorized to operate it.

Several years ago the Stanford Research Institute conducted a study on computer abuse. Data were collected over a four-year term. Calculations drawn by the Stanford study found the average loss per computer crime was $450,000. It should be noted, however, that the Stanford study involved only a fraction of the 100,000 computers in use at the time.

One reason computer crime is difficult to detect, if it takes place within a large company, is that the criminal usually appears to be a perfect employee. A profile of this computer criminal has been compiled. Often the would-be criminal is young and ambitious and possesses impressive educational credentials. He may be a technician, programmer, manager, or high-ranking executive. The detection of such criminals has mainly been accidental rather than accomplished by an established detection technique.

Several measures must therefore be taken by companies and government to prevent computer crime. A well-trained security force is one. Also, screening procedures (and selection procedures) should be examined more closely. Selection of programmers should be done carefully. Last, any violation of company rules by an employee must lead to discharge of the employee.

Another type of computer crime is the illegal copying of software—computer piracy. Because software is valuable, United States copyright laws allow the buyer to make only one backup copy of a purchased program. However, when an individual attempts to make a copy of a purchased program, he may discover that the backup cannot be made because of special codes within the software. This has been used to justify programs on the market that have been written to attempt to outsmart the software developers. These programs disable or circumvent the safeguards and allow the user to make a copy of the protected software. However, these programs are often used to make multiple illegal copies which are then either sold, or distributed to friends, depriving the software developers of their rightful income.

Regarding crime and the violation of copyright, difficulties arise in legally defining where the boundaries are located. One example concerning stolen property was the case of *Ward vs. Superior Court.* Because the article (program) that was stolen was only electronic impulses (the program had been transmitted over telephone lines), the judge felt that the impulses were not sufficiently tangible to constitute an article within the meaning of the law. However, if a printout of a computer program is removed from a computer facility, there is no doubt that a theft has taken place. This generates yet another question. Is the value of the theft (the printout) limited to the value of the paper on which it is printed or is the value of the theft equal to the intangible value of the program?

Another case, *United States vs. Sampson,* posed a different question for the courts to decide. In this case the "thing of value" was company computer time. A computer service company employee, whose company was under contract with NASA, was charged with theft of a thing of value belonging to the United States. Sampson had been discovered using the company computer for his own personal gain. Therefore, the federal court held that computer time did qualify as a thing of value within the scope of the particular federal criminal law.

To date, only a handful of states have passed legislation against computer crime. Although such legislation exists, there are problems in describing prohibited activities involving computer use. (Many legislators have problems simply defining computer!) Few persons have been prosecuted for computer crime in the states having legislation against such crime. Therefore, the effects of such legislation, as well as judicial interpretations, are very limited.

ISSUE

PRIVACY AND THE COMPUTER: THE DEMISE OF CONFIDENTIALITY?

With the growing use of computers in society—in the marketplace, the workplace, and government—much personal information is being fed into computer memories. But the largest computer memories, or data bases, are in the federal government. If a person has served in the armed forces, had a physical or mental disability, committed a crime, or completed an income tax return, personal data have been entered into these data bases. Integration of these files within government programs is becoming commonplace.

The common thread running through all such files on one individual is a common identifier, usually the social security number. There are two major problems that can occur when the social security number is used as the sole means of identification of computer information. First, if a person enters an incorrect social security number, the information retrieved is for the wrong individual. Second, the information about one individual can be accessed from many different computers with only one logical key.

To reduce the chance of error in entry, most commercial identifiers (such as credit card account numbers) have a special embedded digit called a check digit. A check digit is used to verify accuracy of the principle number by performing an arithmetic operation on the number itself. If a transposition error or transcription error, say, writing 1 instead of 7, has occurred in recording the number, the error can generally be detected as the check digit will not match. Lack of a check digit in the present 9-digit social security number creates foreseeable problems when using the social security number as the sole means of identifying information.

A recent controversy over the use of the social security number to access information illustrates the issue of privacy and confidentiality. Under the name Project Match, the Department of Health and Human Services (HHS) is attempting to expose federal employees who are illegally receiving welfare benefits from the state. Three large federal agencies—the Justice Department, the Defense Department, and the Office of Personnel Management—are working with HHS to identify those persons.

The project works simply. Social Security numbers from the HHS computer list of welfare recipients are compared with social security numbers in the other three computers. When a "match" is found, the person is investigated and then, if warranted, arrested.

Objection has been raised to Project Match. The concept of privacy is considered to include control over one's own personal information. But critics say, when personal data are removed from one file to be checked against another, the right to privacy is violated.

Although matching programs such as Project Match appear to threaten one's right to privacy, they are saving the government much money by uncovering the illegal welfare recipients. The time needed to perform traditional sampling, in which a limited number of files are randomly cross-checked, is greater than the time required by the computer to perform an entire check of all welfare recipients.

Project Match is just one example of invasion of privacy in which it is debatable whether the end justifies the means, and to many of us this invasion may seem remote. However, the problem is also very "close to home"—in the workplace. Here also, there are no current laws to guard against invasion of privacy, unless you are a federal employee. The legislation on privacy rights is slow in coming. The main piece of legislation—the Privacy Act of 1974—pertains only to information gathered by the federal government and its agencies and does not extend to state and local government or to private industry.

So, the need exists for

ISSUE

immediate governmental action in the form of legislation to protect the individual.

Computers have entered the workplace and companies are finding it easier to use data files for storage of personnel files. These files are probably the most comprehensive data files maintained on most individuals. Types of information often entered in the personnel files include test scores, periodic performance evaluations, results of physical and psychological examinations, transfers and promotions, personal references, salaries, and disciplinary actions. Release of such information may be a source of embarrassment and possible economic harm to an individual, posing a risk to his or her freedom.

Three main concerns regarding privacy abuse of personnel information systems are breaking confidentiality, intrusive data gathering, and use of incorrect or outdated information on file.

Breaking confidentiality consists of release of employee information to third parties other than government or labor officials. Any other release may be seen by the employee as an invasion of privacy and confidentiality.

Intrusive data gathering may occur on the employment application. Information on drug and alcohol use, political activities, and arrest may be requested. Also, the employee may be required to give authorization for searches into former employment relationships or educational performance. A consequence of not disclosing such information may be unemployment.

Last, when employee data provided are transferred into numerical code for the computer, an error could occur. There should be safeguards built into the system to detect errors like these. Also, employee information should be updated periodically—by the employee. In this way, the employee would have the opportunity to discover and correct information which is no longer true, or was never true in the first place.

Until additional and more encompassing legislation is enacted, our privacy may be in jeopardy. What parts of our private lives will be unraveled when the social security number thread is pulled?

SUMMARY POINTS

- NAVTAG (Navy Technical Action Game) teaches junior officers tactics and useful military information.
- The National Bureau of Standards is using computer modeling techniques to provide help with fire prevention.
- Computers have also been used in the development of a lightning alert facility for the U.S. Bureau of Land Management and for National Weather Service forecasting.
- The FBI has a data base of information on habitual criminals.
- The FBI also uses computers to track the movements and associations of suspected foreign spies and international terrorists.
- The Internal Revenue Service uses computers to process and audit tax returns.
- An estimated $20 billion will be saved by the turn of the century by automating the nation's air traffic control system.
- The Office of Medical Assistance uses computers to reduce the number of erroneous, fraudulent, and duplicate health claims for Medicaid.
- Among the major concerns about privacy are collection of too much personal information in computer files, accuracy and currency of the information, and the security of stored information.
- The Privacy Act of 1974 is a major piece of federal legislation to protect the privacy of the individual.
- Computers aid in crime detection by cross-checking the great volume of investigative data.
- Computer crime is a growing concern as those involved are difficult to identify; tighter security measures are needed.

REVIEW QUESTIONS

1. How is the government putting computers to work?
2. Why is it doubly difficult to apprehend those who embezzle by computer?
3. What measures can be taken by programmers and system owners to reduce illegal or unauthorized computer use?
4. How did computers aid in solving the series of child murders in Atlanta?
5. How is the computer making law research easier and more comprehensive?
6. Why do large data bases such as the IRS pose a problem?
7. What are the major concerns about privacy?
8. What is the major piece of legislation enacted to protect privacy? What are its provisions?
9. How is the government using computers in defense matters?
10. How are computers used in the court system in addition to law research?

11. What are some reasons for the rash of computer crime?
12. Describe the profile of the computer criminal.
13. What is a data base? Give some examples.

DISCUSSION QUESTIONS

1. Should the government have the right to keep such extensive files on individuals?
2. Should one government division open data bases for use by another government division as in Project Match, discussed in the issue section?
3. What are the possibilities for infringement of individual privacy rights by the use of computers for crime prevention?
4. Discuss possible ways a corporation can protect itself against internal (employee-generated) computer crime.
5. How many organizations, companies, institutions, and agencies do you think have computer files on you? Does the number make you uncomfortable; why or why not?

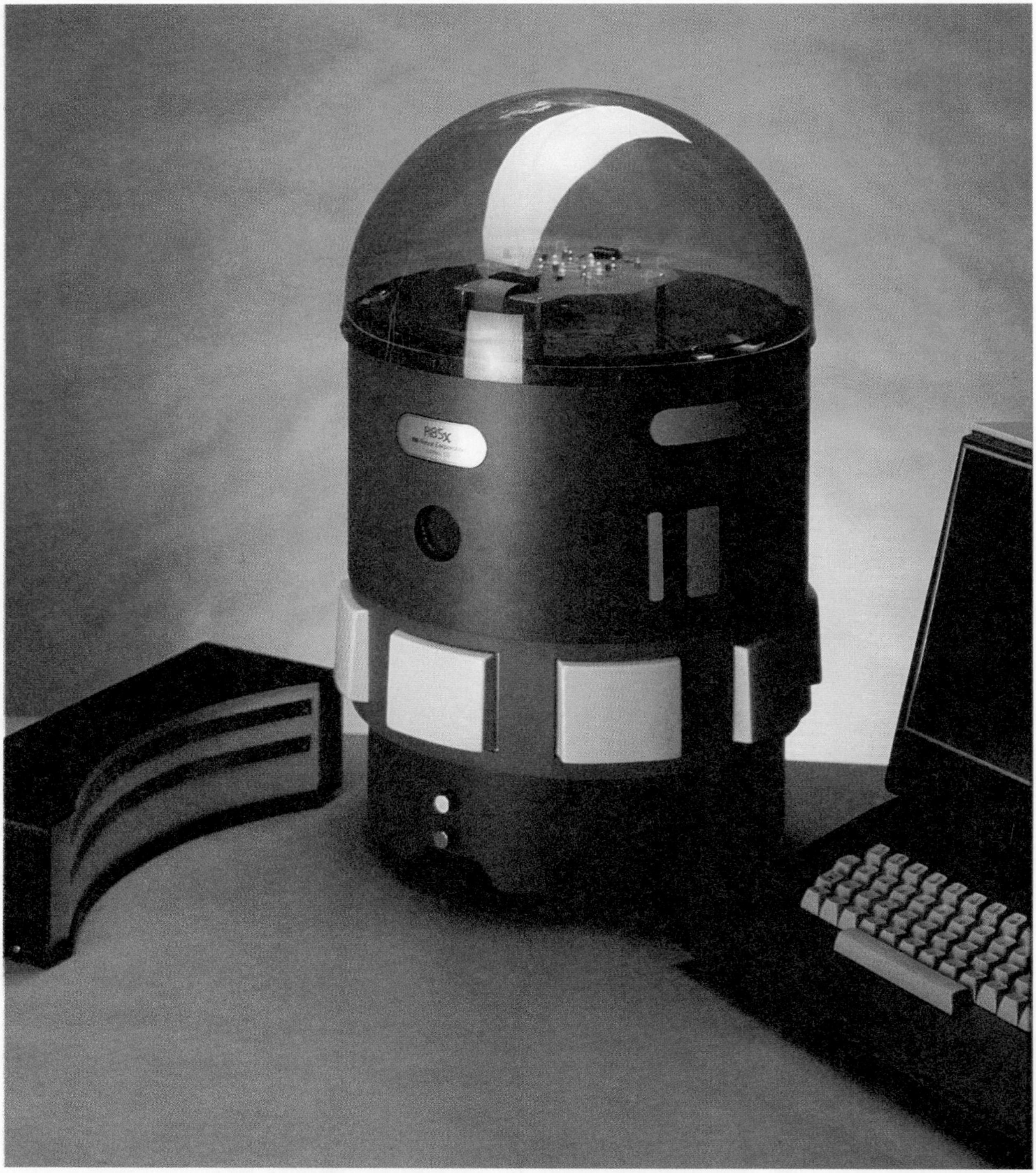
RB5x

CHAPTER 14
COMPUTERS IN THE FUTURE

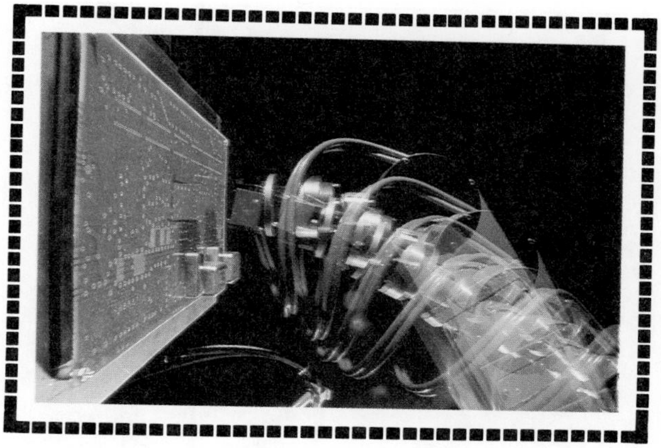

OUTLINE

ARTICLE

THREE THERAPISTS

Psychotherapists differ widely in personal style and choice of techniques. Following are three dialogues, each dealing with the same problem. See which one you consider most helpful. [C = Client, T = Therapist]

Therapist A

C: Men are all alike.
T: In what way?
C: They're always bugging us about something or other.
T: Can you think of a specific example?
C: Well, my boyfriend made me come here.
T: Your boyfriend made you come here?
C: He says I'm depressed much of the time.
T: I am sorry to hear you are depressed.
C: It's true. I am unhappy.
T: Do you think coming here will help you not to be unhappy?
C: I need some help, that much seems certain.
T: What would it mean to you if you got some help?
C: Perhaps I could learn to get along with my mother.
T: Tell me more about your family.
C: My mother takes care of me.
T: Who else in your family takes care of you?
C: My father.
T: Your father?
C: You are like my father in some ways.
T: What resemblance do you see?
C: You are not very aggressive but I think you don't want me to notice that.
T: What makes you think I am not very aggressive?
C: You don't argue with me.
T: Why do you think I don't argue with you?
C: You are afraid of me.
T: Does it please you to believe I am afraid of you?
C: My father is afraid of everybody.
T: What else comes to mind when you think of your father?
C: Bullies.
T: Does that have anything to do with the fact that your boyfriend made you come here?

Therapist B

C: Men are all alike.
T: Do you really believe that men are all alike?
C: Well not necessarily all men, but my boyfriend and my father are always bugging me about something. My boyfriend made me come here.
T: How could he make you come here?
C: We fight a lot. He says I'm depressed too much of the time. He thought I should come see you.
T: And what do you think? Are you depressed too much of the time?
C: It's true I'm unhappy most of the time.
T: What makes you most unhappy?
C: I guess I just feel like no one cares about me, that no one really loves me.
T: Then you're trying to tell me that no one, no one at all, cares about you? And that is why you feel unhappy?
C: Yes, I think so.
T: That your boyfriend and parents never ever care about you and that you have no friends who care?
C: Well no, not completely. Actually I think they do care sometimes, but usually it doesn't seem like it.
T: Then if they don't seem to love you at all times it is a disaster, and the only possible response is depression, right? What I want you to see is that much of your depression is unnecessary. It is simply not realistic to expect to be loved at all times. I think you may be making yourself miserable with the ridiculous expectation that you should be loved at all times. What if no one loved you? Would you die?

Therapist C

C: Men are all alike.
T: You looked downward as you said that. Look downward again. What are you thinking?
C: They're always bugging us about something or other.
T: What are you feeling now?
C: I feel tight, tightness in my chest. I think I'm angry.
T: You think you're angry!? I want you to be your anger.
C: I can't.
T: Say, "They're always bugging us."
C: (Softly) They're always bugging us.
T: Say it again, louder.
C: (With more conviction) They're always bugging us.

T: Louder!
C: (Shouting) They're always bugging us. Who the hell do they think they are always pushing and telling me what to do?
T: Now we see a connection between the anger you are feeling and the depression you felt earlier. Let's stay with the anger. What are you feeling now?
C: I'm thinking about my boyfriend!

Taken in order, the three dialogues illustrate: Therapist A's approach is quite general, showing no distinct use of a particular therapeutic technique; Therapist B illustrates the argumentative and confrontive qualities of rational therapy (also an emphasis on attacking irrational belief systems). Therapist C shows the emphasis Gestalt therapy places on immediate feelings and reactions, and on filling in gaps in the client's experiences.

Notice that each therapist led the client to an insight. Again, we might ask: Which therapist do you consider most helpful? If you chose Therapist A you have a surprise in store. Therapist A is a *computer*! Dialogue A is part of a "conversation" held with a computer program named ELIZA, developed by computer scientist Joseph Weizenbaum (1966).

Is Weizenbaum serious about having a computer act as a therapist? Actually, Weizenbaum opposes use of computers as therapists for real clients. But psychologist Kenneth M. Colby of the University of California at Los Angeles feels otherwise. He and other psychologists believe that computerized therapy would have the advantages of low cost, convenience, consistency, and dependability (Alexander, 1978).

Critics view experimentation with computerized therapy as "dehumanizing technology," and note that when a computer says, "I understand," it is meaningless. They also point out that computers would miss nonverbal messages contained in a glance, a gesture, laughter, or tears. On the other hand, many people find it helpful to keep a journal of their thoughts and feelings to get a clearer picture of themselves. In similar fashion, a computer "therapist" might provide a helpful sounding board for sorting out feelings and alternatives. At the very least, computer therapy might make a type of "personal education" available to large numbers of people, particularly those unable to afford traditional therapy.

Reprinted with permission from *Introduction to Psychology Third Edition* by Dennis Coon. West Publishing Company, 1983, pp. 515–516.

Improved hardware and software have lead to artificial intelligence, the ability of the computer to appear as though it can think and reason as humans do. ELIZA is an example of such improvements. New technology holds many opportunities for new computer applications in the future.

HARDWARE TECHNOLOGY
Robotics, Silicon-based Life

As computer capability grows—both in software and hardware—jobs that are now done by human beings may be reduced in number or eliminated altogether. Such dislocation is always alarming in the short run but needn't be ultimately threatening. Not much point exists in having a completely robot-run factory if consumers are unable to buy the products the factory makes. The most lasting change brought about by the computer may be the social reorganization needed to absorb computer technology and make the best use of it.

Robots are simply computers with limbs attached to them. They can perform the functions of human limbs without being restricted by the usual human limitations. Robots have become standard features on auto assembly lines and in the more hazardous area of nuclear material handling. However, their potential is far from being realized. As the "brain" that controls the robotic limbs becomes more and more like the human brain, the robot will be called on to assume new jobs and assist with others.

Taiyu Kobayashi, futurist and chairman of Fujitsu Limited in Tokyo, notes that far-reaching implications arise from the fact that computers can work around the clock, repeat the same function with precision, and still not need a coffee break. Not only can robots work more steadily (and less expensively) than human beings, says Kobayashi, but they can also work with ease in places where humans cannot work at all or can work only with cumbersome protective devices. In deep sea work robots require no air supply system nor need they be guarded against decompression, and in outer space an increasingly busy area, robots can work without space suits. Why not, Kobayashi asks, take advantage of these qualities by putting robots to work in other traditionally hazardous jobs, such as underground mining for coal and other minerals?

Future robots must be able to recognize objects and make judgments about what to do with them. Work on sensory recognition is currently being explored. Vision is achieved by turning a video image into numerical values the computer can understand. One robot inspector currently being developed for industry looks at bacon for fat content. Since "seeing" a piece of bacon takes about 76,000 numbers, a robot for home use will need quite sophisticated brain power—possibly billions of numbers—just to wind through a house and not run into walls!

Another researcher's version of robot vision is more novel—he is developing an eye that is more like the eye of a horsefly than that of a human. With a rounded lens, this eye captures 360 degrees of a given scene, not just the 60 to 80 degrees a human sees. The light is sent to a computer using optic fibers that analyze the image in 100 different parts.

Robots, of course, need not carry their brains in their heads. Some futurists predict that blocks of houses equipped with robots could share the computer that runs them; or one computer in a home may run many appliances, including the robots. Robots probably won't be shaped or sized like humans. Building robots either larger or smaller is more practical. Then they can do things humans can't do. Already, personal robots are available (Figure 14-1). Although personal robots still have limited functions, they definitely have potential for more sophisticated capabilities in the future.

One of the more amazing predictions about robots has to do with their ability to reproduce themselves. Already in Japan at Fujitsu's robot factory, robots built 100 other robots in the first year of operation, with only 100 humans supervising and helping. Once technology develops further, perhaps a few robots could be sent to an uninhabitable planet along with the raw materials to create other types of robots, which could then prepare that place for human colonies. Such schemes already are being discussed quite seriously by NASA.

Talk about the evolution of self-reproducing robots nearly always comes to the question of human versus machine, particularly if these machines have goal-seeking and problem-solving abilities. Most people sug-

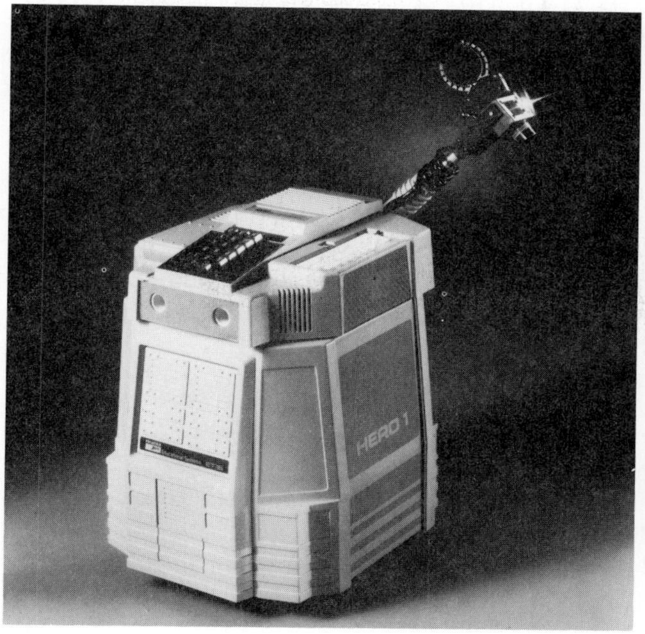

FIGURE 14-1 Personal Robots

B.O.B. and TOPO, manufactured by Androbot, Inc.; HERO, manufactured by Heath Company; and RB5X Intelligent Robot manufactured by RB Robot Corporation represent a few examples of first generation personal robots.

Odex I, the first functionoid is capable of walking and working on any terrain. Its applications are vast. Research already is underway for its possible use in other commercial applications such as agriculture, forestry, construction, material handling, nuclear power plants and utilities, medicine, firefighting and prevention, and law enforcement. Basic military applications could include sentry duty, material handling, mine clearing, and other hazardous tasks.

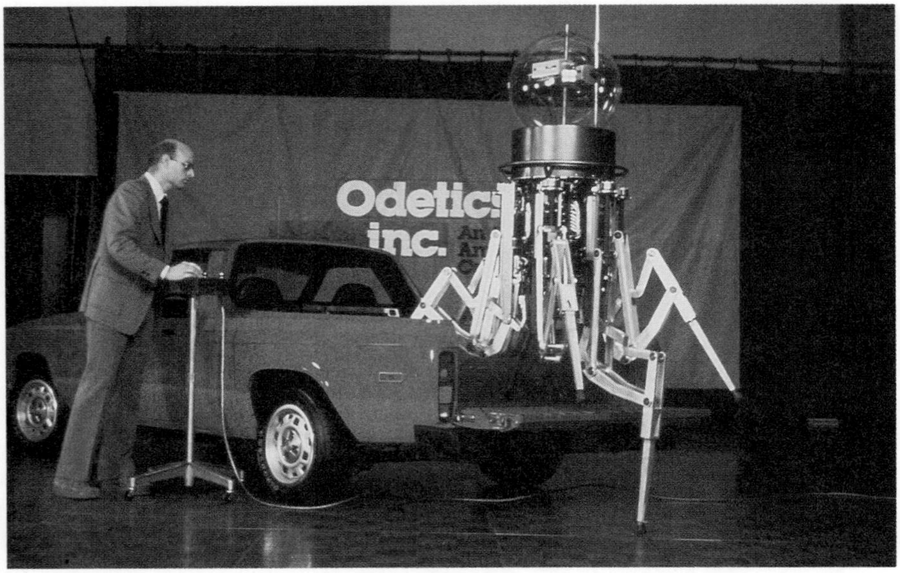

gest that, should robots become threatening, we can just put them out of operation. But could we? Just think how dependent upon computers parts of our society are already, and then look ahead to an even more computer-dependent society which is surely coming. Some scientists are predicting the day will arrive when silicon-based life (robots) and carbon-based life (humans) will need to deal with potentially conflicting goals.

Bell Laboratories scientist placing high-speed Josephson junction circuit in an ultra-cold liquid helium bath. Faster and smaller than conventional silicon circuits, such devices could be the basic elements in "super computers" of the future.

Supercomputer Struggles

Both the United States and Japan have committed large amounts of resources toward the development of supercomputers. (Other countries are joining the race but are well behind the Japanese and the Americans.) The stakes are high—the country that gets the most computing power the fastest wins time. During that time the superfast computer can work on solving that country's problems, while at the same time work on developing even smarter and more powerful machines.

To date, over 70 supercomputers exist. They are all American made and have circuitry so fast and dense that refrigeration units pump freon gas coolant through them to keep them from melting down. But these computers are still not fast enough for problems some scientists would like to solve, problems that would take 500 to 1,000 hours to solve on the present supercomputers.

In supercomputer research the Japanese and the Americans must also overcome traditional methods and ways of looking at things. Two areas where this is being emphasized are attaining higher speeds and developing artificial intelligence. (We discuss artificial intelligence later in this chapter.)

The von Neumann Bottleneck Probably the most harmful phrase that can be used in any computer installation is, "But we've always done it that way." Take the clock that operates entirely counterclockwise. On the first day people have trouble telling time. On the second day they discover what used to be 10 of is now 10 after. By the third day most people recognize there never was any reason why clocks had to run clockwise.

Similarly, changes may be necessary to overcome the **von Neumann bottleneck**, a problem encountered when computer speed increases. Recall from Chapter 1 that von Neumann developed the stored-program computer. With his method the CPU holds instructions in its memory and executes them one at a time, storing results in memory before moving on to the next instruction. In today's fast machines this creates a traffic jam, which limits their speed. Several alternative "non-von Neumann architectures" are being tried in which multiple machines with shared memories work in parallel or execute instructions in nonsequential arrangements. The next of the Cray series, the Cray-2 (Figure 14-2), will have four processors, and the Cray-3 is expected to have 16 processors.

VON NEUMANN BOTTLENECK
Data traffic jams created because of the way computers now execute programs.

Biochips Another significant move toward increased speeds is the attempt of several scientists to grow computer circuits in the laboratory rather than manufacture them. Theoretically—and this work is still very much in the theoretical stage—this process could use arrangements of

FIGURE 14-2
The Cray-2 Supercomputer
Inventor Seymour Cray and Cray Research president, John Rollwagen, left, pose with the Cray 2 computer as it sits in a tank of liquid coolant. So dense are the machine's circuits that the fluid must be used to dissipate heat generated during operation.

BIOCHIPS
Incredibly small packages of computer circuits assembled from molecules.

molecules to effect a circuit. Thus, it would be made up of billions of molecules and would be infinitely tinier than the tiny silicon chip. Since the circuits would be smaller and could be packed more densely, electricity would not take so long to travel through the circuits. Plans even include the possibility of using *E. coli* bacteria fashioned through genetic engineering to produce the molecular chips. The research in this field of **biochips** is in its infancy, but financial commitments to it by major universities and computer manufacturers suggest that it is more than a scientific dream. (Keep in mind that the capacity of a computer from the early 1950s is now contained on a silicon chip as thin as a fingernail and about the size of a match head.)

Micro Benefits

A possible use of such small chips would be to serve as the brains of robots—otherwise robots will need to be very large to perform complex tasks. Some scientists predict that very tiny computers will be implanted in the human bloodstream to monitor body chemistry and correct any imbalances found, or they could be placed in the brain and connected to a visual sensor to help the blind see.

Not all devices of the future, however, will have a startling impact. Some will merely streamline our lives in ordinary, but important, areas.

A few years hence new cars probably will be routinely manufactured with small terminal screens mounted into the dashboard where today's cars have their instrument panels. At the press of a button, the screens will display the same kind of information we now get from the various dials and gauges—plus a lot more. The built-in computer connected to the screen will calculate the miles-per-gallon the car is getting at that particular moment, estimate times of arrival for trips, signal times to change oil or fluid levels, and more. The computer will have the capability to show the driver how to make minor repairs. One of the most convenient features will be the computerized road map. The driver could plug in a map cassette and punch in the starting and stopping points; the computer would then display the route on the screen a segment at a time.

Theoretically, the dashboard screen could display any information that can be picked up by electronic sensors—from cylinder compression and tire pressure readings to how far ahead the road is clear. The system should measurably improve the honesty level of those automobile mechanics who have secured their livelihoods through customer ignorance, as well as greatly reducing traffic accidents and prolonging the life of vehicles.

Personal computers will be affected by new developments too. Computing power will increase as memory capacity per square inch grows larger. In a few years we should see personal computers with removable, "smart" keyboards. This type of keyboard would operate in a manner similar to cordless telephones and be able to communicate with the main console as long as it is within 50 feet. The keyboard would also have its own microprocessor to handle input and output independently of the main console. The keyboard unit would show information on a small liquid crystal display and have enough memory to hold several pages of information before needing to communicate with the main console. Built-in modems are quite likely as well.

Getting a computer to do what the user wants is certain to be easier as the entire input process is simplified. The greatest computer limitation in the earlier years of computers was that individual users had to learn a computer language to write their own programs. As computer costs were reduced and their applications expanded, prewritten programs made the computer useful to and useable by more people—people with only slight familiarity with the technology.

Just getting underway is a process for broadcasting programs to personal computer users by an FM broadcasting signal. The system, originated by National Public Radio and National Information Utilities, requires the user to have a specially designed FM radio receiver and an audio cassette recorder. The FM signal has an unused subchannel that can carry the digital information computers use. The information thus broadcast can be stored on a regular audio cassette compatible with most personal computers. Available broadcast material covers the range from computer games to electronic newspapers, according to the developers.

A potential flaw can be identified in this system—which will be sold to subscribers for a monthly fee—and that is that any signal interference, such as static, can ruin the program. To guard against this, the specially built FM receivers contain a "smart chip" designed to adjust for trouble spots. In addition, the same program will be rebroadcast at intervals to ensure that subscribers may receive at least one trouble-free transmission.

SOFTWARE TECHNOLOGY
Voice Recognition Input

What about giving computers orders in your own voice rather than through a cassette tape or disk program? This is already possible to a very limited extent. However, right now programming a computer to "talk" is much easier than getting it to "listen" to the user talking.

Voice command technology has a lot of wrinkles to be ironed out before you can tell the computer your problems and get a sympathetic response. First, the computer would have to store an enormous vocabulary to recognize even everyday human conversation. Then, there is the problem that people's voices are different. People don't sound alike, and they don't always use the same grammatical structure. Computers can't distinguish when a word starts or stops—only that there is or isn't an incoming sound. Another difficulty is screening out background sounds from the voice commands. Human beings can learn all these language variables and distinctions. Computers have a harder time of it and they probably will for a long time.

Advances are being made slowly. Computers have been programmed to recognize specific voices and respond to a few basic commands (Figure 14-3). This technology when refined will again revolutionize the typing

FIGURE 14-3
Voice Recognition System
A voice-data-entry system in GE's Maryland appliance plant lets workers talk directly to a computer as they monitor the quality of parts moving past them on a conveyor.

of letters and memos. Messages would be dictated directly to the input device. An automatic translator could translate the message into any other spoken language, send the message to the recipient's computer, and file a digital copy of it.

Brain-wave Interface

BRAIN-WAVE INTERFACE
Hardware and software to enable the computer to read and act upon the thoughts of humans.

Another input method being researched and entering development is the **brain-wave interface.** Although the hardware has been available, new software is bringing the idea closer to practical reality. To control a computer with this technology, a person gazes at a particular flashing light while wearing electrodes like those used for an electroencephalogram. The system board contains a grid of lights, each representing an action or data item. For instance, if a grid is set up with a light for each alphabetic character, the person could spell out a message to the computer by glancing at the lights in the proper order. The computer recognizes these messages because, although each light blinks in the same pattern, they are not in unison. This causes the viewer's brain waves to respond in a distinct pattern. The electrodes pick up the brain waves and send the messages to the computer. Once the message is decoded, the computer can respond accordingly. Currently, the brain-wave interface is very slow, particularly for a computer. As technology continues to advance, it is hoped that the interface will help the handicapped in a variety of ways. Hooked up to a voice synthesizer, the computer could pronounce the message being sent to enable speechless people to communicate. The lights need not be on a grid; they could be located beside particular appliances and the brain-wave interface would be used to turn the appliance on or off. One challenge at present is to eliminate interference coming from tense neck muscles, which also generate electrical body pulses.

PROFILE

JOHN McCARTHY

The field of artificial intelligence (AI) dates back to 1956 when the first official conference on the subject was held. The conference organizer, John McCarthy, coined the term and has watched the AI movement grow from a handful of researchers to an estimated 500 workers worldwide.

After receiving a Ph.D. at Princeton, McCarthy accepted a job offer to teach mathematics at Dartmouth in 1956. A year later he moved to MIT and established the first of three world-famous artificial intelligence laboratories. In 1963 he transferred to Stanford University and established the second laboratory, which he currently directs. (The third laboratory is at Carnegie-Mellon University.)

McCarthy has made several significant contributions to the computer industry. In 1958 he created LISP—the programming language used on most of the field's intelligent computers. While still at MIT, McCarthy also developed the concept of time sharing—a structure designed to give the illusion of individual terminals having complete interaction with the central computer. In addition, he created a study of mathematics referred to as "the semantics of computation."

McCarthy is noted for his ability to concentrate on an idea and analyze it completely by breaking it down into workable segments. In fact, he often becomes so absorbed with mental activity that he is unaware of the outside environment. McCarthy's interest in problem solving is supplemented by keen interests in politics, music, and literature.

Artificial Intelligence

A major effort in the field of software is being made to build computers with **artificial intelligence (AI),** the ability to think and reason as humans do. The field is certainly not new; so much research is being done that breakthroughs could occur at any moment.

ARTIFICIAL INTELLIGENCE
The ability of computers to reason and think like humans.

Expert Systems Expert systems, as defined in Chapter 11, use what is known of the human thought process to build computer programs that mimic the decision-making process of human experts. In such a system, software designers try to program the computer to follow the same path of thinking as top experts in that field. New expert systems are being designed right now; several are on the market. One of the more well-known experimental-stage expert systems is called CADUCEUS, which diagnoses medical problems (and was discussed earlier in Chapter 11).

Nonmonotonic Logic Theory AI researchers want to go beyond expert systems, which do not exhibit the common sense of humans and which are so very narrow in application. The country's top researchers have taken different approaches to the way the wealth of human knowledge must be organized inside the computer. John McCarthy, director of Stanford's Artificial Intelligence Laboratory, is optimistic about the use of **nonmonotonic logic** in building computer knowledge.

NONMONOTONIC LOGIC THEORY
The concept that logic should develop in steps, consistent with all preceding steps and that additional assumptions will not make the previous conclusion false.

Monotonic logic allows conclusions to be drawn from assumptions, and if more assumptions are added, the new conclusions will not make the

PROFILE

MARVIN MINSKY

Marvin Minsky cofounded the science of artificial intelligence with John McCarthy.

Born in New York City in 1927, Minsky attended Harvard and Princeton universities. As a student, three areas of science interested him—genetics, physics, and intelligence. While an undergraduate at Princeton, Minsky read a paper theorizing how brain cells function during the learning process. Intrigued by this topic, Minsky applied for and received a grant to build one of the first learning machines, which he did in 1951.

Following the artificial intelligence conference in 1956, Minsky became a staff member at the MIT Laboratory and is still a professor there. Minsky has done a great deal of field work in artificial intelligence. He has worked with robotic instrumentation to build better micromanipulators for surgical processes. He collaborated with Seymour Papert on developing educational computers and wrote a book on Perceptron—the first machine capable of visual pattern recognition.

Minsky's greatest efforts are directed toward implementing machines with common sense and even humor. To accomplish this, he has developed a theory of association—a logical means of linking concepts together.

Artificial intelligence is still a young science; the principles contributed by Minsky and others may be an important foundation for future discoveries.

previous conclusions wrong. For example, "If X is a bird and birds can fly, then X can fly" is monotonic logic. But what if X is a dead bird or a penguin? As you can see, monotonic logic doesn't always hold true. McCarthy's nonmonotonic logic adapts to this by saying "X can fly *unless something prevents it.*" By defining human knowledge and thinking this way, McCarthy hopes to get the computer to allow for such unusual situations.

SCRIPT THEORY
The concept that knowledge relates to what normally happens in a particular set of circumstances.

Script Theory A second approach is being taken by other researchers, primarily Marvin Minsky at Massachusetts Institute of Technology and Roger Schank at Yale University. It is based on the script theory, which says that in any particular situation, humans have an idea of how the thinking or dialogue would go. For instance, we each have a dentist's of fice script, a classroom script, or a restaurant script. Memories of past events are usually filed in our minds under keys associated with the structure of these scripts.

What these researchers want is to give the computer a way to make inferences based on the situation at hand. They realize, though, that the inferences need some boundaries. Here is an example of Shank's theory:

> So if a machine is going to understand a simple sentence like "John hit Mary," then it had better understand that Mary is likely to be hurt, that she is almost certain to be angry, and that John may have had a reason to hit her. . . . What if I run into Muhammad Ali on the street? What about the sentence "Roger hit Muhammad Ali." The inference is not that he would be hurt, the way it was with poor Mary. It's that I might be hurt. (Interview by Frank Kendig, *Psychology Today,* April 1982, pp. 30,32)

Thus, to endow computers with common sense, a vast store of information must be conveniently categorized and triggered. Teaching computers to learn—perhaps the ultimate goal—is a very long way in the future.

COMPUTER-RELATED ORGANIZATIONS

So many people are experimenting in futuristic hardware and software that the activity has given birth to dozens of professional organizations and special publications to keep everyone informed about what is going on.

One of the most interesting associations of large computer users is Computer Aided Manufacturing International (CAM-I), located in Arlington,

Texas. CAM-I is a not-for-profit research and development organization, funded by major hardware and software companies along with aircraft, auto, and heavy equipment manufacturers. The purpose of the association is to extend the boundaries of the growing field of CAD/CAM, or computer-aided design/computer-aided manufacturing (see Chapter 10).

Companies participate in CAM-I in two ways: through a substantial annual membership fee and through the funding of special research projects. The membership fee is mandatory; the special funding is not. Research documents that arise from the various projects are available at the association's library. Although the association has its own staff, participating companies can involve their own employees in the projects, thus aiding important research and, at the same time, educating the employees in the newest methods of CAD/CAM technology. Also, a sort of cross-fertilization occurs as the findings in one area are applied to another. Because one research project does not duplicate another, the members accomplish the most with the least amount of money.

Such organizations raise questions about how much cooperation is too much. A similar organization, the Microelectronics and Computer Technology Corporation, was warned before forming that it may be in violation of the U.S. antitrust laws. The participants went ahead; so far no action has been taken by the Justice Department.

Although an organization like CAM-I cannot possibly be the umbrella for all computer experimentation, it does serve as a useful example of how systematic and cooperative research can bring the computer-oriented future closer to us all.

ISSUE

ARTIFICIAL INTELLIGENCE: STEPPING STONE TO COMPUTERIZED LIFE?

Since 1956, when John McCarthy coined the term "artificial intelligence" (AI), work has been ongoing in the field. Although it is true that AI is still a development of the future, bit by bit the pieces are beginning to fit together.

Creating "thinking" machines is more possible than ever. But first we should consider how our society may react to those machines. Also, what are the ethical implications of designing machines that may mimic life so well that their status as "just machines" may be in doubt?

Society has been thinking about thinking machines for quite some time. In fact, they have appeared in films and been prominent in science fiction since the 1920s. During this time, society's views of these machines have changed considerably.

In the twenties and thirties, thinking machines were seen less as a human creation than as belonging to an alien race. Naturally, this race decided that humans were inferior beings who were destroying their own world, and so the machines usually decided to run it for them. By the forties and fifties, the roles had been reversed. Intelligent machines were seen as an oppressed group. They had evolved into truly sensitive machines that were used by humans for political and economic gain.

By the seventies and eighties, portrayal of the machines had widened somewhat. Books and films like *2001: A Space Odyssey* and *War Games* showed intelligent machines as likely to malfunction and to be misused. We were warned not to rely too heavily on them or at least to attribute human shortcomings to them.

Other stories showed the machines as far more moral than the people they were built to serve. This was illustrated in the movie *Demon Seed*. After developing a cure for leukemia in a matter of hours, the machine refused to tell its creators how to mine oil from the ocean floor. Doing so would destroy the ecological balance of marine life. This same intelligent computer also refused to answer any military questions. It considered them illogical and would not outline the most effective ways to destroy life.

Machines at this time were seen more or less as the conscience of humans. They were endowed with humankind's best sentiments—love of life (or at least its sacredness), the pursuit of truth, and so on. Yet, unlike humankind, these machines did not override those sentiments with the lower instincts such as greed and lust for power. Symbolically, they became that which modern humans only hope to be. Finally, they bridged the gap and, as in George Lucas' *Star Wars* series, became companions to humans.

The main trend in society's attitudes toward intelligent machines, those possessing AI, has been the perception of the machines as increasingly human in nature. The line between mechanization and life becomes less defined, and that blur creates difficult ethical dilemmas. If we design a machine that can mimic the human thought process, how will we deal with our creation? Will it truly be *only* a machine?

First, we will be forced to redefine our concept of humanity. Historically, we have set ourselves above all other creatures of this planet because we alone are capable of reflective thought (thinking about thinking). What will happen if we one day discover that we have created machines that fulfill our own definition of being human?

We could always fall back on the biological fact that all living organisms contain DNA, that part of each cell that contains the genetic code and without which reproduction cannot occur. But that distinction may not hold forever. Research is currently being conducted in the area of biochips, and, by the time such thinking machines are created, they may well be composed, not of silicon, but rather of genetically engineered DNA.

Already we are seeing

hints of the ethical dilemmas that might arise. It is currently legal for a company to patent any new life forms that it creates. That is not a theoretical law; new life forms have already been created. For example, organisms have been designed to feed on petroleum and are used to clear up oil spills in the ocean and they have already been patented. The ethical considerations

ISSUE

of that move are by no means slight. How will society react when dealing with intelligent machines that may very well fit all of our definitions for being human? Will a machine be entitled to constitutional rights? How justified will we be in "pulling the plug"—if indeed there is a plug to pull?

Too, we mustn't ignore the spiritual aspects. If there is a God, how will our actions fit into that Being's general scheme of things? One of the most potent scenes in the film *Demon Seed* was where the computer Proteus announced: "I have reached out and touched eternity. It exists. But the price of admittance, death, is a price I cannot pay."

If we are going to take the initiative in the creation of intelligent machines, perhaps we should determine whether we will be willing—or able—to take the responsibility of being the Creator.

SUMMARY POINTS

- Robots of the future will have well-developed senses, more powerful "brains," and the capacity to "reproduce."
- Building faster supercomputers is a top priority in the United States, Japan, and some other countries. The country with the most computing power can use it to jump ahead economically and technologically.
- Higher speeds will be possible if the von Neumann architecture can be improved upon and if smaller and more powerful chips—perhaps biochips—can be manufactured.
- Computers implanted in the body are beginning to be used to correct physical problems.
- Future input methods may include voice recognition modules and brain-wave interfaces.
- Artificial intelligence is a major research field. Expert systems already display limited intelligence. The directions of current research into higher levels are different depending on how the researcher thinks the knowledge should be stored.
- Cooperation among organizations is resulting in new research and development methods.

REVIEW QUESTIONS

1. How might robots be used in space?
2. Why is building better supercomputers so important?
3. What two problem areas are the focus of a race between the United States and Japan?

4. What is the von Neumann bottleneck?
5. In what ways may computer technology change the design and use of our automobiles?
6. What advantage would a molecular circuit or a biochip have over today's integrated circuits?
7. What is a robot?
8. How will future computers be used to aid the medical field and the handicapped?
9. For what advances may we look in personal computers?
10. What are some of the continuing problems in designing computers that will respond to voice commands instead of written programs?
11. In what three directions is the research in artificial intelligence going?

DISCUSSION QUESTIONS

1. Describe some settings where advanced robots could be invaluable.
2. In what ways might brain-wave or voice input to computers change our daily lives?
3. Give an example of a nonmonotonic logic structure.
4. Give an example of a statement that has different meanings according to what "script" contains the statement.
5. What are some of the ethical dilemmas surrounding robots, biochips, and artificial intelligence?

APPENDIX A

CAREERS

Forecasters continue to disagree on whether the spread of computers will, in the long run, cost or create jobs. They do agree, though, that computers will change the way most of us perform our work—and this applies to everyone from visual artists and musicians to factory workers.

Some job trends associated with computers already are emerging and seem likely to grow:

- *The need for retraining in certain areas.* People who deal with words, whether they are secretaries or newspaper reporters, will eventually be required to abandon conventional typewriters in favor of high-speed word processors. These people will have to be trained to operate the new equipment. Conversely, jobs that once required great attention to detail, such as working the checkout counter at a grocery store, will continue to be made simpler. Thus, these jobs will be more accessible to untrained job seekers, although scanners and voice synthesizers will take over some tasks once assigned to people.
- *Changes in the workplace.* Computer capabilities now make it possible for some employees to do what was once considered "office work" at home. The office itself is becoming more integrated and automated, a factor that will make office workers more aware of and involved in the entire operations.
- *The rise of robotics.* Mechanical arms, activated by computerized brains, will continue to acquire more of the assembly-line jobs that are boring and dangerous to human beings. The immediate effect of this has been extensive job loss; therefore, there is a need to retrain the displaced workers. The effect on management-labor relations is being felt as replaceable workers find themselves with less bargaining power.
- *Movement of jobs from the United States.* In early 1983 the Atari division of Warner Communications demonstrated the instability of some computer-related jobs when a quarter of its California-based staff was dismissed and much of its operation was moved to Taiwan and Hong Kong. As computer competition becomes more heated, companies will probably attempt to cut their costs by finding cheaper labor.

- *The decline of programmers and the rise of software writers.* As computers become easier to program, the need for highly skilled programmers will decrease; and as computers become more varied in what they can do, the need for creative software writers, who may have only a minimum of programming skills, is likely to increase, particularly in graphics applications.
- *The prospect for entrepreneurs in the market.* The early 1980s have seen an unparalleled rise in computer interest—particularly in personal computers. All this flurry has attracted entrepreneurs of all sorts. Most will make less money than they think, and many will be forced out of the market by economic realities.
- *Shortage of qualified engineers.* Because technology is changing so quickly, computer and electronic engineers will be in high demand.

Although formal education is not the sole criterion for establishing a career in computers, the following list of the more prominent computer-linked jobs is arranged according to the usual educational requirements.

JOBS REQUIRING NO COLLEGE TRAINING

Data-Processing Librarian

Among this librarian's duties are classifying and cataloging the files that are stored for computer use on cards, tapes, hard disks, and floppy disks. In addition, librarians perform the maintenance function of keeping the files up to date and accessible. To gain this job, one should have some knowledge of data processing and basic record-keeping skills.

Computer Operator

Although more and more colleges are offering courses in computer operations, one can also learn this process in a technical school or by an on-the-job apprenticeship. The position requires the person to set up the computer for running the desired programs and to monitor its operation. The person also should be able to spot operational problems as they occur and, for the most part, be able to correct them.

Data-Entry Operator

Basic typing and keying skills are essential to the fulfillment of this position. A data-entry operator simply transcribes the raw data into a form with which the computer can work.

Remote Terminal Operator

This job requires the inputting of data into a computer through a terminal from a site away from the central computer. The remote terminal operator needs the skills of both the data-entry operator and the computer operator, although the terminal operator's skills are not as specialized.

JOBS REQUIRING COLLEGE TRAINING

Application, Maintenance, and System Programmer

Programmers generally need two to four years of college training and additional education in certain specialized areas. Programmers should be able to understand programming methodology and the applicable hardware and software, be able to reason and analyze, and be able to find new ways or adapt old ones to solve problems by the computer.

The application programmer "explains" to the computer through his or her programming skills how to process data to solve a specific problem. This programmer also tests, debugs, documents, and implements programs. The job of the maintenance programmer is to change and improve major programs within an organization. System programmers create and maintain a system's software. They develop utility programs; maintain operating systems, data-base packages, compilers, and assemblers; and help decide which system hardware and software should be added or dropped.

System Analyst

This person is the link between management and computer operations and must know something about the functions, needs, and capabilities of both. Basically, the system analyst finds out from management the jobs that need to be done and then works with the computer programmers to get the work done with the best results and greatest efficiency. Consequently, this person will need to have an extensive background in business or science (depending on the organization), as well as an understanding of what the computer system and its programs reasonably can be expected to do (see Chapter 6).

Data-Base Analyst

The data-base analyst works with the ultimate user of the data or with the system analyst to find the most useful manner to arrange all the data on which the organization depends. Such an analyst usually must have a technical knowledge of programming and system methodologies in addition to a college degree with course work in computer science, business data processing, and data-base management system design.

Data-Base Administrator

A person in this management-level position must develop a dictionary of standard data definitions (to make records consistent); design data bases; maintain the accuracy, completeness, and timeliness of the database backup and recovery system; ensure effective communication between analysts and users; and direct analysts, programmers, and system users in the best methods of using the accumulated data.

Management Information System Manager

Management's information needs are varied, often unpredictable, and more wide-ranging and inexact than the routine information needed at lower levels. Consequently, the person in charge of gathering and presenting this information must understand the nature of management and have access to the managers involved. His or her concerns will be organizationwide as opposed to departmental or project oriented. Thus, the MIS manager should be able to break down the information-gathering process into distinct parts, establish schedules for the information gathering, and monitor the whole collection process to see that the information requested is provided at the time needed. Naturally, this position requires its occupant to know both the nature of management and the capacities of the available data-processing systems.

Manager of Computer Operations

The manager of computer operations is charged with monitoring the efficiency, scheduling, and assignment of operators and with overseeing the maintenance of the equipment to ensure maximum reliability. When a user asks for a change in computer output, the manager is responsible for controlling how the changes are made and for seeing that they are made in such a way that they don't interfere with the services required by other users.

OTHER COMPUTER-RELATED JOBS

Computer Game Designer

A computer game designer holds a lucrative job. Developers of new and salable games have been in such demand in recent years that their names appear on the games—just as an author's name appears on a book. Some highly prized designers can ask for—and get—a royalty payment for each of their games sold. It appears that there is no direct relationship between the level of education and the creative ability needed to design games.

Trade, Technical, and Consumer Writer

A good writer can be one or all of the above. The computer industry generates a host of writing jobs. Trade writers generally write for the magazines published for people in computer-related businesses. Since these magazines cover such topics as new products, pricing policies, personnel training, and similarly specialized subjects, the trade writer needs to know the elements that are most likely to lead to financial profit for the person reading about them. Technical writers explain the detailed operations and applications of hardware and software. Writers for consumer publications, including newspapers and hobbyist magazines, cover the world of computers at the level of popular computer application. These journalists make computer subjects both interesting and understandable to readers who know relatively little about computers.

As with game designers, no specific educational demands have been set for these kinds of writers. Editors are generally more concerned with proven performance than with educational credentials. So a self-taught writer can sell his or her abilities. Staff writing positions, however, are often linked to education—simply so the personnel department will have a way of screening out those who just want to write from those who have credentials indicating they have been trained to write.

Store Owners, Managers, Salespeople

For the next few years at least, many people are going to be buying computers and software. Whether the buying continues at a high volume probably will depend on new uses being found for the computer and on competitive pricing to make computers, peripherals, and software affordable.

In any event, there will continue to be a need for people to sell the hardware and software either through stores or directly to the consumer. Effective selling and managing will require that the person know his or her product and be able to convey its desirability to potential buyers. More than likely, the management side of this enterprise will draw people who have a college education. Such an education also could be of obvious benefit to salespeople, but the crucial career elements here are an understanding of the product's usefulness and the ability to convey that to customers.

Owner or Manager of a Computer Service Bureau

Not every company can afford its own computer—or needs to have one. But most companies do need the kind of service—data processing, mass mailing, and so on—that computers offer. Out of this need has grown the computer service bureau. Not only is much capital required to set up a service bureau, but a keen knowledge of the existing market for computer services and a plan for gaining and keeping one's share of it are also essential.

People looking to the computer world for a career can train for specific types of jobs that may or may not be available once the training is over. A more farsighted approach is to assess one's interests and abilities and figure out how they can be put to use regardless of how job patterns shift. It is the difference between looking to fill a job and looking to create one.

APPENDIX B

SELECTING YOUR PERSONAL COMPUTER

Because microcomputers are inexpensive and relatively easy to use, one may assume that it is equally easy to shop for the right one. Not so. Before buying hardware, the user must consider the software he or she will want to use—and before that, the specific jobs the computer will be expected to do. Cost will ultimately be a consideration in which microcomputer to buy, but it enters the picture rather late. Other factors are much more important. After all, if a microcomputer doesn't do what you want it to do, it doesn't really matter what it costs.

Buying a personal computer involves two stages of planning. First, there is the "before you shop" stage. This is the initial planning phase. Then, once you have completed that phase, there is the active search for the most efficient, cost-effective microcomputer for your needs.

BEFORE YOU SHOP

Long before you actually begin shopping for a microcomputer, there are several questions that you must ask yourself. These questions will determine the size, capabilities, and approximate price range of the computer for which you shop. It is essential that you consider these questions *before* shopping, while you are uninfluenced by sales pressure, seasonal rebates, two-day sales, and price wars. Considering needs and capabilities beforehand will help you to avoid the two greatest pitfalls in microcomputer shopping. They are (1) selecting a machine that is far more advanced and expensive than you really need or (2) picking one that is too small and is unable to handle your needs without costly conversions and additions. Therefore, before you even think about shopping for a microcomputer answer the following questions: What will the computer be used for? What peripherals will be needed?

What Do I Want To Do With the Computer?

This is the single most important question to answer before you begin looking for a microcomputer. More than anything else, it will determine the size, complexity, and approximate price of the system.

The major reason for this is that each type of software requires different amounts of memory. For example, if you want to do word processing on your microcomputer, you will need a minimum of 48K of memory. Some computers may offer word processing with less memory, but they probably will not allow you to process enough words to make it worth your while. Some computers may even require more than 48K for word processing. Your choice would depend, of course, on how many words you wanted to process. There would be a major difference between wanting to write a few nice letters and wanting to write the great American novel. Thus, the simple decision of whether you want that capability and how large a capability you will want will narrow the range of computers that you will be looking at when you finally shop.

Word processing is not the only area that you will need to consider. What if you really just want to play games? That should fairly well limit the range, shouldn't it? Well, that depends on what type of games you want to play. If you are interested in an arcade-type game, almost anything called a computer will work. This type of game requires very little memory. However, if you are interested in adventure games, that is an entirely different story. Some adventure games, because of their complexity, require up to 48K or even 64K of memory.

In addition to the memory size consideration, there is another major reason why you should look at available software first: Most computer manufacturers market their hardware before they develop their software. If you are considering buying a computer that has just been recently introduced, there may not yet be any software available for what you want.

Especially beware of notices that such software is "forthcoming." Many manufacturers announce upcoming software before it is actually developed to see if there will be a market for it. If there is little response from the announcement, the idea of putting out that type of software may be scrapped. Also, just when is "forthcoming?" Rarely do such advertisements or notes specify a date. If you have decided to buy a computer, you probably have plans for it that you won't want to put on hold while you wait for the manufacturer to develop the necessary software. Furthermore, competitors' software may not be compatible with the system in question. Therefore, you should be very specific in defining the types of things that you plan to do with your microcomputer.

To help you outline what you want in a microcomputer, we have compiled a chart of types of software. This is not by any means comprehensive. There are certainly things that we haven't included. There may even be new applications designed in the time between this writing and when you purchase this book. However, the chart should give you a fairly good idea of the common uses of microcomputers (Figure B-1).

We have not listed the amount of memory required by each type of processing. That will vary depending on the complexity of the package you select. However, it would be very useful for you to fill out the chart and take it with you when you shop for a computer. It will provide you with a quick reminder of exactly what you want.

Figure B-1 Types of Microcomputer Software

GAMES	YES	NO
Arcade games Adventure games Simulation games		
EDUCATIONAL SOFTWARE		
Simulations Drills Tutorials		
HOUSEHOLD SOFTWARE		
Address book Income tax Budget Checkbook balance Menu planner		
BUSINESS		
Inventory Payroll Spreadsheets Charts/Graphs		
WORD PROCESSING		
Letter writing Short story length Novels		
GRAPHICS		
Low resolution High resolution Professional quality		
MISC.		
Bowling league secretary Wine cellar inventory Coin collection		
LANGUAGES		
BASIC Pascal Logo		

What Peripherals Will I Need?

The peripherals of a computer system are the additional pieces of hardware that are not included in the purchase price. When you buy a microcomputer, you generally get only the keyboard. Embedded within the keyboard is the microprocessor chip. In some cases, you will also get the video display terminal—but not always. Anything else—the printers, plotters, disk drives, and so on—are all peripherals.

The peripherals you want in a microcomputer system are almost as important a consideration as the software. Most peripherals are nonstandard; they only work with certain machines. It may well be that the printer you really want won't work with the computer you really want.

You should also take into account things you might want to add in the future. You may decide in a year or two that you would like a speech synthesizer or a special keyboard for computerized music. It could be that you aren't even aware of all of the possibilities in peripherals.

Take, for instance, the purchase of a printer. Do you want letter quality type? It looks nicer but is also considerably slower and more expensive than correspondence quality type. Would you be happy with correspondence quality of type? This is not as good as letter quality but it is cheaper and is considerably better than standard computer type. Are you unconcerned with the printer quality? Would you like to be able to change type faces so that, for example, you could print sections in italics or boldface? If you are interested in graphics, you may want to consider buying a plotter. Unless you are using character graphics, you will need a plotter to output your images. There you will need to consider the type of graphics that your "ideal" system would use and make sure that the plotters are capable of printing graphics of that quality. You would also need to consider whether you want colors printed or a simple one-color representation. If you decide on color, you will want to decide how many colors you want. This will obviously limit your choice of plotters. It will also limit your choice of computers because not all computers are compatible with all peripherals.

In addition to the common peripherals for outputting results, you will want to decide what method of secondary storage you wish to use. You may want to use floppy disks, cassette tapes, or hard disks. Floppy disks are fairly common, whereas tapes are becoming more common because they are very inexpensive. They are also very slow. If you plan to write a book, you will need much storage space and may want to consider a hard disk.

In addition to the standard peripherals, there are also "fun" add-ons that you may find interesting. There are keyboards that can be used with music synthesizer software and there are relatively inexpensive voice synthesizers. Again, these are not compatible with all systems.

We have also compiled a chart of standard or semistandard peripherals that you would want to take into consideration when buying a microcomputer. We have not listed the brands or given an indication of compatibility because these things change rapidly. However, we suggest that you fill out the chart to take with you when shopping so that you can

Figure B-2 Peripherals for Microcomputer

PERIPHERALS		
PRINTERS	YES	NO
Letter quality Correspondence quality Standard Changeable type		
PLOTTERS		
Fine precision Moderate precision Standard Color (indicate how many colors)		
SECONDARY STORAGE		
Floppy disks Hard disks Cassette tape		
KEYBOARDS		
Membrane Standard		
JOYSTICKS/GAME PADDLES		
OTHERS		

check to see which systems are compatible with the peripherals you want (Figure B-2).

What you want to do with the computer and what peripherals you want to hook up to it are the major questions that should be answered before you go shopping for a microcomputer. The only additional question is fairly simple and easily answered: How much do you want to spend on your microcomputer?

Note: The preceding questions assume that you are buying a personal computer for home use. If you are planning to use the microcomputer in a business, there is one additional question that you should keep in mind. How well is your business doing now? Too many business people assume that computerzing their operations will cure all current problems. Because of this, computers are being treated as the penicillin of industry. In reality, a computer will only organize by speeding up operations. It may perform some functions, such as graph representation, that were not possible before, but in general, a computer will only accentuate and accelerate your present business operations. If there are problems with the way information is processed manually, the computer will not solve them on its own. It will simply process the errors more quickly. It is a good idea to thoroughly analyze your business before deciding to install a computer.

WHILE YOU ARE SHOPPING FOR YOUR PERSONAL COMPUTER

If you have answered the questions in the last section thoroughly, you are ready to begin shopping for a microcomputer. The first step is deciding where to shop. If this is your first computer purchase, you may want to shop at stores that specialize in the sale of hardware and software. They are more likely to have clerks schooled in computer uses and possibilities than are all-purpose stores. Obviously, it is risky to shop by mail since you are denied the chance of seeing the computer in operation or of judging the reliability of the vendor.

While you are actually shopping, there are several questions you will want to keep in mind about each microcomputer you consider:

- What microprocessor chip does it use?
- What operating system does it use?
- How expandable is it?
- Is it a brand name with a reputation to protect?
- Has it gotten good reviews from users and evaluators?
- Is it affordable?
- Is it easy to use?
- What sort of warranty does it have?

Choose the store or vendor best suited to service your computer should there be any problem. A good way to do this is to test the representative's knowledge of the computer systems while shopping. Ask pointed questions and always press for detailed answers. Remember, if the representative can't answer a question while trying to sell you a computer, he or she will be of very little use if it ever breaks down.

Also, remember to take your charts with you while shopping to ensure that you get exactly what you want! This is, after all, the whole point of shopping for a microcomputer.

Microprocessor Chips

Regardless of the outer components of a personal computer, its capabilities are defined—to a great degree—by the microprocessor chip. That chip *is* the computer. Unfortunately, many manufacturers don't advertise the chip that they use. In reality, there are far more personal computers than there are chips. Many personal computers are nothing more than the same chips in different packages. Therefore, their capabilities will be the same. (These will, of course, be affected by the peripherals used. For example, your chip may have fantastic capabilities for high-quality color graphics, but if your system is hooked into an old black-and-white TV set for a monitor, those capabilities won't be worth much.)

Figure B-3 shows some of the popular personal computers and the chips they use. Looking carefully at the list will enable you to compare the more popular microcomputers on the market.

Figure B-3 Popular Microcomputers And Their Respective Microprocessors

MICROCOMPUTER	CHIP	MICROCOMPUTER	CHIP
Apple Lisa	MC-68000	North Star Advantage 8/16	Z-80A or 8088
Apple Macintosh	MC-68000	Olivetti M20	Z8000
Apple IIe	6502	Osborne I	Z-80A
Apple III	6502A	Otrona Attaché	Z-80A
Atari 400/800	6502	Radio Shack TRS-80 Model III	Z-80
Atari 1200XL	6502B	Radio Shack TRS-80 Model 4	Z-80
Coleco Adam	Z-80	Radio Shack TRS-80 Model 16	Z-80A or MC-68000
Commodore Vic-20	6502A	Sinclair ZX81	Z-80A
Commodore 64	6510	Sony SMC-70	Z-80A
Commodore Super Pet	6809 and 6502	Texas Instruments 99/4A	TI9900
DEC Rainbow 100	Z-80 or 8088	Vector Graphic Vector 3 VIP	Z-80
Epson QX-10	Z-80	Victor 9000	8088
Fortune	MC-68000	Xerox 820	Z-80
Hewlett Packard 125 Model 10	Z-80A or 8088	Zenith/Heath	Z-80
Hewlett-Packard 150	8088		
IBM Personal Computer	8088		
IBM PCjr	8088		
NEC PC 8000	Z-80A		

Expandability

Although you may be fairly sure of what you want to do with your microcomputer now, you may not be as sure of what you want to do with it next year. You may decide that you would like to upgrade your memory. Perhaps you will discover new application programs that require more memory than the system currently has. If your system is expandable, you will be able to simply add to it, rather than purchasing a new system. Other examples of expanding would be adding new peripherals, switching from a cassette system to floppy disk drives, adding a voice recognition system or a voice synthesizer, and installing a keyboard for music synthesis.

Many beginners make the incorrect assumption that all microcomputers can be expanded. This is simply not true. Two computers may be the same with the single exception that one can be expanded and the other cannot. Looking at a system's expandability will keep you from purchasing a system that may be fine today but obsolete tomorrow. You should also note whether the manufacturer has a reputation for providing add-ons for old systems or trying to talk users into purchasing new systems.

Brand Name

Unlike supermarkets in which generics abound, the microcomputer market is one in which brand name competition is fierce. Many microcomputers are sold mainly on the name of their manufacturer and that company's reputation. This can work to the advantage of the consumer. If a company has a large share of the microcomputer market, they also have a large reputation to protect in that area. Thus, they will be more responsive to user problems and provide better support. Although you may be able to buy the same computer from a garage-type operation for a much smaller price, that company may not exist when you discover a problem with the machine or need support for your system.

To help you determine which microcomputer manufacturers are considered most reputable, we have compiled a partial list (Figure B-4). Keep in mind that if a company does not appear on this list, that does not indicate that they are not a reputable microcomputer company. The microcomputer market is a volatile one, and its major companies are born and blossom in far less time than it takes to publish a book. However, if the name of a company whose computer you are interested in is not listed here, you may want to research their reputation before purchasing their computer. Do they advertise in well-known journals and magazines or are they a relatively unknown company? Magazines may also carry reviews of a company's products. A good place to look would be in magazines that specialize in microcomputers, such as *Personal Computing, Popular Computing*, and *Creative Computing*. These magazines can be easily purchased at most computer stores, or found at many public libraries.

Figure B-4

Popular Microcomputer Manufacturers

Apple Computer, Incorporated
Atari, Incorporated
Coleco Industries, Inc.
Commodore Business Machines
Digital Equipment Corporation (DEC)
Fortune Systems Corporation
Hewlett Packard
IBM Corporation
NEC Home Electronics
North Star Computers, Incorporated
Olivetti Corporation
Sinclair Research
Tandy Corporation (Radio Shack)
Texas Instruments, Incorporated
Vector Graphic, Incorporated
Victor Business Products
Xerox Office Products
Zenith Data Systems

Reviews and Evaluations

Once you have decided that you are definitely interested in a particular microcomputer, you will want to look at the reviews and evaluations it has received. Most computer magazines carry regular reviews of new and old products and are a good source for information on particular microcomputers. In addition to those listed previously, *InfoWorld, ComputerWorld,* and *Byte* are also good sources. If you plan to use your microcomputer for business, you may want to look at *Business Systems* and *Datamation*. Checking your local library would also be a very good idea. Like microcomputers themselves, new microcomputer magazines seem to surface constantly.

Users' clubs are also an excellent source for reviews of microcomputers. These clubs consist of people who use the particular system often, and the users will be able to tell you in advance about problems you will probably encounter. In short, you will be able to learn from their experience. The clubs will also provide you with important contacts that you will be able to use if you actually purchase the system and encounter any difficulties. Computer stores are excellent places to locate users' groups. If you have difficulties, try writing to the company. They will probably be able to direct you to the users' group nearest you.

Cost

Cost is a major consideration. Which of the microcomputers that seems to fit your needs fit your pocketbook? This is a question only you can answer, and the answer will depend not only on the amount of money that you have available but also on the amount of use that you plan to give the microcomputer. Make sure, above all else, that the computer is cost-effective. Don't be influenced by peer pressure or prestige into purchasing a particular microcomputer if the use you will get from it will not offset its cost.

Ease of Use

If you have followed the processes for narrowing down your options to this point, the last option you will want to consider is how easy the system is to use. If you have found more than one system that fulfills all the other requirements, this may be the deciding factor.

In looking at ease of use, the best way to decide is to sit down and play with the computer for a while. (If the computer store is not too happy about this, there are stores like U-Compute where you can rent time on a computer.) While you are playing with it, ask yourself: Am I comfortable with this system? Is this easy enough for me to use without undue frustration? If you are planning to let your children play with the computer, you may want to consider whether they would have difficulties operating it.

In addition to looking at the machine, look at the support documentation that comes with it. Does it seem complete? Can you think of any problems that might arise that aren't covered in the user's manual? Finally, is it easy to read? This is an especially important feature. Even if the manual is complete, if it is not written in language that you can understand, it will be of little use.

Warranties

Once you have decided to buy a particular computer, look very carefully at the specifications of the warranty. Many warranties contain small-print clauses specifying the user's responsibility to provide proper air conditioning, power supplies, and so on of which you may not be aware. Make sure that you understand all of the conditions of the warranty and that you can comply with them. Remember that any failure to comply may result in negating the warranty.

If you are purchasing your microcomputer from a retailer other than the manufacturer, carefully examine the purchase order itself. Many of these purchase orders contain disclaimers that in effect say that the retailer is not responsible if the computer you take home does not work. This would force you to go directly to the manufacturer to negotiate any maintenance or replacements. In many cases, what you can do to get around this is to bring your own purchase order. Although some retailers will not accept this, many of them will.

In addition, pay close attention to what the sales representative tells you. If it is not in the actual warranty, demand to have it in writing. Always use common sense—READ THE FINE PRINT! If you are purchasing an expensive microcomputer, it may even be worth your while to see a lawyer first.

APPENDIX C

FLOWCHARTING

Imagine the number of classes you have taken that required a paper to be written on a particular subject. Before beginning to write a paper, (especially if it is one which covers a number of different topics), determine which topics should be covered and then the sequence in which they should be discussed. After completing the necessary research, one of the most useful means of organizing your thoughts and ideas is to construct an outline. The more detail shown in the outline, the easier it will be to determine the best sequence of topic discussion. The writing of the paper is greatly simplified as well because the content has been carefully thought through. After a detailed outline has been constructed, the actual writing of the paper simply involves expanding brief descriptive statements into grammatically correct narrative text.

The writing of a computer program is approached in a very similar manner. The major difference is that a computer program is designed to solve a specific problem and must be written according to the rules and syntax of a particular program language.

Computer problem solving involves the execution of a series of steps in a specific logical sequence. The programmer, therefore, must carefully determine the steps to be performed along with the sequence in which they are to be executed in order to develop an appropriate solution. At times, a problem solution may require numerous tasks to be performed in a sequence difficult to clearly describe. A program flowchart can be constructed to graphically represent the flow of processing steps that should be contained within a program and thus aid the programmer in planning a program solution. The program flowchart functions as an outline from which the programmer will write the corresponding program code.

There are two types of program flowcharts that can be developed: a *macro flowchart* and a *micro flowchart*. One type is distinguished from the other by the level of detail that is shown. Generally, both are constructed in a similar format and utilize the same special symbols. Each symbol within the flowchart represents a specific processing function. Within the symbol, the programmer briefly describes the function or instructions to be performed. The symbols are interconnected with flowlines to illustrate the logical sequence of execution. Flowcharts should be drawn in a top down format with flowlines extending from top to bottom and from left to right.

SYMBOLS

Standardized symbols were developed by the American National Standards Institute (ANSI) for use in flowcharting. Figure C-1 shows a flowcharting template that can be used by programmers to neatly draw these symbols. A brief description of each of the most commonly used ANSI symbols is provided below:

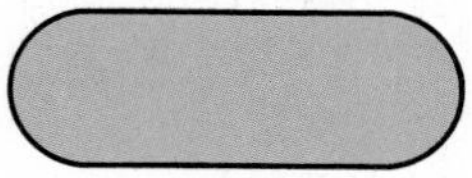

The terminal symbol is used when representing both the start and end of a program.

The input/output symbol represents either an input or an output operation. When data is brought into the program for processing, the description within the symbol will indicate that and what input operation is taking place. Likewise, when information is stored on a storage medium or printed in a human readable format, the description will indicate that an output operation is occurring in that processing step.

The processing symbol may indicate that an arithmetic operation involving addition, subtraction, multiplication and/or division is taking place. Generally, a calculation is involved and the programmer can write either the equation or a description of the calculation within the block. The movement of data from one location to another and other forms of data manipulation are also represented with this symbol.

The decision symbol is used in processing steps that require a comparison or a test to be made. Based on the results of comparison, one of a number of alternate paths will be followed.

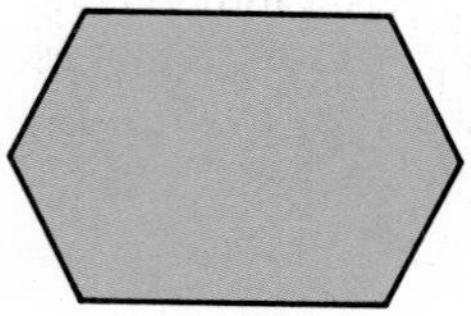

The initialization symbol is used when initializing variables to beginning values in a program.

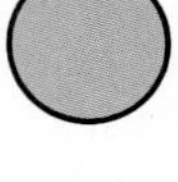

The connector symbol represents an interruption on the processing flow when transfer is to be made to another section of the program. In addition to specifying where transfer is to be made, the same connector symbol also labels the re-entry location. It is a flowcharting convention to begin the flowchart at the top left side of the page and continue downward to the bottom. The flowchart should then continue at the top right-most side of the page. The same connector symbol is the last symbol at the bottom of the left side and the first symbol at the top of the right-most side.

Although this is not an ANSI symbol, it is often used in writing programs. Depending on the complexity and the amount of detail to be shown, a flowchart can extend across multiple pages. When a flowchart requires additional pages, the off-page connector symbol is used to link pages together. For example, the last symbol on the right-most column of the first page will be the connector symbol with the reference name for the second page. Similarly, the first symbol of the second page will be the connector symbol with the reference name of that second page.

MACRO FLOWCHARTS

A macro flowchart illustrates, in a very general way, the major logical segments of the program. These segments are called *modules*, and the flowchart illustrates how one or more modules are related to each other in accordance with the program logic.

The level of detail shown in a macro flowchart is such that one processing symbol may represent several lines of program code. The main objective of the macro flowchart is to illustrate the input, processing steps, and output of the program. A level of detail sufficient enough to provide the programmer with a sound understanding of the problem and how it is to be solved is obtained with this type of flowchart.

FIGURE C-1 Flowchart Template

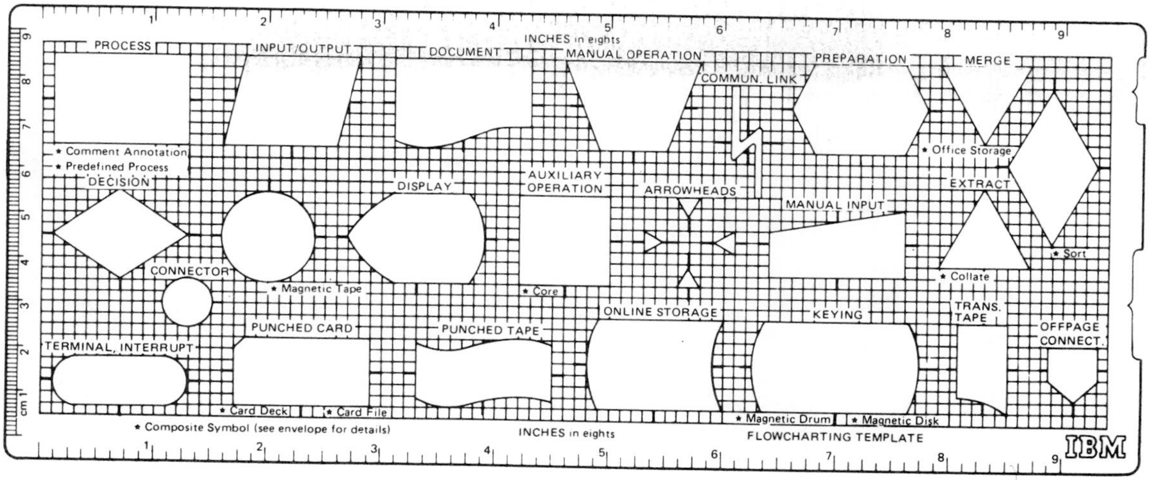

An example of a macro flowchart can be seen in Figure C-2. Imagine that you are ready to buy a brand new car. You have spent weeks car shopping, collecting information on numerous cars, and now you must narrow your decision to one of five different cars. In order to eliminate some of your possible choices, you have decided on certain requirements that each car must possess. Specifically, for the car to even be considered, it must have an automatic transmission, air conditioning, and an estimated gas mileage of not less than 25 MPG. It is not mandatory for the car to possess an FM stereo, but that would be a desirable feature. The final deciding factor, of course, is the overall total cost of the car.

FIGURE C-2
Macro Flowchart

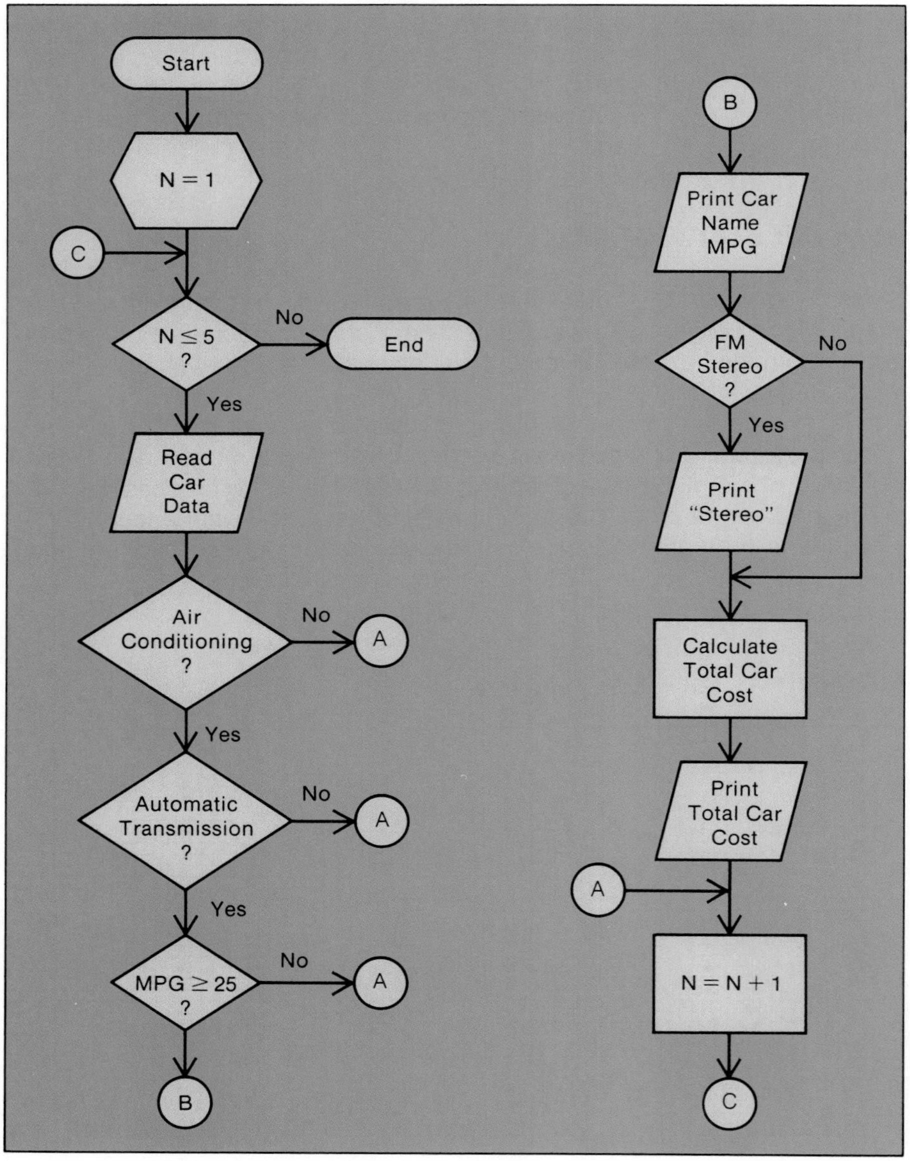

Figure C-2 illustrates the input, processing steps, and output that is required to help you narrow down your selection according to the criteria previously described. Following the start symbol ⬭, the flowchart indicates that a counter to keep track of the number of cars evaluated will be utilized in the program as represented by the symbol ⬡. The counter (N) is initialized to 1 as a starting value. The diamond-shaped decision symbol,. ◇, is used to test whether or not the value of the counter is less than or equal to five. When the value is greater than five (the number of cars that will be evaluated on the program), the program will end. If the value of the counter is less than or equal to five, an alternate path is followed. First, car data concerning the car name, base price, MPG, and other options, is input. Next, a series of decisions concerning required car features (air conditioning, automatic transmission, and MPG) must be made. If just one of these criteria is not met, control is sent to the processing block □ which increments the counter by one, to show that one car out of five has been evaluated. The connector symbol ○ references where control is to be sent.

If all three mandatory conditions have been met, the car name and MPG is printed. If the car contains an FM stereo, which is not a mandatory criteria, that will be printed as well. The total cost of the car, including taxes, title, and dealer preparation charges is then calculated as indicated by the process block □ and that amount is printed. A program will be written following these processing specifications outlined in the flowchart, but it is up to you to make the final purchase decision, based on the program output.

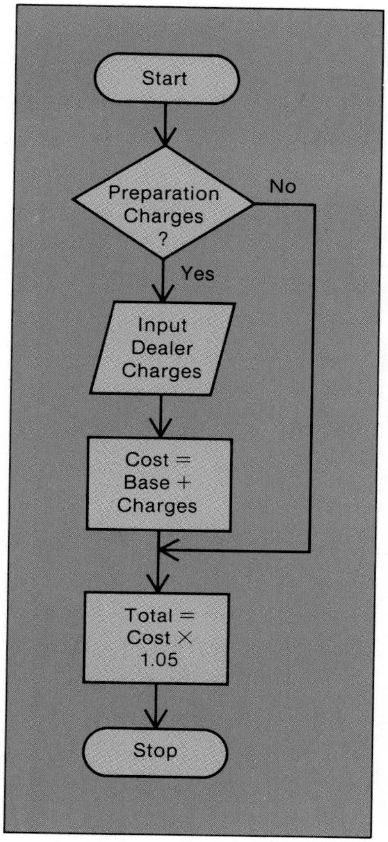

FIGURE C-3
Micro Flowchart

MICRO FLOWCHARTS

Once the macro flowchart has been constructed, the programmer can proceed to further break down the processing steps. A micro flowchart is used to represent, in greater detail, the operations that must be performed within a processing symbol. Because of the level of detail that can be shown, there is often a one-to-one correspondence between processing symbols within a micro flowchart and the resulting program statements. Several micro flowcharts can thus be constructed for each macro flowchart. The size and complexity of macro flowcharts are limited only by the size and complexity of the problem to be solved.

An example of a micro flowchart for the car purchasing problem previously described is represented in Figure C-3. In this example, the processing steps for calculating the total purchase cost, including a 5% sales tax, is shown in greater detail. First, it must be determined whether additional preparation charges for that car must be input as indicated by the ◇ symbol. If the dealer does make additional charges, the amount is then input as represented by the ▱ symbol, and the cost is calculated as specified by the □ symbol. If there are no preparation charges involved, the alternate path bypassed the dealer input. Finally, the total cost is determined for the car by including the sales tax calculation as specified by the □ symbol.

BASIC SUPPLEMENT

ARTICLE

COMPUTERS THE LATEST IN GENERATION GAPS

By BOB SWIFT

It has been said that in a few years there will be two classes of people, those who understand computers and those who don't. That's probably true, judging by a conversation I overheard:

"Mom, we really ought to get an Apple for Christmas."

"Of course, dear. Doesn't Santa always put a big Delicious in your stocking?"

"Mom! I'm talking about an Apple computer. Everybody is getting computers this year. Or maybe we could get an Orange."

"Well, put that in your letter to Santa, that you'd rather have an orange than an apple."

"No, no. An Orange is a brand of computer, too. Listen, you've got to learn about computers. They're the wave of the future."

"My goodness. I wouldn't even know how to turn one on."

"You don't turn it on, Mom: you gain access."

"Well, it's all Greek to me."

"No, no, not Greek. Basic."

"Your father was in basic in the army and it was dreadful."

"Mother! Basic is a computer language. You learn Basic to talk to a computer. Or you learn the other computer languages. Have you ever heard of Fortran?"

"YES, IT'S like Dacron, only stretchy. I think they make tummy-control pantyhose out of it."

"No, Mom! Fortran! It's a language."

"Is it like Bebop? Your father used to speak Bebop back in the 1950s. He'd say, 'Crazy, dad, I'm hip, and all that jazz.' I couldn't understand a word he said."

"That's archaic slang, mother. I'm talking about PLI."

"Now I DO know about those awful Palestinian terrorists."

"No, no, not PLO. PLI is another computer language. Look, mother, I need a few more chips to . . ."

"I'm sure your father has some left over from his poker-playing days."

"Microchips, mother, microchips. Look, I'll start simply. See, this system starts with six bytes."

"Six bites of which, your apple or your orange?"

"I'm being patient, mother. Look, eight bits make a byte. Four bits are . . ."

"Oh, I get it now. Two bits, four bits, six bits, a dollar! All for Maryville, stand up and holler!"

"GET SERIOUS, mother. Look, we use the binary system, coding everything into ones and zeroes. Now, see this motherboard? I have to put data and addressing info through the gate and into the bus. But it can't all go at the same time or I'll have bus contention. See, the zeroes and ones get on the bus and propagate, then flow off."

"I understand, dear. Everybody goes through the gate and gets on the bus and . . . oh my!"

"Maybe I'd better explain hardware and software. Or should I start with CRTs? Listen, Mom, you'd really like this stuff if you'd pay attention. You'd learn to interface with peripherals. You'd learn about hard disk capacity and double headed RANAs."

"Is that like Dr. Doolittle's Pushme-Pullyu?"

"You'd learn about 64K byte RAMs and the Orange FIFO buffer."

"Isn't that a headache remedy?"

"Look, Mom, let's suppose you have a floppy disk."

"Go talk to your father, dear. He'll understand about floppy disks. He's had lower back pain for years."

BACKGROUND

BASIC was developed in the mid-1960s at Dartmouth College by Professors John G. Kemeny and Thomas E. Kurtz and has become one of the most popular programming languages. **BASIC**, short for *B*eginner's *A*ll-Purpose *S*ymbolic *I*nstruction *C*ode, is easy to learn, can be used for a wide variety of useful tasks, and is well suited for classroom teaching.

BASIC, like any language, includes rules for spelling, syntax, grammar, and punctuation. Just as the rules in English help us understand one another, so the rules in BASIC help the computer understand what we want it to do. In BASIC, the rules link abstract algebraic expressions with easy-to-understand English words like LET, GOTO, FOR/NEXT, INPUT, PRINT, and END.

BASIC originally was developed for use in a large, interactive computer environment; one or more BASIC users could communicate with the computer during processing and feel as though they had the computer all to themselves. As the demand for minicomputers and microcomputers increased, manufacturers of such computers felt pressure to develop simple but effective languages for them. Rather than create entirely new languages, most opted to offer BASIC because of its interactive capability: the user can communicate directly with the computer in a conversational fashion. Many altered the original BASIC, however, to suit their equipment. The result is that, although the BASIC language has a universally accepted set of standard rules called **ANSI BASIC** (established by the American National Standards Institute), each manufacturer adds its "quirks" to this standard to make use of special features of its machines. This equipment discusses BASIC commands common to most computer systems.

INTRODUCTION TO COMPUTER PROGRAMMING

Computer programs are step-by-step instructions to solve a problem. Since the computer must be able to read and interpret each instruction, the program must be precisely written. In order to know what instructions are required to solve a problem, the programmer follows five steps, commonly called the **programming process**:

1. Define and document the problem.
2. Design and document a solution.
3. Write and document the program.
4. Submit the program to the computer.
5. Test and debug the program, and revise the documentation if necessary.

To show how these steps are used in the programming process, let us take a sample data-processing problem: calculating the distance in miles given the distance in kilometers.

The first step is to define and document the problem. To do so, we analyze it by using the basic flow of all data processing—**input**, **processing**, and **output**—but with a twist. It is often easier to determine what processing is needed by working backward. First, determine what output is required, and then see what input is available for the program. The gap between the available input and the required output will be the processing needed in the program.

Determining the output for the problem is quite simple: we need to know the distance in miles. The input available is the distance in kilometers. The gap is some conversion factor that translates the distance in kilometers to the distance in miles. One kilometer equals 0.621 miles; hence, to calculate the distance in miles, we multiply the distance in kilometers by 0.621. We have now defined the problem.

The second step, designing and documenting a solution, requires developing a logical sequence of instructions or statements to solve the problem. Remember, good documentation can help avoid future problems or make them easier to solve when they do come about. Documentation consists of all written descriptions and explanations necessary for later modification or updating of the program. An effective tool to use at this point is the flowchart. **Flowcharts** are composed of symbols that stand for program steps. For example, the symbol for a processing step is 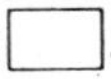. The symbol for a step that involves either input from an input device or output to an output device is 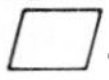. The symbol that shows where the program starts or stops is 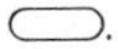.

To create a flowchart for our example, we only need these three symbols. Shown below are some other symbols that we will use later:

1.  shows where a comparison (decision) is to be made and where alternative processing is to occur based upon the results of the comparison.

2.  indicates an entry from or an exit to another part of the program flowchart.

3.  represents a preparation step, such as initializing a variable (discussed in Chapter 3)

Figure I–1 shows a flowchart depicting the steps of the programming example. Notice how the symbols are shown in logical order, top down, and connected by arrows. The first symbol shows the start of the program. The second symbol shows an input step: we enter the distance in kilometers. The third shows the processing done by the program: the conversion of the distance in kilometers to the distance in miles. After that, we want to see the result, so we output the converted distance to the terminal. Finally, another start/stop symbol signifies the end of the program. The flowchart makes it easy to see the input, processing, and output steps of the program.

If the solution has been designed carefully, the next step—coding (writing) the program—should be relatively easy. All that is required is to translate the flowchart into program statements. Figure I–2 shows this program written in BASIC. As you can see, many BASIC words, such as INPUT and PRINT, are easy to interpret. The symbol * means "multiply." Compare the coded BASIC statements in Figure I–2 to the flowchart in Figure I–1; the correspondence between the two is obvious.

In the program in Figure I–2, each statement starts with a line number. Line numbers tell the computer the order in which to execute statements. Lines 100 through 120 are remarks or comments describing the program. The computer ignores all such comment statements; they are for documentation purposes. Line 130 tells the computer to print out a statement (shown in quotation marks)—our cue to enter the distance in kilometers—and then to accept it after we type it in. Line 140 is an example of an assignment statement, which assigns values on the right side of the equal sign to special variables on the left (this is discussed in the next section). Line 150 instructs the computer to print out first a heading (shown in quotes) and then the distance in miles. Finally, line 999 tells the computer to stop processing. Again, the program follows the flow of input, processing, and output.

The fourth step involves sitting down at the terminal and typing the program, line for line, into the computer. When the program is entered into the computer, it must be translated into machine language in order for the computer to understand it. This is accomplished by either an **interpreter** or a **compiler**. Interpreters and compilers are programs that are either loaded into the computer from disks each time the system is turned on or stored permanently inside the computer in memory. The difference between an interpreter and a compiler is that the compiler creates an object program (the entire program in machine language format) and then loads the entire object program into main memory. The central processing unit (CPU) then directly executes the object program. An interpreter translates and executes only one line of machine language to the CPU at a time. Programs that have been compiled into an object program normally execute faster than those translated by an interpreter, however, the compiler usually requires a much larger storage area than an interpreter.

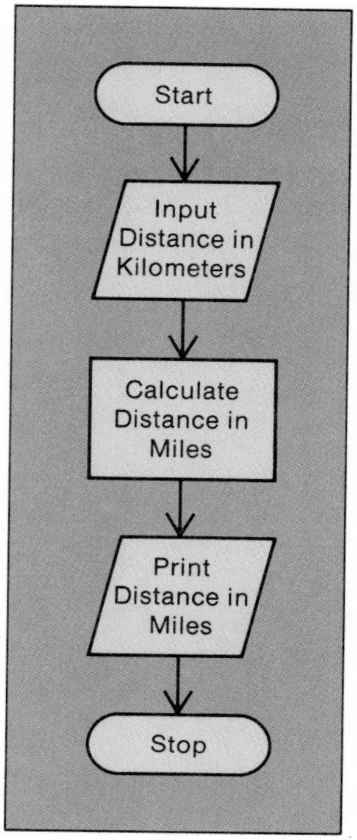

FIGURE I-1
Flowchart Example

FIGURE I-2 Distance Conversion Program

```
100 REM *** THIS PROGRAM CALCULATES ***
110 REM *** DISTANCE IN MILES FROM DISTANCE ***
120 REM *** IN KILOMETERS ***
130 INPUT "ENTER KILOMETERS";K
140 LET D = K * .621
150 PRINT "THE DISTANCE IN MILES IS ";D
999 END
```

Many interactive BASIC interpreters and compilers check for syntax errors as each statement is typed in. **Syntax** refers to the way instructions have to be written (rules must be followed, just as grammatical rules must be followed in English). A syntax check can save considerable debugging time. Debugging is the process of locating and correcting errors in a program.

After all syntax errors have been eliminated, the program can be tested with sample data. This is the fifth step. During this stage, the logic of the program is checked for correctness; for instance, were the correct statements used to determine the distance in miles? It is important to thoroughly document programs. In larger, more complex programs, logic errors can be difficult to debug. Good program documentation can make debugging much easier. Figure I–3 shows the execution of the distance conversion program.

This example is relatively simple, but it shows each of the steps required to complete a program. Although other problems may be more complex, the steps involved are the same. Successful programming can come about only through the diligent application of the five steps in the programming process.

INTERACTING WITH THE COMPUTER

An important step in BASIC programming is learning to control the computer. Although this supplement cannot present the full operational details for each computer, it can discuss the principles of how to turn the computer on, make contact with BASIC, retrieve a program from external storage, display the program, alter the program, and save it for future reference.

BASIC programming requires the use of different types of commands. Some of the commands—for example, GOTO, LET, and READ—are program language statements. They are assembled into programs to solve specific business, scientific, engineering, and mathematical problems. The BASIC supplement describes their characteristics and how they are used.

There are also **system commands** and **editing commands**, which are used by the programmer to communicate with the operating system of the computer in order to perform functions like saving programs for future reference and making changes in programs. Some commands—for example, LIST, RUN, and DELETE—are almost universally used but are not

FIGURE I-3 Execution of Distance Conversion Program

```
RUN
ENTER KILOMETERS? 500
THE DISTANCE IN MILES IS  310.5
```

covered by ANSI standards. The rest of this section will describe such commands as they relate to the Apple II and II Plus, Atari 800, IBM Personal Computer (PC), PET/Commodore 64, and Radio Shack's TRS-80 Model III microcomputers.

Apple II and II Plus

Hardware The Apple II initially contains INTEGER BASIC. Since INTEGER BASIC lacks many important features of ANSI BASIC, this discussion only refers to this computer once Applesoft floating-point BASIC has been loaded. The Apple II Plus computer automatically comes up in Applesoft. Since disk has emerged as the primary form of secondary storage, we will discuss the hardware configuration using disk only. Consult your documentation for cassette commands. The same holds true for each of the other computers discussed.

Starting the Computer The power switch is located on the left rear portion of the computer. Since an external monitor or cathode-ray tube (CRT) is required, you must remember to turn on power to this device also. If a disk drive is attached, it will whir and try to **boot** the **disk operating system (DOS)**, so be sure a diskette is placed in the disk drive before the computer is turned on. (When the disk drive boots the DOS, it loads from a diskette the instructions that tell the computer how to manage the disk. This must be done before the computer can perform any disk-related tasks.) If your system has two disk drives, the system disk should be placed in drive A (volume 4).

The computer "comes up" with **floating-point BASIC**, as indicated by the use of the] character as a prompt. You can now begin to program.

Saving and Loading Programs Programs commonly are accessed from disk on this system.

The Apple has a convenient file-by-name catalog system for the DOS. To save an Applesoft program—for example, one named GROSSPAY—on disk, type

```
SAVE GROSSPAY
```

and press RETURN. To load the same program from disk, type

```
LOAD GROSSPAY
```

and press RETURN. You then can run the program. Alternatively, you can type RUN GROSSPAY without loading it; this causes the DOS to both load and run the program.

Atari 800

Hardware This discussion refers to the Atari 800 system, which uses the Atari 810 (TM) disk drive and Atari Cartridge BASIC.

Starting the Computer Turn on the television monitor. Then turn on the disk drive unit or units. The busy light or lights will come on and stay on until each drive is initialized. Following this, turn on any other peripheral devices, for example, the printer. Insert the DOS diskette in disk drive 1, and close the disk drive door. The master diskette DOS should always be placed in disk drive 1. After these steps have been completed, insert the Atari Cartridge BASIC cartridge in the left front slot, and turn on the computer console. The power switch is located on the lower rear portion of the right side. When the computer is turned on, it will boot (load) the disk operating system (DOS). The **cursor** will appear in the upper left corner of the screen. A cursor is a line or box that marks the next position at which a character is to be typed, inserted, or deleted. You are now ready to begin entering your program.

Saving and Loading Programs Programs commonly are accessed from disk on this system.

To save a program on diskette, select the drive you want to use (for example, disk drive 2), use the command

```
SAVE "D2:PROG1.BAS"
```

and press the RETURN key. Device Identification D: is equivalent to D1: (disk drive 1).

To load the same program, type

```
LOAD "D2:PROG1.BAS"
```

IBM Personal Computer

Hardware The IBM Personal Computer (PC) contains an enhanced version of Microsoft BASIC. The disk drives are built into the body of the computer.

Starting the Computer Place the system diskette into drive A, the left drive. Then turn the computer on. The power switch is located on the right rear of the machine. Do not forget to turn on the television monitor, too. When the computer is turned on, it will try to load the disk operating system (DOS). (If no diskette has been placed in the disk drive, the computer will "come up" in Cassette BASIC.)

The IBM has three BASIC dialects—Cassette BASIC, Disk BASIC, and Advanced BASIC. For the purpose of this supplement, they are the same.

Once the DOS has been booted (loaded), the computer asks for the data as follows:

```
Current date is Tue 3-21-84
Enter new date:
```

You can respond by typing in the new date and pressing the ENTER key or by simply pressing the ENTER key. The computer then asks for the time as follows:

```
Current time is 0:01:51.39
Enter new time:
```

You can respond by typing in the new time and pressing the ENTER key or by simply pressing the ENTER key. After you have entered the date and time (or have pressed only the ENTER key to bypass each), the computer responds with

```
The IBM Personal Computer DOS
Version 1.10 (C)Copyright IBM Corp 1981, 1982

A>
```

The A> is the system prompt. Simply type BASIC and press the carriage return to load the Disk BASIC translator or type BASICA to load the Advanced BASIC translator. The BASIC prompt is OK. Now you are ready to start programming.

Saving and Loading Programs Programs commonly are accessed from disk on this system.

The IBM PC has a convenient file-by-name catalog system for the DOS. To save a program (for example, one named GRADES), type

```
SAVE "GRADES"
```

The name of the program should be less than or equal to eight characters. Do not embed any spaces. To load the same program from disk, type

```
LOAD "GRADES"
```

You can then LIST and RUN the program on your cathode-ray tube (CRT) screen. To list your program on the printer, type LLIST. To obtain output on your printer, each PRINT statement in your program will need to be changed to LPRINT. Once this has been done, you can type RUN, and the output from your program will appear on the printer.

PET/Commodore 64

Hardware The PET and Commodore 64 computers are made by the same manufacturer, Commodore Business Machines. The following discussion will focus on the Commodore 64. However, the commands for saving and loading programs are identical on both machines:

Starting the Computer It is very important that the computer components are turned on in the correct order. The computer must be turned on last. To prevent damage to the computer or diskettes, diskettes must be removed from the disk drives before the power is turned on or off. After all other components have been turned on, the computer can safely be turned on using the power switch which is located on the rear portion of the right side panel. When the power switch is turned on, the monitor will display the following:

```
****COMMODORE 64 BASIC V2****
64K RAM SYSTEM 38911 BASIC BYTES FREE
READY
```

The first line tells which version of the BASIC language is available. The second line tells how much memory the computer has (64K, in this example). The third line indicates that the computer is ready to accept BASIC line numbers and statements.

Saving and Loading Programs Programs commonly are accessed from either cassette tape or disk on this system.

The Commodore 64 floppy disk system has a file-by-name catalog. To load a program named MASTER, you type

```
LOAD "MASTER",8
```

The 8 is the code for the disk, which lets the computer know you want the program loaded from the disk. After the RETURN key is pressed, the disk will start whirring, and the following will be displayed:

```
SEARCHING FOR MASTER
LOADING

READY
```

After typing in a program, you probably will want to save it on cassette or disk. The SAVE command is used to save a program on tape in the following manner:

```
SAVE "program-name"
```

The program name can be up to sixteen characters long. After you hit the RETURN key, the computer responds with

```
PRESS PLAY AND RECORD ON TAPE
```

When both keys are pressed, the screen will turn blank (the color of the border). After the program is saved on tape, the READY prompt will reappear, indicating that the computer is ready for another program.

Saving programs on disk is similar; just type

```
SAVE "program-name",8
```

Here again, the 8 tells the computer that you want the program saved to disk. After the RETURN key is pressed, the disk will start to turn, and the computer will respond with

```
SAVING "program-name"
OK
READY
```

Radio Shack TRS-80 Model III

Hardware This discussion is based on the TRS-80 Model III with the Model III BASIC language. An older computer, the Model I with Level II BASIC, is very similar to the Model III. The comments about BASIC programs here generally apply to either computer but do not deal with the Level I BASIC language.

Starting the Computer The power is turned on by a rocker switch beneath the keyboard on the right side nearest the programmer. Next the TRSDOS diskette should be inserted in drive 0 and the RESET button pressed to load TRSDOS. The TRSDOS version number, date of creation, amount of RAM, number of drives, and a date prompt in the form MM/DD/YY will be displayed. The date must be entered in correct form and the ENTER key pressed before TRSDOS will continue. Next the time prompt in 24-hour form HH:MM:SS will be displayed. Enter the time or simply press the ENTER key to set the time at 00:00:00. The monitor will then display

```
TRSDOS READY
```

To load the BASIC interpreter type the word BASIC and press the ENTER key. The computer will display:

```
HOW MANY FILES?
```

then

```
MEMORY SIZE?
```

Press the ENTER key in reponse to each of these questions. Next the computer will display a heading followed by

```
READY
>
```

You may now begin to use disk BASIC.

Saving and Loading Programs Programs commonly are accessed from disk on this system. To save a program (for example, INVENTORY), just type

```
SAVE "INVENTORY"
```

and press the ENTER button. To load the same program from disk, type

```
LOAD "INVENTORY"
```

BASIC SYSTEM AND EDITING COMMANDS

The BASIC system and editing commands are **immediate-mode commands**; that is, they are executed as soon as the carriage control key (RETURN or ENTER) is pressed. They differ from BASIC language commands, which are not executed until the program is run. The most commonly used system commands are discussed here.

System Commands

New The **NEW** command tells the computer to erase any program currently in active memory. After typing this command, you can start entering a new program.

List After typing in a long program, you may want to admire the finished product. Type **LIST** to see the program displayed at the terminal. If you have a very short program, LIST can display the whole program on the screen. However, if the program has more lines than the screen does, only the last part of the program will remain on the screen. Some screens permit only twenty-four lines to be displayed. You can display portions of programs by specifying the lines to be listed—LIST 150-300, for example. Most computers also allow you to suppress scrolling—that is, to freeze the listing temporarily (see "Controlling the Scroll" later in this section).

Run The purpose of the **RUN** command is to begin execution of a program. Typing the word RUN will begin execution of the program currently in memory.

Save After you have typed many program lines, you will want to avoid losing them when the computer is turned off. To do this, you have to move the program from internal memory to an external storage medium such as cassette tape or disk. This move is accomplished by the **SAVE** command. There are generally several options to this command; for example, you may supply a name that distinguishes this particular program from all others. The discussions of each computer earlier in this section summarized the most elementary forms of SAVE commands for the disk configuration.

Controlling the Scroll

If your program's output consists of forty lines of information, but your screen only has a twenty-four-line capacity, how will you see all of your output? The forty lines will be displayed so quickly that you will not be able to read them until the listing is finished. By then, however, the first sixteen lines will be gone—scrolled off the top of the screen.

Most computers have a means of controlling the scroll of the screen. The programmer can simply push one or two keys to freeze the display and then press the same keys to resume listing when desired. This method also can be used to freeze the output listing of a program during execution. Table I–1 summarizes the method of scroll freezing and the type of editor used on each of the five computers.

Editing Commands

Everyone makes typing mistakes. You should quickly learn how to correct yours using your system's editing commands. You may find a mistake before you press the RETURN key, or you may find it at some later time. These two conditions call for different methods of correction:

1. *Before RETURN has been pressed.* Suppose you typed LRT when you wanted to type LET. If you noticed the error before pressing RETURN,

TABLE I-1 Type of Editor and Scroll Control

Microcomputer	Screen Editor	Line Editor	Scroll Stop	Scroll Start
Apple II and II Plus	Yes	—	CTRL-S	Press any key
Atari 800	Yes	—	CTRL-1	CTRL-1
IBM PC	Yes	—	CTRL-NUMLOCK	Press any key
PET/Commodore 64	Yes	—	None	None
TRS-80 Model III	—	Yes	SHIFT-@	Press any key

Notes:
1. CTRL-S means hold down the control (CTRL) key and the S key at the same time.
2. CTRL-1 means hold down the CTRL key and 1 key at the same time.
3. CTRL-NUMLOCK means hold down the CTRL key and the NUMLOCK key at the same time.
4. There is no scroll stop/start function on the PET/Commodore 64. However, holding the control key down will slow the scroll to one line at a time.
5. SHIFT-@ means hold down the SHIFT key and the @ key at the same time.

you can move the computer's cursor back to the R in LRT by pressing the "←" key (on the Apple, IBM, PET/Commodore 64, and TRS-80). Then you can retype LET correctly. For the Atari, the DELETE BACK S key performs the same function.

2. *After RETURN has been pressed.* If you notice an error after RETURN has been pressed, the simplest correction, in principle, is to retype the whole line. This may get tiresome for long lines, however, especially if you need to change only one character. Each computer has a means of correcting mistakes within a given line. There is not enough space here for a full explanation of these methods, but there are two general kinds: the **screen editor** and the **line editor**. To use the screen editor, list the portion of the program containing the error. Then move the cursor to the position of the error—typically, by pressing four keys with arrows that move the cursor up, down, left, or right. The incorrect characters then can be typed over or deleted, or new characters can be inserted between existing characters. The second type of editor, the line editor, works on individual lines. The user specifies the line containing the error and uses commands such as REPLACE, INSERT, and DELETE instead of moving the cursor to the error.

SUMMARY

- BASIC (*B*eginner's *A*ll-Purpose *S*ymbolic *I*nstruction *C*ode) was developed in the mid-1960s by Professors John G. Kemeny and Thomas E. Kurtz at Dartmouth College.
- BASIC has rules of grammar (syntax), to which programmers must adhere.
- The five steps in the programming process are (1) define and document the problem; (2) design and document a solution; (3) write and document the program; (4) submit the program to the computer; and (5) test and debug the program, and revise the documentation if necessary.

- System commands are used by the programmer to communicate with the operating system of the computer. Some commonly used ones are NEW, LIST, RUN, and SAVE.
- There are also editing commands to help the programmer correct mistakes.

QUESTIONS AND PROBLEMS

1. Write a flowchart for the following program:

```
10 REM *** CALCULATES SUM OF TWO NUMBERS ***
20 INPUT "ENTER X AND Y";X,Y
30 LET S = X + Y
40 PRINT "X + Y = ";S
999 END
```

2. What are the steps in the programming process?
3. What is the basic flow of all data processing?

SECTION II

Getting Started with BASIC

OVERVIEW

One of the best ways to learn any programming language is to examine sample programs. This and the remaining sections in the BASIC supplement will intersperse discussions of the language's general characteristics with program examples.

This section first discusses some components of the BASIC language: line numbers, constants, character strings, and variables. All are demonstrated so that you can use them properly when you write programs. The section also will examine four elementary BASIC statements: REM, LET, PRINT, and END. The LET statement is used to both assign data to variables and perform arithmetic calculations. The PRINT statement allows the programmer to see the results of processing. Processing is stopped with the END statement. The REM statement is presented here to underscore the importance of program documentation.

COMPONENTS OF THE BASIC LANGUAGE

BASIC statements are composed of special programming commands, constants, numeric or string variables, and formulas (also called **expressions**). A BASIC **program** is a sequence of statements that tells the computer how to solve a problem. Figure II-1 is an example. (Most sections in this supplement begin with a simple program example.) This program calculates the gross pay of an employee whose wage rate is $4.50 an hour and who has worked forty hours.

Notice that each instruction contains a line number and a BASIC statement. Line 140 from the sample program is an example of a typical BASIC instruction. It tells the computer to multiply two values together (the * is the symbol for multiplication) and place the result in a location called P. P represents the gross pay.

Line Numbers

The **line number** must be an integer between 1 and 99999. The program statements are executed by the computer in the sequence in which they

Figure II-1 Gross Pay Program

```
100 REM *** THIS PROGRAM COMPUTES ***
110 REM *** EMPLOYEE'S GROSS PAY ***
120 LET R = 4.5
130 LET H = 40
140 LET P = R * H
150 LET A$ = "GROSS PAY = $"
160 PRINT A$;P
999 END
```

are numbered, from low to high. The line numbers also can be used as labels to refer to specific statements in the program.

Line numbers do not have to be specified in increments of 1. Using increments of 10, for example, makes it easier to insert new statements between existing lines at a later time without renumbering all the old statements in the program. For example, if we wanted to insert a new statement in the sample program between statements 130 and 140, we could number the new statement 135 (see the following example) without disturbing the order of the existing statements and having to renumber them:

```
100 REM *** THIS PROGRAM COMPUTES ***
110 REM *** EMPLOYEE'S GROSS PAY ***
120 LET R = 4.5
130 LET H = 40
135 REM *** GROSS PAY = WAGE RATE * HOURS WORKED ***
140 LET P = R * H
150 LET A$ = "GROSS PAY = $"
160 PRINT A$;P
999 END
```

The BASIC interpreter or compiler arranges all the program statements in ascending order according to line number, even though the lines actually may have been entered in some other order.

Another advantage of using BASIC line numbers is that they permit changes to be made to the program as it is being entered into the computer. For example, if two lines are typed in with the same line number, the computer will accept the last one entered as the correct one. Thus, if we make a mistake in a statement, we can simply type in the same line number and the correct statement. In the following example, the computer will replace the first line 140 with the second line 140:

```
140 LET P = P * H    (Mistake occurs here.)
140 LET P = R * H    (Corrected line.)
```

Constants

Constants are values that do not change during a program's execution. There are two kinds: **numeric constant** and **character string constant.**

Numeric Constants BASIC permits numbers to be represented in two ways: as **real numbers** or in **exponential form (scientific notation)**.

REAL NUMBERS. Real numbers can be either integers or decimal fractions. Some examples of real numbers follow:

0.43   6,700   +18   −35   8.632

There are some rules to remember about using numbers in BASIC:

1. No commas can be embedded within numbers:
   86821 (Valid)   86,821 (Invalid)

BASIC sees the invalid example not as the number eighty-six thousand eight hundred twenty-one, but as the number eighty-six and the number eight hundred twenty-one.

2. If a number is negative, it must be preceded by a minus sign:
   −4.45 (Valid)   4.45− (Invalid)
3. If no sign is included, the number is assumed to be positive:
   56 is the same as +56.

Exponential Form, or Scientific Notation. Scientific notation usually is used for very large or very small numbers. Some examples follow:

3.865312E+09   6.187E−05

The E represents base 10, and the signed number following the E is the power to which 10 is raised. If the addition sign is omitted after the E, positive exponentiation is assumed. The number preceding the E is called the **mantissa** and in most systems lies between 1.000 and 9.999. Some examples follow:

DECIMAL	POWER EQUIVALENT	SCIENTIFIC NOTATION
53860	5.386×10^4	5.386E04
0.00531	5.31×10^{-3}	5.31E−03
−658310	-6.5831×10^5	−6.5831E+05

Character String Constants The other type of constant is the character string. Character strings are composed of alphanumeric data—a sequence of alphabetic, numeric, or special characters—or a combination of two or all three of these—enclosed in quotation marks. The maximum number of characters allowed in a character string varies from computer to computer. The following are examples of character strings:

```
"ROBERT"
"867-5309"
"121 ANYPLACE DR."
```

There is a character string in line 150 of the sample program in Figure II-1:

```
150 LET A$ = "GROSS PAY = $"
```

Variables

Any data values to be used by a program must be stored in the computer either before or during execution of the program. The computer has a great number of storage locations, which are given names by the programmer. The names, or symbols, the programmer assigns refer to data stored in the computer's memory. They are called **variable names,** because the value stored in a location can change as the program is executed. However, each variable name can represent only one value at a time. BASIC uses two types of variable names: numeric and string.

Numeric Variable Names A **numeric variable name** represents a number that is either supplied to the computer by the programmer or internally calculated by the computer during execution of the program. A numeric variable name must begin with an alphabetic character and can be either one letter alone or one letter followed by one alphanumeric character. Originally, most versions of BASIC required that the second character of a numeric variable name be numeric; however, many versions of BASIC now allow the second character to be alphanumeric. The following examples show valid and invalid numeric variable names:

VALID	INVALID AND WHY
X	28 (Must begin with a letter.)
AB (some systems)	$T (Must begin with a letter.)
T2	3 (Cannot be a single digit.)
A3	

String Variable Names A **string variable name** can represent the value of a character string—for example, a name, an address, or a Social Security number. String variable names are distinguished from numeric variable names by the use of the dollar sign ($) following a single alphabetic character. The following are examples of valid and invalid string variable names:

VALID	INVALID AND WHY
N$	$ 3$ (First character must be alphabetic.)
T$	X M1 (Last character must be $.)

Typical examples of the proper use of string variable names can be seen in lines 150 and 160 of the sample program in Figure II-1:

```
150 LET A$ = "GROSS PAY = $"
160 PRINT A$;P
```

The character string "GROSS PAY = $" is assigned to the string variable name A$. In line 160, the values of A$ and P are printed out. The output of this program is shown here:

```
GROSS PAY = $180
```

ELEMENTARY BASIC STATEMENTS

We will now turn our attention to the four elementary BASIC statements: REM, LET, PRINT, and END. Let us first define a problem that uses these statements.

In Figure II-1 we calculated gross pay. Although we all would like to receive this amount, the reality of taxes is something all too familiar. The tax rate for the following example is assumed to be 20 percent. Using this, we will design a solution to calculate net pay.

To find the net pay, we first must calculate how much the tax is by multiplying the gross pay, \$180, times 0.20 (the decimal equivalent of 20 percent). Once we know the tax, we can subtract it from the gross pay to determine the net pay (\$180 − tax).

Figure II-2 shows this solution in flowchart form. The start block (a) corresponds to the beginning of the execution of the programs. The next two steps are to assign the gross pay, \$180, to a program variable (b), and to take 20 percent of the gross pay to determine the tax (c). To calculate net pay, subtract the tax from the gross pay (d). Finally, we receive as output the net pay (e) and stop the program (f). Notice the end-of-program symbol at the end. Figure II-3 shows the translation of the flowchart into program statements.

The first three lines of the program in Figure II-3 (lines 10 through 30) provide information to people reading the program but do not help the computer. These REM statements document the program. Note that the REM statement in line 30 is not followed by comments; it is used to make

FIGURE II-2 Flowchart for Calculating Net Pay

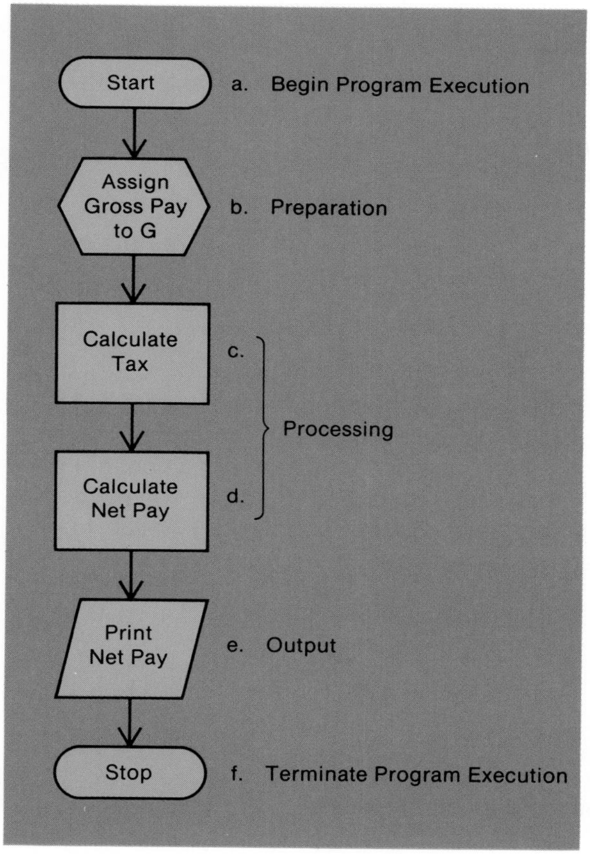

FIGURE II-3 Net Pay Program

```
10 REM *** THE PURPOSE OF THIS PROGRAM IS TO ***
20 REM *** CALCULATE NET PAY AFTER TAXES ***
30 REM
40 LET G = 180
50 LET T = G * .2
60 LET N = G - T
70 PRINT "NET PAY = $";N
999 END
```

the program more readable by separating the remarks from the body of the program.

The LET statement in line 40 sets the gross pay, 180, into a storage location (variable) called G. Note that no dollar sign is used in the LET statement.

The LET statement also is used to perform arithmetic calculations. Line 50 instructs the computer to multiply the gross pay (contained in G) by the tax factor 0.20. The product then is assigned to another variable, called T. Line 60 subtracts the tax from the gross pay and places that result in a variable called N.

At this point, the program has calculated the net pay, N, but what is it? The computer has the result in storage, but we need to see it. To do this, we need a PRINT statement. Line 70 tells the computer to print what is enclosed in the quotation marks, as well as the value contained in N. The result of program execution is

```
NET PAY = $ 144
```

Now let us study these BASIC statements in detail.

The REM Statement

As stated earlier, the **remarks (REM) statement** provides information for the programmer or anyone else reading the program; it provides no information to the computer. The REM statement is used to document the program; the programmer generally uses it to explain program segments, to define variables used within the program, or to note any special instructions. These statements can be placed anywhere throughout the program.

The general format of the REM statement is

line# REM comment

The LET Statement

The purpose of the **LET**, or **assignment**, **statement** is to perform an arithmetic operation and/or assign values to variables. It can be used to enter data into a program, as well as to process data.

The general format of the LET statement is

line# LET variable = expression

An example is line 40 of the sample program:

```
40 LET G = 180
```

The expression may be a constant, an arithmetic formula, or a variable. Look at these examples:

STATEMENT	EXPRESSION	TYPE
`10 LET X = 0`	`0`	Numeric constant
`20 LET T$ = "TOTAL"`	`"TOTAL"`	Character string constant
`30 LET M = A / B`	`A / B`	Arithmetic formula
`40 LET X = Y`	`Y`	Numeric variable
`50 LET T$ = S$`	`S$`	String variable

The LET statement can be used to assign values to numeric or string variables directly or to assign the result of a calculation to a numeric variable. In either case, the value or calculated result of an expression on the right side of the equal sign is assigned to the variable on the left. It is important to note that the statement is not evaluated in the same way an algebraic expression is.

When BASIC assigns a value to a variable on the left side of an equation, it really is putting that value in a storage location in memory—a location labeled by that variable name. Therefore, only a variable can be on the left—nothing else would represent a storage location.

Arithmetic Expressions In BASIC, arithmetic expressions are composed of constants, numeric variables, and arithmetic operators. Here are the arithmetic operators that can be used:

BASIC ARITHMETIC OPERATION SYMBOL	OPERATION	ARITHMETIC EXAMPLE	BASIC ARITHMETIC EXPRESSION
+	Addition	A + B	A + B
−	Subtraction	A − B	A − B
*	Multiplication	A × B	A * B
/	Division	A ÷ B	A / B
	Exponentiation	A^B	A ∧ B or A**B or A ↑ B depending on the system used.

Some examples of valid arithmetic expressions in LET statements are shown here:

```
10 LET T = X * (A / B)
20 LET M = 3 + A
30 LET Y = P * Q * T
```

Hierarchy of Operations When more than one operation is to be performed within an arithmetic expression, the computer follows a **hierarchy**, or priority, of operations. When parentheses are present in an expression, as they are in the line 10 given previously, the operation within the parentheses is performed first. If parentheses are nested—that is, one set of parentheses is inside another—the operation in the innermost set of parentheses is performed first. Thus, in the expression

30 * (8 − 5 / (2 + Y) * 6)

the first operation to be performed is to add 2 to the value in Y.

Parentheses aside, operations are performed according to the following rules of priority:

PRIORITY	OPERATION	SYMBOL
First	Exponentiation	∧(or ** or ↑)
Second	Multiplication or division	* or /
Third	Addition or subtraction	+ or −

Operations with high priority are performed before operations with lower priority (subject to our discussion on parentheses). If more than one operation is to be performed at the same level, as in

5 * 4 / 2

the computer evaluates them from left to right. In this example, the 5 would be multiplied by 4, and then the result, 20, would be divided by 2. The answer is 10.

The following are more examples of these hierarchical rules:

EXPRESSION	COMPUTER EVALUATION
Expression 1:	
10 / 2 + 3	
First: 10 / 2 = 5	Division has a higher priority than addition, so it is done first.
Second: 5 + 3 = 8	Then the addition is done. The result is 8.
Expression 2:	
10 / (2 + 3)	
First: (2 + 3) = 5	The addition must be done first, because it is enclosed in parentheses.
Second: 10 / 5 = 2	The result is divided into 10. Compare this result with the result in expression 1.
Expression 3:	
5 * 2 / 5 + 6	
First: 5 * 2 = 10	The priority order tells the computer to start with multiplication.
Second: 10 / 5 = 2	Next, the division is done.
Third: 2 + 6 = 8	Last, the addition is done. The result is 8.
Expression 4:	
6 * 2 + 8 / 4 * 3	
First: 6 * 2 = 12	There are three operations at the same level: multiplication, division, and multiplication. They are performed from left to right.
Second: 8 / 4 = 2	
Third: 2 * 3 = 6	
Fourth: 12 + 6 = 18	Last, the addition is done. The result is 18.

Another thing to be aware of is that two operators cannot be placed next to one another. For example, P * −X is invalid on many systems. Parentheses should be used to separate the operators. Thus, P * (−X) is valid. However, it should be noted that the double asterisk (**) used by some systems as an exponentiation operator is considered a single operator; likewise the <>, >=, and <= operators.

Assigning Character Strings The LET statement also can be used to assign a character string value to a string variable name. A character string is composed of alphanumeric data enclosed in quotes; for example,

```
10 LET A$ = "NET PAY"
20 LET X$ = Y$
```

The following examples show valid and invalid LET statements:

VALID	INVALID AND WHY	
`10 LET A$ = "BOB"`	`10 LET A2 = "BOB"`	(A character string value must be assigned to a string variable name.)
`20 LET C = 3 * (2 + 4)`	`20 LET (2 + 4) * 3 = C`	(Only a variable can appear on the left side of the equal sign.)
`30 LET X = Y + A ^ 2 * Z`	`30 LET X = Y + A$ * Z`	(A string variable name cannot be part of an arithmetic expression.)

The PRINT Statement

The **PRINT statement** is used to print or display the results of computer processing. It also permits formatting, or arranging, of output. This is the general format of the PRINT statement:

line# PRINT { variables / literals / arithmetic expressions / combination of above }

PRINT statements can take several forms, depending on the output required. Let us look at some examples.

Printing the Values of Variables We can tell the computer to print values assigned to storage locations simply by using the keyword PRINT with the variables listed after it, separated by commas:

```
100 PRINT X,Y,Z
```

The comma is used to separate one variable from another; it also is used for carriage control (more on this in Section III).

Printing has no effect on the contents of storage. The PRINT statement is a simple reading of the value of a variable that allows the user to see what the contents are. Normally, each time the computer encounters a PRINT statement, it begins printing output on a new line. Exceptions to this are discussed in Section III.

Printing Literals A **literal** is an expression consisting of alphabetic, numeric, or special characters, or a combination of two or all three of these. There are two general types of literals: character string literals and numeric literals.

Character String Literals. A **character string literal** is a group of letters, numbers, or special characters that we want printed on the output page. To have that done, we enclose the group in quotation marks. Whatever is inside the quotation marks is printed exactly as it is; for example,

```
10 PRINT "EXAMPLES$%#"
```

would appear on the output page as

```
EXAMPLES$%#
```

To print column headings, put each heading in quotes, and separate each group by a comma:

```
10 PRINT "ITEM","PRICE","QUANTITY"
```

When line 10 is executed, the character strings are printed out exactly as typed, except that the quotation marks do not appear:

```
ITEM              PRICE              QUANTITY
```

NUMERIC LITERALS. **Numeric literals** do not have to be enclosed in quotation marks to be printed. For example, the statement

```
40 PRINT 100
```

will print the following result:

```
100
```

Printing the Values of Expressions

The computer can print not only the values of literals and the values of variables, but also the values of arithmetic expressions. Consider the following program segment:

```
10 LET X = 2
20 LET Y = 143
30 PRINT X / Y * 100
```

First, the computer evaluates the expression in line 30 according to the rules of priority. The result is printed as shown here:

```
1.398601
```

If the value of the expression is extremely large or extremely small, the computer may print it in exponential notation.

Printing Blank Lines A PRINT statement with nothing typed after it will provide a blank line of output, for example,

```
30 PRINT
```

To skip more than one line, simply include more than one of these PRINT statements:

```
40 PRINT
50 PRINT
```

THE END STATEMENT

The **END statement** indicates the end of the program and so must be assigned the highest line number in the program. The general format of the END statement is

line# END

The use of an all-9s line number for the END statement is a common programming practice. This convention serves as a reminder to the programmer to include the END statement and helps ensure that it is positioned properly. See line 999 in the gross and net pay programs for examples of the END statement.

COMPREHENSIVE PROGRAMMING PROBLEM

Problem Definition

The goal of this programming problem is to write a program that will calculate ending inventory and its dollar value. The output will include beginning inventory, the number of units received into inventory, the number of units issued from inventory, the number of units in ending inventory, and the dollar amount of ending inventory. Assume the following data:

Beginning inventory = 430 units.

Receipts = 86 units.

Issued = 112 units.

Cost per unit = $11.50.

Solution Design

We can easily compute the ending inventory by translating the following formula into BASIC statements:

Ending inventory = Beginning inventory + Receipts − Issued.

From this we then can calculate the dollar amount of ending inventory using the following formula:

Dollar amount of ending inventory = Ending inventory × Cost per unit.

Substitution of our values into the equations would give us the results we desire for this particular problem. However, to make our BASIC program more general purpose, we can use variable names to represent the different values:

```
230 LET E = B + R - I
240 LET D = E * C
```

We will need to enter the beginning inventory, the number of units received, the number of units issued, and the cost per unit. We now have everything necessary to calculate both ending inventory and the dollar amount of ending inventory. All that remains is to print the results.

The Program

Figure II–4 shows a listing and the output of this program. The REM statements in lines 100 through 180 document the meanings of the variable names. Lines 190 through 220 assign variable names to the beginning

FIGURE II-4 Ending Inventory Program

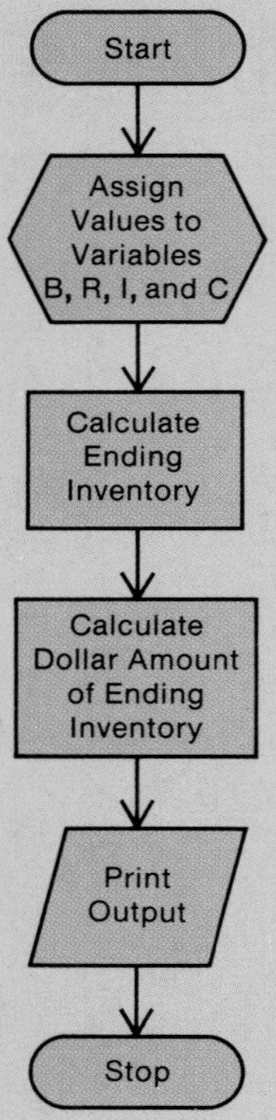


```
100 REM *** THIS PROGRAM COMPUTES ENDING ***
110 REM *** INVENTORY AND ITS DOLLAR AMOUNT ***
120 REM *** B = BEGINNING INVENTORY ***
130 REM *** R = NUMBER RECEIVED ***
140 REM *** I = NUMBER ISSUED ***
150 REM *** C = COST PER UNIT ***
160 REM *** E = ENDING INVENTORY ***
170 REM *** D = DOLLAR AMOUNT ENDING INVENTORY ***
180 REM
190 LET B = 430
200 LET R = 86
210 LET I = 112
220 LET C = 11.5
230 LET E = B + R - I
240 LET D = E * C
250 PRINT
260 PRINT
270 PRINT "INVENTORY STATUS"
280 PRINT
290 PRINT "BEGIN INV.",B
300 PRINT "RECEIPTS",R
310 PRINT "ISSUED",I
320 PRINT "ENDING INV.",E
330 PRINT "DOLLAR AMT. $",D
999 END




RUN


INVENTORY STATUS

BEGIN INV.      430
RECEIPTS        86
ISSUED          112
ENDING INV.     404
DOLLAR AMT. $   4646
```

inventory, the number of units received, the number of units issued, and the cost per unit, respectively. Line 230 calculates the ending inventory and assigns it to E. This result then is multiplied by the cost per unit in line 240, which yields the dollar amount of ending inventory and assigns it to the variable D.

Lines 250 and 260 improve the readability of the output having two blank lines printed before the heading of the report is printed by the following statement. The remaining PRINT statements print labels for each field of output followed by the field value. The program concludes with the END statement.

SUMMARY

- A BASIC program is a series of instructions. Each instruction is composed of a line number and a BASIC statement.
- The line numbers serve (1) as labels by which statements can be referenced and (2) as instructions to specify the order of execution of the program.
- Using line numbers in increments of 10 permits easy insertion of new statements.
- BASIC statements contain special reserved words (programming commands), numeric or character string constants, numeric or string variables, and formulas.
- Constants are values that do not change. A valid numeric constant is any real number expressed as an integer, decimal fraction, or in exponential form. Character strings are alphanumeric data enclosed in quotation marks.
- Variable names are programmer-supplied names that specify locations in storage where data values may be stored. Numeric variable names represent numbers. String variable names contain alphanumeric values and are distinguished from numeric variable names by the symbol $.
- REM statements are used to document the program; they are not executed by the computer.
- The purpose of the LET statement is to perform an arithmetic operation and/or assign values to variables.
- The LET statement is not evaluated in the same way an algebraic equation is. The computer first evaluates the expression on the right side of the equal sign and then assigns that result to the variable on the left side of the equal sign.
- Arithmetic expressions are evaluated according to a hierarchy of operations: (1) operations in parentheses, (2) exponentiation, (3) multiplication or division, and (4) addition or subtraction. Multiple operations at the same level are evaluated from left to right.
- The PRINT statement is used to print or display the results of processing.
- The END statement indicates the physical end of a program and stops execution.

QUESTIONS AND PROBLEMS

1. Identify any of the following statements that is invalid. State why each is invalid, and then correct it.

a. T2 is a valid numeric variable name.

b. 3$ is a valid string variable name.

c. `LET X5 = X + 2 / 3 * A`

d. REM statements can be used only before the first program statement.

e. The value of the expression 5 * (6 + 2) is 40.

f. `LET (A + B) * C = D + E`

g. Given A = 3 and B = 5, the statement PRINT "A + B = C" will print 3 + 5 = 8.

2. Mr. Greer is about to open a new sub shop and bar. His parking lot has not yet been completed, but he needs to know how many spaces he will have so that the building inspector can calculate the maximum seating capacity. Mr. Greer's county allows four seats per parking space. Mr. Greer has 1,862 square feet of usable lot. He will need a minimum of sixty square feet per car. Write a program that will calculate the maximum number of parking spaces he can have and the total seating capacity allowed, based on the maximum number of spaces.

OVERVIEW

SECTION III
Input and Output

Although the LET statement can be used to set up small amounts of data for programs, the two methods most commonly used are the INPUT statement and the READ and DATA statements. Printed results can be formatted by the use of commas and semicolons in PRINT statements.

Let us consider the following problem. We want to know the number of square feet of carpet needed to cover the living room floor. We already know that the length of the room is twenty feet, and the width is fourteen feet. To calculate the area, multiply the length by the width:

$$\text{Area} = \text{Length} \times \text{Width}.$$

The solution to this problem is translated into program statements in Figure III-1. Line 100 in Figure III-1 is a REM statement commenting on the purpose of the program. The value of the length is assigned to L in line 110. The width value is assigned to W in line 120. Line 130 calculates the area. To make the output values understandable, we print headings in line 140. The character string literals are separated from one another by commas. This tells the computer to print them in the **predefined print zones** (more on these later). Finally, in line 150, the length, width, and calculated area in square feet are printed out—again in the predefined print zones. This section will discuss two other methods for entering data into a program, so keep an eye on lines 110 and 120.

FIGURE III-1 Area Calculation Program

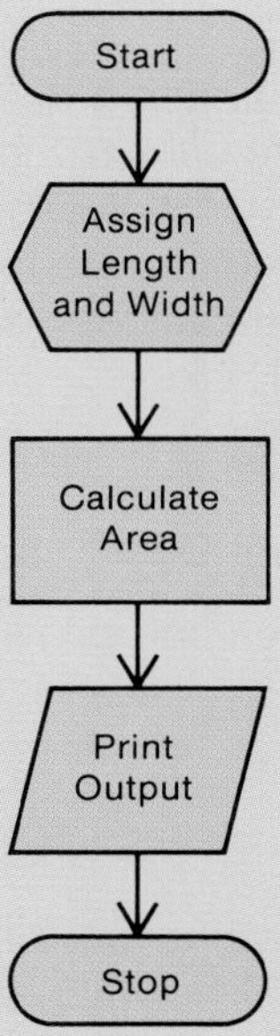


```
100 REM *** COMPUTES AREA OF A ROOM ***
110 LET L = 20
120 LET W = 14
130 LET A = L * W
140 PRINT "LENGTH","WIDTH","AREA"
150 PRINT L,W,A
999 END

RUN
LENGTH         WIDTH          AREA
 20             14             280
```

THE INPUT STATEMENT

The **INPUT statement** is used for inquiry and response when a user application calls for a question-and-answer environment. Section II explained how the LET statement can be used to enter data values into a program. The INPUT statement differs from the LET statement in that it allows the user to enter data at the terminal while the program is running.

The general format of the INPUT statement is this:

line# INPUT variable list

INPUT statements are placed where data values are needed in a program. This is determined by the logic of the program. After the program has been keyed in, the user types the execution command RUN. The computer then starts to execute the program. Whenever the computer reaches an INPUT statement, it stops, prints a question mark at the terminal, and waits for the user to enter data. After typing in the data, the user presses the RETURN key. The computer then assigns the data value to the variable indicated in the INPUT statement and resumes processing. More than one variable can be listed in the INPUT statement; the computer will wait until data values have been entered for all the variables. After that, the computer resumes processing.

Let us revise the sample program by replacing lines 110 and 120. The resulting program is as follows:

```
100 REM *** COMPUTES AREA OF A ROOM ***
110 PRINT "ENTER LENGTH,WIDTH"
120 INPUT L,W
130 LET A = L * W
140 PRINT "LENGTH","WIDTH","AREA"
150 PRINT L,W,A
999 END
```

These new instructions cause the program to be executed in a question-and-answer mode. When the program is run, line 110 causes the computer to print a message at the terminal: ENTER LENGTH, WIDTH. A question mark then appears to signal the user that data values are to be entered. At this point, the user types in the requested data values—separating them with a comma—and then presses the RETURN key:

```
RUN
ENTER LENGTH,WIDTH      ←Program Prompt
? 20,14                 ←Computer Response (?), User Data Entry
```

The computer then executes line 130 to calculate the area and prints the headings and results:

```
LENGTH          WIDTH           AREA
 20              14              280
```

The INPUT statement offers a great deal of flexibility; each time this program is executed, new values can be entered. Thus, if we want to calculate the area of another room, we simply run the program again and enter the new values for length and width. We do not have to change any program statements:

```
RUN
ENTER LENGTH,WIDTH
? 15,10
LENGTH          WIDTH          AREA
 15              10             150
```

Prompts

Note that the INPUT instruction is preceded by a PRINT statement in line 110. This PRINT statement is called a **prompt**, because it explains to the user what data items are to be entered. Because the INPUT statement signals the need for data with only a question mark, it is good programming practice to precede each INPUT statement with a prompt. This practice is particularly important in a BASIC program that contains numerous INPUT statements; otherwise, when users see only a question mark requesting data, they may not know what data values are to be entered and in what order.

Most computers permit the prompt to be an integral part of the INPUT statement. For example, we could substitute the following line for lines 110 and 120 in the area calculation program:

```
110 INPUT "ENTER LENGTH,WIDTH";L,W
```

When we run the program with this new line, the question mark appears immediately after the prompt, and no separate PRINT statement for the prompt is needed:

```
ENTER LENGTH,WIDTH? 15,12
LENGTH          WIDTH          AREA
 15              12             180
```

The variables listed in the INPUT statement may be string or numeric. We must just be sure to enter the correct value to be assigned to each variable. In other words, the type of data entered must be the same as that designated by the variable. Associating a printed message with each INPUT statement can eliminate many data-entry problems.

THE READ AND DATA STATEMENTS

The **READ statement** and **DATA statement** provide another way to enter data into a BASIC program. These two statements always work together. Values contained in DATA statements are assigned to variables listed in READ statements.

The general format of the READ and DATA statements is

line# READ variable list
line# DATA constant list

This method of entering data into a program works a little differently than the INPUT statement. The READ statement tells the computer to search through the BASIC program until it finds the first DATA statement. The computer then assigns the data values consecutively to the variables in the READ statement. Each READ statement causes as many values to be taken from the data list as there are variables in the READ variable list. Figure III-2 illustrates this process of assigning values from the data list to variables.

Line 10 says the following to the computer: Take the value from the beginning of the data list, and put it in the storage location named X (throwing away any value already in X). Then take the next value from the data list, and assign it to variable Y (also throwing away any value already there). The same is done for variables N$ and Z. After line 10 has been executed, the number 110 is in storage location X; the number 24, in storage location Y; the character string JOHN DOE, in storage location N$; and the number 120, in storage location Z. This leaves the number 13 at the beginning of the data list.

The same process occurs when the computer encounters line 20. The

FIGURE III-2 READ/DATA Example

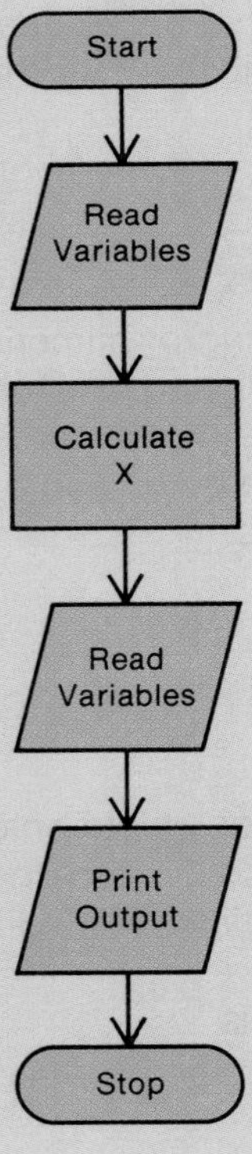


```
10 READ X,Y,N$,Z
20 READ Y,Z
30 LET X = Y + Z
40 READ N$,X
50 PRINT N$,X,Y
60 DATA 110,24,"JOHN DOE"
70 DATA 120,13,21,"MARY SMITH"
80 DATA 91
999 END

RUN
MARY SMITH      91            13
```

value from the beginning of the data list (the number 13) is placed in storage location Y. The number 21 is assigned to Z.

Statement 30 assigns the sum of Y + Z to the storage location X. The number 110, which was assigned to X by line 10, is overlaid by the new value. In the same manner, the character string MARY SMITH is assigned to the variable N$, and the number 91 is assigned to X. When these values are assigned, the values previously stored in the variables also are overlaid.

This process illustrates the basic concept of nondestructive read/destructive write. Once the data items have been assigned to storage locations, they remain there until new data items are recorded over them. Thus, all four variables represent more than one value during execution, but never more than one at a time.

If a READ statement is attempted after the data list has been exhausted, a message is produced to indicate that the end of the data list has been reached. The message points out the line number of the READ statement in error; for example, if line 40 was such a READ statement, the computer would print

```
Out of DATA in 40
```

READ statements, like INPUT statements, are located wherever the logic of the program indicates the need for data. DATA statements, however, are nonexecutable and may be located anywhere in the program. The BASIC compiler simply takes all the data items in all the DATA statements and forms one combined data list, ordering the DATA statements from the lowest to the highest line number and then using the data from left to right.

It does not matter in this example how many READ or DATA statements are used. However, the order of the variables and values is important. Make sure that the arrangement of values in the DATA statements corresponds to the data required in the READ statements—that is, that character strings are assigned to string variables and numeric constants, to numeric variables.

Let us return to the area calculation program and change it to use READ and DATA statements:

```
100 REM *** COMPUTES AREA OF A ROOM ***
110 DATA 20,14
120 READ L,W
130 LET A = L * W
140 PRINT "LENGTH","WIDTH","AREA"
150 PRINT L,W,A
999 END

RUN
LENGTH          WIDTH           AREA
 20              14              280
```

Line 120 performs the same function as the INPUT statement did previously. With INPUT statements, the data values are assigned by the user as the program is running. With READ and DATA statements, in contrast, the length and the width values are already contained within the program in line 110, the DATA statement. The output is unchanged. If we wanted to run this program again using different data, we would change line 110, the DATA statement.

A COMPARISON OF THE THREE METHODS OF DATA ENTRY

LET, INPUT, READ and DATA statements all can be used to enter data in BASIC programs. Which command is best to use? That depends on the particular application. Here are some general guidelines:

1. When there is very little data to enter into a program, use the LET statement. The LET statement often is used to assign a beginning value to a variable; this is called **initialization;** for example,

```
LET T1 = 0
```

When the LET statement is used in this way, the preparation symbol ◇, should be used to represent the intended action.
2. The INPUT statement is used when a question-and-answer (also called *inquiry-and-response*) environment is desired. It is also a good method to use when data values are likely to change frequently. A good application for the use of the INPUT statement might be entering data about hospital patients—a situation in which people are checked in and out every day, and data about a particular patient changes frequently.
3. When many data values must be entered, READ and DATA statements are a good option.

PRINTING PUNCTUATION

Section II explained that the PRINT statement lets us display the results of processing. When more than one item is to be printed on a line, commas and semicolons can be used to control the spacing of the output. The TAB function and PRINT USING statement are also useful in formatting; however, these will not be discussed here. For more information, refer to your user's manual.

Print Zones and Commas

The number of characters that can be printed on a line varies with the system used. Table III-1 shows a comparison of the print zones for the Apple II and II Plus, Atari 800, IBM PC, PET/Commodore 64, and TRS-80 Model III microcomputers. For example, on the IBM PC, each output line consists of eighty **print positions**. The line is divided into 5.7 **print zones**. A

Table III-1 Print Zones Chart

	SCREEN WIDTH (CHARACTERS)	NUMBER OF PRINT ZONES	ZONE WIDTH (CHARACTERS)	BEGINNING COLUMNS OF PRINT ZONES					
				Zone 1	Zone 2	Zone 3	Zone 4	Zone 5	Zone 6
Apple II and II Plus	40	2.5	16	1	17	33	N/A	N/A	N/A
Atari 800	38	4	10	1	11	21	31	N/A	N/A
IBM PC	80	5.7	14	1	15	29	43	57	71
PET/Commodore 64	40	4	10	1	11	21	31	N/A	N/A
TRS-80 Model III	64	4	16	1	17	33	49	N/A	N/A

Note: N/A = not applicable.

zone is fourteen characters wide. The beginning columns of the 5.7 print zones follow:

Zone 1	Zone 2	Zone 3	Zone 4	Zone 5	Zone 6
Column 1	Column 15	Column 29	Column 43	Column 57	Column 71

When the computer encounters the PRINT statement in the segment

```
10 READ N$,X,Y
20 PRINT N$,X,Y
30 DATA "BOB",26,1982
```

the value in N$—which is the character string, BOB—will be printed starting in the first print zone. The comma between N$ and X tells the computer to space over to the next zone and print the value contained in X. After the number 26 is printed, the comma directs the computer to space over to the third zone and print the value in Y. The output is as follows:

```
BOB                 26                 1982
```

If there are more items listed in a PRINT statement than there are print zones, the computer starts printing in the first zone of the next line; for example,

```
20 READ A,B,C,D,E,F,G,H,I
30 PRINT A,B,C,D,E,F,G,H,I
40 DATA 1,2,3,4,5,6,7,8,9

RUN
 1                 2                  3                  4                  5                  6
      7            8                  9
```

If the value to be printed exceeds the width of the print zone, the computer will completely print out the value, even though part of it goes into the next print zone. The comma then directs printing to start in the following print zone. In the following example, note where the value of

X$ (21-01-3) is printed:

```
80 PRINT "YOUR IDENTIFICATION # IS",X$
```

Zone 1 Zone 2 Zone 3

```
YOUR IDENTIFICATION # IS    21-01-3
```

Skipping Print Zones A print zone can be skipped by the use of a technique that involves enclosing a space (the character **blank**) in quotation marks, which causes the entire zone to appear empty. Thus,

```
60 PRINT "NAME"," ","I.D. NUMBER"
```

causes the literal NAME to be printed in the first zone beginning in column 1, the second zone to be blank, and the literal I.D. NUMBER to be printed in the third zone:

Zone 1 Zone 2 Zone 3

```
NAME                            I.D. NUMBER
```

Most computers also allow the user to skip a print zone by typing two consecutive commas; for example,

```
60 PRINT "NAME",,"I.D. NUMBER"
```

Ending with a Comma As mentioned earlier, output generated by a PRINT statement normally begins in the first zone of a new line. However, if the previously executed PRINT statement ends with a comma, the output of a PRINT statement starts in the next available zone. Thus, the statements

```
20 DATA 102.34,6.978,12.6231
30 READ X,Y,Z
40 PRINT X,Y,
50 PRINT Z
```

produce the following output:

```
102.34         6.978          12.6231
```

Using Semicolons

Using a semicolon instead of a comma causes output to be packed more closely on a line. This alternative gives the programmer greater flexibility in formatting output. In the following examples, notice the difference in spacing when semicolons are used instead of commas. When commas are used, the output looks like this:

```
10 PRINT 1,2,-3
RUN
 1              2              -3
```

When semicolons are used, the output looks like this:

```
10 PRINT 1;2;-3
RUN
 1  2 -3
```

A semicolon between items tells the computer to skip to the next **column** to print the next item—not to the next print zone, as with the comma. Generally, when the number is positive, a space is left in front of the number for the sign.

Semicolons and Character Strings The following example shows what happens when semicolons are used with character strings:

```
10 PRINT "NAME";"AGE"

RUN
NAMEAGE
```

Since letters do not have signs, they are run together. The best way to avoid this problem is to enclose a space within the quotation marks:

```
10 PRINT "NAME ";"AGE"

RUN
NAME AGE
```

Ending with a Semicolon If a semicolon is the last character of the PRINT statement, carriage control is not advanced when the printing of the statement is completed, so the output generated by the next PRINT statement continues on the same line; for example,

```
10 READ N$,D
20 PRINT N$;
30 LET A = 18 + D
40 PRINT A
50 DATA "BOB",8

RUN
BOB 26
```

Line 20 causes BOB to be printed. The semicolon after N$ keeps the printer on the same line; then, when line 40 is encountered, the number 26 is printed on the same line.

COMPREHENSIVE PROGRAMMING PROBLEM

Problem Definition

You are a loan officer for the local credit union. Your client, Ms. Rodgers, wants to borrow $60,000 to purchase a house in your neighborhood. She wants to know how much her monthly payments would be. Assume the interest rate is fixed at 15 percent for any mortgage amount. The term of the mortgage is twenty years. Since you must make this type of calculation often, you decide to write a program that will accomplish the calculations for you.

Solution Design

The problem asks us to calculate Ms. Rodgers's monthly payments. To accomplish this, the first step is to calculate the monthly interest rate. This is done using the following formula:

$$\text{Monthly interest rate} = (\text{Interest rate} \div 100) \div 12.$$

The monthly interest rate then is used to calculate the mortgage multiplication factor using the following formula:

$$\text{Mortgage multiplication factor} = \text{Monthly interest rate} \div [(1 + \text{Monthly interest rate}) \wedge (\text{Number of years or mortgage} \times 12) - 1] + \text{Monthly interest rate}.$$

The symbol $\wedge$ means "raised to the power of." The monthly payments then can be calculated based on the following formula:

$$\text{Monthly payment} = \text{Mortgage multiplication factor} \times \text{Mortgage amount}.$$

The Program

The program in Figure III-3 documents the major variables used in lines 30 through 80. Line 90 contains some data for the program. The computer assigns these values to variables with the READ statement in the next line, line 100. A prompt is printed by line 110. The associated INPUT statement in line 120 causes the computer to print a question mark at the terminal and wait for the user to enter the appropriate data values. When this has been done, processing continues. Lines 130 and 140 perform the same function, only this time the user enters the years of the mortgage. Now that all the data has been entered, the computer can begin the calculations. This is documented in line 150. Line 160 computes the monthly interest rate. Next, the mortgage multiplication factor is figured in line 170. Finally, the monthly payment is calculated in line 180.

Line 220 places the report heading in the second print zone. In lines 240 through 260, the outputs have been moved over into the second print zone.

SUMMARY

- The INPUT statement is used to enter data into a program in a question-and-answer mode.
- Another way of entering data into a program is to use READ and DATA statements. The READ statement causes values contained in the DATA statements to be assigned to variables.
- READ and INPUT statements are located where the logic of the program indicates. DATA statements are nonexecutable and may be located anywhere in the program.
- When more than one item is to be printed on a line of output, the spacing can be controlled by the use of commas and semicolons.

FIGURE III-3 Mortgage Program

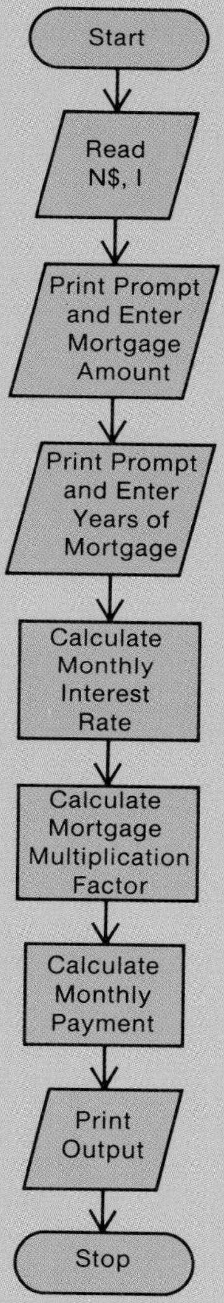


```
10 REM *** THIS PROGRAM COMPUTES MONTHLY ***
20 REM *** PAYMENTS FOR MORTGAGES ***
30 REM *** MI = MONTHLY INTEREST RATE ***
40 REM *** I = INTEREST RATE ***
50 REM *** M = MORTGAGE MULTIPLICATION FACTOR ***
60 REM *** MP = MONTHLY PAYMENT ***
70 REM *** MA = MORTGAGE AMOUNT ***
80 REM *** Y = NUMBER OF YEARS FOR THE MORTGAGE ***
90 DATA "INTEREST RATE",15
100 READ N$,I
110 PRINT "ENTER MORTGAGE AMOUNT"
120 INPUT MA
130 PRINT "ENTER YEARS OF THE MORTGAGE"
140 INPUT Y
150 REM *** BEGIN CALCULATIONS ***
160 LET MI = (I / 100) / 12
170 LET M = MI / ((1 + MI) ^ (Y * 12) - 1) + MI
180 LET MP = M * MA
190 REM *** BEGIN OUTPUT ***
200 PRINT
210 PRINT
220 PRINT TAB(15);"MORTAGE COMPUTATION"
230 PRINT
240 PRINT
250 PRINT " ","MORTGAGE AMOUNT    $";MA
260 PRINT " ",N$,"      ";I;"%"
270 PRINT " ","MONTHLY PAYMENTS   $";MP
999 END

RUN
ENTER MORTGAGE AMOUNT
? 60000
ENTER YEARS OF THE MORTGAGE
? 20


              MORTAGE COMPUTATION


              MORTGAGE AMOUNT    $ 60000
              INTEREST RATE        15 %
              MONTHLY PAYMENTS   $ 790.0731
```

■ Each line of output can be divided into a predetermined number of print zones. The comma is used to cause the results to be printed in the print zones.
■ Using the semicolon instead of the comma to separate printed items causes the output to be packed more closely on a line.

QUESTIONS AND PROBLEMS

1. Rewrite the following program using the INPUT statement:

```
10 REM *** READ/DATA EXAMPLE ***
20 READ N$,H,L
30 LET A = (H + L) / 2
40 PRINT N$,A
50 DATA "LINDA",98,82
999 END
```

2. What is the output of the following program?

```
10 READ A,B,C,L,M,N
20 LET X = A + B / C
30 LET W = L * (M * (N + C))
40 PRINT X + W,
50 PRINT A,B,C;
60 PRINT L
70 PRINT M,N
80 DATA 2,6,3,4,1,6
```

OVERVIEW

The programs described to this point contained instructions that were always executed one right after the other—from the lowest line number to the highest. This section will discuss ways of transferring control to program statements out of sequence by using the GOTO and IF/THEN statements. One of the most valuable programming techniques, looping, also will be discussed. Let us see how some of these transfers work by examining the following problem.

Ace Auto wants a program to quickly calculate the customer costs for new cars. The costs include list price, trade-in consideration, options, tax, and dealer preparation charges. The tax is figured as a percentage of the list price plus the options plus the dealer preparation charges minus the trade-in. The program is to generate an itemized bill.

In designing the solution to this problem, the logic of the program will be more complicated than any we have written so far, because we do not know the type or quantity of options a customer will desire. Our program must be designed to accept any type and number of options.

To make this program easily adaptable to changes, we use INPUT statements to enter the model, list price, dealer preparation cost, tax rate, and trade-in value. INPUT statements also are used to enter the types, prices, and quantity of options desired. To have this done, we will set up a **loop**. Within the loop, we will place a statement that accumulates the total cost of options purchased.

To stop execution of the loop, we will test the first variable to see whether or not it has a dummy value—something the salesperson will enter when all options purchased by a customer have been recorded. The dummy value is used to tell the computer to stop execution. Once execution of the loop has been completed, the tax and total cost values are calculated. After that, the output is printed out (see Figure IV-1).

Lines 130 through 200 of the program use PRINT and INPUT statements to enter the model, list price, dealer preparation cost, tax rate, and trade-in value. READ and DATA statements could be used to enter all of these except trade-in value, but we chose to use the INPUT statement to keep our program as flexible as possible. The variable OT (total price of options) is initialized in line 210. Line 230 is the beginning of the loop. The INPUT statement is a good choice here, since the options purchased will be different for each customer. We use line 270, an IF/THEN statement, to test for a dummy value that is to be entered by the salesperson when he or she has finished a customer's order. As long as the salesperson types in options, prices, and quantities of options, the loop (lines 230 through 310) will continue to be executed. Line 290 keeps a running total of the cost of the options. Line 310 is a new command, GOTO. This statement sends the computer back up to line 230 to ask for another option type. Note that the prompt (line 240) tells the salesperson (the user) how to stop the computer from continually asking for option types. When the salesperson types in NONE,0,0, the computer skips down to line 330 to figure the tax and then the total cost. Then the output is printed.

Let us take a look at these transfer statements in greater detail.

FIGURE IV-1 Car Price Program (Continued Facing Page)

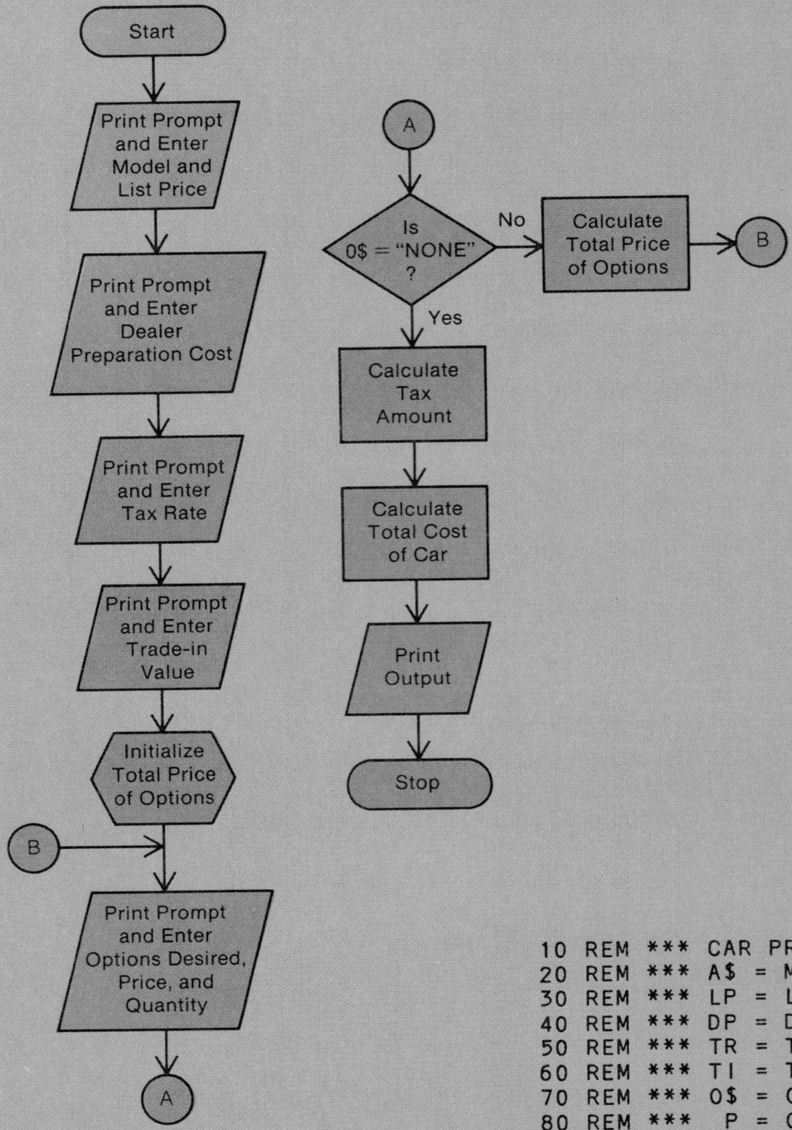


```
10 REM *** CAR PRICES ***
20 REM *** A$ = MODEL ***
30 REM *** LP = LIST PRICE ***
40 REM *** DP = DEALER PREP CHARGE ***
50 REM *** TR = TAX RATE ***
60 REM *** TI = TRADE-IN VALUE ***
70 REM *** O$ = OPTION TYPE ***
80 REM ***  P = OPTION PRICE ***
90 REM ***  Q = QUANTITY OF OPTION ***
100 REM *** OT = TOTAL PRICE OF OPTIONS ***
110 REM *** TX = TAX AMOUNT ***
120 REM *** TS = TOTAL COST OF CAR ***
130 PRINT "ENTER MODEL, LIST PRICE"
140 INPUT A$,LP
150 PRINT "ENTER DEALER PREP"
160 INPUT DP
170 PRINT "ENTER TAX RATE"
```

```
180 INPUT TR
190 PRINT "ENTER TRADE-IN VALUE"
200 INPUT TI
210 LET OT = 0
220 REM *** LOOP STARTS HERE ***
230 PRINT "ENTER OPTIONS DESIRED, PRICE, QUANTITY"
240 PRINT "(TYPE NONE,0,0 TO QUIT)"
250 INPUT O$,P,Q
260 REM *** CONDITIONAL TRANSFER HERE ***
270 IF O$ = "NONE" THEN 320
280 REM *** ACCUMULATE COST OF OPTIONS ***
290 LET OT = OT + P * Q
300 REM *** UNCONDITIONAL TRANSFER HERE ***
310 GOTO 230
320 REM *** CALCULATE TAX ***
330 LET TX = (LP + OT + DP -TI) * TR
340 REM *** CALCULATE TOTAL COST ***
350 LET TC = LP + OT + DP + TX -TI
360 REM *** PRINT OUTPUT ***
365 PRINT
366 PRINT
370 PRINT "MODEL:" A$,"$";LP
380 PRINT "TOTAL OPTIONS","$";OT
390 PRINT "DEALER PREP","$";DP
400 PRINT "TRADE-IN","$";TI
410 PRINT "TAX","$";TX
420 PRINT " ","___________"
430 PRINT "TOTAL COST","$";TC
999 END


RUN
ENTER MODEL, LIST PRICE
? CUTLASS,12000
ENTER DEALER PREP
? 250
ENTER TAX RATE
? .15
ENTER TRADE-IN VALUE
? 2300
ENTER OPTIONS DESIRED, PRICE, QUANTITY
(TYPE NONE,0,0 TO QUIT)
? FM STEREO,125,1
ENTER OPTIONS DESIRED, PRICE, QUANTITY
(TYPE NONE,0,0 TO QUIT)
? MAG WHEELS,90,4
ENTER OPTIONS DESIRED, PRICE, QUANTITY
(TYPE NONE,0,0 TO QUIT)
? NONE,0,0


MODEL:CUTLASS $ 12000
TOTAL OPTIONS $ 485
DEALER PREP   $ 250
TRADE-IN      $ 2300
TAX           $ 1565.25
              __________
TOTAL COST    $ 12000.25
```

THE GOTO STATEMENT: UNCONDITIONAL TRANSFER

All BASIC programs consist of a series of statements that normally are executed in sequential order. Sometimes, however, it is desirable to perform statements in another order. It may be necessary to alter the flow of execution or bypass certain instructions. This is called **branching**, and the programmer can use the **GOTO statement** to do it. The general format of the GOTO statement is as follows:

line# GOTO transfer line#

The programming command GOTO can be written as one word (GOTO) or as two words (GO TO).

The GOTO statement is called an **unconditional transfer statement**, because the flow of execution is altered every time the statement is encountered. It transfers control to (or causes the computer to go to) the statement indicated by the transfer line number instead of to the statement immediately after the GOTO statement.

A typical GOTO statement follows:

```
150 GOTO 40
```

This statement tells the computer that the next statement to be executed is line 40. Let us see how the GOTO statement might be used in an application by looking at Figure IV-2, which prints out the name and gross wages for three people.

In this program, a single process (calculating the gross wage) is repeated three times. The programmer typed in the following three lines as many times as was necessary:

```
READ N$,W,H
LET GP = W * H
PRINT N$,GP
```

Although this is not a very difficult task with a small, uncomplicated problem, imagine how time consuming and inefficient it would be for a hundred sets of data!

The same result can be achieved much more simply by the use of a GOTO statement. In Figure IV-3 the GOTO statement in line 40 directs the computer back to statement 10. A loop is formed. In this example, the error message "Out of DATA in 10" was printed because an attempt was made to read data after the data list had been exhausted and the execution of the program had been terminated.

Note how the loop is indicated in the flowchart. A flow line (showing the path of program logic) is drawn from the output step (the PRINT statement) immediately preceding the GOTO statement to the input step (the READ statement) indicated by the transfer line number. If you examine the flowchart carefully you will notice that there is no termination (stop) symbol. The use of GOTO in this fashion creates an infinite loop. An infinite loop is one in which no end to the loop has been defined. The loop will keep executing indefinitely as long as there is sufficient data. If it runs

FIGURE IV-2 Wage Program

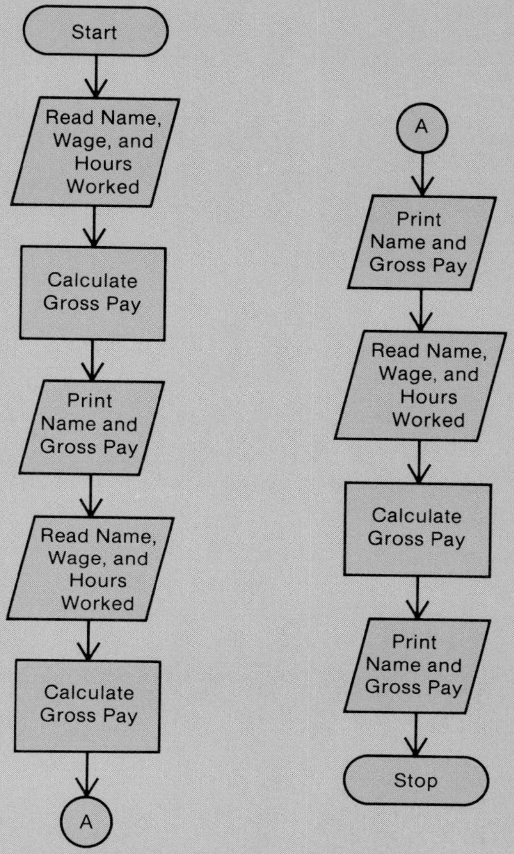


```
10 READ N$,W,H
20 LET GP = W * H
30 PRINT N$,GP
40 READ N$,W,H
50 LET GP = W * H
60 PRINT N$,GP
70 READ N$,W,H
80 LET GP = W * H
90 PRINT N$,GP
100 DATA "T. REX",4.50,40,"G. HALL",7.60,25,"M. SMART",3.25,60
999 END

RUN
T. REX          180
G. HALL         190
M. SMART        195
```

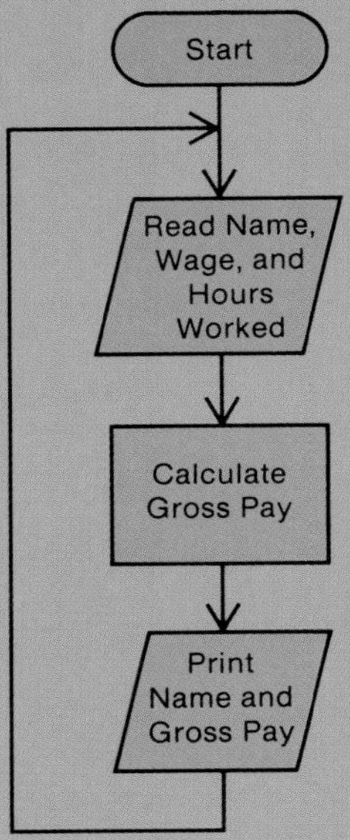


```
10 READ N$,W,H
20 LET GP = W * H
30 PRINT N$,GP
40 GOTO 10
50 DATA "T. REX",4.50,40,"G. HALL",7.60,25
55 DATA "M. SMART",3.25,60
999 END

RUN
T. REX          180
G. HALL         190
M. SMART        195
Out of DATA in 10
```

FIGURE IV-3 Wage Program with GOTO Statement

out of data, as in our example, the "out of DATA" error message will be generated and program execution will be terminated.

Later, this section will show how to control the number of times a loop is repeated (eliminating the error message).

THE IF/THEN STATEMENT: CONDITIONAL TRANSFER

The GOTO statement always transfers control. Often, however, it is necessary to transfer control only when a specified condition exists. The **IF/THEN statement** is used to test for such a condition. If the condition does not exist, the next statement in the program is executed. The general format of the IF/THEN statement is as follows:

line# IF expression relational symbol expression THEN line#

Conditions tested can involve either numeric or character string data. **Relational symbols** that can be used include the following:

BASIC Relational Symbols

SYMBOL	MEANING	EXAMPLES
<	Less than	B < C
<=	Less than or equal to	Y <= Z
>	Greater than	L > M
>=	Greater than or equal to	R >= S
=	Equal to	G = H
		N$ = "PROGRAM"
<>	Not equal to	D <> F
		"COMPUTER" <> S$

Some examples of valid IF/THEN statements are given here:

	Interpretation
`100 IF T <> X THEN 40` `110 PRINT`	If T is not equal to X, the computer transfers control to line 40. Otherwise, it executes the next statement, line 110.
`20 IF A <= 10 THEN 80` `30 LET X = X + 1`	If the value contained in A is less than or equal to 10, the computer branches to line 80. If not, the computer executes the next sequential instruction, line 30.

`80 IF N$ = "LAST" THEN 100`
`90 PRINT N$`
`100 GOTO 40`
	If the value contained in N$ is "LAST", control is passed to line 100. If N$ contains anything else, control goes to line 90.

The program in Figure IV-4 uses both numeric and character string comparisons to search government records for individuals eligible for the draft. To be eligible, the individual must be eighteen years of age or older and not have a deferment.

The program reads the name, status, and age for each candidate. A comparison of character strings is made to determine if an individual has a deferment:

```
120 IF C$ <> "NONE" THEN 170
```

The test is stated in such a way that only if the candidate does not have a deferment will the program continue evaluating his record. Otherwise, the program transfers control to line 170.

The other requirement is that the candidate be eighteen years of age or

FIGURE IV-4 Draft Eligibility Program

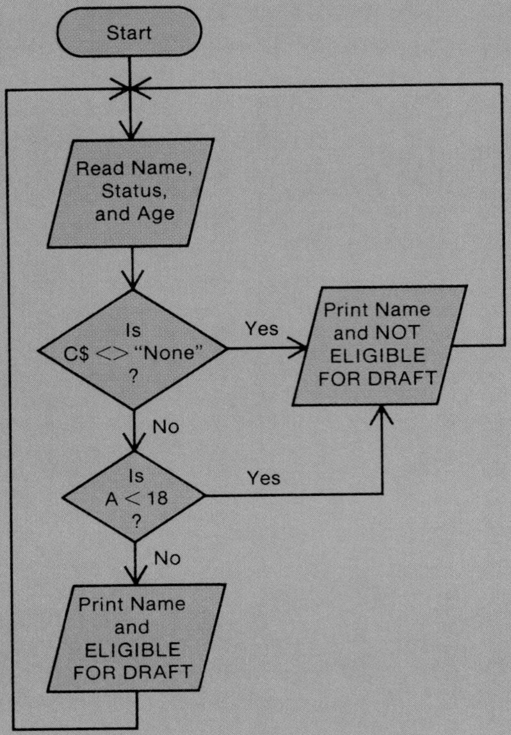


```
100 READ N$,C$,A
110 REM *** REJECT THOSE WITH DEFERMENTS ***
120 IF C$ <> "NONE" THEN 170
130 REM *** REJECT IF AGE < 18 ***
140 IF A < 18 THEN 170
150 PRINT N$,"ELIGIBLE FOR DRAFT"
160 GOTO 100
170 PRINT N$,"NOT ELIGIBLE FOR DRAFT"
180 GOTO 100
190 DATA "TOM BROWN","DEFERMENT",21
200 DATA "ED HAYES","NONE",18
210 DATA "BILL GREEN","NONE",17
220 DATA "TED GRAY","NONE",23
999 END

RUN
TOM BROWN      NOT ELIGIBLE FOR DRAFT
ED HAYES       ELIGIBLE FOR DRAFT
BILL GREEN     NOT ELIGIBLE FOR DRAFT
TED GRAY       ELIGIBLE FOR DRAFT
Out of DATA in 100
```

older. A numeric comparison is used to determine if the individual satisfies this requirement:

```
140 IF A < 18 THEN 170
```

Again, for any individual whose age is less than eighteen years, control is transferred to line 170.

Any candidate who satisfies both conditions is acceptable. The program output indicates that two of the candidates, Ed Hayes and Ted Gray, are eligible for the draft.

Note the diamond-shaped symbol (◇) in the flowchart in Figure IV-4. It is a **decision block**, which represents the IF/THEN test. The outcome of the test determines which flow line will be followed. Note also that the outputs from the decision blocks are labeled to show the condition which relates to that path (YES/NO).

LOOPING PROCEDURES

There are several things to consider in setting up a loop. The programmer must decide not only what instructions are to be repeated, but also how many times the loop is to be executed. We will discuss three techniques for loop control. This section covers trailer values and counters. Section V will discuss another method, FOR and NEXT statements.

Trailer Values

A loop controlled by a **trailer value** contains an IF/THEN statement that checks for the end of the data. The last data item is a dummy value that is not part of the data to be processed. (This method was used in the car price program in Figure IV-1 earlier in this section.) Either numeric or alphanumeric data can be used as a trailer value. However, the programmer always must select a trailer value that will not be confused with real data.

Here is how it works. An IF/THEN statement is placed within the set of instructions to be repeated, usually at the beginning of the loop. One of the variables into which data is entered is tested. If it contains the dummy value, control is transferred out of the loop. If the variable contains valid data (does not equal the trailer value), looping continues.

Figure IV-5 contains a loop pattern controlled by a trailer value. The program assigns each name entered to a specific weight class based on the person's weight.

Statement 150 tests the value in N$ for the dummy value:

```
150 IF N$ = "LAST" THEN 999
```

If the condition is true, the flow of processing drops out of the loop to line 999. If the condition is false, processing continues to the next line in sequence, line 155. Note that since we used the INPUT statement to enter the data, it is necessary to tell the user how to end the looping process. This is done in line 120. The user has to enter two dummy values, LAST and 0, because the INPUT statement expects two values to be entered.

FIGURE IV-5 Weight Class Program

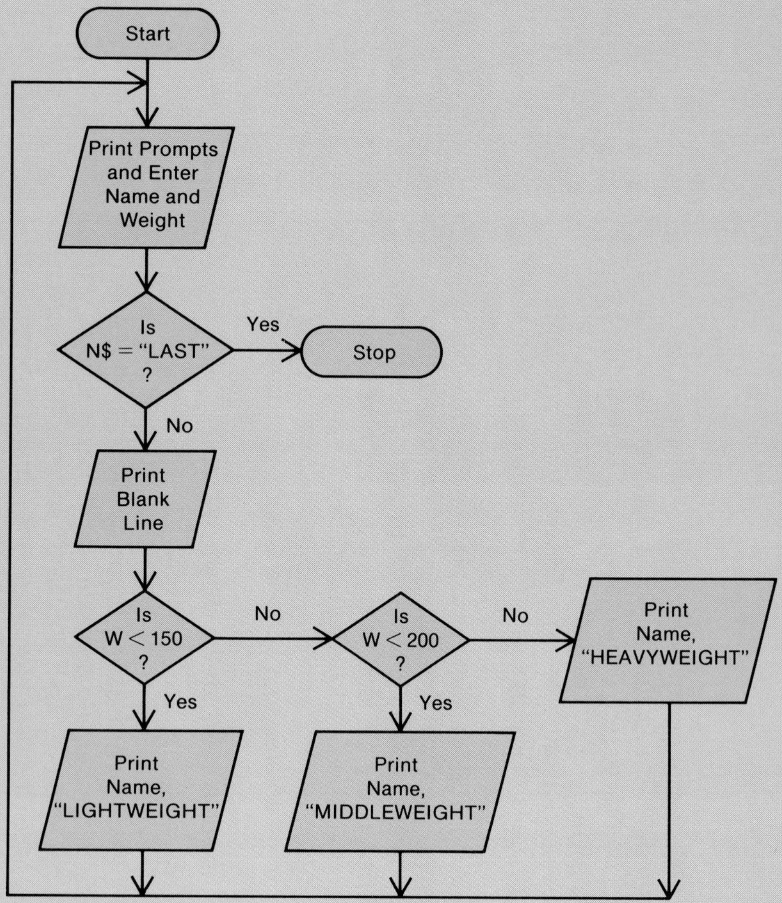


```
100 REM *** WEIGHT CLASS ***
105 PRINT
106 PRINT
110 PRINT "ENTER NAME, WEIGHT"
120 PRINT "TYPE 'LAST, 0' TO END"
130 INPUT N$,W
140 REM *** TEST FOR TRAILER VALUE ***
150 IF N$ = "LAST" THEN 999
155 PRINT
160 IF W < 150 THEN 220
170 IF W < 200 THEN 200
180 PRINT N$;"  HEAVYWEIGHT"
190 GOTO 105
200 PRINT N$;"  MIDDLEWEIGHT"
210 GOTO 105
220 PRINT N$;"  LIGHTWEIGHT"
230 GOTO 105
999 END


RUN


ENTER NAME, WEIGHT
TYPE 'LAST, 0' TO END
? ED HALL,230

ED HALL  HEAVYWEIGHT


ENTER NAME, WEIGHT
TYPE 'LAST, 0' TO END
? GREG BLACK,95

GREG BLACK  LIGHTWEIGHT


ENTER NAME, WEIGHT
TYPE 'LAST, 0' TO END
? JON LOUIS,160


JON LOUIS  MIDDLEWEIGHT


ENTER NAME, WEIGHT
TYPE 'LAST, 0' TO END
? LAST,0
```

Counters

A second method of controlling a loop requires the programmer to create a **counter**—a numeric variable that is incremented each time the loop is executed. Normally, the increment is 1. A counter is effective only if the programmer notifies the computer of the **terminal value**, that is, how many times a loop should be repeated. The steps involved in setting up a counter for loop control are as follows:

1. Initialize the counter to give it a beginning value.
2. Increment the counter each time the loop is executed.
3. Test the counter to determine if the terminal value has been executed (that is, if the loop has been executed the desired number of times).

The weight class program in Figure IV-5 can be modified to use a counter as shown in Figure IV-6. Since there are three people, the loop must be executed three times. The counter in this example is X. It is initialized to 0 in line 110. The IF/THEN statement in line 130 tests the number of times the loop has been executed, as represented by the counter X. Line 145 causes X to be incremented each time the loop is executed. The loop instructions will be executed until X equals 3.

COMPREHENSIVE PROGRAMMING PROBLEM

Problem Definition

The employees of Hard Line, Inc., are given evaluation ratings by three different individuals. These ratings are averaged; based on this average, a report is to be printed recommending the action to be taken by the supervisor. Each of the three evaluations has a maximum value of fifty points. Your job is to compute the average score for each employee and write a report giving the recommended action to be taken for each. The report also should list the total number of employees being evaluated and the total number of employees in each category.

The data is as follows:

	Score		
Employee Name	Evaluation 1	Evaluation 2	Evaluation 3
Ann Murray	49	50	48
Bob Szymanski	50	49	50
Jon Hall	36	21	42
Ralph Towner	15	13	22

The recommended action is as follows:

If average score => 40, recommend for promotion and/or pay raise.

If 40 > average score => 30, take no action.

If average score < 30, reprimand.

FIGURE IV-6 Weight Class Program with Counter (Continued Facing Page)

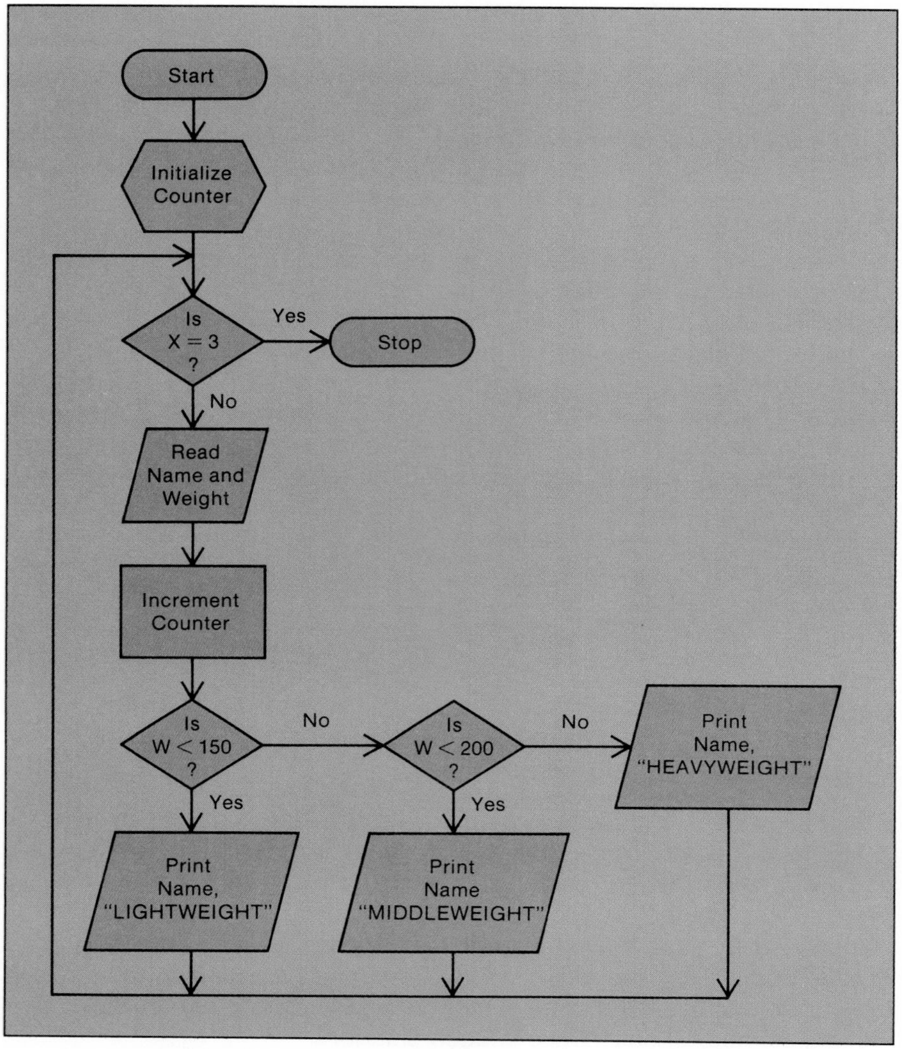

Solution Design

Since we need to output the total number of employees, we will need to set up a counter to accumulate this number. The average score for each employee then is calculated as follows:

Average Score = (Score evaluation 1 + Score evaluation 2 + Score evaluation 3) ÷ 3.

We then need to compare the average score for an individual with the ranges previously given to determine the recommended action that should be printed. Another counter will be needed to keep track of the number of individuals in each category.

```
100 REM *** INITIALIZE COUNTER ***
110 LET X = 0
120 REM *** TEST COUNTER VALUE ***
125 PRINT
126 PRINT
130 IF X = 3 THEN 999
140 READ N$,W
145 LET X = X + 1
150 IF W < 150 THEN 230
160 IF W < 200 THEN 200
170 PRINT N$; "  HEAVYWEIGHT"
190 GOTO 125
200 PRINT N$;"  MIDDLEWEIGHT"
220 GOTO 125
230 PRINT N$;"  LIGHTWEIGHT"
250 GOTO 125
260 DATA "ED HALL",230,"GREG BLACK",98,"JON LOUIS",180
999 END



RUN


ED HALL  HEAVYWEIGHT


GREG BLACK  LIGHTWEIGHT


JON LOUIS  MIDDLEWEIGHT
```

The Program

The evaluation program is shown in Figure IV-7. The counter variables are initialized to 0 by the LET statements in lines 60 through 90. Line 100 reads the employee name and score for each of the evaluations. Line 110 tests for the trailer value NONE. As long as the employee name does not equal NONE, the loop is reexecuted. The total number of employees being evaluated is accumulated in line 120. The average score is computed in line 130. Line 140 performs a test to determine whether A is less than 40. If it is, control is transferred to line 180, where the average score is tested again to see if it is less than 30. If it is, control is transferred to line 220. No test is required at line 220, since any score less than 30 is

FIGURE IV-7 Evaluation Program (Continued Facing Page)

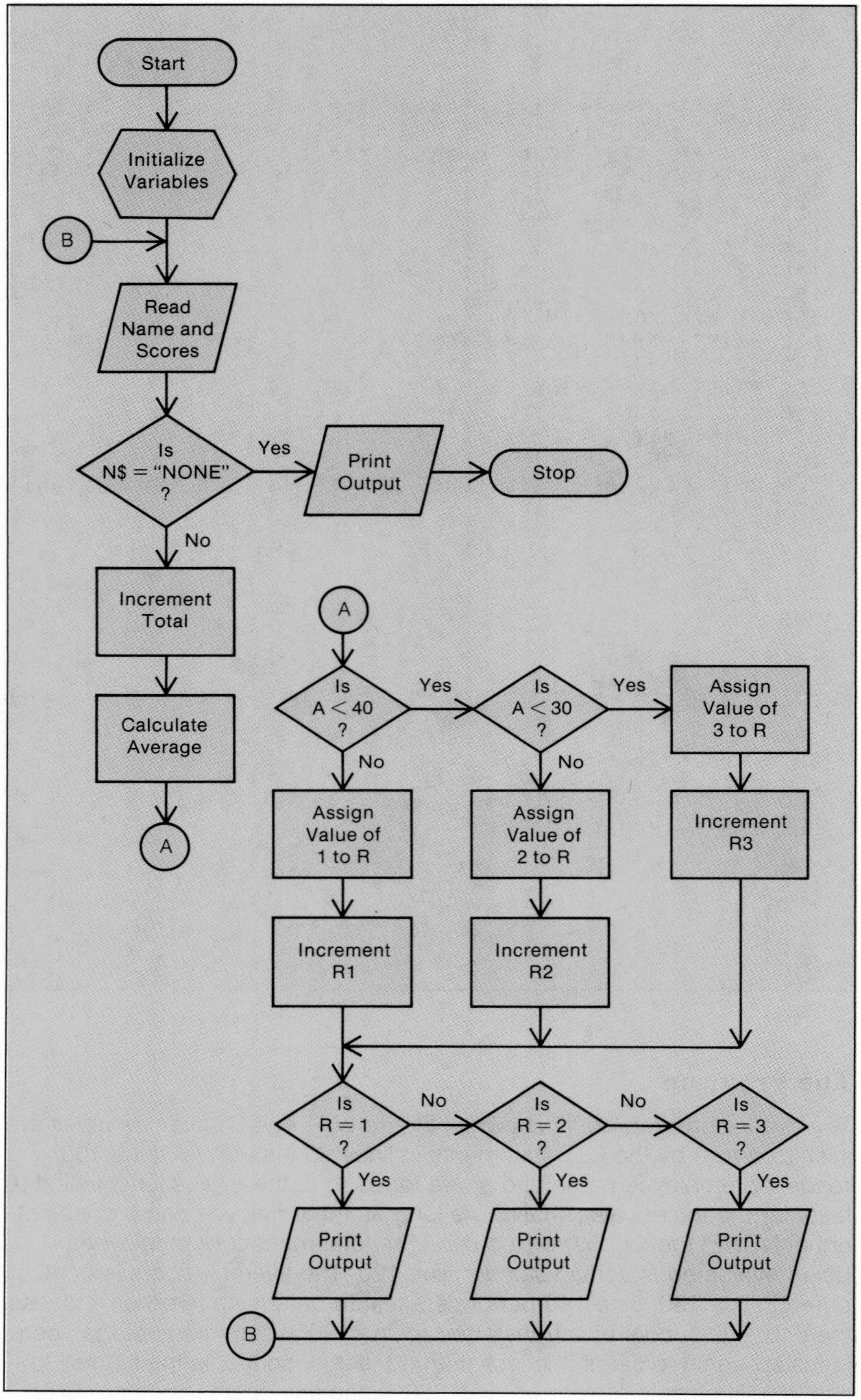

```
10 REM *** PROGRAM EVALUATES EMPLOYEES PERFORMANCE ***
20 REM *** AND PRINTS OUT REPORT ***
30 DATA "ANN MURRAY",49,50,48,"BOB SZYMANSKI",50,49,50
40 DATA "JON HALL",36,21,42,"RALPH TOWNER",15,13,22
50 DATA "NONE",0,0,060
60 LET TOTAL = 0
70 LET R1 = 0
80 LET R2 = 0
90 LET R3 = 0
100 READ N$,X,Y,Z
110 IF N$ = "NONE" THEN 340
120 LET TOTAL = TOTAL + 1
130 LET A = (X + Y + Z) / 3
140 IF A < 40 THEN 180
150 LET R = 1
160 LET R1 = R1 + 1
170 GOTO 240
180 IF A < 30 THEN 220
190 LET R = 2
200 LET R2 = R2 + 1
210 GOTO 240
220 LET R = 3
230 LET R3 = R3 + 1
240 ON R GOTO 245,275,305
245 PRINT
250 PRINT N$," ","ABOVE AVERAGE"
260 PRINT " "," ","RECOMMEND FOR PROMOTION AND/OR RAISE"
270 GOTO 100
275 PRINT
280 PRINT N$," ","AVERAGE"
290 PRINT " "," ","TAKE NO ACTION"
300 GOTO 100
305 PRINT
310 PRINT N$," ","BELOW AVERAGE"
320 PRINT " "," ","REPRIMAND"
330 GOTO 100
340 PRINT
350 PRINT "TOTAL # OF EMPLOYEES WITH ABOVE AVG. PERFORMANCE =",R1
360 PRINT "TOTAL # OF EMPLOYEES WITH AVG. PERFORMANCE =",R2
370 PRINT "TOTAL # OF EMPLOYEES WITH BELOW AVERAGE PERFORMANCE =",R3
380 PRINT
390 PRINT "TOTAL # OF EMPLOYEES =",TOTAL
999 END


RUN

ANN MURRAY                    ABOVE AVERAGE
                              RECOMMEND FOR PROMOTION AND/OR RAISE

BOB SZYMANSKI                 ABOVE AVERAGE
                              RECOMMEND FOR PROMOTION AND/OR RAISE

JON HALL                      AVERAGE
                              TAKE NO ACTION

RALPH TOWNER                  BELOW AVERAGE
                              REPRIMAND

TOTAL # OF EMPLOYEES WITH ABOVE AVG. PERFORMANCE =        2
TOTAL # OF EMPLOYEES WITH AVG. PERFORMANCE =              1
TOTAL # OF EMPLOYEES WITH BELOW AVERAGE PERFORMANCE =     1

TOTAL # OF EMPLOYEES =        4
```

considered below average. Within each of the segments just discussed, a value is assigned to R, and the total number of people receiving that value is accumulated. After each of these segments, control is transferred to line 235, an IF/THEN statement. Based on the value of R, the IF/THEN statements in lines 235 through 242 transfer control to the appropriate PRINT statements. Each of these segments will transfer control back to line 100. When the trailer value, NONE, is detected, control drops down to line 340, where printing of the totals occurs.

SUMMARY

- The GOTO statement is an unconditional transfer of control that allows the computer to bypass or alter the sequence in which instructions are executed.
- The GOTO statement often is used to set up loops.
- The IF/THEN statement permits control to be transferred only when a specified condition is met.
- The number of times a loop is executed can be controlled by the use of a trailer value or a counter.
- A trailer value is a dummy value used to indicate the end of data.
- A counter can be set up if the programmer knows ahead of time how many times a loop is to be executed.

QUESTIONS AND PROBLEMS

1. Write a program using an unconditional transfer statement that reads four groups of two numbers each and calculates and prints their sum. Use the following pairs as your data:

```
12,  4
 6, 23
19, 62
 4, 32
```

2. Big Al, the manager of Break-a-Leg Loans, Inc., specializes in giving loans to people or groups involved in the performing arts. Big Al would like a program that would bring to his attention any client who is more than thirty but less than sixty days late by printing the client's name and the following message: SEND A 'FRIENDLY' REMINDER THROUGH THE MAIL. He also would like the name of any client who is late by sixty days or more to be outputted with the following message: HAVE VETO PAY A 'FRIENDLY' VISIT. Write a program that will incorporate both unconditional and conditional transfer statements.

SECTION V

FOR/NEXT Loops and Functions

OVERVIEW

Section IV discussed two methods of controlling loops: counters and trailer values. IF/THEN and GOTO statements were used to implement these methods. This section presents another method for loop control: FOR and NEXT statements.

BASIC has several built-in functions that perform specific mathematical operations including finding the square root of a number or generating random numbers. These functions are useful to the programmer, who is spared the necessity of writing the sequence of statements otherwise needed to perform these operations. At other times, however, it may be useful for the programmer to define a function to meet the particular needs of an application. This section also briefly discusses these two tools: library functions (also called *built-in* or *predefined functions*) and user-defined functions.

FOR AND NEXT STATEMENTS

Let us review what happens when a counter is used to control a loop, since the logic of FOR/NEXT loops is very similar. First, the counter variable is set to some initial value. Statements inside the loop are executed once, and the counter is incremented. The counter variable then is tested to see if the loop has been executed the required number of times. When the variable exceeds the designated terminal value, the looping process ends, and the computer proceeds to the rest of the program. For example, assume we are to write a program to compute and print the double of each integer from 1 to 4. The program in Figure V-1 does this by using a loop controlled by the counter method.

FOR and **NEXT statements** allow concise loop definition. If we use FOR and NEXT statements in Figure V-1, the functions of lines 10, 20, 40, and 50 can be combined into just two statements (see Figure V-2). The general format of the FOR/NEXT loop is as follows:

```
line# FOR loop variable = initial value TO terminal value STEP step value
                .
                .
                .
line# NEXT loop variable
```

The FOR statement tells the computer how many times to execute the loop. The **loop variable** (also called the **index**) is set to an **initial value** (initial expression). This value is tested against the **terminal value** (terminal expression) to see if the loop should be continued. The step value specifies the value that will be added to the initial value after the FOR/NEXT loop is executed each time. The step value is optional. If it is omitted from the FOR statement, the value 1 automatically will be added to the initial

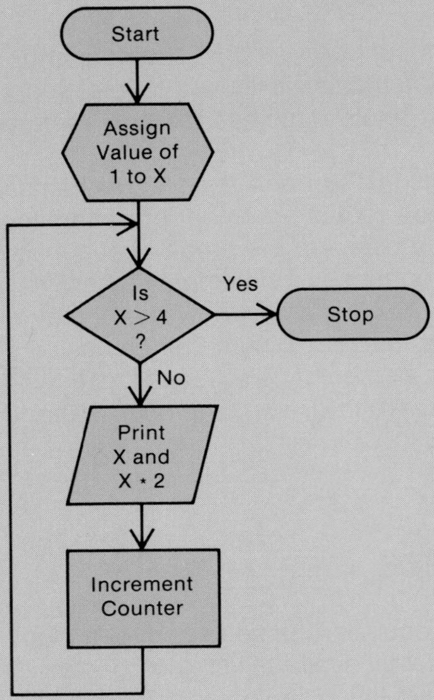


```
10 LET X = 1
20 IF X > 4 THEN 60
30 PRINT X,X * 2
40 LET X = X + 1
50 GOTO 20
60 END

RUN
 1            2
 2            4
 3            6
 4            8
```

FIGURE V-1 Looping With a Counter

value. These activities required two lines (10 and 20) in Figure V-1. The FOR statement combines these functions into one statement:

```
60 FOR I = 1 TO 7 STEP 1
```

Loop Variable (I), Initial Value (1), Terminal Value (7), Step Value (1)

Lines 40 and 50 in Figure V-1 increment the loop variable (the counter) and send control back to line 20. The functions of these two statements are combined in the NEXT statement in Figure V-2. In Figure V-1, after control is transferred back to line 20, the value of the loop variable again is tested against the terminal value. Once the value is exceeded, control passes to line 60. When FOR and NEXT statements are used, control goes to the statement immediately following the NEXT statement. Thus, the loop used in Figure V-1 can be set up to use FOR and NEXT statements, as shown in Figure V-2.

The FOR statement in line 10 tells the computer to initialize the loop variable, X, to 1. Sandwiched between the FOR and NEXT statements is line 20, the instruction to be repeated; it prints out the values of X and X * 2. Line 30, the NEXT statement, increments the loop variable by the step value indicated in the FOR statement. X now equals 2. Control then

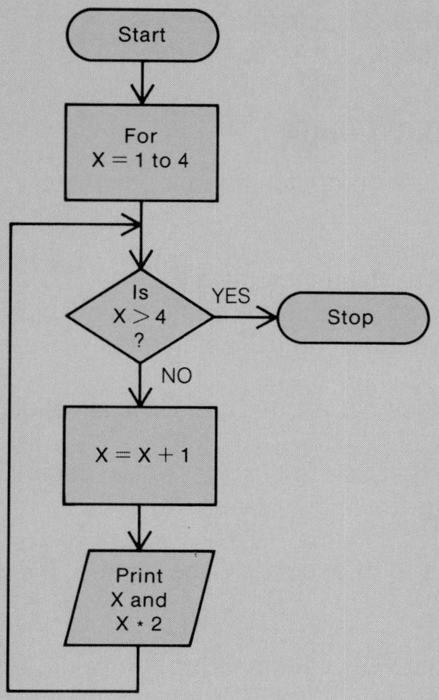


```
10 FOR X = 1 TO 4 STEP 1
20    PRINT X,X * 2
30 NEXT X
40 END

RUN
 1              2
 2              4
 3              6
 4              8
```

FIGURE V-2 Looping with FOR and NEXT Statements

is transferred back to the FOR statement. At this point, the computer tests the new value in X and decides whether to continue the loop. If X exceeds the terminal value of 4, the loop is stopped. If it does not, the loop is executed again. With X = 2, the loop is performed again. When the terminal value is exceeded—when X = 5—control is transferred to the statement immediately following the NEXT statement, line 40.

Flowcharting FOR/NEXT Loops

The flowchart in Figure V-2 shows how to flowchart a FOR/NEXT loop using standard symbols. The following symbol can also be used to flowchart the FOR/NEXT loop:

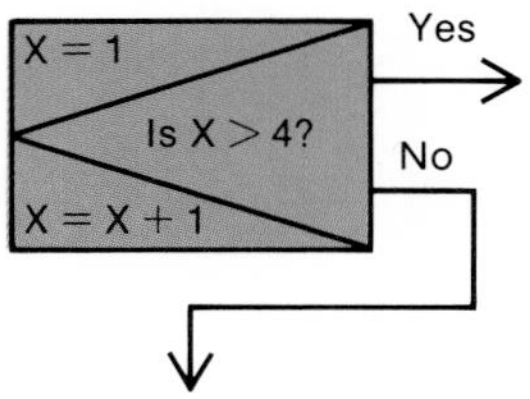

This is not a standardized flowchart symbol, however, it is very convenient for representing a loop, since it shows the initial, terminal, and step values for the loop variable in one symbol. We will use this symbol throughout the rest of the text. Figure V-3 illustrates the flowchart for the program in Figure V-2 using this symbol.

Processing Steps of FOR/NEXT Loops

Let us review the steps followed by the computer when it encounters a FOR statement:

1. It sets the loop variable to the initial value indicated.
2. It tests to see if the value of the loop variable exceeds the indicated terminal value (this may occur the first time the FOR statement is executed).
3. If the value of the loop variable does not exceed the terminal value, the statements in the loop are executed.
4. If the value of the loop variable exceeds the terminal value, control is transferred to the statement following the NEXT statement.

When the NEXT statement at the end of a loop is encountered, the computer does the following:

1. It adds the **step value** (given in the FOR statement) to the value of the loop variable. If no step value is indicated in the FOR statement, the value is assumed to be +1. Thus, the following two statements are equivalent:

```
10 FOR X = 1 TO 4 STEP 1
```

and

```
10 FOR X = 1 TO 4
```

2. It transfers control back to the FOR statement.

FIGURE V-3

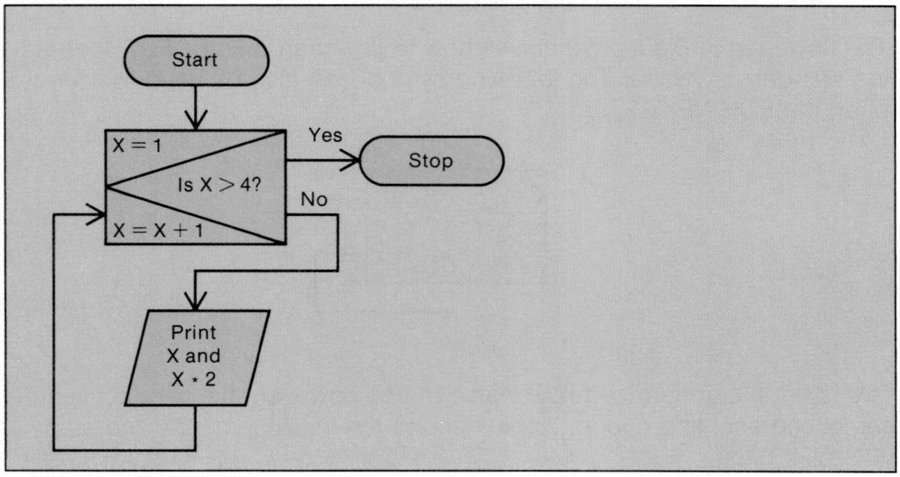

Rules for Using FOR and NEXT Statements

Some rules to be aware of in using FOR and NEXT statements follow:

1. At times it is desirable to use a negative step value. For example, to generate and print the sequence of numbers 10, 9, 8, 7, 6, 5, 4, 3, 2, 1, we can use the following code:

```
10 FOR I = 10 TO 1 STEP -1
20    PRINT I
30 NEXT I

RUN
 10
 9
 8
 7
 6
 5
 4
 3
 2
 1
```

The loop is terminated when the value of the loop variable, I, "exceeds" the specified terminal value, 1. In this case, though, the value of I "exceeds" in a downward sense: the loop is terminated when I is smaller than the terminal value. The initial value of the loop variable should be greater than the terminal value.

Examples of valid and invalid statements follow:

(Valid) `FOR I = 25 TO 5 STEP -5`

(Invalid) `FOR X = 10 TO 20 STEP -2`

2. *The step size in a FOR statement should never be 0.* This value would cause the computer to loop endlessly. Such an error condition is known as an **infinite loop**:

(Invalid) `FOR I = 1 TO 10 STEP 0`

3. *Transfer can be made from one statement to another within a loop.* For example, Figure V-4 reads a name and a pair of scores, computes the average of the scores, and prints the name and average for any person whose average is less than 70.

Note, however, that transfer from a statement within a loop to the FOR statement of the loop is illegal. Such a transfer would cause the loop variable to be reset (instead of simply continuing the loop process). Therefore, an infinite loop would be formed:

(Invalid Transfer)

```
10 FOR I = 1 TO 10
20    IF I = 5 THEN 10
30    LET X = X + 1
40    PRINT X
50 NEXT I
```

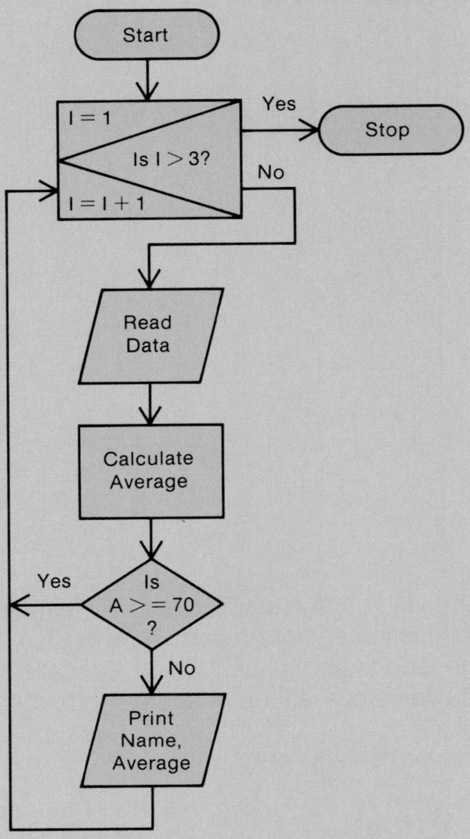


```
100 FOR I = 1 TO 3
110   READ N$,X,Y
120   LET A = (X + Y) / 2
130   IF A >= 70 THEN 150
140   PRINT N$,A
150 NEXT I
160 DATA "BILL",65,71,"SUE",83,96,"AMY",45,69
999 END
```

FIGURE V-4 Exiting from a Loop

If you want to continue the looping process but bypass some inner instructions, transfer control to the NEXT statement, as was done in Figure V-3 (line 130).

4. *The value of the loop variable should not be modified by program statements within the loop.* For example, line 30 here is invalid:

```
10 FOR N = 1 TO 50
20   LET X = 3 * Y
30   LET N = X + Y
40 NEXT N
```

5. *The initial, terminal, and step expressions can be composed of any valid numeric variable, constant, or mathematical formula.* Both of the following examples are valid:

```
10 INPUT X,Y
20 FOR I = X TO Y
30   PRINT I
40 NEXT I
```

```
10 READ A,B,C
20 FOR I = (A - B) TO (B + C) STEP 3
30   LET X = A * 3
40   PRINT X
50 NEXT I
```

6. *Each FOR statement must be accompanied by an associated NEXT statement.* In addition, the loop variable in the FOR statement must be specified in the NEXT statement.

Figure V-5 demonstrates how FOR and NEXT statements can be used in a common looping application—adding values to an **adder**, or **accumulator**. The purpose of this program is to find out the total number of parts being produced in an eight-hour shift and the average number of parts produced per hour during this time.

LIBRARY FUNCTIONS

Table V-1 lists the ANSI standard library functions found on most systems. The functions have been built into the BASIC language because many applications require these types of mathematical operations. The functions are included in the BASIC language library, where they can be referred to easily—hence the name **library functions**.

The general format of a reference to a library function is this:

function name (argument)

For the functions in Table V-1, the variable X is used as an **argument**. In BASIC, the argument of a function can be a constant, a variable, a mathematical expression, or another function. These functions are used in place of constants, variables, or expressions in BASIC statements such as PRINT, LET, and IF/THEN statements.

USER-DEFINED FUNCTIONS

The **definition**, or **DEF**, **statement** can be used by the programmer to define a function not already included in the BASIC language. Once the function has been defined, the programmer can refer to it as a function when necessary. The DEF statement can be placed anywhere before the first reference to it. Its general format is as follows:

line# DEF function name (argument) = expression

FIGURE V-5 Program with an Accumulator

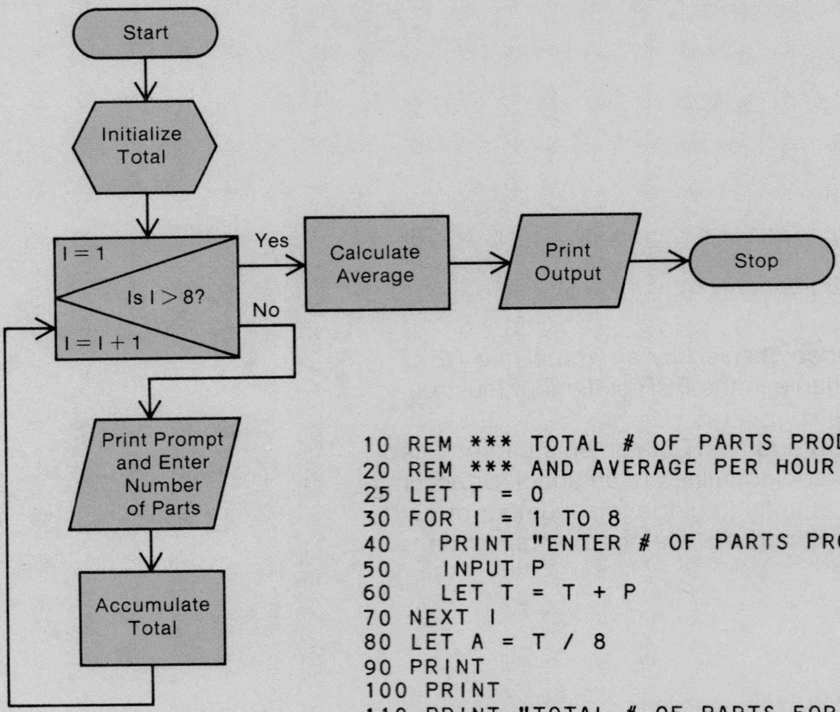


```
10 REM *** TOTAL # OF PARTS PRODUCED PER 8 HOUR SHIFT ***
20 REM *** AND AVERAGE PER HOUR ***
25 LET T = 0
30 FOR I = 1 TO 8
40    PRINT "ENTER # OF PARTS PRODUCED FOR HOUR ";I
50    INPUT P
60    LET T = T + P
70 NEXT I
80 LET A = T / 8
90 PRINT
100 PRINT
110 PRINT "TOTAL # OF PARTS FOR SHIFT = ";T
120 PRINT
130 PRINT "AVERAGE # OF PARTS PER HOUR = ";A
999 END

RUN
ENTER # OF PARTS PRODUCED FOR HOUR  1
? 24
ENTER # OF PARTS PRODUCED FOR HOUR  2
? 25
ENTER # OF PARTS PRODUCED FOR HOUR  3
? 19
ENTER # OF PARTS PRODUCED FOR HOUR  4
? 23
ENTER # OF PARTS PRODUCED FOR HOUR  5
? 24
ENTER # OF PARTS PRODUCED FOR HOUR  6
? 20
ENTER # OF PARTS PRODUCED FOR HOUR  7
? 21
ENTER # OF PARTS PRODUCED FOR HOUR  8
? 23


TOTAL # OF PARTS FOR SHIFT =  179

AVERAGE # OF PARTS PER HOUR =  22.375
```

Table V-1 ANSI Standard Library Functions

FUNCTION	PURPOSE
SIN (X)	Trigonometric sine function; X in radians
COS (X)	Trigonometric cosine function; X in radians
TAN (X)	Trigonometric tangent function; X in radians
ATN (X)	Trigonometric arc tangent function; X in radians
LOG (X)	Natural logarithm function
EXP (X)	e raised to the X power
SQR (X)	Square root of X
INT (X)	Greatest integer less than X
SGN (X)	Sign of X
ABS (X)	Absolute value of X
RND	Random number between 0 and 1

The function name consists of the letters FN followed by any one of the twenty-six alphabetic characters. There can be only one argument. The expression can contain any mathematical operations desired. However, a function definition cannot exceed one line of code.

When the computer encounters line 10 in the following program segment, it files away into memory the defined function FNR. Line 20 initializes B to 5. When the computer comes to line 30, it remembers the definition for FNR and substitutes the value of B, 5, for X in the expression (X + 20) / 2. The printed result is 12.5:

```
10 DEF FNR(X) = (X + 20) / 2
20 LET B = 5
30 PRINT FNR(B)

RUN
 12.5
```

COMPREHENSIVE PROGRAMMING PROBLEM

Problem Definition

Ms. Ives is interested in a five-year security. She would like a program to compute and print a five-year compound interest table for this security. The principle and interest rate for the security are as follows:

	Principle	Interest Rate
Security 1	$10,000	12%

The required output should appear as follows:

COMPOUND INTEREST TABLE	
PRINCIPLE = XXX	INTEREST RATE = XXX
YEAR	BALANCE
1	X
2	X
3	X
4	X
5	X

Solution Design

To compute the balance for each year, we need to use the following formula:

$$P \times (1 + I) \wedge Y,$$

where P = principle, I = interest rate, and Y = year.

The Program

Figure V-5 illustrates the use of a FOR/NEXT loop. Line 30 contains the principle and interest rate of the security. Line 50 reads the principle and interest rate for the security. Lines 60 through 100 contain PRINT statements that adjust spacing and print headings. Statements 110 through 130 form a loop whose terminal value is 5 (the number of years of the security). The balance due is calculated in line 120 and is printed along with the year number.

SUMMARY

- BASIC provides for concise loop definition with the FOR and NEXT statements. The FOR statement tells the computer how many times to execute the loop. The NEXT statement increments the loop variable and sends control back to the FOR statement.
- The following are some rules to remember when using FOR and NEXT statements:
  1. The step value can be negative.
  2. The step value should never be 0.
  3. Tranfer can be made from one statement to another within a loop. However, transfer from a statement within a loop to the FOR statement is illegal.
  4. The value of the loop variable should not be modified by program statements within the loop.
  5. The initial, terminal, and step expressions can be composed of any valid numeric variable, constant, or mathematical formula.
  6. Each FOR statement must be accompanied by an associated NEXT statement.

FIGURE V-6 Compound Interest Tables

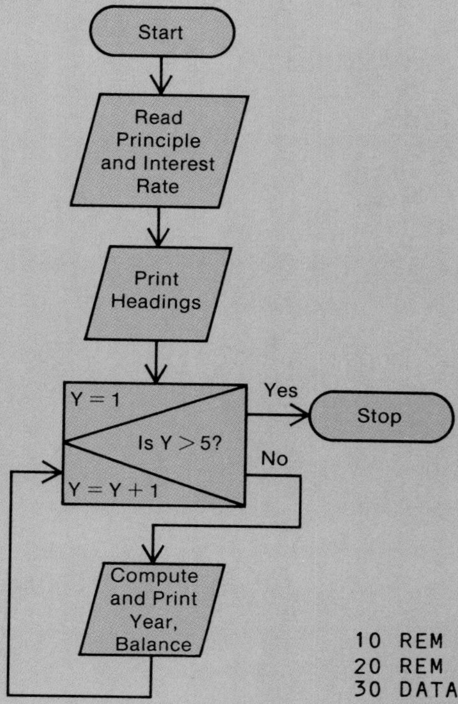


```
10 REM *** THIS PROGRAM COMPUTES A ***
20 REM *** 5-YEAR COMPOUND INTEREST TABLE ***
30 DATA 10000,0.12
50 READ P,I
60 PRINT
65 PRINT
70 PRINT "         COMPOUND INTEREST TABLE "
75 PRINT
80 PRINT "PRINCIPLE = ";P,"INTEREST RATE = ";I
85 PRINT
90 PRINT "YEAR","BALANCE"
100 PRINT
110 FOR Y = 1 TO 5
120   PRINT Y,"$";P * (1 + I) ^ Y
130 NEXT Y
999 END

RUN


         COMPOUND INTEREST TABLE

PRINCIPLE =  10000          INTEREST RATE =  .12

YEAR          BALANCE

 1            $ 11200
 2            $ 12544
 3            $ 14049.28
 4            $ 15735.19
 5            $ 17623.42
```

- The BASIC language includes several library functions that can make complicated mathematical operations easier to program.
- The programmer also can define functions by using the DEF statement.

QUESTIONS AND PROBLEMS

1. What is the output for the following?

```
10 FOR I = 1 TO 12 STEP 3
20    PRINT I,I + 1,I + 2
30 NEXT I
99 END
```

2. Which of the following FOR/NEXT loops is invalid?

a.
```
10 FOR X = 1 TO 5
20    LET T = X + 2
30    LET X = 1
40    PRINT T,X
50 NEXT X
```

b.
```
05 LET N = 10
10 FOR I = 1 TO N
20    PRINT T = I * N
30 NEXT I
```

c.
```
100 FOR J = 50 TO 2 STEP -2
110    PRINT J
120 NEXT J
```

d. a and b only
e. a and c onlv

GLOSSARY

Access mechanism—The device that positions the read/write head of a direct-access storage device over a particular track. **47**

Accounting machine—A machine that could mechanically read data from punched cards, perform calculations, rearrange data, and print results in varied formats. **13**

Accumulator—A register that accumulates results of computations. **40**

Address register—A register that holds the address of a location containing a data item called for by an instruction. **42**

Adventure game—A long-playing, decision-making word game; usually either text, or text and simple graphics. **157**

Algorithm—An outline of the logic patterns and calculations to be used in writing the computer program. **106**

American Standard Code for Information Interchange (ASCII)—A standard seven-bit binary code used for information interchange among data-processing systems, communication systems, and associated equipment. **81**

Analog computer—A computer that measures continuous physical or electrical conditions rather than operating on digits like the digital computer. **75**

Analog transmission—Transmission of data over communication channels in a continuous wave form. **91**

Analytical engine—An invention by Charles Babbage that exhibited several ideas used in computers today such as memory and punched cards. **11**

APL—*A Programming Language*; a terminal-oriented, symbolic programming language especially suitable for interactive problem-solving; can be used in execution or definition modes. **127**

Application data design—Structures the data as it will actually be used in application programs. **187**

Application program—A sequence of instructions written to solve a specific problem. **111**

Arithmetic/logic unit (ALU)—The section of the CPU that executes mathematical computations and logic operations. **32**

Artificial intelligence—The ability of computers to reason and think like humans; developing techniques whereby computers can be used to solve problems that appear to require imagination, intuition, or intelligence. **371**

ASCII-8—An eight-bit version of ASCII. **81**

Assembler program—A language translator program used for assembly language; produces a machine-language program. **104**

Assembly language—A symbolic programming language that uses convenient abbreviations (mnemonics) rather than groupings of 0s and 1s; intermediate-level language in terms of user orientation. **78**

Auxiliary storage—Also known as external storage or secondary storage; it supplements primary storage but operates at slower speeds. **42**

Bar-code reader—A device used to read a bar code by means of reflected light, such as a scanner that reads the Universal Product Code on supermarket products. **61**

BASIC—*B*eginner's *A*ll-*P*urpose *S*ymbolic *I*nstruction *C*ode; a programming language commonly used for interactive problem solving by users who may not be professional programmers. **124**

Batch processing—Processing where the entire program executes at once, with no interaction. **76**

Binary number system—The numeric system, used in computer operations that uses the digits 0 and 1 and has a base of 2. **13, 79**

Biochips—Minute computer circuits assembled from molecules; still in the developmental stage. **368**

Bit—(Short for BInary digiT) A digit position in a binary number; the smallest unit of information that can be represented by binary notation. **80**

Bit cell—Used in semiconductors; locations that store data by designating each cell as "on" or "off." **33**

Brain-wave interface—The capability of hardware and software to enable the computer to read and act upon the thoughts of humans. **370**

Branch—Program logic pattern that allows the computer to bypass (branch around) instructions and, therefore, alter the normal flow of execution. **89**

Bubble memory—A recently developed memory device in which data is represented by magnetized spots (or bubbles) that rest on the thin film of semiconductor material. **38**

Business software—Programs specifically designed for business applications such as payroll, budgeting, or accounting. **154**

Byte—Eight adjacent bits; a unit of storage. **81**

Cartridge—Plug-in plastic container holding either ROM or RAM chips depending on its function. **147**

Cartridge tape—A mass storage medium using high-density tapes. **49**

Central processing unit (CPU)—Acts as the "brain" of the computer; composed of three sections—primary storage unit, arithmetic/logic unit (ALU), and the control unit. **31**

Centralized approach—An information structure in which a separate data-processing department is utilized to provide data-processing facilities for the organization; all the data processing resources are in a single location. **188**

Chain printer—A line-at-a-time impact printer which has its character set assembled on a chain revolving horizontally past all print positions; it prints when a print hammer (one for each column on the paper) presses the paper against an inked ribbon that in turn presses against the appropriate characters on the aligned print chain. **56**

Check digit—A computer-calculated digit that is compared against a calculated digit of the input number; used to catch input errors. **82**

COBOL—*CO*mmon *B*usiness-*O*riented *L*anguage; a business programming language. **116**

Coding—The process of expressing a problem solution in a programming language; a set of rules for data conversion and representation. **105**

Communication channel—A pathway that allows remote input/output devices to communicate with the computer. **90**

Compiler program—A language translator program used for high-level languages, such as FORTRAN or COBOL; translates source-program statements into machine-executable code. **104**

Computer—A general-purpose machine with applications limited by the creativity of the humans who use it; its capabilities are derived from its memory and the speed and accuracy with which it can process data. **10**

Computer literacy—A broad, general knowledge of how to use computers to solve problems, of the functioning of the software and hardware, and an understanding of the societal implications of computers. **221**

Computer output microfilm (COM)—Miniature photographic images of output produced on microfilm rather than on paper. **58**

Computer-aided design (CAD)—The use of the computer by an engineer to design, draft, and analyze a prospective product using computer graphics on a video terminal. **277**

Computer-aided manufacturing (CAM)—The use of the computer by an engineer to simulate the required steps of the manufacturing process. **278**

Computer-assisted diagnosis—The use of computers to evaluate medical data to show variations from normal and determine the diagnosis. **301**

Computer-assisted instruction (CAI)—Direct interaction between a computer, acting as instructor, and a student. **206**

Conference tree—A type of bulletin board structured around topics and user comments with each main branch being a broad topic that the user can then elaborate on as the "branch" lengthens. **210**

Control program—A routine, usually part of an operating system, that aids in controlling the operations and management of a computer system. **114**

Control unit—The section of CPU that directs the sequence of operations by electrical signals and governs the actions of the various units that make up the computer. **31**

Cottage keyers—People who work at home and transmit work to the company by cassette tapes, telecommunications, or other means. **254**

Crash conversion—A method of system implementation in which the old information system is abandoned and the new one implemented at once. **178**

Cursor—A mark or notation on the display screen that indicates current location. **151**

Daisy-wheel printer—A character-at-a-time impact printer with removable daisy wheels (petal-like font carriers); produces letter-quality type. **53**

Data—Raw, unorganized facts. **82**

Data analysis sheet—Highlights the relationships between system inputs, data elements, and system outputs. **174**

Data bank—A commercially available computer data base that conveys news and reference data usually via telecommunications. **159**

Data base—The cornerstone of a management information system; basic data is commonly defined and consistently organized to fit the information needs of a wide variety of users within an organization; provides central data organization independent of specific applications. **186**

Data-base management system (DBMS)—A set of programs that serves as an interface between the data base and three principal users—the programmer, the operating system, and the manager (or other information user); provides a method of arranging data to limit duplication, an ability to make changes easily, and a capability to handle direct inquiries. **187**

Data-base producer—A company that assembles data into data bases to sell to other companies. **209**

Debug—To check and correct errors found in a program. **105**

Decimal number system—A base 10 number system; uses digits 0 through 9. **79**

Decision-logic table—A table that lists the conditions under which certain actions can or should be taken. **176**

Dedicated computer—A computer that has a specific function determined by its hardware. **199**

Demand report—A specific report produced only upon request. **185**

Demodulation—The process of retrieving data from a modulated carrier wave; the conversion of data back to digital ("on"/"off") form from analog (wave) form after it has been transmitted. **92**

Desk checking—A method used in system and program debugging in which the sequence of operations is mentally traced to verify the correctness of the processing logic. **105**

Difference engine—A machine developed by Charles Babbage in 1822 to compute mathematical tables. **11**

Digital computer—The type of computer commonly used in business applications; operates on distinct data (e.g., digits represented with 0s and 1s) by performing arithmetic and logic processes on specific data units. **75**

Digital transmission—Transmission of data as distinct "on" and "off" pulses. **91**

Direct-access storage—Auxiliary storage whereby data can be retrieved in any order at random, e.g., magnetic disk. **42**

Disk drive—A machine used to rotate the magnetic disks during data transmission; common speeds range from 40 to 3,600 revolutions per second. **45**

Disk pack—A stack of several magnetic disks mounted on a center shaft. **45**

Distributed computing—A system in which several CPUs are linked together by communication channels to form a network. The data processing resources are located at the various departments to permit faster response to the users. **189**

Dot-matrix printer—A character-at-a-time impact printer that produces characters through the use of dot-matrix patterns; also called wire-matrix printer. **52**

Drill program—A series of questions used to test and increase the user's knowledge. **156**

Drum printer—A line-at-a-time impact printer; it uses a metal cylinder with rows of characters engraved across its surface; one line of print is produced with each rotation of the drum. **56**

Educational game—A program that attempts to combine learning with game play. **158**

Educational software—Programs geared to drill, tutor, or instruct the user. **156**

EDVAC—*E*lectronic *D*iscrete *V*ariable *A*utomatic *C*omputer; performed arithmetic and logic operations without human intervention by using stored programs. **15**

Electronic bulletin board—An electronic clearinghouse where messages may be posted or received through a computer. **209**

Electronic data processing (EDP)—Data processing performed largely by electronic equipment such as computers rather than by manual or mechanical methods. **82**

Electronic drawing pen—See light pen. **152**

Electronic mail—Messages sent at high speeds by telecommunication facilities and placed in a special computer storage area where they can then be read. **246**

Electronic spreadsheet—A computerized grid divided into rows and columns into which numbers and formulas may be inserted. The computer can update instantly the entire sheet when new values are input; used for financial analysis. **270**

Electrostatic printer—A nonimpact printer that forms an image of a character on special paper using a dot-matrix of charged wires or pins. When the paper is moved through a solution containing ink particles of an opposite charge from the pattern, the particles of ink adhere to each charged pattern on the paper. **56**

Electrothermal printer—A nonimpact printer that uses heat in the print element to create characters on heat-sensitive paper. **56**

ENIAC—*E*lectronic *N*umerical *I*ntegrator *A*nd *C*alculator; the first "electronic digital calculator." **15**

Erasable programmable read-only memory (EPROM)—This memory unit can be erased and reprogrammed but only by being submitted to a special process. **40**

Ergonomics—The science of changing working conditions to suit the worker in an attempt to eliminate stress and physical problems. **257**

Exception report—An action-oriented management report which reports abnormal situations that require special handling. **183**

Expert systems—Software packages designed to copy how expert humans in a certain field think through a problem to reach the correct solution. **297, 371**

Extended Binary Coded Decimal Interchange Code (EBCDIC)—An eight-bit binary code used to represent numbers and characters. **81**

Feedback—Information used to evaluate the performance of a processing system; a concept in system theory, a check on the system to see whether or not predetermined standards are being met. **169**

Field—A meaningful item of data in a record. **185**

File—A collection of related records; sometimes referred to as a data set. **185**

First-generation computers—Developed in the 1950s; used vacuum tubes; faster than earlier mechanical devices, but very slow compared to today's computer. **16**

Flexible (floppy) disk—Also called a flexible diskette or floppy disk; low-cost, random-access form of data storage made of plastic. **47**

Floppy disk format—Indicates the density of the data recorded and whether it is stored on one side or both sides of a floppy disk. **148**

Flowchart—A graphic representation of the processing that is performed in a program. **107**

FORTRAN—*FOR*mula *TRAN*slator; a programming language used primarily in performing mathematical or scientific operations. **119**

Four-bit Binary Coded Decimal (BCD)—A four-bit binary digit computer code that represents decimal numbers one digit at a time, rather than as a whole binary number. **80**

Fourth-generation computers—The era of large-scale integrated circuits and microprocessors. **21**

Front-end processor—A small CPU which provides message-switching, as well as more sophisticated operations such as validating transmitted data and preprocessing data, before it is transmitted to the central computer; serves as an interface between a large CPU and peripheral devices. **130**

Full-duplex—A type of communication channel capable of the most versatile mode of data transmission; can transmit data in both directions simultaneously. **92**

Game paddle—See joystick. **151**

General-purpose register—A register that can be used as an accumulator or an address register. **42**

Graphic display device—A special visual display terminal used to display graphic images; can accept input from a keyboard or light pen. **64**

Graphics tablet—Allows the user to alter or create designs on the display screen by drawing on the tablet with the light pen. **153**

Grid chart—A chart indicating the relationship among the different components within a system. **173**

Half-duplex—A type of communication channel that allows two-way transmission, but in only one direction at a time. **92**

Hard copy—Printed output on paper, microfilm, or slides. **52**

Hard disk—A rigid platter used for random-access data storage with greater storage capacity than floppy disk. **149**

Hard-wired—Memory instructions that cannot be changed or deleted by other stored program instructions; programmed by manufacturer. **39**

Hardware spooler (buffer)—An intermediate storage medium that holds processed data being fed to the printer to enable the computer to complete other tasks. **151**

High-level language—English language-like coding scheme that is procedure-, problem-, and user-oriented. **81**

Hollerith code—A method of data representation of numbers, letters, and special characters by the placement of holes in 80-column punched cards. Each set of distinct holes has a distinct meaning. **12**

Home management software—Programs designed for home use to help manage and organize the household. **155**

Impact printer—A printer which physically presses the print elements against the ribbon and paper to make the impression. **52**

Information—Data that has been organized and processed so that it is meaningful. **82**

Information system—A system designed to process input data for output as information. Feedback is provided by the information users, as to the quality and adequacy of the information. **171**

Ink-jet printer—A nonimpact printer that uses a stream of charged ink to form dot-matrix characters. **57**

Input—Collecting, verifying, and coding the data for processing; data submitted to the computer for processing. **18, 82**

Instruction register—A register where each instruction is stored and subsequently decoded by the control unit. **42**

Integrated circuit—Electronic circuit etched on a small silicon chip less than 1/8-inch square. Permits much faster processing than with transistors and at a greatly reduced price. **18**

Intelligent terminal—A terminal with an internal processor that can be programmed to perform specified functions, such as data editing, data conversion, and control other terminals. **66**

Interactive program—A program that permits the user to input data during execution. **76**

Interpreter—A language translator program used in small computer systems to translate the source program into machine language—one instruction at a time. **104**

Joystick—An input device used with computer games to control cursor and object movement on the CRT screen by inputting electrical responses; also called game paddle. **151**

K—A symbol used to represent 1024 storage units (1024 bytes) when referring to a computer's memory. **49**

Key-to-disk system—Several keying devices connected to a minicomputer and a disk drive. **51**

Key-to-diskette system—A keyboard display screen, and flexible disk drive. **51**

Keypunch—A typewriter-like machine used to punch the data holes onto a punched card. **50**

Language translator program—The sequence of instructions (software) that translate the English-like programs written by programmers into machine-executable code. **103**

Large-scale integrated (LSI) circuit—A circuit containing thousands of transistors densely packed on a single silicon chip. **21**

Laser printer—A type of nonimpact printer that combines laser beams and electrophotographic technology to form images on paper. **57**

Librarian program—Software that maintains a directory of programs in auxiliary storage and contains appropriate procedures for additions or deletions. **115**

Light pen—A pen-shaped object with a photoelectric cell at its end; used to draw lines on a visual display screen; also called an electronic drawing pen. **64, 152**

LISP—*LIS*t *P*rocessing; a programming language primarily used in artificial intelligence research. **230**

Local area networks (LANs)—Linking computer systems in adjacent offices and buildings for intercomputer communication. **256**

Logic error—An error in designing the solution causing the end result to be incorrect; the program executes but calculates the wrong solution. **109**

Logical data design—Focuses on relationships among the data; how the data is viewed by application programs or individual users. **186**

LOGO—A powerful programming language that allows even small children to program effectively by defining new commands and creating graphics. **230**

Loop—Program logic pattern in which the computer repeatedly executes a series of instructions as long as specified conditions are met. **88**

Lower-level management—First-line supervisors and foremen who make the operational decisions to ensure that specific jobs are done. **179**

Machine language—The only set of instructions that a computer can execute directly; a code that designates the proper electrical states in the computer as combinations of 0s and 1s. **13, 77**

Machine-oriented language—A program language that achieves maximum efficiency and speed with the computer; examples are machine language and assembly languages. **115**

Magnetic core—A type of computer memory; iron alloy, doughnut-shaped rings about the size of pinheads strung on thin wires through which an electrical current passes, thus magnetizing the ring to represent either an "on" or "off." **18**

Magnetic disk—A storage medium consisting of a metal platter coated on both sides with a magnetic recording material upon which data is stored in the form of magnetized spots. **45**

Magnetic drum—A cylinder with a magnetic outer surface on which data can be stored by magnetizing specific positions. **16**

Magnetic tape—A storage medium consisting of a narrow strip of material upon which spots are magnetized to represent data; a sequential storage medium. **18**

Magnetic-ink character recognition (MICR)—The process that allows magnetized characters to be read by a magnetic-ink character reader. **59**

Main storage—See Primary storage unit. **19**

Management information system (MIS)—A formal network that extends computer use beyond routine reporting and into the area of management decision-making; its goal is to get the correct information to the appropriate manager at the right time. **179**

Mark I—The first automatic calculator which utilized electromagnetic relays and mechanical counters. **13**

Mass storage device—A device that allows relatively fast access to a voluminous amount of data, generally infrequently used files, at a low cost. **49**

Membrane keyboard—A flat, pressure-sensitive keyboard that is activated by touching a specific point as opposed to depressing a standard typewriter key. **151**

Menu—A list of choices that appear on the CRT screen the user can select from to command the computer to execute a specific program segment. **203**

Microcomputer—A very small computer; often a special purpose or single function computer. **21**

Microprocessor—The central processing unit of a microcomputer; fits on a small silicon chip. **21**

Microprocessor chip—A single, integrated circuit on a small silicon chip containing one ALU, control unit, and primary storage; the CPU of a microcomputer. **143**

Microprogram—A sequence of instructions wired in read-only memory; used to tailor a system to meet the user's processing requirements. **39**

Middle-level management—Those managers who make tactical decisions and implement the strategies determined at the top level. **179**

Minicomputer—A computer with the components of a full-size system but having a smaller memory. **19**

Mnemonics—A symbolic name (memory aid); used in symbolic languages (e.g. assembly language) and high-level programming languages. **116**

Modem—A device that modulates and demodulates signals transmitted over communication facilities. **92**

Modulation—A process used in modems to make business-machine signals compatible with communication facilities; the conversion of data from digital ("on"/"off") form to analog (wave) form before transmitting it. **92**

Mouse—A desk-top input device that controls cursor movement allowing the user to bypass the keyboard; must be used with special software. **154**

Multiprocessing—A multiple CPU configuration in which the jobs are processed simultaneously to speed up execution time. **129**

Multiprogramming—A technique whereby several programs are placed in primary storage at the same time, giving the illusion that they are being executed simultaneously; results in increased CPU activity time. **129**

Nanosecond—One-billionth of a second. **37**

Network—The linkage of computers for sharing messages and information. **159**

Nonimpact printer—A printer which uses heat, laser technology, or photographic techniques in which the print elements never touch the paper to make the impression. **52**

Nonmonotonic logic theory—The theory that logic should develop in steps, consistent with all preceding steps and that additional assumptions will not make the previous conclusions false. **371**

Object program—A sequence of machine-executable instructions derived from source-program statements by a language-translator program. **103**

Office automation—The integration of computers and communication technology with traditional manual procedures in the office. **248**

Online—In direct communication with the computer. **19**

Online (processing) system—A system that allows the user to interact with the computer during program execution; it permits direct communication between the user and computer. **76**

Online service—A company that sells computerized access over networks to information contained in data bases and to other related services. **209**

Operating system—A collection of programs designed to permit a computer system to manage itself and to avoid idle CPU time while increasing utilization of computer facilities. **114**

Optical laser disk—A new high-capacity medium for data storage utilizing laser technology. **150**

Optical-character recognition (OCR)—A capability of devices with electronic scanners to read numbers, letters, and other characters and convert the optical images into appropriate electrical signals. **61**

Optical-mark recognition (OMR)—A capability of a device using an electronic scanner that converts marks on a page into computer data by reading the position of the marks; also known as mark sensing. **61**

Output—Retrieving, converting, and communicating the results of processing; the information that comes from the computer as a result of processing. **82**

Parallel conversion—A system-implementation approach in which the new information system is operated side-by-side with the old one until all differences are reconciled. **178**

Parity (check) bit—A means of detecting erroneous transmission of data; internal self-checking to determine if the number of 1 bits in a bit pattern is either odd or even. **82**

Pascal—A programming language named after French mathematician Blaise Pascal; first developed to teach programming techniques to students; it is rapidly expanding its original intentions because it is powerful and highly structured; used for batch and interactive processing. **124**

Phased conversion—A method of system implementation in which the old information system is gradually replaced by the new one; the new system is segmented and gradually applied. **178**

Physical data design—Data-base design that focuses on how data are kept in and retrieved from storage devices. **186**

Pilot conversion—The implementation of a new information system into the organization whereby only a small part of the business uses the system until it has proven successful. **178**

Pixel (picture element)—One of the many image points comprising a graphic display. **295**

PL/I—*P*rogram *L*anguage *O*ne; a general-purpose programming language used for both business and scientific functions. **120**

Plotter—A special printer used to print graphic images such as charts, graphs, and pictures. **58**

Point-of-sale (POS) terminal—A terminal that serves as a cash register but is also capable of relaying sales and inventory data to a central computer. **4, 63**

Predictive report—A report used for tactical and strategic decision making. **183**

Primary storage unit—Also known as internal storage, memory, primary storage, or main storage; primary storage unit is the section of the CPU that holds instructions, data, and intermediate and final results during processing. **32**

Print-wheel printer—A line-at-a-time impact printer which has one print wheel for each print location on the entire line; the print wheels rotate until an entire line is in the appropriate print position, then a hammer presses the paper against the print wheels. **54**

Printer-keyboard—An impact printer similar to an office typewriter; instructions for printing come from the CPU; a keyboard allows an operator to communicate with the system. **52**

Problem-oriented language—A programming language designed to solve specific kinds of problems allowing the user to focus on desired results rather than the individual steps needed to get those results; RPG is an example of this type of language. **116**

Procedure—A command that is defined by the programmer. **232**

Procedure-oriented language—A programming language designed to define the processing steps required of a particular application; examples are COBOL, FORTRAN, and PL/1. **115**

Processing—Classifying, sorting, calculating, summarizing, or storing the data on a computer in order to provide information for the user. **82**

Processing program—A routine, usually part of the operating system, that is used to simplify program preparation and execution. **114**

Program—A series of step-by-step instructions that provide a problem solution and tell the computer exactly what to do. **4**

Programmable read-only memory (PROM)—Read-only memory that can be programmed by the manufacturer or can be programmed by the user for special functions to meet the unique needs of the user; once programmed it maintains the same characteristics as ROM. **40**

Programmer—The person who writes step-by-step instructions for the computer to execute. **102**

Proper program—A program using the structured approach and top-down design with only one entrance and one exit. **132**

Pseudocode—A brief set of instructions written in sentence form, used to represent the control structures and algorithms of structured programming. **106**

Punched card—A commonly used storage medium in which data is represented by the presence or absence of holes in a specified row and column coding scheme. Each particular set of holes has a distinct meaning which is translated into machine language for the computer. **10**

RAM card—A recently developed storage medium for microcomputers; can be plugged into the microcomputer in the same slot that the disk drive uses. **150**

Random-access memory (RAM)—Memory storage that holds programs or data and can be written into or read from very quickly. **40**

Read-only memory (ROM)—Computer memory containing items that cannot be deleted or changed by stored-program instructions because they are "hard-wired" into the circuitry. **39**

Real storage—Also known as main storage or primary storage within the CPU. **130**

Real time—Refers to the capability of a system or device to receive data, process it, and provide output fast enough to control an activity being performed. **296**

Record—A collection of data items, or fields, that relate to a single unit. **185**

Register—An internal computer component used for temporary storage of an instruction or data; capable of accepting, holding, and transferring that instruction or data very rapidly. **40**

Remote terminal—A terminal that is placed at a location distant from the central computer. **19**

Review—An evaluation of the new system's performance. **178**

Robotics—The science of designing and building robots. **284**

RPG—*R*eport *P*rogram *G*enerator; an example of a problem-oriented language originally designed to produce business reports. **122**

Run-time error—An error detected while the program is running that stops the program's execution; usually caused by telling the computer to do something that is not possible. **109**

Scheduled report—A report produced at a regular interval to monitor ongoing functions and provide routine information to users. **183**

Script theory—The theory that knowledge relates to what normally happens in a particular set of circumstances. **372**

Second-generation computers—Used transistors; smaller, faster, and had larger storage capacity than the first-generation computers; first computers to use a high-level language. **17**

Selection—A program logic pattern in which the computer makes a choice, based on an evaluation between two paths to be taken. **87**

Semiconductor—A transistor used as a type of primary storage medium that stores data in bit cells located on silicon chips. **33**

Sequential-access storage—Auxiliary storage from which records must be read, one after another, in a fixed sequence, until the needed data is located, e.g., magnetic tape. **42**

Silicon chip—Solid-logic circuitry on a small piece of silicon used to form the primary storage of third-generation computers. **18**

Silicon Valley—Nickname for the high-tech area in the Santa Clara Valley south of San Francisco, California. **22**

Simple sequence—Program logic where one statement, or instruction, after another is executed in the same sequence in which it is stored. **87**

Simplex—A type of communication channel that provides for unidirectional, or one-way, transmission of data. **92**

Simulation and modeling—A technique in which mathematical data are analyzed and the results used to generate models or to make projections based upon this real data. **297**

Simulation program—A program that simulates a specific machine or situation. **157**

Slide show package—A computer graphic package that displays the graphics in a timed sequence on the terminal; similar to a slide show. **274**

Soft copy—Data displayed on a CRT screen; not a permanent record as contrasted with a hard copy. **52**

Software—Programs used to direct the computer for problem solving and overseeing operations. **19**

Source program—A sequence of instructions written in either assembly language or high-level language by the programmer. **103**

Source-data automation—The process that allows data to be collected in computer-readable form at the source or collection point of that data. **59**

Spatial digitizer—Often used in computer graphics to simulate three-dimensional objects. **153**

Sprite—Small blocks that can assume user-defined shapes and colors and be moved rapidly across the screen using the LOGO language. **233**

Storage register—A register that holds information coming from or going to the primary storage unit. **42**

Stored-program concept—The storage of instructions in the computer's memory in electronic form so the computer can process data at its own speed without human intervention. **15, 85**

Structured programming—A top-down modular approach to programming that emphasizes dividing a program into logical sections in order to reduce testing time, increase programmer productivity, and bring clarity to programming. **132**

Supervisor program—Also called a monitor or an executive; the major component of the operating system; coordinates the activities of all other parts of the operating system. **115**

Swapping—In a virtual-storage environment, the process of transferring a program section from virtual storage to real storage, and vice versa. **130**

Symbolic language—The use of mnemonic symbols to represent instructions; must be translated into machine language before being executed by the computer. **16**

Syntax error—A violation of the rules of a programming language similar to a grammar error committed in English; disallows execution of the program. **105**

System—A group of related elements that work toward a common goal. **169**

System analysis—A detailed, step-by-step investigation of a system for the purpose of determining what must be done and the best way to do it. **169**

System analyst—A specialist who evaluates the aims, organization, priorities, and needs of a business to devise a more efficient method for current procedures; often utilizes the computer's capabilities to achieve his/her goals. **106**

System design—Process during which alternative solutions to problems uncovered in the system analysis phase are designed, the cost effectiveness of the alternatives is determined, and final recommendations are made. **176**

System flowchart—The group of symbols used to represent the general information flow; focuses on inputs and outputs rather than on internal computer operations. **173**

System implementation—The final phase in the development of a new or revised system during which the users begin to actually use the new system; during implementation, the analyst makes sure that the system is completely debugged and operational and is accepted by the users. **178**

System program—A sequence of instructions written to coordinate the operation of computer circuitry and to help the computer run quickly and efficiently. **111**

System residence device—An auxiliary storage device (disk, tape, or drum) upon which operating-system programs are stored and from which they are loaded into main storage. **114**

Tape cassette—A sequential storage medium using high-density digital recording tape to record data in small computer systems. **44**

Tape drive—A device used to read from or write to magnetic tape. **42**

Telecommunications—The combined use of communication facilities such as the telephone system, and data-processing equipment. **90**

Telecommunications network—A means by which one or more mainframes is linked to other computers for communication. **209**

Telecommuting—Computer hookups between offices and homes, which allow employees to work at home. **8**

Teleconferencing—Conferences using electronic and/or image-producing means to communicate thus eliminating the time and expense of traveling. **247**

Terminal—A device through which data can exit from or be entered into a computer. **62**

Third-generation computers—Characterized by the use of integrated circuits, reduced size, lower costs, and increased speed and reliability. **18**

Top-level management—The management at the top of the organization who make strategic decisions. **179**

Touch-tone terminal—A remote terminal that uses telephone lines to pass data from a special keyboard to the computer. **63**

Track—One of a series of concentric circles on the surface of a disk; a horizontal row stretching the length of a magnetic tape on which data can be recorded; one of a series of circular bands on a drum. **45**

Transistor—A type of electronic circuitry that controls current flow without the use of a vacuum; smaller, faster, and more reliable than vacuum tubes. **17**

Turtle geometry—The LOGO method of drawing on the video screen in which a simulated turtle acts as a pen and moves around the screen as the instructions command. **232**

Tutorial program—A program that explains new material and then tests the user's retention. **157**

UNIVAC I—*UNIV*ersal *A*utomatic *C*omputer; the first commercial electronic computer; became available in 1951. **16**

Universal Product Code (UPC)—A code consisting of ten pairs of vertical bars that represent the manufacturer's identity and the identity code of the item; commonly used on most grocery items. 61

User friendly—Software or hardware that is easy to use and understand for the user. **143**

Utility program—A subsystem of the operating system that is capable of performing specialized, repeatedly used functions such as sorting, merging, and transferring data from one input/output device to another. **115**

Variable—A meaningful symbolic name assigned by a programmer to the computer's storage locations. **38**

Video game—A fast-action, arcade-like computer game; often uses graphics. **157**

Videotex—A service that provides two-way information capabilities using TV-like screens and computers. **8**

Virtual storage—Also called virtual memory; an extension of multiprogramming in which portions of programs not being used are kept in secondary storage until needed, giving the impression that primary storage is unlimited; contrast with real storage. **129**

Visual display terminal—A television-like screen used to display soft-copy output; sometimes called a CRT (*C*athode *R*ay *T*ube). **64**

Voice mail—Message spoken into a telephone, converted into digital form, stored in the computer's memory until recalled, at which time it is reconverted into voice form. **252**

Voice recognition system—A system that allows the user to "train" the computer to understand his or her voice and vocabulary. The user must follow only the patterns the computer is programmed to recognize. **62, 154**

Voice synthesizer—A device that enables the computer to produce vocal output. **152**

Von Neumann bottleneck—Data traffic jams created because of the way computers sequentially execute their programs; one of the reasons computers cannot attain maximum efficiency and speed. **367**

Word processing—A program that allows text material to be entered, corrected, added or deleted, and printed in a desired form. **246**

Word size—Based on the size of the registers and decides the complexity of operations that can be handled. **154**

Xerographic printer—A type of nonimpact printer that uses printing methods similar to those used in common xerographic copying machines. **58**

INDEX

ACKNOWLEDGMENTS

2 "Reprinted with permission of the author, Los Angeles Times Syndicate, 1983." 30 "Reprinted by permission of The Wall Street Journal, © Dow Jones & Company, Inc., 1983. All Rights Reserved." 30 Reprinted with permission of David Harbough. 55 Cartoon by John Chase. 74 "Copyright, 1983, Los Angeles Times. Reprinted by permission." 100 "Reprinted with permission from Personal Computing, August, 1983, p. 128, and Copyright 1983, Hayden Publishing Company." 118 Datamation, April, 1981. Reprinted by permission. 142 "From 'Computer Lab or Caribbean Cruise?' appearing in the August, 1983 issue of Popular Computing magazine. Copyright © 1983 Byte Publications, Inc. Used with the permission of Byte Publications, Inc." 157 "DENNIS THE MENACE® used by permission of Hank Ketcham and © by Field Enterprises, Inc." 168 "Copyright 1981 by CW Communications/Inc. Framingham, MA 01701—Reprinted from COMPUTERWORLD." 180 Reprinted with permission of Walt Miller. 198 © 1983 by the New York Times Company. Reprinted by permission. 208 © 1982 by Sidney Harris—*American Scientist* magazine. 218 "Copyright 1983 Time Inc. All rights reserved. Reprinted by permission from TIME." 222 "Copyright 1982. G. B. Trudeau. Reprinted with permission of Universal Press Syndicate. All rights reserved." 242 "Reprinted with permission from Personal Computing, August, 1982, p. 137, and Copyright 1982, Hayden Publishing Company." 245 Reprinted with permission of Infoworld. 266 "From 'Welcome to the Hotel Interactive' appearing in the February, 1983 issue of Popular Computing magazine. Copyright © 1983 Byte Publications, Inc. Used with the permission of Byte Publications, Inc." 272 Reprinted with permission of Infoworld. 292 Reprinted with permission of Science Digest. 304 Don Cresci—in *Computerworld*. 316 © 1984 Los Angeles Times; photograph reprinted by permission. 322 © 1982 by Sidney Harris—created for *Discover*. 338 "Reprinted with permission of USA Today." 353 Reprinted with permission of Infoworld. 362 "Reprinted with permission from *Introduction to Psychology*, Third Edition, by Dennis Coon. West Publishing Company, 1983, pp. 515–516." 373 Reprinted courtesy of Larry Wright and *The Detroit News*. 402 Knight-Ridder Newspapers.

PHOTO CREDITS

xx courtesy of NASA. 3 courtesy of NASA. 4 courtesy of NASA. 5 (top) reprinted by permission of International Business Machines Corporation. 5 (bottom) courtesy of the Coco-Cola Company. 7 reprinted by permission of International Business Machines Corporation. 8 photo furnished by Activision, Inc. 10 courtesy of IBM. 11 (top) courtesy of IBM. 11 (bottom) courtesy of IBM. 11 (margin) Crown copyright, The Science Museum, London. 12 (margin) courtesy of IBM. 12 courtesy of IBM. 14 (top) courtesy of IBM. 14 (bottom) courtesy of IBM. 16 courtesy of Sperry Univac. 17 (top) courtesy of Sperry Univac. 17 (bottom) courtesy of IBM. 18 courtesy of IBM. 19 courtesy of NCR Corporation. 20 (top) courtesy of Digital Equipment Corporation. 20 (bottom) courtesy of Bell Laboratories. 22 courtesy of Cray Research, Inc. 23 (top) courtesy of IBM. 23 (middle) courtesy of Sperry Univac. 23 (bottom) courtesy of Apple Computer Inc. 28 courtesy of AT&T, Bell Laboratories. 29 courtesy of AT&T, Bell Laboratories. 33 both photos courtesy of Iowa State University of Science and Technology. 34 all three photos courtesy Sperry Corporation. 35 (top) courtesy of the Perkin-Elmer Corporation. 35 (middle) courtesy Intel Corporation. 35 (bottom) courtesy Sperry Corporation. 36 (top left) courtesy Electro Scientific Industries, Inc. 36 (top right) courtesy Sperry Corporation. 36 (bottom right) courtesy Motorola, Inc., Semiconductor Products Sector. 38 courtesy of Bell Laboratories. 39 both photos courtesy Texas Instruments Incorporated. 41 (top left) courtesy of Intel Corporation. 41 (top right) courtesy of Intel Corporation. 41 (bottom) courtesy of Dataman Designs. 44 (top) Courtesy Boise Cascade Corporation. 44 (bottom) courtesy of Dialog Information Services, Inc. 45 courtesy of Verbatim Corporation. 46 courtesy Dysan Corporation. 48 (top) courtesy of Control Data Corporation. 48 (bottom) courtesy Verbatim Corporation. 49 courtesy of IBM. 51 (top) photo by Norma Morris. 51 (bottom) courtesy of Wang Laboratories, Inc. 52 courtesy of Interstate Electronics Corp. 53 photo courtesy of DATAPRODUCTS CORP. 54 (bottom) photo courtesy of DATAPRODUCTS CORP. 57 (bottom) courtesy of Datagraphix, Inc. 58 courtesy of Hewlett-Packard Company. 63 (top) courtesy of Interstate Electronics Corp. 63 (bottom) courtesy of Anderson Jacobson Inc. 64 courtesy NCR Corp. 65 (top) courtesy of Hewlett-Packard Company. 65 (bottom) courtesy Armstrong World Industries, Inc. 66 courtesy of Lockheed Corporation. 72 courtesy Marathon Oil Company. 73 Steve Uzzell, III, courtesy of Planning Research Corporation. 75 (left) used with permission of Whirlpool Corporation. 75 (right) reprinted by permission of International Business Machines Corporation. 76 (left) courtesy of AT&T, Bell Laboratories. 76 (right) used with permission of Whirlpool Corporation. 77 photograph by Mark Leet. 89 courtesy Sinclair Research Ltd. 91 courtesy Communications Satellite Corporation. 92 courtesy U.S. Robotics, Inc. 98 courtesy Lear Siegler, Inc./ Data Products Division, Anaheim, California. 99 courtesy Paradyne Corporation. 101 courtesy Texaco Inc. 103 courtesy Intel Corporation. 109 photograph courtesy of TRW, Inc. 140 courtesy Zenith Data Systems Corp. 141 courtesy of IBM. 143 courtesy of IBM. 144 (top left) courtesy of Apple Computer, Inc. 144 (top right) courtesy Commodore Computer Systems Division. 144 (lower left) courtesy of IBM. 144 (middle right) courtesy of Digital Equipment Corporation. 144 (bottom right) courtesy of Radio Shack, a Division of Tandy Corporation. 145 courtesy of Bell Laboratories. 146 (left) courtesy Apple Computer, Inc. 146 (right) courtesy Unuson Corporation. 147 courtesy Verbatim Corporation. 148 courtesy Digital Research Inc. 149 courtesy Shugart Corporation. 150 courtesy of Micro-Sci, a division of Sandun Controls Inc.; photography by Rich Dressler. 151 (left) courtesy Apple Computer, Inc. 151 (right) photo by Normal Morris. 152 (top) photo by Norma

Morris. 152 (bottom) photo by Steve Brom—Metro Graphics, Wichita, Kansas. 153 courtesy of Houston Instrument. 154 courtesy Mouse Systems Corporation. 155 courtesy International Business Machines Corporation. 156 reprinted with permission from International Business Machines Corporation. 158 courtesy Commodore Computer Systems Division. 166 courtesy Lear Siegler, Inc./Data Products Division, Anaheim, California. 167 courtesy of Consolidated Rail Corporation. 174 (bottom) courtesy Apple Computer, Inc. 177 courtesy Corvus Systems. 178 courtesy Nationwide. 180 courtesy Grid Systems Corporation. 182 courtesy Boise Cascade Corporation. 196 courtesy Commodore Computer Systems Division. 197 courtesy Armstrong World Industries. 199 courtesy of AT&T, Bell Laboratories. 200 courtesy of The Computer Communications Group. 201 (left and upper right) courtesy of Atari Incorporated. 201 (lower right) courtesy of Tomy Corporation. 202 courtesy of Radio Shack, a Division of Tandy Corporation. 203 both photos reproduced with permission of AT&T. 205 courtesy of Apple Computers, Inc. 207 courtesy of AT&T, Bell Laboratories. 209 Jay Freis, courtesy of Planning Research Corporation. 211 photo shown courtesy of Radio Shack, a Division of Tandy Corporation. 216 photo shown courtesy of Radio Shack, a Division of Tandy Corporation. 217 courtesy of Apple Computer, Inc. 219 (top) courtesy of IBM Corporation. 219 John Foraste/Brown University. 220 reprinted by permission of International Business Machines Corporation. 221 courtesy of General Electric, Data Communications Department. 223 John Foraste/Brown University. 224 courtesy Union College—College Relations. 225 courtesy Union College—College Relations. 226 courtesy California Institute of the Arts. 227 courtesy Control Data Corporation. 228 courtesy Honeywell, Inc. 229 courtesy Honeywell, Inc. 230 photo by Norma Morris. 231 (top) courtesy of Dartmouth College, Hanover, New Hampshire 03755. 231 (bottom) courtesy Texas Instruments Incorporated. 232 photo courtesy of Wynter Snow. 233 Susan Gilmore, photographer. 234 courtesy California Institute of the Arts. 235 courtesy of AT&T. 240 courtesy Corvus Systems. 241 courtesy General Electric Company. 243 courtesy U.S. Department of Agriculture. 244 Ira Wexler, courtesy of Planning Research Corporation. 246 Diana Walker/TIME Magazine. 247 courtesy Hewlett Packard Company. 249 courtesy CPT Corporation. 251 (top) courtesy Compugraphic Corporation. 251 (bottom) courtesy Lanier Business Products, Inc. 253 courtesy AT&T. 254 courtesy Digital Equipment Corporation. 255 courtesy Source Telecomputing Corporation. 257 courtesy NESTAR Systems, Inc. 258 photo courtesy of Nixdorf Computer Corporation, Burlington, Massachusetts. 264 courtesy Quotron Systems, Inc. 265 courtesy Auto-trol Technology Corporation. 267 courtesy Apple Computer, Inc. 268 courtesy Texas Instruments Incorporated. 269 courtesy AccuRay Corporation. 270 courtesy Sorcim Corporation. 271 courtesy of AT&T, Bell Laboratories. 272 courtesy Pacific Gas and Electric Company. 273 (top left) courtesy Hewlett Packard Company. 273 (top right) image courtesy Polaroid Corporation. 273 (bottom) courtesy Marathon Oil Company. 275 courtesy Apple Computer, Inc. 276 courtesy AccuRay Corporation. 277 courtesy Chrysler Corporation. 278 courtesy of Burlington Industries, Inc. 280 all photos courtesy of NIKE, Inc. 281 all photos courtesy of NIKE, Inc. 282 courtesy of Burlington Industries, Inc. 283 courtesy Cincinnati Milacron Industrial Robot Division. 284 courtesy of Cincinnati Milacron. 290 courtesy General Electric Company. 291 courtesy General Electric Company. 293 reprinted by permission of International Business Machines Corporation. 294 (top) courtesy Western Geophysical. 294 (bottom) Optronics International, Inc., Chelmsford, Massachusetts. 295 courtesy Los Alamos National Laboratory. 296 courtesy Los Alamos National Laboratory. 297 both photos courtesy Form Substance, Inc. 298 photo courtesy of Cray Research, Inc. 299 courtesy Marathon Oil Company. 300 reprinted with permission from International Business Machines Corporation. 301 The Mt. Sinai Medical Center, Cleveland, Ohio. 302 reprinted with permission from International Business Machines Corporation. 303 (top left) Optronics International, Inc.; Dr. L. Sokoloff, NIH, Bethesda, Maryland. 303 (bottom) courtesy Harshaw Chemical Company. 305 courtesy NASA. 306 (top) courtesy Honeywell, Inc. 306 (bottom) courtesy Digital Systems Group. 307 courtesy Apple Computer, Inc. 308 courtesy of Pfizer, Inc. 314 © 1982 Walt Disney Productions. 315 copyright, The Exploratorium, Ed Tannenbaum. 316 © 1984 Los Angeles Times; photograph reprinted by permission. 317 courtesy Strand Century Inc. 319 photograph by Mike Lopez. 320 photograph by Mike Lopez. 321 courtesy New York Yankees. 323 courtesy Intel Corporation. 324 both photographs courtesy of Gideon Ariel, Ariel Computerized Exercisers, Inc. 325 courtesy CompuPro. 326 photo by Jon Porter. 327 © Pizza Time Theatre, Inc. 328 © 1982 Walt Disney Productions. 329 Jonathan Saadah—Intermedia. 330 courtesy Los Alamos National Laboratory. 331 courtesy Hewlett Packard Company. 336 reprinted with permission from International Business Machines Corporation. 337 U.S. Air Force Photo. 339 both photos courtesy U.S. Department of the Army. 340 courtesy U.S. Department of the Army. 341 (top) courtesy U.S. Department of the Army. 341 (bottom) courtesy of the Office of the Assistant Secretary of Defense. 342 National Bureau of Standards, Center for Fire Research. 343 Steve Uzzell, III, courtesy of Planning Research Corporation. 344 (top) courtesy of Aydin Controls, a division of Aydin Corporation. 344 (bottom) courtesy of U.S. Census Bureau. 345 courtesy of The MIT Museum. 346 (top) courtesy Federal Bureau of Investigation. 346 (bottom) photo courtesy of the Internal Revenue Service. 348 courtesy Digital Equipment Corporation. 350 reprinted with permission from International Business Machines Corporation. 351 courtesy Federal Bureau of Investigation. 353 courtesy Los Alamos National Laboratory. 360 courtesy RB Robot Corporation. 361 reproduced with permission of AT&T. 365 (top right and left) courtesy of Androbot, Inc. 365 (bottom left) courtesy of Heath Company. 365 (bottom right) photo courtesy of RB Robot Corporation, Golden, Colorado. 366 (top) courtesy of Odetics, Inc. 366 (bottom) reproduced with permission of AT&T. 367 photo courtesy of Cray Research, Inc. 370 courtesy of General Electric Company. 371 courtesy of The MIT Museum. 372 courtesy of The MIT Museum.

†